COMPETITION LAW AND POLI

COMPETITION LAW AND POLICY

Cases, Materials and Commentary

TIM FRAZER
Professor of Law, Newcastle Law School, University of Newcastle upon Tyne
Consultant, Watson Burton, Newcastle upon Tyne

AND

MICHAEL WATERSON
Professor of Economics
The University of Warwick

HARVESTER
WHEATSHEAF

New York London Toronto Sydney Tokyo Singapore

First published 1994 by
Harvester Wheatsheaf
Campus 400, Maylands Avenue
Hemel Hempstead
Hertfordshire, HP2 7EZ
A division of
Simon & Schuster International Group

Typeset in 9/10pt Times and Helvetica
by Keyset Composition, Colchester, Essex
Printed and bound in Great Britain by
The University Press, Cambridge

British Library Cataloguing in Publication Data

A catalogue record for this book is available from the British Library

ISBN 0 7450 1440 2 (pbk)

1 2 3 4 5 98 97 96 95 94

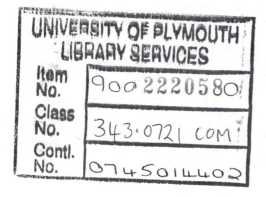

CONTENTS

9 HORIZONTAL AGREEMENTS: PRICE FIXING

10 VERTICAL AGREEMENTS: DISTRIBUTION

11 VERTICAL AGREEMENTS: EXCLUSIVE DISTRIBUTION

18 THE PROCESS OF ASSESSMENT

19 MONOPOLY PRACTICES AND THE PUBLIC INTEREST

PART FIVE MERGERS

20 MERGER TRANSACTIONS

PART SIX EXTRATERRITORIALITY

23 EXTRATERRITORIALITY

PREFACE

There are already excellent texts on competition law. In preparing this book we have not sought to add directly to their number in an evangelical attempt to demonstrate the competitive process at work. Instead we have tried to produce a differentiated product. The aim is to present a workable library of excerpts from cases, statutes and articles bearing on competition law and policy, which will serve as a research tool for students and researchers, as well as a teaching medium. It is intended that the book contains a self-sufficient explanation of the law and its underlying economic policies, though it cannot be as fully detailed as a text aimed primarily at practitioners. The advantage of the materials format is, we hope, that it gives a better flavour of how the law actually works to those who are not practising, whilst suggesting appropriate precedents to those who are. References enable readers to follow up on particular points of economics or the law in more detail.

The book covers the legal systems and underlying policies of the UK, the EC and the USA. The individual legal systems of the other member States of the EC are not included, and the law and policy of the USA is not covered in the same detail; it is mainly included to provide a point of reference for the other two systems. As many readers will be aware, even in purely domestic competition policy issues, the framework of UK law increasingly reflects Community legislation. Throughout, we have attempted to provide an economic rationale for the legal framework, where one exists, or at least to present economic analysis which bears on the issue in straightforward terms. As far as possible, we have tried to let the extracts speak for themselves, and we have been fairly careful in editing them in order to have the points made as crisply as possible. The commentary merely provides a few signposts.

Competition law is somewhat more heavily involved in restrictive practices (RTPs) than it is in, say, mergers. This balance is reflected in the contents. Parts 2 and 3 both contain material on RTPs, firstly some general issues then applications to horizontal and vertical market agreements. Part 4 covers monopoly, including anticompetitive practices, whilst Part 5 deals with mergers. Remedies are covered as they arise. Finally, Part 6 considers some issues of extraterritoriality. Before the substantive legal matters are dealt with, some underlying issues are considered in Part 1.

Of course the law is subject to change. It has changed substantially over the period in which we have been thinking of producing this book, which has its origins in a course taught jointly at the University of Newcastle some years ago. We have for some time used the excuse that further changes were imminent to postpone the evil day when the book had to be delivered to the publishers. Now that the excuse has worn thin we hope change will not be too rapid, but expect the opposite.

ACKNOWLEDGEMENTS

P. McNulty, 'Economic Theory and the Meaning of Competition', reprinted from *Quarterly Journal of Economics*, Vol. 82, p. 639 (1968) by permission of the MIT Press, Cambridge, Massachusetts, Copyright © 1968 by the President and Fellows of Harvard College and the Massachusetts Institute of Technology. K. George and C. Joll, 'A Review of the Main Economic Issues', reproduced from *Competition Policy in the UK and EEC*, eds K. George and C. Joll (Cambridge University Press, Cambridge, 1975), by permission of the Economic and Social Research Council. W. Hirsch, *Law and Economics: An Introductory Analysis*, 2nd edn (Academic Press, London, 1988), reprinted by permission of the author and Academic Press, Inc. Copyright © 1979, 1988 by Academic Press, Inc. The following are all reproduced by permission of the Office for Official Publications of the European Communities: Commission of the European Communities, *Ninth Report on Competition Policy*, (Commission of the European Communities, Brussels, 1979); Treaty of Rome; Commission of the European Communities, *Commission Notice of 3rd September 1986 on Agreements of Minor Importance Which Do Not Fall Under Article 85(1) of the Treaty Establishing the European Economic Community* OJ 1986, No. C 231/2; Commission Regulation (EEC) No. 17/62 OJ Sp. Ed. 1962 No. 204/62, p. 87; *UK Agricultural Tractor Registration Exchange*, Decision of the Commission of the European Communities OJ 1992 No. L68/19; Commission Regulation (EEC) No. 1983/83 on the Application of Article 85(3) to Categories of Exclusive Distribution Agreements OJ 1983 No. L173/1; Commission Regulation (EEC) No. 1984/83 on the Application of Article 85(3) to Categories of Exclusive Purchasing Agreements OJ 1983 No. L173/5; Commission of the European Communities, *Commission Notice of 22 June 1983 Concerning Commission Regulations (EEC) No. 1983/83 and (EEC) No. 1984/83* OJ 1984 No. C101/2; *Yves Saint Laurent Parfums*, Decision of the Commission of the European Communities OJ 1992 No. L12/24; Commission Regulation (EEC) No. 556/89 on the Application of Article 85(3) to Certain Categories of Know-How Licensing Agreements OJ 1989 No. L61/1; Commission Regulation (EEC) No. 4087/88 on the Application of Article 85(3) to Categories of Franchise Agreements OJ 1988 No. L359/46; Council Regulation (EEC) No. 4064/89 on the Control of Concentrations Between Undertakings OJ 1989 No. L395/1; Commission of the European Communities, *Notice Regarding the Concentrative and Co-Operative Operations under Council Regulation 4064/89* OJ 1990 No. C203/10; *Nestlé/Perrier*, Decision of the Commission of the European Communities OJ 1992 No. L356/1; *Aerospatiale-Alenia/de Havilland*, Decision of the Commission of the European Communities OJ 1991 No. L334/42; Commission of the European Communities, *Notice on co-operation between national courts and the Commission in applying Articles 85 and 86 of the EEC Treaty*. OJ 1993 No. C39/6. The following are all reproduced with the permission of the Controller of Her Majesty's Stationery Office: Department of Trade and Industry, *Review of Restrictive Trade Practices Policy* Cm 331 (HMSO, London, 1988); Department of Trade and Industry, *Opening Markets: New Policy on Restrictive Trade Practices* Cm. 729 (HMSO, London, 1989); Restrictive Trade Practices Act 1976; Supply of Beer (Tied Estate) Order 1989 (SI 1989 No. 2390); Supply of Beer (Loan Ties, Licensed Premises and Wholesale Prices) Order 1989 (SI 1989 No. 2258); Resale Prices Act 1976; Fair Trading Act 1973; Department of Trade and Industry, *Abuse of Market Power: A Consultative Document on Possible Legislative Options* Cm. 2100 (HMSO, London, 1992); Competition Act 1980; Anti-Competitive Practices (Exclusions) Order 1980 (SI 1980 No. 979); Monopolies and Mergers Commission, *White Salt* Cmnd. 9778 (HMSO, London, 1986); Monopolies and Mergers Commission, *Soluble Coffee* Cm. 1459 (HMSO, London, 1991); Monopolies and Mergers Commission, *Plasterboard* Cm. 1224 (HMSO, London, 1990); Trade and Industry Committee, *First Report on Takeovers and Mergers*, HC Paper 90, Session 1991–92; Monopolies and Mergers Commission, *Report on the Proposed Joint Venture: Allied-Lyons PLC/Carlsberg A/S* Cm. 2029 (HMSO, London, 1992); Monopolies and Mergers Commission, *Report on the Proposed Merger between Credit Lyonnais and Woodchester* Cm. 1404 (HMSO, London, 1991); Department of Trade and Industry, *Merger Policy: A Department of Trade and Industry Paper on the policy and procedures of merger control* (HMSO, London, 1988); Protection of Trading Interests Act 1980; Aide-Memoire of the British Government to the Commission of the European Communities, 20 October 1969. The following are all reproduced from Common Market Law Reports with permission from Sweet and Maxwell Ltd: *Metro SB-Grossmarkte GmbH and Co KG* v. *Commission of the European Communities* European Court of Justice [1978] 2 CMLR 1; *Pronuptia de Paris GmbH, Frankfurt am Main* v. *Rosalinde Irmgard Schillgalis* European Court of Justice [1986] 1 CMLR 414; *Re The Polypropylene Cartel: Hercules NV* v. *Commission of the European Communities* European Court of First Instance [1992] 4 CMLR 84; *Delimitis* v. *Henninger Brau AG* European Court of Justice, [1992] 5 CMLR 210; *Metro SB-Grossmarkte GmbH and Co KG* v. *Commission of the European Communities* (No. 2) European Court of Justice [1987] 1 CMLR 118; *Publishers Association – Net Book Agreements* Decision of the Commission of the European Communities [1989] 4 CMLR 825; *Maize Seeds: L C Nungesser KG, and Kurt Eisele* v. *Commission of the European Communities* European Court of Justice [1983] 1 CMLR 278; *United Brands Company* v. *Commission of the European Communities* European Court of Justice [1978] 3 CMLR 83; *Tetra Pak Rausing SA* v. *Commission of the European Communities* European Court of First Instance [1991] 4 CMLR 334;

Italian Flat Glass: Società Italiano Vetro SpA v. *Commission of the European Communities* European Court of First Instance [1992] 5 CMLR 302; *Re Wood Pulp Cartel: A Ahlstrom Oy and Others* v. *Commission of the European Communities* European Court of Justice [1988] 4 CMLR 901; *Napier Brown – British Sugar* Decision of the Commission of the European Communities [1990] 4 CMLR 196; *The European Sugar Cartel* Decision of the Commission of the European Communities OJ 1973 No. L140/17. J. Kay, 'Identifying the Strategic Market', 1 *Business Strategy Review*, 2 (1990) and R. Rees, 'Tacit Collusion', 9 *Oxford Review of Economic Policy* (1993) reproduced by permission of Oxford University Press. *Royal Institution of Chartered Surveyors* v. *Director General of Fair Trading* Court of Appeal [1986] ICR 550 reproduced by permission of the Incorporated Council of Law Reporting for England and Wales. Sir Gordon Borrie, 'Restrictive Practices Control in the United Kingdom: Big Bangs and Lesser Detonations', 1986 *J Business Law*, 358 and W. Sibree, 'EEC Merger Control and Joint Ventures', 17 *European Law Rev.*, 91 (1992) reproduced by permission of Sweet and Maxwell Ltd. B. Hawk, 'The American (Anti-Trust) Revolution: Lessons for the EEC?', 1988 *European Competition Law Rev.*, 53 reproduced by permission of the author and Sweet and Maxwell Ltd. G. Matthewson and R. Winter, 'The Economics of Vertical Restraints in Distribution', in *New Developments in the Analysis of Market Structure* eds J. Stiglitz and G. Mathewson (Macmillan, London, 1986), Copyright © International Economic Association, reproduced by permission of Macmillan Ltd and the MIT Press, Cambridge, Massachusetts. E. Glynn, 'Distribution under EEC Law', 59 *Antitrust Law Journal*, 473 (1991), Copyright © 1991 American Bar Association, reprinted by permission of the American Bar Association. Scherer, F M and David Ross, *Industrial Market Structure and Economic Performance*, Third Edition, Copyright © 1990 by Houghton Mifflin Company, used with permission of Houghton Mifflin Company. M. Waterson, 'Allocative Efficiency and Monopoly as a Basis for Regulation', in *Industrial Economic Regulation* ed. R. Sugden (Routledge, London, 1993), Copyright © 1993 Roger Sugden, reproduced by permission of the editor and Routledge. R. Posner, 'The Social Costs of Monopoly and Regulation', *Journal of Political Economy*, 807 (1975), Copyright © 1975 by The University of Chicago, reproduced by permission of The University of Chicago Press. W. Sharkey, *The Theory of Natural Monopoly* (Cambridge University Press, Cambridge, 1982), Copyright © 1982 Bell Telephone Laboratories, Incorporated, reproduced by permission of AT & T. E G West 'Monopoly' in *The New Palgrave: A Dictionary of Economics*, J. Eatwell, M. Milgate, P. Newman (eds), Macmillan, London, 1987, Copyright © The Macmillan Press Limited, 1987, reproduced by permission of Macmillan Press Limited. R Schmalensee, 'Another Look at Market Power', 95 *Harvard Law Review*, 1789 (1982) Copyright © 1982 by the Harvard Law Review Association. *R.* v. *Monopolies and Mergers Commission, Secretary of State for Trade and Industry, Director General of Fair Trading ex p. Visa International Services Assoc.* Court of Appeal (1991) 10 Trad. L. R. 97, reproduced by permission of Barry Rose Law Periodicals. *R.* v.

Monopolies and Mergers Commission ex p. South Yorkshire Transport Limited House of Lords *The Times*, 17 December 1982 © Times Newspapers Limited 1992, reproduced by permission of Times Newspapers Ltd. M. Utton, 'Anticompetitive Practices and the Competition Act 1980', *Antitrust Bulletin* (1993), Copyright © 1992 by Federal Legal Publications, Inc., reproduced by permission of Federal Legal Publications, Inc. M. Waterson, 'Takeovers', 7 *The Economic Review*, 2 (1989), Copyright © Philip Allan Publishers Limited 1989, reproduced by permission of Philip Allan Publishers Limited.

PART ONE

INTRODUCTION

1

COMPETITION AND COMPETITION POLICY

Achieving a perfectly competitive economy is impossible. Indeed, it might also be undesirable. What, then, are the goals of competition policy? What is the meaning of competition? Few economists pause for long to think about such questions. The extract from **McNulty** is an example of a relatively philosophical discussion along these lines. **George and Joll** point out that the importance of competition policy differs between the frameworks underlying UK and EC legislation. Such differences in philosophy will, of course, come out in more detail later in specific policy areas. The extract from **Hirsch** continues these themes, introducing differences between lawyers' and economists' views. He also provides a very brief survey of methods of monopolisation, together with a short discussion of remedies, including promotion of information.

It is well known that UK competition law and policy are concerned with an ill-defined focus on 'the public interest'. The Fair Trading Act 1973, for example, refers to five criteria, only two of which are concerned directly with competition. The rather more explicit focus of EC and US legal frameworks is covered in more detail in the extracts from the EC **Competition Policy Report** and the **Attorney General's Report** respectively.

1.1 P. McNulty, 'Economic theory and the meaning of competition', 82 *Quarterly Journal of Economics*, 639 (1968)

There is probably no concept in all of economics that is at once more fundamental and pervasive, yet less satisfactorily developed, than the concept of competition. Although the hesitancy and inconsistency which has characterized the history of American competitive policy is doubtless partly due, as is often emphasized, to the fact that competition is, in our system, a political and social *desideratum* no less than an economic one, with some possible resulting conflict between these various values, surely it is due also to the failure of economists adequately to define competition. Not the least among the many achievements of economic science has been the ability to erect a rigorous analytical system on the principle of competition – a principle so basic to economic reasoning that not even such powerful yet diverse critics of orthodox theory as Marx and Keynes could avoid relying upon it – without ever clearly specifying what, exactly, competition is. [. . .]

Probably the most general tendency concerning the meaning of competition in economic theory is to regard it as the opposite of monopoly. An unfortunate result of this way of thinking has been no little confusion concerning the relationship between economic efficiency and business behavior. There is a striking contrast in economic literature between the analytical rigor and precision of competition when it is described as a market structure, and the ambiguity surrounding the idea of competition whenever it is discussed in behavioral terms. Since, as Hayek has rightly noted, 'the law cannot effectively prohibit states of affairs but only kinds of action', a concept of economic competition, if it is to be significant for economic policy, ought to relate to patterns of business behavior such as might reasonably be associated with the verb 'to compete'. That was the case with the competition which Adam Smith made the central organizing principle of economic society in the *Wealth of Nations*, and with the competition whose effects Cournot, in the first formal statement of the idea of 'perfect' competition, could accurately claim to be 'realized, in social economy, for a multitude of products, and, among them, for the most important products'. Whether it was seen as price undercutting by sellers, the bidding up of prices by buyers, or the entry of new firms into profitable industries, the fact is that competition entered economics as a concept which had empirical relevance and operational meaning in terms of contemporary business behavior. Yet on the question of whether such common current practices as advertising, product variation, price undercutting, or other forms of business activity do or do not constitute competition, modern economic theory offers the clarification that they are 'monopolistically' competitive. While this is a useful way of illustrating the truth that most markets are in some degree both controlled and controlling, it is less useful as a guide in implementing a policy, such as our antitrust policy, which seeks at once to restrain monopoly and promote competition. It is too late in the history of economics, and it is surely not in any way here the purpose, to de-emphasize the truly monumental character of E. H. Chamberlin's great achievement [. . .] in reconciling economic theory with the undeniable fact that much of the business world was really a mixture of competition and monopoly, as those concepts were then defined in economics, which fitted neither of those traditional economic models of business enterprise. But it is not, perhaps, too late to suggest that the traditional distinction between competition and monopoly was, in a fundamental sense, inappropriate to begin with, and that the merging of the concepts in a theory of monopolistic competition, while representing a profound improvement over the simplicity of the older classification, and giving microeconomics a new vitality almost comparable to that which Keynes was at the same time bringing to employment theory, has, nonetheless, allowed us to avoid defining a concept of competition, *as distinct from the concept of a competitive market*, which is at once relevant and adequate both for economic analysis and for economic policy.

Clearly, the failure to distinguish between the idea of competition and the idea of market structure is at the root of much of the ambiguity concerning the meaning of competition. As far as market structure, conceived of in terms of the paucity or plethora of sellers (buyers), is the appropriate focus of analysis, consistency would suggest relying on terms such as monopoly (sony), duopoly, triopoly, oligopoly, polypoly, and, perhaps, a newly-coined term ending in 'poly', the prefix of which means an indefinitely large number. Such a classification, although it would add to an already cumbersome body of technical jargon, would nonetheless retain for market taxonomy the analytical usefulness it currently possesses, while having the further advantage of eliminating much of the confusion that now exists between competition and monopoly. As it is, it is one of the great paradoxes of economic science that every *act* of competition on the part of a businessman is evidence, in economic theory, of some degree of monopoly power, while the concepts of monopoly and perfect competition have this important common feature: both are situations in which the possibility of any competitive behavior has been ruled out by definition.

That perfect competition is an ideal state, incapable of actual realization, is a familiar theme of economic literature. That for various reasons it would be less than altogether desirable, even if it were attainable, is also widely acknowledged. But that perfect competition is a state of affairs quite incompatible with the idea of any and all competition has been insufficiently emphasized. It is this last feature of perfect competition, and not, as is sometimes incorrectly claimed, its high level of abstraction or the 'unreality' of its assumptions, which limits its usefulness, especially for economic policy. What needs more stress than it has generally received is not the inescapably abstract and 'unreal' nature of theory but, rather, the fact that while all other forms of competition represent, in economic theory, an *admixture* of monopoly and competition, perfect competition itself means the *absence* of competition in quite as complete a sense, although for different reasons, as does pure monopoly. Monopoly is a market situation in which intraindustry competition has been defined away by identifying the firm as the industry. Perfect competition, on the other hand, is a market situation which, although itself the *result* of the free entry of a large number of formerly competing firms, has evolved or progressed to the point (of equilibrium) where no *further* competition within the industry is possible, or, in the words of A. A. Cournot, its intellectual parent, to the point where 'the effects of competition have reached their limit'. It is for this reason that Frank Knight can correctly stress, as he often has, that perfect competition involves 'no presumption of psychological competition, emulation, or rivalry', and can rightly assert that '"atomism" is a better term for the idea.' Perfect competition, the only clearly and rigorously defined concept of competition to be found in the corpus of economic theory, which is free of all traces of business behavior associated with 'monopolistic' elements, means simply the *existence* of an indefinitely large number of noncompeting firms. Economists have sometimes criticized American competitive policy for its not infrequently manifested tendency over the years to identify the maintenance of competition with the maintenance of competitors. But economic theory offers no clear guide for distinguishing between them. To the extent that we look to economics for an answer to the question 'What are the advantages of competition over monopoly?', we ought also to be able to look to economics for an answer to the question 'How may a business firm be expected to compete without monopolizing?' And the critical reader will search economic literature in vain for a clear answer to that question.

[. . .]

1.2 K. George and C. Joll, 'A review of the main economic issues', in K. George and C. Joll (eds), *Competition Policy in the UK and EEC* (Cambridge University Press, Cambridge, 1975)

[. . .]

It is universally agreed by commentators in this area that competition as such has a higher priority among the aims of the EEC than of the UK. Thus 'the institution of a system ensuring that competition in the Common Market is not distorted' is given in Article 3 of the Treaty of Rome as one of the ways of achieving the fundamental purposes of the EEC, which are themselves laid down in Article 2 of the Treaty [. . .]. [A] passage from the EEC Commission's *First Report on Competition Policy* [. . .] may be said to express the philosophy on which EEC competition policy is based. This states that competition is regarded as desirable because it will guarantee freedom of action and choice, ensure efficiency and the optimal allocation of resources and so on. Thus the EEC's position may be regarded as intermediate between that of the USA, which provides a frame of reference for the discussion of competition policy where competition, for cultural and political as well as economic reasons, is regarded as a 'way of life' or an 'end in itself', and that of the UK. In the UK, competition is certainly seen as a means to an end, where the end is variously described in terms of efficiency in production and distribution, development of technical improvements, distribution of industry and employment etc. [. . .]. However, competition is not seen as invariably the best or only way of achieving these primarily economic aims and UK policy has contained very little presumption in favour of competition. The 1973 Fair Trading Act was the first piece of UK legislation to contain specific mention of competition as desirable on its own account rather than as one of a number of alternative means of achieving the aims of policy, all to be considered on an equal basis. Thus, although the pointers to the public interest contained in this Act include 'the desirability of maintaining and promoting effective competition between persons supplying goods and services in the UK' taken as a whole they are [. . .] something of a mixture of means and ends.

If we accept that the philosophy of the EEC's policy is more strongly in favour of competition than that of the UK, then how does this difference show through in legislation on competition policy and in the way in which this legislation is enforced in practice? It is possible to point out ways in which the different provisions of legislation on monopolies, mergers and restrictive practices in the UK and the EEC reflect a greater commitment to competition in the latter. In the field of restrictive practices, UK and EEC policies are broadly similar in that a wide range of restrictive practices are prohibited but agreements may be permitted on certain conditions. It is in the specification of these conditions that the difference between the UK and EEC attitudes manifests itself. Thus in the UK [. . .] an agreement may be upheld by the Restrictive Practices Court if it has beneficial consequences which outweigh the detriment to competition, and also agreements which are considered by the Government to be 'on balance in the public interest' or to be anti-inflationary can be licensed by the Government without the anti-competitive effects of the agreement being weighed up by the Court. In these cases there is plainly no presumption in favour of competition operating. In the EEC, however, a restrictive agreement must simultaneously fulfil four conditions in order to be exempt, and one of these conditions is that competition must not be eliminated from a substantial proportion of the product in question. Thus an agreement with a 'substantially' anti-competitive effect cannot be licensed in the EEC under any circumstances whatever or, to put it in UK terms, could never be considered 'in the public interest'.

UK legislation on monopolies and mergers expresses a less favourable attitude towards competition than that on restrictive practices, which are after all initially presumed to be against the public interest. Towards monopoly situations and mergers, however, the UK approach is basically to assess the effects of each situation separately and pronounce on whether these are against the public interest. The 'cons' to be assessed will consist of adverse effects on competition, but UK policy has given little guidance to the Monopolies Commission, which is responsible for this exercise, as to how these effects should be weighed in the balance against the beneficial consequences claimed for the monopoly situation or merger. EEC monopoly policy, that is Article 86, prohibits the abuse of dominant position and there is no provision for exemption. Much depends on the interpretation of this Article, but it could be taken as prohibiting any conduct which would not have occurred in a competitive situation, e.g. price fixing or restrictions on output. This would undoubtedly express a stronger determination to regulate the behaviour of large firms and make them behave 'as if' they were in a competitive situation, than can be deduced from the UK legislation which prohibits nothing and assesses anew in each case the effects of monopolistic practices to see whether the practice can be said to operate against the public interest in these circumstances.

[. . .]

We can say, therefore, that EEC legislation does, on the face of it, show a greater commitment to competition and a tougher line on monopolies mergers and restrictive practices as offences against competition than UK legislation. However, it must be stressed that both systems leave a substantial amount of scope for discretion in interpreting the legislation [. . .]

1.3 W. Hirsch, *Law and Economics: An introductory analysis*, 2nd edn (Academic Press, London, 1988)

Contract law [. . .] is based on the premise that all parties to a transaction are reasonably equal in bargaining power. This equality of bargaining power is a prerequisite – a necessary though not sufficient condition – for a competitive market, where important characteristics of a competitive market are:

1. A large number of firms.
2. Homogeneous products.
3. Free entry into and exit from the market.
4. Independence of decisions among firms.
5. Perfect knowledge.

Economists differentiate between perfect and pure competition. *Perfect competition* requires all five characteristics; for *pure competition*, some economists consider the first four characteristics essential; others, merely the first two. In the absence of pure or perfect competition, markets are monopolistic or oligopolistic to varying degrees, depending on whether the industry has one or a small number of members.

However [. . .] lawyers and economists use the word *monopoly* (and therefore the word *competition*) in distinctly different ways. For lawyers, the term *monopoly* is use as 'a standard of evaluation', designating a situation not in the public interest. *Competition*, in comparison, designates situations in the public interest. For the lawyer, monopoly means a restriction of the freedom of business to engage in legitimate economic activities.

To an economist, the distinction between monopoly and pure competition is the differing ways in which market transactions occur and resources are allocated under the two. A monopolist (or oligopolist) is able to influence the market price. Consequently, firm output decisions are made keeping in mind their potential effect on price. A (pure) competitor, conversely, cannot affect the market price; as a result, in the abstract, he seeks to maximize profits by producing until marginal cost equals price.

A firm with monopoly power will produce at a lower output level and charge a higher price than an identical firm in a competitive market. Clearly, total surplus could be increased by forcing a monopolist to act like a competitive firm, yet whether such coercion could or should be adopted is a difficult question. It is imperative to ask not only whether a firm has market power but also why it has such power.

Besides questions of efficiency, issues of social justice and equity may also be relevant in evaluating the effects of monopolies. The domination of an industry by a single firm may be undesirable, apart from effects on efficiency. For instance, to allow a single firm to dominate an industry vital to national security may grant the firm's owners more political power than is in society's interest.

Both on efficiency and equity grounds, antimonopoly laws could conceivably improve upon outcomes in markets devoid of government intervention. Economists who seek to evaluate antimonopoly laws can raise some major questions: Have these laws produced consistent, socially desirable results? Does the precedent-setting nature of decisions cause justices to overlook case-specific factors in order to establish market-wide rules to the detriment of the pursuit of the objectives of the law?

Why should government interfere with the sanctity of a contract? The reason is simple. When there exists great inequality in bargaining power, a contract, even if freely arrived at, can have major ill effects on others who are not parties to it. Government intervention, it can be argued, is then needed to champion resource-allocation, and even social, efficiency.

Some authors have expressed strong opinions on these issues. For example, R. H. Bork [has argued that]

> The present misshapen look of antitrust doctrine is due in large measure to the Supreme Court's habit of regarding business efficiency as either irrelevant or harmful. Insufficient regard for efficient methods of production and distribution meant that hardly any business practice challenged could survive.

Clearly, [. . .] this is not the only view of antimonopoly laws.

Much of the difficulty perhaps stems from the fact that the benchmark to which economists tend to compare real-life markets is a highly theoretical construct – the purely or perfectly competitive market. It has never been shown to exist and is a most improbable phenomenon. Therefore, we cannot be sure that rigorous economic theory of pure or perfect competition can, as is often claimed, provide powerful policy guidelines. [. . .]

This issue is recognized by H. Demsetz when he states, 'The proper issue for antitrust, then, is not the degree to which a market descriptively diverges from perfect competition, but the degree to which it diverges in either direction from that intensity of competition which takes account of the real social costs of competing.'

There are many legal scholars and economists who hold positive views of antitrust laws and action. For example, in 1981, Ernest Gellhorn concluded, 'The past five years have seen a remarkable growth of sophisticated antitrust scholarship and a widespread effort to integrate economic theory into antitrust.' In his view and that of many others, the application of microeconomic theory together with empirical analysis has made important contributions. He recognizes that Richard Posner and Robert Bork have been generally dissatisfied with the application of economics to case law. But, then, their predominant concern has been the efficiency results of antitrust action. Both of these legal scholars have been appointed in the meantime to federal appeals courts. They now have the opportunity to improve upon the courts' use of economics. [. . .]

[. . .] Firms have traveled different roads toward enhanced monopoly power. Perhaps the single most direct one is consolidation, be it through merger or creation of conglomerates. Thus, for example, one study found that in 17 West German (four-digit) manufacturing industries, between 1958 and 1971, mergers were the single most important factor increasing market concentration. Internal growth was of secondary importance, and exit and entry were relatively insignificant. Mergers rarely if ever lead to a complete monopolization of the industry; more often they lead to oligopoly.

A second method often employed to monopolize markets involves various forms, often secret, of cooperation among competitors. The outstanding example is the cartel that engages in price fixing and/or market division.

Third, firms can engage in predatory pricing (threatening to or actually pricing goods below average cost) to foreclose entry. Fourth, market power can be increased through vertical integration or other vertical restraints on prices or output. Last, the government may allocate the power to restrict entry to individuals within the industry. [. . .]

[. . .]

Clearly, as long as monopoly means something distinctly different to lawyers and economists [. . .] consistent remedies are difficult to come by. Various sanctions have been imposed once a violation of law has been established. Matters are complicated because the economic problem posed by monopoly is often independent of business conduct in any particular situation. Thus, resource misallocation and increased prices appear to stem more from the power of monopolists than from specific business strategies they may pursue. One might therefore argue that criminal fines, imprisonment, and treble damages in private suits are often inappropriate. Divestiture, instead, would deal with the more basic structural problems of the industry.

Thus, in [US] criminal cases, frequently involving conspiracy, those who are found guilty can be fined or even incarcerated. Fines are usually small in comparison to the wealth of the firm, and prison sentences are infrequent.

Once an illegal act has been found to have taken place, the court often issues an injunction to discontinue the practice in question. Such a restriction, even if combined with positive conduct requirements, is frequently insufficient. Moreover, there is no mechanism for policing the firm to see whether the court ruling is indeed consistently and fully implemented. Therefore, rather than insisting on divestiture, courts have in some cases threatened divestiture within a given time period unless satisfactory structural changes are carried out. For example, in *United States* v. *Eastman Kodak Co.*, consent decrees were entered requiring that the company split the tie-in between its color film and color-film-processing activities. Eastman Kodak was to divest itself in seven years of any processing facilities in excess of 50% of national capacity, but divestiture would *not* be required if in six years it was shown that purchasers of Eastman color film had easy access to processors other than Eastman. When, in 1961, the government and the company agreed that independent processors had captured more than 50% of the market, divestiture was set aside.

Class action has been permitted in those cases where the effects of violation are so widely diffused among consumers that none has an incentive to bear the costs of a suit. Class action permits persons who would be affected by a decree, but are so numerous that it would be impossible or at least impracticable to bring them all in as parties, to seek judgment as a 'class'; though only some members of the class may be parties to the suit, the judicial opinion may bind all members of that class. Class action provides economies of scale as well as enhanced power to plaintiffs. But class action can also lead to frivolous harassment of defendants. The importance of class actions has been rapidly increasing, though admittedly only some cases relate to antimonopoly action. [. . .]

A further remedy is to bring about more equal knowledge available to buyer and seller. The central purpose of the provision of the Federal Trade Commission Act prohibiting false advertising is to abolish the rule of *caveat emptor* and give consumers the right to rely on the representations of fact as truths. The Fair Packaging and Labeling Program makes it unlawful to distribute commodities that fail to conform to the act's provisions. Conspicuously visible labels must specify the identity of the commodity, the name and place of business of the manufacturer, packer, or distributor, and the net quantity of content, which should be separately and accurately stated in a uniform location on the label.

[. . .]

Economists have worked with lawyers in antimonopoly matters for longer than in any other legal field, but one would be wrong to assume that antimonopoly law is therefore clear and implemented in an unambiguous manner. Dissatisfaction with the status of antimonopoly law is widespread. In part, this stems from major disagreements about the purposes of antimonopoly laws. As seen, for example, by Chief Justice Warren, the congressional mandate often is to promote competition by protecting 'viable, small, locally owned businesses', and it is the court's duty to implement this mandate. Others see the purpose of antimonopoly laws to be the promotion of consumer welfare. [. . .]

The objectives of EEC competition policy were clearly enunciated in the Commission's **Ninth Report on Competition Policy**. The more recent enactment of the Council's **Merger Regulation** (4064/89) has made these objectives more attainable. They should, perhaps, be supplemented by the Commission's desire to establish a strong technology base for European industry, an objective which may conflict with other 'competition' objectives (see the extract from **Frazer**, '*Vorsprung durch Technik*', Section 14.4. As the Single Market becomes more established, the 'first fundamental objective' of the policy (to keep the common market open and unified) may give way to more efficiency-based objectives (see T. Frazer, 'Competition policy: the next step', 53 *Mod Law Review*, 609 (1990)). In the USA, the **Attorney General's Report**, although an old document, reveals a more ideological basis for the antitrust policy of the Sherman Act. This has now become overlaid with more pressing concerns for efficiency, although the objectives of US antitrust law are still subject to fierce debate.

1.4 Commission of the European Communities, *Ninth Report on Competition Policy* (Commission of the European Communities, Brussels, 1979)

The persistence of conditions of crisis prompts questions as to the role that competition policy should play and as to the respective merits of rigidity and flexibility in its application. In the case of the Community, delineation of the general thrust of its competition policy must not be based on a dogmatic approach but requires reference back to the fundamental provisions of the EEC Treaty. The Treaty stipulates that the Community's primary task is, by establishing a common market, to promote the harmonious development of economic activities throughout the Community. The methods prescribed for accomplishing this task include the institution of a system for ensuring undistorted competition, a prerequisite for the proper functioning of the common market, which is the rock on which economic integration is to be founded.

It follows that the Community's competition policy must persist in its pursuit of a group of basic objectives.

The first fundamental objective is to keep the common market open and unified. The metamorphosis of a heterogeneous collection of isolated national markets into a single vast market could not succeed without the establishment of some basic rules. The fear was that obstacles to freedom of movement and long-standing differences in firms' business environments, which were present to a disproportionate extent when the common market was formed, would tempt member governments to take measures to protect certain firms or aggravate the tendency to engage in defensive restrictive practices on the part of the firms themselves. The same protectionist reflexes are still raising their heads particularly at times of economic difficulty, even in an enlarged and unified market which reproduces as far as it can the characteristics of a domestic market. There is accordingly a continuing need – and this is the primary task of the Community's competition policy – to forestall and suppress restrictive or abusive practices of firms attempting to divide up the market again so as to apply artificial price differences or impose unfair terms on their customers. This duty is translated into action by the bulk of the Community's general rules on restrictive practices and State aids and equally by a lengthy series of decisions in individual cases. In the period covered by the present report we can see this policy continued in the Commission's efforts to draw up new rules on exclusive dealing agreements, selective distribution systems and patent licensing agreements.

Nevertheless, the perpetual struggle to unify the common market is not the only objective of the system to ensure undistorted competition. It is an established fact that competition carries within it the seeds of its own destruction. An excessive concentration of economic, financial and commercial power can produce such far-reaching structural changes that free competition is no longer able to fulfil its role as an effective regulator of economic activity. Consequently, the second fundamental objective of the Community's competition policy must be to ensure that at all stages of the common market's development there exists the right amount of competition in order for the Treaty's requirements to be met and its aims attained. The desire to maintain a competitive structure dictates the Commission's constant vigilance over abuses by dominant firms and over mergers which result in abrupt and substantial increases in the market shares of such firms. In a similar way, the establishment of a systematic control over large-scale mergers continues to be indispensable if the Community is to be able to react effectively against structural changes that may jeopardize the continuance of effective competition in the common market.

Thirdly, the competition system instituted by the Treaty requires that the conditions under which competition takes place remain subject to the principle of fairness in the market place. In the Commission's view, this principle is of prime importance in the present economic circumstances. In its application to the Commission's activities three main aspects emerge.

First, equality of opportunity must be preserved for all commercial operators in the common market. This means in the first place, that the Member States of an active and constantly evolving Community must refrain from granting aids or other measures of assistance to favour firms in their own countries to the detriment of other firms. Secondly it implies that the financial relationships between these States and undertakings in the public sector should be of such transparency that it can readily be ascertained whether or not the latter are operating on an equal footing with their competitors in the private sector, provided that this does not prejudice the carrying out of services of general economic interest. Lastly, the preservation of equality of opportunity means that firms from outside the Community which operate within it, whether directly or through subsidiaries, must be subject to the same rules as firms of Community origin.

A second aspect of the principle of fairness in the market place is the need to have regard to the great variety of situations in which firms carry on business. So far as competition policy is concerned, this factor makes it necessary to adapt the Community competition rules so as to pay special regard in particular to small and medium firms that lack market strength.

Finally, equity demands that the Commission's competition policy takes account of the legitimate interests of workers, users and consumers. These persons should be allowed a fair share of the benefits derived by firms from agreements that restrict competition between themselves. The same considerations, particularly the development of employment prospects, play an important part in the Commission's assessment of proposals for State aids.

The three fundamental objectives of the system of undistorted competition and the operational rules which they entail represent the effective contribution of Community competition law to the harmonious development of economic activities in the common market. But the proper functioning of the market mechanism is not in itself sufficient to ensure that other objectives are attained beyond those of greater productivity and competitiveness of Community firms.

If we are to advance towards greater economic and social justice, other Community policies must be pressed into service, always of course ensuring that they are consistent with the competition policy. Generally speaking, however, the harmonization of the various policies is most effectively guaranteed by the fact that every Community policy is required to adapt itself in order to fit into the perspective of a common market that is both unified and outward-looking at the same time. While it is virtually impossible to assess accurately the true contribution of the Community system of undistorted competition to the competitiveness of the European economy, it is worth pointing out that on aggregate there has been no appreciable deterioration in the competitive strength of the Community and its Member States *vis-à-vis* their major trading partners in the world. This is no mean achievement when one considers that the Community's heavy dependence on certain imported products which have risen steeply in price makes it extremely vulnerable to the current crisis. Irrevocably committed to international trade, the Community must maintain its drive to adapt its industrial structures to the changing world order, notably by encouraging its industries in the use of the new technologies.

The sheer scale of the common market and its inextricable enmeshment in world trade dictate that the need for a universal regulator of economic activity throughout the Community can only be answered by a Community competition policy. To yield to the persuasions of those who would respond to the crisis by a retreat into self-sufficient isolation would simply aggravate the situation beyond redemption by deepening the trauma of the structural changes thrust upon Europe by the shifting patterns of world trade. If we delude ourselves that we can dispense with the forces of competition and a decentralized economy and can steer through the necessary restructuring by purely legislative means, we run the irremediable risk of cutting our Community off from the economic reality of its surroundings.

1.5 Attorney General, *Report of the Attorney General's National Committee to Study the Antitrust Laws* (US Government Printing Office, Washington, DC, 1955)

The general objective of the antitrust laws is promotion of competition in open markets. This policy is a primary feature of private enterprise. Most Americans have long recognized that opportunity for market access and fostering of market rivalry are basic tenets of our faith in competition as a form of economic organization.

Sixty-four years have elapsed since Congress passed the Sherman Act of 1890, a basic statute known as a charter of economic freedom. In 1914, this statute was supplemented by the Federal Trade Commission Act and the Clayton Act. These three statutes are the core of the present antitrust policy on which we have focused.

In addition, at various times since 1890, Congress has specified a policy favoring competition as an essential ingredient in a wide variety of regulatory statutes dealing, for example, with banking, transportation, communications, and the disposal of Government surplus property. As recently as 1946, Congress has reiterated its belief in competition as an indispensable means of safeguarding our market economy from severe booms and slumps and for insuring its capacity for sustained growth.

Opinions have varied regarding the extent to which the antitrust laws have fulfilled their expectations at any particular period of their history. There have undoubtedly been fluctuations in the vitality and wisdom of antitrust administration and enforcement as well as occasional setbacks in Congress and in the courts. Nonetheless, a backward look across the 64 years since the Sherman Act reveals on the whole a healthy process of growth through which antitrust fundamentals have gained in strength and effectiveness.

By now the courts and other agencies of the Federal Government – especially the Antitrust Division of the Department of Justice and the Federal Trade Commission – have considered antitrust aspects of innumerable problems. A large body of antitrust doctrine has thus developed. A principal task of the Committee is to analyze the main course of this antitrust policy, its interpretation, and decisions. From this analysis, an evaluation of antitrust developments is made in light of established antitrust goals. On this evaluation the Committee bases its conclusions and recommendations as future guides to enforcement agencies, Congress, and the courts.

Initially, a preliminary sketch of this Report's content and scope may be helpful. We turn, first, to the basic concepts in sections 1 and 2 of the Sherman Act of restraint of trade and monopolization, both parts of the dominant Policy Against 'Undue Limitations on Competitive Conditions'. Topics here include arrangements controlling price and production as well as the range of activities which may unduly limit market entry or other commercial freedom. We consider application of that policy in both Domestic and Foreign Commerce. We next discuss Mergers, primarily under amended section 7 of the Clayton Act. Then we turn to sections 2 and 3 of the Clayton Act – Antitrust is a distinctive American means for assuring the competitive economy on which our political and social freedom under representative government in part depend. These laws have helped release energies essential to our leadership in industrial productivity and technological development. They reinforce our ideal of careers open to superior skills and talent, a crucial index of a free society. As a result, the essentials of antitrust are today proclaimed by both political parties as necessary to assure economic opportunity and some limitation on economic power incompatible with the maintenance of competitive conditions.

Louis B. Schwartz and some other members would, in addition, emphasize that competition 'is also desirable on principle and for its own sake, like political liberty and because political liberty is jeopardized if economic power drifts into relatively few hands.' Antitrust 'also performs the function of keeping governing power in the hands of politically responsible persons. Power to exclude someone from trade, to regulate prices, to determine what shall be produced, is governing power, whether exercised by public officials or by private groups. In a democracy, such powers are entrusted only to elected representatives of the governed' . . . . He points out, moreover, that 'Antitrust opposition to overwhelming Bigness serves still another purpose. Intellectual and artistic creativeness can be imperiled by the quality of sameness imposed on us when standards of thought and form are delivered into the hands of a few businessmen' . . .

The Committee unanimously adheres to antitrust fundamentals with full vigor. Although many forces and other Government policies have materially promoted our creative American economy, we believe the antitrust laws remain one of the most important. [. . .]

FURTHER READING

See the following works on the issues raised above.

Cowling, K. and Mueller, D. (1978), 'The social costs of monopoly power', 88 *Economic Journal*, 727.

Dansby, R. E. and Willig, R. D. (1979), 'Industry performance gradient indices', 69 *American Economic Review*, 249.

Harberger, A. C. (1954), 'Monopoly and resource allocation', 44 *American Economic Review*, 77.
Hay, D. A. (1987), 'Competition and industrial policies', 3(3) *Oxford Review of Economic Policy*, 27.
Kay, J. A. (1983), 'A general equilibrium approach to the measurement of monopoly welfare loss', 1 *International Journal of Industrial Organisation*, 317.
Sawyer, M. (1980), 'Monopoly welfare loss in the United Kingdom', 48 *Manchester School*, 331.

2

COMPETITION AND COMPETITION LAW

This section provides a comparison of the different methods of legal control of business through competition policy. The Green Paper, **Review of Restrictive Trade Practices Policy** puts arguments for moving to an effects-based system rather than the current form-based system (one based upon the legal form of agreements between firms, with some forms of agreement being proscribed) which currently exists for restrictive trade practices (RTPs) in the UK. But it notes the counter-arguments. It also sketches out links between UK and EC policy. **Metro** returns to themes raised by McNulty and others in Chapter 1. Restrictions on competition (e.g. selective distribution) may be essential to allowing competition to prosper. **Pronuptia** makes a similar point, as well as providing useful comparisons between legal schemes. **Superior Court Trial Lawyers** deals with the justiciability of antitrust policy and the restraints on freedom potentially created by RTPs, but ultimately concludes that the freedom of the market mechanism is a higher freedom than that of the right to associate in order to fix prices.

Legislative frameworks differ in the extent to which they allow or encourage private action on antitrust matters. Clearly the injured parties in any particular case may have a greater incentive to pursue an offending action than has the competition authority. But a private harm is not necessarily a social harm. The remaining extracts in this section touch on these questions. The White Paper **Opening Markets** outlines a proposed change in policy in the UK, whilst the **US Code** and the **American Stores** case illustrate the considerable (but necessarily ultimately constrained) scope for private action afforded by the US legal framework.

2.1 Department of Trade and Industry, *Review of Restrictive Trade Practices Policy*, Cm. 331 (HMSO, London, 1988)

IS EC LAW SUFFICIENT?

3.10 Article 85 of the Treaty of Rome prohibits anti-competitive agreements if they affect trade between Member States of the EC. The boundaries of Community jurisdiction are difficult to draw because of this inherently uncertain criterion [. . .].

Agreements which appear purely domestic may still fall within the scope of Community law. For example, an agreement between two or more UK parties may affect trade between Member States because it makes it more difficult for competing manufacturers from other Member States to sell into the UK market. Furthermore, the need for UK companies to take account of EC competition law has grown as business has become increasingly international.

3.11 There will, nevertheless, always be a large number of restrictive agreements which fall outside the scope of Article 85 but which national authorities may well want to regulate. The Government are concerned to be able to control those agreements and practices which, though small in terms of their effect on intra-Community trade, have a big anti-competitive effect in national, regional or local markets and which affect the ordinary consumer.

3.12 A second, practical consideration is the lack of resources for this task within the European Commission. This means that there are considerable delays in dealing with agreements and practices which fall within the scope of Article 85. It is therefore desirable to retain the ability to take speedier action at national level against restrictive agreements.

3.13 In short, the Government believe that on its own EC law does not constitute a complete instrument for the effective and comprehensive control of restrictive practices in the UK. Notably, there will be many instances of agreements which are unlikely to be regarded as affecting trade between Member States or, while affecting trade between Member States, national considerations suggest need to be tackled with a higher degree of priority than the European Commission's resources alone will permit.

3.14 There is therefore an overwhelming case for new national legislation to complement the powers under EC legislation. Other EC Member States have their own national laws and France, for example, has recently reformed its law for the same reasons.

COMPATIBILITY WITH EC LAW

3.15 The effects-based prohibition which the Government propose has the added benefit of alignment with existing EC law for the sake of consistency and simplicity. Increasingly UK companies must have close regard to EC competition rules. Much greater compatibility between EC and UK law than the present system affords will make the latter more easily comprehensible and workable for the business community.

3.16 The Community's focus in domestic agreements and practices inevitably entails an overlap between Community and national law. If agreements have been prohibited under EC law, the UK cannot grant an exemption. But there is a potential for conflict in decisions – for example in the case of agreements which have been exempted under Community law but which the UK authorities may wish to prohibit under domestic law. Furthermore, businesses will still have to deal with two laws and two authorities.

3.17 Maximising compatibility should reduce both the potential for conflict and the burden on firms. Potential conflicts can also be minimised by continuing close liaison between the UK and EC authorities and by incorporating into UK law as much of the principles of Community law as seems appropriate. Similarly the burden on business ought to be reduced not least since firms will be operating under a more harmonised regime.

The **Metro** case, below, demonstrates the nature of Article 85. The case concerned a selective dealing agreement which, although depressing price competition, did facilitate enhanced non-price competition. Given the circumstances of the market, such competition was found to be within the objectives of

Article 85. In the **Pronuptia** case, the Advocate General at the European Court of Justice assesses a franchise agreement by way of a comparative study of other antitrust systems. A clear distinction is made between inter-brand, and intra-brand, competition, a distinction crucial to the proper evaluation of vertical agreements. In the **Superior Court Trial Lawyers** case, the Supreme Court of the USA reviews the dangers to society which the antitrust laws are designed to repel.

2.2 *Metro SB-Grossmarkte GmbH & Co. KG* v. *Commission of the European Communities* Case 26/76, Court of Justice of the European Communities [1977] ECR 1875, [1978] 2 CMLR 1, [1978] FSR 400

[. . .]
20. The requirement contained in Articles 3 and 85 of the EEC Treaty that competition shall not be distorted implies the existence on the market of workable competition, that is to say the degree of competition necessary to ensure the observance of the basic requirements and the attainment of the objectives of the Treaty, in particular the creation of a single market achieving conditions similar to those of a domestic market.

In accordance with this requirement the nature and intensiveness of competition may vary to an extent dictated by the products or services in question and the economic structure of the relevant market sectors.

In the sector covering the production of high quality and technically advanced consumer durables, where a relatively small number of large- and medium-scale producers offer a varied range of items which, or so consumers may consider, are readily interchangeable, the structure of the market does not preclude the existence of a variety of channels of distribution adapted to the peculiar characteristics of the various producers and to the requirements of the various categories of consumers.

On this view the Commission was justified in recognizing that selective distribution systems constituted, together with others, an aspect of competition which accords with Article 85(1), provided that resellers are chosen on the basis of objective criteria of a qualitative nature relating to the technical qualifications of the reseller and his staff and the suitability of his trading premises and that such conditions are laid down uniformly for all potential resellers and are not applied in a discriminatory fashion.

It is true that in such systems of distribution price competition is not generally emphasized either as an exclusive or indeed as a principal factor.

This is particularly so when, as in the present case, access to the distribution network is subject to conditions exceeding the requirements of an appropriate distribution of the products.

However, although price competition is so important that it can never be eliminated it does not constitute the only effective form of competition or that to which absolute priority must in all circumstances be accorded. The powers conferred upon the Commission under Article 85(3) show that the requirements for the maintenance of workable competition may be reconciled with the safeguarding of objectives of a different nature and that to this end certain restrictions on competition are permissible, provided that they are essential to the attainment of those objectives and that they do not result in the elimination of competition for a substantial part of the Common Market.

For specialist wholesalers and retailers the desire to maintain a certain price level, which corresponds to the desire to preserve, in the interests of consumers, the possibility of the continued existence of this channel of distribution in conjunction with new methods of distribution based on a different type of competition policy, forms one of the objectives which may be pursued without necessarily falling under the prohibition contained in Article 85(1), and, if it does fall thereunder, either wholly or in part, coming within the framework of Article 85(3).

This argument is strengthened if, in addition, such conditions promote improved competition inasmuch as it relates to factors rather than prices. [. . .]

2.3 *Pronuptia de Paris GmbH, Frankfurt am Main* v. *Rosalinde Irmgard Schillgalis, carrying on business under the name Pronuptia de Paris Irmgard Schillgalis, Hamburg* Case 161/84, Court of Justice of the European Communities [1986] ECR 353, [1986] 1 CMLR 414

[For the facts of this case, see Section 15.1.]

Opinion of the Advocate General:

[. . .]

Within the Community it is only in the judgment of the Bundesgerichtshof of 23 March 1982 (Meierei-Zentrale, Wirtschaft und Wettbewerb 1982, p. 781) that I have been able to find a judicial ruling on the competition law aspects of franchise agreements. In that judgment the prohibition of resale maintenance laid down in Article 15 of the Gesetz gegen Wettbewerbsbeschränkungen [German Law on restrictive trade practices] was considered applicable to a franchise agreement in which resale prices were fixed. In its 1981 report *Full-line Forcing and Tie-In-Sales*, however, the British Monopolies and Mergers Commission did take the view that exclusive supply obligations could in certain circumstances be significant from the point of view of competition law.

[I]n the United States the term franchise agreement was initially used in a very wide sense. According to the more recent restricted use of the term (which served as a model for the European development) a franchise is defined as a licence from the owner of a trade-mark or trade-name permitting another to sell a product or service under that mark or name (*Black's Law Dictionary*, 5th edn., 1979; Von Kalinowski, *Antitrust Laws and Trade Regulation*, vol. 2, paragraph 6H.01/1981 supplement).

In the United States, as in the United Kingdom, exclusive purchase obligations contained in a franchise agreement are not automatically regarded as 'tying arrangements' prohibited by competition law. In appropriate market conditions they may however fall under that prohibition. Since the 1977 *Sylvania* judgment the 'rule of reason' has been applied to vertical territorial restriction clauses in order to ascertain whether there is restriction of competition (in particular horizontal restriction). Contract provisions regarding resale prices are regarded as prohibited *per se* where it appears that the franchisor, not content with mere price recommendations, is attempting one way or another to force the franchisee to apply his suggestions or recommendations. In the *Sylvania* judgment the 'rule of reason' was applied to territorial restrictions, in particular restrictions on premises, such as those at issue in the *Pronuptia* case, notwithstanding the resulting restrictions on competition between retailers of Sylvania products. Despite the concomitant restrictions on 'intra-brand' competition, vertical restrictions on competition such as those at issue in the *Sylvania* case were regarded as beneficial for 'inter-brand' competition. Only in certain cases and on the basis of their actual economic consequences may such vertical restrictions of competition be held to be caught by the *per se* prohibition contained in American anti-trust legislation. Having regard to the later American legal practice the decisive question seems to be whether or not there is effective competition with other products on the relevant market. In speaking of the American practice I should point out that in the United States the problem peculiar to the EEC of separate national markets with prices which are often widely divergent does not exist. A single internal market was achieved long ago in the United States, so that the problem of obstacles to parallel imports does not arise.

[. . .]

In the American case-law it seems that the market position of the undertakings concerned and the distinction between the vertical relationship between the franchisor and franchisee and the horizontal relationship between each of the franchisees and their competitors are of particular importance in assessing such agreements from the point of view of competition law. Except in extraordinary market conditions, it seems that inter-brand competition is considered more important for the maintenance of effective competition than intra-brand competition. In the United States the imposition of fixed prices by franchisors seems to be regarded as automatically contrary to the prohibition of price agreements, just as it is in the Federal Republic of Germany. For the rest, the judicial practice in the United States and in three of the larger Member States of the EEC seems to be to judge each agreement on its own merits, taking into account its specific provisions and, in so far as competition aspects are to be dealt with, the specific circumstances of the relevant market. The last mentioned factor is particularly relevant with regard to the various exclusivity clauses to be found in franchise agreements.

[. . .]

I think the following criteria [are] relevant to the assessment of franchise agreements [. . .].

(a) Since the important point for the application of Article 85(1) is, according to all the judgments referred to, the horizontal effects of vertical agreements (for instance the exclusion of certain competitors, such as parallel importers), it seems to me that the question whether or not a franchise agreement results in a fair division of costs and benefits as between franchisor and franchisee is not in itself relevant to the question of whether Article 85(1) is applicable. The same is true in principle of specific obligations of the franchisee, such as the obligation of specialization [. . .] the obligation to advertise [. . .] and the obligation to set up and run the shop in a particular manner [. . .]. With regard to the vertical obligations I think Article 85(1) can only apply when it can be shown in a particular case that they cause injury to third parties (competitors, suppliers or purchasers), which will seldom be the case where there are adequate alternative chains of distribution for similar products.

(b) If the main issue is thus the 'horizontal' effects, or more correctly the results of the agreement for third parties, then [. . .] particular attention must be paid to the questions whether (i) parallel imports remain possible [. . .] (ii) whether, having regard to the market position of the suppliers concerned, access to the market for other suppliers or dealers is restricted [. . .] and (iii) whether the agreement results in price increases [. . .] or involves price-fixing by means of contractual obligations or concerted practices on the part of the franchisor, its subsidiaries and its various franchisees.

With regard to this last criterion I am of the view, contrary to the American and German case-law referred to, that the Court's judgments regarding resale price maintenance and other forms of price agreement need only be applied in a case where a party is in a position of economic strength on the local markets concerned, or where price maintenance is also applied by competitors [. . .].

2.4 *Federal Trade Commission* v. *Superior Court Trial Lawyers Association* Supreme Court of the United States 493 U.S. 411, 110 S. Ct. 768; 1990 U.S. LEXIS 638,1; 107 L. Ed. 2d 851

[. . .]

A group of lawyers in private practice who regularly acted as court-appointed counsel for indigent defendants in District of Columbia criminal cases agreed at a meeting of the Superior Court Trial Lawyers Association (SCTLA) to stop providing such representation until the District increased group members' compensation. The boycott had a severe impact on the District's criminal justice system, and the District government capitulated to the lawyers' demands. After the lawyers returned to work, petitioner Federal Trade Commission (FTC) filed a complaint against SCTLA and four of its officers (respondents), alleging that they had entered into a conspiracy to fix prices and to conduct a boycott that constituted unfair methods of competition in violation of section 5 of the FTC Act [. . .] [T]he FTC ruled that the boycott was illegal *per se* and entered an order prohibiting respondents from initiating future such boycotts. The Court of Appeals, although acknowledging that the boycott was a 'classic restraint of trade' in violation of section 1 of the Sherman Act, vacated the FTC order. Noting that the boycott was meant to convey a political message to the public, the court concluded that it contained an element of expression warranting First Amendment protection and that, under *United States* v. *O'Brien*, 391 U.S. 367, an incidental restriction on such expression could not be justified unless it was no greater than was essential to an important governmental interest. Reasoning that this test could not be satisfied by the application of an otherwise appropriate *per se* rule, but instead requires the enforcement agency to prove rather than presume that the evil against which the antitrust laws are directed looms in the conduct it condemns, the court remanded for a determination whether respondents possessed 'significant market power'.

Justice Stevens:

The FTC characterized respondents' conduct as 'a conspiracy to fix prices and to conduct a boycott' and concluded that they were engaged in 'unfair methods of competition in violation of section 5 of the Federal Trade Commission Act'.

The [Administrative Law Judge – a quasi-judicial official in the Federal Trade Commission] nevertheless concluded that the complaint should be dismissed because the District officials, who presumably represented the victim of the boycott, recognized that its net effect was beneficial. The increase in fees would attract more [trial] lawyers, enabling them to reduce their caseloads and provide better representation for their clients. 'I see no point', he concluded, 'in striving resolutely for an antitrust triumph in this sensitive area when the particular case can be disposed of on a more pragmatic basis – there was no harm done.' The ALJ's pragmatic moderation found no favor with the FTC. Like the ALJ, the FTC rejected each of respondents' defenses. It held that their 'coercive, concerted refusal to deal' had the 'purpose and effect of raising prices' and was illegal *per se* [. . .].

The Court of Appeals vacated the FTC order and remanded for a determination whether respondents possessed 'significant market power'. The court began its analysis by recognizing that absent any special First Amendment protection, the boycott, 'constituted a classic restraint of trade within the meaning of Section 1 of the Sherman Act' [. . .]. The Court of Appeals [. . .] concluded [. . .] that 'the [. . .] boycott did contain an element of expression warranting First Amendment protection.' [. . .] It noted that boycotts have historically been used as a dramatic means of expression and that respondents intended to convey a political message to the public at large. It therefore concluded that under *United*

States v. *O'Brien*, 391 U.S. 367 (1968), a restriction on this form of expression could not be justified unless it is no greater than is essential to an important governmental interest. This test, the court reasoned, could not be satisfied by the application of an otherwise appropriate *per se* rule, but instead required the enforcement agency to 'prove rather than presume that the evil against which the Sherman Act is directed looms in the conduct it condemns.' [. . .]

[. . .]

[I]t is not our task to pass judgment upon the social utility or political wisdom of price-fixing agreements. [The] respondents' boycott 'constituted a classic restraint of trade within the meaning of Section 1 of the Sherman Act'. [. . .] As such, it also violated the prohibition against unfair methods of competition in section 5 of the FTC Act [. . .]. Prior to the boycott [trial] lawyers were in competition with one another, each deciding independently whether and how often to offer to provide services to the District at [the previous] rates. The agreement among the [. . .] lawyers was designed to obtain higher prices for their services and was implemented by a concerted refusal to serve an important customer in the market for legal services and, indeed, the only customer in the market for the particular services that [such lawyers] offered. 'This constriction of supply is the essence of "price-fixing", whether it be accomplished by agreeing upon a price, which will decrease the quantity demanded, or by agreeing upon an output, which will increase the price offered.' [. . .]

[. . .] The horizontal arrangement among these competitors was unquestionably a 'naked restraint' on price and output: see *National Collegiate Athletic Assn.* v. *Board of Regents of Univ. of Okla.*, 468 U.S. 85, 110 (1984).

It is of course true that the city purchases respondents' services because it has a constitutional duty to provide representation to indigent defendants. It is likewise true that the quality of representation may improve when rates are increased. Yet neither of these facts is an acceptable justification for an otherwise unlawful restraint of trade. As we have remarked before, the 'Sherman Act reflects a legislative judgment that ultimately competition will produce not only lower prices, but also better goods and services': *National Soc. of Professional Engineers* v. *United States*, 435 U.S. 679, 695 (1978). This judgment 'recognizes that all elements of a bargain – quality, service, safety, and durability – and not just the immediate cost, are favourably affected by the free opportunity to select among alternative offers.' [. . .] That is equally so when the quality of legal advocacy, rather than engineering design, is at issue.

The social justifications proffered for respondents' restraint of trade thus do not make it any less unlawful. The statutory policy underlying the Sherman Act 'precludes inquiry into the question whether competition is good or bad' (*ibid*). [. . .] Respondents' argument, like that made by the petitioners in *Professional Engineers*, ultimately asks us to find that their boycott is permissible because the price it seeks to set is reasonable. But it was settled shortly after the Sherman Act was passed that it 'is no excuse that the prices fixed are themselves reasonable. See, e.g. *United States* v. *Trenton Potteries Co.*, 273 U.S. 392, 397–398 (1927); *United States* v. *Trans-Missouri Freight Assn.*, 166 U.S. 290, 340–341 (1897); *Catalano, Inc.* v. *Target Sales, Inc.*, 446 U.S. 643, 647 (1980). Respondents' agreement is not outside the coverage of the Sherman Act simply because its objective was the enactment of favorable legislation.

[. . .]

It of course remains true that 'no violation of the Act can be predicated upon mere attempts to influence the passage or enforcement of laws' (*Noerr* case [356 U.S. 127 (1961)] at 135) even if the defendants' sole purpose is to impose a restraint upon the trade of their competitors: *ibid.*, at 138–140. But in the *Noerr* case the alleged restraint of trade was the intended consequence of public action; in this case the boycott was the means by which respondents sought to obtain favorable legislation. The restraint of trade that was implemented while the boycott lasted would have had precisely the same anticompetitive consequences during that period even if no legislation had been enacted. In *Noerr*, the desired legislation would have created the restraint on the truckers' competition; in this case the emergency legislative response to the boycott put an end to the restraint.

Indeed, respondents' theory of *Noerr* was largely disposed of by our opinion in *Allied Tube and Conduit Corp.* v. *Indian Head, Inc.*, 486 U.S. 492 (1988). We held that the *Noerr* doctrine does not extend to 'every concerted effort that is genuinely intended to influence governmental action': 486 U.S., at 503. We explained:

> If all such conduct were immunized then, for example, competitors would be free to enter into horizontal price agreements as long as they wished to propose that price as an appropriate level for governmental rate-making or price supports. But see *Georgia* v. *Pennsylvania R. Co.* 324 U.S. 439, 456–463 (1945). Horizontal conspiracies or boycotts designed to exact higher prices or other economic advantages from the government would be immunized on the ground that they are genuinely intended to influence the government to agree to the conspirators' terms. But see *Georgia* v. *Evans*, 316 U.S. 159 (1942). Firms could claim immunity for boycotts or horizontal output restrictions on the ground that they are intended to dramatize the plight of their industry and spur legislative action. (*ibid.*)

[. . .]

SCTLA argues that if its conduct would otherwise be prohibited by the Sherman Act and the Federal Trade Commission Act, it is nonetheless protected by the First Amendment rights recognized in *NAACP* v. *Claiborne Hardware Co.*, 458 U.S. 886 (1982). That case arose after black citizens boycotted white merchants in Claiborne County, Mississippi. The white merchants sued under state law to recover losses from the boycott. We found that the 'right of the States to regulate economic activity could not justify a complete prohibition against a nonviolent, politically motivated boycott designed to force governmental and economic change and to effectuate rights guaranteed by the Constitution itself': *ibid.*, at 914. We accordingly held that 'the nonviolent elements of petitioners' activities are entitled to the protection of the First Amendment': *ibid.*, at 915.

[. . .]

[. . .] Respondents' concerted action in refusing to accept further [. . .] assignments until their fees were increased was thus a plain violation of the antitrust laws.

The *per se* rules are, of course, the product of judicial interpretations of the Sherman Act, but the rules nevertheless have the same force and effect as any other statutory commands. Moreover, while the *per se* rule against price fixing and boycotts is indeed justified in part by 'administrative convenience', the Court of Appeals erred in describing the prohibition as justified only by such concerns. The *per se* rules also reflect a long-standing judgment that the prohibited practices by their nature have 'a substantial potential for impact on competition', *Jefferson Parish Hospital District No. 2* v. *Hyde*, 466 U.S. 2, 16 (1984). . . . In our opinion in *Jefferson Parish Hospital District No. 2* v. *Hyde*, 466 U.S. 2 (1984), we noted that 'the rationale for *per se* rules in part is to avoid a burdensome inquiry into actual market conditions in situations where the likelihood of anticompetitive conduct is so great as to render unjustified the costs of determining whether the particular case at bar involves anticompetitive conduct. See, e.g. *Arizona* v. *Maricopa County Medical Society*, 457 U.S. 332, 350–351 (1982)'; *ibid.*, at 15–16, n. 25. The Court of Appeals overlooked the words 'in part' in that footnote, and also overlooked the statement in text that 'there must be a substantial potential for impact on competition in order to justify *per se* condemnation': *ibid.*, at 16. As we explained in *Professional Engineers*, the rule of reason in antitrust law generates

> two complementary categories of antitrust analysis. In the first category are agreements whose nature and necessary effect are so plainly anticompetitive that no elaborate study of the industry is needed to establish their illegality – they are 'illegal *per se*'. In the second category are agreements whose competitive effect can only be evaluated by analyzing the facts peculiar to

> the business, the history of the restraint, and the reason why it was imposed. (435 U.S., at 692)

'Once experience with a particular kind of restraint enables the Court to predict with confidence that the rule of reason will condemn it, it has applied a conclusive presumption that the restraint is unreasonable': *Arizona* v. *Maricopa County Medical Society*, 457 U.S. 332, 344 (1982).

The *per se* rules in antitrust law serve purposes analogous to *per se* restrictions upon, for example, stunt flying in congested areas or speeding. Laws prohibiting stunt flying or setting speed limits are justified by the State's interest in protecting human life and property. Perhaps most violations of such rules actually cause no harm. No doubt many experienced drivers and pilots can operate much more safely, even at prohibited speeds, than the average citizen.

If the especially skilled drivers and pilots were to paint messages on their cars, or attach streamers to their planes, their conduct would have an expressive component. High speeds and unusual maneuvers would help to draw attention to their messages. Yet the laws may nonetheless be enforced against these skilled persons without proof that their conduct was actually harmful or dangerous.

In part, the justification for these *per se* rules is rooted in administrative convenience. They are also supported, however, by the observation that every speeder and every stunt pilot poses some threat to the community. An unpredictable event may overwhelm the skills of the best driver or pilot, even if the proposed course of action was entirely prudent when initiated. A bad driver going slowly may be more dangerous that a good driver going quickly, but a good driver who obeys the law is safer still.

So it is with boycotts and price fixing. Every such horizontal arrangement among competitors poses some threat to the free market. A small participant in the market is, obviously, less likely to cause persistent damage than a large participant. Other participants in the market may act quickly and effectively to take the small participant's place. For reasons including market inertia and information failures, however, a small conspirator may be able to impede competition over some period of time. Given an appropriate set of circumstances and some luck, the period can be long enough to inflict real injury upon particular consumers or competitors.

As Justice Douglas observed in an oft-quoted footnote to his *United States* v. *Socony-Vacuum Oil Co.*, 310 U.S. 150 (1940), opinion:

> Price-fixing agreements may or may not be aimed at complete elimination of price competition. The group making those agreements may or may not have power to control the market. But the fact that the group cannot control the market prices does not necessarily mean that the agreement as to prices has no utility to the members of the combination. The effectiveness of price-fixing agreements is dependent on many factors, such as competitive tactics, position in the industry, the formula underlying pricing policies. Whatever economic justification particular price-fixing agreements may be thought to have, the law does not permit an inquiry into their reasonableness. They are all banned because of their actual or potential threat to the central nervous system of the economy. (*ibid.*, at 225–226, n. 59)

[. . .]

Of course, some boycotts and some price-fixing agreements are more pernicious than others; some are only partly successful, and some may only succeed when they are buttressed by other causative factors, such as political influence. But an assumption that, absent proof of market power, the boycott disclosed by this record was totally harmless – when overwhelming testimony demonstrated that it almost produced a crisis in the administration of criminal justice in the District and when it achieved its economic goal – is flatly inconsistent with the clear course of our antitrust jurisprudence.

Conspirators need not achieve the dimensions of a monopoly, or even a degree of market power any greater than that already disclosed by this record, to warrant condemnation under the antitrust laws.

FURTHER READING

For a commentary on this case, see:

Calkins, S. (1991) 'The October 1989 Supreme Court Term and antitrust: power access and legitimacy', 59 *Antitrust Law Journal*, 339.

On the application of the Sherman Act to boycotts, see the extensive discussion in:

Mattern, S. (1992), 'Free speech, free markets and the *per se* rule of antitrust', 21 *Southwestern University Law Review*, 1443.

As mentioned above, an important aspect of competition law regimes concerns the access allowed to private plaintiffs. In the USA, private enforcement comprises the great majority of antitrust litigation. Private plaintiffs are encouraged by the **Clayton Act** to bring such actions; the reward of treble damages will often justify the heavy investment in antitrust litigation. Private actions were further facilitated by the **American Stores** judgment, which gave private plaintiffs the right to seek the divestment of an anticompetitive merger. The UK White Paper, **Opening Markets: New Policy on Restrictive Trade Practices**, acknowledges the advantages of private actions, as does a more recent Green Paper on monopoly control, **Abuse of Market Power: A Consultative Document on Possible Legislative Options**, Cm. 2100 (HMSO, London, 1992).

2.5 Department of Trade and Industry, *Opening Markets: New Policy on Restrictive Trade Practices*, Cm. 729 (HMSO, London, 1989)

[. . .]

5.15 The Government's proposal that the new legislation should make it a duty not to operate a prohibited agreement, owed by the parties to all those who may be affected by a contravention of the law, has attracted support but also some criticism. Any person adversely affected by the operation of an unregistered agreement may bring an action under the RTPA and the Government remain convinced that those who suffer loss as a result of failure by others to comply with the law should continue to have access to compensation under the new legislation. Businesses which contravene the law will therefore face the dual cost of penalties and damages.

5.16 The Government hope that the part played by private actions will grow over time to form a significant part of the enforcement system. The threat of such actions, with the risk of damages, would add to the deterrent effect of the new system. There are signs of a growing interest in the possibility of taking action under existing RTP law and the Government are considering whether there are positive steps which could be taken to encourage this trend under the new law.

5.17 The Government's consideration of which measures to take to promote private actions under RTP legislation, such as making provision for class actions or the introduction of contingency fees, will be completed in the context of other decisions yet to be taken, for instance, on aspects of reform of the legal profession. However, it is likely that, where a litigant has incurred costs to establish that an agreement is anti-competitive, the legislation will permit these to be included in any damages claim.

5.18 The Green Paper *Contingency Fees* (Cm. 571) published earlier this year explained that experience in the US of litigation for damages differs for several reasons from that in England and Wales, and that the impact of each of these is difficult to establish. The proposed RTP legislation will involve a further difference: the law will be based on the EC system in which all anti-competitive agreements are caught by the prohibition and can generally only be exempted by the EC Commission, whereas in the US these two steps are taken together and the courts reach decisions on the net effect of an agreement on competition. Private actions are therefore unlikely to become as significant a feature of the law as they are in the US and it is likely that in most cases, one or other party will seek a decision from the DGFT to support its arguments. This will not be a necessity but the legislation will recognise the situation by requiring the judge in a private action to order a stay in proceedings where an exemption decision is pending. The courts will also have a discretion to ask the DGFT to submit an opinion in a private case.

5.19 The Government are in addition exploring what organisational measures could be taken to ensure a high level of consistency in court proceedings arising from RTP law, whether arising from a case heard by the tribunal or from a private action. The further possibility of such measures encompassing cases brought in UK courts under Articles 85 and 86 of the EEC Treaty will be considered.

[. . .]

2.6 United States Code (Clayton Act) 15 USC [Section] 15 (1993)

15. SUITS BY PERSONS INJURED

[. . .] any person who shall be injured in his business or property by reason of anything forbidden in the antitrust laws may sue therefor in any district court of the United States in the district in which the defendant resides or is found or has an agent, without respect to the amount in controversy, and shall recover threefold the damages by him sustained, and the cost of suit, including a reasonable attorney's fee [. . .].

2.7 *California* v. *American Stores Co.* No. 89-258 Supreme Court of the United States 495 U.S. 271; 110 S. Ct. 1853; 1990 U.S. LEXIS 2214; 109 L. Ed. 2d 240; 58 U.S.L.W. 4529; 1990-1 Trade Cas. (CCH) P69,003

STEVENS, J., delivered the opinion for a unanimous Supreme Court:

By merging with a major competitor, American Stores Co. (American) more than doubled the number of supermarkets that it owns in California. The State sued, claiming that the merger violates the federal antitrust laws and will harm consumers in 62 California cities. The complainant prayed for a preliminary injunction requiring

American to operate the acquired stores separately until the case is decided, and then to divest itself of all of the acquired assets located in California. The District Court granted a preliminary injunction preventing American from integrating the operations of the two companies. The Court of Appeals for the Ninth Circuit agreed with the District Court's conclusion that California had made an adequate showing of probable success on the merits, but held that the relief granted by the District Court exceeded its authority under [section] 16 of the Clayton Act, 38 Stat. 737, as amended, 15 U.S.C. [section] 26. In its view, the 'injunctive relief [. . .] against threatened loss or damage' authorized by [section] 16 does not encompass divestiture, and therefore the 'indirect divestiture' effected by the preliminary injunction was impermissible.

[. . .]

Section 15 [of the Clayton Act] grants the federal district courts jurisdiction 'to prevent and restrain violations of this Act' when United States attorneys 'institute proceedings in equity to prevent and restrain such violations' through petitions 'praying that such violation shall be enjoined or otherwise prohibited.'

Section 16 entitles '[a]ny person, firm, corporation, or association [. . .] to sue for and have injunctive relief [. . .] against threatened loss or damage by a violation of the antitrust laws [. . .] when and under the same conditions and principles as injunctive relief against threatened conduct that will cause loss or damage is granted by courts of equity.'

[. . .]

It is agreed that the general language of [section] 15, which provides that antitrust violations 'shall be enjoined or otherwise prohibited', is broad enough to authorize divestiture. Indeed, in Government actions divestiture is the preferred remedy for an illegal merger or acquisition. As we wrote in the Du Pont case:

> Divestiture or dissolution has traditionally been the remedy for Sherman Act violations whose heart is intercorporate combination and control, and it is reasonable to think immediately of the same remedy when [section] 7 of the Clayton Act, which particularizes the Sherman Act standard of illegality, is involved. Of the very few litigated [section] 7 cases which have been reported, most decreed divestiture as a matter of course. Divestiture has been called the most important of antitrust remedies. It is simple, relatively easy to administer, and sure. It should always be in the forefront of a court's mind when a violation of [section] 7 has been found. (*United States* v. *E. I. du Pont de Nemours and Co.*, 366 U.S. 316, 329-331 (1961))

On its face, the simple grant of authority in [section] 16 to 'have injunctive relief' would seem to encompass divestiture just as plainly as the comparable language in [section] 15. Certainly [section] 16's reference to 'injunctive relief [. . .] against threatened loss or damage' differs from [section] 15's grant of jurisdiction to 'prevent and restrain violations', but it obviously does not follow that one grant encompasses remedies excluded from the other. Indeed, we think it could plausibly be argued that [section] 16's terms are the more expansive. In any event, however, as the Court of Appeals for the First Circuit correctly observed, [section] 16 'states no restrictions or exceptions to the forms of injunctive relief a private plaintiff may seek, or that a court may order [. . .]. Rather, the statutory language indicates Congress' intention that traditional principles of equity govern the grant of injunctive relief (754 F. 2d, at 416). We agree that the plain text of [section] 16 authorizes divestiture decrees to remedy [section] 7 violations.

If we assume that the merger violated the antitrust laws, and if we agree with the District Court's finding that the conduct of the merged enterprise threatens economic harm to California consumers, the literal text of [section] 16 is plainly sufficient to authorize injunctive relief, including an order of divestiture, that will prohibit that conduct from causing that harm. This interpretation is consistent with our precedents, which have upheld injunctions issued pursuant to [section] 16 regardless of whether they were mandatory or prohibitory in character. See *Zenith Radio Corp.* v. *Hazeltine Research, Inc.*, 395 U.S. 100, 129–133 (1969) (reinstating injunction that required defendants to withdraw from patent pools); see also *Silver* v. *New York Stock Exchange*, 373 U.S. 341,345, 365 (1963) (reinstating judgment for defendants in suit to compel installation of wire services). We have recognized when construing [section] 16 that it was enacted 'not merely to provide private relief, but [. . .] to serve as well the high purpose of enforcing the antitrust laws': *Zenith Radio Corp.*, 395 U.S., at 130–131. We have accordingly applied the section 'with this purpose in mind, and with the knowledge that the remedy it affords, like other equitable remedies, is flexible and capable of nice "adjustment and reconciliation between the public interest and private needs as well as between competing private claims": *ibid.*, quoting *Hecht Co.* v. *Bowles*, 321 U.S. 321, 329–330 (1944). Finally, by construing [section] 16 to encompass divestiture decrees we are better able than is American to harmonize the section with its statutory context. The Act's other provisions manifest a clear intent to encourage vigorous private litigation against anticompetitive mergers. Section 7 itself creates a relatively expansive definition of antitrust liability: To show that a merger is unlawful, a plaintiff need only prove that its effect 'may be substantially to lessen competition': Clayton Act [section] 7, 38 Stat. 731, 15 U.S.C. [section] 18 [. . .]. See *Brown Shoe Co.* v. *United States*, 370 U.S. 294, 323 (1962) [. . .].

Section 16, construed to authorize a private divestiture remedy when appropriate in light of equitable principles, fits well in a statutory scheme that favors private enforcement, subjects mergers to searching scrutiny, and regards divestiture as the remedy best suited to redress the ills of an anticompetitive merger.

Although we do not believe the statutory language is ambiguous, we nonetheless consider the legislative history that persuaded the Ninth Circuit to place a narrow construction on [section] 16. To understand that history, however, it is necessary to place the statute in its historical perspective.

The Sherman Act became law just a century ago. It matured some 15 years later, when, under the administration of Theodore Roosevelt, the Sherman Act 'was finally being used against trusts of the dimension that had called it into being, and with enough energy to justify the boast that the President was using a Big Stick': W. Letwin, *Law and Economic Policy in America*, 240 (1965). Two of the most famous prosecutions concluded in 1911, with decisions from this Court endorsing the 'Rule of Reason' as the principal guide to the construction of the Sherman Act's general language: *Standard Oil Co. of New Jersey* v. *United States*, 221 U.S. 1; *United States* v. *American Tobacco Co.*, 221 U.S. 106. In consequence of the violations found in those two cases, wide-ranging injunctions were entered requiring the separation of the 'oil trust' and the 'tobacco trust' into a number of independent, but still significant, companies. The relief granted received mixed reviews. In some quarters, the cases were hailed as great triumphs over the forces of monopoly; in others, they were regarded as Pyrrhic victories.

Concern about the adequacy of the Sherman Act's prohibition against combinations in restraint of trade prompted President Wilson to make a special address to Congress in 1914 recommending that the antitrust laws be strengthened: *The New Democracy: The public papers of Woodrow Wilson '81–89* (R. Baker and W. Dodd (eds.) 1926). Congressman Clayton, the Chairman of the House Judiciary Committee, promptly appointed a subcommittee to prepare the legislation. The bill drafted by the subcommittee contained most of the provisions that were eventually enacted into the law now known as the Clayton Act. The statute reenacted certain provisions of the Sherman Act and added new provisions of both a substantive and procedural character: Letwin, *Law and Economic Policy in America*, at 272–273; A. Link, Wilson: *The New Freedom*, 426 (1956). Thus, [section] 4 of the Sherman Act, which authorizes equitable relief in actions brought by the United States, was reenacted as [section] 15 of the Clayton Act, while [section] 16 filled a gap in the Sherman Act by authorizing equitable relief in private actions. Section 7 of the Clayton Act made stock acquisitions of competing companies more vulnerable, and [sections] 4 and 5 gave special procedural advantages to private litigants. The reform project had broad social significance, and it is obvious that the Act as a whole is fairly characterized as important remedial legislation. Some proponents of reform, however, were critical of the bill for not going further.

Thus, for example, proposals that were never enacted would have expressly authorized private individuals to bring suit for the dissolution of corporations adjudged to have violated the law and for appointment of receivers to wind up the corporation's affairs. Samuel Untermyer, a New York lawyer who urged Congress to give private plaintiffs express authority to seek dissolution decrees, stated his views in a colloquy with Congressman John Floyd during a hearing on the bill before a subcommittee of the House Judiciary Committee. Floyd told Untermyer that 'We did not intend by section 13 to give the individual the same power to bring a suit to dissolve the corporation that the Government has', and added that the committee Members had discussed the matter very thoroughly. Untermyer replied that 'the very relief that the man needs nine times out of ten is the dissolution of the corporation, because [. . .] it may not be doing any specific act of illegality, but its very existence, in violation of law, is the thing that is injuring him': Hearings on Trust Legislation before the House Committee on the Judiciary, 63d Cong., 2d Sess. 842-846 (1914) (House Hearings).

Two weeks later, Louis Brandeis, testifying on behalf of the administration before the same committee, was asked whether he favored a proposal 'to give the individual the right to file a bill in equity for the dissolution of one of these combinations, the same right which the Government now has and which it is its duty to perform.' Brandeis responded that the proposal was not sound and added:

> It seems to me that the right to change the status [of the combination], which is the right of dissolution, is a right which ought to be exercised only by the Government, although the right for full redress for grievances and protection against future wrongs is a right which every individual ought to enjoy.
>
> Now, all of this procedure ought to be made so as to facilitate, so far as possible, the enforcement of the law in aid, on the one hand, of the Government, and in aid, on the other hand, of the individual. But that fundamental principle is correct, that the Government ought to have the right, and the sole right, to determine whether the circumstances are such as to call for a dissolution of an alleged trust. (*ibid.*, at 649-650)

[. . .] We have already concluded that the suggested distinction between divestiture and injunctions that prohibit future conduct is illusory. These excerpts, moreover, from the legislative history provide even less support for such a categorical distinction than does the text of [section] 16 itself.

[. . .] As the New York Court of Appeals ominously declared before affirming a decree against the North River Sugar Refining Company, dissolution was a 'judgment [. . .] of corporate death', which 'represent[ed] the extreme rigor of the law.' This meaning is evident from the text of the Senate amendment proposing private dissolution suits, which provided for a receiver to administer the doomed corporation's assets.

The concept of dissolution, of course, also encompassed remedies comparable to divestiture, or to our present-day understanding of dissolution. It was one thing to dissolve a pool, trust, combination, or merger, and quite another to atomize, or to revoke the charter of, a large corporation. In the early part of this century, however, new forms of corporate organization were arising at a pace that outstripped the vocabulary used to describe them. Concern about monopoly and competition dominated domestic politics, but people disagreed about what these things were, and about why, and to what extent, they were good or bad. Men like McReynolds, Wilson's Attorney General, and Brandeis, the President's chief adviser on antitrust policy, could concur upon the need for forceful antitrust legislation and prosecution while finding themselves parted – as their later battles in this Court made clear – by a vast gulf in their understandings of economic theory and marketplace ethics. Absent agreement on the terms of debate, dissolution could mean the corporate death sentence, or the decrees of the *Standard Oil* and *American Tobacco* cases, or something else. So long as this ambiguity persisted, dissolution had to be considered a public remedy, one that encompassed a power peculiarly suited to transgressions so 'material and serious' as to 'harm or menace the public welfare' in a manner transcending the 'quarrels of private litigants'. For those like Brandeis, who viewed dissolution as desirable only if treated not as a moral penalty but rather as a necessary economic remedy, it would be imprudent to allow private parties to control a weapon potentially so lethal. Although it may now be second nature to conceive of dissolution in economic terms compatible with the policy Brandeis championed, this view was anything but uncontroversial when the Act was drafted [. . .] The rejection of a proposed remedy that would terminate the corporate existence of American and appoint a receiver to supervise the disposition of its assets is surely not the equivalent of the rejection of a remedy that would merely rescind a purchase of stock or assets. Dissolution was too vague and ill defined a remedy to be either incorporated into or excluded from [section] 16 as such; Congress instead sensibly avoided the problematic word and spoke in terms of equitable relief drawn to redress damage or loss which a private party might suffer by consequence of the Act's violation. That divestiture was encompassed within the concept of dissolution as understood at the time of the Clayton Act's framing does not imply that the equitable formulation of [section] 16 cannot permit divestiture while excluding more severe sanctions that also traveled under the name 'dissolution'.

FURTHER READING

Kurr, E. C. (1992), 'Granting divestiture to private parties as a remedy for anticompetitive mergers after *California* v. *American Stores Co.*,' 26 *University of San Francisco Law Review*, 319.

(1990) 'Report of the American Bar Association Section of Antitrust Law Task Force to review the Supreme Court's decision in *California* v. *ARC America*', 59 *Antitrust Law Journal*, 273.

Rearden, J. A. (1987), *Theoretical and Empirical Analysis of Public and Private Antitrust Enforcement* (Michigan University Microfilms, Ann Arbor, MI).

White, L. (ed.) (1988), *Private Antitrust Litigation: New evidence, new learning* (MIT Press, Cambridge).

3

FIRMS AND MARKETS

One of the fundamental issues which has to be considered by a competition authority is the extent of the market. Drawing the market boundaries tightly enough, almost any firm with a presence could be construed as having substantial market power; power to raise prices and gain at the expense of consumers. On the other hand, this power will be substantially attenuated by the presence of closely competitive goods – the market power of a steel can manufacturer is heavily influenced by competition from aluminium, somewhat influenced by competition from plastic containers. Any view of the relevant market will be conditioned by the initial definitions a competition authority adopts. The extract from **Kay**, although written for a quite different purpose, is nevertheless very useful in clarifying thinking on what constitutes a market and an industry, and covers the governmental statistical definition of markets. A comprehensive attempt to codify the concept for antitrust purposes is extracted in **Department of Justice**, Section 22.7.

The extract from **Schmalensee** is extremely useful in explaining the underlying rationale behind competition policy from an economic point of view. This amplifies the discussion in, say, Hirsch, making clear the nature of deadweight loss. An additional presentation is provided in the **Waterson** extract, Section 16.1. Schmalensee goes on to make the point that other factors will intervene to influence the size of monopoly welfare loss in any particular instance. Hence he provides, in effect, a rationale for the complex process outlined in the Department of Justice extract referred to earlier.

3.1 J. Kay, 'Identifying the strategic market', 1 *Business Strategy Review*, 2 (1990)

It is [. . .] important to distinguish the geographical scope of the industry and the market. The most striking example is the way in which the European Commission's programme for removing trade barriers within the Community has been given the title of 'the single European market'. The programme does very little, in fact, to create a single European market: more often it promotes measures to create a single European industry. The one does not imply the other. In popular discussion, the elision is almost complete. I discuss this example more specifically below.

THE ECONOMIC MARKET

The concept of the economic market was well established by the 19th century. 'Originally a market was a public place in a town where provisions and other objects were exposed for sale; but the word has been generalised, so as to mean any body of persons who are in intimate business relations and carry on extensive transactions in any commodity' (Jevons, 1871) [. . .] And so 'economists understand by the term market, not any particular market place in which things are bought and sold, but the whole of any region in which buyers and sellers are in such free intercourse with one another that the prices of the same goods tend to equality easily and quickly' (Cournot, 1838) [. . .] Thus the boundaries of the market are determined by 'the law of one price'. There could only be one price for any commodity within a single market: if similar goods sold at different prices, then it would be necessary to talk about distinct commodities or distinct markets. 'The more nearly perfect a market is, the stronger is the tendency for the same price to be paid for the same thing at the same time in all parts of the market' (Marshall, 1927).

To what extent do so-called 'global markets' meet Marshall's condition? Table 1 shows price differentials across Europe for four commodities – cars, pharmaceuticals, life insurance and domestic appliances. Pharmaceutical prices in West Germany are around twice those of Italy or France. Life insurance is almost three times as expensive in Italy as in the UK. Even for cars and domestic appliances, the differential between the cheapest and most expensive market is of the order of 40%. The commodities illustrated are all – by deliberate choice – ones for which production is highly integrated internationally, and in three of the four (insurance is the exception) both trade and multinational operation are very extensive. Although confusion is very widespread, there is a clear distinction between a global market and a global industry: and for those commodities, at least, there may be a single European industry but there is no single European market.

Indeed there is, at present, a single European market for very few branded consumer products of the type described in Table 1. Truly international markets are mainly to be found for intermediate goods – aircraft, steel, many electrical components – and for commodity products – oil, minerals and (subject to a variety of distortions produced by agricultural support policies) for unprocessed foodstuffs.

A single product market can be identified in much the same way. A Ford Sierra and a Vauxhall Cavalier are clearly part of the same economic product market, because they sell at prices which are similar to each other in all the different geographical markets in which they are to be found. A Mini and a Rolls-Royce, however, are equally clearly in different product markets, even though they are both called cars and are both produced by members of the same trade association.

Although Marshall's condition is helpful in focusing attention on the concept of the single economic market, it is necessary to look behind it and to ask what creates, or fails to create, a single market. Two markets become one when customers, or their agents, are able to substitute products from one market to another. Product markets are determined mainly by the degree of substitutability perceived by consumers themselves. The Sierra and the Cavalier are seen as very similar cars, and the manufacturer's recognition of this ensures that their prices cannot diverge by very much. However, consumers cannot readily substitute a haircut in Bangor for a haircut in Bognor and even though these products are, in some respects, identical, they compete in different economic markets.

In the main, substitution between different geographical markets by individual consumers is prohibitively costly unless the geographical markets are in very close proximity. Cars are a product of high unit

Table 3.1 Prices in European markets (Belgium = 100)

	German cars	Pharmaceuticals	Life insurance	Domestic appliances
Belgium	100	100	100	100
France	115	78	75	130
West Germany	127	174	59	117
Italy	129	80	102	110
Netherlands	n.a.	164	51	105
UK	142	114	39	93

Source: *European Economy*, March 1988; Nicolaides & Baden Fuller, 1987 [no explicit citation].

value and uniquely easy to transport. But personal import into the UK is very small even in the face of the price differentials shown in Table 3.1. It is even less common to find a French purchaser accompanying his new washing machine on a cross channel ferry. Price equalization across geographic markets depends on the possibility of commercial, rather than personal arbitrage. If wholesalers or retailers can buy in the low price market and sell in the high, they will do so until the price differential is reduced or eliminated. This is generally easy for homogeneous products, which is why there have long been international markets in commodity products such as oil or copper. There is considerably greater difficulty in arbitraging heterogeneous goods, and particularly branded commodities. For these it is important for manufacturers to identify as many distinct markets as possible and to take steps to keep them apart: through control of the distribution chain, the exploitation of non-tariff barriers to trade and other devices. [. . .]

But how do we know whether we are dealing with one market, or many? This question has been particularly important for the implementation of anti-trust policy. The existence of a monopoly position, or the acceptability of a merger, routinely turns on the view that Courts or Commissions take of the dimensions of the market. [. . .] [There are] two primary themes. One is concerned with the cross-elasticity of demand – to what extent does a price movement in market A influence the quantity which is demanded in market B? If the effect is sufficiently large, then price differentials between the two markets are, necessarily, severely constrained and it is appropriate to talk about one market rather than two. [. . .] A second approach emphasizes price relatedness. It looks at the behaviour of prices in two markets. Do movements in prices in market A follow closely movements in prices in market B? If the answer is yes, then A and B constitute a single market. [. . .]

Careful identification of the relevant economic market is critical to corporate strategy. Far from it being desirable to create global markets where none presently exist, it is important to maintain as many distinct economic markets, in both the geographical and product sense, as possible. There is little exaggeration in observing that the profitability of the European car industry over the last decade, and at times of the worldwide operations of the Ford Motor Company, have depended on realizations from the UK car market. The relatively high levels of pharmaceutical prices in Britain and Germany reflect the anxiety of the governments of these countries to support their strong domestic pharmaceutical industries. The governments of France and Italy do not have similar concerns. The pattern of price discrimination which results is sustained by differences in national registration requirements and by the packaging adopted by manufacturers and wholesalers. Keeping markets apart in this way is necessary if profitability in

Germany and the UK is to remain high enough to finance research and development spending.

Market segmentation is a key strategic tool in the product market also. Airline profitability turns on the ability to sell the same, or similar, seats at different prices to different users. Goods as different as cosmetics, books and washing machines are sold in ways which depend on distinguishing high value from price sensitive consumers. These patterns of price discrimination are important to the producers involved and wider markets mean lower returns. The potential benefits to producers from internationalization come not from the creation of international *markets*, but from the creation of international *industries*. To this I now turn.

DEFINING THE INDUSTRY

Like the market, the industry has both a geographic and a product dimension. We might talk about the car market, or the luxury car market; about the car industry or the luxury car industry. We might talk about the British car market, or the European car market; about the British car industry, or the European car industry. Some of these phrases trip more readily off the tongue than others. I now consider why.

Careful analysis of the extent of the market has mostly been a matter for the anti-trust authorities. Discussion of the definition of an industry has mostly been aimed at a quite different audience – the compilers of official statistics. National statistical offices have to procure and publish information on the structure of production and to do so they need to classify it by industry.

The US and UK describe industrial production in broadly similar ways. Two, three and four digit levels correspond to progressively greater degrees of disaggregation (Table 3.2). Food, drink and tobacco is a two digit industry. Confectionery represents a lower level of disaggregation, while sugar confectionery is lower still. The classification is essentially production based, in that activities are grouped together if they are frequently undertaken by the same firms. Hence washing machines are grouped with refrigerators because they are commonly made by the same firms, use related technologies, employ similar components, and are marketed and distributed in similar ways. Refrigerators are, however, useless for cleaning clothes: laundries do a better job.

This epitomizes the essential distinction between the industry and the market. There is a domestic appliance industry but there is no domestic appliance market: there is a market for methods of cleaning clothes but there is no clothes care industry. If the market is defined by cross elasticities of *demand*, the scope of the industry is influenced by cross elasticities of *supply*. Processes are part of the same industry if they are closely associated, or closely substitutable. It is relatively easy for a manufacturer of washing machines to diversify into refrigerators: both are white boxes with motors in. It is relatively difficult for him to diversify into laundry services, which is why the manufacturers of

Table 3.2 The Standard Industrial Classification

	Number	Description
Division	4	Other manufacturing industry
Class	41/42	Food, drink and tobacco manufacturing
Group	421	Ice cream, cocoa, chocolate and sugar confectionery
Activity	4214	Cocoa, chocolate and sugar confectionery

washing machines have not done so, and why we define these as distinct industries.

We begin thinking of the boundaries of the industry by reference to the degree to which manufacturers can choose to substitute one line of production for another. The definition of the geographical scope of the industry may be approached in very much the same way. What is the geographical area within which production at one location can effectively be substituted for another? The geographic dimension of the industry is the area within which the location of production can be determined independently of the location of consumption. For haircuts or newsagency, this domain is extremely limited. If I want these services in central London, they have to be produced in central London with all the costs that entails. But for watches or cutlery there is a world industry. The goods you buy could have been produced anywhere and are in fact likely to have been produced wherever in the world costs are lowest. For beer, the relationship between the location of production and the location of consumption lies somewhere in between. It is now rare to brew beer on the premises, but shipping it from Australia is prohibitively expensive for mass market products. That is why there are local hairdressing industries, regional and national brewing industries and a world cutlery industry. The assessment of the geographical boundaries of the industries is generally a quite distinct question from that of whether the areas concerned form part of the same economic market. To return to Table 3.1, there are European industries, but no European markets, for domestic appliances, for cars, and for pharmaceuticals.

THE INDUSTRY AND THE STRUCTURE OF THE FIRM

The validity of industrial classification is conventionally assessed by reference to homogeneity – the extent to which there is a one-to-one mapping between the activities, as defined by the official statistician, and the structure of production between and within firms. The classification breaks down if multiple activities are seen to be undertaken in the same plants, or many plants which are very differently configured are grouped under the same heading.

Official statistics define industrial production at three or four levels of disaggregation. This is largely an *ad hoc* procedure motivated by administrative convenience. It is, however, potentially useful both to the corporate strategist and to statisticians to relate this kind of disaggregation to that which is characteristic of the firm itself. If we envisage the large modern corporation as operating at the level of the firm, the strategic business unit, and the plant or establishment, there is a loose correspondence between these layers of organization and the two, three and four digit categorizations of the Census of Production.

In Table 3.3 we undertake this comparison for a specific diversified firm – Nestlé SA. Nine of Nestlé's product groups, accounting for over 95% of its sales, fall within the single class (two digit industry) of food, drink and tobacco manufacturing. The SIC classification of the group broadly corresponds to Nestlé's own categorization of product group: no Nestlé business unit covers more than three SIC groups and only three SIC groups are split over business groups. The activity corresponds broadly to plant organization. At present, the statisticians' 'tests of heterogeneity' are conducted principally at the four digit level (do the activities of the plant and the classification correspond) but it is apparent that related analyses could be applied at two and three digit levels. The decision as to whether cocoa should be grouped with confectionery, or with other beverages, is one which needs to be made both by the firm and by the Census of Production and the criteria which should govern that choice are similar.

These choices are not simply administrative matters: they are the product of both the level and type of scale and scope economies within the firm and industry. The level of production should be that at which technical economies of scale and

Table 3.3 Nestlé's main product groups

Nestlé	SIC Categorization		
Main Product Group	Class	Group	Activity
1 Drinks	41/42 Food, drink, tobacco	423 Other foods 426 Wine and cider 428 Beverages	4239 Other foods 4261/1 Wines 4283 Soft drinks
2 Dairy products	41/42 Food, drink, tobacco	413 Milk products	4130 Milk products
3 Chocolate and confectionery	41/42 Food, drink, tobacco	419 Flour products 421 Confectionery	4197 Biscuits 4213 Ice cream 4214 Sweets
4 Culinary products	41/42 Food, drink, tobacco	423 Other foods	4239 Other foods
5 Frozen foods and ice cream	41/42 Food, drink, tobacco	412 Meat production 414 Fruit & Veg processing 415 Fish processing 421 Confectionery	4122/2 Meet freezing 4123/2 Poultry freezing 4147/1 Frozen vegetables 4150/1 Fish freezing 4213 Ice cream 4214 Sweets
6 Refrigerated products	41/42 Food, drink, tobacco	412 Meat production 413 Milk products	4122 Meat chilling 4130 Milk products
7 Infant foods and dietetic products	41/42 Food, drink, tobacco	423 Other foods	4239 Other foods
8 Pet foods	41/42 Food, drink, tobacco	422 Pet foods	4222 Pet foods
9 Pharmaceutical and cosmetic products	25 Chemicals	257 Pharmaceuticals 258 Toiletries	2570 Pharmaceuticals 2582 Perfumes, cosmetics
10 Subsidiary products and activities			
11 Hotels and restaurants	66 Hotels, catering	661 Restaurants 665 Hotels	6611 Restaurants 6650 Hotels

scope are exhausted. But if there are economies in marketing and purchasing the definition of the strategic business unit will generally require a higher level of aggregation.

[. . .]

3.2 R. Schmalensee, 'Another look at market power', 95 *Harvard Law Review*, 1789 (1982)

[. . .]

A perfectly competitive market is defined in part as an arena in which no seller or buyer can influence the price at which transactions occur. If a seller can affect the terms of its sales – in the words of Landes and Posner, 'raise price above the competitive level without losing so many sales so rapidly that the price increase is unprofitable and must be rescinded' – the seller is said to possess market power. Perfect competition is rarely encountered outside textbooks; almost all firms have some market power, though most have very little. Accordingly, the relevant question in antitrust cases is not whether market power is present, but whether it is important. I begin by examining this question in the context of a

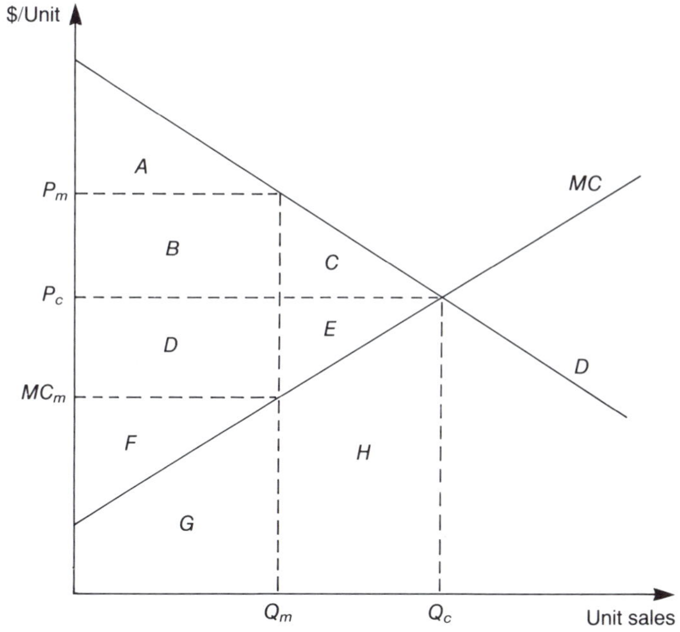

Figure 3.1

static, single-firm model, then discuss some important dynamic complications, and conclude this Part by considering the relation between analysis of a single firm and analysis of a market as an aggregate.

THE FIRM IN THE SHORT RUN

For a single-product firm facing a well-defined demand curve and maximizing its short-run profits, the following condition holds:

$$L = (P - MC)/P = 1/\varepsilon_f \qquad (1)$$

L is the Lerner index of monopoly power, P is price, MC is marginal cost, and ε_f is the elasticity of the *firm's* demand curve. [. . .] Landes and Posner ['Market power in antitrust cases', 94 *Harvard Law Review* 937 (1981)] treat L as 'a precise economic definition of market power' and examine its theoretical determinants by relating the firm demand elasticity, ε_f, to other quantities (for example, market share). [Later in the same article], however, when addressing applications of their market power theory, Landes and Posner shift their focus to the deadweight loss caused by monopoly pricing.

The deadweight loss is the sum of areas C and E in Figure 3.1. D is the firm's demand curve; MC is its marginal cost schedule. Deadweight loss is the dollar cost to society of the monopolist's failure to increase output from Q_m, assumed to be the profit-maximizing level, to Q_c, the competitive level. If the MC and D curves are linear, the deadweight loss is given by the following equation:

$$DW = L(P_m Q_m)K/2. \qquad (2)$$

K is a constant between zero and one that reflects the slope of the marginal cost curve;

it equals one if the marginal cost is constant. P_m and Q_m are the price charged and quantity sold by the monopolist.

Equation (2) clarifies the main difference between L and DW. DW reflects the amount of commerce affected by a firm's market power and therefore is measured in dollars of loss, whereas the L is a dimensionless figure. It is thus quite appropriate [. . .] to turn from L to DW when considering the degree of market power sufficient to warrant antitrust concern: a small firm with a high L causes insubstantial social losses. A firm must have *both* a high L (or, equivalently, face a low ε_f) *and* significant dollar revenues to impose significant costs on society.

Equation (2) also demonstrates [. . .] that the firm's sales volume, and not the size of the 'relevant market', is the most direct indication of the need for antitrust intervention. Because defining 'the relevant market' is usually difficult and sometimes impossible, this result is reassuring. If available, information on a single firm's costs and revenues is sufficient to assess the magnitude of the costs the firm imposes on society.

Other social costs that may result from market power are the loss of resources expended to obtain or maintain such power and the waste of resources by managers not subject to the discipline of effective competition. In such cases, deadweight-loss estimates based on observed firm costs will understate the total costs of market power.

Single-product firms are common in textbooks but uncommon in reality. To use, in the more realistic multiple-product case, the apparatus developed by Landes and Posner and discussed above, one must aggregate L's or (more importantly) DW's across products.

[. . .]

THE DYNAMICS OF MARKET POWER

The formal analysis [above] [. . .] focuses on the short-term consequences of monopoly power. As an analysis of real world behavior, it is strictly valid only if cost and demand conditions never change. Under this extreme assumption, DW gives the annual net social cost caused by the monopoly's exercise of market power. To obtain the net present value of those costs – the true measure of the cost to society of market power – the future stream of deadweight losses would be capitalized by dividing DW by an appropriate discount rate.

A simple capitalization of constant deadweight losses, however, implicitly assumes a static market with identical short-run and long-run conditions. Real world markets are much more complex. In the short run, the set of producers of any particular product, and the producers' investment in plant and equipment, is taken to be fixed (unless there exist nonproducers who could begin production without significant new investment). In the long run, firms are assumed to enter any market in which they expect to earn adequate returns. Market power, therefore, is likely to be more important in the short run, when the range of competition is limited by the fixed assets already in place, than in the long run, when market entrants may create sufficient competition to force prices down. In other words, the individual firm's demand curve is more elastic in the long run than in the short run, because the loss of sales from any increase in price should increase over time as competitors enter the market.

[It] has [been] demonstrated that the deadweight loss from market power depends in part on a firm's Lerner index (equation (2)), which is itself determined by the firm's demand elasticity (equation (1)). A lower long-run demand elasticity, therefore, indicates that the long-run deadweight loss from the exercise of market power will be lower than the short-run deadweight loss. The true cost to society of the exercise of market power cannot be determined by capitalizing the short-run loss alone, but must also reflect reductions in deadweight loss over the long run. If γ represents the annual fractional reduction in the gap between short-run and long-run DW – in effect, the decay rate for market power – and if r is defined to be the interest rate used to discount future costs, the total deadweight loss (TDW) is given by:

$$TDW = \frac{1}{r}\left[\frac{r(DW_S) + \gamma(DW_L)}{r + \gamma}\right]. \qquad (3)$$

Equation (3) emphasizes that the measurement of the social cost of market power is a quantitative exercise that involves both short-run and long-run deadweight losses (DW_S and DW_L), the discount rate (r), and the decay rate for market power (γ). Precise estimates of the variables in equation (3) will rarely be feasible. But the equation does provide a framework for integrating judgments about the magnitude of each variable in a particular problem of market analysis. For example, even the approximate ratio of γ to r provides a quantitative indication of the relevant importance of DW_L and DW_S. If γ is large relative to r – indicating, perhaps, low barriers to entry – then DW_L will be much more important than DW_S in determining TDW.

[. . .]

Market power has two conceptually distinct dimensions. The power to control prices in the short run leads to a high value of DW_S, whereas the power to exclude competition over the long run is reflected in positive values of DW_L. Confusion [. . .] arises [in the view] that '[t]he supply elasticity of the competitive fringe is determined by both the ability of existing firms to expand output and the ability of new firms to enter the market.' The first of these two determinants is all that matters in the short run, whereas the conditions of entry are a key element affecting the long-run elasticity. The distinction is important because entry can be expected to occur more slowly than expansion, and because different techniques are required to analyze the two mechanisms.

The most serious risk of confusion, however, arises [in arguing] that firms of average profitability do not possess significant market power, even if they have high Lerner indices. A firm that has developed a desirable product will enjoy short-run discretion over the price it charges, even if free entry prevents any significant degree of long-run power. For example, if no entry barriers hinder the development and marketing of new prescription drugs, the drug industry as a whole will not enjoy persistent excess profits. But each individual firm will have considerable discretion over the price charged for unique and desirable drugs that it develops and patents. The absence of long-run power does not by itself imply that the social cost of market power is insufficient to justify antitrust action. To determine whether antitrust action is warranted, one must consider the dynamics of the industry involved (as indicated by product lifetimes) along with the importance of short-run power.

Product lifetimes relate to the speed with which short-run power decays – the parameter γ in equation (3). If the decay is slow enough, the absence of long-run power has no quantitative importance. For example, the expected lifetime of a patented product is at least as long as the patent grant; thus, the TDW associated with such a product may be sizeable (because γ is effectively very low) even though DW_L is zero. After all, in the very long run all patents expire; it is nonetheless appropriate to be concerned with the conduct of any particular patent holder that has monopoly power. As always in the assessment of market power, the issues are fundamentally quantitative.

The absence of long-run power may also be relatively unimportant if one is considering relief designed to alter an industry's prevailing mode of conduct. In the popular-song industry, for instance, the effective lifetime of an average individual product is probably so short (γ is probably so large) that TDW is very small for any individual song. There may be little reason, therefore, for concern over the pricing of any *particular* popular song, but the aggregate deadweight loss associated with *all* popular songs may be significant. Further, even though the market power associated with any one song may vanish rapidly, the industry may be marked by the continued exercise of short-run power even in long-run equilibrium.

[. . .]

The demand conditions a firm faces are central to an assessment of its market power. Since firm demand curves are rarely observable, however, their characteristics are generally inferred from other data. [Under some circumstances one can] relate a single-product firm's demand elasticity, ε_f in equation (1), to such parameters as market share. But those assumptions and the market model they imply do not describe all markets, and their use may significantly understate market power for some industries that are of particular concern to antitrust lawyers.

[. . .]

As Landes and Posner state, '[t]he standard method of proving market power in antitrust cases involves first defining a relevant market in which to compute the defendant's market share, next computing that share, and then deciding whether it is large enough to support an inference of the required degree of market power.' This approach focuses attention on market definition, not on the fundamental question of market power. It has a number of intrinsic weaknesses, some of which are noted by Landes and Posner, and thus is not always reliable or even usable.

[. . .]

The market share approach can yield useful results only when there exists a good approximation to a standard textbook market. Such a market is bounded by a 'marked gap in the chain of substitutes' for a particular firm's output, such that the supply of, and demand for, the products within the defined market are independent of the supply of, and demand for, products outside the market.

The market share approach depends on the implicit assumption that 'marked gaps in the chain of substitutes' generally occur in convenient places. That is, the approach assumes not only that the gaps separating included from excluded products are sufficiently wide that all excluded products may be neglected in an analysis of market power, but also that all products within 'the relevant market' defined by those gaps are very close substitutes.

It is easy to think of examples in which 'marked gaps in the chain of substitutes' do not occur in convenient locations. For instance, a Chevrolet and a Mercedes-Benz are not especially close substitutes in demand, though some substitutability undoubtedly exists. On the other hand, in the array of automobiles of intermediate price there are no obvious 'marked gaps' across which little substitution takes place. Similar problems seem likely to exist in cameras (consider the spectrum of products between a Kodak Instamatic and a Hasselblad), in computers (in which the products range from a small Apple to a large IBM mainframe computer), and in other lines of business.

Exactly the same problem may be encountered in the context of geographic market definition. On Interstate 55 between Chicago and St Louis there are (or at least there used to be) a large number of gasoline stations, distributed more or less evenly along the way. Should one attempt to measure the share of 'the relevant market' accounted for by a hypothetical group of colluding stations near Springfield, one would not find a 'marked gap in the chain of substitutes' by proceeding either north or south. But it would clearly make little sense to compute the ratio of the sales of the hypothetical colluding group to total gasoline sales between Chicago and St Louis.

When a sizeable number of differentiated products are involved, 'marked gaps in the chain of substitutes' will seldom occur in convenient places, and the market share measure of market power is not likely to be reliable. There is no general, universally applicable model of the competitive relationships among differentiated products. A low market share does not necessarily establish that market power is negligible, for competition may be 'localized': a particular firm or brand may have only a few effective rivals even though a large number of generally similar brands are marketed, or firms may have long-run market power by virtue of membership in 'strategic groups' protected by 'mobility barriers'. A large share of a market of differentiated products provides evidence of substantial market power only if the market definition is not excessively narrow.

Regardless of the number of brands considered, if all plausible definitions of 'the relevant market' require grouping products that are significantly differentiated, one can say nothing about the relation between a firm's demand elasticity and that firm's share of the market. If substantial differentiation can be demonstrated, market share computation is unlikely to yield reliable information, and other tests must be employed to diagnose the importance of market power.

[. . .]

[. . .] [M]arket share is of interest only to the extent that it provides accurate information about market power [. . .]. An immediate corollary of th[is] argument is that other evidence of market power deserves equal standing with market share data. Two broad categories of such evidence deserve mention here: evidence of profitability and evidence derived from patterns of conduct.

[. . .]

Under the simple assumptions made above [. . .] the excess profit earned by a single-product firm exercising market power is directly proportional to the deadweight loss (*DW*) the firm imposes on society. When demand is linear and marginal costs constant, *DW* is equal to exactly half of the firm's excess profits. In simple models, therefore, profitability data are *exactly* as informative about *DW* as is information about price-cost margins or firms' demand elasticities. Because elasticities of demand and marginal costs are generally difficult to establish, profitability is likely to be considerably easier to use in cases in which a firm sells a number of different products.

There are, however, three serious problems with using profitability to gauge market power. First, it is very difficult in practice to measure actual profitability, and it may be even more difficult to measure excess profits. There are no simple, generally valid techniques for obtaining accurate estimates of these quantities, though advances have been made in this area recently and continued progress is likely. Second, the absence of significant excess profit does not establish the absence of significant market power. The costs of obtaining or keeping such power, as well as waste caused by managers not subject to competitive pressures, reduce observed profits but represent real social costs of market power. Finally, substantial excess profits can arise in the short run even in perfectly competitive markets. Such profits provide essential signals to guide the flow of investment funds in market economies.

Even if all measurement problems are solved, therefore, profitability is an unreliable measure of short-run market power. Nevertheless, *persistent* excess profits provide a good indication of long-run power; they show clearly that there is some impediment to effective imitation of the firm in question. The deadweight loss caused by such a breakdown in competition, and the resulting market power available to individual firms, can be roughly estimated from the observed excess profits.

[. . .]

Evidence that competitors have conspired to fix prices or divide markets is treated as very good evidence that those competitors have market power. Other kinds of evidence of a firm's conduct may also provide useful information about the firm's market power.

It is, for example, a standard textbook proposition that '[f]or a seller to practice price discrimination profitably', it 'must have some control over price – some monopoly power.' If the same product is sold to different customers at different prices and if it is reasonable to assume that no sales are made below cost, one can obtain a lower bound on the extent of market power by using the lowest price as an estimate of marginal cost. In general, however, it is difficult to proceed from the fact of price discrimination to estimates of the degree of market power. Thus, evidence of price discrimination is probably most useful in cases in which only some minimum quantum of market power is required.

In a similar vein, one can argue that proof of predatory conduct should in principle suffice to establish market power. Predation has been defined as:

> a firm's deliberate aggression against one or more rivals through the employment of business practices that would not be considered profit maximizing except for the expectation either that (1) rivals will be driven from the market . . . or (2) rivals will be chastened sufficiently to abandon competitive behavior the predator finds inconvenient or threatening.

Without a material effect from the exit or passivity of the prey, predation could not be profitable. If one assumes that firms rarely engage in strategies that present negligible chances of success, one may conclude that a predatory firm has (or at least thinks it has) the ability to affect market conditions materially. Predatory behavior, therefore, implies some degree of market power, although evidence of such behavior cannot lead directly to any estimate of the extent of market power.

Finally, a firm's price and output decisions may yield direct evidence of the presence of market power. Documentation of recognition of market power in a firm's price setting and other marketing decisions, coupled with the market's acceptance of those decisions, provides evidence of some market power. Unless such evidence is unusually strong, it may be insufficient by itself in a monopolization case. But if comprehensive high-quality data are available, skillful econometric analysis may permit rigorous testing of hypotheses about market power or collusive conduct. This issue is a particularly interesting area of current research in industrial economics.

[. . .]

[. . .] The deadweight loss (*DW*) associated with a firm's price and output decisions is in principle a good measure of the short-run significance of the firm's market power. Fundamentally, this measure depends on the net demand curve of the firm, not on its share of the relevant market or on any other aggregate. [. . .] The analysis of deadweight loss can be improved by explicitly recognizing that market power erodes over time; information on the likely speed and extent of that erosion can be used to assess the total deadweight loss (*TDW*) imposed by the exercise of market power.

Computation of market share can provide information about the importance of market power, but markets differ considerably and shares should be interpreted in light of evidence on market demand elasticities and other conditions. Mechanical adjustments to ordinary share computations can be misleading. In particular, I do not think that excess-capacity estimates should be used to adjust market shares. In situations in which 'gaps in the chain of substitutes' do not occur in convenient places, whether because of product differentiation or other reasons, the absence of a 'standard' market may cripple the reliability of the market share approach. Other approaches to proving the existence of substantial market power are no less valid than the market share approach. Depending on the facts of the case at hand, data on profitability or on patterns of conduct may be more informative than are market shares.

[. . .]

FURTHER READING

See the following works on the issues raised in this chapter. Some of the works listed on pages 13–14 above are also relevant to these issues.

Horowitz, T. (1981), 'Market definition in antitrust analysis: a regression-based approach', 48 *Southern Economic Journal*, 1.

National Economic Research Associates (1993), *Market definition in UK competition policy* (Office of Fair Trading, London).

PART TWO

RESTRICTIVE TRADE PRACTICES: GENERAL MATTERS

4

THE NATURE OF COLLUSION

Collusion may be viewed as an attempt by a group of firms to coordinate their actions in order to achieve an outcome equivalent to the situation of a multiplant monopolist, each plant (or group of plants) being a firm party to the collusion. Thus the colluding act is designed to create benefits for the parties involved, at the expense of consumers. In the course of so doing deadweight welfare loss arises (see **Schmalensee**, Section 3.2; **Waterson**, Section 16.1). It might be argued that a merger among a group of firms in powerful positions within an industry would have similar effects, and should therefore attract similar penalties. But a merger may create a much more general expectation of efficiency benefits – see Chapter 22 – whereas the efficiency benefits of a cartel action are generally thought to be few. Hence the law pursues the cartel far more rigorously than the merger.

How, though, does one recognise the cartel? If they are proscribed, people will not openly admit to joining. There also exist problems of members reneging on their agreement to participate. The **Rees** paper discusses the problematic question of tacit collusion – collusion which does not proclaim itself openly.

Collusion between firms may be based on written agreements covering all aspects of the parties' relationship, or on oral understandings where no detail is committed to paper, but where the participants are aware of their mutual obligations. The legal regimes in the UK, EEC and USA all provide for a wide remit, through an extended definition of 'agreement' or 'conspiracy' or through the concept of 'arrangement' or concerted practice.

4.1 Restrictive Trade Practices Act 1976

6 RESTRICTIVE AGREEMENTS AS TO GOODS

(1) This Act applies to agreements (whenever made) between two or more persons carrying on business within the United Kingdom in the production or supply of goods, or in the application to goods of any process of manufacture, whether with or without other parties, being agreements under which restrictions are accepted by two or more parties in respect of any of the following matters:

(*a*) the prices to be charged, quoted or

paid for goods supplied, offered or acquired, or for the application of any process of manufacture to goods:

(*b*) the prices to be recommended or suggested as the prices to be charged or quoted in respect of the resale of goods supplied;

(*c*) the terms or conditions on or subject to which goods are to be supplied or acquired or any such process is to be applied to goods;

(*d*) the quantities or descriptions of goods to be produced, supplied or acquired;

(*e*) the processes of manufacture to be applied to any goods, or the quantities or descriptions of goods to which any such process is to be applied; or

(*f*) the persons or classes of persons to, for or from whom, or the areas or places in or from which, goods are to be supplied or acquired, or any such process applied.

(2) For the purposes of subsection (1) above it is immaterial:

(*a*) whether any restrictions accepted by parties to an agreement relate to the same or different matters specified in that subsection, or have the same or different effect in relation to any matter so specified, and

(*b*) whether the parties accepting any restrictions carry on the same class or different classes of business.

(3) For the purposes of this Part of this Act an agreement which:

(*a*) confers privileges or benefits only upon such parties as comply with conditions as to any such matters as are described in subsection (1)(*a*) to (*f*) above; or

(*b*) imposes obligations upon parties who do not comply with such conditions; shall be treated as an agreement under which restrictions are accepted by each of the parties in respect of those matters.

(4) Without prejudice to subsection (3) above, an obligation on the part of any party to an agreement to make payments calculated by reference:

(*a*) to the quantity of goods produced or supplied by him, or to which any process of manufacture is applied by him: or

(*b*) to the quantity of materials acquired or used by him for the purpose of or in the production of any goods or the application of any such process to goods;

being payments calculated, or calculated at an increased rate, in respect of quantities of goods or materials exceeding any quantity specified in or ascertained in accordance with the agreement, shall be treated for the purposes of this Act as a restriction in respect of the quantities of those goods to be produced or supplied, or to which that process is to be applied.

This subsection does not apply to any obligation on the part of any person to make payments to a trade association of which he is a member, if the payments are to consist only of bona fide subscriptions for membership of the association.

7 INFORMATION AGREEMENTS AS TO GOODS

(1) The Secretary of State may by statutory instrument make an order directing that this Act shall apply to information agreements (whenever made) of any class described in the order; and in this section 'information agreement' means an agreement between two or more persons carrying on within the United Kingdom any such business as is described in section 6(1) above, whether with or without other parties, being an agreement under which provision is made for or in relation to the furnishing by two or more parties to each other or to other persons (whether parties or not) of information in respect of any of the following matters:

(*a*) the prices charged, quoted or paid or to be charged, quoted or paid for goods which have been or are to be supplied, offered or acquired or for the application of any process of manufacture to goods;

(*b*) the prices to be recommended or suggested as the prices to be charged or quoted in respect of the resale of goods supplied;
(*c*) the terms or conditions on or subject to which goods have been or are to be supplied or acquired or any such process has been or is to be applied to goods;
(*d*) the quantities or descriptions of goods produced, supplied or acquired or to be produced, supplied or acquired;
(*e*) the costs incurred or to be incurred in producing, supplying or acquiring goods or in applying any such process to goods;
(*f*) the processes of manufacture which have been or are to be applied to any goods or the quantities or descriptions of goods to which any such process has been or is to be applied;
(*g*) the persons or classes of persons to or for whom goods have been or are to be supplied, or from or for whom goods have been or are to be acquired, or for whom any such process has been or is to be applied;
(*h*) the areas or places in or from which goods have been or are to be supplied or acquired or in which any such process has been or is to be applied to goods.

(2) For the purposes of subsection (1) above it is immaterial:

(*a*) whether any information provisions made by the parties to an agreement relate to the same or different matters specified in that subsection, or have the same or different effect in relation to any matter so specified, and
(*b*) whether the parties by whom any information is to be furnished carry on the same class or different classes of business.

(3) An order under this section may describe the classes of information agreements to which it applies by reference to one or more of the following matters:

(*a*) the trade or industry in which the persons to whom the information provision made by the agreement applies are engaged, or the class of business carried on by such persons;
(*b*) the character of the information provision made by the agreement, or the goods, processes, transactions, areas, places or other matters with respect to which that provision relates;
(*c*) any other features which appear to the Secretary of State to be expedient.

(3A) An order under this section may specify matters (in addition to those mentioned in section 9) which are to be disregarded in determining whether an agreement is one to which this Act applies by virtue of the order.

(4) No order shall be made under this section unless a draft of the order has been laid before, and approved by resolution of, each House of Parliament.

(5) The Secretary of State shall, before laying before Parliament the draft of an order under this section for applying this Act in relation to information agreements of any class, publish in such manner as he thinks appropriate a notice:

(*a*) describing the classes of arrangements to which the proposed order would apply; and
(*b*) specifying a period (not being less than 28 days) within which representations with respect to the proposed order may be made to the Secretary of State; and in settling the draft to be laid before Parliament shall take into consideration any such representations received by him within that period.

8 TRADE ASSOCIATIONS

(1) This Act has effect in relation to an agreement made by a trade association as if the agreement were made between all persons who are members of the association or are represented on it by such members and, where any restriction is accepted or information provision made in the agreement on the part of the association, as if the like restriction or the like information provision

were accepted or made by each of those persons.

(2) Where:

(*a*) specific recommendations (whether express or implied) are made or on behalf of an association to its members, or to any class of its members, and
(*b*) those recommendations are as to the action to be taken or not to be taken by them in relation to any particular class of goods or process of manufacture in respect of any matters described in section 6(1) above,

this Act has effect in relation to the agreement for the constitution of the association (notwithstanding any provision in the agreement to the contrary) as if that agreement contained the term mentioned in subsection (3) below.

(3) The term referred to in subsection (2) above is one by which each such member, and any person represented on the association by any such member, agrees to comply with those recommendations and with any subsequent recommendations made to them by or on behalf of the association as to the action to be taken by them in relation to the same class of goods or process of manufacture and in respect of the same matters.

(4) In the case of an order under section 7 above, where:

(*a*) specific recommendations (whether express or implied) are made by or on behalf of an association to its members, or to any class of its members, and
(*b*) those recommendations are as to the furnishing of information in relation to any particular class of goods or process of manufacture in respect of any matters described in subsection (1) of that section.

this Act has effect in relation to the agreement for the constitution of the association (notwithstanding any provision in the agreement to the contrary) as if that agreement contained the term mentioned in subsection (5) below.

(5) The term referred to in subsection (4) above is one by which each such member, and any person represented on the association by any such member, agrees to comply with those recommendations and with any subsequent recommendations made to them by or on behalf of the association as to the furnishing of information in relation to the same class of goods or process of manufacture and in respect of the same matters.

10 PRESUMPTION UNDER PART II AS TO THE PUBLIC INTEREST

(1) For the purposes of any proceedings before the Court under Part I of this Act, a restriction accepted or information provision made in pursuance of an agreement to which this Act applies by virtue of this Part shall be deemed to be contrary to the public interest unless the Court is satisfied of any one or more of the following circumstances:

(*a*) that the restriction or information provision is reasonably necessary having regard to the character of the goods to which it applies, to protect the public against injury (whether to persons or to premises) in connection with the consumption, installation or use of those goods;
(*b*) that the removal of the restriction or information provision would deny to the public as purchasers, consumers or users of any goods other specific and substantial benefits or advantages enjoyed or likely to be enjoyed by them as such, whether by virtue of the restriction or information provision itself or of any arrangements or operations resulting therefrom;
(*c*) that the restriction or information provision is reasonably necessary to counteract measures taken by any one person not party to the agreement with a view to preventing or restricting competition in or in relation to the trade or business in which the persons party thereto are engaged;
(*d*) that the restriction or information provision is reasonably necessary to enable

the persons party to the agreement to negotiate fair terms for the supply of goods to, or the acquisition of goods from, any one person not party thereto who controls a preponderant part of the trade or business of acquiring or supplying such goods, or for the supply of goods to any person not party to the agreement and not carrying on such a trade or business who, either alone or in combination with any other such person, controls a preponderant part of the market for such goods;

(*e*) that, having regard to the conditions actually obtaining or reasonably foreseen at the time of the application, the removal of the restriction or information provision would be likely to have a serious and persistent adverse effect on the general level of unemployment in an area, or in areas taken together, in which a substantial proportion of the trade or industry to which the agreement relates is situated;

(*f*) that, having regard to the conditions actually obtaining or reasonably foreseen at the time of the application, the removal of the restriction or information provision would be likely to cause a reduction in the volume or earnings of the export business which is substantial either in relation to the whole export business of the United Kingdom or in relation to the whole business (including export business) of the said trade or industry;

(*g*) that the restriction or information provision is reasonably required for purposes connected with the maintenance of any other restriction accepted or information provision made by the parties, whether under the same agreement or under any other agreement between them, being a restriction or information provision which is found by the Court not to be contrary to the public interest upon grounds other than those specified in this paragraph, or has been so found in previous proceedings before the Court; or

(*h*) that the restriction or information provision does not directly or indirectly restrict or discourage competition to any material degree in any relevant trade or industry and is not likely to do so;

and is further satisfied (in any such case) that the restriction or information provision is not unreasonable having regard to the balance between those circumstances and any detriment to the public or to persons not parties to the agreement (being purchasers, consumers or users of goods produced or sold by such parties, or persons engaged or seeking to become engaged in the trade or business of selling such goods or of producing or selling similar goods) resulting or likely to result from the operation of the restriction or the information provision.

(2) In this section:

(*a*) 'purchasers', 'consumers' and 'users' include persons purchasing, consuming or using for the purpose or in the course of trade or business or for public purposes; and

(*b*) references to any one person include references to any two or more persons being interconnected bodies corporate or individuals carrying on business in partnership with each other.

11 RESTRICTIVE AGREEMENTS AS TO SERVICES

(1) The Secretary of State may by statutory instrument make an order in respect of a class of services described in the order (in this Act referred to, in relation to an order under this section, as 'services brought under control by the order') and direct by the order that this Act shall apply to agreements (whenever made) which:

(*a*) are agreements between two or more persons carrying on business within the United Kingdom in the supply of services brought under control by the order, or between two or more such persons together with one or more other parties; and

(*b*) are agreements under which restrictions, in respect of matters specified in the order for the purposes of this paragraph, are accepted by two or more parties.

(2) The matters which may be specified in such an order for the purposes of subsection (1)(*b*) above are any of the following:

(*a*) the charges to be made, quoted or paid for designated services supplied, offered or obtained;
(*b*) the terms or conditions on or subject to which designated services are to be supplied or obtained;
(*c*) the extent (if any) to which, or the scale (if any) on which, designated services are to be made available, supplied or obtained;
(*d*) the form or manner in which designated services are to be made available, supplied or obtained;
(*e*) the persons or classes of persons for whom or from whom, or the areas or places in or from which, designated services are to be made available or supplied or are to be obtained.

43 INTERPRETATION AND CONSTRUCTION

(1) In this Act:

'agreement' includes any agreement or arrangement, whether or not it is or is intended to be enforceable (apart from any provision of this Act) by legal proceedings, and references in this Act to restrictions accepted or information provisions made under an agreement shall be construed accordingly [. . .].

4.2 *Royal Institution of Chartered Surveyors* v. *Director General of Fair Trading*, Court of Appeal (Civil Division) [1986] ICR 550

May LJ:

[. . .]

A multilateral agreement, such as was held to exist in *British Basic Slag Ltd.* v. *Registrar of Restrictive Trading Agreements* (1962) LR 3 RP 178 (in the Chancery Division) and (1963) 4 RP 116 (in the Court of Appeal), is to be contrasted with a series of bilateral agreements, that is to say a situation in which each of a number of persons agrees with a single person but not with each other, as was held to exist in *Fisher* v. *Director General of Fair Trading* [1982] ICR 71 [. . .]

In the Basic Slag case [*British Basic Slag Ltd.* v. *Registrar of Restrictive Trading Agreements*, LR 3 RP 178; LR 4 RP 116] Cross J [stated:] 'As I see it, all that is required to constitute an arrangement not enforceable in law is that the parties to it shall have communicated with one another in some way, and that as a result of the communication each has intentionally aroused in the other an expectation that he will act in a certain way.' This decision was upheld by the Court of Appeal, LR 4 RP 116. Willmer LJ considered the meaning of 'arrangement' and said, at pp. 145–146:

> I think it is highly significant that Parliament did not see fit to include any definition of 'arrangement'. I infer from this that it was intended that the word should be construed in its ordinary or popular sense. Though it may not be easy to put into words, everybody knows what is meant by an arrangement between two or more parties. If the arrangement is intended to be enforceable by legal proceedings, as in the case where it is made for good consideration, it may no doubt properly be described as an agreement. But the Act of 1956 clearly contemplates that there may be arrangements which are not enforceable by legal proceedings, but which create only moral obligations or obligations binding in honour. This seems to me to be entirely

consistent with the dictum of Upjohn J in *In re Austin Motor Co. Ltd's Agreements* (1957) LR 1 RP 6, 19 [. . .] Nor do I consider that there is any inconsistency between that and the view expressed by the judge in the present case. For when each of two or more parties intentionally arouses in the others an expectation that he will act in a certain way, it seems to me that he incurs at least a moral obligation to do so. An arrangement as so defined is therefore something 'whereby the parties to it accept mutual rights and obligations'.

Dankwerts LJ underlined the difficulties that there are in considering cases such as this when he said, at p. 149:

> However, the provisions of the [Restrictive Trade Practice Act 1956], in this respect, seem to me to be calculated to drive any accurately minded lawyer to despair. Once the ascertainable ambit of arrangements, rights or obligations, which are legally enforceable is left behind, one flounders in a morass of inexactitudes. There is no path or guide which can be followed except that it must be an arrangement 'between two or more persons carrying on business in the United Kingdom'. What is the limit of looseness of association which may be tolerated in the application of the Act? It may be that it is impossible to lay down any principle for application and that each case must be decided on the particular circumstances of the case; and heaven help the lawyer who has to advise a client – a form of assistance which I gather has not always been at hand in the present case.

Finally, Diplock LJ did not attempt a comprehensive definition of the word 'arrangement'. He quoted the dictum from the judgment of Cross J at first instance, to which I have referred, and continued, at p. 155:

> I think that I am only expressing the same concept in slightly different terms if I say without attempting an exhaustive definition, for there are many ways in which arrangements may be made, that it is sufficient to constitute an arrangement between A and B, if (1) A makes a representation as to his future conduct with the expectation and intention that such conduct on his part will operate as an inducement to B to act in a particular way, (2) such representation is communicated to B, who has knowledge that A so expected and intended, and (3) such representation or A's conduct in fulfilment of it operates as an inducement, whether among other inducements or not, to B to act in that particular way.

The multilateral arrangement that the courts held that there was in the *Basic Slag* case is [. . .] to be contrasted with a series of merely bilateral agreements or arrangements as was held to exist in *Fisher* v. *Director General of Fair Trading* [1982] ICR 71. That case concerned the management of greyhound racing and the activities of the National Greyhound Racing Club Ltd. That was a limited company whose objects included acting as the judicial body for the discipline and conduct of greyhound racing in England, Wales and Scotland and to license greyhound racecourses, trainers, kennel hands and officials. Fisher was a licensed trainer and he applied to the Restrictive Practices Court for a declaration that the agreement between persons licensed by the stewards of the club and others was one to which the Act of 1976 applied and was subject to registration under the Act. The court held that it was not so and its decision was upheld on appeal. In his judgment, Waller LJ referred to the earlier judgments on the meaning of 'arrangement' which I have quoted and commented on. He said, at p. 79: 'The essential part of all those definitions is mutuality, and, as Diplock LJ emphasises in the passage which I have just quoted from the *Basic Slag* case, there has to be a meeting of minds.' Later on the same page Waller LJ quoted a passage from a judgment of Megaw J in an earlier case, *In re Mileage Conference Group of the Tyre Manufacturers' Conference Ltd.'s Agreement* (1966) LR 6 RP 49, 95, and pointed out that in it the latter had also emphasised the existence of 'reciprocity'.

Kerr LJ pointed out, at p. 81, that the basic structure of the participants, the club and licensees in Fisher's case was 'an extremely common one; indeed, the subjection of members or participants to certain rules must be virtually inevitable in any kind of organisation whose aims are to promote and regulate some kind of activity.' A little later he continued, at pp. 81–82:

> I do not think that the mere existence of a structure of rules, which bind persons who voluntarily engage in activities covered by the rules, *ipso facto* leads to the inference that all the persons bound by the rules have also made an agreement or arrangement between themselves, even if only binding in honour, that they will mutually abide by the rules. I think that more is required. An essential requirement of the legislation, as it seems to me, is some evidence of a consensus *inter se*, among the persons who are alleged to be engaged in restrictive practices falling within the legislation, to engage in the restrictive activities in question. It is therefore necessary, in addition, to establish some manifestation of the common will of such persons to make an agreement or arrangement *inter se*, albeit binding in honour only, to engage in the practices in question and mutually to abide by the restrictions.

In his judgment the other member of the court, Sir David Cairns, also stressed the contract between a number of bilateral agreements on the one hand and a multilateral agreement on the other. He said, at p. 83:

> Even if it could be shown that it is a regular practice of trainers and racecourse executives to contract with each other on terms which contain a provision incorporating the rules of the club, I should not regard that as going to show that the whole body of licensees in the club were agreeing together to adhere to those rules. Whether there are bipartite agreements between any parties who are the holders of licences which might be registrable under the Restrictive Practices Act 1976 is immaterial for the purposes of this case. The agreement or arrangement which Mr Fisher alleges and seeks to have registered is one between those licensed by the stewards of the NGRC and others, which clearly envisages a multilateral agreement – an agreement between a considerable number of persons, of whom Mr Fisher himself must be one, because otherwise he would have no right under section 26 of the Act to make the application. The existence of agreements between A and B, A and C, B and D, C and E, etc., does not begin to establish that there is an agreement between A and B and C and D and E. For there to be an agreement between all the parties, there must be a meeting together of all their minds.

As concepts, the multilateral agreement which is within the Restrictive Trade Practices legislation and the bilateral agreements which are not are, in my judgment, readily appreciable. What is much more difficult is to lay down any more precise criteria than those to which I have already referred to decide with which one is concerned in any given case, or to set out a logical step by step argument to guide one to the correct conclusion. As with so many construction problems, and the present is only a particular example of this type of problem, the answer may largely be a matter of first impression, supported by the concepts of mutuality, reciprocity and perhaps equitable estoppel (see *British Basic Slag Ltd.* v. *Registrar of Restrictive Trading Agreements*, LR 4 RP 116, 155 per Diplock LJ) which have been referred to in the decided cases [. . .].

4.3 Treaty of Rome, Article 85

[. . .]

1. The following shall be prohibited as incompatible with the common market: all agreements between undertakings, decisions by associations of undertakings and concerted practices which may affect trade between Member States and which have as their object or effect the prevention, res-

triction or distortion of competition within the common market, and in particular those which:

(*a*) directly or indirectly fix purchase or selling prices or any other trading conditions;
(*b*) limit or control production, markets, technical development, or investment;
(*c*) share markets or sources of supply;
(*d*) apply dissimilar conditions to equivalent transactions with other trading parties, thereby placing them at a competitive disadvantage;
(*e*) make the conclusion of contracts subject to acceptance by the other parties of supplementary obligations which, by their nature or according to commercial usage, have no connection with the subject of such contracts.

2. Any agreements or decisions prohibited pursuant to this article shall be automatically void.

3. The provisions of paragraph 1 may, however, be declared inapplicable in the case of:

- any agreement or category of agreements between undertakings;
- any decision or category of decisions by associations of undertakings;
- any concerted practice or category of concerted practices;

which contributes to improving the production or distribution of goods or to promoting technical or economic progress, while allowing consumers a fair share of the resulting benefit, and which does not:

(*a*) impose on the undertakings concerned restrictions which are not indispensable to the attainment of these objectives;
(*b*) afford such undertakings the possibility of eliminating competition in respect of a substantial part of the products in question.

[. . .]

4.4 Commission of the European Communities, *Commission Notice of 3 September 1986 on Agreements of Minor Importance which do not fall under Article 85(1) of the Treaty Establishing the European Economic Community* OJ 1986, No. C 231/2

1. The Commission considers it important to facilitate cooperation between undertakings where such cooperation is economically desirable without presenting difficulties from the point of view of competition policy, which is particularly true of cooperation between small and medium-sized undertakings. To this end it published the 'Notice concerning agreements, decisions and concerted practices in the field of cooperation between undertakings' listing a number of agreements that by their nature cannot be regarded as restraints of competition. Furthermore, in the Notice concerning its assessment of certain subcontracting agreements the Commission considered that this type of contract which offers opportunities for development, in particular, to small and medium-sized undertakings is not in itself caught by the prohibition in Article 85(1). By issuing the present Notice, the Commission is taking a further step towards defining the field of application of Article 85(1), in order to facilitate cooperation between small and medium-sized undertakings.

2. In the Commission's opinion, agreements whose effects on trade between Member States or on competition are negligible do not fall under the ban on restrictive agreements contained in Article 85(1). Only those agreements are prohibited which have an appreciable impact on market conditions, in that they appreciably

alter the market position, in other words the sales or supply possibilities, of third undertakings and of users.

3. In the present Notice the Commission, by setting quantitative criteria and by explaining their application, has given a sufficiently concrete meaning to the concept 'appreciable' for undertakings to be able to judge for themselves whether the agreements they have concluded with other undertakings, being of minor importance, do not fall under Article 85(1). The quantitative definition of 'appreciable' given by the Commission is, however, no absolute yardstick; in fact, in individual cases even agreements between undertakings which exceed these limits may still have only a negligible effect on trade between Member States or on competition, and are therefore not caught by Article 85(1).

4. As a result of this Notice, there should no longer be any point in undertakings obtaining negative clearance, as defined by Article 2 of the Council Regulation No. 17, for the agreements covered, nor should it be necessary to have the legal position established through Commission decisions in individual cases; notification with this end in view will no longer be necessary for such agreements. However, if it is doubtful whether in an individual case an agreement appreciably affects trade between Member States or competition, the undertakings are free to apply for negative clearance or to notify the agreement.

5. In cases covered by the present Notice the Commission, as a general rule, will not open proceedings under Regulation No. 17, either upon application or upon its own initiative. Where, due to exceptional circumstances, an agreement which is covered by the present Notice nevertheless falls under Article 85(1), the Commission will not impose fines. Where undertakings have failed to notify an agreement falling under Article 85(1) because they wrongly assumed, owing to a mistake in calculating their market share or aggregate turnover, that the agreement was covered by the present Notice, the Commission will not consider imposing fines unless the mistake was due to negligence.

6. This Notice is without prejudice to the competence of national courts to apply Article 85(1) on the basis of their own jurisdiction, although it constitutes a factor which such courts may take into account when deciding a pending case. It is also without prejudice to any interpretation which may be given by the Court of Justice of the European Communities.

[. . .]

7. The Commission holds the view that agreements between undertakings engaged in the production or distribution of goods or in the provision of services generally do not fall under the prohibition of Article 81(1) if:

- the goods or services which are the subject of the agreement (hereinafter referred to as 'the contract products') together with the participating undertakings' other goods or services which are considered by users to be equivalent in view of their characteristics, price and intended use, do not represent more than 5% of the total market for such goods or services (hereinafter referred to as 'products') in the area of the common market affected by the agreement and
- the aggregate annual turnover of the participating undertakings does not exceed 200 million ECU.

8. The Commission also holds the view that the said agreements do not fall under the prohibition of Article 85(1) if the above-mentioned market share or turnover is exceeded by not more than one tenth during two successive financial years.

9. For the purposes of this Notice, participating undertakings are:

(*a*) undertakings party to the agreement;
(*b*) undertakings in which a party to the agreement, directly or indirectly,
  - owns more than half the capital or business assets or
  - has the power to exercise more than half the voting rights, or
  - has the power to appoint more than half the members of the supervisory board, board of management or

bodies legally representing the undertakings, or
- has the right to manage the affairs;

(*c*) undertakings which directly or indirectly have in or over a party to the agreement the rights or powers listed in (*b*);

(*d*) undertakings in or over which an undertaking referred to in (*c*) directly or indirectly has the rights or powers listed in (*b*).

Undertakings in which several undertakings as referred to in (*a*) to (*d*) jointly have, directly or indirectly, the rights or powers set out in (*b*) shall also be considered to be participating undertakings.

10. In order to calculate the market share, it is necessary to determine the relevant market. This implies the definition of the relevant product market and the relevant geographical market.

11. The relevant product market includes besides the contract products any other products which are identical or equivalent to them. This rule applies to the products of the participating undertakings as well as to the market for such products. The products in question must be interchangeable. Whether or not this is the case must be judged from the vantage point of the user, normally taking the characteristics, price and intended use of the goods together. In certain cases, however, products can form a separate market on the basis of their characteristics, their price or their intended use alone. This is true especially where consumer preferences have developed.

12. Where the contract products are components which are incorporated into another product by the participating undertakings, reference should be made to the market for the latter product, provided that the components represent a significant part of it. Where the contract products are components which are sold to third undertakings, reference should be made to the market for the components. In cases where both conditions apply, both markets should be considered separately.

13. The relevant geographical market is the area within the Community in which the agreement produces its effects. This area will be the whole common market where the contract products are regularly bought and sold in all Member States. Where the contract products cannot be bought and sold in a part of the common market, or are bought and sold only in limited quantities or at irregular intervals in such a part, that part should be disregarded.

14. The relevant geographical market will be narrower than the whole common market in particular where:

- the nature and characteristics of the contract product, e.g. high transport costs in relation to the value of the product, restrict its mobility; or
- movement of the contract products within the common market is hindered by barriers to entry to national markets resulting from State intervention, such as quantitative restrictions, severe taxation differentials and non-tariff barriers, e.g. type approvals or safety standard certifications.

In such cases the national territory may have to be considered as the relevant geographical market. However, this will only be justified if the existing barriers to entry cannot be overcome by reasonable effort and at an acceptable cost.

15. Aggregate turnover includes the turnover in all goods and services, excluding tax, achieved during the last financial year by the participating undertaking. In cases where an undertaking has concluded similar agreements with various other undertakings in the relevant market, the turnover of all participating undertakings should be taken together. The aggregate turnover shall not include dealings between participating undertakings.

16. The present Notice shall not apply where in a relevant market competition is restricted by the cumulative effects of parallel networks of similar agreements established by several manufacturers or dealers.

17. The present Notice is likewise applicable to decisions by associations of undertakings and to concerted practices.

[. . .]

The nature of agreements and concerted practices was explored by the Advocate General in the case of the ***Polypropylene Cartel.*** Here, several firms organised regular meetings of management and technical staff over an extended period.

4.5 *Re The Polypropylene Cartel: Hercules NV* v. *Commission of the European Communities*, European Court of First Instance [1992] 4 CMLR 84

Opinion of the Advocate General:

[. . .]

Article 85(1) prohibits all agreements between undertakings and all concerted practices which may affect trade between member States and which have as their object or effect the prevention, restriction or distortion of competition within the Common Market. Article 85(1) (*a*) to (*e*) enumerates, non-exhaustively, the forms of conduct of which the applicants in the present cases are guilty in the Commission's view. According to Article 85(2), any agreements or decisions prohibited pursuant to Article 85(1) are to be automatically void.

In the cases now before the Court, the interpretation of Article 85 has given rise to argument on the interpretation of the concept of 'concerted practice' and on the question of the extent to which a plurality of acts or, in some circumstances, omissions, which are partly quite heterogeneous in character can properly be regarded as a single agreement or as a concerted practice within the meaning of Article 85(1).

Another question which, conceptually, can be considered independently from the problem referred to above but which is closely allied to it is whether the prohibition in Article 85 covers participation *per se* in a cartel with the result that the participants, by virtue of their participation, can be held responsible for all the infringements committed in the cartel. In the present cases, the question has been discussed under the heading 'collective responsibility'.

Before I go any further into the question of the interpretation of 'concerted practice', it might be useful to begin with a few observations on the interpretation of the concept of 'agreement' within the meaning of Article 85.

[. . .]

The case law of the Court of Justice enables the concept of 'agreement' to be defined with relative precision. An agreement covered by Article 85 can, of course, have been concluded in such a way that it would be legally binding on the parties but for the fact that it is invalid under Article 85(2). However, it is clear from the case law of the Court of Justice that an agreement within the meaning of Article 85 may also consist of a 'gentlemen's agreement', the binding and rule-making character of which is not due to legal factors but to social psychological factors. An agreement may consist of a continuous contractual relationship and it can probably also be tacit so that it need not be set down in writing.

Anti-competitive agreements are prohibited as soon as they have as their 'object' the restriction of competition. This has been quite clear since the judgment in *Grundig* [1966] CMLR 418. The detailed requirements to be satisfied in order for an agreement to have as its object the restriction of competition will be dealt with below in the section devoted to the argument that the agreements in question did not have the restriction of competition as their 'objective' object.

It is important to emphasise, as the Court has done most recently in the *Sandoz* case, [*Sandoz Prodotti Farmaceutici SpA* v. *Commission of the European Communities* (Case 277/87) European Court of Justice, 11 January 1990] that the offence involved is a pure 'conduct' offence so that it is not necessary to attempt to explain the actual effects of the agreement. This form of infringement of Article 85(1) has rightly been described as an '*abstraktes Gefährdungsdelikt*'.

An agreement within the meaning of Article 85 ('agreements [. . .] which have as their [. . .] effect [. . .]') may, however, also display the characteristics of pure 'result' offences; in such cases, it is unnecessary to prove an anti-competitive object. On the other hand, it is clear that a particular set of facts may at one and the same time contain the constituent elements of both types of offence.

In the present cases, it is not, however, the concept of 'agreement' which causes difficulties in the realm of interpretation. Rather, as mentioned above, it is the concept of 'concerted practice' which raises considerable problems of interpretation.

THE CONCEPT OF CONCERTED PRACTICE

The problem defined

The cases in which the Court of Justice has had to consider the question of the interpretation of the concept of 'concerted practices' contained in the prohibition laid down in Article 85 are very few. As will be seen later, owing in particular to the different factual situations in the relevant cases, only limited assistance in the task of interpretation is to be found in that case law for the purposes of resolving the specific problems arising in the complex of cases now before the Court.

As is apparent from the proceedings in these cases, there are considerable difficulties in arriving at anything like a clear definition of the conceptual content of, on the one hand, the offence consisting of a concerted practice having an unlawful object, and, on the other hand, a concerted practice having an unlawful effect.

Much of the debate in academic circles and in the present cases has left the impression that many commentators have in fact reached the conclusion that the concerted practice/object combination may if anything be described as a conceptual anomaly, which has virtually led to the explaining away of this type of offence. It must also be recognised that a type of offence which appears to combine elements of both a 'conduct' offence (object) and a 'result' offence (practice which is concerted) may be a difficult concept to handle.

The Commission maintains that there is evidence proving that the alleged concerted practice was put into effect by the initiation of parallel measures. It also believes that there was an effect on the market. In the Commission's view, however, in order for an infringement of Article 85 to be found it need only be proved that concertation took place. So, in the Commission's view – as expounded in these proceedings – the concerted practice is constituted by the concertation *per se*.

The Court might conceivably find that there is evidence that the elements in the case which might rightly be described as a concerted practice had an appreciable effect on the market or at least that there is evidence proving the initiation of parallel measures. It is also possible, however, that the Court might come to the conclusion that it is not possible to establish, with the required degree of certainty, either perceptible effects on the market or at least conduct which can be traced back to concertation of some sort.

It would then be a matter of interest unto itself to know how to judge the situation when one knows that collusion has taken place but cannot establish exactly what happened thereafter.

There is now before the Court a complex of cases in which the factual circumstances are such that the Court will have to decide for the first time whether the term concerted practices appearing in Article 85 can also cover cases in which there is no proof of specific, concrete acts on the market but only of meetings between the market operators at which information on prices, production volumes and so forth, which are normally regarded as matters of business secrecy, was exchanged, and whose object, judging by the subject-matter of the discussions which took place between the parties, must have been to co-ordinate subsequent conduct on the market. In other words, the question is whether a concerted practice within the meaning of Article 85 presupposed manifestation on the market as a constituent element of the infringement or whether the actual conduct, formed by the concertation itself at the meetings, can be regarded as unlawful under the provision, even if after the concertation no actual conduct, causally related to it, on the part of the undertakings which took part in the concertation can be proved.

The pleadings submitted by the parties in the present cases may also give rise to considerations as to whether an attempt falls within the ambit of Article 85; in other words, whether under Article 85 'concerted practices [. . .] which have as their object' constitute an offence in themselves and not only attempts to commit the offence of adopting concerted practices having an unlawful effect.

[. . .]

The Commission [. . .] contends that 'agreements' and 'concerted practices' within the meaning of the Treaty cover all types of arrangements by which producers mutually accept a limitation of their freedom of action instead of determining their future competitive conduct in complete independence. Such arrangements always presuppose direct or indirect contacts between competitors, whether these take the form of formal contracts, informal agreements of the kind known as 'gentlemen's agreements,' or simply practical co-operation. The purpose of having the two concepts, agreement and concerted practices, in Article 85 is, in the Commission's view, to avoid any lacuna in the scope of application of the provision. Article 85 can thus be applied to all agreements, express as well as implicit, formal or informal. It can also apply to purely *de facto* or practical co-operation. Such cooperation is not necessarily identical with a common pattern of behaviour on the market, because the prohibition in Article 85 also covers the mere object of distorting competition.

The Commission then describes the various degrees of co-operation. First, agreements which do not need to be legally binding – which by virtue of Article 85(2) they never actually are if they fall under Article 85(1). Whether one chooses to regard non-binding arrangements as agreements within the meaning of Article 85 or to reserve the term concerted practices for practical co-operation which has not been given formal expression, it is the whole gamut of anti-competitive arrangements which is caught by Article 85. The term 'concerted practices' refers to practical co-operation of a merely factual nature and co-operation that need not arise from a plan or concertation properly so called. According to the Commission, the judgments of the Court in *Suiker Unie* [1976] 1 CMLR 295 and *Zuchner* [1982] 1 CMLR 313 show that there can be a concerted practice once contact between competitors takes place prior to their behaviour on the market. This contact may, according to the circumstances, consist in exchanges of information without its being necessary for there to be an agreement on such exchanges. There may conceivably be an agreement to exchange information which can itself be caught by Article 85 if it has the object or effect of restricting competition. In order for such an exchange of information to be regarded as a concerted practice having at least the object of restricting competition, the information exchanged must relate to the parties' intentions regarding their future conduct on the market and must not be available to competitors by mere observation of the market. The object underlying such an exchange of information is to enable each of the undertakings to determine its own market conduct in reliance on its competitors behaving in parallel. Such an exchange of information cannot be explained except on the assumption that there exists a legitimate expectation between the information exchanging parties that the others will behave as they previously indicated they would.

When, for their part, the applicants contend that a concerted practice must have manifested itself on the market, this indicates to the Commission that they are confusing the question of the proof of the existence of a concerted practice with the concerted practice itself.

In my view, there is little indication that in general the applicants are confusing the concepts or have otherwise misunderstood the problem. They simply disagree with the Commission's point of view.

The most succinct account of the applicants' point of view is to be found in Mr Hermann's oral argument presented at the hearing before the Court. He stated *inter alia* that in the case of concerted practices the minimum requirement for Article 85(1) to be regarded as infringed is that it should be proved that (a) at least two undertakings entered into concertation by whatever means; (b) the concertation was followed by a corresponding practice on the market; (c) that practice had an anti-competitive effect; and (d) in the case of an anti-competitive effect, this effect was foreseeable.

The applicants also recognise that a concerted practice within the meaning of Article 85(1) can consist in a concerted practice having only the object of restricting competition without such an effect having to be proved; according to the applicants, this may be where the undertakings pursue an anti-competitive purpose through specific conduct on the market but without being in a position to fulfil their project.

In their submissions both sides examine closely the case law of the Court of Justice but arrive at completely different results. It will therefore be useful first to look at the background to the provision and at what can be deduced from the Court's case law which, as already stated, is sparse [. . .] academic literature is of some assistance in the task of interpretation.

Historical background

As is well known, in drafting Article 85(1) the authors of the Treaty were influenced by the concepts 'concerted actions', 'concerts of actions' and 'concerted practices', those concepts having originated in American case law on the basis of Section 1 of the Sherman Act and notably the concept of 'conspiracy' contained therein.

It is important from American case law, that anti-competitive effects are not necessary as a constituent element of 'conspiracy,' just as no acts other than the conspiracy need be committed.

As Joliet has remarked [R. Joliet (1974) *Cahiers de Droit Européen*, 258], the concept of 'concerted action' was of significance for the determination of the legal meaning of conscious parallelism of action, when there was no direct evidence of 'conspiracy'. The concept has thus been important in cases where the problem has been examined from the market aspect and where on the basis of an assessment of the market compared with other evidence it was necessary to determine whether the alleged practice could be presumed to have been 'concerted unlawfully'. Direct evidence of 'conspiracy' is, however, as stated, sufficient to constitute an infringement of the Sherman Act.

In the present cases, the applicants, in their arguments concerning the genesis of Article 85, assume that the authors of the Treaty, under the influence *inter alia* of the Allies' somewhat vague post-war decartelisation legislation in Germany, did not wish to adopt the American concept of 'conspiracy', which, in the applicants' view, was also rather imprecise. For reasons of legal certainty, the concepts of 'agreement', a term with a fairly well-defined meaning, and 'concerted practices' were preferred. The latter concept, I understand, was in fact inspired by American case law, being a component of 'conspiracy', which concerns conduct on the market.

The interpretation of the Treaties on the basis of the *travaux préparatoires* is a notoriously difficult area in Community law, one reason for this being that a large number of the preparatory documents have not been published. In the area of competition law, the difficulties are illustrated, for example, by Ellis's examination of the known, more or less official, preparatory documents relating to Article 85 [J. Ellis, (1963) 'Source material for Article 85(1) EEC', 32 *Fordham Law Review*, 247]. It is probably also indicative that the applicants have not pointed to any specific, written elements in the genesis of Article 85 in support of their view.

It is certainly not improbable that the applicants may well be right in their observations on the historical background, but the significance which can be attached to them is hardly decisive. When one considers the wording of the provision, which is plainly intended to embrace all anti-competitive activity incompatible with the common market, it cannot be presumed without very solid evidence that the authors of the Treaty wished to exclude from the scope of the provision a whole category of questionable business initiatives. The Court of Justice has made no such assumption in the cases in which it has had occasion to address this matter, as is clear from the judgments cited below. Nor do I see any decisive criteria for interpretation which would compel the Court to limit the scope of Article 85 in that way. On the other hand, historical considerations do not support the Commission's view either.

The dicta of the Court of Justice concerning the concept of 'concerted practice'

The Court's first judgments on this subject [concerted practice] were delivered in [*ICI* v. *EC Commission* [1972] CMLR 557]. They were later to become the subject of a wide, and in part critical, debate, which will be discussed below [. . .].

In those cases the facts differed significantly from the cases now under review. It was price increases implemented on the market which in themselves made the Commission suspect co-ordination of a practice which had unquestionably been implemented on the market. The dispute was about the extent to which the uniformity of the price rises could be explained by the oligopolistic structure of the market and the judgment refers (in paragraph [96]) to only one meeting at which the undertakings could have had the opportunity to arrange the concertation which is the central issue in the present case.

With regard to the definition of the concept, the Court began by resolving a question which had previously been controversial, namely whether the term 'concerted practice' within the meaning of Article 85(1) had an independent scope of application or whether it was simply a kind of legal rule lessening the evidential burden in cases in which essentially there is only market observation to go on and in which the evidence of an agreement will often be impossible to adduce unless the concept of agreement is to be emptied of all meaning.

In paragraphs [64] and [65] the Court stated:

> Article 85 draws a distinction between the concept of 'concerted practices' and that of 'agreements between undertakings' or of 'decisions by associations of undertakings'; the object is to bring within the prohibition of that article a form of co-ordination between undertakings which, without having reached the stage where an agreement properly so-called has been concluded, knowingly substitutes practical co-operation between them for the risks of competition.

By its very nature, then, a concerted practice does not have all the elements of a contract but may *inter alia* arise out of co-ordination which becomes apparent from the behaviour of the participants.

The concept of 'concerted practice' has then, according to the Court of Justice, an independent scope which may be described as covering co-operation which is not an agreement. The key word here is co-ordination and the question in the present cases is whether it is co-ordination as such or 'co-ordination which becomes apparent from the behaviour of the participants' which is decisive.

It should also be mentioned that in paragraphs [118] and [119] of the judgment the Court stated:

> Although every producer is free to change his prices, taking into account in so doing the present or foreseeable conduct of his competitors, nevertheless it is contrary to the rules on competition contained in the Treaty for a producer to co-operate with his competitors, in any way whatsoever, in order to determine a co-ordinated course of action relating to a price increase and to ensure its success by prior elimination of all

uncertainty as to each other's conduct regarding the essential elements of that action, such as the amount, subject-matter, date and place of the increases.

In these circumstances and taking into account the nature of the market in the products in question, the conduct of the applicant, in conjunction with other undertakings against which proceedings have been taken, was designed to replace the risks of competition and the hazards of competitors' spontaneous reactions by co-operation constituting a concerted practice prohibited by Article 85(1) of the Treaty.

The dicta set forth immediately above relate to the examination of the market and the Court's own view of the nature of the publicly announced price increases. However, the question once again is whether it is solely co-operation in establishing a co-ordinated course of action or in addition the ensuring of its success which was decisive in the Court's view.

Considering that the Court was, of course, speaking in the context of the cases then before it, in which the question was precisely whether particular conduct on the market found to be *de facto* uniform was due to collusion and there is nothing else in the judgment to indicate that in setting forth those grounds the Court also had in view situations such as that existing in the polypropylene cases, the judgment can hardly be relied upon in support of either the applicants' view or the Commission's view in the present cases.

The Court's judgment in the *Sugar* cases [*Suiker Unie* [1976] 1 CMLR 295] comes perhaps somewhat closer to the view now put forward by the Commission. It was stated in paragraphs [172] to [176] [. . .] that since the concept of 'concerted practices' presupposes a plan and the aim of removing in advance any doubt as to the future conduct of competitors, the reciprocal knowledge which the parties concerned could have of the parallel or complementary nature of their respective decisions cannot in itself be sufficient to establish a concerted practice; otherwise every attempt by an undertaking to react as intelligently as possible to the acts of its competitors would be an offence.

The criteria of co-ordination and co-operation laid down by the case law of the Court, which in no way require the working out of an actual plan, must be understood in the light of the concept inherent in the provisions of the Treaty relating to competition that each economic operator must determine independently the policy which he intends to adopt on the common market including the choice of the persons and undertakings to which he makes offers or sells.

Although it is correct to say that this requirement of independence does not deprive economic operators of the right to adapt themselves intelligently to the existing and anticipated conduct of their competitors, it does however strictly preclude any direct or indirect contact between such operators, the object or effect whereof is either to influence the conduct on the market of an actual or potential competitor or to disclose to such a competitor the course of conduct which they themselves have decided to adopt or contemplate adopting on the market.

The documents quoted show that the applicants contacted each other and that they in fact pursued the aim of removing in advance any uncertainty as to the future conduct of their competitors.

Therefore the applicants' argument cannot be upheld.

In that case, therefore, the argument was about how far it was necessary to find that there was a 'plan' for the purposes of Article 85(1). The Court held that this was not necessary. However, it only addressed itself to the nature of the co-operation which can be caught by the provision and not to the question of the time from which an infringement may be considered to have been committed.

[. . .]

In view of the foregoing, I consider that nothing can be inferred from the case law of the Court of Justice directly contradicting the Commission's view, but the facts of the cases decided hitherto by the Court have been significantly different from the facts in the cases now before us. The

Court's description of a concerted practice must necessarily be seen against that background and thus cannot be assumed to provide any answer to the question whether the offence of a concerted practice referred to in Article 85(1) is constituted by concertation alone or whether subsequent *de facto* and causally related conduct on the part of the undertakings involved is required.
[. . .]

Academic writing

In this section, which is not intended to be exhaustive, reference is made to a number of writers whose observations on the matter highlight the nature of the problem.

Probably the most thorough commentary to be found on the *Dyestuffs* judgments is the article by Joliet [R. Joliet (1974) *Cahiers de Droit Européen*, 258] who emphasises in particular that any confusion between the concept of concerted practice and proof thereof should be avoided. His own definition of a concerted practice (set forth on p. 285, and see p. 271) was the reciprocal communication of intentions by competitors prior to any action on the market by which each of the undertakings concerned leads the others to expect that it will act in a certain way, thus reducing the uncertainty prevailing on the market. In Joliet's view, there is thus a concerted practice as soon as concertation takes place, that is to say whether or not implementing action is later taken by the parties engaged in the concertation and whether or not the concertation had effects detrimental to competition, provided that it was capable of having such effects.

J. A. van Damme [*La Politique de la Concurrence dans la CEE* (L'Institut Universitaire International, Luxembourg, 1977)] endorses Joliet's view, emphasising that a concerted practice can be disassociated from the actual effects on market conditions. He bases his argument on the fact that Article 85(1) also covers concerted practices having the distortion of competition as their object. It is, however, interesting to note that van Damme appears to make a distinction only between, on the one hand, cases in which only concertation itself is proved and, on the other hand, cases in which concertation which has affected market conditions is proved. The last category mentioned by Van Damme is really collusion having as its effect and not only as its object the impairment of competition. He does not therefore distinguish an intermediate category of concertation which has such an object and is followed by subsequent implementing action but which does not succeed and thus has no actual effects on competition.

In contrast, Schapira, Le Tallet and Blaise [*Droit Européen des Affaires* (Presses Universitaires de France, Paris, 1990)] state that if one wishes to remain within the bounds of a literal interpretation, due consideration must be given to the term 'practice', which would appear to exclude mere intention. In the view of these writers, it is necessary to prove not only concertation but also the taking of steps to give effect to the concertation.

Goldman [(1973) *Journal de Droit International*, 925] states in his commentary on the *Dyestuffs* case when discussing the definition of concerted practices that the concept can be understood either as an exchange of declarations of intent which the participants did not however intend to be legally binding (or as obligations from which they can unilaterally discharge themselves) or as an arrangement under which concerted participation follows upon exchanges of information and mutual consultations between undertakings but is ultimately freely decided upon by each individual undertaking. Goldman goes on to state that not only may gentlemen's agreements and agreements which can be terminated unilaterally be included in the concept of concerted practices, it is also possible for practices decided upon individually, but following exchanges of information and consultation, to be regarded as 'concerted'. It thus appears from Goldman's description of the concept of concerted practice that he would consider the constituent elements of a concerted practice having the impairment of competition as its object to be present when (i) collusion is proved, for example in the form of consultations and exchanges of information, and (ii) action is subsequently taken, even if that subsequent action is freely decided upon by each of the participating undertakings. It is not therefore necessary for the action to be determined in common; it need simply follow the collusion. In Goldman's view, 'concerted practices' may, therefore, be quite different as well as parallel. Concertation having the restriction of competition as its object is thus not sufficient *per se*: it must be followed by action.

Piriou [(1973) *Cahiers de Droit Européen*, 50] in her commentary on the *Dyestuffs* judgments, takes the view that the Court of Justice attached decisive weight to the effect which the concertation has on competition. From this she concludes that concertation must in practice result in the elimination of the risks of competition. She is thus dubious about Mayras AG's suggestion that the potential effect of a concerted practice, that is to say an attempt *per se* to mount a concerted practice, could be caught by Article 85(1). Piriou concludes (p. 58) that it can be inferred from the judgments that inasmuch as the Court does not lay down a minimum requirement as to the degree of co-operation needed in order for it to fall foul of Article 85, exchanges of information on prices may, for example, be caught, provided, however, that the concertation also manifests itself in an alteration in the actual competitive situation. Piriou thus appears to overlook the intermediate category in which steps have been taken to implement the concertation but they have not succeeded in bringing about the intended effects. Her description seems rather to imply that in her interpretation she ignores the category of concertation having an anti-competitive object because she considers the concertation must manifest itself in an alteration in the actual competitive situation, in other words that the concertation must have produced effects.

Eric Colmant [(1973) *Revue de Marché Commun*, 17] expresses a view which comes close to that of the applicants in the present cases, namely that a concerted practice may have an unlawful object without having an unlawful effect. According to Colmant, that is the case where the effects of the undertakings' conduct are insufficient to damage competition but are sufficiently clear for it to be concluded that there must have been an intention to enter into anti-competitive activity. Colmant maintains that the existence of a concerted practice presupposes a combination of two factors: first, concertation, the subjective factor; secondly, certain *de facto* conduct, the objective factor; between those two factors there must be a link.

Van Gervan [*Kartelrecht*, 1986] stresses the importance of proving the anti-competitive activity ensuing from the concertation.

Schroter in Groeben/Boech [*Handbuch des Europäischen Rechts*] aligns himself essentially with Joliet and J. A. van Damme. He states *inter alia* that the prohibition against cartels operates as soon as co-ordination of the participating undertakings' future conduct occurs, thus even before the intended conduct is translated into action.

Koch in Grabitz [*Kommentar zum EWG-Vertrag*] likewise states, without providing detailed explanation, that concertation *per se* can constitute an infringement of Article 85(1).

Bellamy and Child [*Common Market Law of Competition* 3rd edn (Sweet and Maxwell, London, 1987)] also consider that contact between undertakings, often consisting of meetings, discussions, exchanges of information or 'soundings out', when their object is to influence market behaviour, falls within the concept of concerted practices.

Kovar [Clunet 1977, p. 219] interprets the *Dyestuffs* judgments as laying down a definition with two components: one, objective, the parallel conduct, the other, subjective, its intentional character.

Druesne [*Droit Materiel et Politique de la Communauté Européenne*, 1986] considers that a concerted practice comprises two aspects: the conduct itself and the intention to act together. According to Druesne, the mere exchange of information can, however, constitute a concerted practice, inasmuch as the undertakings, by making their intentions known to their competitors, exert an influence on their decision-making autonomy.

Deringer [*Das Wettbewerbsrecht der Europäischen Wirtschaftsgemeinschaft*] is doubtful whether Article 85(1) relates solely to concerted conduct or also covers collusion as an attempt.

As will be seen from this brief examination of some of the academic literature dating from 1973 to this day, there is considerable disagreement about the interpretation of the concept of 'concerted practice'. Some writers regard the concept as meaning that concertation itself is sufficient, thus overlooking the word 'practice', or consider concertation to be a practice in itself. Other academic writers, particularly the most recent, insist that there must be both concertation and a practice, described by some as subjective and objective elements respectively. It appears clear, however, that it is the concertation which is universally regarded as the crucial element. All the commentators are unanimous that a practice on the market which cannot be traced back to any concertation is manifestly outside the scope of Article 85.

However, it also appears from an examination of the academic literature that those commentators who say that there should also be a practice seem to suppose in some way that evidence must be adduced of an effect on the market and not solely of conduct, even if it has not actually affected competition. Consequently, in my view a study of the relevant academic literature does not give any clear, or more convincing, support for either the Commission's or the applicants' interpretation of the concept of concerted practice.

The starting point for interpretation

If one considers the actual wording of Article 85, a concerted practice within the meaning of that provision comprises *a priori* exactly the same elements as an agreement, namely there is a prohibition of concerted practices which have as their object the prevention, restriction or distortion of competition and an equivalent prohibition against concerted practices which have such an effect. A literal and grammatical interpretation thus clearly leads to the conclusion that a separate category may be identified comprising concerted practices having an (unlawful) object.

If, like some academic writers and, it would appear, the Advocates General, and in accordance with the wording of Article 85, one takes the view that, besides concertation, a proven practice causally related thereto is required, the problem which arises is to decide how much or how little is needed for there to be a 'practice' in a case involving a concerted practice having an unlawful object. Whether a possible proven practice has had actual consequential effects on competition is unimportant in this regard. On the other hand, in the present cases the Commission is in difficulty in explaining what form is taken by that element of the offence covered by the provision which is called 'a practice' since, in its view, concertation having the restriction of competition as its object constitutes *per se* a concerted practice.

As I shall endeavour to demonstrate below, the problem can, I believe, be reduced to one question: when is an infringement of the law committed? As will be seen, all this boils down to, in my view, is that the point in the course of events at which one can speak of a completed infringement called a concerted practice having an unlawful object is later than the corresponding point for agreements having an unlawful object.

Do 'concerted practices' require conduct on the market?

. . . [I]n my opinions no support for the Commission's point of view can be found in the case law of the Court of Justice [. . .]. Nor do the wording and historical background of Article 85 lend support to the theory that a concerted practice may be assumed to exist immediately upon, and by virtue of, the exchange of information of competitive significance or if concertation is ensured in any other way.

If we look at the available case law [. . .] it will be seen that the cases have been considered from the perspective of the market. Hitherto the task has been to decide whether, on the basis of an observation of *de facto* conduct on the market and on the basis of the often slender documentary evidence available, it was possible to consider it established that the reason for the observed conduct on the market was collusion between the undertakings in question. It is also clear that when the market behaves in a way which is hard to explain, when one or more meetings take place between undertakings normally in competition, when more or less similar telexes are sent out with, for example, price instructions and so on, these happenings will typically be strong indications that everything is not as it should be, even if there is no conclusive direct evidence.

When one considers a situation from the perspective of the market, it is evident that it will normally be conspicuously uniform behaviour on the market which will arouse the Commission's suspicions. However, a concerted practice can quite conceivably consist in a mutual understanding between the participating undertakings that A will do X (for example, charge a particular price) while B, C, D and E will do Y (for example, charge a particular price less 5 pence). In that case, too, there is a concerted practice. If, for the sake of the argument, we ignore the fact that it is scarcely conceivable for such a sophisticated arrangement to come into existence without something that can best be described as an agreement and we suppose that A is to do *a*, B is to do *b*, C is to do *c* and so on, it is, however, quite obvious that such a concertation may be extraordinarily difficult to prove unless it has also been possible to obtain other, fairly direct, evidence of what has taken place. Nevertheless, there is clearly a concerted practice which simply does not manifest itself in the form of uniform parallel action.

If one is confronted with a market which is behaving in a conspicuous way, displaying other indications of unlawful concertation, the relevant factors must, of course, be concordant. If the market inexplicably shows an actual price which is the 'right' market price plus 15 per cent, then, as far as the evidential situation is concerned, it does not help to have a telex which states the 'right' price minus 15 per cent or, for that matter, the 'right' price plus 150 per cent. It must be possible to prove a connection upon the evidence; it must be possible to infer safely from the behaviour of the market, on the basis of evidence pointing in the same direction, that there was concertation and what form it took.

But how does the situation appear from the other side? How does the matter stand if one is aware of 'concertation' but the other factors are somewhat less clear? Is it sufficient, as the Commission believes, that there is proof of concertation, that is to say, is the co-ordination or the exchange of information sufficient? Or, in other words, does the concertation constitute in itself a concerted practice?

As explained above, there is little support to be found for assuming that such an interpretation of the concept of 'concerted practice' is correct. That interpretation might perhaps be desirable from the point of view of legal policy but it is difficult to reconcile with the ordinary meaning of the words of the provision; nor is it corroborated by the history of the provision, I therefore consider that such an interpretation should be rejected.

We have to ask ourselves, however, what it is that happens when undertakings have entered into concertation? Why is the concertation something so crucial that, in the view of the Court of Justice, it follows from Article 85 that 'any direct or indirect contact between such operators, the object or effect whereof is [. . .] to influence the conduct on the market of an actual or potential competitor' is categorically prohibited, as it stated in the more recent *Sugar* and *Zuchner* cases cited above? In my view, the reason is that such undertakings will then necessarily, and normally unavoidably, act on the market in the light of the knowledge and on the basis of the discussions which have taken place in connection with the concertation. They will have received information about the way in which others are thinking; they will be aware that the other undertakings now know something about their own circumstances and they will be fairly confident about what they can expect, or at least what they should be able to expect, from the others in the light of the discussions they have had. They will negotiate with their customers and arrange their production and so forth possessing a different body of knowledge and being in a different state of awareness than if they had only their own experience, general knowledge and perception of the market to rely on.

In my opinion, it can therefore be maintained that in principle concertation will automatically trigger subsequent action on the market which will be determined by the concertation, whether the undertakings do one thing or another with regard to their market policy, that is to say regardless whether they subsequently behave in a more or less uniform way on the market. Something of this sort will, in my view, also occur if concertation in the form of exchanges of information of competitive significance, for example about actual or anticipated prices, takes place without any further co-ordination between the undertakings, that is to say merely on the understanding between the undertakings that all are presumed to react rationally in relation to their own and the other participants' situation. Thus, in such a case, the undertakings are in a position to assess the market situation with considerably more certainty and to act accordingly. The exchange of information will, all else being equal, entail at all events a considerable risk that market conditions will not be the same as they would otherwise have been. It is obvious that in such a case it will not normally be possible to prove any concrete, specific causal link between the acts (practice) and the concertation (the exchange of information for an unlawful purpose).

According to Article 85(1), all concerted practices are prohibited. That part of the provision is thus in the nature of a 'catch-all' provision, which in its broad terms is intended to cover all forms of competitive co-operation between undertakings other than just those belonging to the concept of agreements. The passage from the judgment of the Court of Justice referred to above in section (*e*) in which it is stated

> a form of co-ordination between undertakings which, without having reached the stage where an agreement properly so-called has been concluded, knowingly substitutes practical co-operation between them for the risks of competition may be understood in the same way.

In those circumstances if it is certain that concertation having an unlawful object has taken place and if, as I stated above, it can be assumed that the undertakings have acted on the basis of that concertation even if the Commission adduces no evidence of the concrete acts (practice), there is in my opinion nothing to prevent it from being said that there is a concerted practice with an unlawful object covered by Article 85. When undertakings act with greater knowledge and more or less justified expectations about other undertakings than they should have had and normally would have, there is always a clear risk that competition will be less intense than it otherwise would have been. Such a danger is distinctly present where market conditions are such that wholly free competition would lead to drastic falls in prices. If, as stated above [. . .], agreements having an object which is unlawful under Article 85 have the character of an *abstraktes Gefährdungsdelikt*, I find it difficult to see what is to prevent the infringement called a concerted practice having an unlawful object, which is completely parallel in that regard, from being interpreted in a more or less comparable way. The infringements have exactly the same character. In the case of a concerted practice, there must and will be, in addition to the concertation, *de facto* conduct subsequent to and connected with the concertation. Nothing like that is required in the case of agreements. However, in both cases the essential thing about the infringement is that traders in those cases no longer determine independently the policies they will pursue and there thus arises a very considerable risk that conditions of competition not corresponding to the normal conditions on the relevant market will be created.

Contrary to what would follow from the Commission's argument, it is therefore necessary, in my view, for action to be taken with the knowledge and the awareness that results from the concertation. The difference is, firstly, that if no action is taken at all there is no infringement. If, therefore, directly after the concertation, an undertaking has to leave the market for unconnected, extraneous reasons such as the destruction of its production plant, Article 85 cannot apply. It would, however, apply if there was evidence of an agreement having an unlawful object. Secondly, the view contended for here means that it remains at least theoretically possible to prove that the practice being pursued is not concerted in the sense that in some circumstances a party will be able to show that it has cast off the ties or bonds ensuing from the concertation and closed its mind to the knowledge gained from it. This might be conceivable where, for example, an undertaking is taken over and the new management seeks to clean up the business or is simply unaware of the collusion which had taken place. In a continuous process such as existed in the formation of the alleged polypropylene cartel, it is, of course, clear that in practice it may be difficult to argue plausibly that after collusion occurred the previous course of action was changed before the knowledge obtained from the meetings was put to use.

It is evident that, as far as the practical consequences are concerned, there will not normally be any great differences between the Commission's view and the concept of concerted practice for which I am contending. If it is assumed that concertation will have and must have a kind of automatic effect, it will generally be sufficient for there to be proof of the concertation and of subsequent conduct on the market pursued in the knowledge ensuing from the concertation. The Commission need not therefore specifically prove individual, causally related acts. As far as the undertakings are concerned, it follows from my argument that there is in fact incumbent on the undertakings a certain burden of proof or at least a very broad obligation to provide information if it is to be accepted that the knowledge obtained from the concertation was not used in the determination of the undertaking's policy. It is also worth pointing out in this regard that the applicants admitted during the hearing before the Court that the information obtained in the meetings was useful.

The interpretation of the concept of concerted practice which I am advocating and which, as I have stated, finds no direct or express support in the case law of the Court of Justice, is, however, in my view congruent or in line with that case law. My interpretation of the concept is in fact consistent with the opinion of a considerable number of academic commentators and in particular with the ordinary and natural meaning of the words used in the provision. It is to be observed in this regard that there is no question of an extensive interpretation of the provision, which, because of its quasi-penal nature, would be difficult to reconcile with generally accepted legal safeguards, as the Court of Justice also indicated in its judgment in the *Parke Davis* case [*Parke Davis and Co.* v. *Probel and Others* [1968] CMLR 47]. Finally, it is to be observed that the interpretation advocated here ensures that the *effet utile* of the provision is not neglected, which would be one result of the interpretation which the applicants have sought to persuade the Court is correct.

[. . .]

FURTHER READING

Puttler, A. (1989), 'EEC competition law – applicability to concerted practices of non-EC companies and trade associations affecting prices within the Community – territoriality and noninterference – consultation under EEC-Finnish Free Trade Agreement', 83 *American Journal of International Law*, 357–361.
Ris, M. (1990), 'The European Community rules on competition: the concerted practices doctrine', 13 *Boston College International and Comparative Law Review*, 465–481.
Shaw, J. (1989), 'Collective dominance or concerted practices?', 14 *European Law Review*, 96–99.

Merely parallel behaviour will not amount to a concerted practice. Firms are entirely free to pursue 'conscious parallelism', so long as it is not dependent on any tacit understanding between them. This pattern of parallel but non-collusive behaviour is most likely to occur in oligopoly markets (see page 70). The problem for the European Commission (or a private plaintiff in court proceedings based on Article 85) is to prove, in the absence of an agreement, that parallel behaviour is the result of a concertation.

The European Commission's decision in **Wood Pulp** (Commission Decision 85/202/EEC of 19 December 1984, OJ 1985 L85/1) was the first occasion on which economic analysis was relied on to prove the existence of a concerted practice (see the extract in Section 23.1). For the use of economic evidence in EEC antitrust cases, see J. M. Joshua, 'Proof in contested EEC competition cases: a comparison with the rules of evidence in common law', 12 *European Law Review*, 315 (1987), especially at page 334 *et seq*. For a comparative viewpoint, see W. Môschel, 'Use of economic evidence in antitrust litigation in the Federal Republic of Germany', 32 *Antitrust Bulletin*, 523 (1987). See also J. F. Zellmer, 'Detecting collusion in oligopolistic industries: a comparison and proposal', 6 *Hastings International and Comparative Law Review*, 829 (1983).

4.6 Section 1 of the Sherman Act

The apparent breadth of the Sherman Act's prohibition has given rise to a debate over the meaning of 'contract or conspiracy', requiring the nature of the transaction and the method of its analysis to be conflated.

The Act provides:

> Every contract, combination in the form of trust or otherwise, or conspiracy, in restraint of trade or commerce among the several States, or with foreign nations, is declared to be illegal [. . .].

4.7 *National Society of Professional Engineers* v. *United States*, Supreme Court of The United States 435 U.S. 679; 98 S. Ct. 1355; 1978 U.S. LEXIS 47; 55 L. Ed. 2d. 637; 1978-1 Trade Cas. (CCH) P61,990

Justice Stevens:

One problem presented by the language of section 1 of the Sherman Act is that it cannot mean what it says. The statute says that 'every' contract that restrains trade is unlawful. But, as Mr Justice Brandeis perceptively noted [in *Chicago Board of Trade* v. *United States*, 246 U.S. 231, 238], restraint is the very essence of every contract; read literally, section 1 would outlaw the entire body of private contract law. Yet is is that body of law that establishes the enforceability of commercial agreements and enables competitive markets – indeed, a competitive economy – to function effectively.

Congress, however, did not intend the text of the Sherman Act to delineate the full meaning of the statute or its application in concrete situations. The legislative history makes it perfectly clear that it expected the courts to give shape to the statute's broad mandate by drawing on common-law tradition [. . .]. The Rule of Reason, with its origins in common-law precedents long antedating the Sherman Act, has served that purpose. It has been used to give the Act both flexibility and definition, and its central principle of antitrust analysis has remained constant. Contrary to its name, the Rule does not open the field of antitrust inquiry to any argument in favor of a challenged restraint that may fall within the realm of reason. Instead, it focuses directly on the challenged restraint's impact on competitive conditions.

This principle is apparent in even the earliest of cases applying the Rule of Reason, *Mitchel* v. *Reynolds* [1 P. Wms. 181 (1711)]. *Mitchel* involved the enforceability of a promise by the seller of a bakery that he would not compete with the purchaser of his business. The covenant was for a limited time and applied only to the area in which the bakery had operated. It was therefore upheld as reasonable, even though it deprived the public of the benefit of potential competition. The long-run benefit of enhancing the marketability of the business itself – and thereby providing incentives to develop such an enterprise – outweighed the temporary and limited loss of competition [. . .].

The Rule of Reason suggested by *Mitchel* v. *Reynolds* has been regarded as a standard for testing the enforceability of covenants in restraint of trade which are ancillary to a legitimate transaction, such as an employment contract or the sale of a going business. Judge (later Mr Chief Justice) Taft so interpreted the Rule in his classic rejection of the argument that competitors may lawfully agree to sell their goods at the same price as long as the agreed-upon price is reasonable: *United States* v. *Addyston Pipe and Steel Co.*, 85 F. 271, 282–283 (CA6 1898), aff'd, 175 U.S. 211. That case, and subsequent decisions by this Court, unequivocally foreclose an interpretation of the Rule as permitting an inquiry into the reasonableness of the prices set by private agreement. The early cases also foreclose the argument that because of the special characteristics of a particular industry, monopolistic arrangements will better promote trade and commerce than competition: *United States* v. *Trans-Missouri Freight Assn.*, 166 U.S. 290; *United States* v. *Joint Traffic Assn.*, 171 U.S. 505, 573–577). That kind of argument is properly addressed to Congress and may justify an exemption from the statute for specific industries, but it is not permitted by the Rule of Reason. As the Court observed in *Standard Oil Co.* v. *United States*, 221 U.S., at 65, 'restraints of trade within the purview of the statute [. . .] [cannot] be taken out of that category by indulging in general reasoning as to the expediency or nonexpediency of having made the contracts or the wisdom or want of wisdom of the statute which prohibited their being made.'

The test prescribed in *Standard Oil* is whether the challenged contracts or acts 'were unreasonably restrictive of competitive conditions'. Unreasonableness under that test could be based either (1) on the nature or character of the contracts, or (2) on surrounding circumstances giving rise to the inference or presumption that they were intended to restrain trade and enhance prices. Under either branch of the test, the inquiry is confined to a consideration of impact on competitive conditions.

In this respect the Rule of Reason has remained faithful to its origins. From Mr Justice Brandeis's opinion for the Court in *Chicago Board of Trade* to the Court opinion written by Mr Justice Powell in *Continental T.V., Inc.*, 433 U.S. at 49 the Court has adhered to the position that the inquiry mandated by the Rule of Reason is whether the challenged agreement is one that promotes competition or one that suppresses competition. 'The true test of legality is whether the restraint imposed is such as merely regulates and perhaps thereby promotes competition or whether it is such as may suppress or even destroy competition.'

There are, thus, two complementary categories of antitrust analysis. In the first category are agreements whose nature and necessary effect are so plainly anticompetitive that no elaborate study of the industry is needed to establish their illegality – they are 'illegal *per se*'. In the second category are agreements whose competitive effect can only be evaluated by analyzing the facts peculiar to the business, the history of the restraint, and the reasons why it was imposed. In either event, the purpose of the analysis is to form a judgment about the competitive significance of the restraint; it is not to decide whether a policy favoring competition is in the public interest, or in the interest of the members of an industry. Subject to the exceptions defined by statute, that policy decision has been made by the Congress.

4.8 R. Rees, 'Tacit collusion', 9 *Oxford Review of Economic Policy*, 27 (1993)

The word collusion describes a type of conduct or form of behaviour whereby decision-takers agree to co-ordinate their actions. This in general would seem to involve two elements: a process of communication, discussion, and exchange of information with the aim of reaching an agreement; and, where there are gains to reneging on the agreement given that the others comply, some kind of mechanism for punishing such violations and so enforcing the agreement. In the economics of oligopolistic markets the distinction between 'explicit' and 'tacit' collusion turns on the first of these elements. It is possible that firms could agree to co-ordinate their actions in some way without explicit communication and discussion. For example, it may become tacitly accepted practice in a market exactly to match the price changes of the largest firm. All firms are aware of this 'tacit agreement' or 'conscious parallelism', and no process for reaching agreement is strictly necessary. However, the second element must always be present: typically there are at least short-run gains from reneging on an agreement and so tacit collusion requires the perception that to do so would in the end turn out to be unprofitable because of punitive reactions by the other firms.

Indeed, at the extreme, it could be argued that whether or not there is explicit communication is irrelevant: what matters is whether a collusive agreement, however arrived at, can be sustained by the self-interest of the parties involved. If this is not the case, then explicit communication is simply 'cheap talk'. This is most easily seen in the context of a market which takes place only once. For example, suppose that a government wishes to sell off, once and for all, the mineral rights on a tract of land and invites sealed bids which will specify required acreage and a price per acre. There are just two firms which will bid, though the minerals extracted will subsequently be sold on a competitive world market. Each firm knows that the value of the land is £100 per acre, and knows the other knows this and that the government does not. The government places a reservation value of £10 an acre on the land. If the firms bid competitively, they will each bid £100 an acre for the entire acreage. It would clearly be in their interests for them to agree to bid £10 an acre for one-half the acreage each. Such an agreement would not, of course, be legally enforceable. Moreover, it is not sustainable by the self-interest of the firms. If one firm believed that the other would bid according to the agreement, it is in its interest to bid slightly more than £10 an acre for the entire acreage. But then it would realize that the other firm would have also worked that out, and it should raise its bid. But the other firm will also have worked this out . . . and so on. Whatever the firms may have discussed and agreed, this is merely cheap talk if the agreement cannot be enforced: under the conditions of this example, the firms will end up making competitive bids.

The enforceability of collusive agreements by some means can, therefore, be taken as a necessary condition for their existence. We shall consider at some length below circumstances under which this condition is met even when enforcement through the courts is not available. If the distinction between tacit and explicit collusion is to mean anything, it must also be shown that the ability to communicate in some way affects the likely existence and stability of collusion. Is collusion indeed *ever really* 'tacit', or is it the case that what may appear to be tacit collusion is actually explicit collusion in which the process of agreement is simply concealed? The statement by Adam Smith that businessmen's meetings, even for 'merriment and diversion', usually end up in connivance to restrict competition, is often quoted, but the sentence which follows it is equally perceptive: 'It is impossible indeed to prevent such meetings, by any law which either could be executed, or would be consistent with liberty and justice.' Moreover, short of methods of surveillance which are also not 'consistent with liberty and justice' it may be impossible to obtain evidence on what transpired at such meetings.

Turning now to antitrust policy [. . .] among [t]he problem[s] here is that, quite apart from the possibility that collusion might be concealed, the observation that firms communicated and appeared to reach agreement need not imply that the collusive outcome was actually achieved (as in the above bidding example), while if collusion is tacit there will be no evidence of communication and negotiation. The observation of communication is neither necessary nor sufficient for existence of collusion.

EQUILIBRIUM CONCEPTS

Until relatively recently, oligopoly theory was typically presented as a collection of models each based on a particular *ad hoc* set of assumptions about firms' perceptions of their rivals' reactions to their own choices of prices or outputs. The leading models in the literature are:

The Cournot model: in the traditional story firms independently choose outputs on the assumption that their rivals make no response to their choices – even though this assumption may be continually falsified – and market equilibrium is achieved through a sequence of alternating output choices which converges over time.

The Stackelberg model: a leader makes a choice of output, the other firms act as followers and make their profit-maximizing response to this output. The leader takes account of these responses in choosing its output and is able to do better than it would under

Cournot reactions – there is a 'first mover' or precommitment advantage.

The 'kinked demand curve' model: each firm believes that an increase in its output (reduction in its price) will be matched by its rivals, while a reduction in output (increase in price) will not be followed. This creates a kink in the firm's perceived demand curve at its current price–output pair (the levels of which are, however, unexplained) which then tends to remain the same despite changes in marginal cost, because of a discontinuity in the firm's marginal revenue at the kink.

The Bertrand model: again in the traditional story firms independently choose prices, on the assumption that their rivals make no response to their choices. Where firms produce identical outputs and have identical constant marginal costs equilibrium price ends up equal to this common cost. If the constant marginal costs differ, then only the firm with the lowest marginal cost is left in the market and it sets a price just below the marginal cost of the next-to-lowest cost firm. If marginal costs are non-constant then no equilibrium price exists unless outputs are non-homogeneous, i.e. there is product differentiation.

The Edgeworth model: firms choose prices as in the Bertrand model, with identical constant marginal costs, but with fixed output capacities. There is a range of possible types of outcome, including those of the Cournot and Bertrand models, but the novel possibility is that of 'price cycles'. There is a range of prices the upper and lower limits of which are determined by demand, cost, and capacity parameters. As firms set prices alternately over consecutive periods, price falls by small steps from the upper limit of the interval until it reaches the lower limit and then jumps back to the upper limit and the cycle begins again.

Recent developments in game theory have had an important impact on the way we interpret these models. Game theory forces us to be precise about three sets of assumptions on which a model rests.

(i) the possibility of binding commitments. If it is possible for firms to make binding commitments, for example legally enforceable contracts, to carry out certain agreed actions, then this raises a fundamentally different set of issues than if no such commitments are possible. In the former case the firms are involved in a *co-operative game*, the problem is to reach agreement on division of the gains from co-operation. In the latter case, whether or not explicit communication takes place, each firm has to decide on the choice of action which is in its own best interest in the light of the fact that the others are behaving in the same way: we have a *non-co-operative game*. All the oligopoly models just discussed are examples of non-co-operative games, and in the light of the antitrust laws in most advanced industrial countries this would seem to be appropriate.

(ii) The frequency of market interaction. This is something that is often somewhat ambiguously specified in the traditional economic models. The models are usually formulated as 'one-shot games': firms are making their choices relative to market and cost conditions at a given point in time as if there were no past and no future. Nevertheless, time enters through the back door in the discussion of reaction patterns. The very concept of 'action' and 'reaction' must presuppose at least two points in time, but the discussions underlying the Cournot and Bertrand models implicitly require much more, possibly an infinity of time periods as the processes of convergence to an equilibrium work themselves out. Likewise the price cycles in the Edgeworth model take place through real time. If market interaction takes place repeatedly, however, why is it that firms are assumed to ignore this and treat each decision as if it were a move in a 'one-shot' game? Surely if the market is held repeatedly firms would realize this and formulate strategies that determine their actions over time. But then, as we shall see, it may become possible to rationalize the kind of collusive behaviour which is simply not contemplated in the standard models.

(iii) The way in which firms form their expectations of their rivals' choices. A rational player in a game cannot be thought of as simply taking his rivals' actions as given by some *ad hoc* assumption. The analysis of a game is concerned precisely with the question of the expectations of the behaviour of his rivals it is rational for any one player to form. The general answer game theory gives to this question is contained in the concept of Nash Equilibrium (NE). The choices made by players in a game must be mutually consistent in the sense that each player's choice is the best for him given the choices made by the others. The NE choices have the property that if each player knows the others will make their NE choices, he has no reason to deviate from making his own NE choice. The argument to suggest that a non-NE set of choices cannot be an equilibrium outcome of the game proceeds as follows. Suppose player 1 assumes that player 2 will choose action A, and that 1's best (most profitable) response to this is action B. Suppose, further, that 2's best response to B is *not* A. Should 1 continue to assume that 2 will choose A? If 2 *had* been going to choose A, she would work out that 1 would plan to choose B, in which case she would change her planned action to whatever is the best response to B, so falsifying the initial assumption that she would choose A. Thus 1 cannot persist in believing 2 will choose A if he knows that she is as rational and well-informed as he is. Only the NE choices are immune to this kind of contradiction.

The classic oligopoly models can then be thought of as one-shot, non-co-operative games to which the NE concept can be applied to find a solution. They differ not in respect of reaction patterns but in the economic characteristics of the market concerned, and it is a matter of fact, not logic, to decide which model is appropriate for any particular market under study. An interesting point is that in the three leading models, those of Cournot, Bertrand, and Stackelberg, the NE outcomes are identical to those traditionally derived; only the reasoning underlying the derivation of those equilibria changes. Since the games are played just once, with the firms making output or price choices simultaneously, the equilibria cannot be rationalized by appeal to a process of action and reaction through time. The explanation of the equilibrium outcomes is that they *are* the NE outcomes in these games.

It is useful to consider the antitrust implications of the outcomes in these three market games. First, firms are behaving non-co-operatively and, it seems safe to say, non-collusively. Communication between firms is unnecessary to achieve the market equilibrium, since this is done by the firms independently thinking through the logic of the situation.[1] In the absence of the ability to make binding agreements any such communication would in any case be cheap talk – the only outcomes that are sustainable by the self-interest of the firms are the NE outcomes, and any agreement to choose non-NE outcomes would be reneged upon, as in our earlier example. Thus a charge of collusion could not be made to stick. At the same time, in two of the three models the equilibrium outcomes could be quite bad from the welfare point of view. In the Bertrand case with constant identical marginal costs we have, in fact, the perfectly competitive market outcome, with price equal to marginal cost and no excess profit, but in the Cournot and Stackelberg cases prices exceed marginal costs and the firms make excess profit. Moreover, in these models, if the firms have different and non-constant marginal costs, a further source of inefficiency is that total market output will be produced at more than minimum total cost – the marginal costs of firms are not equalized at the equilibrium. It is certainly true that the Cournot and Stackelberg equilibria in general involve smaller welfare losses, and lower levels of excess profit, than would be the case if the firms acted as a joint profit-maximizing monopoly or cartel but, none the less, contingent on market parameters, allocative inefficiency could still be quite large.

It seems clear then that an antitrust policy based on the behaviour of firms, in particular on whether or not this is collusive, could come to different conclusions to one which was based upon appraisal of the inefficiency and extent of excess profits associated with the market outcome. Except in the special Bertrand case, even if the self-interest of the firms does not lead them to collude, it would not lead them to behave as perfectly competitive firms either.

The assumption that the market takes place just once is, of course, patently unrealistic: repeated market interaction among firms would appear to be the rule. Some care has to be taken, however, in specifying the time horizon in a model of a multiperiod market. To simplify the dynamics of the model, it is usual to assume that the market situation in each period is the same: the same population of firms faces the same market demand with the same cost conditions in each period. The key distinction is that between the case in which there is a known, finite number of periods in which firms will choose prices or outputs, and those in which either the number of periods, though finite, is not known with certainty, or the time horizon can be regarded as infinite. When there is a known, finite number of periods, an argument based on backward induction can be constructed, to the effect that the equilibrium strategies for the multi-period game consist simply of repetitions of the single-period NE, for example the one-period Cournot equilibrium outputs in a market in which firms make output choices.[2] Nothing of substance, therefore, is added by analysing the market in a multi-period setting. On the other hand, if there is no known, certain last period from which this backward induction argument can begin, it makes sense to discuss the conditions under which *collusive* behaviour can be sustained as a *non-co-operative* equilibrium of the repeated game.

The intuitive argument is straightforward. If firms agree to set outputs or prices which give them higher profits than those they would earn in a one-shot NE, and one of them reneges on this agreement, then in the following period(s) punitive actions can be undertaken, for example a price war, to wipe out the gains from the deviation. The threat of this *ex ante* can then be used to ensure adherence to the agreement. The existence of a future in which to apply punishment allows current collusion to be sustained by the self-interest of the firms.

There are two respects in which this intuition must be taken more rigorously. First, it must be established that sufficiently large future losses can be threatened so that, when discounted to a present value, they offset the gain from reneging in the current period. Second, the threat to inflict these losses must be credible. We consider each of these points in turn.

The fact that future losses from punishment have to be set against current gains to defection implies that the rate at which a firm discounts the future will be important. This rate will in general reflect a firm's (marginal) cost of capital. In an imperfect capital market it need not be the same for all firms, and in an economy subject to cyclical fluctuations in economic activity it need not be the same over time. In general, the more heavily firms discount the future (i.e. the higher their cost of capital) the smaller will be the present value of future losses of profit caused by punishment, relative to the immediate gains from cheating on an agreement. In a particular market, given its underlying cost and demand parameters, it will usually be possible to define a range of discount rates over which agreement on some collusive set of outputs or prices can be sustained by some threatened punishment strategy. In general this range will vary with the set of outputs or prices to be sustained, the punishment strategy and the characteristics of the individual firm. We shall explore how these factors interact more fully below. It suffices to note here that the more heavily firms discount the future the less likely is it that collusion among them can be sustained.

The gain to a firm from reneging on the collusive agreement will depend partly on cost, demand, and capacity parameters and partly on the length of time for which a higher profit than that realized under the agreement can be earned before retaliation by the other firms takes place. For example, if technology is such that production is subject to a fixed maximum rate of capacity output, and for each firm its output under the collusive agreement is just about at capacity, then there would be virtually no short-run gain to reneging on the agreement. On the other hand, if there is significant excess capacity at the agreed output, and the agreed price is well above marginal cost, then a significant output expansion would be both feasible and profitable and so reneging on the agreement could appear attractive. The longer the other firms take to detect a deviation and implement a punitive response, the greater will be the duration of the flow of profit from reneging and the further into the future the losses from punishment will be delayed, thus reducing their present value.

The extent of losses from punishment of course depends on the form of punishment adopted (we consider the question of the *credibility* of this punishment below, here we examine only its extent). In the literature three main types of punishment strategy have been analysed.

(i) *Nash reversion*: it is generally expected that the profits firms receive as a result of collusion exceed those they would earn in the one-shot NE, otherwise they might as well not collude. In that case, one way of inflicting a loss of profit in retaliation for reneging on the agreement would be to revert to the NE of the one-shot game, either permanently or for a number of periods sufficient to wipe out the gains from reneging, if that is possible. One limitation of this as a punishment is that it may not be very severe – it may imply a moderate loss of profit relative to the collusive agreement – and so may support collusion only for a small set of discount rates. A second limitation, at least if the joint profit-maximizing (cartel) allocation is thought to be a likely objective of the collusion, is that this allocation may not be sustainable by threats of reversion to a Cournot–Nash equilibrium. It is not difficult to construct cases in which firms have unequal marginal costs and some firms earn higher profits at the Nash equilibrium than at the joint profit-maximizing allocation.

(ii) *Minimax punishment*: for each firm in the market, it is possible to define its profit-maximizing action (an output or price) or *best response* given the actions of all other firms. We can then find the values of the latter which make the firm's best-response profit as small as possible. This is the firm's minimax profit, and it is also often referred to as its 'security level', since the firm cannot be forced to take a lower profit than that. Clearly the most drastic punishment for a firm that has reneged on the collusive agreement would be for the other firms to force it to its security level, either forever or for some specified number of time periods. It is straightforward to show that the threat of minimax punishment forever is always capable of enforcing a collusive agreement which gives a firm a higher profit than its security level for *some* set of interest rates. Thus denote the firm's security level profit by π^s, the profit level under the agreement by $\pi^* > \pi^s$, and the maximum profit the firm can earn when it reneges on the agreement in a single period by $\pi^R > \pi^*$. Then in contemplating reneging the firm must weigh up the one-off gain $\pi^R - \pi^*$, against the present value of the infinite future stream of profit it loses as a result of punishment, $(\pi^* - \pi^s)/r$, where r is the per-period interest rate. The firm will not renege if

$$\pi^R - \pi^* \leq (\pi^* - \pi^s)/r$$

or

$$r \leq (\pi^* - \pi^s)/(\pi^R - \pi^*)$$

and since the right-hand side is always positive there must be some set of interest rates for which this will hold. This proposition goes under the name of the Folk theorem in the theory of repeated games. In a given market, the set of profits which can be sustained by minimax punishments could be very large indeed.

(iii) *Simple penal codes*: Abreu's theory of simple penal codes involves a 'stick and carrot' form of punishment. For each firm that is party to the agreement, a 'punishment path' is formulated, which specifies outputs (or prices) for each firm to be adopted if the firm in question deviates from the agreement. This punishment path involves two phases: a phase of expanded outputs (lower prices) which inflicts loss of profit on the deviant; then the remainder of the path consists of a return to the original collusive outputs. Thus the path could be thought of as a period of price warfare followed by reversion to collusion. The loss of profit in the punishment phase must be enough to wipe out the gain from reneging. If the deviant reneges again in the punishment phase, this is met with a reimposition of the punishment phase *from its beginning*, thus postponing the date of reversion to the more profitable collusive phase. This reversion to collusion is the carrot to induce the deviant to accept whatever is meted out to it in the punishment phase. If one of the non-deviant firms fails to carry out its role in punishing the cheat by producing its punishment output, it in turn is treated as having reneged and the firms adopt the punishment path for this firm. It can be shown that again a large set of collusive allocations can be supported by threats of punishment of this kind provided firms do not discount the future 'too heavily'.

These three types of punishment strategy will sustain different sets of collusive allocations, but the main point of interest in comparing them is that of the credibility of the strategies. Clearly, if a threat of punishment is to be effective in sustaining collusion the firms must believe that the punishment would actually be carried out if the need arose. This not only requires the firm reneging on the agreement to 'accept its punishment'. Since in general inflicting punishment may be costly to the non-reneging firms, it must be credible that they would in fact do so. In the case of the first two of the above punishment strategies, Nash reversion and minimax, the acceptance of punishment by the deviant is not an issue. In each case the punishment profit corresponds to its best response to the actions of the other firms. In the case of a simple penal code, acceptance of its punishment is the best action by the deviant given that the alternative is reimposition of the punishment path: punishment outputs are so chosen that it is better not to postpone the date of reversion to collusion than to make a short-term gain from deviating from the punishment path. We shall, therefore, focus on the question of the credibility of the threat that the non-deviating firms will actually carry out the punishment.

Study of the general question of credibility of threats in dynamic games has led to the formulation of the 'refinement' of the Nash equilibrium concept termed 'subgame perfect equilibrium'. We can illustrate with the case of minimax punishment and, for simplicity, assume that there are just two firms. If each firm believes the other's threat to minimax forever following a defection, its best response is not to defect. Now, consider what would be the situation at the beginning of the period immediately following a defection. In the game beginning at that time, which is a proper subgame of the original game, it is not in the best interest of the non-deviating firm actually to minimax the other. For suppose this firm believes that the deviant believes that it will be minimaxed, and so will produce the corresponding output. Then the punishing firm's best response to this is *not to* carry out the punishment but to produce its corresponding profit-maximizing output. There is nothing to make it in the firm's best interests actually to follow through with the punishment in the *period following* a deviation, given the game that then presents itself. This will then be perceived in the previous period, and so the threat of minimax punishment will not be credible. To be credible, it must be in a firm's best interest to carry out the threat at the time it is called upon to do so. This criterion of credibility is more formally embodied in Selten's equilibrium concept of *subgame perfection*. According to this, a subgame perfect equilibrium strategy for a game is one which gives a Nash equilibrium strategy for *every subgame* of the game. The above example of a minimax punishment strategy was not subgame perfect because, in the subgame beginning in the period just after a defection, the minimax choices did not constitute a Nash equilibrium.

Both Nash reversion and Abreu's simple penal codes are subgame perfect equilibrium strategies and so satisfy this criterion of credibility. The former does so because a strategy of playing Nash equilibrium in every constituent game is also a Nash equilibrium of an entire repeated game. In the case of the simple penal code, the essential reason it is in the interest of a firm in this case to carry out the threat of punishment is that it believes that if it does not it itself will be punished. This in turn is credible because if any other firm does not join in this punishment it will be punished, and so on. Thus belief in the credibility of punishment is sustained by the expectation that each firm will prefer to be the punisher than the punished. This can be put in its least intuitively reasonable light if we assume just two firms. If firm 1 reneges, firm 2 in the next period must punish it. If firm 2 reneges on punishment, then in the following period firm 1 must punish firm 2 for not having punished it in the previous period, and so on.

This reliance on 'self-lacerating' punishment strategies has led a number of authors to propose an alternative criterion of credibility, known as 'renegotiation proofness'. [. . .] They begin by asking the question: in the period immediately following a defection, what would stop the firms getting together and, instead of actually carrying out the punishment, agreeing to reinstitute the collusive agreement? The game from that period looks just as it did when the original agreement was concluded – because of the infinite horizon assumption every subgame is identical to the original game – and so if it was in the firms' interests to negotiate that agreement initially it will be in their interests now to renegotiate that agreement. But if firms perceive that a deviation will be followed by renegotiation rather than punishment this means that punishment would never be carried out, and so agreement to collude could not be reached in the first place. Abreu's strategies appear to rule out such renegotiation possibilities – an agreement is made once and for all and can never be reopened.

This argument leads to the *renegotiation proofness* criterion of credibility of threats. Punishment strategies are credible only if they are not only subgame perfect but also not capable of being pre-empted by renegotiation of the agreement if the occasion arises that they must be implemented. Informally put, in the case of an oligopolistic market this can be achieved by an agreement which specifies that the punishing firms choose outputs or prices which yield them higher profit than at the collusive allocation, so that they would actually gain in the punishment phase. This ensures that they would not be prepared to renegotiate back to the original agreement.

These theories suggest that collusion may or may not be successful in a particular market: that depends on the values taken by a set of market or firm-specific parameters. The assumption that the same constituent game is repeated period after period also implies that collusion, if achieved, is perfectly stable and never breaks down. Although the non-co-operative collusive equilibrium is sustained by threats, those threats never have to be implemented because they are successful. Thus we would never observe price wars. Given that price wars *are* observed, the question arises of how to explain them within this type of approach. [. . .]

Stigler's insight was that randomness in demand provides scope for cheating on a collusive agreement, and creates a problem of statistical inference in enforcing that agreement. In Green and Porter's model it is assumed that a firm's choice of output cannot be observed by another firm, and the sum of all outputs determines market price according to a demand function which is subject to unobservable random shocks. Then, when price is low firms do not know for sure whether it was because someone cheated (produced a larger than agreed output), or because demand was low. The strategy for maintaining collusion consists of choosing a critical level of price such that, if market price falls below that level, firms infer cheating and enter a punishment phase, a price war. It is always possible (for one set of discount rates) to find a critical price level that will fully enforce adherence to the agreement – no one cheats. There is now, however, a non-zero probability that in any time period a price war will break out, and in an infinitely repeated market it is virtually certain that one will be observed. The interesting, though not necessarily plausible, feature of this result is that firms know that when the price falls below the critical level this is due to a random shock, because they know it pays no one to cheat, but nevertheless they must still go into the punishment phase to enforce the collusive agreement. This is clearly very much open to the critique based upon renegotiation-proofness, even more so than in the case without uncertainty. From the point of view of this paper, an important aspect of the model is that it shows the costs that can be imposed (in the form of probable price wars) when firms' outputs are unknown to each other and demand is stochastic. We return to this point when we consider the subject of information agreements later.

[. . .]

FACILITATING TACIT COLLUSION

Many theorists see the models surveyed in the previous section as giving analytical precision to the idea of tacit collusion.

[. . .]

[. . .] 'Collusion' should, certainly for antitrust purposes, refer to a form of conduct, not the value of an outcome: collusive behaviour might well result in less than monopoly profits. It is tacit not simply because of the absence of a binding (legally enforceable) agreement, but because of the absence of any explicit agreement whatsoever. Explicit collusion would involve the firms in talking to each other, explicitly agreeing to produce half the monopoly output each, and, quite possibly, agreeing also that deviation by one would be punished by a price war. The fact that the agreement is sustained by threats of market sanctions rather than a binding contract makes it no less explicit, at least in the eyes of antitrust law. Tacit collusion, on the other hand, would involve no explicit agreement but simply the unspoken acceptance by the two firms that it was in their best interests each to produce half the monopoly output on the understanding that failure to do so would provoke a price war.

As with non-co-operative playing of the one-shot game, the tacitly collusive equilibrium still requires information. [Even in the simplest homogeneous output-setting duopoly each] firm must know that the other's costs are identical to its own, and must know that they have the same beliefs about the market demand function as well as in the credibility of the punishment that would result from a deviation. It is easy to see that these information requirements expand considerably with the number of firms, product heterogeneity, spatial dispersion of markets, uncertainty about future demands and costs, rate of technological change, and the extent of threats from entry of new firms. If firms are to collude tacitly, they must somehow choose prices and outputs which are sustainable by a credible punishment strategy that also has to be tacitly agreed upon. We have seen that there may be many punishment strategies, and relative to any one of them there may be a very large set of sustainable price–output configurations. The firms must somehow define the set of feasible agreements, reach a point within it, preserve stability of the agreement, and make the threat of punishment as effective and credible as possible.

It is, therefore, natural that in real-world markets many so-called 'facilitating devices' would have been developed. These are arrangements or practices which can be construed as helping firms in at least one of the four steps to stable, successful tacit collusion: defining the possible agreements; focusing upon one; preserving it; and providing for credible effective punishment. It should also be noted that in many cases they would also facilitate explicit collusion, and so their use does not rule out the (possibly concealed) existence of this. We shall consider them in order of increasing specificity.

Information exchange: a flow of information among firms is clearly essential for all four aspects of successful collusion. Firms may enter into formal information agreements, under which they undertake to exchange information on costs, outputs, prices, and discounts. Exchange of cost information is clearly important in defining the set of possible agreements and arriving at one. Exchange of price and output data is important in detecting deviation: the shorter the lag between cheating and detection, the smaller the incentive to cheat. Such exchange of information is, of course, possible in the absence of a formal information agreement.

Trade associations: many industries have a central organization which may function fairly innocuously, handling public relations at the industry-wide level and organizing conventions, trade fairs, etc. However, they may also act as facilitating devices, collecting and disseminating information on costs, outputs, and prices, suggesting price lists (for example, the professional associations for lawyers, doctors, and architects publish 'recommended fee scales') and policing the (tacit) agreement. For example, the trade association in the nut and bolt industry actually employed individuals who posed as buyers and tried to obtain discounts on prices from sellers suspected of cheating. Trade associations may also carry out services such as demand forecasting and capacity planning for the market as a whole. This can be important both in achieving agreement on prices in the short run, and in preventing the development of excess capacity, which can pose a serious threat to collusion in the long run. At the very least, trade associations often provide the opportunities for the 'meeting of merriment and diversion' mentioned in Adam Smith's famous remark.

Price leadership: it is usual to distinguish between 'dominant firm' and 'barometric' price leadership. In the former, the largest firm first announces price changes and the other firms then follow within a short space of time; in the latter, some non-dominant firm, which presumably is considered the best at judging the market conditions, plays this role. In many markets, however, the identity of the firm initiating a price change may vary over time, possibly to avoid the impression that there *is* a price leader, or to spread more equitably the unpopularity of being the first firm to raise prices. Clearly, the practice of price leadership is a way of solving the problem of choosing one price agreement in the set of possible agreements. If the leader is good at finding mutually acceptable prices, or has the market power to punish deviants from its prices sufficiently, agreement can be entirely tacit. For many writers the 'conscious parallelism' in prices associated with price leadership is the very essence of tacit collusion.[3]

Collaborative research and cross-licensing of patents: for sound reasons – high fixed costs, economies of scale, and risk-sharing – firms may pool research and development (R&D) resources and set up a common R&D agency. This obviously limits competition in product design and innovation and facilitates uniform pricing of the resulting products. In the case of cross-licensing on the other hand, firms license use of the results of their own research out to their competitors. It is legal under the terms of these licences to specify selling prices and to place other restrictions on sale, for example geographical area. Thus what may at first sight appear to be something that facilitates competition can actually be a form of legal collusion.

MFN and MC clauses in buyer–seller contracts: Salop [has] pointed out that 'most favoured nation' (MFN) and 'meeting competition' (MC) clauses in contracts between buyers and sellers can act to facilitate collusion among sellers. A MFN clause guarantees to a buyer that if, when the contract is concluded or within some specified time period later, the seller makes a sale to another buyer at a lower price, then the buyer in question will also receive that lower price. A MC clause guarantees that if the buyer can find another seller offering a lower price, then the seller in question will match that price upon presentation of appropriate evidence. Salop argues convincingly that both these types of clauses help sustain collusion. Note first that since they form part of a contract between buyer and seller they are legally enforceable and that in itself is an important advantage because it reduces the cost of enforcing collusion. Moreover, the buyer has an incentive to detect and report deviations from the price agreement, either by the seller in question (under MFN) or by other sellers (under MC). A MFN clause sustains collusion because it makes it costly for a seller to reduce price in a discriminatory way, which is how secret cheating on a price agreement often takes place. If price cuts have to be paid to all buyers this reduces their profitability as well as increasing their detectability. A MC clause obviously sustains collusion by creating an incentive for a buyer to report to a seller keeping to the agreement the prices of a seller who may be cheating on the agreement, at the same time nullifying the effect of the latter.

Resale price maintenance: this is a system under which manufacturers contractually control the minimum level of prices charged by retailers. This obviously stops collusion at the manufacturing stage being undone by price competition at the point of sale to the ultimate buyer.

Basing point pricing: this is a pricing system often encountered in industries, such as steel and cement, where transport costs are high relative to production costs and buyers and sellers are spatially dispersed. In one variant, manufacturing plants of each seller are designated as bases, and a 'base price' is set at each of them. There is also a standard table of transport charges. Then, a buyer at any given location will be quoted a price by each seller, equal to the base price at the nearest base plus the standard charge for transporting the product from the base to the buyer's location. The result is then that *delivered* prices to any buyer are always uniform across sellers, and there is no price competition. Clearly sellers must exchange information – the list of bases and base prices, the standard transport charges – but no *explicit* agreement to collude on prices need be made.

Common costing books: in some industries where there may be variation in the form of the finished product because of variation in the buyer's specifications (for example, industrial engines, building services) a book may be circulated by a trade association which shows how the overall cost of the specific product variant can be calculated. This encourages price uniformity among sellers and makes it less easy to label price-cutting a computational mistake.

This list covers the most generally encountered facilitating devices. Particular markets may provide examples of practices specific to them. For example, if airlines share a computerized reservation system this makes it easy to monitor and collude on prices. Insurance companies may collaborate in working out loss probabilities and this leads to uniformity in premium rates. It should also be noted that there are many opportunities for company representatives to make their views known to each other on the state of the market and the direction prices should take, for example, in after-dinner speeches, newspaper interviews, articles in trade publications as well as while doing lunch.

POLICY IMPLICATIONS

[. . .]

[. . .] [T]here have been cases in which 'the inference of illegal conspiracy' has been drawn from 'detailed similarity of behaviour'. From the economic point of view, the problem is that in most cases the US antitrust process is concerned with deciding whether *conduct* has been illegal, rather than with the appraisal of the economic consequences of whatever conduct may have taken place. In this respect the UK system, though it also has substantial defects, is [arguably] superior. [. . .]

In theoretical language, we could state the core of the problem as being that tacit collusion is a form of non-co-operative equilibrium, just as is Nash equilibrium in a one-shot oligopoly game (which, as we argued earlier, would never be regarded as collusive). The equilibrium results from rational pursuit of individual self-interest in a situation of perceived mutual interdependence. The behaviour of firms need not be conspiratorial in the legal sense. Therefore a conduct-based approach such as that underlying US antitrust law inevitably encounters difficulties.

[. . .]

NOTES

1 Note, however, that the firms are assumed to have full knowledge of each other's profit functions, which, at the least, requires knowledge of each other's cost functions. There is clearly a role for exchange of information to achieve this, as we discuss more fully below.

2 Even in finite horizon games, there are cases in which collusive behaviour may constitute a non-co-operative equilibrium. If there are multiple Nash equilibria of the constituent game, over which players have strict preferences, then collusion can be sustained by threats to play less-preferred Nash equilibrium strategies. If the end-period of the finite horizon game is not known with certainty, then at each period there is a probability there will be a next period in which punishment can take place, and by factoring this probability into the discount rate the model becomes similar to the infinite horizon case. Finally, if each player believes that there is a non-zero probability that the other will play co-operatively, because she is 'crazy' or not individually rational, [then it can be shown that], even in a finite horizon game, if the horizon is long enough, firms may play co-operatively. In the interests of simplicity, and since similar issues arise, we subsume all these cases under the 'infinite horizon' case.

3 At the same time, price leadership may also be a way of implementing an agreement arrived at by explicit, though secret, negotiations. Colluding firms may well choose to announce price increases in a non-simultaneous way.

FURTHER READING

See the following works on the economic issues raised in this chapter. Some of these works are also relevant to issues relating to horizontal agreements in Part 3.

Abreu, D. (1986), 'Extremal equilibria of oligopolistic supergames', 39 *Journal of Economic Theory*, 191.

Brock, W. A. and Scheinkman, J. A. (1985), 'Price-setting supergames with capacity constraints', 52 *Review of Economic Studies*, 371.

Deneckre, R. and Kovenock, D. (1992), 'Price leadership', *59 Review of Economic Studies*, 143.

Dixon, H. (1989), 'Oligopoly theory made simple', in S. Davies, B. Lyons with H. Dixon, P. Geroski, *Economics of Industrial Organisation* (Longman, London).

Donsimoni, M. P., Economides, N. S. and Polemarchakis, H. M. (1986), 'Stable Cartels', *27 International Economic Review*, 317.

Friedman, J. W. (1971), 'A non-cooperative equilibrium for supergames', 38 *Review of Economic Studies*, 1.

Fudenberg, D. and Maskin, E. (1986), 'The Folk theorem in repeated games with discounting or with incomplete information', 54 *Econometrica*, 533.

Hay, G. A. and Kelley, D. (1974), 'An empirical survey of price fixing conspiracies', 17 *Journal of Law and Economics*, 13.

Lambson, V. (1987), 'Optimal penal codes in price-setting supergames with capacity constraints', 54 *Review of Economic Studies*, 385.

Osborne, D. K. (1976), 'Cartel problems', 66 *American Economic Review*, 835.

Porter, R. H. (1983), 'Optimal cartel trigger-price strategies', 29 *Journal of Economic Theory*, 313.

Salop, S. (1986), 'Practices that credibly facilitate oligopoly coordination', in J. Stiglitz and F. Mathewson (eds), *New Developments in the Analysis of Market Structure* (MIT Press, Cambridge).

Slade, M. E. (1987), 'Interfirm rivalry in a repeated game: an empirical test of tacit collusion', 35 *Journal of Industrial Economics*, 499.

Stigler, G. J. (1964), 'A theory of oligopoly', 72 *Journal of Political Economy*, 44.

Tirole, J. (1988), *The Theory of Industrial Organization* (MIT Press, London), Chapter 6.

5

REGULATED PRACTICES: FORM AND EFFECT

One of the principal differences between the respective approaches of EEC and UK law lies in the distinction between a form-based approach and an effects-based approach. There has been a debate in the UK as to the relative merits of such approaches. The consultative process, conducted through the Green Paper extracted below, resulted in the publication of a White Paper (**Opening Markets: New Policy on Restrictive Trade Practices**, Cm. 729). The UK government has signalled its intention to move over to an effects-based system for the regulation of restrictive trade agreements. A parallel debate on the approach of the legislation has been taking place in relation to the control of monopoly practices (see the extract from the Green Paper **Abuse of Market Power**, Section 18.1).

5.1 Department of Trade and Industry, *Review of Restrictive Trade Practices Policy*, Cm. 331 (HMSO, London, 1988)

2.3 The existing legislation defines the class of agreements to which it applies and therefore it catches all agreements of a specified form (i.e. it adopts the 'form-based' approach). Consequently, a large number of agreements are caught, and have to be dealt with, although they do not significantly restrict competition. This UK approach differs from the legislation in many other countries and, importantly, also from the competition provisions of the Treaty of Rome where it is the effect or purpose of agreements in respect of competition which determines whether they are covered by the legislation or not (an 'effects-based' approach). These effects-based systems have the considerable advantage that the scope of the legislation is consistent with its objective. It is, of course, true that under the RTPA, the effects of registered agreements are considered by the Restrictive Practices Court (RPC) when agreements are referred to it for assessment of whether they operate against the public interest. A change from a form-based to an effects-based system therefore only relates to the stage of registration. But it is the registration criteria that determine which agreements come forward for evaluation and it is this stage therefore which is of vital importance.

[. . .]

AN EFFECTS-BASED PROHIBITION

3.2 The Government propose to prohibit agreements and concerted practices which are anti-competitive. But this does not necessarily include agreements which only affect the ability of an individual competitor to compete. The agreements must adversely affect competition in the relevant market taken as a whole to fall within the scope of the prohibition; it is the potential effect on the customer – or supplier – which is important. The size of the total relevant market will, of course, vary according to circumstances including the type of product or service involved.

3.3 An effects-based system would focus on agreements and practices which had an effect on the market as a whole. It would therefore release businesses and associations from the burden of registering all agreements which contain restrictions regardless of their effect on competition and, at the same time, it would bring under control anti-competitive agreements which at present fall outside the scope of the present legislation.

3.4 There are disadvantages. The changes will undoubtedly introduce a period of uncertainty for industry. But the Government believe that the change will be considerably less disruptive than it would have been when first considered during the inquiry into restrictive trade practices in 1979 [. . .] because industry has now gained experience with the operation of EC competition rules.

3.5 It has also been argued that an effects-based system might make it more difficult for lawyers to give clear and reliable advice to their clients, for example, in relation to the anti-competitive effect of an agreement. Again, experience gained by UK industry of EC rules should reduce this problem. In any case, the Government envisage reducing the level of uncertainty as much as possible through the publication of guidelines. The authority will also be able to deal with informal enquiries and requests for guidance. The Government are aware that this will entail a considerable change for UK business. But given the overall benefits of clarified scope, consistency with the EC system and the reduced burden resulting from the removal of the present registration system, such a change is now worthwhile.

3.6 Two main options for drawing up a new effects-based law were considered: a statutory prohibition of agreements which have anti-competitive effects (and, as the next chapter shows, this itself breaks down into two options) or a system which bans agreements with anti-competitive effects after they have been found upon investigation to be against the public interest. The Government have concluded that the second option is too weak.

3.7 The reasons for this judgment are as follows. Weighing up the public interest involves a careful balancing act. The promotion or maintenance of competition may only be one of a number of other factors and policy objectives which the authority is expected to take into account. But it is the promotion of competition which is at the root of the Government's economic philosophy; and since it is anti-competitive agreements which have to be suppressed, the law should be targeted on these from the outset.

3.8 The Government are clear that any new system will need to be a strong deterrent against anti-competitive agreements. A weakness of the present legislation which has been identified by a number of commentators is the lack of sanctions against transgressors. A system which relies on registration followed by a public interest test means that companies can operate anti-competitive agreements without their being positively prohibited by law and then argue their public interest case in due course. This gives companies the opportunity to operate such agreements, even if only for a limited period, with impunity. Furthermore, since those firms which were found to have acted against the public interest would not have behaved unlawfully, it is doubtful whether tough enough penalties could be imposed. In other words, such a system would be a less effective deterrent. In addition, it is more difficult to envisage a private action being brought against something which is not illegal *ab initio* and private actions could be a useful supplement to enforcement of the new law. (Private actions and powers and sanctions are considered further in Chapter 7.)

3.9 This is not to say that everything

about a prohibition system is straightforward. The authority will need to weigh up cases under this system too: companies will no doubt advance arguments involving the definition of the market or concerning the long-term pro-competitive advantages of short-term anti-competitive restrictions. But, in that its central thrust is clear and that there is less danger of ineffective enforcement, the prohibition system has the advantage.

5.2 B. Hawk, 'The American (anti-trust) revolution: lessons for the EEC?', 9, *European Competition Law Review*, 53 (1988)

[. . .]

A major dispute under EEC law concerns the definition of prevention, restriction or distortion of competition under Article 85(1). Many commentators criticise the Commission's penchant to avoid any serious analysis of an agreement's actual competitive harms and benefits (for example effect on prices or output) by finding that 85(1) applies simply on the basis of a restriction on the freedom of one of the parties and/or third parties. This debate has significant practical implications and raises questions about the relative importance and roles of the Commission, national courts and anti-trust counsel in the interpretation of Article 85(1). A broad definition of restriction of competition under Article 85(1) shifts most of the inquiry over to Article 85(3) where only the Commission has the power to grant exemptions, thus requiring notification and excluding national courts from the more important part of the anti-trust analysis.

United States anti-trust law is relevant to this debate not only because it may offer useful lessons to the EEC. US anti-trust law has also been made relevant by critics who call for a 'rule of reason' under Article 85(1). As seen below, the long history of the rule of reason in the United States reveals numerous ambiguities and analytical problems many of which US courts have only begun to address. These ambiguities and problems do not argue against a fuller economic inquiry under Article 85(1). They do counsel that the debate about Article 85(1) will produce more heat than light if the participants propose a rule of reason solution without taking the US experience into account.

The United States and the EEC take very different approaches to defining respectively restraint of trade under section 1 of the Sherman Act and restriction of competition under Article 85(1). US courts generally reject restraint on freedom of the parties to a contract or third parties as sufficient to establish a section 1 restraint of trade. The Supreme Court reasons that such a definition would be overly broad and could literally cover most if not all contractual agreements on the reasoning that the contract contains provisions which limit or 'restrict' the freedom of the parties as it existed prior to the contract. An effect on competition is necessary; harm to the plaintiff or a particular trader is not sufficient. This is clearly accepted. Less clear is what must be proved or is meant by effect on competition. This in turn leads to the US distinction between *per se* unlawful restraints of trade and agreements subject to the rule of reason under which agreements can be adjudged reasonable or unreasonable. Certain agreements are deemed *per se* unreasonable restraints of trade under any circumstances on the ground that they almost invariably harm competition through higher prices and reduced output without any redeeming pro-competitive benefits. The list of *per se* offences has been reduced to price fixing (both horizontal and vertical) and horizontal market division and customer allocation. Boycotts and tie-ins are now *per se* unlawful only under certain limited conditions. Moreover, some recent decisions indicate an increasing reluctance to condemn as *per se* unlawful restrictions concerning prices and markets even among competitors where the restrictions are not 'naked' – that is, where they are ancillary to an efficiency-enhancing arrangement. Under the *per se* rule no inquiry is made into the actual competitive effects of the challenged agreement which is declared unlawful on its face. More specifically, the court does not examine defendant firms' market power, does not define the market (at least not with any precision) and does not evaluate asserted benefits of the agreement. Thus the *per se* rule provides several advantages, notably predictability of legal rules, provision of a bright-line deterrent to undesirable conduct and reduced judicial and enforcement costs. The *per se* rule also partially rests on the notion that courts may be inappropriate fora to resolve the complex economic issues involved.

The rule of reason analysis is far more complex and less defined. As 'classically' formulated in 1918 in *Chicago Board of Trade*, an elaborate inquiry must be made, including the history of the industry, the parties' intent, benefits and harms of the challenged practices, etc. This open-ended definition of the rule of reason permits consideration of so-called economic evidence and more traditional evidence such as the intent of the parties. The tests applied under the general rubric of the rule of reason have varied considerably as to the comprehensiveness of the market analysis required. Many decisions formulate the rule of reason primarily in terms of purpose, effect and less restrictive alternatives. Other decisions speak in terms of benefits and harms, with less or no emphasis on intent or purpose.

Courts continue to struggle with the rule of reason. The shift away from *per se* rules to rule of reason analyses has intensified this struggle. Much of the doctrinal confusion arises from the Supreme Court's failure to re-examine the rule of reason for many decades. This situation has changed in the last ten years. In 1978 the Court declared that the rule of reason inquiry 'is confined to a consideration of impact on competitive conditions'. Thus health and safety justifications or considerations unrelated to effects on the marketplace would appear irrelevant under the rule of reason. More importantly, the Supreme Court has emphasised that there is frequently no clear bright line between the rule of reason and *per se* rules. Thus the distinction between a *per se* rule and the rule of reason has been blurred considerably.

The shift away from *per se* rules has increased the complexity and costs of litigation and has reduced legal certainty. This has prompted courts, commentators and the Justice Department to formulate truncated rules of reason which obviate the necessity of the court engaging in an elaborate market analysis in every case. In most cases this has worked in favour of defendants. For example, many lower courts use market power as a filter and dismiss rule of reason claims before trial where plaintiff fails to show that defendant(s) has significant market power. However, the most recent two Supreme Court decisions to apply a quick look or truncated rule of reason affirmed that the challenged agreements were unreasonable. In so doing, the Court held that plaintiff does not have to prove defendant's market power (or probably define the relevant market) under certain not entirely clear circumstances.

In *NCAA* the Court refused to apply a *per se* rule to certain provisions in an agreement between an association of universities and television networks concerning the telecasts of college football games. The contracts imposed, among other things, limitations on the number of televised appearances by one school during the season and an absolute maximum on the number of televised games. The contracts also provided for minimum aggregate compensation which resulted in each school receiving the same fee for each national or regional television appearance. Several popular football powers challenged the restrictions. The Court held first that although agreements among competitors to restrict output are ordinarily subject to a *per se* rule, this was inappropriate because some restrictions were essential in order that the product (televised college football) be available at all. The Court went on to apply a truncated or 'quick look' rule of reason analysis under which the agreements were found to constitute unreasonable restraints of trade.

In applying its truncated rule of reason, the Court first found anti-competitive effects notably restrictions on output, higher prices and limitation of consumer choice. The Court then stated that no inquiry into market power is required where the challenged practice is a 'naked' restraint (that is, without redeeming competitive benefits). Finally, if anti-competitive effects are proved (and market power in the case of a non-naked restraint), then defendants bear a heavy burden of establishing competitive benefits as an affirmative defence – a burden that was not met.

A truncated rule of reason was also made in *Dentists* where the Court upheld a Federal Trade Commission decision that an agreement by dentists not to provide X-rays to third party insurers as part of a fee review system was unreasonable. A *per se* rule was rejected on the grounds that the courts are slow to condemn rules of professional associations and the impact of the challenged practice was not immediately obvious. Under the rule of reason the Court asked first whether plaintiff had proved actual anti-competitive effects. The Court affirmed the finding of actual harms, although it emphasised primarily the limitation on consumer choice and the possible future effect on insurance premiums and medical cost-containment programmes. The Court declared further that no elaborate inquiry into market power was necessary both on the *NCAA* rationale that the refusal was a 'naked' restraint and on a more persuasive rationale – that is, market power and market definition are relevant to determine whether conduct has the potential for causing genuine harm; if actual harms have been otherwise proved, then it is unnecessary to inquire into market power. Finally, the Court held that no efficiency-enhancing benefits or other justifications had been proved.

Two principal conclusions can be drawn about the recent US decisions. First, the line between the *per se* rule and the rule of reason is increasingly blurred with courts applying 'quick look' *per se* rules and 'quick look' rules of reason. Second, the major issue in the cases surrounds the circumstances in which inquiry into market power and market definition can be avoided. This issue is frequently addressed in the context of interpreting the Supreme Court opinions in *NCAA* and *Dentists*, particularly the definition of 'naked' restraint and the question whether 'naked' restraints are the only exception to the rule that market power (and market definition) are essential elements of the rule of reason analysis. These questions are often dispositive in cases involving horizontal restraints where characterisation of the challenged provision as not 'naked' may defeat plaintiff's claim where defendants lack market power. Non-price vertical restraints are usually viewed as ancillary or non-'naked' and thus lack of the supplier's market power will preclude a finding of unreasonableness.

Despite the ambiguities seen above, the struggle to refine the test for a restraint of trade under US law nevertheless compares favourably with the near anarchy under Article 85 engendered by inconsistent Commission and Court interpretations of restriction of competition under Article 85(1) and the bifurcation of what ideally should be a single anti-trust analysis into the double tests of Article 85(1) and Article 85(3). This *maudite* bifurcation presents a more serious obstacle to predictable and coherent rules than the current doctrinal confusion in the United States which may be a transitional phenomenon.

FURTHER READING

Borrie, G. (1986), 'Restrictive practices control in the United Kingdom', *Journal of Business Law*, 358 (extracted in section 6.2).

Forrester, I. and Norall, C. (1984), 'The laicization of Community law', 21 *Common Market Law Review*, 11.

Korah, V. (1992), 'The judgment in *Delimitis*: a milestone towards a realistic assessment of the effects of an agreement or a damp squib?', *European Intellectual Property Review*, 167.

6

INSTITUTIONS AND PROCESSES

6.1 Department of Trade and Industry, *Review of Restrictive Trade Practices Policy*, Cm. 331 (HMSO, London, 1988)

[. . .]

1. The Restrictive Trade Practices Act 1976 (RTPA) is the key instrument in the control of restrictive trade practices within the UK. It is the most resource intensive of the competition laws for the OFT and currently involves some 30 administrative, professional and support staff out of a total competition staff of 100. Under the Act details of certain kinds of agreements which restrict the freedom of action of parties to the agreement are required to be furnished within specified time limits to the Director General of Fair Trading (DGFT) and are entered on a public register of restrictive agreements. The primary purpose of the public register is to inform third parties who might be affected by the operation of a registrable agreement of its existence and conditions: at the present time there are about 6,600 such agreements on the register; many of these are no longer operative and many have been modified and no longer have anti-competitive effect.

2. The Act provides that an agreement is registrable if it is between two or more parties carrying on business within the UK in the production or supply of goods and if, under the agreement, certain kinds of restriction are accepted by two or more parties. The restrictions concerned include: prices to be charged; terms or conditions on which goods will be supplied and quantities or descriptions of goods to be supplied. Similar provisions apply to agreements between suppliers of services, and agreements between producers or suppliers of goods who agree to exchange information as to certain matters.

3. The DGFT is under a statutory duty to refer registrable agreements to the Restrictive Practices Court (RPC) for a decision as to whether the restrictions they contain are contrary to the public interest. In most cases, however, court proceedings are now unnecessary: the DGFT will usually refrain from taking proceedings if he considers it appropriate to do so having regard to any relevant EC decision or if the agreement has ended or if all the restrictions which make it registrable have been removed, or have ceased to have effect. Most commonly, if the restrictions in an agreement are not of such significance as to call for investigation by the RPC, the Secretary of State may issue a direction under Section 21(2) of the Act discharging the DGFT from referring the agreement to the RPC.

4. Where a registered agreement is referred to the RPC by the DGFT, parties may or may not choose to defend the restrictions in the agreement as being not against the public interest; the Court proceedings centre on an examination of each of the specific restrictions and not on the whole agreement. Unless the RPC on certain criteria laid down in the RTPA decides that the restrictions are not against the public interest it has a duty to strike them

down. Breach of any order prohibiting the giving of effect to any restriction or prohibiting the making of any other similar agreement (to the 'like effect') in the future is contempt of court.

5. A main conclusion of the last major inquiry into restrictive trade practices control (*A Review of Restrictive Trade Practices Policy: A Consultative Document*, March 1979, Cmnd. 7512) was that the RTPA had been 'very effective' in controlling the more formal kinds of price fixing and market sharing agreements which had been endemic in UK industry up to the late 1950s. The available economic evidence suggested that the abandonment of such agreements had generally led to an increase in competition, to lower prices and to an improvement in efficiency and that the legislation had 'achieved its primary objective by contributing to improved industrial efficiency'. But this conclusion was reached with two qualifications in mind: (i) 'growing evidence of evasion by failure to register' and the scope for avoidance of the legislation by drafting agreements in ways that made them non-registrable; (ii) the possibility that the legislation may have inhibited the making of agreements which would have improved efficiency and been in the public interest.

6. The 1979 review also looked at the way the legislation operated and concluded that a number of changes were desirable with the following objectives: firstly, to make it easier for desirable agreements to be made which may be unintentionally deterred or prevented by the legislation; secondly to simplify the operation of the legislation and its comprehensibility; and thirdly to strengthen the means of enforcement.

7. The 1979 review also considered whether there should be a fundamental change in restrictive practices control from the present form-based to an effects-based system. But it concluded that at that time the likely benefits from such a change would not offset the disadvantages likely from the resultant upheaval. However, it should be pointed out here that the conclusion that this change would lead to disruption was in part underpinned by a belief that the comparatively minor changes proposed would be sufficient at least to reduce the inflexibility of the existing system.

8. Following the change of Government, the recommendations from that Review relating to restrictive trade practices were not taken up. On the other hand, as we shall see, the criticisms that were aired in the 1979 review still exist; indeed some problems have increased. But had the 1979 recommendations been implemented, it is not at all certain that the need for further change now would have been avoided; the essential form-based structure of the legislation would not have been affected.

9. The legislation remains very much the same as it was at the time of the previous review and therefore the review of the effectiveness of the legislation has inevitably covered much of the same ground as in 1979. But there have been additional factors to take into account, particularly the significant changes to the scope of the law since 1979. Some exemptions have been removed, for example for agreements between operators of bus services in Great Britain following bus deregulation, agreements relating to banking services in Northern Ireland and agreements on interest rates between building societies. At the same time, new exemptions have been introduced, such as those for insolvency services with the introduction of the Insolvency Act 1985 and those for financial services with the introduction of the Financial Services Act 1987. The scope of the Act therefore has been constantly modified and the present structure and extent of exemptions (including those for certain professional services in Schedule 1 of the Act) is clearly overdue for an overhaul. (Annex D indicates the range of exemptions.) Another consideration is that in 1979 the RTPA had applied to the service sector for only a short time; the additional experience of the 1980s has been invaluable in reviewing the effectiveness of the law.

10. Furthermore, when the last review took place the UK had been a member of the EC for only a relatively short time. Meanwhile, the impact of European com-

petition law and policy has increased. Companies have become much more used to having to deal with European law not only because of the passage of time but also because of the increasing internationalisation of business. It is against all these changes and additional considerations that the legislation has been reviewed once more.

REGISTRATION

11. Agreements continue to be registered in sizeable numbers each year, the cumulative total at the end of 1987 being 4,882 goods agreements and 1,771 services agreements. Until very recently, the number of unprocessed cases had been growing at almost 100 a year. About 1,500 agreements remain to be dealt with, reflecting the upsurge in the numbers being furnished by companies to the OFT following the 1976 Services Order.

12. Comparison of the first 200 services agreements put on the register with the last 200 at the end of 1986 suggests that fewer of the services agreements now going on to the register are obviously restrictive of competition: 58.5 per cent of the first 200 contained restrictions relating to charges compared with only 16 per cent of the 1986 sample. Of the last 200 registered in 1986, 21 per cent concerned the sale and purchase of businesses, 14 per cent terms and conditions of sale other than charges and 31 per cent franchising (a rapidly growing area). The requirement to register is based on the precise legal form of an agreement, and is not concerned at that stage with its actual or potential effect on competition.

13. This formalistic approach to restrictive trade practices control means that very large numbers of agreements without anti-competitive effects – indeed, they may even be pro-competitive – have to be registered. At the same time, certain agreements with anti-competitive effects might be drafted so as to avoid the law. This 'catch-all' characteristic and the resulting indiscriminate nature of the Act is unnecessarily burdensome on business and one of the prominent weaknesses of the present legislation.

14. The more obviously anti-competitive horizontal price-fixing or market-sharing agreements cannot easily be drafted in a way to avoid registration, given the very wide interpretation which the law gives to 'acceptance of a restriction'. With these agreements the problem is evasion rather than avoidance of the law.

EVASION AND DETERRENCE

15. It is impossible to assess the extent of deliberate evasion. The competitive pressures within much of UK industry since 1979 might have increased the desire to collude since collusion is frequently defensive. At the same time, the business climate in recent years may also have reduced the chance of collusion being successful: companies are tempted to break cartels in order to gain market share at the expense of their rivals. Examples of registrable but unregistered agreements continue to be unearthed and, in due course, are referred to the RPC. These have been concentrated in relatively few industries; many have been local collusive tendering agreements in the construction industry. No-one is likely to furnish details of collusive tendering and bid rigging and it would be naïve to assume it does not go on in other industries. Similarly meetings and discussions between businessmen may give rise to more informal understandings on prices or contracts which might well be registrable but which the parties will not see, or will not want to see, in that light.

16. Failure to furnish a registrable agreement is not an offence. However, if particulars of a registrable agreement are not furnished as required by the legislation, the restrictions in that agreement are void, it is unlawful for any party to the agreement to give effect to the restrictions or purport to enforce compliance with them, and any person affected by the agreement may bring an action for breach of statutory duty. But the deterrent effect of such actions has been slight since there have been no cases,

as far as the Government are aware, other than those settled out of court.

17. Where an unfurnished agreement is discovered and brought before the RPC the Court will normally make an order restraining the parties from giving effect to the agreement (in respect of the void restrictions) or to any other agreement details of which have not been properly furnished. Breach of the order would be contempt of court and can lead to the imposition of fines but it is difficult to prove and even then it is questionable whether the fines have been sufficiently heavy.

18. Perhaps the main reason for concern about evasion and enforcement is the general impression given by the Act. Whatever the impact of the early judgments of the RPC, the Act must now appear a relatively weak piece of legislation. Potential colluders will appreciate that the chances of being found out are low; even when agreements are detected, the penalty is unlikely to be a sufficient deterrent.

BENEFICIAL AGREEMENTS

19. The 'gateways' in the present legislation provide a wide variety of arguments that the parties may use to demonstrate to the RPC that restrictions in an agreement are not contrary to the public interest. The gateways are sufficiently wide that there is no need to spell out particular types of agreement such as agreements to co-operate on R&D, or other agreements which might in particular circumstances be found to be in the public interest. Parties to agreements have been unwilling to defend them in the Court, in part no doubt because the early cases before the RPC virtually all failed; and also to some extent because of the costs involved. Since the 1960s there have only been two cases where the parties have been prepared to argue on public interest grounds: the *ABTA* (travel agents) case and the *Stock Exchange*. In the former the Court did accept that the 'stabiliser' or the exclusive dealing arrangement by which ABTA tour operators and travel agency members would only deal with each other was not against the public interest because it enabled ABTA to put in place consumer protection arrangements that could not be provided so effectively in any other way. In the case of the *Stock Exchange*, the Restrictive Trade Practices (Stock Exchange) Act 1984 exempted the rules of the Stock Exchange from the RTPA and hence the court case was terminated.

20. From time to time, there are claims that the legislation as it has evolved inhibits desirable agreements, particularly in industries requiring structural reorganisation; but there is little evidence to back these claims. There have been few applications for exemption by the Secretary of State under section 29 for agreements 'of substantial importance to the national economy' (admittedly, a demanding requirement). It is true that rationalisation agreements may escape registration under the exemption for capital reconstruction schemes provided in Schedule 3 paragraph 1(2). But it is surprising, to put it no higher, that over the recent years of contraction in the manufacturing sector, more rationalisation-type agreements have not been furnished to the OFT. It is not clear whether this is because the legislation has inhibited industry from making such agreements or whether the agreements have been made but not registered. It may be of interest that in the Federal Republic of Germany where agreements which restrict competition are prohibited but where rationalisation and other types of 'beneficial' agreement can be exempt from the prohibition in particular circumstances, the number of such exemptions is not trivial.

SECTION 21(2)

21. As mentioned in paragraph 3 above, section 21(2) of the RTPA provides a means of dealing administratively with agreements which are registrable but are not of such significance as to call for inspection by the Court. If an agreement is registered, which has restrictions of suf-

ficient significance that the DGFT cannot make a section 21(2) representation, he has no option but to refer the agreement to the Court even if, in his view, the agreement is likely to be in the public interest.

22. There has been increased use of the section 21(2) procedure since the last review and indeed it now dominates the whole process. Significant restrictions, including price restrictions, have been removed from a large number of agreements by negotiation against the threat of Court proceedings. Where the agreement has not then been 'filleted' of all restrictions it has often been possible to obtain a section 21(2) direction for those that remain. By the end of 1987 680 section 21(2) representations had been made on goods agreements and 434 on services agreements.

23. Section 21(2) has been particularly effective in dealing with a wide range of services agreements brought within the scope of the Act since 1976. Price restrictions have been removed in agreements in the road haulage, cold storage, house removal, and freight forwarding sectors, for example, and a host of restrictions in agreements relating to professional and financial services. Given the dominance of franchise and sale and purchase agreements in recent times, many agreements can be dealt with under section 21(2) straight away. But some still involve negotiation.

24. There are disadvantages in this. The Act does not set out the test or criteria to be applied by the authorities in judging whether a restriction is significant enough to warrant investigation by the Court. Decisions are published in the DGFT's *Annual Report* and some guidance is contained in the OFT's Guide to the Act but businessmen may feel this is insufficient.

25. A major disadvantage is the time that can elapse before significant restrictions are negotiated away. There can be much toing and froing between lawyers. Representative bodies may need to await occasional Council meetings or get the approval of the membership for rule changes. From a sample of eighty-six cases in 1985 the average time for registration to section 21(2) direction was two years and nine months with forty-one cases taking less than one year and nine cases taking longer than eight years.

26. Nevertheless Court proceedings too are time-consuming and costly. From a sample of thirty-one Court cases since 1976 the average time between registration and judgment was three years and two months, the longest eight years. However, the Court is now little used except for undefended cases. Its primary function is to hear arguments and make public interest judgments on agreements yet it is hardly ever called into action for this purpose.

6.2 Sir Gordon Borrie, 'Restrictive practices control in the United Kingdom: big bangs and lesser detonations', *Journal of Business Law*, 358 (1986)

[. . .]

The Restrictive Trade Practices Act [1976] is certainly the most complex of the various United Kingdom competition statutes. It is concerned with registrable restrictive agreements and imposes a general duty on the Director General of Fair Trading to take all such agreements to the Restrictive Practices Court for a ruling on whether the restrictions they contain are against the public interest. The term 'agreement' has a very broad meaning. It covers both written and oral agreements, whether or not they are legally enforceable, and it covers arrangements and understandings, however informal. In short, it extends from binding legal agreements concluded after months of negotiation to understandings between business friends reached over a drink. An agreement is registrable (subject to certain fairly narrow exemptions) if it is between two or more firms operating in the United

Kingdom and if more than one party accepts restrictions (i.e. some limitations on his freedom to make his own decisions) relating to such matters as prices, terms and conditions of sale, the persons to whom, or areas in which, goods or services are sold, and the quantities and kinds of goods or services to be bought or sold. Details of registrable agreements must be furnished to the Director General of Fair Trading within specified time periods (broadly before they come into operation) for entry on the public register. Failure to provide details of an agreement is not an offence but the restrictions in the agreement are void and the agreement unenforceable. It is because the whole system turns on the registration requirement that it is commonly described as a *form*-based rather than an *effects*-based system. Thus, the first question for us to consider is whether an agreement is registrable, a question often requiring complicated legal analysis, rather than whether the agreement has any detrimental effect upon competition [. . .]

As is well know[n], thousands of agreements were duly registered with the predecessor of the Director General of Fair Trading, the Registrar of Restrictive Trading Agreements. Under the 1956 [Restrictive Trade Practices] Act it was the duty of the Registrar to refer registrable agreements to the Restrictive Practices Court; he had virtually no discretion not to refer. As is also well known, the legislation contains a presumption that restrictions in registrable agreements are against the public interest and there is a heavy burden of proof on the parties to counter that presumption. Not surprisingly perhaps, most of the early judgments of the court went against the parties. With the precedents of these judgments staring them in the face, the vast majority of the agreements registered in the early years of the legislation were voluntarily abandoned. [. . .]

More important, of course, than the number of agreements struck down by the court or voluntarily abandoned by the parties is the effect that this had upon the efficiency of the industries concerned and on users of their products. Some early academic research found little change in prices or increase in competition in as many as two-thirds of the cases examined. Evidence was unearthed of the substitution in many industries of information-sharing agreements for previous price-fixing agreements. My predecessor, the Registrar, also commented upon this development and in 1968 steps were taken to try to block what seemed to be becoming an increasingly serious loophole in the law, particularly where the information agreement was to exchange information about price changes before those changes came into effect. Mergers between companies, which were not subject to any statutory control in this country until 1965, were also a common response to the abolition or abandonment of restrictive agreements.

I must not give the impression, however, that the benefits to be expected from the disbandment of formal collusive agreements in the 1960s were insignificant. The most searching investigation of the effects of the legislation (published in 1974) looked at 18 industries in depth and 22 in rather less detail. [Swann *et al.*, *Competition in British Industry*.] In over half the cases studied there was evidence of increased competition following the termination of agreements, mainly in the form of lower prices or higher discounts; in some cases price reductions were substantial. The research showed that, as well as the direct effect on prices of increased competition, there was an indirect effect from improvements in efficiency and the elimination of excess capacity. In the longer term, enhanced competitive pressures were sustained in some industries though in others they were stifled by mergers or by more tacit forms of collusive behaviour. Generalising from the 40 industries investigated, the researchers concluded that the restrictive trade practices legislation had led to a significant improvement in efficiency.

Although now rather dated, these are important findings. They support the basic thrust of the legislation that restrictive agreements are likely to operate against the public interest. But I have to admit to some doubt as to whether the legislation is *cur-*

rently as effective in that parties to price-fixing or market-sharing agreements may now decide *not* to furnish details as required by the law. The penalties for failure to furnish details of registrable agreements are neither immediate nor serious. It is *not* an offence to fail to provide details to the Director General of Fair Trading. Non-registration *does* mean that the agreement is void in respect of all registrable restrictions and any person who suffers loss may bring an action for damages for breach of statutory duty but this right has been little used (and, of course, is far less a sanction than it would be if the damages suffered were tripled as is the practice with private anti-trust actions in the United States) [. . .]

The main sanctions against non-registration are those which flow from legal action that *I* may take when secret unregistered agreements come to light. The sanctions depend, therefore, on a public official going to court at public expense. My normal practice is to apply to the Restrictive Practices Court for an order to stop any of the parties from operating the agreement *and* from operating any other registrable agreement to which they might be party, details of which have not been properly furnished to us.

If the court finds a registrable agreement against the public interest (whether it has been properly registered or not) the agreement is, of course, declared void (in respect of the registrable restrictions). The court will usually make an order restraining the parties from giving effect to the condemned restrictions *and* from making any other agreement to 'like effect'. Breach of *any* orders of the Restrictive Practices Court or of any undertakings given in lieu of an order may result in proceedings for contempt of court [see now *DGFT* v. *Smith's Concrete Ltd.* [1991] 4All Er150]. [. . .]

My powers to investigate suspected unregistered agreements are somewhat limited (they are only exercisable when I already have reasonable grounds for believing that an unregistered and therefore unlawful agreement exists), a catch 22 situation if ever there was one, and I have long felt that there is a clear case for strengthening them. This is particularly so where our information consists of unconfirmed accounts of what may have taken place at meetings or in telephone conversations.

Nevertheless, with all the difficulties, my Office has uncovered unlawful restrictive agreements in a number of industries, mainly as a result of whistle blowing by erstwhile parties or by persons adversely affected by the agreement. Disclosure by one party has often led to hundreds of other agreements coming to light [. . .].

It is unusual for parties to agreements which have not been properly registered to seek to defend the agreement before the court. Hence the court hearings and judgments do not receive as much publicity as the celebrated defended cases of the 1960s. Yet the orders made by the court in these undefended cases represent an important contribution of the Restrictive Trade Practices Act to the promotion of competition.

Since unregistered agreements continue to be uncovered, there is obviously a problem of evasion though we cannot know how many unlawful agreements go undetected as a result of a conscious decision by the parties to flout the law, or how important they are in economic terms. [. . .]

I am sometimes told that desirable restrictive agreements are frustrated because the parties are not prepared to register them and then defend them before the court. I must say I am rather suspicious of the notion of a benign restrictive trading agreement and I would add that precious little concrete evidence has ever been brought to my attention to show that the Act is having this sort of potentially damaging effect. Nevertheless I do recognise that Restrictive Practices Court proceedings, as with any High Court proceedings, can be long and expensive. [. . .]

I said earlier that, under the original Act, the Registrar had to all intents and purposes no authority *not* to refer a registrable agreement to the court. The law was changed in 1968 and under the present 1976 Act I can seek a direction from the Secretary of State for Trade and Industry discharging me from my normal duty to refer a restrictive trading agreement to the court if I am satisfied that the restrictions in the agreement are 'not of such significance as to call for investigation by the court'. This is the so-called section 21(2) procedure. It has proved to be an extremely important innovation, especially since 1976 when the legislation was extended to services agreements. By the end of 1985, 1,153 services agreements had been entered upon the register. Most of those agreements, either current at the time of registration or still current, have been considered or will be considered by my Office for possible section 21(2) treatment. In recent years indeed, the court has become something of a long stop to be used only when it would be quite inappropriate for me to seek a section 21(2) direction.

What happens first is that my officials discuss with the parties whether they would be willing to drop or modify any restrictions which we consider have significant adverse effects upon competition or customers. This can lead to complicated negotiations with much toing and froing between the two sides and their lawyers. If we are satisfied that the restrictions, or any remaining restrictions, after a filleting out process, are insignificant in their effects then the way is open for a section 21(2) direction rather than reference to the court. In many areas this procedure had led to the removal of major restrictions including, most obviously, restrictions on prices. Examples are agreements in the fields of cold storage, commercial home removals, freight forwarding, and road haulage, to mention a few. In each of these cases, clauses specifying minimum charges were abandoned under the threat of reference to the court leaving a balance of less significant restrictions (in these cases largely recommended standard terms and conditions of sale) which were capable in due course of receiving section 21(2) treatment. [. . .]

A problem is that the negotiations can be protracted. The parties are rarely in a hurry to bring these to a conclusion. In the future, we shall need to be more prepared to refer agreements to the court if there is any suggestion that the parties are stringing us along in negotiations for the removal or modification of significant restrictions. A problem for the parties under the present arrangements is uncertainty over whether or not we shall regard a restriction as significant enough to warrant investigation by the court. There is no definition of 'significance' in the Act and no court interpretation of its meaning. The task of my Office is to consider whether the restriction has any detrimental effect of the kind which the court would take into account if the agreement was referred to it. We can only deal with this hypothesis by asking whether the agreement reduces competition in any material way to the disadvantage of users, and whether it has any discriminatory or other adverse effects. We are likely to look particularly carefully at restrictions which create entry barriers; prohibitions on advertising; rules, recommendations or agreements which have the effect of imposing a uniform level of charges for goods or services; restrictions on soliciting or touting for business; and any form of market sharing agreement. The assessment has to be made in the light of the individual circumstances.[. . .]

I would strenuously resist any suggestion that the Act is a spent force. [. . .] The Act certainly catches some forms of restrictive trading agreement which have little impact on competition, while it may encourage the skilful (or the skilfully advised) to draft anti-competitive agreements in ways which get round the Act: avoidance rather than evasion. And, of course, an anti-competitive agreement which is outside the restrictive trade practices legislation may instead be the subject of investigation under the Fair Trading Act or the Competition Act, or of action under the Resale Prices Act. It does not entirely escape our scrutiny.

A highly complicated competition law, as the Restrictive Trade Practices Act undoubtedly is, is not likely to be the most effective competition law. I do wonder whether the whole concept of a public register on which people are supposed to volunteer details of their agreements, innocuous or otherwise, is any longer appropriate. I wonder too whether it is appropriate to have a system which merely asserts a presumption that a restrictive trading agreement is against the public interest rather than prohibits them, subject to exemptions. [. . .] An alternative model which will obviously have to be studied is Article 85 of the Treaty of Rome which prohibits anti-competitive agreements and concerted practices while providing for exemption from that prohibition in specified circumstances. Article 85 is, of course, already part of United Kingdom law through our membership of the EEC, but only in so far as agreements affect inter-State trade. Where it does apply, substantial monetary sanctions are available at the instance of either the EEC Commission or private persons and businesses. Also part of United Kingdom law are the various powers of EEC officials to search for contraventions of Article 85. If there were in United Kingdom law generally a system based on prohibition of certain categories of agreement, then it would be appropriate to introduce wider powers and tougher sanctions than are provided under the Restrictive Trade Practices Act and to provide for greater scope for private rights of action. I am not here advocating the Article 85 model about which there can be as many arguments as about our own statute. What is indisputable is that an effective means of controlling restrictive trading agreements, wherever they are found, is a *sine qua non* for an effective competition policy and therefore for an efficiently functioning market economy.

[. . .]

6.3 Commission Regulation (EEC) No. 17/62 OJ Sp. Ed. 1962 No. 204/62, p. 87

THE COUNCIL OF THE EUROPEAN ECONOMIC COMMUNITY

[. . .]

Whereas, in order to establish a system ensuring that competition shall not be distorted in the common market, it is necessary to provide for balanced application of Article 85 and 86 in a uniform manner in the Member Sates;

Whereas in establishing the rules for applying Article 85(3) account must be taken of the need to ensure effective supervision and to simplify administration to the greatest possible extent;

Whereas it is accordingly necessary to make it obligatory, as a general principle, for undertakings which seek application of Article 85(3) to notify to the Commission their agreements, decisions and concerted practices;

Whereas, on the one hand, such agreements, decisions and concerted practices are probably very numerous and cannot therefore all be examined at the same time and, on the other hand, some of them have special features which may make them less prejudicial to the development of the common market;

Whereas there is consequently a need to make more flexible arrangements for the time being in respect of certain categories of agreement, decision and concerted practice without prejudging their validity under Article 85;

Whereas it may be in the interest of undertakings to know whether any agreements, decisions or practices to which they are party, or propose to become party, may lead to action on the part of the Commission pursuant to Article 85(1) or Article 86;

Whereas, in order to secure uniform application of Articles 85 and 86 in the common market, rules must be made under which the Commission, acting in close and constant liaison with the competent authorities of the Member States, may take the requisite measures for applying those Articles;

Whereas for this purpose the Commission must have the co-operation of the competent authorities of the Member States and be empowered, throughout the common market, to require such information to be supplied and to undertake such investigations as are necessary to bring to light any agreement, decision or concerted practice prohibited by Article 85(1) or any abuse of a dominant position prohibited by Article 86;

Whereas, in order to carry out its duty of ensuring that the provisions of the Treaty are applied, the Commission must be empowered to address to undertakings or associations of undertakings recommendations and decisions for the purpose of bringing to an end infringements of Articles 85 and 86;

Whereas compliance with Articles 85 and 86 and the fulfilment of obligations imposed on undertakings and associations of undertakings under this Regulation must be enforceable by means of fines and periodic penalty payments;

Whereas undertakings concerned must be accorded the right to be heard by the Commission, third parties whose interests may be affected by a decision must be given the opportunity of submitting their comments beforehand, and it must be ensured that wide publicity is given to decisions taken;

Whereas all decisions taken by the Commission under this Regulation are subject to review by the Court of Justice under the conditions specified in the Treaty;

Whereas it is moreover desirable to confer upon the Court of Justice, pursuant to Article 172, unlimited jurisdiction in respect of decisions under which the Commission imposes fines or periodic penalty payments;

Whereas this Regulation may enter into force without prejudice to any other provisions that may hereafter be adopted pursuant to Article 87;

HAS ADOPTED THIS REGULATION:

Article 1 – Basic provision

Without prejudice to Articles 6, 7 and 23 of this Regulation, agreements, decisions and concerted practices of the kind described in Article 85(1) of the Treaty and the abuse of a dominant position in the market, within the meaning of Article 86 of the Treaty, shall be prohibited, no prior decision to that effect being required.

Article 2 – Negative clearance

Upon application by the undertakings or associations of undertakings concerned, the Commission may certify that, on the basis of the facts in its possession, there are no grounds under Article 85(1) or Article 86 of the Treaty for action on its part in respect of an agreement, decision or practice.

Article 3 – Termination of infringements

1. Where the Commission, upon application or upon its own initiative, finds that there is infringement of Article 85 or Article 86 of the Treaty, it may by decision require the undertakings or associations of undertakings concerned to bring such infringement to an end.

2. Those entitled to make application are:

(*a*) Member States;
(*b*) natural or legal persons who claim a legitimate interest.

3. Without prejudice to the other provisions of this Regulation, the Commission may, before taking a decision under paragraph 1, address to the undertakings or associations of undertakings concerned recommendations for termination of the infringement.

Article 4 – Notification of new agreements, decisions and practices

1. Agreements, decisions and concerted practices of the kind described in Article 85(1) of the Treaty which come into existence after the entry into force of this Regulation and in respect of which the parties seek application of Article 85(3) must be notified to the Commission. Until they have been notified, no decision in application of Article 85(3) may be taken.

2. Paragraph 1 shall not apply to agreements, decisions or concerted practices where:

(1) the only parties thereto are under-

takings from one Member State and the agreements, decisions or practices do not relate either to imports or to exports between Member States;

(2) not more than two undertakings are party thereto, and the agreements only;
   (*a*) restrict the freedom of one party to the contract in determining the prices or conditions of business upon which the goods which he has obtained from the other party to the contract may be resold; or
   (*b*) impose restrictions on the exercise of the rights of the assignee or user of industrial property rights – in particular patents, utility models, designs or trade marks – or of the person entitled under a contract to the assignment, or grant, of the right to use a method of manufacture or knowledge relating to the use and to the application of industrial processes;

(3) they have as their sole object:
   (*a*) the development or uniform application of standards or types; or
   (*b*) joint research and development;
   (*c*) specialisation in the manufacture of products, including agreements necessary for the achievement thereof;
      – where the products which are the object of specialisation do not, in a substantial part of the common market, represent more than 15 per cent of the volume of business done in identical products or those considered by the consumers to be similar by reason of their characteristics, price and use, and
      – where the total annual turnover of the participating undertakings does not exceed 200 million units of account.

These agreements decisions and concerted practices may be notified to the Commission.

Article 5 – Notification of existing agreements, decisions and practices

1. Agreements, decisions and concerted practices of the kind described in Article 85(1) of the Treaty which are in existence at the date of entry into force of this Regulation and in respect of which the parties seek application of Article 85(3) shall be notified to the Commission before 1 November 1962. However, notwithstanding the foregoing provisions, any agreements, decisions and concerted practices to which not more than two undertakings are party shall be notified before 1 February 1963.

2. Paragraph 1 shall not apply to agreements, decisions or concerted practices falling within Article 4(2); these may be notified to the Commission.

[. . .]

Article 6 – Decisions pursuant to Article 85(3)

1. Whenever the Commission takes a decision pursuant to Article 85(3) of the Treaty, it shall specify therein the date from which the decision shall take effect. Such date shall not be earlier than the date of notification.

2. The second sentence of paragraph 1 shall not apply to agreements, decisions or concerted practices falling within Article 4(2) and Article 5(2), nor to those falling within Article 5(1) which have been notified within the time limit specified in Article 5(1).

Article 7 – Special provisions for existing agreements, decisions and practices

1. Where agreements, decisions and concerted practices in existence at the date of

entry into force of this Regulation and notified within the limits specified in Article 5(1) do not satisfy the requirements of Article 85(3) of the Treaty and the undertakings or associations of undertakings concerned cease to give effect to them or modify them in such manner that they no longer fall within the prohibition contained in Article 85(1) or that they satisfy the requirements of Article 85(3), the prohibition contained in Article 85(1) shall apply only for a period fixed by the Commission. A decision by the Commission pursuant to the foregoing sentence shall not apply as against undertakings and associations of undertakings which did not expressly consent to the notification.

2. Paragraph 1 shall apply to agreements, decisions and concerted practices falling within Article 4(2) which are in existence at the date of entry into force of this Regulation if they are notified before 1 January 1967.

Article 8 – Duration and revocation of decisions under Article 85(3)

1. A decision on application of Article 85(3) of the Treaty shall be issued for a specified period and conditions and obligations may be attached thereto.

2. A decision may on application be renewed if the requirements of Article 85(3) of the Treaty continue to be satisfied.

3. The Commission may revoke or amend its decision or prohibit specified acts by the parties:

(*a*) where there has been a change in any of the facts which were basic to the making of the decision;
(*b*) where the parties commit a breach of any obligation attached to the decision;
(*c*) where the decision is based on incorrect information or was induced by deceit;
(*d*) where the parties abuse the exemption from the provisions of Article 85(1) of the Treaty granted to them by the decision.

In cases to which subparagraphs (*b*), (*c*) or (*d*) apply, the decision may be revoked with retroactive effect.

Article 9 – Powers

1. Subject to review of its decision by the Court of Justice, the Commission shall have sole power to declare Article 85(1) inapplicable pursuant to Article 85(3) of the Treaty.

2. The Commission shall have power to apply Article 85(1) and Article 86 of the Treaty; this power may be exercised notwithstanding that the time limits specified in Article 5(1) and in Article 7(2) relating to notification have not expired.

3. As long as the Commission has not initiated any procedure under Articles 2, 3 or 6, the authorities of the Member States shall remain competent to apply Article 85(1) and Article 86 in accordance with Article 88 of the Treaty; they shall remain competent in this respect notwithstanding that the time limits specified in Article 5(1) and in Article 7(2) relating to notification have not expired.

Article 10 – Liaison with the authorities of the Member States

1. The Commission shall forthwith transmit to the competent authorities of the Member States a copy of the applications and notifications together with copies of the most important documents lodged with the Commission for the purpose of establishing the existence of infringements of Articles 85 or 86 of the Treaty or of obtaining negative clearance or a decision in application of Article 85(3).

2. The Commission shall carry out the procedure set out in paragraph 1 in close and constant liaison with the competent authorities of the Member States; such authorities shall have the right to express their views upon that procedure.

3. An Advisory Committee on Restrictive Practices and Monopolies shall be consulted prior to the taking of any decision following upon a procedure under paragraph 1, and of any decision concerning the renewal, amendment or revocation of a decision pursuant to Article 85(3) of the Treaty.

4. The Advisory Committee shall be

composed of officials competent in the matter of restrictive practices and monopolies. Each Member State shall appoint an official to represent it who, if prevented from attending, may be replaced by another official.

5. The consultation shall take place at a joint meeting convened by the Commission; such meeting shall be held not earlier than fourteen days after dispatch of the notice convening it. The notice shall, in respect of each case to be examined, be accompanied by a summary of the case together with an indication of the most important documents, and a preliminary draft decision.

6. The Advisory Committee may deliver an opinion notwithstanding that some of its members or their alternates are not present. A report of the outcome of the consultative proceedings shall be annexed to the draft decision. It shall not be made public.

Article 11 – Requests for information

1. In carrying out the duties assigned to it by Article 89 and by provisions adopted under Article 87 of the Treaty, the Commission may obtain all necessary information from the Governments and competent authorities of the Member States and from undertakings and associations of undertakings.

2. When sending a request for information to an undertaking or association of undertakings, the Commission shall at the same time forward a copy of the request to the competent authority of the Member State in whose territory the seat of the undertaking or association of undertakings is situated.

3. In its request the Commission shall state the legal basis and the purpose of the request and also the penalties provided for in Article 15(1)(*b*) for supplying incorrect information.

4. The owners of the undertakings or their representatives and, in the case of legal persons, companies or firms, or of associations having no legal personality, the persons authorised to represent them by law or by their constitution shall supply the information requested.

5. Where an undertaking or association of undertakings does not supply the information requested within the time limit fixed by the Commission, or supplies incomplete information, the Commission shall by decision require the information to be supplied. The decision shall specify what information is required, fix an appropriate time limit within which it is to be supplied and indicate the penalties provided for in Article 15(1)(*b*) and Article 16(1)(*c*) and the right to have the decision reviewed by the Court of Justice.

6. The Commission shall at the same time forward a copy of its decision to the competent authority of the Member State in whose territory the seat of the undertaking or association of undertakings is situated.

Article 12 – Inquiry into sectors of the economy

1. If in any sector of the economy the trend of trade between Member States, price movements, inflexibility of prices or other circumstances suggest that in the economic sector concerned competition is being restricted or distorted within the common market, the Commission may decide to conduct a general inquiry into that economic sector and in the course thereof may request undertakings in the sector concerned to supply the information necessary for giving effect to the principles formulated in Articles 85 and 86 of the Treaty and for carrying out the duties entrusted to the Commission.

2. The Commission may in particular request every undertaking or association of undertakings in the economic sector concerned to communicate to it all agreements, decisions and concerted practices which are exempt from notification by virtue of Article 4(2) and Article 5(2).

3. When making inquiries pursuant to paragraph 2, the Commission shall also request undertakings or groups of undertakings whose size suggests that they occupy a dominant position within the

common market or a substantial part thereof to supply to the Commission such particulars of the structure of the undertakings and of their behaviour as are requisite to an appraisal of their position in the light of Article 86 of the Treaty.

4. Article 10(3) to (6) and Articles 11, 13 and 14 shall apply correspondingly.

Article 13 – Investigations by the authorities of the Member States

1. At the request of the Commission, the competent authorities of the Member States shall undertake the investigations which the Commission considers to be necessary under Article 14(1), or which it has ordered by decision pursuant to Article 14(3). The officials of the competent authorities of the Member States responsible for conducting these investigations shall exercise their powers upon production of an authorisation in writing issued by the competent authority of the Member State in whose territory the investigation is to be made. Such authorisation shall specify the subject matter and purpose of the investigation.

2. If so requested by the Commission or by the competent authority of the Member State in whose territory the investigation is to be made, the officials of the Commission may assist the officials of such authorities in carrying out their duties.

Article 14 – Investigating powers of the Commission

1. In carrying out the duties assigned to it by Article 89 and by provisions adopted under Article 87 of the Treaty, the Commission may undertake all necessary investigations into undertakings and associations of undertakings. To this end the officials authorised by the Commission are empowered:

(*a*) to examine the books and other business records;
(*b*) to take copies of or extracts from the books and business records;
(*c*) to ask for oral explanations on the spot;
(*d*) to enter any premises, land and means of transport of undertakings.

2. The officials of the Commission authorised for the purpose of these investigations shall exercise their powers upon production of an authorisation in writing specifying the subject matter and purpose of the investigation and the penalties provided for in Article 15(1)(*c*) in cases where production of the required books or other business records is incomplete. In good time before the investigation, the Commission shall inform the competent authority of the Member State in whose territory the same is to be made of the investigation and of the identity of the authorised officials.

3. Undertakings and associations of undertakings shall submit to investigations ordered by decision of the Commission. The decision shall specify the subject matter and purpose of the investigation, appoint the date on which it is to begin and indicate the penalties provided for in Article 15(1)(*c*) and Article 16(1)(*d*) and the right to have the decision reviewed by the Court of Justice.

4. The Commission shall take decisions referred to in paragraph 3 after consultation with the competent authority of the Member State in whose territory the investigation is to be made.

5. Officials of the competent authority of the Member State in whose territory the investigation is to be made may, at the request of such authority or of the Commission, assist the officials of the Commission in carrying out their duties.

6. Where an undertaking opposes an investigation ordered pursuant to this Article, the Member State concerned shall afford the necessary assistance to the officials authorised by the Commission to enable them to make their investigation. Member States shall, after consultation with the Commission, take the necessary measures to this end before 1 October 1962.

Article 15 – Fines

1. The Commission may by decision impose on undertakings or associations of

undertakings fines of from 100 to 5000 units of account where, intentionally or negligently:

(*a*) they supply incorrect or misleading information in an application pursuant to Article 2 or in a notification pursuant to Articles 4 and 5; or
(*b*) they supply incorrect information in response to a request made pursuant to Article 11(3) or (5) or to Article 12, or do not supply information within the time limit fixed by a decision taken under Article 11(5); or
(*c*) they produce the required books or other business records in incomplete form during investigations under Article 13 or 14, or refuse to submit to an investigation ordered by decision issued in implementation of Article 14(3).

2. The Commission may by decision impose on undertakings or associations of undertakings fines of from 1000 to 1 000 000 units of account, or a sum in excess thereof but not exceeding 10% of the turnover in the preceding business year of each of the undertakings participating in the infringement where, either intentionally or negligently:

(*a*) they infringe Article 85(1) or Article 86 of the Treaty; or
(*b*) they commit a breach of any obligation imposed pursuant to Article 8(1).

In fixing the amount of the fine, regard shall be had both to the gravity and to the duration of the infringement.

3. Article 10(3) to (6) shall apply.

4. Decisions taken pursuant to paragraphs 1 and 2 shall not be of a criminal law nature.

5. The fines provided for in paragraph 2(*a*) shall not be imposed in respect of acts taking place:

(*a*) after notification to the Commission and before its decision in application of Article 85(3) of the Treaty, provided they fall within the limits of the activity described in the notification;
(*b*) before notification and in the course of agreements, decisions or concerted practices in existence at the date of entry into force of this Regulation, provided that notification was effected within the time limits specified in Article 5(1) and Article 7(2).

6. Paragraph 5 shall not have effect where the Commission has informed the undertakings concerned that after preliminary examination it is of opinion that Article 85(1) of the Treaty applies and that application of Article 85(3) is not justified.

Article 16 – Periodic penalty payments

1. The Commission may by decision impose on undertakings or associations of undertakings periodic penalty payments of from 50 to 1000 units of account per day, calculated from the date appointed by the decision, in order to compel them:

(*a*) to put an end to an infringement of Article 85 or 86 of the Treaty, in accordance with a decision taken pursuant to Article 3 of this Regulation;
(*b*) to refrain from any act prohibited under Article 8(3);
(*c*) to supply complete and correct information which it has requested by decision taken pursuant to Article 11(5);
(*d*) to submit to an investigation which it has ordered by decision taken pursuant to Article 14(3).

2. Where the undertakings or associations of undertakings have satisfied the obligation which it was the purpose of the periodic penalty payment to enforce, the Commission may fix the total amount of the periodic penalty payment at a lower figure than that which would arise under the original decision.

3. Article 10(3) to (6) shall apply.

Article 17 – Review by the Court of Justice

The Court of Justice shall have unlimited jurisdiction within the meaning of Article 172 of the Treaty to review decisions whereby the Commission has fixed a fine or periodic penalty payment; it may cancel, reduce or increase the fine or periodic penalty payment imposed.

Article 18 – Unit of account

For the purposes of applying Articles 15 to 17 the unit of account shall be that adopted in drawing up the budget of the Community in accordance with Articles 207 and 209 of the Treaty.

Article 19 – Hearing of the parties and of third persons

1. Before taking decisions as provided for in Articles 2, 3, 6, 7, 8, 15 and 16, the Commission shall give the undertakings or associations of undertakings concerned the opportunity of being heard on the matters to which the Commission has taken objection.

2. If the Commission or the competent authorities of the Member States consider it necessary, they may also hear other natural or legal persons. Applications to be heard on the part of such persons shall, where they show a sufficient interest, be granted.

3. Where the Commission intends to give negative clearance pursuant to Article 2 or take a decision in application of Article 85(3) of the Treaty, it shall publish a summary of the relevant application or notification and invite all interested third parties to submit their observations within a time limit which it shall fix being not less than one month. Publication shall have regard to the legitimate interest of undertakings in the protection of their business secrets.

Article 20 – Professional secrecy

1. Information acquired as a result of the application of Articles 11, 12, 13 and 14 shall be used only for the purpose of the relevant request or investigation.

2. Without prejudice to the provisions of Articles 19 and 21, the Commission and the competent authorities of the Member States, their officials and other servants shall not disclose information acquired by them as a result of the application of this Regulation and of the kind covered by the obligation of professional secrecy.

3. The provisions of paragraphs 1 and 2 shall not prevent publication of general information or surveys which do not contain information relating to particular undertakings or associations of undertakings.

Article 21 – Publication of decisions

1. The Commission shall publish the decisions which it takes pursuant to Articles 2, 3, 6, 7 and 8.

2. The publication shall state the names of the parties and the main content of the decision; it shall have regard to the legitimate interest of undertakings in the protection of their business secrets.

Article 22 – Special provisions

1. The Commission shall submit to the Council proposals for making certain categories of agreement, decision and concerted practice falling within Article 4(2) or Article 5(2) compulsorily notifiable under Article 4 or 5.

2. Within one year from the date of entry into force of this Regulation, the Council shall examine, on a proposal from the Commission, what special provisions might be made for exempting from the provisions of this Regulation agreements, decisions and concerted practices falling within Article 4(2) or Article 5(2).

Article 23 – Transitional provisions applicable to decisions of authorities of the Member States

1. Agreements, decisions and concerted practices of the kind described in Article 85(1) of the Treaty to which, before the entry into force of this Regulation, the competent authority of a Member State has declared Article 85(1) to be inapplicable pursuant to Article 85(3) shall not be subject to compulsory notification under Article 5. The decision of the competent authority of the Member State shall be

deemed to be a decision within the meaning of Article 6; it shall cease to be valid upon expiration of the period fixed by such authority but in any event not more than three years after the entry into force of this Regulation. Article 8(3) shall apply.

2. Applications for renewal of decisions of the kind described in paragraph 1 shall be decided upon by the Commission in accordance with Article 8(2).

Article 24 – Implementing provisions

The Commission shall have power to adopt implementing provisions concerning the form, content and other details of applications pursuant to Articles 2 and 3 and of notifications pursuant to Articles 4 and 5, and concerning hearings pursuant to Article 19(1) and (2).

Article 25

1. As regards agreements, decisions and concerted practices to which Article 85 of the Treaty applies by virtue of accession, the date of accession shall be substituted for the date of entry into force of this regulation in every place where reference is made in this Regulation to this latter date.

2. Agreements, decisions and concerted practices existing at the date of accession to which Article 85 of the Treaty applies by virtue of accession shall be notified pursuant to Article 5(1) or Article 7(1) and (2) within six months from the date of accession.

3. Fines under Article 15(2)(*a*) shall not be imposed in respect of any act prior to notification of the agreements, decisions and practices to which paragraph 2 applies and which have been notified within the period therein specified.

4. New Member States shall take the measures referred to in Article 14(6) within six months from the date of accession after consulting the Commission.

5. The provisions of paragraphs (1) to (4) above still apply in the same way in the case of accession of the Hellenic Republic, the Kingdom of Spain and of the Portuguese Republic.

This Regulation shall be binding in its entirety and directly applicable in all Member States.
Done at Brussels, 6 February 1962.

6.4 *Re The Polypropylene Cartel: Hercules NV* v. *Commission of the European Communities*, European Court of First Instance [1992] 4 CMLR 84

Opinion of the Advocate General:
[. . .]

In various connections the applicants have directed rather general criticism at the Commission's handling of competition cases. This question touches upon one of the major difficulties which arises in the handling of competition cases and which to some extent is manifest in this instance in connection with the handling of the procedural objections and to an even greater extent in connection with the handling of the issues of substantive law. I have in mind the tension which can clearly be felt – perhaps even more so in the present cases than in any previous competition case which has come before the Court of Justice – between the procedural framework of the cases, consisting of an administrative procedure followed by judicial review of legality, and the substance of the cases, which all broadly exhibit the characteristics of a criminal law case. In many instances, the parties' submissions can only be understood with the help of the terminology and concepts used in criminal law and procedure.

The Court of Justice has held that the procedure for dealing with cases before the Commission is an administrative procedure. I would refer here to Case 45/69, *Boehrin-*

ger Mannheim v. *EC Commission* [1970] ECR 769 where it was held that the procedure before the Commission concerning the application of Article 85 EEC is an administrative procedure, even where it can lead to the imposition of fines. This means, as far as the present case is concerned, that the Commission's decision was not unlawful notwithstanding the fact that the members of the Commission themselves did not take part in the hearings but left this task to officials pursuant to Article 9(1) of Regulation 99/63.

Furthermore, the Commission is not a tribunal in the sense in which that term is used in Article 6 of the European Convention for the Protection of Human Rights. This point has been made several times by the Court of Justice and it has not been gainsaid by the bodies set up under the Human Rights Convention [. . .]. However, as the Court of Justice expressly emphasised in the said judgments, the Commission is bound to observe the procedural safeguards provided for by Community law. It follows, on the one hand, that no institutional claims, that is to say claims relating to the established system, can be advanced concerning the Commission's handling of competition cases but that the Commission – and this is self-evident – must in any event respect not only the written rules but also the unwritten principles laid down in the case law of the Court of Justice. In the *Pioneer* cases [1983] 3 CMLR 221, the Court of Justice considered Article 6(1) of the European Convention for the Protection of Human Rights in connection with an allegation that the decision in those cases was unlawful because the Commission exercised the function of both judge and prosecutor, whilst in the FEDETAB cases [1981] 3 CMLR 134 it addressed the question in connection with alleged infringements of a number of procedural rules. The arguments of the undertakings were not accepted in any of the cases.

In view of the fact [. . .] that the fines which may be imposed on undertakings pursuant to Article 15 of Regulation 17 do in fact, notwithstanding what is stated in Article 15(4), have a criminal law character, it is vitally important that the Court should seek to bring about a state of legal affairs not susceptible of any justified criticism with reference to the European Convention for the Protection of Human Rights. At all events, within the framework formed by the existing body of rules and the judgments handed down hitherto it must therefore be sought to ensure that legal protection within the Community meets the standard otherwise regarded as reasonable in Europe [. . .]

THE COMMISSION'S INTERNAL WORKING PROCEDURES

The internal organisation of the Commission's work

Shell has contended both in the procedure before the Commission and in the proceedings before the Court that the Commission disregarded essential legal safeguards during the procedure. Arguing that the Commission failed to fulfil its 'duty to act fairly', Shell states that the Commission's working procedures should be so organised, first, to ensure as reasonably as is practicable that that duty can be observed and, secondly, to afford the undertakings involved in cases before the Commission as well as the public a reasonable degree of confidence in the Commission as an impartial adjudicator. In this connection, Shell claims that in dealing with cases pursuant to Regulations 17 and 99/63 the Commission has a duty to adopt an objective and impartial position with regard to all the evidence and to listen to arguments put forward by the applicants which may cast serious doubts upon the provisional views expressed in the statement of objections. Shell expresses the view that the said objective can only be attained if there is a functional separation between the 'investigative' stage and the 'prosecutorial' stage within the Commission. According to Shell, there was no such separation at the time when the present cases were being investigated and assessed, at any event not before the time when the statements of objections were sent out. Shell cites a number of concrete examples from the procedure, which, in its view, demonstrate such a biased and unbalanced assessment of some of the facts that it would be warrantable to conclude that the working procedure in Directorate-General IV was in itself capable of affecting the decisions to the applicants' detriment.

After explaining the reorganisation of the Directorate-General which took place in 1984 and 1985 and which, in the defendant's opinion, was apt to allay the criticism expressed, the Commission states that in this regard there are no rules anywhere stipulating how the Commission should organise its internal working procedures. Furthermore, the Commission denies that it is possible to trace back the origin of any mistakes or errors of judgment to a specific way of organising its work. In its view, the examples advanced by the applicants must therefore be dealt with as a whole, together with the substantive issues. Finally, the Commission points out that more than 20 of its staff worked on the case.

In my view, the first thing which must be said in response to those points is that as a rule it is not possible in any individual case to conclude from possible mistakes or possibly poor work that there is something generally wrong with the way in which the Commission's work is organised internally. Even administrative authorities organised in the best way conceivable, incorporating all possible procedural guarantees, can make mistakes. Conversely, organisations whose internal working arrangements perhaps leave something to be desired can perform outstanding work. I therefore agree with the Commission that any errors made in dealing with the present complex of cases do not warrant the conclusion that the internal organisation of the Commission was arranged in a way that it may be assumed from the outset that it leads to mistakes of the sort the applicant considers it has demonstrated.

On the other hand, as suggested in the previous paragraph, Shell is right in pointing out that generally problems may arise if the same administrative authority has such wide-ranging powers that, in addition to investigating and prosecuting, it may also impose fines of such considerable amounts as in these cases. According to the case law of the Court of Justice [. . .] it is, however, quite clear that Article 6 of the Convention for the Protection of Human Rights can provide no specific legal underpinning for the call for the Commission's work to be organised in a particular way. It would appear that Shell, in referring to the normal requirements of good administrative practice, objectivity and impartiality, with which no one can disagree and which Shell rightly considers should form the guidelines for dealing with competition cases, is seeking to establish a principle that administrative working procedures should be organised in a particular way; however such a principle cannot be derived from the Treaty, from the rules laid down pursuant thereto for the handling of competition cases, or from any other source of law. Shell's submissions concerning the Commission's internal working procedures should therefore be dismissed [. . .].

6.5 Commission of the European Communities, *Notice on cooperation between national courts and the Commission in applying Articles 85 and 86 of the EEC Treaty*, OJ 1993 No. C39/6

I. INTRODUCTION

1. The abolition of internal frontiers enables firms in the Community to embark on new activities and Community consumers to benefit from increased competition. The Commission considers that these advantages must not be jeopardized by restrictive

or abusive practices of undertakings and that the completion of the internal market thus reaffirms the importance of the Community's competition policy and competition law.

2. A number of national and Community institutions have contributed to the formulation of Community competition law and are responsible for its day-to-day application. For this purpose, the national competition authorities, national and Community courts and the Commission each assume their own tasks and responsibilities, in line with the principles developed by the case-law of the Court of Justice of the European Communities.

3. If the competition process is to work well in the internal market, effective cooperation between these institutions must be ensured. The purpose of this Notice is to achieve this in relations between national courts and the Commission. It spells out how the Commission intends to assist national courts by closer cooperation in the application of Articles 85 and 86 of the EEC Treaty in individual cases.

II. POWERS

4. The Commission is the administrative authority responsible for the implementation and for the thrust of competition policy in the Community and for this purpose has to act in the public interest. National courts, on the other hand, have the task of safeguarding the subjective rights of private individuals in their relations with one another.

5. In performing these different tasks, national courts and the Commission possess concurrent powers for the application of Article 85(1) and Article 86 of the Treaty. In the case of the Commission, the power is conferred by Article 89 and by the provisions adopted pursuant to Article 87. In the case of the national courts, the power derives from the direct effect of the relevant Community rules. In *BRT* v. *Sabam*, the Court of Justice considered that 'as the prohibitions of Articles 85(1) and 86 tend by their very nature to produce direct effects in relations between individuals, these Articles create direct rights in respect of the individuals concerned which the national courts must safeguard'.

6. In this way, national courts are able to ensure, at the request of the litigants or on their own initiative, that the competition rules will be respected for the benefit of private individuals. In addition, Article 85(2) enables them to determine, in accordance with the national procedural law applicable, the civil law effects of the prohibition set out in Article 85.

7. However, the Commission, pursuant to Article 9 of Regulation No. 17, has sole power to exempt certain types of agreements, decisions and concerted practices from this prohibition. The Commission may exercise this power in two ways. It may take a decision exempting a specific agreement in an individual case. It may also adopt regulations granting block exemptions for certain categories of agreements, decisions or concerted practices, where it is authorized to do so by the Council, in accordance with Article 87.

8. Although national courts are not competent to apply Article 85(3), they may nevertheless apply the decisions and regulations adopted by the Commission pursuant to that provision. The Court has on several occasions confirmed that the provisions of a regulation are directly applicable. The Commission considers that the same is true for the substantive provisions of an individual exemption decision.

9. The powers of the Commission and those of national courts differ not only in their objective and content, but also in the ways in which they are exercised. The Commission exercises its powers according to the procedural rules laid down by Regulation No. 17, whereas national courts exercise theirs in the context of national procedural law.

10. In this connection, the Court of Justice has laid down the principles which govern procedures and remedies for invoking directly applicable Community law.

> Although the Treaty has made it possible in a number of instances for private persons to bring a direct action, where appropriate,

before the Court of Justice, it was not intended to create new remedies in the national courts to ensure the observance of Community law other than those already laid down by national law. On the other hand . . . it must be possible for every type of action provided for by national law to be available for the purpose of ensuring observance of Community provisions having direct effect, on the same conditions concerning the admissibility and procedure as would apply were it a question of ensuring observance of national law.

11. The Commission considers that these principles apply in the event of breach of the Community competition rules; individuals and companies have access to all procedural remedies provided for by national law on the same conditions as would apply if a comparable breach of national law were involved. This equality of treatment concerns not only the definitive finding of a breach of competition rules, but embraces all the legal means capable of contributing to effective legal protection. Consequently, it is the right of parties subject to Community law that national courts should take provisional measures, that an effective end should be brought, by injunction, to the infringement of Community competition rules of which they are victims, and that compensation should be awarded for the damage suffered as a result of infringements, where such remedies are available in proceedings relating to similar national law.

12. Here the Commission would like to make it clear that the simultaneous application of national competition law is compatible with the application of Community law, provided that it does not impair the effectiveness and uniformity of Community competition rules and the measures taken to enforce them. Any conflicts which may arise when national and Community competition law are applied simultaneously must be resolved in accordance with the principle of the precedence of Community law. The purpose of this principle is to rule out any national measure which could jeopardize the full effectiveness of the provisions of Community law.

III. THE EXERCISE OF POWERS BY THE COMMISSION

13. As the administrative authority responsible for the Community's competition policy, the Commission must serve the Community's general interest. The administrative resources at the Commission's disposal to perform its task are necessarily limited and cannot be used to deal with all the cases brought to its attention. The Commission is therefore obliged, in general, to take all organizational measures necessary for the performance of its task and, in particular, to establish priorities.

14. The Commission intends, in implementing its decision-making powers, to concentrate on notifications, complaints and own-initiative proceedings having particular political, economic or legal significance for the Community. Where these features are absent in a particular case, notifications will normally be dealt with by means of comfort letter and complaints should, as a rule, be handled by national courts or authorities.

15. The Commission considers that there is not normally a sufficient Community interest in examining a case when the plaintiff is able to secure adequate protection of his rights before the national courts. In these circumstances the complaint will normally be filed.

16. In this respect the Commission would like to make it clear that the application of Community competition law by the national courts has considerable advantages for individuals and companies:

- the Commission cannot award compensation for loss suffered as a result of an infringement of Article 85 or Article 86. Such claims may be brought only before the national courts. Companies are more likely to avoid infringements of the Community competition rules if they risk having to pay damages or interest in such an event,
- national courts can usually adopt interim measures and order the ending of infringements more quickly than the Commission is able to do,

- before national courts, it is possible to combine a claim under Community law with a claim under national law. This is not possible in a procedure before the Commission,
- in some Member States, the courts have the power to award legal costs to the successful applicant. This is never possible in the administrative procedure before the Commission.

IV. APPLICATION OF ARTICLES 85 AND 86 BY NATIONAL COURTS

17. The national court may have to reach a decision on the application of Articles 85 and 86 in several procedural situations. In the case of civil law proceedings, two types of action are particularly frequent: actions relating to contracts and actions for damages. Under the former, the defendant usually relies on Article 85(2) to dispute the contractual obligations invoked by the plaintiff. Under the latter, the prohibitions contained in Articles 85 and 86 are generally relevant in determining whether the conduct which has given rise to the alleged injury is illegal.

18. In such situations, the direct effect of Article 85 (1) and Article 86 gives national courts sufficient powers to comply with their obligation to hand down judgment. Nevertheless, when exercising these powers, they must take account of the Commission's powers in order to avoid decisions which could conflict with those taken or envisaged by the Commission in applying Article 85(1) and Article 86, and also Article 85(3).

19. In its case-law the Court of Justice has developed a number of principles which make it possible for such contradictory decisions to be avoided. The Commission feels that national courts could take account of these principles in the following manner.

1. Application of Article 85(1) and (2) and Article 86

20. The first question which national courts have to answer is whether the agreement, decision or concerted practice at issue infringes the prohibitions laid down in Article 85(1) or Article 86. Before answering this question, national courts should ascertain whether the agreement, decision or concerted practice has already been the subject of a decision, opinion or other official statement issued by an administrative authority and in particular by the Commission. Such statements provide national courts with significant information for reaching a judgment, even if they are not formally bound by them. It should be noted in this respect that not all procedures before the Commission lead to an official decision, but that cases can also be closed by comfort letters. Whilst it is true that the Court of Justice has ruled that this type of letter does not bind national courts, it has nevertheless stated that the opinion expressed by the Commission constitutes a factor which the national courts may take into account in examining whether the agreements or conduct in question are in accordance with the provisions of Article 85.

21. If the Commission has not ruled on the same agreement, decision or concerted practice, the national courts can always be guided, in interpreting the Community law in question, by the case-law of the Court of Justice and the existing decisions of the Commission. It is with this in view that the Commission has, in a number of general notices, specified categories of agreements that are not caught by the ban laid down in Article 85(1).

22. On these bases, national courts should generally be able to decide whether the conduct at issue is compatible with Article 85(1) and Article 86. Nevertheless, if the Commission has initiated a procedure in a case relating to the same conduct, they may, if they consider it necessary for reasons of legal certainty, stay the proceedings while awaiting the outcome of the Commission's action. A stay of proceedings may also be envisaged where national courts wish to seek the Commission's views in accordance with the arrangements referred to in this Notice. Finally, where national courts have persistent doubts on

questions of compatibility, they may stay proceedings in order to bring the matter before the Court of Justice, in accordance with Article 177 of the Treaty.

23. However, where national courts decide to give judgment and find that the conditions for applying Article 85(1) or Article 86 are not met, they should pursue their proceedings on the basis of such a finding, even if the agreement, decision or concerted practice at issue has been notified to the Commission. Where the assessment of the facts shows that the conditions for applying the said Articles are met, national courts must rule that the conduct at issue infringes Community competition law and take the appropriate measures, including those relating to the consequences that attach to infringement of a statutory prohibition under the civil law applicable.

2. Application of Article 85(3)

24. If the national court concludes that an agreement, decision or concerted practice is prohibited by Article 85(1), it must check whether it is or will be the subject of an exemption by the Commission under Article 85(3). Here several situations may arise.

25. (*a*) The national court is required to respect the exemption decisions taken by the Commission. Consequently, it must treat the agreement, decision or concerted practice at issue as compatible with Community law and fully recognize its civil law effects. In this respect mention should be made of comfort letters in which the Commission services state that the conditions for applying Article 85(3) have been met. The Commission considers that national courts may take account of these letters as factual elements.

26. (*b*) Agreements, decisions and concerted practices which fall within the scope of application of a block exemption regulation are automatically exempted from the prohibition laid down in Article 85(1) without the need for a Commission decision or comfort letter.

27. (*c*) Agreements, decisions and concerted practices which are not covered by a block exemption regulation and which have not been the subject of an individual exemption decision or a comfort letter must, in the Commission's view, be examined in the following manner.

28. The national court must first examine whether the procedural conditions necessary for securing exemption are fulfilled, notably whether the agreement, decision or concerted practice has been duly notified in accordance with Article 4(1) of Regulation No. 17. Where no such notification has been made, and subject to Article 4(2) of Regulation No. 17, exemption under Article 85(3) is ruled out, so that the national court may decide, pursuant to Article 85(2), that the agreement, decision or concerted practice is void.

29. Where the agreement, decision or concerted practice has been duly notified to the Commission, the national court will assess the likelihood of an exemption being granted in the case in question in the light of the relevant criteria developed by the case law of the Court of Justice and the Court of the First Instance and by previous regulations and decisions of the Commission.

30. Where the national court has in this way ascertained that the agreement, decision or concerted practice at issue cannot be the subject of an individual exemption, it will take the measures necessary to comply with the requirements of Article 85(1) and (2). On the other hand, if it takes the view that individual exemption is possible, the national court should suspend the proceedings while awaiting the Commission's decision. If the national court does suspend the proceedings, it nevertheless remains free, according to the rules of the applicable national law, to adopt any interim measures it deems necessary.

31. In this connection, it should be made clear that these principles do not apply to agreements, decisions and concerted prac-

tices which existed before Regulation No. 17 entered into force or before that Regulation became applicable as a result of the accession of a new Member State and which were duly notified to the Commission. The national courts must consider such agreements, decisions and concerted practices to be valid so long as the Commission or the authorities of the Member States have not taken a prohibition decision or sent a comfort letter to the parties informing them that the file has been closed.

32. The Commission realizes that the principles set out above for the application of Articles 85 and 86 by national courts are complex and sometimes insufficient to enable those courts to perform their judicial function properly. This is particularly so where the practical application of Article 85(1) and Article 86 gives rise to legal or economic difficulties, where the Commission has initiated a procedure in the same case or where the agreement, decision or concerted practice concerned may become the subject of an individual exemption within the meaning of Article 85(3). National courts may bring such cases before the Court of Justice for a preliminary ruling, in accordance with Article 177. They may also avail themselves of the Commission's assistance according to the procedures set out below.

V. COOPERATION BETWEEN NATIONAL COURTS AND THE COMMISSION

33. Article 5 of the EEC Treaty establishes the principle of constant and sincere cooperation between the Community and the Member States with a view to attaining the objectives of the Treaty, including implementation of Article 3(*f*), which refers to the establishment of a system ensuring that competition in the common market is not distorted. This principle involves obligations and duties of mutual assistance, both for the Member States and for the Community institutions. The Court has thus ruled that, under Article 5 of the EEC Treaty, the Commission has a duty of sincere cooperation *vis-à-vis* judicial authorities of the Member States, who are responsible for ensuring that Community law is applied and respected in the national legal system.

34. The Commission considers that such cooperation is essential in order to guarantee the strict, effective and consistent application of Community competition law. In addition, more effective participation by the national courts in the day-to-day application of competition law gives the Commission more time to perform its administrative task, namely to steer competition policy in the Community.

35. In the light of these considerations, the Commission intends to work towards closer cooperation with national courts in the following manner.

36. The Commission conducts its policy so as to give the parties concerned useful pointers to the application of competition rules. To this end, it will continue its policy in relation to block exemption regulations and general notices. These general texts, the case-law of the Court of Justice and the Court of First Instance, the decisions previously taken by the Commission and the annual reports on competition policy are all elements of secondary legislation or explanations which may assist national courts in examining individual cases.

37. If these general pointers are insufficient, national courts may, within the limits of their national procedural law, ask the Commission and in particular its Directorate-General for Competition for the following information.

First, they may ask for information of a procedural nature to enable them to discover whether a certain case is pending before the Commission, whether a case has been the subject of a notification, whether the Commission has officially initiated a procedure or whether it has already taken a position through an official decision or through a comfort letter sent by its services. If necessary, national courts may also ask the Commission to give an opinion as to how much time is likely to be required for granting or refusing individual exemption for notified agreements or practices, so as to be able to determine the conditions for any decision to suspend proceedings or whether interim measures need to be adopted. The Commission, for its part, will endeavour to give priority to cases which are the subject of national proceedings suspended in this way, in particular when the outcome of a civil dispute depends on them.

38. Next, national courts may consult the Commission on points of law. Where the application of Article 85(1) and Article 86 causes them particular difficulties, national courts may consult the Commission on its customary practice in relation to the Community law at issue. As far as Articles 85 and 86 are concerned, these difficulties relate in particular to the conditions for applying these Articles as regards the effect on trade between Member States and as regards the extent to which the restriction of competition resulting from the practices specified in these provisions is appreciable. In its replies, the Commission does not consider the merits of the case. In addition, where they have doubts as to whether a contested agreement, decision or concerted practice is eligible for an individual exemption, they may ask the Commission to provide them with an interim opinion. If the Commission says that the case in question is unlikely to qualify for an exemption, national courts will be able to waive a stay of proceedings and rule on the validity of the agreement, decision or concerted practice.

39. The answers given by the Commission are not binding on the courts which have requested them. In its replies the Commission makes it clear that its view is not definitive and that the right of the national court to refer to the Court of Justice, pursuant to Article 177, is not affected. Nevertheless, the Commission considers that it gives them useful guidance for resolving disputes.

40. Lastly, national courts can obtain information from the Commission regarding factual data: statistics, market studies and economic analyses. The Commission will endeavour to communicate these data, within the limits laid down in the following paragraph, or will indicate the source from which they can be obtained.

41. It is in the interests of the proper administration of justice that the Commission should answer requests for legal and factual information in the shortest possible time. Nevertheless, the Commission cannot accede to such requests unless several conditions are met. First, the requisite data must actually be at its disposal. Secondly, the Commission may communicate this data only in so far as permitted by the general principle of sound administrative practice.

42. For example, Article 214 of the Treaty, as spelt out in Article 20 of Regulation No. 17 for the purposes of the competition rules, requires the Commission not to disclose information of a confidential nature. In addition, the duty of sincere cooperation deriving from Article 5 is one applying to the relationship between national courts and the Commission and cannot concern the position of the parties to the dispute pending before those courts. As *amicus curiae*, the Commission is obliged to respect legal neutrality and objectivity. Consequently, it will not accede to requests for information unless they come from a national court, either directly, or indirectly through parties which have been ordered by the court concerned to provide certain information. In the latter case, the Commission will ensure that its answer reaches all the parties to the proceedings.

43. Over and above such exchange of information, required in specific cases, the Commission is anxious to develop as far as possible a more general information policy. To this end, the Commission intends to publish an explanatory booklet regarding the application of the competition rules at national level.

44. Lastly, the Commission also wishes to reinforce the effect of national competition judgments. To this end, it will study the possibility of extending the scope of the Convention on jurisdiction and the enforcement of judgments in civil and commercial matters to competition cases assigned to

administrative courts. It should be noted that, in the Commission's view, competition judgments are already governed by this Convention where they are handed down in cases of a civil and commercial nature.

VI. FINAL REMARKS

45. This Notice does not relate to the competition rules governing the transport sector. Nor does it relate to the competition rules laid down in the Treaty establishing the European Coal and Steel Community.

46. This Notice is issued for guidance and does not in any way restrict the rights conferred on individuals or companies by Community law.

47. This Notice is without prejudice to any interpretation of the Community competition rules which may be given by the Court of Justice of the European Communities.

48. A summary of the answers given by the Commission pursuant to this Notice will be published annually in the Competition Report.

ANNEX

BLOCK EXEMPTIONS

A. ENABLING COUNCIL REGULATIONS

I. **Vertical agreements** (see under B.I and B.II)

Council Regulation No 19/65/EEC of 2 March 1965 on the application of Article 85(3) of the Treaty to certain categories of agreements and concerted practices (OJ, Special Edition 1965-66, p. 35).

II. **Horizontal agreements** (see under B.III)

Council Regulation (EEC) No 2821/71 of 20 December 1971 on the application of Article 85(3) of the Treaty to categories of agreements, decisions and concerted practices (OJ, Special Edition 1971-III, p. 1032), modified by Regulation (EEC) No 2743/72 of 19 December 1972 (OJ, Special Edition 1972, 28-30. 12. 1972, p. 60).

B. COMMISSION BLOCK EXEMPTION REGULATIONS AND EXPLANATORY NOTICES

I. **Distribution agreements**

1. Commission Regulation (EEC) No 1983/83 of 22 June 1983 concerning exclusive distribution agreements (OJ No L 173, 30. 6. 1983, p. 1).
2. Commission Regulation (EEC) No 1984/83 of 22 June 1983 concerning exclusive purchasing agreements (OJ No L 173, 30. 6. 1983, p. 5).
3. Commission Notice concerning Commission Regulations (EEC) No 1983/83 and (EEC) No 1984/83 (OJ No C 101, 13. 4. 1984, p. 2).
4. Commission Regulation (EEC) No 123/85 of 12 December 1984 concerning motor vehicle distribution and servicing agreements (OJ No L 15, 18. 1. 1985, p. 16).
5. Commission Notice concerning Regulation (EEC) No 123/85 (OJ No C 17, 18. 1. 1985, p. 4).
6. Commission Notice on the clarification of the activities of motor vehicle intermediaries (OJ No C 329, 18. 12. 1991, p. 20).

II. **Licensing and franchising agreements**

1. Commission Regulation (EEC) No 2349/84 of 23 July 1984 con-

cerning patent licensing agreements (OJ No L 219, 16. 8. 1984, p. 15; corrigendum OJ No L 280, 22. 10. 1985, p. 32).

2. Commission Regulation (EEC) No 4087/88 of 30 November 1988 concerning franchising agreements (OJ No L 359, 28. 12. 1988, p. 46).
3. Commission Regulation (EEC) No 556/89 of 30 November 1988 concerning know-how licensing agreements (OJ No L 61, 4. 3. 1989, p. 1).

III. **Cooperative agreements**

1. Commission Regulation (EEC) No 417/85 of 19 December 1984 concerning specialization agreements (OJ No L 53, 22. 2. 1985, p. 1).
2. Commission Regulation (EEC) No 418/85 of 19 December 1984 concerning research and development agreements (OJ No L 53, 22. 2. 1985, p. 5).

PART THREE

RESTRICTIVE TRADE PRACTICES: APPLICATIONS

7

HORIZONTAL AGREEMENTS: MARKET SHARING

Although the competitive effects of price-fixing and market-sharing agreements between competitors may be clear, the nature of such transactions is often rather complex. Examples of such agreements include the **Polypropylene Cartel** (Section 6.4), **Wood Pulp** (Section 23.1), and the cartel, described below, between sugar producers and sellers in the Community.

7.1 *The European Sugar Cartel*, Decision of the Commission of the European Communities OJ L 140, 26.5.73, p 17, [1973] CMLR D 65

[. . .]

[. . .] The main producers and sellers of sugar in the Community have, from the 1968–69 season onwards, engaged in concerted practices to control the trade in sugar between member-States with the aim of ensuring the protection of their respective markets and of thus considerably restraining competition between particular groups of producers and sellers of sugar. These concerted practices have been implemented mainly by applying the following measures:

- deliveries between competing producers;
- measures relating to intra-Community deliveries made to buyers other than competing producers (consent of the producers in the market of destination, increased prices or alignment with the prices in the country of destination);
- measures adopted with regard to distributors, intended to impede or prevent free imports or exports within the Common Market [. . .] to compel them to observe the practices concerted between producers;
- concerting tenders submitted for subsidies for exports to non-member countries.

[The Commission decision describes in detail the nature of the horizontal agreements in each of the countries affected. In relation to the Dutch market, the concerted practice was engaged in between Suiker Unie (SU) and Central Suiker Mij (CSM) on the one hand, and Raffinerie Tirlemontoise (RT) and Pfeifer and Langen on the other. The concerted practice consisted]

[. . .] in the fact that Dutch producers have bought sugar directly from Belgian and German producers, and have re-sold it at the same prices and under the same conditions of sale as sugar produced domestically. This concerted practice by those concerned is revealed, as regards deliveries of Belgian sugar, in the business correspondence, which clearly shows that RT cannot make any deliveries to the Netherlands without the consent of the Dutch industry, and also in the way in which RT has obliged its exporters not to deliver to the Netherlands except with the consent of the Dutch producers or for certain specified purposes not only the sugar it produces itself but also that of other Belgian producers.

All the deliveries of Belgian sugar to the Netherlands have, by agreement between the producers, only been made to specified purchasers [. . .]. As regards deliveries of German sugar, the concerted practice consists in the fact that Pfeifer and Langen have carried out deliveries to Dutch producers systematically and in increasing quantities, without there having been any other deliveries of appreciable amounts.

The basic principle of the concerted practice of RT and the two Dutch producers SU and CSM, whereby RT wished to avoid making sugar available for export to the Netherlands during the marketing years 1968/69 and 1969/70 except for deliveries to its competitors, was reaffirmed several times, and is stated thus in a letter from RT to [a Belgian exporter]: 'As regards Holland, the basic principle is that we do not want to do anything that would upset Suiker Unie or CSM, just as they do not want to do anything which would disturb us.' This concerted practice has as its object and effect the prevention, restriction and distortion of competition within the Common Market.

All competition on the Dutch market between the [. . .] Belgian and German suppliers and Dutch producers has been eliminated. Without these sales among producers, the Belgian and German undertakings in question, which are geographically the best placed, would sell their sugar individually on the Dutch market, fixing the prices and conditions themselves and using their own trade marks. In respect of the quantities sold to their competitors the producers have thus given up independent commercial activity on the Dutch market.

These sales among producers allow the Dutch producers to have at their disposal much larger quantities of sugar and to re-sell them later, as it is a matter of a largely homogeneous product, at the same prices and on the same terms as the sugar they produce themselves.

[. . .]

Other sales by RT help to complete the range of qualities of sugar sold by CSM. However RT has given up selling these qualities of sugar in the Netherlands. Consequently Dutch consumers have no chance to choose such sugars since they are deprived of direct supply from RT. Apart from deliveries of special qualities of sugar, RT also delivers considerable quantities of white sugar to CSM which resells it on the same terms as the sugar it produces itself. As regards deliveries of sugar from RT to SU, those concerned have pointed out that part of these deliveries is of sugar for denaturing. However, even if the use of sugar sold in this way is limited to part of the animal feeding stuffs market, the number of offers made to the sugar users on this market is restricted, and therefore their choice is limited, if not non-existent. Only a very small part of RT's sales to SU is of sugar for denaturing. However, most of the sugar sold by RT to SU is white sugar delivered in bags which are provided by SU.

Normally it is not to a producer's advantage to sell large quantities of his products to one or more competitors. He can obtain higher profits by supplying dealers and consumers direct. Deliveries from one producer to another are thus to be explained by the fact that they were an effective means of restricting competition between the parties concerned and preventing the Dutch consumers from obtaining the sugar they need freely from foreign suppliers. The restrictions on competition resulting from the deliveries between producers are particularly serious since they affect a substantial part of the quantities of sugar traded between the countries concerned.

Furthermore, competition on the Dutch market is restricted because RT makes no deliveries of sugar without the consent of its competitors SU and CSM. The Dutch producers have in the main only given their consent to deliveries to the milk producers' industry, since most of the sugars supplied to this industry are used for inclusion in products derived from milk and therefore have no competitive effect on the sale of sugar from Dutch producers.

The concerted practice was continued during marketing years 1970/71 and 1971/72 by including Belgian and Dutch dealers in these concerted deliveries. This is evident from the agreements concluded with the dealers and the way in which they were implemented. From the marketing year 1970/71 onwards the sources of supply for these Dutch dealers and re-consumers was still more restricted by the fact that RT prevented the Belgian dealers from delivering to the Netherlands sugar produced by other Belgian producers.

This concerted practice, aimed at preventing Belgian and German sugar being delivered freely on the Dutch market in competition with Dutch producers, constitutes a restriction to competition likely to affect trade between Member States. It consequently comes under the prohibition in Article 85(1) of the Treaty. This concerted practice cannot be the subject of a declaration of exemption under Article 85(3), from the very fact that it has not been notified to the Commission in accordance with Article 4(1) of Regulation No. 17.

8

HORIZONTAL AGREEMENTS: INFORMATION EXCHANGE

Perfect information is one of the underlying assumptions of purely competitive markets. However, in imperfect markets, especially those which are highly concentrated, the exchange of detailed information removes the possibility for 'hidden competition'. As the Commission states in the following decision, 'active competition in these market conditions becomes possible only if each competitor can keep its actions secret or even succeeds in misleading its rivals'. The decision distinguishes between benign and anticompetitive information exchange.

8.1 *UK Agricultural Tractor Registration Exchange*, Decision of the Commission of the European Communities (*92/157/EEC*) OJ L68, 13.3.92, p 19

[This decision concerned an information exchange agreement (referred to in the decision as 'the Exchange'), entered into by eight manufacturers and importers of agricultural tractors in the UK. The relevant market was highly concentrated, as the Commission's analysis reveals. The Exchange was managed by AEA with the assistance of a computer bureau (SIL).]

[. . .]

AGGREGATE INDUSTRY DATA

(16) Each member may obtain information on aggregate industry sales with or without a breakdown by horsepower groupings or by driveline. This aggregate information can in addition be broken down by geographic areas [. . .] This information is or can be made available for yearly, quarterly, monthly and weekly time periods.

The Commission has not in principle objected to the availability of these aggregate industry data because they do not identify the retail sales of the individual members of the Exchange. However, the Commission objected to the exchange of aggregate industry data to the extent that in respect of specific geographic areas product breakdowns or time periods, the reports supplied by SIL contain less than 10 tractor units sold for any such specific breakdown by territory, product or time period. Below this minimum number of total sales there is a high risk that even aggregate data will allow, directly or indirectly, the identification of the exact sales volume of individual competitors.

DATA IDENTIFYING SALES OF INDIVIDUAL COMPETITORS

(17) In addition to the aggregate industry sales data described above, each member may obtain information identifying the volume of retail sales and market shares of each individual member of the Exchange with detailed breakdowns by model, by product groups [. . .] by geographic areas (including counties, dealer territories and postcode sectors), and by yearly, quarterly, monthly and daily time periods.

(18) The data exchanged between the members via the AEA and SIL identifies in respect of each member the following information:

- the exact volume of the retail sales and market shares of each member-competitor on the United Kingdom market at national, regional, county, dealer territory and postcode sector level: this makes it possible to compare the market penetration and performance of each supplier down to the smallest geographical level; it is possible to compare the performances not only of the manufacturers but also of their dealers in each dealer territory;
- the exact volume of retail sales and the exact market shares of every specific model sold by each member: this permits comparison of the performance of specific models of each member-competitor; the comparison is equally done at the level of geographic zones which can be determined by each member;
- the exact volume of the retail sales and the market shares of specific horsepower groups for each member: this permits comparison of the performance and market penetration of each member-competitor in specific horsepower bands which are usually categories of 10 horsepower grouping; there are also breakdowns by driveline (two-wheel four-wheel/articulated);
- the daily and monthly retail sales and market shares at United Kingdom level for each member: this permits comparison of the latest most up-to-date sales performance of each participating supplier on the United Kingdom market and their evaluation during the current month.

(19) The above information is made available for time periods broken down by year (calendar year, fiscal year, rolling year), year to date, quarter and month, and in respect of total United Kingdom retail sales and figures are even available on a daily basis. This therefore permits each member to follow the sales performance and market penetration of each participating competitor on a yearly, quarterly, monthly and daily basis in respect of all the products, specific products and within the smallest geographic areas.

(20) In addition, the members release to their dealers all this individualized market information as regards each dealer's own territory and information on the units sold and market share of each member at national level. Thus commercially sensitive information is exchanged not only between the manufacturers of tractors but is also made available to the retailers in the market. This creates full transparency between competitors at manufacturer level and at the dealer level within each dealer territory.

(21) Finally, the Exchange provides to each member aggregate data on the retail sales and market shares of non-members (called 'others') with approximately 12% of the United Kingdom market. Sales by the individual non-members are not identified but members of the Exchange nevertheless have access by this means to up-to-date information about changes in the market shares of the 'others' – the data covers the same periods as the identifying information (yearly, quarterly, monthly and daily).

[. . .]

(35) For the assessment of that part of

the Exchange which identifies the sales of the individual members, the Commission takes account of:

- the market structure, i.e.:
  - high concentration: four firms with approximately 80% of the market, seven firms with 87 to 88% of the market, a still higher degree of concentration for smaller geographic areas or product breakdowns, the members are also major suppliers in the other Community markets, and the gap and dispersion of the market shares of the non-members who together hold only about 12% of the market,
  - high barriers to entry: the need for an extensive distribution and service network, the low volume and stagnant/declining market, the advantage of brand loyalty for established suppliers and the effects of the information Exchange, and
  - the absence of significant imports from outside the Community for agricultural tractors above 30 hp;
- the nature of the information exchanged: i.e. the exact quantities of the retail sales and the exact market shares which are trade secrets between genuine competitors in a highly concentrated market,
- the detail of the information exchanged: i.e. detailed product breakdowns, small geographical breakdowns and time periods below one year, i.e. daily, monthly and quarterly market sensitive information on competitors, and,
- the fact that the members meet regularly within the AEA Committee which gives them a forum for contacts.

(36) The Exchange leads to restriction of competition for two reasons.

(a) Prevention of hidden competition in a highly concentrated market

(37) The Exchange restricts competition because it creates a degree of market transparency between the suppliers in a highly concentrated market which is likely to destroy what hidden competition there remains between the suppliers in that market on account of the risk and ease of exposure of independent competitive action. In this highly concentrated market, 'hidden competition' is essentially that element of uncertainty and secrecy between the main suppliers regarding market conditions without which none of them has the necessary scope of action to compete efficiently.

Uncertainty and secrecy between suppliers is a vital element of competition in this kind of market. Indeed active competition in these market conditions becomes possible only if each competitor can keep its actions secret or even succeeds in misleading its rivals.

This reasoning, however, in no way undermines the positive competitive benefits of transparency in a competitive market characterized by many buyers and sellers. Where there is a low degree of concentration, market transparency can increase competition in so far as consumers benefit from choices made in full knowledge of what is on offer. It is emphasized that the United Kingdom tractor market is neither a low concentration market nor is the transparency in question in any way directed towards, or of benefit to, consumers.

On the contrary, the high market transparency between suppliers on the United Kingdom tractor market which is created by the Exchange takes the surprise effect out of a competitor's action thus resulting in a shorter space of time for reactions with the effect that temporary advantages are greatly reduced. Because all competitive actions can immediately be noticed by an increase in sales, the consequences are that in the case of a price reduction or any other marketing incentives by one company the other can react immediately, thus eliminating any advantage of the initiator. This effect of neutralizing and thus stabilizing the market positions of the oligopolists is in this case likely to occur because there are not external competitive pressures on the members of the Exchange except parallel imports which are however also monitored as has been explained above.

(38) The United Kingdom tractor market is clearly a highly concentrated market where competition is already weakened by the fact that:

- four firms dominate the market with a combined market share of approximately 80%,
- these four firms have created an information exchange with four, now three, other well-known suppliers capable of challenging their market position with the effect that the conditions of a narrow oligopoly have been artificially created between the eight, now seven, best established competitors on this market by giving them information on any change in volumes and market shares at manufacturer and dealer level,
- these eight, now seven, suppliers are active in all other Community markets and know the pattern of trade and products supplied on the United Kingdom market for a long period of time; in particular, there is no difficulty knowing the prices charged by each member because in this industry there are list prices and a simple telephone enquiry will readily reveal the general level of discounts applied by each manufacturer's dealer network; this information is also available from customers who inform the dealers of competitors' prices in a given territory,
- the market is protected from competition from outside the United Kingdom by the fact that there are high barriers to entry and that there are only insignificant imports from outside the Community.

(39) In addition, demand is very dispersed. There are numerous buyers, the majority of whom do not have the possibility of purchasing tractors in other Member States (transport difficulties, import formalities, registration, service, trade-ins, etc.). Thus, demand transferability in this market is very low which weakens the competitive pressure from the demand side on the limited number of suppliers established within the United Kingdom and therefore reinforces their economic strength on that market.

(40) On the United Kingdom tractor market, therefore, the only difficult, but very important, market data to obtain is the exact volume of sales of each manufacturer/dealer so as to be able to notice instantly changes in sales volumes and market shares of each member of the oligopoly and of each dealer at the level of dealer territories. This market knowledge allows each member and dealer to react immediately and thus to neutralize whatever initiative any one of the members/dealers of the oligopoly would take to increase its sales (see recital (37)). However, the result in practice is that few such initiatives will be taken precisely because every supplier knows very well what the position of each of the others is and that, thanks to the transparency created by the system, any initiative on his part can be detected at once by the others.

(41) The very detailed product and geographic market information on retail sales (see recitals (17) to (23)) gives each manufacturer and dealer fully reliable market knowledge (100% coverage and 100% accuracy) which is accessible on an instant or very short time basis (daily, monthly or quarterly). It allows them:

- to establish with accuracy the market positions and performances of their rivals and to follow constantly any changes of these market positions,
- to see at once whether there has been any increase in the retail sales of a rival, to see the territory in which such an increase takes place, to detect the models which contribute such an increase and finally to follow whether and to what extent any price or other marketing strategies of rivals are successful,
- to limit price competition as far as possible by allowing suppliers and dealers to react to any price-cutting or other market strategies selectively by

limiting their response to the absolute minimum degree necessary in terms of product and territory and by being sure to hit the right target,
- to react more quickly if the market positions start changing.

(42) The Exchange further helps the established firms and dealers with considerable market shares (i.e. the four biggest firms holding approximately 80% of the United Kingdom market) to defend their market positions more efficiently than they could do without the detailed information on retail sales of their rivals and any changes thereof. By their wider market coverage and sales volume, these firms and dealers already have the advantage of better market knowledge which is further strengthened by the fact that they can react more effectively to any increase in sales by the smaller competitors on the market. This is confirmed by the fact that, during their participation in the Exchange, the main four suppliers have essentially maintained their combined market share *vis-à-vis* the other members of the Exchange on the United Kingdom market.

(43) In the absence of the Exchange, firms would have to compete in a market with some measure of uncertainty as to the exact place, degree and means of attack by rivals. This uncertainty is a normal competitive risk bringing about stronger competition because reaction and reduction of prices cannot be limited to the absolute minimum degree necessary to defend an established position. Uncertainty would lead the firms to compete more strongly than if they knew exactly how much of a response was necessary to meet competition. They would have to exceed a minimum response, for instance by offering more favourable discounts to move their stock or by offering discounts for more products and in more territories. The Exchange reduces uncertainty by revealing the actions and reactions of all participating competitors who represent 87 to 88% of the United Kingdom market. There is thus a prevention of hidden competition which results necessarily from the Exchange.

(b) Increase of barriers to entry for non-members

(44) The Exchange not only lessens competition between members of the Exchange and between their dealers, it also restricts competition between members and non-members of the Exchange even if the Exchange in principle admits any manufacturer or importer to the information Exchange.

(45) If a supplier chooses not to become a member of the Exchange, he is disadvantaged by the fact that he does not have available the detailed and accurate market information about other suppliers which is available to members of the Exchange. Detailed knowledge of the sales pattern for tractors on the United Kingdom market improves the members' ability to defend their positions *vis-à-vis* non-members.

(46) If a supplier chooses to become a member of the Exchange, he must reveal his exact retail sales by product and by every small geographic territory with the result that the Exchange then permits the established suppliers with considerable market shares and extensive dealer networks to become aware of the existence of new entry and to instantly detect the market penetration by any such new member. This market information on any new member will permit the established suppliers to defend their acquired positions by placing selective actions designed to contain the new member.

(47) As a result, for a small supplier it is neither advantageous to become a member of the Exchange nor to stay outside the Exchange. In both cases the Exchange advantages the big suppliers who already belong to it. The presence of the smaller suppliers in the Exchange shows indeed that these suppliers have not been able to contest the position of the four biggest suppliers [. . .] and that market expansion is only possible through acquisition [. . .]. The presence of the four smaller suppliers can therefore only be explained by the fact that the UK Exchange is part of a network of similar Exchanges in other Community countries and that the eight suppliers par-

ticipate in various exchanges on a reciprocal basis [. . .].

(48) In consequence, the Exchange permits its members to effectively prevent new entry and to contain the expansion of other suppliers on the United Kingdom market who are not members of the Exchange. This constitutes a serious restriction on the development of new competition in a highly concentrated market which is already characterized by high barriers to entry with the result that the members of the Exchange can jointly maximize profits to the detriment of farmers. This restriction affects in particular the smaller suppliers from other Community countries who will not be able to penetrate the United Kingdom market if they wanted to sell or increase their sales on that market.

(61) The Commission does not object to the exchange of aggregate industry information with geographic breakdowns by United Kingdom [. . .] region, land use, county, dealer territory and even postcode sector and with product breakdowns by horsepower groupings or driveline provided that the reports contain at any time a minimum of 10 tractor units sold for any such report. The Commission does not object either to the release of own company information except for certain specific reports with clear anticompetitive effects.

Therefore, the parties may have access to detailed and up-to-date industry and own company figures. In addition, in this particular market, the Commission does not object to the annual exchange of one-year-old figures identifying the sales volume and the market shares of individual competitors at United Kingdom [. . .] region and land use levels with a breakdown by models.

All this information permits each member to identify any overall market trends and changes in demand in the industry and also to forecast production needs, to fix sales targets for their dealers and to maintain adequate stocks of tractors and spare parts. It enables each member to judge the performance of its products and its dealers in relation to the industry as a whole.

[. . .]

(63) As regards data on sales by own company dealers which enable manufacturers to interfere with the retail activity of dealers or parallel importers [. . .] neither arrangements for the exchange of these data nor such practices are eligible for an exemption. It is difficult to see how the sharing of such data or such practices could be said to be indispensable for the achievement of better production or distribution of tractors. The performance of a dealer can be assessed by the number of total sales achieved by the dealer without identifying the exact destination of each specific tractor sold.

(64) In conclusion, without having to examine whether all four conditions of Article 85(3) are fulfilled, the condition of indispensability is not in any event fulfilled in respect of either the data identifying sales of individual competitors or the data on dealer sales of own company dealers which enables interference with the retail activity of dealers or parallel importers. Therefore, the notified Exchange cannot benefit from an exemption pursuant to Article 85(3).

9

HORIZONTAL AGREEMENTS: PRICE FIXING

In the UK, the Restrictive Practices Court has upheld price fixing agreements as being in the public interest, on the grounds that they removed the need for consumers to shop around (*Black Bolt and Nut Assoc.'s Agreement*, LR 2 RP 50 (1960)), induced price stability (*Cement Makers Federation Agreement*, LR 2 RP 241 (1961)), permitted technical cooperation (*Permanent Magnet Association Agreement*, LR 3 RP 119 (1962)), or protected the viability of marginal publications (*Net Book Agreement*, LR 3 RP 246 (1963)). Although the latter case persists as a price fixing agreement, the Restrictive Trade Practices Act 1976 cannot generally be used as a vehicle for horizontal price fixing agreements. For an example of the treatment of clandestine agreements of this nature, see *Director General of Fair Trading* v. *Smith's Concrete Ltd.* [1991] 4 All ER 150, especially at pages 156 to 158.

9.1 *Re The Polypropylene Cartel: Hercules NV* v. *Commission of the European Communities*, European Court of First Instance [1992] 4 CMLR 84

[Fifteen petrochemical companies formed a price-fixing cartel through a series of meetings held to fix 'target prices' for the product (polypropylene). The prices were to be achieved through a series of price initiatives.]

Opinion of the Advocate General:
[. . .]

THE ECONOMIC ANALYSES

Economic analyses often make up an important part of the evidence in competition cases and can be of great value to the Court in understanding the relevant economic context. It is thus important to obtain information about how an oligopolistic market might react in different circumstances. But – and this is the important point – the findings of economic experts cannot take the place of legal assessment and adjudication. Thus, when [economists, on behalf of parties to an agreement, make] observations about what target prices might be in an economic context, it must be emphasised that [such] views are not, and cannot form, a legal assessment. Even if it were to be found that there were no significant effects on the market, that does not prove that no agreement was reached or that no exchange of information took place with a view to regulating prices. It is for the Court to consider what is prohibited under Article 85(1) and the evidence for the commitment of prohibited acts, and not for economic theorists.

On the basis of an overall assessment of the evidence, the Court must therefore consider whether what took place constitutes prohibited conduct, even if the expression 'target prices' from the point of view of economic experts might conceivably mean something other than unanimity on the prices which all should strive to obtain. It is the content of the documentary evidence which must show whether the persons attending the meetings had the intention of influencing prices or whether they simply wished to tell each other what they thought were reasonable prices on the basis of market evaluation and it is the Court which must determine where necessary whether it is unlawful for parties to inform one another over a very long period of time about what they think the market can bear. [. . .]

TARGET PRICES AND VOLUMES AS THE SUBJECT MATTER OF AGREEMENTS OR OF CONCERTATION

According to the Commission, it was sought to implement the alleged price initiatives by applying so-called target prices. In assessing the evidence before the Court we must first establish what the term 'target prices' probably means to the undertakings during their discussions at the meetings. Once that meaning is established, it must be decided whether target prices are caught by the prohibition in Article 85(1).

On this question the Commission states, for example, that the 'jargon' used in the documentary evidence relating to the meetings speaks for itself. The Commission is entitled, it says, to take a common sense approach and to interpret the expressions used in the documents in accordance with what they actually say. Target prices, states the Commission further, must ordinarily be understood as reflecting a specific price level which the producers had agreed to attain as far as the market allowed.

In my view, too, there is no other way to interpret the notes of the meetings.

However, it is perhaps the very term 'target prices' which lies at the root of much of the confusion characterising the proceedings in these cases. For, as the Commission says, the term 'target prices,' as used in the notes of the meetings and so on, must precisely be understood as reflecting agreements to the effect that the undertakings should as far as possible attain a certain price level. As proved to be the case, and as the Commission is also aware, it was often difficult, and, according to the applicants, impossible, for them to attain the prices to which they aspired. Indeed, the applicants believe that the market did not allow them to implement any target prices and that the target prices were actually determined by the market.

Hence the interminable debate about whether it was the applicants who were steering the market or the market which was steering them.

It accounts, too, for some of the impressive presentations of evidence by the applicants in the form of audits and reports by economic experts and so forth, which all tend to show that the prices striven after were not obtained.

The next link in the chain of argument of most of the applicants is the attempt to show that they had not come to any agreement or at any rate did not regard themselves as bound by any agreement, which is purportedly proved by the very fact that the prices they were together striving to achieve were not obtained.

The applicants have thus in fact set themselves the very difficult task of conjuring away the very certain and well-documented content of the negotiations and the impression of them created by the notes of the meetings. In my view, they have not succeeded in that task and I think that there need be no hesitation in assuming that target prices and so forth were agreed to, probably in the form of a 'gentlemen's agreement', as alleged by the

Commission and to the extent that is otherwise borne out by the documentary evidence.

The fact that there could be any discussion at all and that the applicants devoted such considerable resources to it is possibly due to the elasticity of the meaning of the term 'target prices' viewed in relation to the rules of competition.

Some would perhaps argue that an agreement solely designed to strive to obtain a specific price as far as the market will bear is not *per se* a manifestation of anticompetitive conduct.

Yet, to judge by the notes, that is not what was intended. On the contrary, the purpose was to obtain a higher price than the participants reckoned on or could have obtained. The intention was clearly to attempt to push the price level upwards. The 'object' within the meaning of Article 85(1) emerges quite clearly.

In view of the foregoing, it cannot matter, in my opinion, that the very term 'target prices' is so conveniently vague that in the mutual relationship between the parties participating in the cartel it would be difficult to determine when a participant had ignored such an agreement. The fact that the agreements were akin to 'gentlemen's agreements' because of their rather uncertain and vague substance and thus could not have served as a basis for determining the parties' reciprocal legal and moral obligations, is, according to the case law of the Court of Justice, not decisive.

Therefore, it can in itself only be of minor importance whether the undertakings themselves considered that they were under any obligation towards the others, since the substance of the obligation was from the outset rather indistinct.

The conclusion to be drawn from the above must be that even a type of agreement which, according to its substance, takes account of actual market conditions, as it undoubtedly must, is covered by Article 85(1). From the evidential point of view, it can, moreover, be concluded that any non-application or incomplete application in practice of the prices striven for is not suitable counter-evidence in the face of agreements of that type.

Many of the applicants do not in fact dispute the factual circumstances, but only their legal consequences. Thus, ICI, for example, states that the targets discussed at the producers' meetings were consensus recommendations to which the producers aspired with different degrees of enthusiasm.

In my view, that explanation lies square with a description of an agreement or concertation prohibited under Article 85, which shows that to a certain extent only a problem of definition or categorisation is involved.

The entire case does in fact show that the undertakings did not feel themselves bound by the agreements entered into or the concertation which took place in the same way in which they would have felt themselves bound by an agreement to deliver a consignment of polypropylene to a particular customer on a particular date. When customers went elsewhere in order to seek a lower price after a price rise had taken place, those in charge of sales could obviously not tolerate a cessation or serious drop in sales. The notes of some of the meetings show quite clearly, however, that to a large extent it was felt necessary to endeavour to work out a common course of conduct, even though there were obviously often some whose solidarity was in doubt.

Generally, it is not possible to establish which undertakings showed a greater or lesser degree of solidarity, even if some individual undertakings were in the spotlight more than others; moreover, they need not always have been the same. It is possible that one or two undertakings demonstrably had more inclination to 'cheat' than the others, but the picture is far from clear and the fact that the undertaking or undertakings in question possibly looked after their own interests at the others' expense cannot, in my opinion, be taken as an indication that they did not take part [. . .].

For a detailed treatment of the competitive impact of a collusive tendering scheme in the construction industry, see the Commission decision of 5 February 1992 (*Dutch Construction Cartel* 1992 OJ L92/1). See also *Suiker Unie* [1976] 1 CMLR 295. For the treatment of such agreements in the UK, see *Water-Tube Boilermakers Association Agreement*, LR 1 RP 285 (1959).

For an example of the treatment of a vertical resale price maintenance agreement under Article 85, see the **Net Book Agreement** decision (Section 13.2).

Horizontal price fixing is *per se* unlawful in US law, although it may be argued that agreements to increase price are not inherently anticompetitive in reasonably contestable markets. For an example of the treatment of a price-fixing agreement: see the extract from **Federal Trade Commission** v. **Superior Court Trial Lawyers** (Section 2.4).

10

VERTICAL AGREEMENTS: DISTRIBUTION

Horizontal agreements are a relatively clear-cut case, and economics papers on collusion refer at least implicitly to horizontal agreement. The situation relating to vertical agreements, that is between suppliers and distributors, is far more problematic from a welfare economic standpoint. Indeed, economists have only relatively recently come to a reasonable understanding of their reason for existence. This coherent 'story' is well told in the **Mathewson and Winter** extract; the more welfare economic aspects which we have omitted reach no firm conclusion and are in any case based upon a very specific model. The extract is relevant also to Chapters 11–13, and in part to Chapter 15.

10.1 G. Mathewson and R. Winter, 'The economics of vertical restraints in distribution', in J. Stiglitz and G. Mathewson (eds), *New Developments in the Analysis of Market Structure* (Macmillan, London, 1986)

[. . .]

ECONOMICS AND PUBLIC POLICY OF VERTICAL RESTRAINTS

Vertical restraints are contractual limitations placed on downstream distributors or retailers of products by manufacturers or wholesalers. These limitations restrict the products offered for sale by the retailers, the prices set by the retailers and the potential clients of the retailers. Specifically, vertical restraints can include:

1. *Vertical price restrictions*: resale price maintenance (RPM) is the establishment of a floor to the retail price. Price ceilings are a possibility as well, although they are observed less frequently in practice.
2. *Vertical territorial arrangements*: these restrictions protect to some degree a retailer's territory or location against intra-brand competition. The extreme form of this restraint is closed territory distribution (CTD), the assignment to each retailer of exclusive rights to all consumers within a territory. (A more general class of restraints restricts each retailer to supplying a set of consumers defined by some characteristics, e.g. size.)
3. *Quantity forcing or volume requirements*: forcing establishes minimum quantities in wholesale transactions with retailers.
4. *Franchise fees*: such fees are lump-sum transfers from the retailer to the manufacturer.

5. *Full-line forcing*: this requires the dealer to carry the full line (as opposed to selected partial lines) of the manufacturer's products.
6. *Exclusive dealing*: exclusive dealing requires the retailers to carry only the manufacturer's brand of the product.

This chapter considers RPM, CTD, quantity forcing and franchise fees. Why would manufacturers impose these restrictions on decisions taken by retailers? The restrictions have been explained both as 'purely vertical' devices used by a manufacturer to control retail prices, product quality, product information and availability at the retail level: and as devices used to coordinate the activities of horizontal cartels. A distinction must be made between the source of monopoly power and the practices of firms with such power. Whether monopoly power occurs at the upstream or downstream level or at both levels, firms should seek to maximise joint profits provided there are appropriate tools to divide the spoils. The critical issue on horizontal cartels is whether the restrictive practice(s) in question facilitate a cartel which would otherwise fail should the practice be declared illegal. If the answer is no, then we shall maintain that the cartel issue is irrelevant. Eventually, we shall examine the welfare effects of permitting an upstream monopolist to achieve the benefits of integration through vertical restrictions. We argue that our results are widely applicable. Nevertheless, considerable insight is gained if we first attempt to delineate the issues contained in each of the arguments.

Vertical restraints as efficiency-enhancing

A necessary condition for the profitability of vertical restraints is price-setting power. But market power alone is not sufficient: If demand in a competitive retail sector depends only on price (and if technology at the retail level involves fixed factor-proportions) then it is well known that an incentive for vertical control does not arise. The common element in most efficiency explanations of vertical control is the recognition that the demand for a manufacturer's product at the retail level may depend upon more than the price.

The classic explanation of resale price maintenance [. . .] assumes that demand depends upon product information provided at the retail level. Because of a free-rider problem, the provision of this information may be inadequate. Discount stores can free ride on the information provided elsewhere, offering no information themselves and cutting price so low as to attract informed customers (with low search-costs for price).

By foreclosing discount houses, RPM prevents this informational free-riding and supports retail price margins to increase retailers incentive to provide information. If the positive impact of the additional point-of-sale information more than offsets any detrimental impact of an increase in average retail price, RPM will be profitable. [. . .]

The potential for RPM to counteract horizontal externalities is not limited to the dimension of product information. For many products, quality is determined at the retail level, especially through retail servicing of the product, but cannot be identified precisely by consumers prior to purchase. In this case, retail demand will depend upon the reputations of the manufacturer and individual retailers for product quality. When an individual retail outlet increases the quality of its service, it contributes not only to its own reputation but to the reputation of the manufacturer's product. This is especially true when the consumer cannot identify precisely the contribution of the retailer to product quality, as in automobile retailing and servicing. Because not all of the benefits from any increase in quality are appropriated by the retailer, the incentive to set high quality-standards is inadequate. By supporting high retail-price margins, RPM can increase retailers' incentive for high-quality retail service. Arguments similar to this formed part of the defence in the Schwinn case in the US [. . .] and the Raleigh case in the UK [. . .].

Demand for a product may depend not

only on the price- and quality-decisions of retail outlets selling the product, but also on the *number* of outlets choosing to stock the product. [. . .]. The dependence of demand upon the number of outlets (e.g. because of increased availability with more stores) is [. . .] suggestive of a spatial model. In this case, the appropriate equilibrium concept for the retail market is monopolistic competition. The profitability of vertical price restrictions in spatial markets, where retailers have price-setting power but earn only competitive returns, are investigated in [several studies. They] suggest that the profitable price-restraint in spatial markets is a price ceiling (which results in retail firms producing at lower average cost) rather than a price floor, which would increase the availability of the product. The price ceiling counteracts the effect of a double mark-up of prices (above the marginal production-cost upstream and then above the wholesale price downstream); [. . .], vertical control may reduce prices.

A traditional explanation of resale price maintenance, that is less persuasive than those discussed above, is the 'product image' or 'loss leader' argument. Price-cutting is said to damage the quality reputation of a product to the extent that consumers base their expectations of quality on price. Restraints against price-cutting are therefore said to be profitable. The single instrument of the wholesale price, however, is sufficient to determine the retail price of a product, rendering the vertical price-restraint unnecessary.

Some of these explanations for vertical price restraints have been offered for territorial restraints as well. Where retailers' incentives for quality (retail servicing) or product promotion are insufficient, the assignment of retail territorial monopoly power may improve retailers' incentives, by protecting a high retail margin against intra-brand competition. For example, in a major [US] anti-trust case involving closed territory distribution, the White Motor Company argued that CTDs provided sufficient incentive for the dealers to contact customers and to promote the product [. . .].

The *White Motor* case also serves to illustrate the price discrimination incentive for customer restrictions. *White Motor* reserved all state and government accounts for itself, forbidding dealers to sell to these customers. If the demand from new accounts was relatively elastic, *White Motor* profited from charging them a lower price (at a given size of sale). Finally, in situations where conditions for price discrimination at the retail level hold, CTD increases the profits of manufacturers and retailers by allowing discrimination which would be impossible in a competitive market.

'Forcing' is a vertical restraint that has received less attention. It is a practice historically used by US automobile manufacturers. [. . .] Where the only retail decision is on pricing, a minimum-quantity restraint is clearly equivalent to a price floor. Where sales effort or service quality influences the quantity demanded at the retail level, a forcing restraint also has the effect of increasing these non-pricing variables, and may be profitable where levels of these variables are insufficient without the restraint.

Horizontal explanations of vertical restraints

Are vertical restraints helpful practices for manufacturer- or dealer-cartels? RPM, in particular, has been explained as an instrument to co-ordinate a cartel at either the manufacturers' or the dealers' level. In the case of a manufacturers' cartel, the standard collusive practice would be the co-ordination of wholesale prices. But where wholesale contracts are complex or where cheating at the wholesale level is difficult to detect, the manufacturers' cartel may co-ordinate through retail prices.

Contrary to common argument, the desire to fix retail prices is not a *sufficient* reason for a manufacturers' cartel to profit from RPM. With a competitive retail market and stable retail-cost conditions, manufacturers could assume agreed-upon retail prices by appropriately fixing their wholesale prices. Vertical price floors would *not* be necessary. However, fixed wholesale prices do not necessarily produce fixed retail prices. Variation in the costs of other retail inputs could cause retail prices to vary. In this case, the stability of a cartel could suffer, since cartel members would have difficulty in distinguishing changes in retail prices that flowed from a variation in retail costs from those changes that would flow from cheating on the cartel. RPM enhances the stability of a cartel here, by eliminating any retail price variation (albeit at a cost to the cartel) and by easily communicating retail prices.

The mere existence of a manufacturers' cartel, or the use of RPM by manufacturers of close-substitute products, does not imply that the price floor is necessarily co-ordinating the cartel. A cartel acting as a multi-plant monopolist may be using vertical price-restrictions for any of the efficiency reasons that we have discussed. Alternatively, competing manufacturers may each be forced to use restraints in order to achieve the most efficient distribution system. In each of these cases, appropriate public policy towards vertical price restraints must follow from the efficiency explanation, rather than the cartel explanation, of the practices.

Resale price maintenance has also been seen as a means of co-ordinating price-fixing among retailers with market power. According to this argument, retailers can circumvent the anti-trust restrictions against explicit horizontal price-fixing by persuading manufacturers to impose a floor on retail prices of their products. The horizontal price-fixing agreement is camouflaged as a vertical price restriction, to the benefit of retailers. (Thus, retailers' associations were strong supporters of the US Fair Trade Laws.) The retail cartel would have to put pressure not only on existing manufacturers but on all entrants as well if it were to fix retail prices at the cartel level. A retailer cartel that successfully co-ordinated a restrictive price-policy through an upstream market characterised by some competitive element, would produce a higher retail price than would otherwise prevail. This result would have the usual negative welfare consequences. Whatever its plausibility, this argument clearly requires the absence of a successful cartel upstream. (A successful manufacturers' cartel would seek efficient contracts to maximise joint profits independently of the competitive nature of downstream retail markets.)

Sometimes, vertical restrictions orchestrated by downstream trade groups do not seek to achieve cartel rents, but to impede new market equilibria harmful to the members of the group. The support of Fair Trade Laws by independent retailers' associations such as the National Druggists' Association may be explained as an attempt to retard the growth in the market share of more efficient (and thus lower-price) chains of retail outlets [. . .].

SPECIFICATION OF THE BASIC MODEL AND AN OUTLINE OF THE POSITIVE RESULTS

Our objective in this section is to outline an explanation for the use of vertical restrictions by manufacturers to control decisions by retailers, a basic principal-agent problem. [. . .] Why do such restrictions improve joint manufacturer–retailer profits? How are these restrictions packaged together, i.e. which instruments are complements and which substitutes?

[. . .] We set forth here two critical assumptions, which are intended to capture the important elements of markets where restraints are used: (1) demand depends upon the availability of the product and (2) retailers have a role in influencing consumers' purchase choices.

1 Spatial retail markets

Potential consumers are uniformly distributed along a circle or line of infinite length; retail outlets incur a fixed cost and buy one product of known quality from a single manufacturer (wholesaler) at a wholesale price; retailers have local price-setting powers, form conjectures on price strategies of their rivals, but earn zero rents as there is free entry into the retail market.

2 Role for local advertising or sales effort

A consumer must be informed of the existence of the product through local advertising or sales effort that is *not* directly monitorable (and therefore cannot be contractually specified) by the manufacturer. Because of the monitoring problem, indirect means must be found to control local advertising. A proportion of the local-advertising messages potentially spills over into neighbouring retail markets (a spatial analogue to retailer free riding). Once informed of the existence of the good, the consumer has free access to information on retail prices and outlet locations and buys from the store where the delivered price is the lowest, whether or not the store informed the consumer.

We define (P) to be the retail price, (R) to be the market radius, (A) to be local advertising expenditure for each (symmetrical) retailer; define (P_w) to be the wholesale price, (c) to be the (constant) marginal production costs, Π to be the manufacturer's level of profits and Π^R to be each retailer's level of profits. Free entry at the retail level means that $\Pi^R = 0$. Knowledge of (P, R, A) is sufficient to determine total retail-demand and costs, both upstream and downstream, and therefore combined upstream and downstream profit. As $\Pi^R = 0$, obviously all of these profits accrue to the monopolist; hence, Π can be written as a function of P, R and A.

Can a manufacturer using the wholesale price alone induce (P^*, R^*, A^*) (the first-best or joint-profit-maximising levels of these variables)? The answer is no, which means that an incentive exists for vertical control. If packages of vertical restrictions, together with the wholesale price, can achieve (P^*, R^*, A^*), then these packages are alternatives to vertical integration. The nature of the alternative restraint packages follows from an understanding of the insufficiency of P_w alone to achieve (P^*, R^*, A^*). At the source of the insufficiency of wholesale price as a single instrument are three potential externalities, which are the consequence of market conditions:

(i) *Vertical externality*: in attracting demand by lowering (P) or increasing (A), the retail firm does not appropriate additional profits flowing upstream through the ($P_w - c$) wedge. As a result, from the viewpoint of joint maximisation, (P) will be too high and (A) will be too low, other things held constant.

(ii) *Information externalities* (define α to be the proportion of local advertising messages that spills over into neighbouring retail areas). Any increase in profit accruing to either neighbouring retail outlets, or through neighbouring retail outlets to the upstream firm (when $\alpha > 0$), are not appropriated by the advertising retailer. As a result, A is too low. Provided retail price-elasticities are independent of A (i.e. the selection of consumer tastes captured by any retailer is independent of the level of advertising), (P) is unaffected. (Again, other variables are held constant.)

(iii) *Horizontal conjectural externality*: a useful separation of potential retailer conjectures is into Loschian and non-Loschian (e.g. Nash) categories. Retailer conjectures are Loschian when each outlet assumes that its market area is invariant to changes in its price, i.e. that price changes by any one retailer are matched by neighbouring retailers; non-Loschian conjectures involve price changes by neighbouring outlets that do not match a price change by a retailer. For example, if a retailer conjectures that neighbouring retailers do not respond to his price change, his conjectures are of the Nash type.

When a non-Loschian firm considers raising its price, it perceives that this would cause consumers at the geographical margin of its market area to switch to neighbouring retail outlets, thus increasing demand at these outlets. This would be a positive (pecuniary) externality. The increase in other retailers' and the manufacturer's profits resulting from a price increase is not appropriated by the non-Loschian retailer. The effect is that (*P*) set by such retailers is too low. Since (*P*) is too low, the marginal value-product of local advertising is also too low and (leaving aside the impact of any information externalities), (*A*) is too low. (Other variables are again held constant.)

The Loschian retailer, by contrast, believes that neighbouring retailers would match any price rises and therefore reciprocate the positive externality. Offsetting externalities mean that Loschian retailer conjectures do not act to the profit detriment of upstream manufacturers.

How do restraints work to remedy these externalities? In this chapter, we shall illustrate only selected packages of restraints, from possible sets of instruments that are just sufficient to achieve (P^*, R^*, A^*). The full set are listed in Table 10.1. [. . .].

Three examples of minimally sufficient restraints

(1) Set $\alpha = 0$ and invoke Loschian retail conjectures. This is the simplest case, since there is only one (vertical) externality at work. Either (fixed) *franchise fees* or *forcing*, together with P_w, is just sufficient.

If we set $P_w = c$, then transfer prices are efficient in the usual sense and incentive-neutral franchise fees may be used to transfer all rents to the upstream firm. Therefore franchise fees and P_w are just sufficient.

The vertical externality between the Loschian retailer and the manufacturer means that the retailer appropriates only a proportion of the total benefits from pricing and advertising decisions. As the proportion of these benefits appropriated by the retail firm is the same in both the retailer's pricing and advertising decisions, the marginal rate of substitution between (*P*) and (*A*), for a given demand by the retailer, is identical to that required to maximise joint profits. In this setting, forcing pushes the outlet to the appropriate demand level, where the retailer uses (P^*, A^*) to sell the product. Meanwhile, P_w is set to elicit R^* (at $\Pi^R = 0$) and acts to transfer rents back to the manufacturer. (Freed from the task of setting the levels of (*P*) and (*A*), P_w becomes here an incentive-neutral channel for rent transfer.)

In this setting, RPM would *not* be used. If retail price were set at P^* (via RPM), then P_w would have to be used to achieve A^*. However, there would then be no instrument to elicit R^* by transferring rents to the manufacturer.

(2) Set $\alpha = 0$, and invoke non-Loschian retail conjectures (i.e. from (1), permit only retailer conjectures to change). Imposing CTDs, effectively rationalises Loschian conjectures, so that CTDs – in addition to either franchise fees or forcing (together with the wholesale price) – would be just sufficient (minimally-sufficient) instruments in this case.

(3) Set $\alpha > 1$, and invoke Loschian retail conjectures (i.e. from (1), permit advertising to spill over into other retail areas). In this case, one possibility involves the upstream manufacturer setting directly the retail price P^* (via RPM) and reducing the wholesale price below marginal production cost ($P_w < c$), to provide the appropriate retailer incentive to advertise the optimal amount A^*. Finally, in this package franchise fees, as usual, could be used to transfer rents to the upstream manufacturer (i.e. to set R^* via $B^R = 0$). Then, RPM and franchise fees (together with the wholesale price) would be minimally-sufficient instruments in this case.

Arguments for the remaining members of the set of minimally sufficient instruments (noted in Table 10.1) proceed in a similar fashion. All of these packages of instruments are potential substitutes for vertical integration. In actual markets, those candidate restraints that achieve maximum joint profits at the lowest transactions costs will be used by manufacturers. We recognise that issues of shirking or monitoring [. . .] and measurement [. . .] loom large in any evaluation of the relative cost effectiveness of contractual arrangements. These are not, however, issues we deal with here.

Contracts that maximise industry profits need not be welfare-improving. The willing-

Table 10.1 Minimally sufficient sets of instruments.

	Retailer conjectures	
	Loschian	Non-Loschian
Local advertising spillovers		
Absent	(1*) FF QF	(1), (2) CTD, FF CTD, QF FF, RPM QF, RPM
Present	(1), (3) FF, RPM QF, RPM	(1), (2), (3) FF, RPM QF, RPM

CTD ≡ Closed Territory Distribution; FF ≡ Franchise Fees; QF ≡ Quantity Forcing; RPM ≡ Resale Price Maintenance.

*Numbers in parentheses refer to externalities present, as follows:
(1) Vertical externality through ($P_w - c$) wedge;
(2) Horizontal pecuniary (conjectural) externality; and
(3) Local advertising spillover.

ness of the manufacturer to trade-off a higher price for greater product information or availability does not give an *a priori* signal of the social desirability of the restraints; for the restraints to be socially-efficient, the movement from the equilibrium *without* restraints to the equilibrium *with* restraints must increase the total surplus, including consumers' surplus, and not only the manufacturers' profit. [. . .]

10.2 Restrictive Trade Practices Act 1976, section 9

9 PROVISIONS TO BE DISREGARDED UNDER PART II

[. . .]

(3) In determining whether an agreement for the supply of goods or for the application of any process of manufacture to goods is an agreement to which this Act applies by virtue of this Part, no account shall be taken of any term which relates exclusively to the goods supplied, or to which the process is applied, in pursuance of the agreement.

(4) Where any such restrictions as are described in section 6(1) above are accepted or any such information provisions as are described in section 7(1) above are made as between two or more persons by whom, or two or more persons to whom, goods are to be supplied, or the process applied, in pursuance of the agreement, subsection (3) above shall not apply to those restrictions or to those information provisions unless accepted or made in pursuance of a previous agreement:

(*a*) in respect of which particulars have been registered under this Act; or
(*b*) which is exempt from registration by virtue of an order under section 29 (agreements important to the national economy) or section 30 (agreements holding down prices) below.

(5) In determining whether an agreement is an agreement to which this Act applies by virtue of this Part, no account shall be taken of any term by which the parties or any of them agree to comply with or apply, in respect of the production, supply or acquisition of any goods or the application to goods of any process of manufacture:

(*a*) standards of dimension, design, quality or performance, or
(*b*) arrangements as to the provision of information or advice to purchasers, consumers or users,

being either standards or arrangements for the time being approved by the British Standards Institution or standards or arrangements prescribed or adopted by any trade association or other body and for the time being approved by order of the Secretary of State made by statutory instrument.

(6) In determining whether an agreement is an agreement to which this Act applies by virtue of this Part, no account shall be taken of any restriction or information provision which affects or otherwise relates to the workers to be employed or not employed by any person, or as to the remuneration, conditions of employment, hours of work or working conditions of such workers.

In this subsection 'worker' means a person who has entered into or works under a contract with an employer whether the contract be by way of manual labour, clerical work, or otherwise, be express or implied, oral or in writing, and whether it be a contract of service or of apprenticeship or a contract personally to execute any work or labour.

(7) Any reference in Schedule 3 to this Act to:

(*a*) such restrictions as are described in section 6(1) above, or
(*b*) such information provisions as are described in section 7(1) above,

shall be construed, in relation to any agreement, as not including references to restrictions or information provisions of which, by virtue of any provision of this section, account cannot be taken in determining whether the agreement is one to which this Act applies by virtue of this Part, or of restrictions accepted or information provisions made by any term of which account cannot be so taken.

10.3 E. Glynn, 'Distribution under EEC law', 59 *Antitrust Law Journal*, 473 (1991)

Perhaps the most useful place to begin [a comparative analysis of US and EEC laws on distribution agreements] is with a brief summary of current American law on distribution. This has been evolving ever since the Supreme Court's 1977 decision in *GTE Sylvania*, [433 US 36 1977] but I think the law can be fairly summarized as follows. In the area of nonprice vertical restraints, a manufacturer having a market share well below the monopoly or dangerous attempt to monopolize level – say below fifty percent – can probably impose just about any restraint on its distributor that it likes. If challenged, the restraint will be measured by the rule of reason, and the elimination of intrabrand competition will be measured against the promotion of interbrand competition. But, by and large, such an exercise is, in almost every instance, going to result in a victory for the defendant. In short, nonprice vertical restraint law these days is increasingly approaching *per se* legality for the restraint, right up to the point where the manufacturer has so much market power that it may be vulnerable to attack under Section 2, rather than Section 1, of the Sherman Act. And where one has a plausible argument related to the provision of point of sale service, the avoidance of free riding, or some other similar justification, vertically imposed territorial and, in many cases, customer limitations will almost always survive antitrust scrutiny.

Most of the interesting case law in the field of vertical restraints has developed in the area of price restraints, which the Supreme Court has repeatedly confirmed as subject to *per se* analysis. Except in the academic journals, which continue to raise questions concerning the illogic of treating price and nonprice vertical restraints by different substantive rules, the development in vertical restraint law generally revolves around evidentiary issues. [. . .]

[. . .]

So long as one is careful to avoid an express agreement on price, one is pretty much free as a manufacturer to distribute one's product through any type of distribution channel that seems likely to advance one's marketing goals. While keeping in mind that the Robinson–Patman Act can constitute a trap for the unwary, one is free to limit distribution of product through boutiques, bare-bones warehouse operations, or mail order houses, or all of the foregoing. And you can keep your distributors tending the patch of garden that they have been allotted.

That is emphatically not the case in Europe. The American exporter that believes that it may sell into the Common Market based on a marketing strategy that depends on geographic and customer limitations may face a rude awakening. But before turning to the substantive antitrust rules relating to distribution in Europe, I think it would be useful to explore briefly the sort of procedures that a US exporter will face. These differ substantially not just in form but in basic approach from the rules that a US antitrust lawyer confronts on this side of the Atlantic. The first thing to keep in mind is that the antitrust articles of the Treaty of Rome – Article 85 and 86 – do not constitute a stand-alone statute but form part of a larger document, the Treaty, whose major purpose is the achievement of market integration. Thus, it has been observed that Article 85 has been interpreted not in the normal fashion in which one would construe a statute but in a far more teleological way, that is, in a manner which will promote the overall purpose of the Treaty itself.

The other major difference between United States and European procedure is in the use of the block exemption, a procedure created by the European Commission's Competition Directorate (DG-IV) to deal with the over-inclusive nature of the illegality clause of Article 85(1). That article prohibits as incompatible with the Common Market, agreements between companies or individuals which may affect trade between Member States and which have as their object or effect the prevention, restriction, or distortion of competition within the Common Market. The important point is to understand how broadly that net is cast. Although the clause contains language suggesting the application of a competitive effects test similar to the US rule of reason, the reality is very different indeed. Even companies with rather small market shares that attempt to impose nonprice vertical restraints can run afoul of Article 85. I think this point is worth underscoring for US lawyers because it reflects a rather fundamental difference in philosophy and approach between the US and European systems of antitrust.

It is fundamental to US antitrust that the law protects competition, not competitors. Other than in the shrinking category of *per se* agreements, before an agreement between parties will be condemned as violative of the Sherman Act, there must be some demonstration that the agreement will have an effect on the market. Increasingly, over the last fifteen to twenty years, that has meant that a plaintiff must demonstrate that the agreement will have the effect of raising price, restricting output, or having some other direct effect on nonprice competition. Since *GTE Sylvania*, courts have assumed with increasing frequency that a manufacturer that voluntarily grants market power to its distributor through an exclusive territorial arrangement generally does so for a procompetitive reason. And where the manufacturer's market share is small, the prospect of competitive harm flowing from the arrangement is usually so remote that the case can be dismissed quickly.

The focus in Europe is different. In

determining whether a particular agreements falls within the coverage of Article 85(1), the Commission focuses on the effect that a particular agreement may have on the freedom of choice of the parties, especially a distributor. Limitation on this freedom of choice can, of course, flow from many sorts of commercial agreements. As Justice Brandeis observed in the *Chicago Board of Trade case*:

> Every agreement concerning trade, every regulation of trade, restrains. To bind, to restrain, is of their very essence. The true test of legality is whether the restraint imposed is such as merely regulates and perhaps thereby promotes competition or whether it is such as may suppress or even destroy competition.

But what appears to be a truism to a US lawyer is not so to the EC Commission, which, under the Treaty of Rome, considers the reasonableness of the restraint only under Article 85(3).

The European Court of Justice has not always agreed with the Commission's robust interpretation of the scope of Article 85(1). For example, in the *Société Technique Minière* decision in 1966, the Court considered an exclusive distributorship agreement and held that a contract whereby a producer grants a single distributor the right to sell its products in a specified territory does not automatically come under the prohibition of Article 85, Paragraph 1. The Court observed that the alteration of competition referred to in Article 85(1) must flow from the clauses of the agreement itself and must restrict competition that would actually exist without the agreement in issue. But, going further in the opinion, it is clear that what the Court has in mind is the effect on the individual competitor, rather than the effect on competition as that term is understood in the United States. And to gamble that the European Court of Justice will find that a particular distribution contract containing restrictive clauses does not fall within Article 85(1) seems a risky way to proceed.

But there is a second option: one can structure a distribution arrangement to fall within a block exemption. [. . .]

[. . .]

The block exemptions are interesting devices with no equivalent, in my view, under American practice. They are emphatically not the equivalent of the enforcement guidelines issued by the Antitrust Division which purport to describe, in various fields, the sort of conduct that is most likely to injure consumers, and the kinds of cases that the government will bring. The block exemptions are more in the nature of recipes, which, if followed, constitute a 'safe harbor' for agreements. If an agreement doesn't follow the recipe of the block exemption in question, the agreement does not receive the safe harbor benefit and, in the absence of an individual exemption under Article 85(3), a party is liable for violating the Treaty of Rome even though it may be able to establish that the economic effect of the agreement in question is indistinguishable from an agreement of the type mandated by block exemption.

[. . .]

A final point of speculation involves the question of whether, as Europe achieves a truly integrated market after 1992, EC distribution policy will change to reflect more closely US consumer welfare policy. Perhaps, but I don't think that the change will come for quite a while. The enforcement staff of DG-IV has a well-established policy backed up by significant case law and block exemptions. Although this is a subject for another day, the system of European antitrust enforcement is not as susceptible as the US system to change based on the evolution of economic theory. Concern over market integration as a goal of antitrust policy in Europe is likely to continue for a long time after substantial market integration has in fact been achieved.

FURTHER READING

See the following works on the issues raised in Part 3 in relation to vertical agreements.

Bonanno, G. and Vickers, J. (1988), 'Vertical separation', 36 *Journal of Industrial Economics*, 257.

Burstein, M. L. (1990), 'The economics of tie-in sales', 42 *Review of Economics and Statistics*, 68.

Gallini, N. T. and Winter, R. A. (1983), 'On vertical control in monopolistic competition', 1 *International Journal of Industrial Organization*, 275.

Gould, J. R. and Preston, L. E. (1965), 'Resale price maintenance and retail outlets', 32 *Economica*, 302.

Kay, J. (1990), 'Vertical restraints in European competition policy', 34 *European Economic Review*, 551.

Marvel, H. R. and McCafferty, S. (1984), 'Resale price maintenance and quality certification', 15 *Rand Journal of Economics*, 346.

Mathewson, G. F. and Winter, R. A. (1984), 'An economic theory of vertical restraints', 15 *Rand Journal of Economics*, 27.

Perry, M. K. and Besanko, D. (1991), 'Resale price maintenance and manufacturer competition for exclusive dealerships', 39 *Journal of Industrial Economics*, 517.

Posner, R. A. (1981), 'The next step in antitrust treatment of restricted distribution: *per se* legality', 48 *University of Chicago Law Review*, 6.

Rey, P. and Tirole, J. (1986), 'The logic of vertical restraints', 76 *American Economic Review*, 921.

Telser, L. G. (1960), 'Why should manufacturers want fair trade?', 3 *Journal of Law and Economics*, 86.

Waterson, M. (1986), 'The economics of vertical restraints on retailers', in G. Norman (ed.), *Spatial Pricing and Differentiated Markets* (Pion, London).

Yamey, B. S. (1954), *The Economics of Resale Price Maintenance* (Sir Isaac Pitman, London).

11

VERTICAL AGREEMENTS: EXCLUSIVE DISTRIBUTION

11.1 Restrictive Trade Practices Act 1976, Schedule 3

[. . .]

EXCLUSIVE DEALING

2. This Act does not apply to an agreement for the supply of goods between two persons, neither of whom is a trade association, being an agreement to which no other person is party and under which no such restrictions as are described in section 6(1) above are accepted or no such information provisions as are described in section 7(1) above are made other than restrictions accepted or provision made for the furnishing of information:

(*a*) by the party supplying the goods, in respect of the supply of goods of the same description to other persons; or
(*b*) by the party acquiring the goods, in respect of the sale, or acquisition for sale, of other goods of the same description.

EXCLUSIVE SUPPLY OF SERVICES

7. This Act does not apply to an agreement to which there are no parties other than one person who agrees to supply services and another person for whom they are to be supplied, where neither of those persons is, in relation to any order under Part III of this Act, a services supply association and, except in respect of the supply of services of the same description to, or obtaining services of the same description from, other persons:

(*a*) in the case of an order under section 11 above, no restrictions are accepted under the agreement by those parties in respect of matters specified in the order for the purposes of subsection (1)(*b*) of that section; or
(*b*) in the case of an order under section 12 above, no information provision is made under the agreement with respect to matters specified in the order for the purposes of subsection (1)(*b*) of that section.

11.2 Commission Regulation (EEC) No. 1983/83 of 22 June 1983 on the Application of Article 85(3) of the Treaty to categories of exclusive distribution agreements OJ 1983 No. L 173/1 The Commission of the European Communities [. . .]

(1) Whereas Regulation No. 19/65/EEC empowers the Commission to apply Article 85(3) of the Treaty by Regulation to certain categories of bilateral exclusive distribution agreements and analogous concerted practices falling within Article 85(1);

(2) Whereas experience to date makes it possible to define a category of agreements and concerted practices which can be regarded as normally satisfying the conditions laid down in Article 85(3);

(3) Whereas exclusive distribution agreements of the category defined in Article 1 of this Regulation may fall within the prohibition contained in Article 85(1) of the Treaty; whereas this will apply only in exceptional cases to exclusive agreements of this kind to which only undertakings from one Member State are party and which concern the resale of goods within that Member State; whereas, however, to the extent that such agreements may affect trade between Member States and also satisfy all the requirements set out in this Regulation there is no reason to withhold from them the benefit of the exemption by category;

(4) Whereas it is not necessary expressly to exclude from the defined category those agreements which do not fulfil the conditions of Article 85(1) of the Treaty;

(5) Whereas exclusive distribution agreements lead in general to an improvement in distribution because the undertaking is able to concentrate its sales activities, does not need to maintain numerous business relations with a larger number of dealers and is able, by dealing with only one dealer, to overcome more easily distribution difficulties in international trade resulting from linguistic, legal and other differences;

(6) Whereas exclusive distribution agreements facilitate the promotion of sales of a product and lead to intensive marketing and to continuity of supplies while at the same time rationalizing distribution; whereas they stimulate competition between the products of different manufacturers; whereas the appointment of an exclusive distributor who will take over sales promotion, customer services and carrying of stocks is often the most effective way, and sometimes indeed the only way, for the manufacturer to enter a market and compete with other manufacturers already present; whereas this is particularly so in the case of small and medium-sized undertakings; whereas it must be left to the contracting parties to decide whether and to what extent they consider it desirable to incorporate in the agreements terms providing for the promotion of sales;

(7) Whereas, as a rule, such exclusive distribution agreements also allow consumers a fair share of the resulting benefit as they gain directly from the improvement in distribution, and their economic and supply position is improved as they can obtain products manufactured in particular in other countries more quickly and more easily;

(8) Whereas this Regulation must define the obligations restricting competition which may be included in exclusive distribution agreements; whereas the other restrictions on competition allowed under this Regulation in addition to the exclusive supply obligation produce a clear division of functions between the parties and compel the exclusive distributor to concentrate his sales efforts on the contract goods and the contract territory; whereas they are, where they are agreed only for the duration of the agreement, generally necessary in order to attain the improvement in the distribution of goods sought through exclusive distribution; whereas it may be left to the contracting parties to decide which of these obliga-

tions they include in their agreements; whereas further restrictive obligations and in particular those which limit the exclusive distributor's choice of customers or his freedom to determine his prices and conditions of sale cannot be exempted under this Regulation;

(9) Whereas the exemption by category should be reserved for agreements for which it can be assumed with sufficient certainty that they satisfy the conditions of Article 85(3) of the Treaty;

(10) Whereas it is not possible, in the absence of a case-by-case examination, to consider that adequate improvements in distribution occur where a manufacturer entrusts the distribution of his goods to another manufacturer with whom he is in competition; whereas such agreements should, therefore, be excluded from the exemption by category; whereas certain derogations from this rule in favour of small and medium-sized undertakings can be allowed;

(11) Whereas consumers will be assured of a fair share of the benefits resulting from exclusive distribution only if parallel imports remain possible; whereas agreements relating to goods which the user can obtain only from the exclusive distributor should therefore be excluded from the exemption by category; whereas the parties cannot be allowed to abuse industrial property rights or other rights in order to create absolute territorial protection; whereas this does not prejudice the relationship between competition law and industrial property rights, since the sole object here is to determine the conditions for exemption by category;

(12) Whereas, since competition at the distribution stage is ensured by the possibility of parallel imports, the exclusive distribution agreements covered by this Regulation will not normally afford any possibility of eliminating competition in respect of a substantial part of the products in question; whereas this is also true of agreements that allot to the exclusive distributor a contract territory covering the whole of the common market;

(13) Whereas, in particular cases in which agreements or concerted practices satisfying the requirements of this Regulation nevertheless have effects incompatible with Article 85(3) of the Treaty, the Commission may withdraw the benefit of the exemption by category from the undertakings party to them;

(14) Whereas agreements and concerted practices which satisfy the conditions set out in this Regulation need not be notified; whereas an undertaking may nonetheless in a particular case where real doubt exists, request the Commission to declare whether its agreements comply with this Regulation;

(15) Whereas this Regulation does not affect the applicability of Commission Regulation (EEC) No. 3604/82 of 23 December 1982 on the application of Article 85(3) of the Treaty to categories of specialization agreements; whereas it does not exclude the application of Article 86 of the Treaty

HAS ADOPTED THIS REGULATION

Article 1

Pursuant to Article 85(3) of the Treaty and subject to the provisions of this Regulation, it is hereby declared that Article 85(1) of the Treaty shall not apply to agreements to which only two undertakings are party and whereby one party agrees with the other to supply certain goods for resale within the whole or a defined area of the common market only to that other.

Article 2

1. Apart from the obligation referred to in Article 1 no restriction on competition shall be imposed on the supplier other than the obligation not to supply the contract goods to users in the contract territory.

(2) No restriction on competition shall be imposed on the exclusive distributor other than:

(*a*) the obligation not to manufacture or distribute goods which compete with the contract goods;
(*b*) the obligation to obtain the contract

goods for resale only from the other party;

(*c*) the obligation to refrain, outside the contract territory and in relation to the contract goods, from seeking customers, from establishing any branch, and from maintaining any distribution depot.

3. Article 1 shall apply notwithstanding that the exclusive distributor undertakes all or any of the following obligations:

(*a*) to purchase complete ranges of goods or minimum quantities;

(*b*) to sell the contract goods under trademarks, or packed and presented as specified by the other party;

(*c*) to take measures for promotion of sales, in particular:
- to advertise,
- to maintain a sales network or stock of goods,
- to provide customer and guarantee services,
- to employ staff having specialized or technical training.

Article 3

Article 1 shall not apply where:

(*a*) manufacturers of identical goods or of goods which are considered by users as equivalent in view of their characteristics, price and intended use enter into reciprocal exclusive distribution agreements between themselves in respect of such goods;

(*b*) manufacturers of identical goods or of goods which are considered by users as equivalent in view of their characteristics, price and intended use enter into a non-reciprocal exclusive distribution agreement between themselves in respect of such goods unless at least one of them has a total annual turnover of no more than 100 million ECU;

(*c*) users can obtain the contract goods in the contract territory only from the exclusive distributor and have no alternative source of supply outside the contract territory;

(*d*) one or both of the parties makes it difficult for intermediaries or users to obtain the contract goods from other dealers inside the common market or, in so far as no alternative source of supply is available there, from outside the common market, in particular where one or both of them:

1. Exercise industrial property rights so as to prevent dealers or users from obtaining outside, or from selling in, the contract territory properly marked or otherwise properly marketed contract goods;
2. Exercises other rights to take other measures so as to prevent dealers or users from obtaining outside, or from selling in, the contract territory contract goods.

Article 4

1. Article 3(*a*) and (*b*) shall also apply where the goods there referred to are manufactured by an undertaking connected with a party to the agreement.

2. Connected undertakings are:

(*a*) undertakings in which a party to the agreement, directly or indirectly
- owns more than half the capital or business assets, or
- has the power to exercise more than half the voting rights, or
- has the power to appoint more than half the members of the supervisory board, board of directors or bodies legally representing the undertaking, or
- has the right to manage the affairs;

(*b*) undertakings which directly or indirectly have in or over a party to the agreement the rights or powers listed in (*a*);

(*c*) undertakings in which an undertaking referred to in (*b*) directly or indirectly has the rights or powers listed in (*a*).

3. Undertakings in which the parties to the agreement or undertakings connected with them jointly have the rights or powers set out in paragraph 2 (*a*) shall be considered to be connected with each of the parties to the agreement.

Article 5

1. For the purpose of Article 3(*b*), the ECU is the unit of account used for drawing up the budget of the community pursuant to Articles 207 and 209 of the Treaty.

2. Article 1 shall remain applicable where during any period of two consecutive financial years the total turnover referred to in Article 3(*b*) is exceeded by no more than 10%.

3. For the purpose of calculating total turnover within the meaning of Article 3(*b*), the turnovers achieved during the last financial year by the party to the agreement and connected undertakings in respect of all goods and services, excluding all taxes and other duties, shall be added together. For this purpose, no account shall be taken of dealings between the parties to the agreement or between these undertakings and undertakings connected with them or between the connected undertakings.

Article 6

The Commission may withdraw the benefit of this Regulation, pursuant to Article 7 of Regulation No. 19/65/EEC, when it finds in a particular case that an agreement which is exempted by this Regulation nevertheless has certain effects which are incompatible with the conditions set out in Article 85(3) of the Treaty, and in particular where:

(*a*) the contract goods are not subject, in the contract territory, to effective competition from identical goods or goods considered by users as equivalent in view of their characteristics, price and intended use;

(*b*) access by other suppliers to the different stages of distribution within the contract territory is made difficult to a significant extent;

(*c*) for reasons other than those referred to in Article 3(*c*) and (*d*) it is not possible for intermediaries or users to obtain supplies of the contract goods from dealers outside the contract territory on the terms there customary;

(*d*) the exclusive distributor:
1. Without any objectively justified reason refuses to supply in the contract territory categories of purchasers who cannot obtain contract goods elsewhere on suitable terms or applies to them differing prices or conditions of sale;
2. Sells the contract goods at excessively high prices.

Article 7

In the period 1 July 1983 to 31 December 1986, the prohibition in Article 85 (1) of the Treaty shall not apply to agreements which were in force on 1 July 1983 or entered into force between 1 July and 31 December 1983 and which satisfy the exemption conditions of Regulation No 67/67/EEC.

Article 8

This Regulation shall not apply to agreements entered into for the resale of drinks in premises used for the sale and consumption of beer or for the resale of petroleum products in service stations.

Article 9

This Regulation shall apply *mutatis mutandis* to concerted practices of the type defined in Article 1.

Article 10

This Regulation shall enter into force on 1 July 1983. It shall expire on 31 December 1997. This Regulation shall be binding in its entirety and directly applicable in all member states.

Done at Brussels, 22 June 1983.

11.3 Commission Regulation (EEC) No. 1984/83 of 22 June 1983 on the Application of Article 85(3) of the Treaty to categories of exclusive purchasing agreements OJ 1983 No. L 173/5

THE COMMISSION OF THE EUROPEAN COMMUNITIES

[. . .]

(1) Whereas Regulation No. 19/65/EEC empowers the Commission to apply Article 85(3) of the Treaty by Regulation to certain categories of bilateral exclusive purchasing agreements entered into for the purpose of the resale of goods and corresponding concerted practices falling within Article 85(1);

(2) Whereas experience to date makes it possible to define three categories of agreements and concerted practices which can be regarded as normally satisfying the conditions laid down in Article 85(3); whereas the first category comprises exclusive purchasing agreements of short and medium duration in all sectors of the economy; whereas the other two categories comprise long-term exclusive purchasing agreements entered into for the resale of beer in premises used for the sale and consumption (beer supply agreements) and of petroleum products in filling stations (service-station agreements);

(3 Whereas exclusive purchasing agreements of the categories defined in this Regulation may fall within the prohibition contained in Article 85(1) of the Treaty; whereas this will often be the case with agreements concluded between undertakings from different member States; whereas an exclusive purchasing agreement to which undertakings from only one member State are party and which concerns the resale of goods within that member State may also be caught by the prohibition; whereas this is in particular the case where it is one of a number of similar agreements which together may affect trade between member States;

(4) Whereas it is not necessary expressly to exclude from the defined categories those agreements which do not fulfil the conditions of Article 85(1) of the Treaty;

(5) Whereas the exclusive purchasing agreements defined in this Regulation lead in general to an improvement in distribution; whereas they enable the supplier to plan the sales of his goods with greater precision and for a longer period and ensure that the reseller's requirements will be met on a regular basis for the duration of the agreement; whereas this allows the parties to limit the risk to them of variations in market conditions and to lower distribution costs;

(6) Whereas such agreements also facilitate the promotion of the sales of a product and lead to intensive marketing because the supplier, in consideration for the exclusive purchasing obligation, is as a rule under an obligation to contribute to the improvement of the structure of the distribution network, the quality of the promotional effort or the sales success; whereas, at the same time, they stimulate competition between the products of different manufacturers; whereas the appointment of several resellers, who are bound to purchase exclusively from the manufacturer and who take over sales promotion, customer services and carrying of stock, is often the most effective way, and sometimes the only way, for the manufacturer to penetrate a market and compete with other manufacturers already present; whereas this is particularly so in the case of small and medium-sized undertakings; whereas it must be left to the contracting parties to decide whether and to what extent they consider it desirable to incorporate in their agreements terms concerning the promotion of sales;

(7) Whereas, as a rule, exclusive purchasing agreements between suppliers and resellers also allow consumers a fair share of the resulting benefit as they gain the

advantages of regular supply and are able to obtain the contract goods more quickly and more easily;

(8) Whereas this Regulation must define the obligations restricting competition which may be included in an exclusive purchasing agreement; whereas the other restrictions of competition allowed under this Regulation in addition to the exclusive purchasing obligation lead to a clear division of functions between the parties and compel the reseller to concentrate his sales efforts on the contract goods; whereas they are, where they are agreed only for the duration of the agreement, generally necessary in order to attain the improvement in the distribution of goods sought through exclusive purchasing; whereas further restrictive obligations and in particular those which limit the reseller's choice of customers or his freedom to determine his prices and conditions of sale cannot be exempted under this Regulation;

(9) Whereas the exemption by categories should be reserved for agreements for which it can be assumed with sufficient certainty that they satisfy the conditions of Article 85(3) of the Treaty;

(10) Whereas it is not possible, in the absence of a case-by-case examination, to consider that adequate improvements in distribution occur where a manufacturer imposes an exclusive purchasing obligation with respect to his goods on a manufacturer with whom he is in competition; whereas such agreements should, therefore, be excluded from the exemption by categories; whereas certain derogations from this rule in favour of small and medium-sized undertakings can be allowed;

(11) Whereas certain conditions must be attached to the exemption by categories so that access by other undertakings to the different stages of distribution can be ensured; whereas, to this end, limits must be set to the scope and to the duration of the exclusive purchasing obligation; whereas it appears appropriate as a general rule to grant the benefit of a general exemption from the prohibition on restrictive agreements only to exclusive purchasing agreements which are concluded for a specified product or range of products and for not more than five years;

(12) Whereas, in the case of beer supply agreements and service-station agreements, different rules should be laid down which take account of the particularities of the markets in question;

(13) Whereas these agreements are generally distinguished by the fact that, on the one hand, the supplier confers on the reseller special commercial or financial advantages by contributing to his financing, granting him or obtaining for him a loan on favourable terms, equipping him with a site or premises for conducting his business, providing him with equipment or fittings, or undertaking other investments for his benefit and that, on the other hand, the reseller enters into a long-term exclusive purchasing obligation which in most cases is accompanied by a ban on dealing in competing products;

(14) Whereas beer supply and service-station agreements, like the other exclusive purchasing agreements dealt with in this Regulation, normally produce an appreciable improvement in distribution in which consumers are allowed a fair share of the resulting benefit;

(15) Whereas the commercial and financial advantages conferred by the supplier on the reseller make it significantly easier to establish, modernize, maintain and operate premises used for the sale and consumption of drinks and service stations; whereas the exclusive purchasing obligation and the ban on dealing in competing products imposed on the reseller incite the reseller to devote all the resources at his disposal to the sale of the contract goods; whereas such agreements lead to durable cooperation between the parties allowing them to improve or maintain the quality of the contract goods and of the services to the customer and sales efforts of the reseller; whereas they allow long-term planning of sales and consequently a cost effective organization of production and distribution; whereas the pressure of competition between products of different makes obliges the undertakings involved to determine the number and character of premises used for

the sale and consumption of drinks and service stations, in accordance with the wishes of customers;

(16) Whereas consumers benefit from the improvements described, in particular because they are ensured supplies of goods of satisfactory quality at fair prices and conditions while being able to choose between the products of different manufacturers;

(17) Whereas the advantages produced by beer supply agreements and service-station agreements cannot otherwise be secured to the same extent and with the same degree of certainty; whereas the exclusive purchasing obligation on the reseller and the non-competition clause imposed on him are essential components of such agreements and thus usually indispensable for the attainment of these advantages; whereas, however, this is true only as long as the reseller's obligation to purchase from the supplier is confined in the case of premises used for the sale and consumption of drinks to beers and other drinks of the types offered by the supplier, and in the case of service stations to petroleum-based fuel for motor vehicles and other petroleum-based fuels; whereas the exclusive purchasing obligation for lubricants and related petroleum-based products can be accepted only on condition that the supplier provides for the reseller or finances the procurement of specific equipment for the carrying out of lubrication work; whereas this obligation should only relate to products intended for use within the service station;

(18) Whereas, in order to maintain the reseller's commercial freedom and to ensure access to the retail level of distribution on the part of other suppliers, not only the scope but also the duration of the exclusive purchasing obligation must be limited; whereas it appears appropriate to allow drinks suppliers a choice between a medium-term exclusive purchasing agreement covering a range of drinks and a long-term exclusive purchasing agreement for beer; whereas it is necessary to provide special rules for those premises used for the sale and consumption of drinks which the supplier lets to the reseller; whereas, in this case, the reseller must have the right to obtain, under the conditions specified in this Regulation, other drinks, except beer, supplied under the agreement or of the same type but bearing a different trademark; whereas a uniform maximum duration should be provided for service-station agreements, with the exception of tenancy agreements between the supplier and the reseller, which takes account of the long-term character of the relationship between the parties;

(19) Whereas to the extent that member States provide, by law or administrative measures, for the same upper limit of duration for the exclusive purchasing obligation upon the reseller as in service-station agreements laid down in this Regulation but provide for a permissible duration which varies in proportion to the consideration provided by the supplier or generally provide for a shorter duration than that permitted by this Regulation, such laws or measures are not contrary to the objectives of this Regulation which, in this respect, merely sets an upper limit to the duration of service-station agreements; whereas the application and enforcement of such national laws or measures must therefore be regarded as compatible with the provisions of this Regulation;

(20) Whereas the limitations and conditions provided for in this Regulation are such as to guarantee effective competition on the markets in question; whereas, therefore, the agreements to which the exemption by category applies do not normally enable the participating undertakings to eliminate competition for a substantial part of the products in question;

(21) Whereas, in particular cases in which agreements or concerted practices satisfying the conditions of this Regulation nevertheless have effects incompatible with Article 85(3) of the Treaty, the Commission may withdraw the benefit of the exemption by category from the undertakings party thereto;

(22) Whereas agreements and concerted practices which satisfy the conditions set out in this Regulation need not be notified; whereas an undertaking may nonetheless, in a particular case where real doubt exists,

request the Commission to declare whether its agreements comply with this Regulation;

(23) Whereas this Regulation does not affect the applicability of Commission Regulation (EEC) No 3604/82 of 23 December 1982 on the application of Article 85(3) of the Treaty to categories of specialization agreements; whereas it does not exclude the application of Article 86 of the Treaty,

HAS ADOPTED THIS REGULATION:

Title I General Provisions

Article 1
Pursuant to Article 85(3) of the Treaty, and subject to the conditions set out in Articles 2 to 5 of this Regulation, it is hereby declared that Article 85(1) of the Treaty shall not apply to agreements to which only two undertakings are party and whereby one party, the reseller, agrees with the other, the supplier, to purchase certain goods specified in the agreement for resale only from the supplier or from a connected undertaking or from another undertaking which the supplier has entrusted with the sale of his goods.

Article 2
1. No other restriction of competition shall be imposed on the supplier than the obligation not to distribute the contract goods or goods which compete with the contract goods in the reseller's principal sales area and at the reseller's level of distribution.

2. Apart from the obligation described in Article 1, no other restriction of competition shall be imposed on the reseller than the obligation not to manufacture or distribute goods which compete with the contract goods.

3. Article 1 shall apply notwithstanding that the reseller undertakes any or all of the following obligations;

(*a*) to purchase complete ranges of goods;
(*b*) to purchase minimum quantities of goods which are subject to the exclusive purchasing obligation;
(*c*) to sell the contract goods under trademarks, or packed and presented as specified by the supplier;
(*d*) to take measures for the promotion of sales, in particular:
- to advertise
- to maintain a sales network or stock of goods,
- to provide customer and guarantee services,
- to employ staff having specialized or technical training.

Article 3
Article 1 shall not apply where:

(*a*) manufacturers of identical goods or of goods which are considered by users as equivalent in view of their characteristics, price and intended use enter into reciprocal exclusive purchasing agreements between themselves in respect of such goods;
(*b*) manufacturers of identical goods or of goods which are considered by users as equivalent in view of their characteristics, price and intended use enter into a non-reciprocal exclusive purchasing agreement between themselves in respect of such goods, unless at least one of them has a total annual turnover of no more than 100 million ECU;
(*c*) the exclusive purchasing obligation is agreed for more than one type of goods where these are neither by their nature nor according to commercial usage connected to each other;
(*d*) the agreement is concluded for an indefinite duration or for a period of more than five years.

Article 4
1. Article 3(*a*) and (*b*) shall also apply where the goods there referred to are manufactured by an undertaking connected with a party to the agreement.

[. . .]

Title II Special Provisions For Beer Supply Agreements

Article 6
1. Pursuant to Article 85(3) of the Treaty, and subject to Articles 7 to 9 of this Regulation, it is hereby declared that Article 85(1) of the Treaty shall not apply to

agreements to which only two undertakings are party and whereby one party, the reseller, agrees with the other, the supplier, in consideration for according special commercial or financial advantages, to purchase only from the supplier, an undertaking connected with the supplier or another undertaking entrusted by the supplier with the distribution of his goods, certain beers, or certain beers and certain other drinks, specified in the agreement for resale in premises used for the sale and consumption of drinks and designated in the agreement.

2. The declaration in paragraph 1 shall also apply where exclusive purchasing obligations of the kind described in paragraph 1 are imposed on the reseller in favour of the supplier by another undertaking which is itself not a supplier.

Article 7

1. Apart from the obligation referred to in Article 6, no restriction on competition shall be imposed on the reseller other than:

(*a*) the obligation not to sell beers and other drinks which are supplied by other undertakings and which are of the same type as the beers or other drinks supplied under the agreement in the premises designated in the agreement;

(*b*) the obligation, in the event that the reseller sells in the premises designated in the agreement beers which are supplied by other undertakings and which are of a different type from the beers supplied under the agreement, to sell such beers only in bottles, cans or other small packages, unless the sale of such beers in draught form is customary or is necessary to satisfy a sufficient demand from consumers;

(*c*) the obligation to advertise goods supplied by other undertakings within or outside the premises designated in the agreement only in proportion to the share of these goods in the total turnover realized in the premises.

2. Beers or other drinks of the same type are those which are not clearly distinguishable in view of their composition, appearance and taste.

Article 8

1. Article 6 shall not apply where:

(*a*) the supplier or a connected undertaking imposes on the reseller exclusive purchasing obligations for goods other than drinks or for services;

(*b*) the supplier restricts the freedom of the reseller to obtain from an undertaking of his choice either services or goods for which neither an exclusive purchasing obligation nor a ban on dealing in competing products may be imposed;

(*c*) the agreement is concluded for an indefinite duration or for a period of more than five years and the exclusive purchasing obligation relates to specified beers and other drinks;

(*d*) the agreement is concluded for an indefinite duration or for a period of more than 10 years and the exclusive purchasing obligation relates only to specified beers;

(*e*) the supplier obliges the reseller to impose the exclusive purchasing obligation on his successor for a longer period than the reseller would himself remain tied to the supplier.

2. Where the agreement relates to premises which the supplier lets to the reseller or allows the reseller to occupy on some other basis in law or in fact, the following provisions shall also apply:

(*a*) notwithstanding paragraphs (1)(*c*) and (*d*), the exclusive purchasing obligations and bans on dealing in competing products specified in this title may be imposed on the reseller for the whole period for which the reseller in fact operates the premises;

(*b*) the agreement must provide for the reseller to have the right to obtain:
– drinks, except beer, supplied under the agreement from other undertakings where these undertakings offer them on more favourable conditions which the supplier does not meet,

- drinks, except beer, which are of the same type as those supplied under the agreement but which bear different trade marks, from other undertakings where the supplier does not offer them.

Article 9
Articles 2(1) and (3), 3(*a*) and (*b*), 4 and 5 shall apply *mutatis mutandis*.
[. . .]

Title IV Miscellaneous Provisions

Article 14
The Commission may withdraw the benefit of this Regulation, pursuant to Article 7 of Regulation No. 19/65/EEC, when it finds in a particular case that an agreement which is exempted by this Regulation nevertheless has certain effects which are incompatible with the conditions set out in Article 85(3) of the Treaty, and in particular where:

(*a*) the contract goods are not subject, in a substantial part of the common market, to effective competition from identical goods or goods considered by users as equivalent in view of their characteristics, price and intended use;
(*b*) access by other suppliers to the different stages of distribution in a substantial part of the common market is made difficult to a significant extent;
(*c*) the supplier without any objectively justified reason:
  1. Refuses to supply categories of resellers who cannot obtain the contract goods elsewhere on suitable terms or applies to them differing prices or conditions of sale;
  2. Applies less favourable prices or conditions of sale to resellers bound by an exclusive purchasing obligation as compared with other resellers at the same level of distribution.

Article 15
[. . .]
3. In the case of agreements of the kinds described in Articles 6 and 10, which were in force on 1 July 1983 and which expire after 31 December 1988, the prohibition in Article 85(1) of the Treaty shall not apply in the period from 1 January 1989 to the expiry of the agreement but at the latest to the expiry of this Regulation to the extent that the supplier releases the reseller, before 1 January 1989, from all obligations which would prevent the application of the exemption under Titles II and III.

Article 16
This Regulation shall not apply to agreements by which the supplier undertakes with the reseller to supply only to the reseller certain goods for resale, in the whole or in a defined part of the Community, and the reseller undertakes with the supplier to purchase these goods only from the supplier.

Article 17
This Regulation shall not apply where the parties or connected undertakings, for the purpose of resale in one and the same premises used for the sale and consumption of drinks or service station, enter into agreements both of the kind referred to in Title I and of a kind referred to in Title II or III.

Article 18
This Regulation shall apply *mutatis mutandis* to the categories of concerted practices defined in Articles 1, 6 and 10. Article 19 of this Regulation shall enter into force on 1 July 1983. It shall expire on 31 December 1997. This Regulattion shall be binding in its entirety and directly applicable in all member States.

Done at Brussels, 22 June 1983.

11.4 Commission Notice of 22 June 1983 Concerning Commission Regulations (EEC) No. 1983/83 and (EEC) No. 1984/83 of 22 June 1983 on the application of Article 85(3) of the Treaty to categories of exclusive distribution and exclusive purchasing agreements

I. INTRODUCTION

1. Commission Regulation No. 67/67/EEC of 22 March 1967 on the application of Article 85(3) of the Treaty to certain categories of exclusive dealing agreements expired on 30 June 1983 after being in force for over 15 years. With Regulations (EEC) No. 1983/83 and (EEC) No. 1984/83, the Commission has adapted the block exemption of exclusive distribution agreements and exclusive purchasing agreements to the intervening developments in the common market and in Community law. Several of the provisions in the new Regulations are new. A certain amount of interpretative guidance is therefore called for. This will assist undertakings in bringing their agreements into line with the new legal requirements and will also help ensure that the Regulations are applied uniformly in all the Member States.

2. In determining how a given provision is to be applied, one must take into account, in addition to the ordinary meaning of the words used, the intention of the provision, as this emerges from the preamble. For further guidance, reference should be made to the principles that have been involved in the case law of the Court of Justice of the European Communities and in the Commission's decisions on individual cases.

3. This notice sets out the main considerations which will determine the Commission's view of whether or not an exclusive distribution or purchasing agreement is covered by the block exemption. The notice is without prejudice to the jurisdiction of national courts to apply the Regulations, although it may well be of persuasive authority in proceedings before such courts. Nor does the notice necessarily indicate the interpretation which might be given to the provisions by the Court of Justice.

II. EXCLUSIVE DISTRIBUTION AND EXCLUSIVE PURCHASING AGREEMENTS (REGULATIONS (EEC) No. 1983/83 AND (EEC) No. 1984/83)

1. Similarities and differences

4. Regulations (EEC) No. 1983/83 and (EEC) No. 1984/83 are both concerned with exclusive agreements between two undertakings for the purpose of the resale of goods. Each deals with a particular type of such agreements. Regulation (EEC) No. 1983/83 applies to exclusive distribution agreements, Regulation (EEC) No. 1984/83 to exclusive purchasing agreements. The distinguishing feature of exclusive distribution agreements is that one party, the supplier, allots to the other, the reseller, a defined territory (the contract territory) on which the reseller has to concentrate his sales effort, and in return undertakes not to supply any other reseller in that territory. In exclusive purchasing agreements, the reseller agrees to purchase the contract goods only from the other party and not from any other supplier. The supplier is entitled to supply other resellers in the same sales area and at the same level of distribution. Unlike an exclusive distributor, the tied reseller is not protected against competition from other resellers who, like himself, receive the contract goods direct from the supplier. On the other hand, he is free of restrictions as to the area over which he may make his sales effort.

5. In keeping with their common starting point, the Regulations have many provisions that are the same or similar in both

Regulations. This is true of the basic provision in Article 1, in which the respective subject-matters of the block exemption, the exclusive supply or purchasing obligation, are defined, and of the exhaustive list of restrictions of competition which may be agreed in addition to the exclusive supply or purchasing obligation (Article 2(1) and (2)), the non-exhaustive enumeration of other obligations which do not prejudice the block exemption (Article 2(3)), the inapplicability of the block exemption in principle to exclusive agreements between competing manufacturers (Article 3(*a*) and (*b*), 4 and 5), the withdrawal of the block exemption in individual cases (Article 6 of Regulation (EEC) No. 1983/83 and Article 14 of Regulation (EEC) No. 1984/83), the transitional provisions (Article 7 of Regulation (EEC) No. 1983/83 and Article 15(1) of Regulation (EEC) No. 1984/83), and the inclusion of concerted practices within the scope of the Regulations (Article 9 of Regulation (EEC) No. 1983/83 and Article 18 of Regulation (EEC) No. 1984/83). In so far as their wording permits, these parallel provisions are to be interpreted in the same way.

6. Different rules are laid down in the Regulations wherever they need to take account of matters which are peculiar to the exclusive distribution agreements or exclusive purchasing agreements respectively. This applies in Regulation (EEC) No. 1983/83, to the provisions regarding the obligation on the exclusive distributor not actively to promote sales outside the contract territory (Article 2(2)(*c*)) and the inapplicability of the block exemption to agreements which give the exclusive distributor absolute territorial protection (Article 3(*c*) and (*d*)) and, in Regulation (EEC) No. 1984/83, to the provisions limiting the scope and duration of the block exemption for exclusive purchasing agreements in general (Article 3(*c*) and (*d*) and for beer-supply and service-station agreements in particular (Titles II and III).

7. The scope of the two Regulations has been defined so as to avoid any overlap (Article 16 of Regulation (EEC) No. 1984/83).

2. Basic provision

(Article 1)

8. Both Regulations apply only to agreements entered into for the purpose of the resale of goods to which not more than two undertakings are party.

(a) 'For resale'

9. The notion of resale requires that the goods concerned be disposed of by the purchasing party to others in return for consideration. Agreements on the supply or purchase of goods which the purchasing party transforms or processes into other goods or uses or consumes in manufacturing other goods are not agreements for resale. The same applies to the supply of components which are combined with other components into a different product. The criterion is that the goods distributed by the reseller are the same as those the other party has supplied to him for that purpose. The economic identity of the goods is not affected if the reseller merely breaks up and packages the goods in smaller quantities, or repackages them, before resale.

10. Where the reseller performs additional operations to improve the quality, durability, appearance or taste of the goods (such as rust-proofing of metals, sterilization of food or the addition of colouring matter or flavourings to drugs), the position will mainly depend on how much value the operation adds to the goods. Only a slight addition in value can be taken not to change the economic identity of the goods. In determining the precise dividing line in individual cases, trade usage in particular must be considered. The Commission applies the same principles to agreements under which the reseller is supplied with a concentrated extract for a drink which he has to dilute with water, pure alcohol or another liquid and to bottle before reselling.

(b) 'Goods'

11. Exclusive agreements for the supply of services rather than the resale of goods are not covered by the Regulations. The block exemption still applies, however, where the

reseller provides customer or after-sales services incidentally to the resale of the goods. Nevertheless, a case where the charge for the service is higher than the price of the goods would fall outside the scope of the Regulations.

12. The hiring out of goods in return for payment comes closer, economically speaking, to a resale of goods than to provision of services. The Commission therefore regards exclusive agreements under which the purchasing party hires out or leases to others the goods supplied to him as covered by the Regulations.

(c) 'Only two undertakings party'

13. To be covered by the block exemption, the exclusive distribution or purchasing agreement must be between only one supplier and one reseller in each case. Several undertakings forming one economic unit count as one undertaking.

14. This limitation on the number of undertakings that may be party relates solely to the individual agreement. A supplier does not lose the benefit of the block exemption if he enters into exclusive distribution or purchasing agreements covering the same goods with several resellers.

15. The supplier may delegate the performance of his contractual obligations to a connected or independent undertaking which he has entrusted with the distribution of his goods, so that the reseller has to purchase the contract goods from the latter undertaking. This principle is expressly mentioned only in Regulation (EEC) No. 1984/83 (Article 1, 6, and 10), because the question of delegation arises mainly in connection with exclusive purchasing agreements. It also applies, however, to exclusive distribution agreements under Regulation (EEC) No. 1983/83.

16. The involvement of undertakings other than the contracting parties must be confined to the execution of deliveries. The parties may accept exclusive supply or purchase obligations only for themselves, and not impose them on third parties, since otherwise more than two undertakings would be party to the agreement. The obligation of the parties to ensure that the obligations they have accepted are respected by connected undertakings is, however, covered by the block exemption.

3. Other restrictions on competition that are exempted

(Article 2(1) and (2))

17. Apart from the exclusive supply obligation (Regulation (EEC) No. 1983/83) or exclusive purchase obligation (Regulation (EEC) No. 1984/83), obligations defined in Article 1 which must be present if the block exemption is to apply, the only other restrictions of competition that may be agreed by the parties are those set out in Article 2(1) and (2). If they agree on further obligations restrictive of competition, the agreement as a whole is no longer covered by the block exemption and requires individual exemption. For example, an agreement will exceed the bounds of the Regulations if the parties relinquish the possibility of independently determining their prices or conditions of business or undertake to refrain from, or even prevent, cross-border trade, which the Regulations expressly state must not be impeded. Among other clauses which in general are not permissible under the Regulations are those which impede the reseller in his free choice of customers.

18. The obligations restrictive of competition that are exempted may be agreed only for the duration of the agreement. This also applies to restrictions accepted by the supplier or reseller on competing with the other party.

4. Obligations upon the reseller which do not prejudice the block exemption

(Article 2(3))

19. The obligations cited in this provision are examples of clauses which generally do not restrict competition. Undertakings are therefore free to include one, several or all of these obligations in their agreements. However, the obligations may not be formulated or applied in such a way as to take on the character of restrictions of competition that are not permitted. To forestall this danger, Article 2(3)(*b*) of

Regulation (EEC) No. 1984/83 expressly allows minimum purchase obligations only for goods that are subject to an exclusive purchasing obligation.

20. As part of the obligation to take measures for promotion of sales and in particular to maintain a distribution network (Article 2(3)(*c*) of Regulation (EEC) No. 1983/83 and Article 2(3)(*d*) of Regulation (EEC) No. 1984/83), the reseller may be forbidden to supply the contract goods to unsuitable dealers. Such clauses are unobjectionable if admission to the distribution network is based on objective criteria of a qualitative nature relating to the professional qualifications of the owner of the business or his staff or the suitability of his business premises, if the criteria are the same for all potential dealers, and if the criteria are actually applied in a non-discriminatory manner. Distribution systems which do not fulfil these conditions are not covered by the block exemption.

5. Inapplicability of the block exemption to exclusive agreements between competing manufacturers

(Articles 3(*a*) and (*b*), 4 and 5)

21. The block exemption does not apply if either the parties themselves or undertakings connected with them are manufacturers, manufacture goods belonging to the same product market, and enter into exclusive distribution or purchasing agreements with one another in respect of those goods. Only identical or equivalent goods are regarded as belonging to the same product market. The goods in question must be interchangeable. Whether or not this is the case must be judged from the vantage point of the user, normally taking the characteristics, price and intended use of the goods together. In certain cases, however, goods can form a separate market on the basis of their characteristics, their price or their intended use alone. This is true especially where consumer preferences have developed. The above provisions are applicable regardless of whether or not the parties or the undertakings connected with them are based in the Community and whether or not they are already actually in competition with one another in the relevant goods inside or outside the Community.

22. In principle, both reciprocal and non-reciprocal exclusive agreements between competing manufacturers are not covered by the block exemption and are therefore subject to individual scrutiny of their compatibility with Article 85 of the Treaty, but there is an exception for non-reciprocal agreements of the abovementioned kind where one or both of the parties are undertakings with a total annual turnover of no more than 100 million ECU (Article 3(*b*)). Annual turnover is used as a measure of the economic strength of the undertakings involved. Therefore, the aggregate turnover from goods and services of all types, and not only from the contract goods, is to be taken. Turnover taxes and other turnover-related levies are not included in turnover. Where a party belongs to a group of connected undertakings, the world-wide turnover of the group, excluding intra-group sales (Article 5(3)), is to be used.

23. The total turnover limit can be exceeded during any period of two successive financial years by up to 10% without loss of the block exemption. The block exemption is lost if, at the end of the second financial year, the total turnover over the preceding two years has been over 220 million ECU (Article 5(2)).

6. Withdrawal of the block exemption in individual cases

(Article 6 of Regulation (EEC) No. 1983/83 and Article 14 of Regulation (EEC) No. 1984/83)

24. The situations described are meant as illustrations of the sort of situations in which the Commission can exercise its powers under Article 7 of Council Regulation No. 19/65/EEC to withdraw a block exemption. The benefit of the block exemption can only be withdrawn by a decision in an individual case following proceedings under Regulation No. 17. Such a decision cannot have retroactive effect. It may be

coupled with an individual exemption subject to conditions or obligations or, in an extreme case, with the finding of an infringement and an order to bring it to an end.

7. Transitional provisions

(Article 7 of Regulation (EEC) No. 1983/83 and Article 15(1) of Regulation (EEC) No. 1984/83)
25. Exclusive distribution or exclusive purchasing agreements which were concluded and entered into force before 1 January 1984 continue to be exempted under the provisions of Regulation No. 67/67/EEC until 31 December 1986. Should the parties wish to apply such agreements beyond 1 January 1987, they will either have to bring them into line with the provisions of the new Regulations or to notify them to the Commission. Special rules apply in the case of beer-supply and service-station agreements (see paragraphs 64 and 65 below).

8. Concerted practices

(Article 9 of Regulation (EEC) No. 1983/83 and Article 18 of Regulation (EEC) No. 1984/83)
26. These provisions bring within the scope of the Regulations exclusive distribution and purchasing arrangements which are operated by undertakings but are not the subject of a legally-binding agreement.

III. EXCLUSIVE DISTRIBUTION AGREEMENTS (REGULATION (EEC) No. 1983/83)

1. Exclusive supply obligation

(Article 1)
27. The exclusive supply obligation does not prevent the supplier from providing the contract goods to other resellers who afterwards sell them in the exclusive distributor's territory. It makes no difference whether the other dealers concerned are established outside or inside the territory. The supplier is not in breach of his obligation to the exclusive distributor provided that he supplies the resellers who wish to sell the contract goods in the territory only at their request and that the goods are handed over outside the territory. It does not matter whether the reseller takes delivery of the goods himself or through an intermediary, such as a freight forwarder. However, supplies of this nature are only permissible if the reseller and not the supplier pays the transport costs of the goods into the contract territory.

28. The goods supplied to the exclusive distributor must be intended for resale in the contract territory. This basic requirement does not, however, mean that the exclusive distributor cannot sell the contract goods to customers outside his contract territory should he receive orders from them. Under Article 2(2)(*c*), the supplier can prohibit him only from seeking customers in other areas, but not from supplying them.

29. It would also be incompatible with the Regulation for the exclusive distributor to be restricted to supplying only certain categories of customers (e.g. specialist retailers) in his contract territory and prohibited from supplying other categories (e.g. department stores), which are supplied by other resellers appointed by the supplier for that purpose.

2. Restriction on competition by the supplier

(Article 2(1))
30. The restriction on the supplier himself supplying the contract goods to final users in the exclusive distributor's contract territory need not be absolute. Clauses permitting the supplier to supply certain customers in the territory – with or without payment of compensation to the exclusive distributor – are compatible with the block exemption provided the customers in question are not resellers. The supplier remains free to supply the contract goods outside the contract territory to final users based in the territory. In this case the position is the

same as for dealers (see paragraph 27 above).

3. Inapplicability of the block exemption in cases of absolute territorial protection

(Articles 3(*c*) and (*d*))
31. The block exemption cannot be claimed for agreements that give the exclusive distributor absolute territorial protection. If the situation described in Article 3(*c*) obtains, the parties must ensure either that the contract goods can be sold in the contract territory by parallel importers or that users have a real possibility of obtaining them from undertakings outside the contract territory, if necessary outside the Community, at the prices and on the terms there prevailing. The supplier can represent an alternative source of supply for the purposes of this provision if he is prepared to supply the contract goods on request to final users located in the contract territory.

32. Article 3(*d*) is chiefly intended to safeguard the freedom of dealers and users to obtain the contract goods in other Member States. Action to impede imports into the Community from third countries will only lead to loss of the block exemption if there are no alternative sources of supply in the Community. This situation can arise especially where the exclusive distributor's contract territory covers the whole or the major part of the Community.

33. The block exemption ceases to apply as from the moment that either of the parties takes measures to impede parallel imports into the contract territory. Agreements in which the supplier undertakes with the exclusive distributor to prevent his other customers from supplying into the contract territory are ineligible for the block exemption from the outset. This is true even if the parties agree only to prevent imports into the Community from third countries. In this case it is immaterial whether or not there are alternative sources of supply in the Community. The inapplicability of the block exemption follows from the mere fact that the agreement contains restrictions on competition which are not covered by Article 2(1).

IV. EXCLUSIVE PURCHASING AGREEMENTS (REGULATION (EEC) No. 1984/83)

1. Structure of the Regulation

34. Title I of the Regulation contains general provisions for exclusive purchasing agreements and Titles II and III special provisions for beer-supply and service-station agreements. The latter types of agreement are governed exclusively by the special provisions, some of which (Articles 9 and 13), however, refer to some of the general provisions, Article 17 also excludes the combination of agreements of the kind referred to in Title I with those of the kind referred to in Titles II or III to which the same undertakings or undertakings connected with them are party. To prevent any avoidance of the special provisions for beer-supply-and service-station agreements, it is also made clear that the provisions governing the exclusive distribution of goods do not apply to agreements entered into for the resale of drinks on premises used for the sale or consumption of beer or for the resale of petroleum products in service stations (Article 8 of Regulation (EEC) No. 1983/83).

2. Exclusive purchasing obligation

(Article 1)
35. The Regulation only covers agreements whereby the reseller agrees to purchase all his requirements for the contract goods from the other party. If the purchasing obligation relates to only part of such requirements, the block exemption does not apply. Clauses which allow the reseller to obtain the contract goods from other suppliers, should these sell them more cheaply or on more favourable terms than the other party are still covered by the block exemption. The same applies to clauses releasing the reseller from his exclusive purchasing obligation should the other party be unable to supply.

36. The contract goods must be specified by brand or denomination in the agreement. Only if this is done will it be possible to determine the precise scope of the resel-

ler's exclusive purchasing obligation (Article 1) and of the ban on dealing in competing products (Article 2(2)).

3. Restriction on competition by the supplier

(Article 2(1))

37. This provision allows the reseller to protect himself against direct competition from the supplier in his principal sales area. The reseller's principal sales area is determined by his normal business activity. It may be more closely defined in the agreement. However, the supplier cannot be forbidden to supply dealers who obtain the contract goods outside this area and afterwards resell them to customers inside it or to appoint other resellers in the area.

4. Limits of the block exemption

(Article 3(*c*) and (*d*))

38. Article 3(*c*) provides that the exclusive purchasing obligation can be agreed for one or more products, but in the latter case the products must be so related as to be thought of as belonging to the same range of goods. The relationship can be founded on technical (e.g., a machine, accessories and spare parts for it) or commercial grounds (e.g. several products used for the same purpose) or on usage in the trade (different goods that are customarily offered for sale together). In the latter case, regard must be had to the usual practice at the reseller's level of distribution on the relevant market, taking into account all relevant dealers and not only particular forms of distribution. Exclusive purchasing agreements covering goods which do not belong together can only be exempted from the competition rules by an individual decision.

39. Under Article 3(*d*), exclusive purchasing agreements concluded for an indefinite period are not covered by the block exemption. Agreements which specify a fixed term but are automatically renewable unless one of the parties gives notice to terminate are to be considered to have been concluded for an indefinite period.

V. BEER-SUPPLY AGREEMENTS (TITLE II OF REGULATION (EEC) No. 1984/83)

1. Agreements of minor importance

40. It is recalled that the Commission's notice on agreements of minor importance states that the Commission holds the view that agreements between undertakings do not fall under the prohibition of Article 85(1) of the EEC Treaty if certain conditions as regards market share and turnover are met by the undertakings concerned. Thus, it is evident that when an undertaking, brewery or wholesaler, surpasses the limits as laid down in the above notice, the agreements concluded by it may fall under Article 85(1) of the EEC Treaty. The notice, however, does not apply where in a relevant market competition is restricted by the cumulative effects of parallel networks of similar agreements which would not individually fall under Article 85(1) of the EEC Treaty if the notice was applicable. Since the markets for beer will frequently be characterized by the existence of cumulative effects, it seems appropriate to determine which agreements can nevertheless be considered *de minimis*.

The Commission is of the opinion that an exclusive beer supply agreement concluded by a brewery, in the sense of Article 6, and including Article 8(2) of Regulation (EEC) 1984/83 does not, in general, fall under Article 85(1) of the EEC Treaty if

- the market share of that brewery is not higher than 1% of the national market for the resale of beer in premises used for the sale and consumption of drinks, and
- if that brewery does not produce more than 200 000 hl of beer per annum.

However, these principles do not apply if the agreement in question is concluded for more than 7 and a half years in as far as it covers beer and other drinks, and for 15 years if it covers only beer.

In order to establish the market share of the brewery and its annual production, the provisions of Article 4(2) of Regulation (EEC) 1984/83 apply.

As regards exclusive beer supply agreements in the sense of Article 6, and including Article 8(2) of Regulation (EEC) 1984/83 which are concluded by wholesalers, the above principles apply *mutatis mutandis* by taking account of the position of the brewery whose beer is the main subject of the agreement in question.

The present communication does not preclude that in individual cases even agreements between undertakings which do not fulfil the above criteria, in particular where the number of outlets tied to them is limited as compared to the number of outlets existing on the market, may still have only a negligible effect on trade between Member States or on competition, and would therefore not be caught by Article 85(1) of the EEC Treaty.

Neither does this communication in any way prejudge the application of national law to the agreements covered by it.

2. Exclusive purchasing obligation

(Article 6)

41. The beers and other drinks covered by the exclusive purchasing obligation must be specified by brand or denomination in the agreement. An exclusive purchasing obligation can only be imposed on the reseller for drinks which the supplier carries at the time the contract takes effect and provided that they are supplied in the quantities required, at sufficiently regular intervals and at prices and on conditions allowing normal sales to the consumer. Any extension of the exclusive purchasing obligation to drinks not specified in the agreement requires an additional agreement, which must likewise satisfy the requirements of Title II of the Regulation. A change in the brand or denomination of a drink which in other respects remains unchanged does not constitute such an extension of the exclusive purchasing obligation.

42. The exclusive purchasing obligation can be agreed in respect of one or more premises used for the sale and consumption of drinks which the reseller runs at the time the contract takes effect. The name and location of the premises must be stated in the agreement. Any extension of the exclusive purchasing obligation to other such premises requires an additional agreement, which must likewise satisfy the provisions of Title II of the Regulation.

43. The concept of 'premises used for the sale and consumption of drinks' covers any licensed premises used for this purpose. Private clubs are also included. Exclusive purchasing agreements between the supplier and the operator of an off-licence shop are governed by the provisions of Title I of the Regulation.

44. Special commercial or financial advantages are those going beyond what the reseller could normally expect under an agreement. The explanations given in the 13th recital are illustrations. Whether or not the supplier is affording the reseller special advantages depends on the nature, extent and duration of the obligations undertaken by the parties. In doubtful cases usage in the trade is the decisive element.

45. The reseller can enter into exclusive purchasing obligations both with a brewery in respect of beers of a certain type and with a drinks wholesaler in respect of beers of another type and/or other drinks. The two agreements can be combined into one document. Article 6 also covers cases where the drinks wholesaler performs several functions at once, signing the first agreement on the brewery's and the second on his own behalf and also undertaking delivery of all the drinks. The provisions of Title II do not apply to the contractual relations between the brewery and the drinks wholesaler.

46. Article 6(2) makes the block exemption also applicable to cases in which the supplier affords the owner of premises financial or other help in equipping them as a public house, restaurant, etc., and in return the owner imposes on the buyer or tenant of the premises an exclusive pur-

chasing obligation in favour of the supplier. A similar situation, economically speaking, is the transmission of an exclusive purchasing obligation from the owner of a public house to his successor. Under Article 8(1)(*e*) this is also, in principle, permissible.

3. Other restrictions of competition that are exempted

(Article 7)
47. The list of permitted obligations given in Article 7 is exhaustive. If any further obligations restricting competition are imposed on the reseller, the exclusive purchasing agreement as a whole is no longer covered by the block exemption.

48. The obligation referred to in paragraph 1(*a*) applies only so long as the supplier is able to supply the beers or other drinks specified in the agreement and subject to the exclusive purchasing obligation in sufficient quantities to cover the demand the reseller anticipates for the products from his customers.

49. Under paragraph 1(*b*), the reseller is entitled to sell beer of other types in draught form if the other party has tolerated this in the past. If this is not the case, the reseller must indicate that there is sufficient demand from his customers to warrant the sale of other draught beers. The demand must be deemed sufficient if it can be satisfied without a simultaneous drop in sales of the beers specified in the exclusive purchasing agreement. It is definitely not sufficient if sales of the additional draught beer turn out to be so slow that there is a danger of its quality deteriorating. It is for the reseller to assess the potential demand of his customers for other types of beer; after all, he bears the risk if his forecasts are wrong.

50. The provision in paragraph 1(*c*) is not only intended to ensure the possibility of advertising products supplied by other undertakings to the minimum extent necessary in any given circumstances. The advertising of such products should also reflect their relative importance *vis-à-vis* the competing products of the supplier who is party to the exclusive purchasing agreement. Advertising for products which the public house has just begun to sell may not be excluded or unduly impeded.

51. The Commission believes that the designations of types customary in inter-State trade and within the individual Member States may afford useful pointers to the interpretation of Article 7(2). Nevertheless the alternative criteria stated in the provision itself are decisive. In doubtful cases, whether or not two beers are clearly distinguishable by their composition, appearance or taste depends on custom at the place where the public house is situated. The parties may, if they wish, jointly appoint an expert to decide the matter.

4. Agreements excluded from the block exemption

(Article 8)
52. The reseller's right to purchase drinks from third parties may be restricted only to the extent allowed by Articles 6 and 7. In his purchases of goods other than drinks and in his procurement of services which are not directly connected with the supply of drinks by the other party, the reseller must remain free to choose his supplier. Under Article 8(1)(*a*) and (*b*), any action by the other party or by an undertaking connected with or appointed by him or acting at his instigation or with his agreement to prevent the reseller exercising his rights in this regard will entail the loss of the block exemption. For the purposes of these provisions it makes no difference whether the reseller's freedom is restricted by contract, informal understanding, economic pressures or other practical measures.

53. The installation of amusement machines in tenanted public houses may by agreement be made subject to the owner's permission. The owner may refuse permission on the ground that this would impair the character of the premises or he may restrict the tenant to particular types of machines. However, the practice of some owners of tenanted public houses to allow the tenant to conclude contracts for the

installation of such machines only with certain undertakings which the owner recommends is, as a rule, incompatible with this Regulation, unless the undertakings are selected on the basis of objective criteria of a qualitative nature that are the same for all potential providers of such equipment and are applied in a non-discriminatory manner. Such criteria may refer to the reliability of the undertaking and its staff and the quality of the services it provides. The supplier may not prevent a public house tenant from purchasing amusement machines rather than renting them.

54. The limitation of the duration of the agreement in Article 8(1)(*c*) and (*d*) does not affect the parties' right to renew their agreement in accordance with the provisions of Title 11 of the Regulation.

55. Article 8(2)(*b*) must be interpreted in the light both of the aims of the Community competition rules and of the general legal principle whereby contracting parties must exercise their rights in good faith.

56. Whether or not a third undertaking offers certain drinks covered by the exclusive purchasing obligation on more favourable terms than the other party for the purposes of the first indent of Article 8(2)(*b*) is to be judged in the first instance on the basis of a comparison of prices. This should take into account the various factors that go to determine the prices. If a more favourable offer is available and the tenant wishes to accept it, he must inform the other party of his intentions without delay so that the other party has an opportunity of matching the terms offered by the third undertaking. If the other party refuses to do so or fails to let the tenant have his decision within a short period, the tenant is entitled to purchase the drinks from the other undertaking. The Commission will ensure that exercise of the brewery's or drinks wholesaler's right to match the prices quoted by another supplier does not make it significantly harder for other suppliers to enter the market.

57. The tenant's right provided for in the second indent of Article 8(2)(*b*) to purchase drinks of another brand or denomination from third undertakings obtains in cases where the other party does not offer them. Here the tenant is not under a duty to inform the other party of his intentions.

58. The tenant's rights arising from Article 8(2)(*b*) override any obligation to purchase minimum quantities imposed upon him under Article 9 in conjunction with Article 2(3)(*b*) to the extent that this is necessary to allow the tenant full exercise of those rights.

VI. SERVICE-STATION AGREEMENTS (TITLE III OF REGULATION (EEC) No. 1984/84)

1. Exclusive purchasing obligation

(Article 10)

59. The exclusive purchasing obligation can cover either motor vehicle fuels (e.g. petrol, diesel fuel, LPG, kerosene) alone or motor vehicle fuels and other fuels (e.g. heating oil, bottled gas, paraffin). All the goods concerned must be petroleum-based products.

60. The motor vehicle fuels covered by the exclusive purchasing obligations must be for use in motor-powered land or water vehicles or aircraft. The term 'service station' is to be interpreted in a correspondingly wide sense.

61. The Regulation applies to petrol stations adjoining public roads and fuelling installations on private property not open to public traffic.

2. Other restrictions on competition that are exempted

(Article 11)

62. Under Article 11(*b*) only the use of lubricants and related petroleum-based products supplied by other undertakings can be prohibited. This provision refers to the servicing and maintenance of motor vehicles, i.e. to the reseller's activity in the field of provision of services. It does not affect the reseller's freedom to purchase the said products from other undertakings for resale in the service station. The petroleum-based products related to lubricants

referred to in paragraph (*b*) are additives and brake fluids.

63. For the interpretation of Article 11(*c*), the considerations stated in paragraph 49 above apply by analogy.

3. Agreements excluded from the block exemption

(Article 12)

64. These provisions are analogous to those of Article 8(1)(*a*), (*b*), (*d*) and (*e*) and 8(2)(*a*). Reference is therefore made to paragraphs 52 and 54 above.

VII. TRANSITIONAL PROVISIONS FOR BEER-SUPPLY AND SERVICE-STATION AGREEMENTS (ARTICLE 15(2) AND (3))

65. Under Article 15(2), all beer-supply and service-station agreements which were concluded and entered into force before 1 January 1984 remain covered by the provisions of Regulation No. 67/67/EEC until 31 December 1988. From 1 January 1989 they must comply with the provisions of Titles II and III of Regulation (EEC) No. 1984/83. Under Article 15(3), in the case of agreements which were in force on 1 July 1983, the same principle applies except that the 10-year maximum duration for such agreements laid down in Article 8(1)(*d*) and Article 12(1)(*c*) may be exceeded.

66. The sole requirement for the eligible beer-supply and service-station agreements to continue to enjoy the block exemption beyond 1 January 1989 is that they be brought into line with the new provisions. It is left to the undertakings concerned how they do so. One way is for the parties to agree to amend the original agreement, another for the supplier unilaterally to release the reseller from all obligations that would prevent the application of the block exemption after 1 January 1989. The latter method is only mentioned in Article 15(3) in relation to agreements in force on 1 July 1983. However, there is no reason why this possibility should not also be open to parties to agreements entered into between 1 July 1983 and 1 January 1984.

67. Parties lose the benefit of application of the transitional provisions if they extend the scope of their agreement as regards persons, places or subject matter, or incorporate into it additional obligations restrictive of competition. The agreement then counts as a new agreement. The same applies if the parties substantially change the nature or extent of their obligations to one another. A substantial change in this sense includes a revision of the purchase price of the goods supplied to the reseller or of the rent for a public house or service station which goes beyond mere adjustment to the changing economic environment.

11.5 *Stergios Delimitis* v. *Henninger Brau AG*, Case C-234/89 Court of Justice of the European Communities [1992] 5 CMLR 210

By an order of 13 July 1989, which was received at the Court on 27 July 1989, the Oberlandesgericht Frankfurt am Main referred to the Court for a preliminary ruling under Article 177 EEC several questions on the interpretation of Article 85 EEC and of Commission Regulation 1984/83 on the application of Article 85(3) EEC to categories of exclusive purchasing agreements [. . .].

Those questions were raised in proceedings between Mr Stergios Delimitis, formerly the licensee of premises for the sale and consumption of drinks in Frankfurt am Main (hereinafter referred to as 'the publican') and the brewery Henninger Brau AG, established in Frankfurt (hereinafter referred to as 'the brewery'). The dispute relates to an amount claimed from the publican by the brewery following the termination at the publican's request of the contract entered into between them on 14 May 1985.

Under Clause 1 of that contract the brewery let to the publican a public house. Clause 6 of the contract required the publican to obtain supplies of draught, bottled and canned beer from the brewery, and soft drinks from the brewery's subsidiaries. The range of products in question was determined on the basis of the current price lists of the brewery and its subsidiaries. However, the publican was permitted to purchase beers and soft drinks offered by undertakings established in other member-States.

Under Clause 6 the publican had to purchase a minimum quantity of 132 hectolitres of beer a year. If he bought less, he was required to pay a penalty for non-performance.

The contract was terminated by the publican on 31 December 1986. The brewery considered that he still owed it the sum of 6,032.15 DM, comprising rent, a lump sum penalty for failure to observe the minimum purchasing requirement and miscellaneous costs. The brewery deducted that amount from the tenant's deposit which had been paid by the publican.

The publican challenged the deduction made by the brewery and brought proceedings against it before the Landgericht (Regional Court) Frankfurt am Main in order to recover the sum deducted. In support of his claim, he contended, *inter alia*, that the contract was automatically void by virtue of Article 85(2) EEC [. . .].

THE COMPATIBILITY OF BEER SUPPLY AGREEMENTS WITH ARTICLE 85(1) EEC

Under the terms of beer supply agreements, the supplier generally affords the reseller certain economic and financial benefits, such as the grant of loans on favourable terms, the letting of premises for the operation of a public house and the provision of technical installations, furniture and other equipment necessary for its operation. In consideration for those benefits, the reseller normally undertakes, for a predetermined period, to obtain supplies of the products covered by the contract only from the supplier. That exclusive purchasing obligation is generally backed by a prohibition on selling competing products in the public house let by the supplier.

Such contracts entail for the supplier the advantage of guaranteed outlets, since, as a result of his exclusive purchasing obligation and the prohibition on competition, the reseller concentrates his sales efforts on the distribution of the contract goods. The supply agreements, moreover, lead to co-operation with the reseller, allowing the supplier to plan his sales over the duration of the agreement and to organise production and distribution effectively.

Beer supply agreements also have advantages for the reseller, inasmuch as they enable him to gain access under favourable conditions and with the guarantee of supplies to the beer distribution market. The reseller's and supplier's shared interest in promoting sales of the contract goods likewise secures for the reseller the benefit of the supplier's assistance in guaranteeing product quality and customer service.

Even if such agreements do not have the object of restricting competition within the meaning of Article 85(1), it is nevertheless necessary to ascertain whether they have the effect of preventing, restricting or distorting competition.

In Case 23/67, *Brasserie De Haecht* v. *Wilkin* [[1967] ECR 407] the Court held that the effects of such an agreement had to be assessed in the context in which they occur and where they might combine with others to have a cumulative effect on competition. It also follows from that judgment that the cumulataive effect of several similar agreements constitutes one factor amongst others in ascertaining whether, by way of a possible alteration of competition, trade between member-States is capable of being affected.

Consequently, in the present case it is necessary to analyse the effects of a beer supply agreement, taken together with other contracts of the same type, on the opportunities of national competitors or those from other member-States, to gain access to the market for beer consumption or to increase their market share and, accordingly, the effects on the range of products offered to consumers.

In making that analysis, the relevant market must first be determined. The relevant market is primarily defined on the basis of the nature of the economic activity in question, in this case the sale of beer. Beer is sold through both retail channels and premises for the sale and consumption of drinks. From the consumer's point of view, the latter sector, comprising in particular public houses and restaurants, may be distinguished from the retail sector on the grounds that the sale of beer in public houses does not solely consist of the purchase of a product but is also linked with the provision of services, and that beer consumption in public houses is not essentially dependent on economic considerations. The specific nature of the public house trade is borne out by the fact that the breweries organise specific distribution systems for this sector which require special installations, and that the prices charged in that sector are generally higher than retail prices.

It follows that in the present case the reference market is that for the distribution of beer in premises for the sale and consumption of drinks. That finding is not affected by the fact that there is a certain overlap between the two distribution networks, namely inasmuch as retail sales allow new competitors to make their brands known and to use their reputation in order to gain access to the market constituted by premises for the sale and consumption of drinks.

Secondly, the relevant market is delimited from a geographical point of view. It should be noted that most beer supply agreements are still entered into at a national level. It follows that, in applying the Community competition rules, account is to be taken of the national market for beer distribution in premises for the sale and consumption of drinks.

In order to assess whether the existence of several beer supply agreements impedes access to the market as so defined, it is further necessary to examine the nature and extent of those agreements in their totality, comprising all similar contracts tying a large number of points of sale to several national producers: Case 43/69, *Bilger* v. *Jehle* [[1970] ECR 127]. The effect of those networks of contracts on access to the market depends specifically on the number of outlets thus tied to national producers in relation to the number of public houses which are not so tied, the duration of the commitments entered into, the quantities of beer to which those commitments relate, and on the proportion between those quantities and the quantities sold by free distributors.

The existence of a bundle of similar contracts, even if it has a considerable effect on the opportunities of gaining access to the market, is not, however, sufficient in itself to support a finding that the relevant market is inaccessible, inasmuch as it is only one factor, amongst others, pertaining to the economic and legal context in which an agreement must be appraised (Case 23/67, *Brasserie De Haecht*, cited above). The other factors to be taken into account are, in the first instance, those also relating to opportunities for access.

In that connection it is necessary to examine whether there are real concrete possibilities for a new competitor to penetrate the bundle of contracts by acquiring a brewery already established on the market together with its network of sales outlets, or to circumvent the bundle of contracts by opening new public houses. For that purpose it is necessary to have regard to the legal rules and agreements on the acquisition of companies and the establishment of outlets, and to the minimum number of outlets necessary for the economic operation of a distribution system. The presence of beer wholesalers not tied to producers who are active on the market is also a factor capable of facilitating a new producer's access to that market since he can make use of those wholesalers' sales networks to distribute his own beer.

Secondly, account must be taken of the conditions under which competitive forces operate on the relevant market. In that connection it is necessary to know not only the number of and the size of producers present on the market, but also the degree of saturation of that market and customer fidelity to existing brands, for it is generally more difficult to penetrate a saturated market in which customers are loyal to a small number of large producers than a market in full expansion in which a large number of small producers are operating without any strong brand names. The trend in beer sales in the retail trade provides useful information on the development of demand and thus an indication of the degree of saturation of the beer market as a whole. The analysis of that trend is, moreover, of interest in evaluating brand loyalty. A steady increase in sales of beer under new brand names may confer on the owners of those brand names a reputation which they may turn to account in gaining access to the public-house market.

If an examination of all similar contracts entered into on the relevant market and the other factors relevant to the economic and legal context in which the contract must be examined shows that those agreements do not have the cumulative effect of denying access to that market to new national and foreign competitors, the individual agreements comprising the bundle of agreements cannot be held to restrict competition within the meaning of Article 85(1) EEC. They do not, therefore, fall under the prohibition laid down in that provision.

If, on the other hand, such examination reveals that it is difficult to gain access to the relevant market, it is necessary to assess the extent to which the agreements entered into by the brewery in question contribute to the cumulative effect produced in that respect by the totality of the similar contracts found on that market. Under the Community rules on competition, responsibility for such an effect of closing off the market must be attributed to the breweries which make an appreciable contribution thereto. Beer supply agreements entered into by breweries whose contribution to the cumulative effect is insignificant do not therefore fall under the prohibition under Article 85(1).

In order to assess the extent of the contribution of the beer supply agreements entered into by a brewery to the cumulative sealing-off effect mentioned above, the market position of the contracting parties must be taken into consideration. That position is not determined solely by the market share held by the brewery and any group to which it may belong, but also by the number of outlets tied to it or to its group, in relation to the total number of premises for the sale and consumption of drinks found in the relevant market.

The contribution of the individual contracts entered into by a brewery to the sealing-off of that market also depends on their duration. If the duration is manifestly excessive in relation to the average duration of beer supply agreements generally entered into on the relevant market, the individual contract falls under the prohibition under Article 85(1). A brewery with a relatively small market share which ties its sales outlets for many years may make as significant a contribution to a sealing-off of the market as a brewery in a relatively strong market position which regularly releases sales outlets at shorter intervals [. . .].

As a result of the *Delimitis* case, the EC Commission amended its approach to beer supply agreements: see the new paragraph 40 of the **Commission's Notice on the interpretation of Regulation 1984/83**, Section 11.4. For an analysis of the wider implications of *Delimitis*, see v. *Korah* (1992), 'The judgment in *Delimitis*: a milestone towards a realistic assessment of the effects of an agreement or a damp squib?', 14 *European Intellectual Property Review*, 167.

The supply of beer in the UK was also subject to scrutiny, under a monopoly enquiry conducted under the Fair Trading Act 1973 (see below, page 273). The report of the MMC – Supply of Beer Cm. 651 – resulted in two **Orders of the Secretary of State** (Sections 11.6 and 11.7). Brewery agreements of a different nature are also examined in the MMC **Report on the Proposed Joint Venture** between two brewers (Section 22.2).

11.6 Supply of Beer (Tied Estate) Order 1989 (SI 1989 No. 2390)

(2) In this Order

- 'beer' includes any beverage of an alcoholic strength exceeding 1.2 per cent which is made with beer;
- 'brewer' means a person who carries on business in the manufacture of beer which is supplied by retail in the United Kingdom;
- 'brewery group' means a group which is

(*a*) a group of interconnected bodies corporate, or

(*b*) a group consisting of a body corporate, or a group of interconnected bodies corporate, all other bodies corporate in which it, or any of them, has a substantial minority holding, and all subsidiaries of those other bodies corporate,

and at least one member of which is a brewer; and a brewery group is a 'large brewery group' if one or more of its members holds interests in licensed premises, and the total number of licensed premises in which members of the group hold interests exceeds two thousand; [. . .]

[. . .]

(6) For the purposes of this Order [. . .]

(*c*) a person shall not be treated as carrying out an agreement by reason only that he refrains from doing something the doing of which is the subject of a prohibition or restriction imposed by the agreement; and

(*d*) an agreement precludes or restricts a relevant purchase whether it does so wholly or only in part, whether that is the object or merely the effect of the agreement, and whether the provisions in question are expressed as negative or positive obligations.

[. . .]

5

(1) This article applies, except as provided in paragraph (4) below, to any agreement which is, or has the effect of, a lease or a licence and under which a brewer who holds interests in more than two thousand licensed premises or a member of a large brewery group permits another person not a member of the same group to occupy licensed premises other than a notified tied house, and to any agreement relating to any such agreement.

(2) Subject to article 8 below:

(*a*) the parties to any agreement to which this article applies made before 1st November 1992 shall terminate it before that date to the extent that it precludes or restricts relevant purchases; and

(*b*) it shall be unlawful on and after 1st November 1992 for any person to make or carry out an agreement to which this article applies to the extent that it does not preclude or restrict any relevant purchase.

(3) For the purposes of this article, an agreement under which one person permits another to occupy premises and which does not preclude use of those premises as licensed premises shall be regarded as an agreement under which one person permits another to occupy licensed premises.

(4) This article does not apply to an agreement made before 1st November 1992

if immediately before that date no party to it is any longer a brewer who holds interests in more than two thousand licensed premises or a member of large brewery group unless subsequently a party to it becomes or, as the case may be, becomes again such a brewer or a member of such a group.

6

(1) This article applies to any agreement which is, or has the effect of, a lease or a licence and to which article 5 above applies, except an agreement:

(*a*) which does not impose upon the brewer or any member of the group, as the case may be, any obligation on or after 1st November 1992 to put or keep all or any part of the premises in repair at any time when the premises are licensed premises, and
(*b*) under which the rent or other consideration for occupation on or after 1st November 1992 is an amount which, at the time when the agreement is (or was) made, might reasonably be (or might have reasonably been) sought and obtained on the open market by a lessor or licensor who was not a brewer or a member of a brewery group.

(2) Subject to article 8 below:

(*a*) the parties to any agreement to which this article applies made after the date on which this Order is made and before 1st November 1992 shall terminate it before the latter date; and
(*b*) it shall be unlawful on and after 1st November 1992 for any person to make an agreement to which this article applies or to carry out such an agreement if it was made after the date on which this Order was made.

7

(1) This article applies, except as provided in paragraph (4) below, to any agreement to which one of the parties is:

(*a*) a brewer who holds interests in more than two thousand licensed premises, or
(*b*) a member of a large brewery group,

and which precludes or restricts relevant purchases.

(2) Subject to article 8 below:

(*a*) the parties to any agreement to which this article applies made before 1st May 1990 shall terminate it before that date:
  (i) so far as it relates to beer of an alcoholic strength exceeding 1.2 per cent, to the extent that the person who is precluded or restricted from making relevant purchases is prevented by the agreement from purchasing from whomsoever he may choose at least one brand of draught cask-conditioned beer selected by him, and
  (ii) so far as it relates to beer of an alcholic strength not exceeding 1.2 per cent or any drink other than beer, to the extent of every provision which precludes or restricts relevant purchases, and
(*b*) it shall be unlawful on and after 1st May 1990 for any person to make or carry out an agreement to which this article applies except to the extent that subparagraph (*a*) above would not require it to be terminated if made before that date.

(3) In this article, 'cask-conditioned beer' means beer which undergoes fermentation in the container from which it is served for consumption; and a person is prevented by an agreement from purchasing from whomsoever he may choose at least one brand of draught cask-conditioned beer selected by him if the agreement imposes any prohibition or restriction on his so doing or if it subjects him to any disadvantage should he do so (including liability to pay as rent, interest or the price of goods or services an amount greater than he would otherwise pay).

(4) This article does not apply to an agreement made before 1st May 1990 if

immediately before that date no party to it is any longer a brewer who holds interests in more than two thousand licensed premises or a member of a large brewery group unless subsequently a party to it becomes or, as the case may be, becomes again such a brewer or a member of such a group.

8

(1) This Order shall not apply in respect of an agreement so far as it is or, if made, would be an agreement to which the Restrictive Trade Practices Act 1976 applies or, as the case may be, would apply.

(2) Articles 5, 6 and 7 above shall not apply in respect of an agreement so long as none of the parties to it is a brewer who holds interests in more than two thousand licensed premises and every member of a large brewery group party to it:

(*a*) is a body corporate, or a subsidiary of a body corporate, in which another member of the group has a substantial minority holding, and
(*b*) would not be a member of a large brewery group if the holding did not exist.

11.7 Supply of Beer (Loan Ties, Licensed Premises and Wholesale Prices) Order 1989 (SI 1989 No. 2258)

[for relevant definitions, see Supply of Beer (Tied Estate) Order 1989 (SI 1989 No. 2390)]

[. . .]

2

(1) This article applies to:

(*a*) any agreement under which a brewer or a member of a brewery group makes a loan or gives any other financial assistance to another person (except a member of the same group), and
(*b*) any agreement relating to any such agreement as is mentioned in subparagraph (*a*) above, if (in either case) it precludes or restricts relevant purchases.

(2) Subject to paragraph (4) and article 6 below:

(*a*) the parties to any agreement to which this article applies shall terminate it before 1st May 1990 to the extent that it is not consistent with paragraph (3) below, and
(*b*) it shall be unlawful for any person to make or carry out an agreement to which this article applies except to the extent that it is consistent with paragraph (3) below.

(3) An agreement is consistent with this paragraph only if:

(*a*) the person to whom the loan is made or other financial assistance is given may at any time repay the loan or make such payment as may be due in respect of the financial assistance, having given more than three months' notice of the repayment or payment, and
(*b*) relevant purchases are no longer precluded or restricted once the loan is repaid or payment made, including payment of all interest due; but it shall not be inconsistent with this paragraph for an agreement to provide that if interest is payable at one rate for an initial period of one year or less and a higher rate for a subsequent period and the loan is repaid or payment made before the end of the initial period, interest at the higher rate is due in respect of all or part of the initial period.

(4) Nothing in paragraph (2) above shall

be taken either to advance the time at which any payment under the agreement is due from the person to whom the loan is made or other financial assistance is given, or to relieve that person from any obligation to make payments under the agreement as they fall due.

3

(1) This article applies to any agreement under which:

(*a*) a brewer or a member of a brewery group ceases to hold an interest in licensed premises or in premises which have been licensed premises at any time since 1st January 1990, or

(*b*) a member of a brewery group one or more members of which hold interests in licensed premises ceases to be a member of the group, and to any agreement relating to any such agreement.

(2) Subject to article 6 below:

(*a*) the parties to any agreement to which this article applies made on or after 1st January 1990 and before 1st May 1990 shall terminate it before the latter date to the extent that it imposes any prohibition or restriction on the use as licensed premises of any such premises as are mentioned in paragraph (1)(*a*) above, and

(*b*) it shall be unlawful for any person to make an agreement to which this article applies, or to carry out such an agreement if it was made on or after 1st January 1990, except (in either case) to the extent that it does not impose any such prohibition or restriction.

4

(1) Every brewer and every member of a brewery group who (in either case) sells beer for resale on licensed premises shall publish a list of the prices charged by him therefor, together with information about any discount allowed where the beer is delivered to the purchaser at a place of business of the seller or an agent of his.

(2) Where a brewer or a member of a brewery group charges prices for sales to tied tenants or tied customers which differ from those charged to purchasers who are not tied tenants or tied customers, the list of prices provided for in paragraph (1) above shall indicate the prices charged to each such class of purchaser.

(3) It shall be unlawful for any brewer or member of a brewery group to charge prices for the sale of beer for resale on licensed premises which differ, except to the extent of any discount which he may allow, from those in the list published by him in accordance with paragraph (1) above.

(4) For the purposes of this article:

(*a*) a 'tied tenant' is a person who, not being a member of the group in question (if any), occupies licensed premises pursuant to an agreement which is, or has the effect of, a lease or a licence granted by the brewer in question or a member of the group in question, as the case may be, and is precluded or restricted, under that agreement or another agreement made with the brewer or a member of the group, as the case may be, from making relevant purchases;

(*b*) a 'tied customer' is a person who, not being a tied tenant or a member of the group in question (if any), is precluded or restricted, under an agreement made with the brewer in question or a member of the group in question, as the case may be, from making relevant purchases; and

(*c*) beer is sold for resale on licensed premises whether such resale is by the purchaser or by a subsequent acquirer of the beer.

5

(1) It shall be unlawful, except to the extent provided in paragraph (2) below, for

any brewer or member of a brewery group to withhold any supplies of beer for resale from any other person (except a member of the same group).

(2) It shall not be unlawful so to withhold such supplies where the person withholding the supplies has reasonable cause to believe:

(*a*) that the price for the supplies may not be duly paid, or
(*b*) that any containers of his, or of which he is bailee, in which the supplies would be made may not be duly returned to him or to such other person as might be appropriate, or
(*c*) that any beer which would be supplied may not be handled or kept properly.

6

(1) This Order shall not apply in respect of an agreement:

(*a*) so far as it is or, if made, would be an agreement to which the Restrictive Trade Practices Act 1976 applies or, as the case may be, would apply, or
(*b*) so long as none of the parties to it is a brewer and every member of a brewery group party to it:
  (i) is a body corporate, or a subsidiary of a body corporate, in which another member of the group has a substantial minority holding, and
  (ii) would not be a member of a brewery group if the holding did not exist.

(2) Articles 4 and 5 above shall impose no obligation on any member of a brewery group which:

(*a*) is not a brewer,
(*b*) is a body corporate, or a subsidiary of a body corporate, in which another member of the group has a substantial minority holding, and
(*c*) would not be a member of a brewery group if the holding did not exist.

12

VERTICAL AGREEMENTS: SELECTIVE DISTRIBUTION

The approach of the European Court of Justice to selective dealing agreements is in contrast to its approach to exclusive dealing agreements. As indicated in the first **Metro** case (Section 2.2), the Court regards selective dealing as falling outside Article 85(1) in certain conditions. The second **Metro** case, extracted below, refines the economic analysis of the relevant market for the purpose of evaluating the competitive effect of such agreements. There then follows an extensive treatment of a selective dealing agreement in the perfume sector. The Commission's decision in **Yves Saint Laurent** is now regarded (together with its decision in *Givenchy* OJ 1992 No. L 236/11) as a definitive guide to its attitude towards selective dealing, in the absence of a generally applicable block exemption.

12.1 *Metro SB-Grossmarkte GmbH & Co. KG* v. *Commission of the European Communities* (No. 2) Case 75/84 Court of Justice of the European Communities [1986] ECR 3021, [1987] 1 CMLR 118

[. . .]

The applicant is a 'self-service' wholesale trading undertaking which operates throughout the Community. It has some forty establishments in the Federal Republic of Germany and a number of outlets in the other member-States. Its activities consist in selling a wide range of products, including consumer electronics equipment, which it obtains directly from producers, both to retailers, who themselves resell the products, and to commercial or industrial undertakings or small businesses which wish to use the goods purchased for commercial purposes. Metro also sells to private customers termed 'institutional consumers', such as hospitals and hotels.

Metro's 'cash and carry' distribution system enables purchasers to serve themselves in sales areas where the goods are stored in such a way that they may be removed easily by the customers themselves, are displayed simply and are paid for in cash. This system results in lower costs and makes it possible for Metro to operate satisfactorily on lower profit margins than those of the traditional wholesale trade.

SABA, whose registered office is in Villingen-Schwenningen, Federal Republic of Germany, manufactures consumer electronics equipment such as radios and television sets, video and hi-fi equipment and tape recorders. It distributes such equipment through a network of contracts and agreements with sole distributors, wholesalers and appointed retailers, all of which constitutes a selective distribution system (hereinafter referred to as the 'SABA distribution system') [. . .]

The operation of the SABA distribution system has been contested by Metro ever since, following its application to SABA for recognition as a wholesaler for the distribution of consumer electronics equipment, it was refused supplies on the ground that it did not fulfil the conditions for admission as a SABA wholesaler.

In a decision of 15 December 1975 ([1975] OJ L28/19, [1976] 1 CMLR D61), the Commission adopted a position on an earlier version of the contracts which make up the SABA system. By that decision, it recognised that certain terms of the contracts did not fall within the prohibition laid down in Article 85(1) of the Treaty, whereas other provisions thereof were entitled to exemption under Article 85(3). The action brought by Metro challenging that decision was dismissed by the Court in its judgment of 25 October 1977 in Case 26/76 *Metro* v. *EC Commission* ([1977] ECR 1875, [1978] 2 CMLR 1, hereinafter referred to as Metro I).

The terms of the various agreements which constitute the present SABA system are essentially the same as those of the old SABA system, apart from certain changes concerning in particular the procedure for the admission of specialist distributors. Whereas under the procedure laid down under the old system SABA was entitled to decide whether or not a retailer fulfilled the criteria for admission, the new admission system empowers any SABA wholesaler to admit to the SABA dealer network any retailer who satisfies the selection criteria and to supply him with goods. In addition, even if wholesalers do not sign the Co-operation Agreement and are therefore not supplied directly by SABA, they may obtain supplies from other SABA wholesalers provided that they satisfy the criteria set out in the Wholesaler Agreement.

[. . .]

Metro has applied to the Court under Article 173 EEC for a declaration that the contested decision is void in so far as it grants an exemption under Article 85(3) to the agreements which make up the SABA system [. . .]

The considerations of the Court upon which Metro relies are the following. First, in finding that the original exemption of the SABA network was properly granted, the Court explained:

> The outcome could be different if, in particular as a result of an increase in selective distribution networks of a nature similar to SABA's, self-service wholesale traders were in fact eliminated as distributors on the market in electronic equipment for leisure purposes. (paragraph 50)

In addition, the Court expressly stated:

> Nevertheless, the Commission must ensure that this structural rigidity [in the case of prices] is not reinforced, as might happen if there were an increase in the number of selective distribution networks for marketing the same product. (paragraph 22)

According to Metro, there have been fundamental changes in the structure of competition on the market in consumer electronics equipment since 1975. In particular, there has been a significant increase in the number of selective distribution systems operated by the major producers both on the German market and throughout the Community. Metro claims that, in addition to the systems of which the Commission has been notified and those for which an application has been made to the Commission for exemption under Article 85(3), there is now a large number of other similar selective distribution systems which have not been notified and which also prevent self-service wholesale traders such as Metro from obtaining direct supplies.

Metro alleges that by granting a new exemption by the contested decision, the Commission failed to take those changes into account even though it was required to do so by the judgment in Metro I. It claims that the Commission ought in particular to have taken into account all the selective distribution systems, even the 'simple' systems, the sole purpose of which is to ensure that goods are supplied only to the specialised trade or to dealers with specialised departments.

The Commission points out first that, according to the judgment in Metro I, selective distribution systems constitute 'together with others, an aspect of competition which accords with Article 85(1), provided that resellers are chosen on the basis of objective criteria of a qualitative nature relating to the technical qualifications of the reseller and his staff and the suitability of his trading premises and that such conditions are laid down uniformly for all potential resellers and are not applied in a discriminatory fashion'. Consequently, the Commission has no authority to take action against the operation of such simple selective distribution systems. An increase in the number of such systems is therefore irrelevant in the context of Article 85(1). However, the existence of such systems should be taken into account in assessing whether Article 85(3) is applicable.

In that regard, the Commission contends that when it granted a renewal of the exemption to the SABA system, it was certain that no other selective distribution networks similar to the SABA network were operated on the relevant market; in particular, the Co-operation Agreement requiring wholesalers to sign supply estimates is a unique feature of the SABA system. Of a total number of thirteen selective distribution systems operated in this sector on the territory of the Community and notified to the Commission, four involve simple obligations to supply only through specialised outlets which do not fall within the scope of Article 85(1). The remaining nine systems required exemption under Article 85(3), but none of them contained obligations pertaining to the promotion of distribution or to co-operation comparable with those in the SABA system.

It should be stated that, as Metro alleges and the Commission recognises, the Commission was obliged, when it examined SABA's application for a renewal of the exemption granted in 1975, to verify whether the competitive situation on the relevant market had changed to such an extent that the preconditions for the grant of an exemption were no longer fulfilled.

It must be borne in mind that, although the Court has held in previous decisions that 'simple' selective distribution systems are capable of constituting an aspect of competition compatible with Article 85(1), there may nevertheless be a restriction or elimination of competition where the existence of a certain number of such systems does not leave any room for other forms of distribution based on a different type of competition policy or results in a rigidity in price structure which is not counterbalanced by other aspects of competition between products of the same brand and by the existence of effective competition between different brands.

Consequently, the existence of a large number of selective distribution systems for a particular product does not in itself permit the conclusion that competition is restricted or distorted. Nor is the existence of such systems decisive as regards the granting or refusal of an exemption under Article 85(3), since the only factor to be taken into consideration in that regard is the effect which such systems actually have on the competitive situation. Therefore the coverage ratio of selective distribution systems for colour television sets, to which Metro refers, cannot in itself be regarded as a factor preventing an exemption from being granted.

It follows that an increase in the number of 'simple' selective distribution systems after an exemption has been granted must be taken into consideration, when an application for renewal of that exemption is being considered, only in the special situation in which the relevant market was already so rigid and structured that the element of competition inherent in 'simple' systems is not sufficient to maintain workable competition. Metro has not been able to show that a special situation of that kind exists in the present case.

As regards the effect on the market of the existence of selective distribution systems other than 'simple' systems, the Commission in renewing the exemption based itself on the relatively small market share covered by the SABA system and on the fact that that system is distinguished from 'simple' systems only by the existence of obligations pertaining to the promotion of sales. By so doing, it did not misdirect itself in exercising its discretion to assess, within the framework of Article 85(3), the economic context in which the SABA system is situated.

It is true that Metro also alleges that, following the proliferation of selective distribution systems, there has been a marked decrease in price competition since 1975, but no support for that allegation is to be found in the papers before the Court. Indeed, it is clear from the studies and information provided by the Commission and SABA that considerable differences may be discerned in prices on the German market, not only between the brands of different manufacturers but also within the same brand. It follows from that, in any event, that for the moment no increase in the rigidity of the price structure can be identified.

Further, the Court recognised in that connection in its judgment in Metro I that some limitation in price competition was to be regarded as inherent in any selective distribution system, because the prices applied by specialist dealers necessarily remained within a much narrower margin than would be expected if there were competition between specialist dealers and non-specialist dealers. It stated that that limitation was counterbalanced by competition as regards the quality of the services supplied to customers, which was not normally possible in the absence of an adequate profit margin covering the higher costs entailed by such services [. . .].

12.2 *Yves Saint Laurent Parfums* Decision of the Commission of the European Communities OJ L12 16. 12 92 p24

[. . .]

(a) Selection criteria

The only retailers admitted into the selective distribution network are those approved by Yves Saint Laurent Parfums or by its exclusive agents on the basis of the selection criteria set out below.

(i) Authorized retailers, or their sales staff, must have a professional qualification in perfumery, in the form of a beauty specialist's diploma or a professional perfumery training certificate issued by a recognized Chamber of Commerce and Industry or at least three years' sales experience in perfumery. In addition, authorized retailers undertake to have their staff attend the training sessions organized by Yves Saint Laurent Parfums and to provide, in their retail outlets, adequate advisory and demonstration service for customers.

(ii) The location, name and fittings of the retail outlet must reflect the prestige of the Yves Saint Laurent Parfums brand. In particular, the quality of the outlet is assessed by reference to the nature, standing and external appearance of the other shops in the immediate neighbourhood and the facade, shop window size and decoration, sales area, lighting, floor, furniture, fixtures and fittings of the shop. If another activity is carried on in the retail outlet, the eligibility of the application for the opening of an account is also assessed in the light of the scale of such other activity, the external and internal presentation and separation of the two activities and the competence of the staff allocated to the sale of Yves Saint Laurent products.

(iii) The retailers are prohibited from offering for sale on their premises any goods whose proximity might detract from the brand image of Yves Saint Laurent.

(iv) The area set aside for the sale of Yves Saint Laurent products must not be disproportionate to the number of brands sold. In addition, it must allow the authorized retailer to provide, having regard to the other brands represented, a location reflecting the prestige of the Yves Saint Laurent brand and allowing it to be identified by the consumer.

(v) Authorized retailers must display and sell Yves Saint Laurent products only on the premises covered by the contracts and must refrain in particular from selling them by mail order. They also agree to sell the products only in their original packaging and not by weight, capacity or otherwise.

(vi) Authorized retailers agree to hold a stock in hand comprising two thirds of the references of each of the ranges marketed by Yves Saint Laurent Parfums and at least one product of each of these references. They also agree to present customers products which are always in a perfect state of freshness and preservation and to ensure an annual rotation in the stock in hand corresponding to the application of a minimum rotation factor of two.

(vii) Authorized retailers are required to promote the image of the Yves Saint Laurent brand, notably by having available within their shops new products launched by Yves Saint Laurent Parfums, by endeavouring to participate in the various promotion activities and by displaying within their shops and the shop windows the advertising material, display units and products of Yves Saint Laurent.

(viii) Authorized retailers agree to achieve in the retail outlets covered by the contracts a minimum amount of annual purchases either from the exclusive agent for Yves Saint Laurent products in the country in which the retail outlet is situated or directly from Yves Saint Laurent Parfums if the retail outlet is situated in France. This condition applies both to the admission and the maintenance of the retailer in the network. The purchase figure is set annually by Yves Saint Laurent Parfums, or, where appropriate, by its exclusive agents, in such a way that its amount does not exceed 40% of the average purchase figure achieved the previous year by all the retail outlets situated within a Member State.

(b) Procedure for admission to the distribution network

In their original version, the general conditions of sale attached to the contract concluded with authorized retailers established in France provided that each application for the opening of an account would, as from its receipt, be entered on a regional (departmental) waiting list. Each application was to be dealt with in the order in which it was entered on the list, but the decision to grant applications was taken only where the opening of a new account was regarded by Yves Saint Laurent Parfums as justified in terms of the economic potential in the area in question. Although the contracts concluded with authorized retailers in Member States other than France did not provide for the establishment of such a system of waiting lists, the opening of a new account was subject in practice to similar considerations of economic opportuneness. In response to comments made by the Commission, Yves Saint Laurent agreed to amend its contracts with effect from 1 June 1991, with the existing waiting lists having to be used up during a transitional period ending on 31 May 1992.

Under the new provisions, which apply to the entire territory of the EEC, receipt of an application for the opening of an account is followed by an inspection of the retail outlet to determine whether it meets the qualitative selection criteria. Yves Saint Laurent Parfums (or, where appropriate, its exclusive agent) undertake to carry out such an inspection within an average period of three months and a maximum of five months as from the date on which the application is made for the opening of an account. Such average period of three months has to be understood as the mathematic average of the duration relating to inspections carried out within each period of reference. Thereafter, if the application does not come anywhere near meeting the qualitative criteria, Yves Saint

Laurent Parfums (or, as the case may be, its exclusive agent) informs the applicant in writing that its application has been rejected, specifying the points that do not comply with the criteria. Conversely, if the application is capable of meeting the qualitative selection criteria subject to certain work being carried out in the retail outlet, the applicant is informed accordingly in writing and, if the work is carried out within a period of three months (which can be extended up to six upon request of the applicant), its account will be opened within a maximum period of nine months from the date of the inspection. Lastly, if the application meets entirely the qualitative selection criteria, the applicant is informed accordingly in writing and its account will be opened within a period of nine months as from the date of inspection.

(c) Freedom of cross supplies between members of the distribution network

In respect to the comments made by the Commission, Yves Saint Laurent Parfums amended some of the provisions in the standard-form contract intended for authorized retailers established in Member States other than France, in so far as such provisions restricted the ability of such authorized retailers to resell Yves Saint Laurent products to network members established in the same country as themselves. The new provisions now provide that, as under the standard-form contract applicable in France, each authorized retailer may resell Yves Saint Laurent products to any other authorized retailer established in any Member State, including the country in which he is himself established. The new provisions also stipulate that each authorized retailer is free to obtain supplies from other authorized retailers or exclusive agents of Yves Saint Laurent Parfums established in any Member State.

Exercise of this right is subject to the following conditions.

(i) Before reselling Yves Saint Laurent products to other network members, authorized retailers must ensure that the purchasers are indeed authorized Yves Saint Laurent Parfums retailers. They undertake to check this under their entire responsibility and to consult Yves Saint Laurent Parfums where there is doubt as to the status of the purchaser.

(ii) Authorized retailers must keep copies of the invoices of such resales for one year. Yves Saint Laurent Parfums (or, where appropriate, its exclusive agent) may consult them only where it has grounds for believing that a retailer is reselling Yves Saint Laurent products outside the authorized retail network. Authorized retailers obtaining supplies from other network members are subject to similar provisions. In response to comments made by the Commission, Yves Saint Laurent Parfums deleted provisions under which authorized retailers had to communicate systematically to Yves Saint Laurent Parfums (or, where appropriate, to its exclusive agents) copies of the invoices or vouchers for each resale to or supply from other authorized retailers.

(iii) Only the value of the orders invoiced by Yves Saint Laurent Parfums (or, where appropriate, by its exclusive agent) is taken into account in calculating the authorized retailer's minimum annual purchases figure. So as to maintain the freedom of cross supplies between network members, Yves Saint Laurent Parfums agreed to delete certain provisions in the agreement under which the amount of the price paid by the authorized retailer to Yves Saint Laurent Parfums (or to its exclusive agent) for the purchase of products subsequently resold to another network member was not taken into account in calculating the abovementioned minimum purchase figure.

(iv) Any authorized retailer on whose territory a new Yves Saint Laurent product has not yet been launched undertakes, so as to avoid adversely affecting the campaigns for the launch of the new product, not to engage in the active sale of the new product for a period of one year as from the date when the new product is first launched in a Member State. In this respect, the standard-form contracts notified provided initially for an export ban applicable during the first year of the official launch of the new product in a Member State. Yves Saint Laurent Parfums amended this clause along the above lines in response to comments made by the Commission.

(d) Closed distribution network

Authorized retailers agree not to sell to or obtain supplies from any wholesaler or retailer not included within the Yves Saint Laurent Parfums distribution network. For its part, Yves Saint Laurent Parfums undertakes to market products bearing the Yves Saint Laurent brand name only in retail outlets which meet the conditions stipulated in the selective distribution contract.

(e) No imposed prices

The standard-form contracts notified provide expressly that authorized retailers are free to set the resale prices of their products.

(f) No ban on competition

Authorized retailers may obtain supplies of articles similar to the articles covered by the contract from competing producers.

(g) Duration of the contracts

The contracts are concluded for a specific term, normally one year. They may be terminated before the end of their term, with or without notice having been given, where authorized retailers do not abide by their contractual obligations or where they cease to be responsible for the actual running of their businesses, subject to the rights of their directly descendant heirs. However, where the operator or owner of an authorized retail outlet ceases to operate his sales outlet, Yves Saint Laurent Parfums undertakes to inform the new owner or operator, within a maximum period of three months, whether he meets the professional criteria [. . .]

A. ARTICLE 85(1) OF THE TREATY

1. Under Article 85(1), all agreements between undertakings which may affect trade between Member States and which have as their object or effect the prevention, restriction or distortion of competition within the common market are prohibited as incompatible with the common market.

2. The standard-form contracts notified, which cover relations between Yves Saint Laurent Parfums or, as the case may be, its exclusive agents and the various authorized retailers established within the common market, provide for arrangements for cooperation between legally independent undertakings and constitute agreements between undertakings within the meaning of Article 85(1).

3. The selective distribution contracts notified by Yves Saint Laurent Parfums impose on the authorized retailers the requirement that they must resell the products covered by the contract only to final consumers or to other members of the Yves Saint Laurent Parfums network. For their part, Yves Saint Laurent Parfums and its exclusive agents undertake not to supply products bearing the Yves Saint Laurent brand name to distribution undertakings not forming part of such network. These obligations constitute restrictions of competition, since access to the Yves Saint Laurent Parfums distribution system is granted exclusively to traders who not only fulfil certain general professional and technical conditions, but are in addition willing to enter into subsequent commitments and to provide special services.

4. As the Court of Justice has pointed out (Case 107/82 *AEG* v. *Commission* (1983) ECR 3151, ground 33), agreements constituting a selective distribution system necessarily affect competition in the common market. However, it has always been recognized that certain products which are not ordinary products or services have properties such that they cannot be properly supplied to the public without the intervention of specialized distributors. A system of selective distribution may thus constitute an element of competition which is in conformity with Article 85(1), if it is established that the properties of the products in question necessitate the establishment of such a system in order to preserve

their quality and ensure their proper use (Case 31/80 *L'Oréal* v. *De Nieuwe* [1980] ECR 3775, ground 16) and provided that resellers are chosen on the basis of objective criteria of a qualitative nature relating to the technical qualifications of the reseller and his staff and the suitability of his trading premises and that such conditions are laid down uniformly for all potential resellers and are not applied in a discriminatory fashion (Case 26/76 *Metro* v. *Commission* [1977] ECR 1875, ground 20).

5. In this instance, the contracts underlying the network for the selective distribution of Yves Saint Laurent Parfums products are not covered by Article 85(1) in so far as they are limited to establishing, for access to distribution, qualitative criteria of a technical and professional nature laid down in a uniform manner for all potential resellers and in so far as such criteria are not applied in a discriminatory manner.

The articles in question are high-quality articles based on specific research, which is reflected in the originality of their creation, the sophistication of the ranges marketed and the qualitative level of the materials used, including their packaging. Their nature as luxury products ultimately derives from the aura of exclusivity and prestige that distinguishes them from similar products falling within other segments of the market and meeting other consumer requirements. This characteristic is, on the one hand, closely linked to the producer's capacity to develop and maintain an up-market brand image and, on the other, depends on appropriate marketing that brings out the specific aesthetic or function quality of each individual product or line of products. This is all the more necessary as there exists, on the luxury cosmetic products market, a considerable number of competing brands and since, as a general rule, each retailer sells a wide range of brands. In this respect, it should be noted that, far from aiming at ensuring exclusive representation of Yves Saint Laurent products, the selective distribution system notified is on the contrary based on Yves Saint Laurent Parfums articles being sold alongside other competing high-quality brands.

Accordingly, having specialized technical advice available in the retail outlet is a legitimate requirement in so far as the knowledge specifically required is necessary in order to help consumers select the products best suited to their tastes and requirements and to provide them with the best information on their use and indeed the preservation of such products.

In addition, the requirement that the authorized retailer undertake to have his staff attend the training sessions organized by Yves Saint Laurent Parfums is intended merely to ensure that they have adequate knowledge of Yves Saint Laurent Parfums products and is not such as to restrict the authorized retailer's freedom to sell or promote competing brands.

Since the maintenance of a prestige brand image is, on the luxury cosmetic products market, an essential factor in competition, no producer can maintain its position on the market without constant promotion activities. Clearly, such promotion activities would be thwarted if, at the retail stage, Yves Saint Laurent products were marketed in a manner that was liable to affect the way consumers perceived them. Thus, the criteria governing the location and aesthetic and functional qualities of the retail outlet constitute legitimate requirements by the producer, since they are aimed at providing the consumer with a setting that is in line with the luxurious and exclusive nature of the products and a presentation which reflects the Yves Saint Laurent brand image. In addition, the criterion relating to the shop-name is designed to ensure that the name of the perfumery or shop or area within which the perfumery counter or perfumery is situated is compatible with the principles governing the distribution of the products in question and thus to exclude any name whose image would be associated with an absence of or restriction in customer service and in standing and with a lack of attention to decoration. It should be stressed in this respect that the down-market nature of a retail outlet or of its name cannot be deduced from the retailer's habitual policy on prices.

The ban on selling goods which, through their proximity, are liable to detract from the Yves Saint Laurent brand image is intended merely to safeguard, in the public's mind, the aura of prestige and exclusivity inherent in the products in question, thus preventing any association with lower-quality goods. A similar objective is also pursued by the selection criteria designed to ensure that, in the retail outlets where a variety of activities are carried out, the area set aside for the sale of perfumery products is proportionate and sufficiently separate from the area intended for the sale of other products. It should be stressed in this respect that, since the Yves Saint Laurent Parfums distribution system is open to shops having a specialized counter, and given the various forms of distribution which Yves Saint Laurent Parfums has authorized at Community level, these criteria are not in themselves such as to exclude certain modern forms of distribution such as department stores.

The requirement that the authorized retailer should set aside for Yves Saint Laurent Parfums products a location which, having regard to the other brands represented, corresponds to the standing of the Yves Saint Laurent brand and allows it to be identified by the consumer is intended to meet the objective of ensuring that the products covered by the contract are presented in an enhancing manner. In addition, since this requirement does not involve either binding contractual specifications as to the identity or number of the brands sold alongside Yves Saint Laurent Parfums products or minimum quantitative requirements regarding the allocation of the space set aside for the sale of the contract products, such a selection criterion is not in itself liable to limit the retailer's freedom to sell and promote competing brands or liable to impede the development of new forms of distribution.

Although the ban on selling Yves Saint Laurent Parfums products by mail order is in itself liable to limit the commercial autonomy of the authorized retailer, it cannot be deemed to be an appreciable restriction of competition. On the one hand, supplying the products under optimum conditions presupposes direct contact between customers and a sales staff that is capable of suggesting a choice between the various products and various brands, taking account of the personal requirements of each consumer. On the other, the requirement in question is a necessary corollary to the criteria designed to ensure that the contract products are presented in as homogeneous a way as possible and that the producer can continuously supervise the qualitative level of its distribution network.

6. However, the selective distribution contracts must be assessed from another angle where they contain authorization requirements and criteria that go beyond the limits indicated above. They are then caught by Article 85(1), although they may, where appropriate, be exempted under Article 85(3) (Case 99/79 *Lancôme* v. *Etos* [1980] ECR 2511). The contracts notified do contain such specific obligations.

(*a*) The procedure for dealing with applications for the opening of an account requires Yves Saint Laurent Parfums to take a decision, within precise deadlines, on any request for authorization sent to it by interested resellers, admitting into its network all qualified retailers or, where appropriate, informing the applicant expressly of the grounds on which its request has been rejected. In this measure, the procedure in question eliminates the risk of arbitrariness that was inherent in the admission system initially provided for in the contracts notified, where the producer had been given an exclusive and discretionary right to decide, as the final arbiter, on whether or not a new reseller should be integrated into its network. Nevertheless, the procedure has the effect of restricting access to the distribution network to resellers who are able and willing to carry out work on their retail outlets, while not being able to sell the contract products until the end of a period whose relative length is likely to discourage certain potentially qualified retailers. Thus, the duration of the periods provided for in this context is liable to affect competition between retailers of Yves Saint Laurent Parfums products.

(*b*) The authorized retailers are required to achieve, in their retail outlets, a minimum annual purchases figure set periodically by Yves Saint Laurent Parfums or, where appropriate, by the exclusive agent of the country in which the retail outlet is situated. This requirement goes beyond the requirements regarding the technical qualification of retailers or their sales staff and the appropriate location and fitting-out of the retail outlet that are necessary for proper distribution of luxury cosmetic products. It restricts competition, both within the Yves Saint Laurent brand and between it and other competing brands, since it has the effect, on the one hand, of restricting access to the Yves Saint Laurent Parfums distribution network to resellers who are able to enter into such a commitment and, on the other, of obliging authorized retailers to devote a significant proportion of their activities to selling the contract products. The requirement in question is in addition liable to affect the freedom of the members of the distribution network to obtain supplies, since only the value of the orders invoiced by Yves Saint Laurent Parfums (or, where appropriate, by its exclusive agent) is taken into account in calculating the minimum purchases figure.

(*c*) The notified contracts also impose on the retailer specific obligations regarding stocks, stock rotation and cooperation in advertising and promotion activities. These requirements constitute restrictions of competition, since they result, on the one hand, in firms which, while meeting the qualitative conditions for authorization, are not able to assume such additional commitments being significantly excluded from the distribution of Yves Saint Laurent products and, on the other, in the autonomy of authorized retailers to determine their commercial policy being restricted.

(*d*) The distribution contracts require authorized retailers on whose territory a new Yves Saint Laurent product has not yet been launched to refrain from engaging in active sale of it for one year as from the date on which the product was first launched in a Member State.

Though the non-export clause initially provided for here has been removed, this requirement nevertheless constitutes a restriction of competition, since it has the effect of limiting authorized retailers' freedom of commercial initiative and of impeding cross supplies between members of the distribution network.

7. The verification requirements imposed on authorized retailers where they buy from or sell to members of the distribution network (checking of the invoices by Yves Saint Laurent Parfums, checking that the customer belongs to the official distribution network) are designed to allow Yves Saint Laurent Parfums to supervise the distribution system. Provided that they do not exceed what is necessary for appropriate verification, such requirements are the corollary of the principal obligation whose fulfilment they must ensure, and must be viewed in legal terms in the same way as such principal obligation (Case 26/76 *Metro* v. *Commission* [1977] ECR 1875, ground 27). Since the ban on authorized retailers obtaining supplies from non-authorized traders must in this instance be deemed to be a restriction of competition, the same also applies to the verification requirements designed to ensure application and supervision of such ban. However, the verification requirements are not in themselves a restriction of competition in so far as they are confined to what is strictly necessary in order to ensure the cohesiveness of the distribution system. In particular:

(i) following the incorporation into the contracts of the amendments requested by the Commission, the checking by Yves Saint Laurent Parfums of the authorized retailer's invoices relating to the resale or purchase of Yves Saint Laurent products to or from other members of the distribution network is expressly limited to cases where the producer has concrete evidence that the retailer has been involved in reselling the contract products outside the authorized distribution network. For the manufacturer, such monitoring is an indispensable means of taking action against possible breaches of the selective distribution contract and of ensuring the homogeneity and tightness of the system.

(ii) Although the contract requires the authorized retailer, before supplying another member of the network, to ensure that the latter is indeed an authorized Yves Saint Laurent Parfums retailer, the choice of appropriate means of fulfilling this requirement is left to the discretion of the authorized retailer. Yves Saint Laurent does not have to be consulted on this matter unless the authorized retailer has been able, by his own means, to establish the status of the purchaser. This does not prejudice the authorized retailer's ability to supply another retailer without the knowledge of Yves Saint Laurent.

8. The Yves Saint Laurent Parfums distribution system covers the whole of the Community. Since it restricts competition, it is liable to affect trade between Member States. As to whether or not the restriction is appreciable, the Court of Justice has ruled that an undertaking which supplies some 5% of a market is in a position to influence intra-Community trade through its conduct (Case 19/77 *Miller* v. *Commission* [1978] ECR 131). It should be recalled in this respect that, given the low degree of substitutability in the consumer's mind between luxury cosmetic products and similar products falling within other segments of the sector, the relevant market is that for luxury cosmetic products. On that market, Yves Saint Laurent Parfums has, in several Member States, market shares well in excess of the abovementioned threshold. Consequently, the view must be taken that the barriers to competition encountered constitute an appreciable restriction of intra-Community trade. It should also be added that the agreements modified form part of an economic context in which selective distribution systems comprising restrictions of competition similar to those described above are the rule and that, consequently, the appreciable nature of the restrictions noted may be said to derive from the cumulative effect inherent in such a distribution structure.

B. ARTICLE 85(3) OF THE TREATY

1. The contracts underlying the Yves Saint Laurent Parfums system of selective distribution in the Community meet the conditions provided for in Article 85(3).

2. Improving production and distribution

Luxury cosmetic products differ from similar products that meet other consumer requirements, *inter alia*, through the image of exclusivity and prestige which, in the consumer's mind, is associated with the brand under which they are sold. The manufacturer's capacity to create and maintain an original and prestigious brand image is thus a key factor in competition. It follows that a luxury cosmetics brand must be distributed on an exclusive basis. Experience shows that generalized distribution of a luxury cosmetic product can affect the consumer's perception of it and in the long term reduce demand for it.

Against this background, the procedure for dealing with applications for the opening of an account, as provided for under the amendments to the contract requested by the Commission, is intended to ensure flexible integration of new retailers into the Yves Saint Laurent Parfums selective distribution network. The periods laid down take account, on the one hand, of the organizational requirements of Yves Saint Laurent as regards in particular the inspection visits to retail outlets, the training sessions for sales staff, the adjustment of its own production programmes and the manufacture, usually by other undertakings, of the various advertising and presentation material for the new retail outlets. On the other hand, the procedure allows the retailer to carry out in a proper manner any refitting of the retail outlet that may be required to meet the qualitative criteria for authorization.

The minimum annual purchase requirement is intended to maintain continuous supplies and allows Yves Saint Laurent Parfums (or, where appropriate, its exclusive agents) to concentrate distribution on the cost effective retail outlets, thus rationalizing the spread of the costs associated with the distribution of its products and with the provision of assistance to retail outlets. In particular, this obligation is a means of ensuring, on the one hand, that the costs borne by the manufacturer will be covered by an adequate volume of business and, on the other, that the authorized retailer will contribute actively to enhancing the brand through customer service that is in line with the reputation of the contract products. The rationalization function inherent in the minimum annual purchase requirement also derives from the limits imposed on its implementation, with the minimum purchases figure being set annually by Yves Saint Laurent Parfums (or by each of its exclusive agents) in such a way that its amount does not exceed 40% of the average purchases, during the previous year, of all the retail outlets operating in the territory of a Member State. Furthermore, given the level of this threshold, the view may be taken that the requirement in question is not such as to restrict unduly the retailer's freedom to sell or promote competing brands.

The requirements on the holding of stocks have the effect of extending the range of Yves Saint Laurent products available through authorized retailers, so that consumers can always find, at each retail outlet, the main products in each of the ranges marketed by Yves Saint Laurent Parfums and rely on the products which they desire being rapidly available. In addition, the requirements relating to stock rotation make it possible to ensure that the products sold are always in a perfect state of freshness and preservation. Proper stock rotation is also necessary in order to ensure that products such as articles of make-up are frequently renewed in line with fashion trends.

The provisions on cooperation in advertising and promotional activities, which are generic obligations to support the Yves Saint Laurent brand, are a necessary corollary, in each retail outlet, to the various advertising measures carried out at national or local level by Yves Saint Laurent Parfums or, where appropriate, by its exclusive agents. The provisions make it possible in particular to coordinate, in the common interest of the contracting parties, the promotional measures taken by the manufacturer and its authorized retailers and thus to plan as rationally as possible coordinated advertising campaigns. Furthermore, the constraints imposed by such requirements are not such as to prevent Yves Saint Laurent retailers from taking advantage of inter-brand competition.

The requirement imposed on authorized retailers on whose territory a new product has not yet been launched to refrain from engaging in active sale of such product for one year enables the manufacturer to test a new product on a given market and to reserve the right, in the light of the results obtained on that market, to extend or stop the marketing of the product.

The launching of a new luxury cosmetic product is a complex industrial and commercial operation entailing large-scale investment and sophisticated advertising promotion. The success of such an operation presupposes close cooperation between the manufacturer and its authorized retailers, who, for their part, require specific training in order to provide final customers with the professional advice they expect.

Viewed as a whole, these benefits clearly outweigh the disadvantage that, amongst qualified traders, the only ones authorized are those who declare that they are willing to assume the additional obligations described above. These restrictions have the effect of ensuring that Yves Saint Laurent products are distributed only under conditions that can preserve the high quality image and exclusivity associated with the fact that they are luxury cosmetic products.

3. Benefits to consumers

Consumers derive direct advantage from the benefits inherent in the Yves Saint Laurent Parfums selective distribution system.

The distribution system notified allows the exclusive character of the contract products to be safeguarded, such exclusive character being the main reason why consumers choose them. The consumer is thus assured that the luxury product will not become an everyday product as a result of a downgrading of its image and a decrease in the level of creation.

In addition, the establishment of such a system has the effect of focusing on factors of competition other than the price, such as the provision of an advisory service for customers and the constant availability of the essential products in the ranges, including new products, marketed by Yves Saint Laurent Parfums. Furthermore, if customers regard as secondary the brand image or the services associated with sale within the selective distribution system, they can choose similar articles falling within an adjacent market and distributed without the use of selective distribution systems, thus penalizing the commercial strategy pursued by the producer. In addition, since the Yves Saint Laurent Parfums distribution system is based on the products being sold alongside other prestige brands, consumers can always decide not to buy the Yves Saint Laurent brand, if the level of its prices are considered no longer to correspond to the quality of its products.

Lastly, in view of the number of authorized retailers currently included in the Yves Saint Laurent Parfums network and in view of the fact that the producer cannot refuse the inclusion of new retailers on the basis of purely quantitative criteria, the view may be taken that the system is not such as to restrict unduly intrabrand competition. Accordingly, consumers are allowed a fair share of the benefits resulting from the rationalization of distribution, particularly since the contracts notified provide for complete freedom in the setting of retail prices by authorized retailers.

4. Indispensable nature of the restriction of competition

The Yves Saint Laurent Parfums distribution system does not contain any restrictive obligation that is not indispensable to the attainment of the above-mentioned benefits.

Prohibiting authorized retailers from obtaining supplies of contract products from traders not previously authorized by Yves Saint Laurent or by one of its exclusive agents is a necessary condition for ensuring the cohesiveness and tightness of the selective distribution system. In this context, the requirement incumbent on Yves Saint Laurent Parfums or, where appropriate, its exclusive agents to market the products bearing the Yves Saint Laurent brand name only in retail outlets that meet the conditions specified in the selective distribution contract is complementary to the specialization requirement imposed on authorized retailers and makes it possible to ensure uniform conditions of competition between resellers of the brand. Otherwise, competition would be distorted if Yves Saint Laurent Parfums supplied traders which, not being subject to the same obligations, had to bear financial charges that were appreciably smaller than those borne by the members of the selective distribution network. In such a situation, it would no longer be possible to require authorized Yves Saint Laurent retailers to continue to carry out their own obligations, with the result that the selective distribution system could no longer be maintained.

As a corollary to the requirements intended to ensure that the distribution network is closed, the verification by Yves Saint Laurent Parfums of the authorized retailer's invoices for the resale or purchase of Yves Saint Laurent products to or from other network members is an indispensable means of taking action against any breaches of the selective distribution contract, provided that such monitoring does not go beyond the limits expressly provided in the contract.

The authorization procedure does not go beyond the limits of what is necessary in order to ensure flexible integration of new resellers into the distribution network. It should be pointed out, in particular, that the procedure is applicable only in the case of requests from new candidates or from former authorized retailers whose distribution contracts have been terminated as a result of a breach of contract which they have committed. Consequently, the procedure cannot give rise to abuses during the periodical renewals of contracts. Furthermore, such a procedure is not liable to affect the retailer's freedom to dispose of his business, notably by selling it to third parties, since the extension of the distribution contract in the name of a new operator is subject only to verification of the latter's professional qualifications, within a maximum period of three months. Lastly, since Yves Saint Laurent is required to inform the retailer of the reasons for any rejection of his application, the retailer will always be able to challenge the implementation of the admission procedure with respect to him, notably where the selection criteria have been applied in a discriminatory manner. In addition, it should be observed that, while the periods presently provided for in the context of the aforesaid procedure are relatively long, they have nevertheless been regarded as acceptable in order to facilitate the transition from a closed distribution system, based on the application of quantitative criteria, to a system subject only to the application of certain qualitative criteria. In the light of this, the Commission considers it necessary to re-examine the question of the duration of the admission procedure, at the end of the period of validity of this Decision.

The requirements regarding minimum annual purchases, the holding of stocks and cooperation in advertising and promotional activities are also indispensable to the attainment of the abovementioned benefits. If there were no provisions specifying minimum purchases of supplies, the authorization given to all the retailers having the professional and technical qualifications required by Yves Saint Laurent Parfums would result in a considerable extension in the distribution network which, however, given the relative stability of the market in question, would not result in a proportionate increase in sales. The producer would then be confronted not only with higher distribution costs, but also with a gradual deterioration in the image of the products. Moreover, the minimum annual purchases requirement may be considered reasonable, in that the amount of purchases which Yves Saint Laurent Parfums has undertaken to require from its retailers cannot exceed 40% of the average purchases figure, during the previous year, of all the retail outlets concerned. Consequently, it may be considered that such limitation of the amount relating to the minimum annual purchases requirement is likely to safeguard the retailer's capacity to market a sufficiently broad range of competing brands as well as the access of new retailers to the network. However, the Commission considers it necessary to re-examine this aspect of the distribution system, at the end of the period of validity of this Decision.

It is also to be feared that, if there were no requirements regarding the holding of stocks and stock rotation, authorized retailers would decide to concentrate their promotion activities only on the brand leader products of each of the lines marketed by Yves Saint Laurent Parfums. In addition, the retailer's cooperation in advertising and promotional activities is indispensable in ensuring maximum effectiveness in promotional campaigns, the cost of which represents a substantial proportion of the producer's investment. Lastly, the clause prohibiting active sale of new products while they are still being launched by Yves Saint Laurent Parfums is necessary in order to allow the producer to limit the territory within which a new product is launched so as to gauge consumer reaction and decide, in the light of the results obtained, whether larger-scale production may be envisaged.

5. Elimination of competition

The contracts on which the Yves Saint Laurent Parfums selective distribution system is based do not afford the undertakings concerned the possibility of eliminating competition in respect of a substantial part of the products in question.

Since, on the one hand, the contracts do not contain any no-competition clauses and since, on the other, the Community market comprises a large number of undertakings manufacturing or marketing luxury cosmetic products, authorized Yves Saint Laurent Parfums retailers are able to take advantage of inter brand competition.

In addition, authorized Yves Saint Laurent Parfums retailers may compete with one another throughout the Community. As a result of the amendments made to the standard-form selective distribution contracts, they have the right to obtain their supplies wherever it is most advantageous to them, since they can procure Yves Saint Laurent products from any exclusive agent within the EEC, and supplies between authorized retailers are now allowed without any restriction within the Community distribution network. The Yves Saint Laurent contracts no longer contain either the clause which prohibited resale between retailers established within one and the same Member State or the clause which provided that amounts relating to products resold by a retailer to other network members had to be deducted in calculating the annual purchases of such retailer. It may thus be hoped that such changes will help to prevent any rigidity in the structure of prices in the common market.

Similarly, the Commission has not been able to establish that the spread of selective distribution systems in the field of luxury cosmetic products impedes in principle certain modern forms of distribution, such as department stores. The selection criteria applied by Yves Saint Laurent Parfums are not such that they cannot also be met by such forms of distribution, even if this requires some change in their particular marketing methods.

All the conditions for exemption under Article 85(3) are thus met.

C. ARTICLES 6 AND 8 OF REGULATION No. 17

All the amendments made by Yves Saint Laurent Parfums to its standard-form authorized retailer contracts entered into force on 1 June 1991. It therefore seems appropriate, pursuant to Article 6 of Regulation No. 17, to give effect to the exemption granted under Article 85(3) of the Treaty as from that date.

So as to be able, at the end of a relatively short period, to re-examine the effects of the Yves Saint Laurent Parfums distribution system on competition, the Commission considers it appropriate, pursuant to Article 8(1) of Regulation No. 17, to make this Decision applicable until 31 May 1997.

Lastly, the Decision should be accompanied by conditions and obligations so as to enable the Commission to check whether the amounts imposed on authorized Yves Saint Laurent Parfums retailers under the minimum annual purchases requirement continue to meet the conditions for exemption laid down Article 85(3) of the Treaty. Accordingly, Yves Saint Laurent Parfums is required to submit, every two years, detailed reports specifying, for each Member State of the Community, the amount set annually by Yves Saint Laurent Parfums and by its exclusive agents in implementation of the above-mentioned requirement and the average purchases of Yves Saint Laurent products achieved by all the retail outlets concerned during each of the previous years. The Decision is based in this respect on Article 8(1) of Regulation No. 17,

HAS ADOPTED THIS DECISION:

ARTICLE 1

The provisions of Article 85(1) of the EEC Treaty are hereby declared inapplicable, pursuant to Article 85(3):

- to the standard-form authorized retailer contract binding Yves Saint Laurent Parfums to its specialized retailers established in France, and to the general conditions of sale annexed thereto;

and

- to the standard-form authorized retailer contract binding the exclusive agents of Yves Saint Laurent Parfums established in a Member State other than France to their specialized retailers, and to the general conditions of sale annexed thereto.

This Decision shall apply from 1 June 1991 to 31 May 1997.

ARTICLE 2

Yves Saint Laurent Parfums SA shall present to the Commission reports every two years, starting on 1 June 1993, specifying:

- the total amount of purchases of Yves Saint Laurent Parfums achieved, during each of the previous years, by all the authorized retail outlets in each Member State of the Community, the increases made in prices and the launching of new products or the withdrawal from the market of old products;
- the number of authorized retail outlets in each Member State as at 31 December of each of the previous years

and

- the amounts set annually by Yves Saint Laurent Parfums or, where appropriate, by its exclusive agents pursuant to the minimum purchases requirement incumbent on authorized retailers.[. . .]

FURTHER READING

Lebel, C. and Aicardi, S. (1990), 'Legal aspects of selective distribution of luxury products in France', 12 *European Intellectual Property Review*, 246.

For discussions on the special selective dealing systems used in the motor industry:

Bright, C. (1992), 'Distribution systems and the motor industry', 136 *Solicitors Journal* 630.

Report of the Monopolies and Mergers Commission (1992), *New Motor Cars*, Cm. 1808.

For a consideration of a selective dealing system under the Competition Act 1980:

Report of the Monopolies and Mergers Commission (1981), *Bicycles* HC 67.

13

VERTICAL AGREEMENTS: PRICE

13.1 Resale Prices Act 1976

1 Collective agreement by suppliers

(1) It is unlawful for any two or more persons carrying on business in the United Kingdom as suppliers of any goods to make or carry out any agreement or arrangement by which they undertake:

(*a*) to withhold supplies of goods for delivery in the United Kingdom from dealers (whether party to the agreement or arrangement or not) who resell or have resold goods in breach of any condition as to the price at which those goods may be resold;
(*b*) to refuse to supply goods for delivery in the United Kingdom to such dealers except on terms and conditions which are less favourable than those applicable in the case of other dealers carrying on business in similar circumstances; or
(*c*) to supply goods only to persons who undertake or have undertaken –
  (i) to withhold supplies of goods as described in paragraph (*a*) above; or
  (ii) to refuse to supply goods as described in paragraph (*b*) above.

(2) It is unlawful for any two or more such persons to make or carry out any agreement or arrangement authorising:

(*a*) the recovery of penalties (however described) by or on behalf of the parties to the agreement or arrangement from dealers who resell or have resold goods in breach of any such condition as is described in paragraph (*a*) of subsection (1) above; or
(*b*) the conduct of any domestic proceedings in connection therewith.

2 Collective agreement by dealers

(1) It is unlawful for any two or more persons carrying on business in the United Kingdom as dealers in any goods to make or carry out any agreement or arrangement by which they undertake:

(*a*) to withhold orders for supplies of goods for delivery in the United Kingdom from suppliers (whether party to the agreement or arrangement or not):
  (i) who supply or have supplied goods otherwise than subject to such a condition as is described in paragraph (*a*) of section 1(1) above; or
  (ii) who refrain or have refrained from taking steps to ensure compliance with such conditions in respect of goods supplied by them; or
(*b*) to discriminate in their handling of goods against goods supplied by such suppliers.

(2) It is unlawful for any two or more such persons to make or carry out any agreement or arrangement authorising:

(*a*) the recovery of penalties (however described) by or on behalf of the parties to the agreement or arrangement from such suppliers; or (*b*) the conduct of any domestic proceedings in connection therewith.

3 RECOMMENDATIONS

It is unlawful for any person carrying on business in the United Kingdom as a supplier of or dealer in any goods to make to any other person carrying on such a business any recommendation to act in such a manner that, if there were an agreement between those persons so to act, the agreement would be unlawful by virtue of section 1 or section 2 above.
[. . .]

5 EXCLUSIVE DEALING

A contract for the sale of goods to which not more than two persons are party is not unlawful under this Part of this Act by reason only of undertakings by the purchaser in relation to the goods sold and by the vendor in relation to other goods of the same description.
[. . .]

9 MINIMUM RESALE PRICES MAINTAINED BY CONTRACT OR AGREEMENT

(1) Any term or condition:

(*a*) of a contract for the sale of goods by a supplier to a dealer, or
(*b*) of any agreement between a supplier and a dealer relating to such a sale, is void in so far as it purports to establish or provide for the establishment of minimum prices to be charged on the resale of the goods in the United Kingdom.

(2) It is unlawful for a supplier of goods (or for an association or person acting on behalf of such suppliers):

(*a*) to include in a contract for sale or agreement relating to the sale of goods a term or condition which is void by virtue of this section;
(*b*) to require, as a condition of supplying goods to a dealer, the inclusion in a contract or agreement of any such term or condition, or the giving of any undertaking to the like effect;
(*c*) to notify to dealers, or otherwise publish on or in relation to any goods, a price stated or calculated to be understood as the minimum price which may be charged on the resale of the goods in the United Kingdom.

Paragraph (*a*) does not affect the enforceability of a contract of sale or other agreement, except in respect of the term or condition which is void by virtue of this section.

Paragraph (*c*) is not to be construed as precluding a supplier (or an association or person acting on behalf of a supplier) from notifying to dealers or otherwise publishing prices recommended as appropriate for the resale of goods supplied or to be supplied by the supplier.
[. . .]

11 MINIMUM RESALE PRICES MAINTAINED BY OTHER MEANS

(1) It is unlawful for a supplier to withhold supplies of any goods from a dealer seeking to obtain them for resale in the United Kingdom on the ground that the dealer:

(*a*) has sold in the United Kingdom at a price below the resale price goods obtained, either directly or indirectly, from that supplier, or has supplied such goods, either directly or indirectly, to a third party who had done so; or
(*b*) is likely, if the goods are supplied to him, to sell them in the United Kingdom at a price below that price, or supply them, either directly or indirectly, to a third party who would be likely to do so.

(2) In this section 'the resale price', in relation to a sale of any description, means:

(*a*) any price notified to the dealer or otherwise published by or on behalf of a supplier of the goods in question (whether lawfully or not) as the price or minimum price which is to be charged on or is recommended as appropriate for a sale of that description; or

(*b*) any price prescribed or purporting to be prescribed for that purpose by a contract or agreement between the dealer and any such supplier.

(3) Where under this section it would be unlawful for a supplier to withhold supplies of goods it is also unlawful for him to cause or procure any other supplier to do so.
[. . .]

13 EXCEPTION FOR MEASURES AGAINST LOSS LEADERS

(1) It is not unlawful by virtue of section 11 above for a supplier to withhold supplies of any goods from a dealer, or to cause or procure another supplier to do so, if he has reasonable cause to believe that within the previous twelve months the dealer or any other dealer to whom the dealer supplies goods has been using as loss leaders any goods of the same or a similar description, whether obtained from that supplier or not.

(2) The reference in this section to the use of goods as loss leaders is a reference to a resale of the goods effected by the dealer, not for the purpose of making a profit on the sale of those goods, but for the purpose of attracting to the establishment at which the goods are sold customers likely to purchase other goods or otherwise for the purpose of advertising the business of the dealer.

(3) A sale of goods shall not be treated for the purposes of this section as the use of those goods as loss leaders:

(*a*) where the goods are sold by the dealer at a genuine seasonal or clearance sale, not having been acquired by the dealer for the purpose of being resold as mentioned in this section; or

(*b*) where the goods are resold as mentioned in this section with the consent of the manufacturer of the goods or, in the case of goods made to the design of a supplier or to the order and bearing the trade mark of a supplier, of that supplier.

14 EXEMPTION OF GOODS BY THE COURT

(1) Upon an application under section 16 or section 17 below the Restrictive Practices Court ('the Court') may make an order in accordance with this section directing that goods of any class shall be exempted goods for the purposes of this Part of this Act.

(2) The order referred to in subsection (1) above may be made if it appears to the Court that in default of a system of maintained minimum resale prices applicable to those goods:

(*a*) the quality of the goods available for sale, or the varieties of the goods so available, would be substantially reduced to the detriment of the public as consumers or users of those goods; or

(b) the number of establishments in which the goods are sold by retail would be substantially reduced to the detriment of the public as such consumers or users; or

(*c*) the prices at which the goods are sold by retail would in general and in the long run be increased to the detriment of the public as such consumers or users; or

(*d*) the goods would be sold by retail under conditions likely to cause danger to health in consequence of their misuse by the public as such consumers or users; or

(*e*) any necessary services actually provided in connection with or after the sale of the goods by retail would cease to be so provided or would be substantially reduced to the detriment of the public as such consumers or users; and

in any such case that the resulting detriment to the public as consumers or users of the goods in question would outweigh any detriment to them as such consumers or users (whether by the restriction of competition or otherwise) resulting from the maintenance of minimum resale prices in respect of the goods.

In this section: 'necessary services', in relation to goods, means services which, having regard to the character of the goods, are required to guard against the risk of injury, whether to persons or to premises, in connection with the consumption, installation or use of the goods, or are otherwise reasonably necessary for the benefit of consumers or users; and 'consumers' and 'users' include persons consuming or using for the purpose or in the course of trade or business or for public purposes.

See the Report of the Monopolies and Mergers Commission, *Black and Decker*, Cm. 805 (1989) for the limitations on the use of the 'loss leader' defence.

13.2 *The Publishers Association – Net Book Agreements*, Decision of the European Communities, [1989] 4 CMLR 825

[. . .]

1. INDISPENSABILITY OF THE RESTRICTIONS

(71) The Association has, in its notification of the agreements, set out that without a common application of the standard conditions by publishers there could be no guarantee that booksellers would be protected, as they are in the case of net books. The arguments put forward to that effect [. . .] however concerned not so much the necessity of a common application of standard conditions in case of fixed book prices but much more the question whether fixed book prices as such are indispensable in order to attain their alleged objectives.

The Commission is of the opinion that both aspects can and should be considered separately.

(72) At the hearing, the Association specified its position in stating that, for the following reasons, the benefits it considered to result from the agreements could not and would not be achieved merely by leaving publishers individually with a legal right to fix the retail prices of the books they publish:

(i) It would not be practicable for publishers individually to give notice to every bookseller of the publishers' individual conditions of sale; according to United Kingdom law, only by so doing can a resale price maintenance condition be enforced in the United Kingdom against not only direct but also indirect purchasers;

(ii) It would not be practicable for booksellers to comply with differing resale price maintenance conditions imposed by hundreds of different publishers; in order to be reasonable and practicable such conditions, when applied to books, must allow for exceptions; booksellers would find it impossible to comply on a basis that varied from book to book according to its publisher, with different conditions providing for different exceptions; the conditions therefore need to be standard conditions;

(iii) In order that the system may confer the benefits that the Association considers it does, each bookseller must be confident that if he buys a book as a net book, his competitors will be subject to the same terms as he is, in relation to that book, so that no-one will enjoy an unfair advantage over the others. The agreements provide booksellers with that confidence;

(iv) The monitoring of compliance with the standard conditions, and their enforcement – in the last resort, through the courts – can in practice be carried out only by the Association acting for all publishers.

(73) In order to assess whether restrictions in agreements are indispensable to the attainment of the objectives of the agreements, it is relevant first to recall the objectives of the present agreements.

The Association argues that to impede the proper functioning of the agreements would cause stockholding booksellers to order fewer copies of the same title and few titles on account of the risk that lower prices elsewhere might leave them with stock which they could not sell. Such conduct would cause the number of stockholding booksellers to decrease. As stocks and display are to be considered essential for sales, sales would therefore fall, publishers would print smaller runs and costs would rise. As a result, and taking into account the higher discounts which would be requested by the trade from the publishers, book prices would therefore rise. At the same time titles with small print runs would possibly not be published at all.

In order to avoid those consequences the Association considers it essential that the retail price of a book is the same in all shops and that no price competition takes place as to the same title.

(74) As may be concluded from the position of the Association as mentioned in (72) above, the Association invokes the arguments mentioned in (72) to show that in order to achieve the objectives of the agreements a collective agreement is necessary and that individual vertical resale price maintenance agreements for books would not suffice.

(75) It is not the subject of this case to decide which kind of distribution system on a particular national market is best suited to achieve the objectives invoked by the Association. The Commission has to deal here with a price fixing system extending to exports to other Member States, in particular to Ireland, as well as to imports and re-imports from other Member States, including Ireland. The system as currently applied precludes price competition resulting from trade between Member States at the level of distribution. The Commission has already stated in Decision 82/123/EEC in case No. IV/428 – VBBB/VBVB (OJ No. L54, 25.2.1982, p. 36) that in order to achieve an improvement in the publication and distribution of the books in question, a collective resale price maintenance scheme entailing the imposition of restrictions on competition in trade between Member States, such as contained in the agreements in question, is not indispensable.

The Commission continues to recognize the important cultural role which books play among other cultural media. However, it is convinced that the parties could use less restrictive means to improve the publication and distribution of books.

(76) As to the first argument of the Association as to the indispensability of a common application of standard conditions, i.e. the impracticability for publishers individually to give notice of the standard conditions to every bookseller, the Commission notes that the condition to give such notice to booksellers in order to enable a publisher to enforce the respect for the standard conditions before the national courts as against indirect purchasers with whom the publisher did not contract directly, is a condition provided for in national law the application of which is confined to the United Kingdom territory. Alleged practical difficulties complying with such a condition, imposed by the law of a Member State and having the effect of rendering the enforcement of individual resale price maintenance agreements within that Member State more difficult, cannot be invoked to argue for the acceptance, under Community law, of more far-reaching restrictions within a collective resale price maintenance agreement covering trade with other Member States.

(77) In this connection, it must be emphasized that the condition to give notice only applies in relation to the enforcement of the agreements within the United Kingdom and not in relation to

Ireland, where the law does not provide for such a condition. In this respect the argument relating to the giving of notice is of no relevance.

(78) In any event, the Commission does not see how an alleged practical need for putting together the individual notices into a common system of giving notice could constitute a justification for much more far-reaching agreements on uniform conditions of sale, which are considered by the Association as the essential means to attain the objectives of the agreements.

Thus, the Commission does not consider the argument to be relevant to the question whether a collective resale price maintenance agreement is indispensable.

(79) As to the second argument of the Association, i.e. the impracticability for booksellers to comply with a large number of different fixed book price conditions, the Commission considers that it comes down to the question of the quantity of administration to be handled by individual booksellers.

(80) In this respect it is to be noted that an important share of total book sales is constituted by books published by a relatively small number of publishers.

Moreover, the large majority of booksellers, in particular tobacconists, newsagents and supermarkets, and even smaller specialist bookshops, only have a limited range of titles.

On account of these factors it may be considered that a majority of booksellers have to deal only with a limited number of publishers and conditions of sale.

The situation may be different for stockholding bookshops but it is difficult to see why those bookshops would not be able to cope with this additional administration.

(81) In this connection, the Commission notes that in Ireland, under the present system of resale price maintenance, booksellers, in order to establish their resale prices for net books, representing a substantial share of total book sales, have to do so by proceeding on a title by title basis, since they have to convert the price fixed in British pounds into Irish punts.

(82) Furthermore, booksellers may not want to sell all books at a lower price than the present net price at the same time, but instead may want to reduce prices only for a certain number of titles at the same time. It is then only in relation to such a limited number of titles that a bookseller would have to take into account the differences which, in case of individual resale price maintenance agreements, may exist as between the conditions of sale of different publishers.

(83) On these grounds the second argument of the Association does not appear convincing to the Commission.

(84) The third argument of the Association, i.e. the agreements provide booksellers with the confidence that, if they buy a book as a net book, their competitors will be subject to the same terms as they are in relation to the book concerned, does not appear convincing to the Commission either.

This argument comes down to the statement that the Association considers that booksellers cannot have the same confidence *vis-à-vis* its individual members when they operate through individual resale price maintenance agreements as when they operate through a collective agreement. The Commission does not in any way understand on what basis the Association so distrusts the individual publishers' behaviour *vis-à-vis* booksellers. This is even more so now that most publishers are members of the Association. The Association's argument becomes even more questionable now that the agreement does not exclude in certain cases that publishers allow booksellers to grant discounts other than the uniform discounts provided for in the agreement.

(85) The fourth argument of the Association, i.e. the monitoring of compliance with the standard conditions and their enforcement can, in practice, be carried out only by the Association, does not explain, in the opinion of the Commission, why a collective agreement on standard conditions of sale is indispensable. Thus, the argument is not relevant in this respect.

2. CONCLUSION

(86) The Commission concludes from the foregoing that the agreements are not indispensable to the attainment of their objectives. Since an agreement, in order to be exempted from the prohibition contained in Article 85(1), has to fulfil all conditions of Article 85(3), the agreements cannot be exempted. It is therefore not necessary to examine whether the agreements meet the other conditions of Article 85(3).

[. . .]

13.3 *Business Electronics Corp.* v. *Sharp Electronics Corp.*, Supreme Court of the United States 485 US 717; 108 S. Ct. 1515

In 1968, [Business Electronics Corp., 'petitioner'] became the exclusive retailer in the Houston, Texas, area of electronic calculators manufactured by respondent Sharp Electronics Corporation. In 1972, respondent appointed [. . .] Hartwell as a second retailer in the Houston area [. . .]. Respondent published a list of suggested minimum retail prices, but its written dealership agreements with petitioner and Hartwell did not obligate either to observe them, or to charge any other specific price. Petitioner's retail prices were often below respondent's suggested retail prices and generally below Hartwell's retail prices, even though Hartwell too sometimes priced below respondent's suggested retail prices. Hartwell complained to respondent on a number of occasions about petitioner's prices. In June 1973, Hartwell gave respondent the ultimatum that Hartwell would terminate his dealership unless respondent ended its relationship with petitioner within 30 days. Respondent terminated petitioner's dealership. Petitioner brought suit in the United States District Court for the Southern District of Texas, alleging that respondent and Hartwell had conspired to terminate petitioner and that such conspiracy was illegal *per se* under section 1 of the Sherman Act [. . .] [The District Court held that] [. . .] 'If a dealer demands that a manufacturer terminate a price cutting dealer, and the manufacturer agrees to do so, the agreement is illegal if the manufacturer's purpose is to eliminate the price cutting.' [. . .] The Fifth Circuit reversed, holding that [. . .] to render illegal *per se* a vertical agreement between a manufacturer and a dealer to terminate a second dealer, the first dealer 'must expressly or impliedly agree to set its prices at some level, though not a specific one. The distributor cannot retain complete freedom to set whatever price it chooses.'

[. . .]

Section 1 of the Sherman Act provides that 'every contract, combination in the form of trust or otherwise, or conspiracy, in restraint of trade or commerce among the several States, or with foreign nations, is declared to be illegal' (15 U. S. C. at 1). Since the earliest decisions of this Court interpreting this provision, we have recognized that it was intended to prohibit only unreasonable restraints of trade: *National Collegiate Athletic Assn.* v. *Board of Regents of University of Oklahoma*, 468 U.S. 85, 98 (1984); see, e.g. *Standard Oil Co.* v. *United States*, 221 U.S. 1, 60 (1911). Ordinarily, whether particular concerted action violates [section] 1 of the Sherman Act is determined through case-by-case application of the so-called rule of reason – that is, 'the factfinder weighs all of the circumstances of a case in deciding whether a restrictive practice should be prohibited as imposing an unreasonable restraint on competition': *Continental T.V., Inc.* v. *GTE Sylvania Inc.*, 433 U.S. 36, 49 (1977). Certain categories of agreements, however, have been held to be *per se* illegal, dispensing with the need for case-by-case evaluation. We have said that *per se* rules are appropriate only for 'conduct that is manifestly anticompetitive' (*ibid.*, at 50), that is, conduct '"that would always or almost always tend to restrict competition and decrease output"': *Northwest Wholesale Stationers, Inc.* v. *Pacific Stationery and Printing Co.*, 472 U.S. 284, 289-290 (1985), quoting *Broadcast Music, Inc.* v. *Columbia Broadcasting System, Inc.*, 441 U.S. 1, 19–20 (1979). See also *FTC* v. *Indiana Federation of Dentists*, 476 U.S. 447, 458–459 (1986) ('We have been slow [. . .] to extend *per se* analysis to restraints imposed in the context of business relationships where the economic impact of certain practices is not immediately obvious'): *National Collegiate Athletic Assn.* v. *Board of Regents of University of Oklahoma, supra*, at 103–104 ('*Per se* rules are invoked when surrounding circumstances make the likelihood of anticompetitive conduct so great as to render unjustified further examination of the challenged conduct'); *National Society of Professional Engineers* v. *United States*, 435 U.S. 679, 692 (1978) (agreements are *per se* illegal only if their 'nature and necessary effect are so plainly anticompetitive that no elaborate study of the industry is needed to establish their illegality').

Although vertical agreements on resale prices have been illegal *per se* since *Dr Miles Medical Co.* v. *John D. Park and Sons Co.*, 220 U.S. 373 (1911), we have recognized that the scope of the *per se* illegality should be narrow in the context of vertical restraints. In *Continental T.V., Inc.* v. *GTE Sylvania, Inc.*, *supra*, we refused to extend *per se* illegality to vertical nonprice restraints, specifically to a manufacturer's termination of one dealer pursuant to an exclusive territory agreement with another. We noted that especially in the vertical restraint context 'departure from the rule-of-reason standard must be based on demonstrable economic effect rather than . . . upon formalistic line drawing': *ibid.*, at 58–59. We concluded that vertical nonprice restraints had not been shown to have such a '"pernicious effect on competition"' and to be so '"lacking [in] [. . .] redeeming value"' as to justify *per se* illegality: *ibid.*, at 58, quoting *Northern Pacific Railway Co.* v. *United States*, 356 U.S. 1, 5 (1958). Rather, we found, they had real potential to stimulate interbrand competition, 'the primary concern of antitrust law': 433 U.S., at 52, n. 19.

New manufacturers and manufacturers entering new markets can use the restrictions in order to induce competent and aggressive retailers to make the kind of investment of capital and labor that is often required in the distribution of products unknown to the consumer. Established manufacturers can use them to induce retailers to engage in promotional activities or to provide service and repair facilities necessary to the efficient marketing of their products. Service and repair are vital for many products [. . .]. The availability and quality of such services affect a manufacturer's goodwill and the competitiveness of his product. Because of market imperfections such as the so-called 'free-rider' effect, these services might not be provided by retailers in a purely competitive situation, despite the fact that each retailer's benefit would be greater if all provided the services than if none did': *ibid.*, at 55.

Moreover, we observed that a rule of *per se* illegality for vertical nonprice restraints was not needed or effective to protect intrabrand competition. First, so long as interbrand competition existed, that would provide a 'significant check' on any attempt to exploit intrabrand market power: *ibid.*, at 52, n. 19; see also *ibid.*, at 54. In fact, in order to meet that interbrand competition, a manufacturer's dominant incentive is to lower resale prices: *ibid.*, at 56, and n. 24. Second, the *per se* illegality of vertical restraints would create a perverse incentive for manufacturers to integrate vertically into distribution, an outcome hardly conducive to fostering the creation and maintenance of small businesses: *ibid.*, at 57, n. 26.

Finally, our opinion in *GTE Sylvania* noted a significant distinction between vertical nonprice and vertical price restraints. That is, there was support for the proposition that vertical price restraints reduce interbrand price competition because they '"facilitate cartelizing"': *ibid.*, at 51, n. 18, quoting Posner, 'Antitrust policy and the Supreme Court: an analysis of the restricted distribution, horizontal merger and potential competition decisions', 75 *Columbia Law Review*, 282, 294 (1975). The authorities cited by the Court suggested how vertical price agreements might assist horizontal price fixing at the manufacturer level (by reducing the manufacturer's incentive to cheat on a cartel, since its retailers could not pass on lower prices to consumers) or might be used to organize cartels at the retailer level: see R. Posner, *Antitrust: Cases, Economic Notes and Other Materials*, 134 (1974); E. Gellhorn, *Antitrust Law and Economics*, 252, 256 (1976); Note, 'Vertical territorial and customer restrictions in the franchising industry', 10 *Columbia Journal of Law and Social Problems*, 497, 498, n. 12 (1974). Similar support for the cartel-facilitating effect of vertical nonprice restraint was and remains lacking.

We have been solicitous to assure that the market-freeing effect of our decision in *GTE Sylvania* is not frustrated by related legal rules. In *Monsanto Co.* v. *Spray-Rite Service Corp.*, 465 U.S. 752, 763 (1984), which addressed the evidentiary showing necessary to establish vertical concerted action, we expressed concern that 'if an inference of such an agreement may be drawn from highly ambiguous evidence, there is considerable danger that the doctrine enunciated in *Sylvania* [. . .] will be seriously eroded.' See also *ibid.*, at 761, n. 6. We eschewed adoption of an evidentiary standard that 'could deter or penalize perfectly legitimate conduct' or 'would create an irrational dislocation in the market' by preventing legitimate communication between a manufacturer and its distributors: *ibid.*, at 763, 764.

Our approach to the question presented in the present case is guided by the premises of *GTE Sylvania* and *Monsanto*: that there is a presumption in favor of a rule-of-reason standard; that departure from that standard must be justified by demonstrable economic effect, such as the facilitation of cartelizing, rather than formalistic distinctions; that interbrand competition is the primary concern of the antitrust laws; and that rules in this area should be formulated with a view towards protecting the doctrine of *GTE Sylvania*. These premises lead us to conclude that the line drawn by the Fifth Circuit is the most appropriate one.

There has been no showing here that an agreement between a manufacturer and a dealer to terminate a 'price cutter', without a further agreement on the price or price levels to be charged by the remaining dealer, almost always tends to restrict competition and reduce output. Any assistance to cartelizing that such an agreement might provide cannot be distinguished from the sort of minimal assistance that might be provided by vertical nonprice agreements like the exclusive territory agreement in *GTE Sylvania*, and is insufficient to justify a *per se* rule. Cartels are neither easy to form nor easy to maintain. Uncertainty over the terms of the cartel, particularly the prices to be charged in the future, obstructs both formation and adherence by making cheating easier: cf. *Maple Flooring Mfrs. Assn.* v. *United States*, 268 U.S. 563 (1925); *Cement Mfrs. Protective Assn.* v. *United States*, 268 U.S. 588 (1925); see generally *Matsushita Electric Industrial Co.* v. *Zenith Radio Corp.*, 475 U.S. 574, 590 (1986). Without an agreement with the remaining dealer on price, the manufacturer both retains its incentive to cheat on any manufacturer-level cartel (since lower prices can still be passed on to consumers) and cannot as easily be used to organize and hold together a retailer-level cartel. [. . .]

The District Court's rule on the scope of *per se* illegality for vertical restraints would threaten to dismantle the doctrine of *GTE Sylvania*. Any agreement between a manufacturer and a dealer to terminate another dealer who happens to have charged lower prices can be alleged to have been directed against the terminated dealer's 'price cutting'. In the vast majority of cases, it will be extremely difficult for the manufacturer to convince a jury that its motivation was to ensure adequate services, since price cutting and some measure of service cutting usually go hand in hand. Accordingly, a manufacturer that agrees to give one dealer an exclusive territory and terminates another dealer pursuant to that agreement, or even a manufacturer that agrees with one dealer to terminate another for failure to provide contractually obligated services, exposes itself to the highly plausible claim that its real motivation was to terminate a price cutter. Moreover, even vertical restraints that do not result in dealer termination, such as the initial granting of an exclusive territory or the requirement that certain services be provided, can be attacked as designed to allow existing dealers to charge higher prices. Manufacturers would be likely to forgo legitimate and competitively useful conduct rather than risk treble damages and perhaps even criminal penalties.

We cannot avoid this difficulty by invalidating as illegal *per se* only those agreements imposing vertical restraints that contain the word 'price', or that affect the 'prices' charged by dealers. Such formalism was explicitly rejected in *GTE Sylvania.* As the above discussion indicates, all vertical restraints, including the exclusive territory agreement held not to be *per se* illegal in *GTE Sylvania*, have the potential to allow dealers to increase 'prices' and can be characterized as intended to achieve just that. In fact, vertical nonprice restraints only accomplish the benefits identified in *GTE Sylvania* because they reduce intrabrand price competition to the point where the dealer's profit margin permits provision of the desired services. As we described it in *Monsanto*: 'The manufacturer often will want to ensure that its distributors earn sufficient profit to pay for programs such as hiring and training additional salesmen or demonstrating the technical features of the product, and will want to see that "free-riders" do not interfere': 465 U.S., at 762–763. See also *GTE Sylvania*, 433 U.S., at 55.

Finally, we do not agree with petitioner's contention that an agreement on the remaining dealer's price or price levels will so often follow from terminating another dealer 'because of [its] price cutting' that prophylaxis against resale price maintenance warrants the District Court's *per se* rule. Petitioner has provided no support for the proposition that vertical price agreements generally underlie agreements to terminate a price cutter. That proposition is simply incompatible with the conclusion of *GTE Sylvania* and *Monsanto* that manufacturers are often motivated by a legitimate desire to have dealers provide services, combined with the reality that price cutting is frequently made possible by 'free riding' on the services provided by other dealers. The District Court's *per se* rule would therefore discourage conduct recognized by *GTE Sylvania* and *Monsanto* as beneficial to consumers [. . .].

14

VERTICAL AGREEMENTS: LICENSING

One of the most complex trade-offs for economists arises in the field of technical change. It is here that the conflict between the structural state of competition and the need to compete in order to maintain efficient outcomes becomes fundamental. Dynamic progress requires some element of monopoly, but how much? A good basic discussion of this trade-off, which has implications for the legal framework, is provided by the extract from **Scherer and Ross**.

14.1 F. Scherer and D. Ross, *Industrial Market Structure and Economic Performance*, 3rd edn, (Houghton Mifflin, Boston, Mass., 1990)

[. . .]

THE BASIC LOGIC [OF PATENT PROTECTION]

The funds supporting invention and the commercial development of inventions are front-end 'sunk' investments; once they have been spent, they are an irretrievable bygone. To warrant making such investments, an individual inventor or corporation must expect that once commercialization occurs, product prices can be held above postinvension production and marketing costs long enough so that the discounted present value of the profits (or more accurately, quasi rents) will exceed the value of the front-end investment. In other words, the investor must expect some degree of protection from competition, or some monopoly power. The patent holder's right to exclude imitating users is intended to create or strengthen that expectation. Patents also confer a property right which the original patent holder can sell, recouping its original investment and letting another entity exclusively commercialize the patented subject matter. Partial 'sale' is also possible, for example, when the patent holder licenses others to exploit the invention and charges a royalty for the right.

The simplest case of a product innovation covered by patent protection is shown in Figure 14.1(a). If the product is really new and useful, it creates a wholly new demand curve D_1 – one that did not exist previously. With an exclusive right to make and sell its product, the patent holder is a monopolist. It derives its marginal revenue MR_1, equates marginal revenue with marginal production and distribution cost MC and sets price OP_1, realizing 'monopoly' profits in the amount of rectangular area P_1AXM. These are not pure profits, however, because the innovator's sunk R&D costs must be taken into account. To make that one-

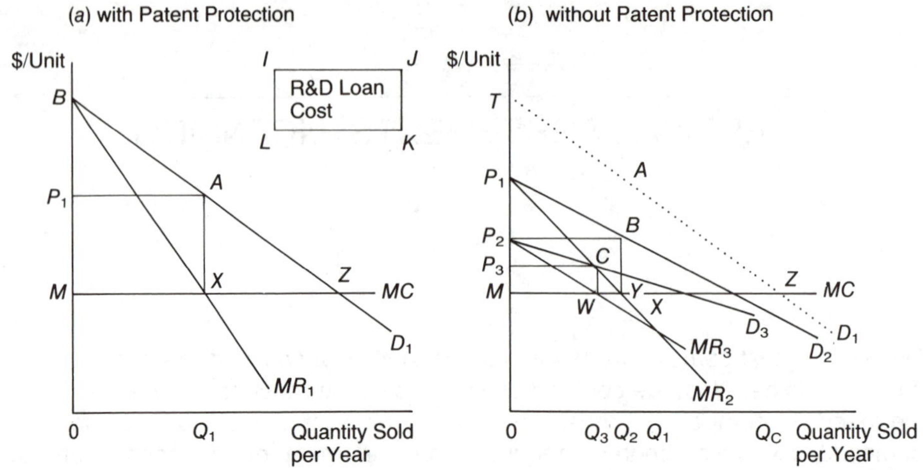

Figure 14.1 New Product Pricing With and Without Patent Protection

time lump sum consistent with Figure 14.1(*a*), which is expressed in annual 'flow' terms, let us assume that the innovator finances its R&D investment by taking out a seventeen-year mortgage whose annual payment obligation is given by the area of the inset rectangle *IJKL*. If the patent monopoly lasts for seventeen years, the annual 'profit' P_1AXM will more than cover the annual R&D debt service cost, and the innovator will be well compensated for its efforts. It is not true, however, that the monopoly innovator is the only one to gain. The ordinates of demand curve D_1 array the values diverse consumers place upon having the new product to consume. The product's availability on monopolized terms generates not only producer's surplus P_1AXM, but also consumers' surplus BAP_1. With linear demand and constant marginal production and distribution costs, as shown in Figure 14.1(*a*), the monopolist is said to 'appropriate' to itself only two-thirds of the total surplus its product creates. The remaining third goes to consumers.

Suppose, however, that there were no patent protection and no other barriers to the imitation of the innovator's invention. Then a scenario like the one shown in panel (b) of Figure 14.1 might unfold. Soon after the new product appears, competing firms will introduce their imitating products, squeezing the demand schedule left for the original innovator to D_2. With less residual demand, the innovator must derive a new marginal revenue function MR_2 and set a new, lower price $0P_2$, which yields profit rectangle P_2BYM barely covering the innovator's R&D debt service cost. However, the imitator firms may have had to incur little or no R&D cost on their own, 'free riding' on the innovator's R&D, and thus, with unit costs of only $0M$, they will realize supra-normal profits at price $0P_2$. More competitors will be drawn in by this price and profit lure, squeezing the innovator's residual demand curve further to D_3. The innovator must reoptimize again, setting profit-maximizing price $0P_3$ and capturing 'profit' rectangle P_3CWM, which is now smaller than the continuing R&D debt service obligations. If this diffusion process were to unfold rapidly and if the innovator correctly foresaw its course, the innovator would perceive that its R&D costs will not be recouped and would therefore choose not to invest in the R&D. Consumers will be deprived of a valuable new product – one that, even under pure monopoly conditions, could yield them a sizable consumers' surplus.

Pursuing the analysis a step further, we see a kind of dilemma. *If* the R&D investment were incurred and the innovation made, imitative entry might, absent patent protection, continue until the price is driven all the way down to the competitive level, ignoring the innovator's front-end costs – that is, to $0M$. If this happens, surplus P_1AXM, originally captured by the innovator, will be transformed into consumers' surplus. In addition, the competitive expansion of output to $0Q_C$ leads to the emergence of still more consumers' surplus, measured by triangle AZX. In this limiting case, the innovator appropriates none of the (now larger) surplus its invention has created – consumers get it all. If the innovator is allowed to monopolize the new product's sale, its profit-maximizing output restriction means that total surplus will be less than it might ideally be by dead-weight loss triangle AZX. In this sense, granting patent monopolies imposes a cost upon society. Seeing this, consumers might urge that the government renege on its patent monopoly grant so they can have the best of all worlds – the new product, competitive pricing, and maximum surplus. But if this occurs with any frequency, would-be innovators will expect rapid imitation to erode their surpluses, causing them to lose money on their R&D investments, so they will not invest in additional new products. The technological well will run dry. The patent system makes a deliberate tradeoff, accepting during the patent grant's life dead-weight surplus losses in order to ensure that new products and processes, along with the surpluses they create, will not be discouraged by fear of rapid imitation. Only after the patent expires, when competitive imitation can run its full course, are consumers able to have their new product along with the extra surplus competitive pricing brings.

COMPLICATIONS

Although devised to solve an important incentive problem, the patent system is a crude and imperfect instrument. Because of diverse real-world complications, the patent protection given an innovator may be too little, too much, or of the wrong kind.

The protection provided is often weak because there can be many viable solutions to a technical problem, so other firms can 'invent around' a given patented solution. Individual patents that solidly protect a whole field of product or process technology are rare, and when such cases occur, the credit is frequently due as much to the skill of the patent attorney as to the breadth of the inventor's vision. To be sure, companies often seek to fence in their technological domain by patenting every conceivable variation on a product or process. Yet fences are also permeable. Du Pont, for example, took out hundreds of patents on variants of its nylon synthetic fiber technology. But even in the directly applicable polyamide molecule family it left a gap into which Germany's I.G. Farben moved with Perlon L, and other companies invented competitive fibers using polyester and polyolefin molecules.

Further complications emerge because the growth of technology is cumulative and richly interactive. Company B may patent an improvement on Company A's invention, or Companies C and D may each hold patents on diverse features, all of which a state-of-the-art product should ideally incorporate. Each might if it wishes block the other from using desired complementary technology. Under Chinese patent law and Japanese practice, firms holding improvement patents on others' inventions can demand a licence to the original patent by reciprocally offering to license their improvement. This logjam-breaking provision, absent from US and European law, engendered considerable conflict between US and Japanese industry leaders during the 1980s. In the United States and Europe, the holders of complementary patents often agree voluntarily to cross license each other. This enables all to achieve state-of-the-art technology but lessens the exclusionary power of patents. However, such cross licensing agreements have sometimes been used as a fulcrum for industry-wide price-fixing and entry-excluding cartels that suppress competition more than would have been possible if each firm independently exploited its own patented technology. In the United States, cartelization through reciprocal licensing of patents has for the most part been dealt with harshly under the antitrust laws.

For smaller and especially less-developed countries (LDCs), patent holders' power to block use of their inventions by others poses a special problem. Multinational corporations commonly patent their most important inventions in dozens of national jurisdictions. The quest for scale economies leads them to produce in one or a few preferred locations, exporting elsewhere and preventing the local exploitation of their technology in export markets by asserting their patent rights. For an LDC, this typically means that high prices will be paid for imported patented products, while opportunities to build a home industry using first-line technology are restricted. Many LDCs and some more industrialized nations have therefore included in their patent laws provisions requiring that the technology on which they issue patents be 'worked' domestically within a few years or be subjected to compulsory licensing. Such provisions have been a focus of conflict between multinational corporations, stressing the rationale of patent incentives and efficiently centralized production, and LDCs, emphasizing their need to escape from backwardness by building dynamic modern industries.

ALTERNATIVE PROTECTION FROM IMITATION

The patent grant is a tradeoff, but if an invention would be made and commercialized without patent protection, the terms are altered. The power to impose monopolistic restrictions remains, but what consumers get in the bargain would have been available on less restrictive terms. There are several reasons why competitive imitation might be impeded even without patents, leaving sufficient incentive for investments in research and development.

For one to imitate, one must know about the innovation and its advantages, and knowledge is almost always imperfect. Firms often protect their technological advances by keeping them secret for as long as they can. Even when patent protection is sought, there is a lag from the time of invention to the time the patent (or under European and Japanese procedures, its application) is published. And once a new technology is made public, it takes time for potential imitators to learn about it and decide whether it is worth copying. [. . .]

Second, free riding on an innovator's technical contribution is often far from free. An appreciable but varying fraction of the original R&D may have to be replicated. At one extreme in this respect are airliners. One can inspect a rival's design, but to build a similar aircraft, one must generate detailed engineering drawings for each part, program machine tools to produce the parts, build prototypes, and subject them to static and dynamic testing to ensure that unnoticed design flaws do not lead to catastrophe. Only the innovator's most basic conceptual work and wind tunnel testing can be circumvented. At the other extreme are new prescription drugs. To introduce a new drug to the U.S. market during the late 1980s entailed research, development, and testing costs of $50 to $100 million. Most of these costs were incurred discovering molecules with desirable therapeutic effects in humans and proving through extensive clinical testing that the substances were effective and safe. Once these formidable information-generating hurdles are surmounted, it typically costs only a few hundred thousand dollars for an able biochemist to develop production methods. Thus, if there is no patent (or regulatory) barrier, imitators can free ride on most of the innovator's investment.

14.2 Restrictive Trade Practices Act 1976, Schedule 3

[. . .]

Know-how about goods

3. This Act does not apply to an agreement between two persons (neither of whom is a trade association) for the exchange of information relating to the operation of processes of manufacture (whether patented or not) where:

(*a*) no other person is party to the agreement; and
(*b*) no such restrictions as are described in section 6(1) above are accepted or no such information provisions as are described in section 7(1) above are made under the agreement except in respect of the descriptions of goods to be produced by those processes or to which those processes are to be applied.

Know-how about services

8. This Act does not apply to an agreement between two persons (neither of whom is a services supply association) for the exchange of information relating to techniques or processes to be applied in the provision of designated services where:

(*a*) no other person is party to the agreement; and
(*b*) all such restrictions as are mentioned in section 11(1)(*b*) above which are accepted under the agreement relate exclusively to the form or manner in which services incorporating those techniques or processes are to be made available or supplied.

[. . .]

Trade marks

4. [. . .]

(1) This Act does not apply to an agreement made in accordance with regulations approved by the Secretary of State under section 37 of the Trade Marks Act 1938 (which makes provision as to certification trade marks) authorising the use of such a trade mark, being an agreement under which no such restrictions as are described in section 6(1) above are accepted or no such information provisions as are described in section 7(1) above are made other than restrictions or information provisions permitted by those regulations.

(2) This Act does not apply to an agreement:

(*a*) between the registered proprietor of a trade mark (other than a certification trade mark) or of a service mark and a person authorised by the agreement to use the mark subject to registration as a registered user under section 28 of the Trade Marks Act 1938 (which makes provision as to registered users); and
(*b*) under which no such restrictions as are described in section 6(1) or 11(2) are accepted or no such information provisions as are described in section 7(1) or 12(2) are made except in respect of:
   (i) the descriptions of goods bearing the mark which are to be produced or supplied; or
   (ii) the processes of manufacture to be applied to such goods or to goods to which the mark is to be applied; or
   (iii) the kinds of services in relation to which the mark is to be used which are to be made available or supplied; or
   (iv) the form or manner in which services in relation to which the mark is used are to be made available or supplied; or
   (v) the descriptions of goods which are to be produced or supplied in connection with the supply of services in relation to which the mark is to be used; or
   (vi) the process of manufacture to be applied to goods which are to be produced or supplied in connec-

tion with the supply of services in relation to which the mark is to be used.

Patents and registered designs

5. (1) Subject to subparagraphs (4) to (8) below, this Act does not apply:

(*a*) to a licence granted by a proprietor or a licensee of a patent or registered design, or by a person who has applied for a patent or for the registration of a design;
(*b*) to an assignment of a patent or registered design, or of the right to apply for a patent or for the registration of a design; or
(*c*) to an agreement for such a licence or assignment;

being a licence, assignment or agreement such as is described in subparagraph (2) or subparagraph (3) below.

(2) The licence, assignment or agreement referred to in subparagraph (1) above is in relation to Part II of this Act one under which no such restrictions as are described in section 6(1) above are accepted or no such information provisions as are described in section 7(1) above are made except in respect of:

(*a*) the invention to which the patent or application for a patent relates, or articles made by the use of that invention; or
(*b*) articles in respect of which the design is or is proposed to be registered and to which it is applied;

as the case may be.

(3) The licence, assignment or agreement referred to in subparagraph (1) above is in relation to Part III of this Act one under which:

(*a*) in the case of an order under section 11 above, no restrictions in respect of matters specified in the order for the purposes of subsection (1)(*b*) of that section are accepted except in respect of the invention to which the patent or application for a patent relates; or
(*b*) in the case of an order under section 12 above, no information provision with respect to matters specified in the order for the purposes of subsection (1)(*b*) of that section is made except in respect of that invention.

(4) No licence, assignment or agreement is by virtue of subparagraph (1) above precluded from being an agreement to which this Act applies if:

(*a*) it is a patent or design pooling agreement; or
(*b*) it is a licence, assignment or agreement granted or made in pursuance (directly or indirectly) of a patent or design pooling agreement.

(5) In this paragraph, subject to subparagraph (8) below, 'patent or design pooling agreement' means an agreement:

(*a*) to which the parties are or include at least three persons (in this and the following subparagraph the 'principal parties') each of whom has an interest in one or more patents or registered designs, and
(*b*) by which each of the principal parties agrees, in respect of patents or registered designs in which he has an interest, or in respect of patents or registered designs in which he has or may during the currency of the agreement acquire an interest, to grant such an interest as is mentioned in subparagraph (6) below.

(6) The grant referred to in subparagraph (5) above is:

(*a*) of an interest in one or more such patents or registered designs to one or more of the other principal parties, or to one or more of those parties and to other persons;
or
(*b*) of an interest in at least one such patent or registered design to a third person for the purpose of enabling that person to grant an interest in it to one or more of the other principal parties, or to one or more of those parties and to other persons;

and 'interest', in relation to a patent or registered design, means an interest as proprietor or licensee of the patent or registered design or an interest consisting of such rights as a person has by virtue of having applied for a patent or for the registration of a design or by virtue of having acquired the right to apply for a patent or for the registration of a design.

(7) For the purposes of subparagraphs (4) to (6) above, a licence, assignment or agreement:

(*a*) shall be taken to be granted or made directly in pursuance of a patent or design pooling agreement if it is granted or made in pursuance of provisions of that agreement such as are mentioned in subparagraph (6)(*a*); and
(*b*) shall be taken to be granted or made indirectly in pursuance of a patent or design pooling agreement if it is granted or made by a third person to whom an interest has been granted in pursuance of provisions of that agreement such as are mentioned in subparagraph (6)(*b*).

(8) In relation to any interest held by or granted to any two or more persons jointly, subparagraphs (5) and (6) apply as if those persons were one person by whom the interest is held or to whom it is granted, and accordingly those persons shall be treated for the purposes of those subparagraphs as together constituting one party.

(9) In this paragraph, references [. . .] to the registration of designs have effect only in relation to Part II.

Copyrights

5A (1) This Act does not apply to:

(*a*) a licence granted by the owner or a licensee of any copyright;
(*b*) an assignment of any copyright; or
(*c*) an agreement for such a licence or assignment;

being a licence, assignment or agreement such as is described in subparagraph (2) or subparagraph (3) below.

(2) The licence, assignment or agreement referred to in subparagraph (1) above is in relation to Part II of this Act one under which no such restrictions as are described in section 6(1) above are accepted or no such information provisions as are described in section 7(1) above are made except in respect of the work or other subject-matter in which the copyright subsists or will subsist.

(3) The licence, assignment or agreement referred to in subparagraph (1) above is in relation to Part III of this Act one under which:

(*a*) in the case of an order under section 11 above, no restrictions in respect of matters specified in the order for the purposes of subsection (1)(*b*) of that section are accepted except in respect of the work or other subject-matter in which the copyright subsists or will subsist; or
(*b*) in the case of an order under section 12 above, no information provision with respect to matters specified in the order for the purposes of subsection (1)(*b*) of that section is made except in respect of that work or other subject-matter.

[. . .]

Design Right

5B (1) This Act does not apply to:

(*a*) a licence granted by the owner or a licensee of any design right,
(*b*) an assignment of design right, or
(*c*) an agreement for such a licence or assignment,

if the licence, assignment or agreement is one under which no such restrictions as are described in section 6(1) above are accepted, or no such information provisions as are described in section 7(1) above are made, except in respect of articles made to the design; but subject to the following provisions.

(2) Subparagraph (1) does not exclude a licence, assignment or agreement which is a design pooling agreement or is granted or made (directly or indirectly) in pursuance of a design pooling agreement.

(3) In this paragraph a 'design pooling agreement' means an agreement:

(*a*) to which the parties are or include at least three persons (the 'principal parties') each of whom has an interest in one or more design rights, and
(*b*) by which each principal party agrees, in respect of design right in which he has, or may during the currency of the agreement acquire, an interest to grant an interest (directly or indirectly) to one or more of the other principal parties, or to one or more of those parties and to other persons.

(4) In this paragraph:
'assignment', in Scotland, means assignation; and 'interest' means an interest as owner or licensee of design right.

(5) This paragraph applies to an interest held by or granted to more than one person jointly as if they were one person.

(6) References in this paragraph to the granting of an interest to a person indirectly are to its being granted to a third person for the purpose of enabling him to make a grant to the person in question.

14.3 *Maize Seeds: L.C. Nungesser KG, and Kurt Eisele* v. *Commission of the European Communities*, Case 258/78 Court of Justice of the European Communities [1982] ECR 2015, [1983] 1 CMLR 278, [1983] FSR 309

By an application lodged at the Court Registry on 27 November 1978, the limited partnership L.C. Nungesser KG (hereinafter referred to as Nungesser) and Kurt Eisele, sole general partner and majority shareholder of that firm, both carrying on business in Darmstadt, brought an action under the second paragraph of Article 173 of the EEC Treaty for a declaration that the Commission's decision of 21 September 1978 relating to a proceeding under Article 85 of the EEC Treaty (IV/28.824 – breeders' rights – maize seed), notified to the applicants on 27 September 1978 and published in the Official Journal (1978, No. L 286, p. 23), is void.

[. . .]

The contested decision found that Article 85(1) of the EEC Treaty had been infringed as a result of the content and application of certain provisions of two contracts entered into between Mr Eisele and the Institut National de la Recherche Agronomique [National Institute for Agricultural Research, hereinafter referred to as INRA], Paris, in 1960 and 1965 concerning respectively the assignment, in respect of the territory of the Federal Republic of Germany, of plant breeders' rights over certain varieties of hybrid maize seeds developed by INRA and the granting of exclusive propagating and selling rights over those seeds for that territory. In addition, it found that the content and application of the settlement reached in 1973 between Mr Eisele and Louis David KG, of Meisenheim (Germany), to prevent that undertaking from importing and selling INRA seeds in the Federal Republic of Germany also constituted an infringement of Article 85(1) of the EEC Treaty (Article 1 of the decision).

The decision also rejected Mr Eisele's application for the exemption of the agreements under Article 85(3) (Article 2 of the decision).

[. . .]

THE APPLICATION OF ARTICLE 85 OF THE EEC TREATY TO EXCLUSIVE LICENCES

By this submission the applicants criticize the Commission for wrongly taking the view that an exclusive licence of breeders' rights must by its very nature be treated as an agreement prohibited by Article 85(1) of the Treaty. They submit that the Commission's opinion in that respect is unfounded in so far as the exclusive licence constitutes the sole means, as regards seeds which have been recently developed in a Member State and which have not yet penetrated the market of another Member State, of promoting competition between the new product and comparable products in that other Member State; indeed, no grower or trader would take the risk of launching the new product on a new market if he were not protected against direct competition from the holder of the breeders' rights and from his other licensees.

This contention is supported by the German and British Governments and by the Caisse de Gestion des Licenses Végétales. In particular, the two Governments claim that the general character of the reasons given for the contested decision is incompatible with the terms of Article 85 of the Treaty and conflicts with a sensible competition policy. The reasons given for the decision are said to be based on the ill-conceived premise that every exclusive licence of an industrial or commercial property right, whatever its nature, must be regarded as an agreement prohibited by Article 85(1) and that it is therefore for the Commission to judge whether, in a given case, the conditions for the grant of an exemption under Article 85(3) are satisfied [. . .].

[. . .] Article 1(*b*) of the [Commission's] decision [. . .] declares the exclusive nature of the licence granted by the 1965 contract to be contrary to Article 85(1) of the Treaty in so far as it imposes:

- An obligation upon INRA or those deriving rights through INRA to refrain from having the relevant seeds produced or sold by other licensees in Germany, and
- An obligation upon INRA or those deriving rights through INRA to refrain from producing or selling the relevant seeds in Germany themselves [. . .]
- An obligation upon INRA or those deriving rights through INRA to prevent third parties from exporting the relevant seeds to Germany without the licensee's authorization for use or sale there, and
- Mr Eisele's concurrent use of his exclusive contractual rights and his own breeder's rights to prevent all imports into Germany or exports to other Member States of the relevant seeds.

It should be observed that those two sets of considerations relate to two legal situations which are not necessarily identical. The first case concerns a so-called open exclusive licence or assignment and the exclusivity of the licence relates solely to the contractual relationship between the owner of the right and the licensee, whereby the owner merely undertakes not to grant other licences in respect of the same territory and not to compete himself with the licensee on that territory. On the other hand, the second case involves an exclusive licence or assignment with absolute territorial protection, under which the parties to the contract propose, as regards the products and the territory in question, to eliminate all competition from third parties, such as parallel importers or licensees for other territories.

That point having been clarified, it is necessary to examine whether, in the present case, the exclusive nature of the licence, in so far as it is an open licence, has the effect of preventing or distorting competition within the meaning of Article 85(1) of the Treaty.

In that respect the Government of the Federal Republic of Germany emphasized that the protection of agricultural innovations by means of breeders' rights constitutes a means of encouraging such innovations and the grant of exclusive rights for a limited period, is capable of providing a further incentive to innovative efforts. From that it infers that a total prohibition of every exclusive licence, even an open one, would cause the interest of undertakings in licences to fall away, which would be prejudicial to the dissemination of knowledge and techniques in the Community.

The exclusive licence which forms the

subject-matter of the contested decision concerns the cultivation and marketing of hybrid maize seeds which were developed by INRA after years of research and experimentation and were unknown to German farmers at the time when the co-operation between INRA and the applicants was taking shape. For that reason the concern shown by the interveners as regards the protection of new technology is justified.

In fact, in the case of a licence of breeders' rights over hybrid maize seeds newly developed in one Member State, an undertaking established in another Member State which was not certain that it would not encounter competition from other licensees for the territory granted to it, or from the owner of the right himself, might be deterred from accepting the risk of cultivating and marketing that product; such a result would be damaging to the dissemination of a new technology and would prejudice competition in the Community between the new product and similar existing products.

Having regard to the specific nature of the products in question, the Court concludes that, in a case such as the present, the grant of an open exclusive licence, that is to say a licence which does not affect the position of third parties such as parallel importers and licensees for other territories, is not in itself incompatible with Article 85(1) of the Treaty [. . .].

As regard to the position of third parties, the Commission in essence criticizes the parties to the contract for having extended the definition of exclusivity to importers who are not bound to the contract, in particular parallel importers [. . .]. The Court has consistently held (cf. Joined Cases 56 and 58/64 *Consten and Grundig* v. *Commission* [1966] ECR 299) that absolute territorial protection granted to a licensee in order to enable parallel imports to be controlled and prevented results in the artificial maintenance of separate national markets, contrary to the Treaty.

The Government of the United Kingdom advanced the view that a contract between two undertakings could not impede the freedom of importers to buy seeds in the country of the owner of the licensee rights with a view to exporting them to the country of the licensee since, according to previous decisions of the Court, a commercial or industrial property right cannot be invoked against the marketing of a product which has been lawfully placed in circulation on the market of another Member State by the owner of that right or with his consent. Therefore such a contract cannot be regarded as an agreement prohibited by Article 85(1) of the Treaty.

However, that view fails to take into account the fact that one of the powers of the Commission is to ensure, pursuant to Article 85 of the Treaty and the regulations adopted in implementation thereof, that agreements and concerted practices between undertaking do not have the object or the effect of restricting or distorting competition, and that that power of the Commission is not affected by the fact that persons or undertakings subject to such restrictions are in a position to rely upon the provisions of the Treaty relating to the free movement of goods in order to escape such restrictions.

See also the judgment of the European Court of Justice in *Louis Erauw-Jacquery Sprl* v. *La Hesbignonne Société Co-operative* 27/87 [1988] ECR 1919, [1988] 4 CMLR 576.

14.4 T. Frazer, '*Vorsprung durch Technik*: the Commission's policy on know-how agreements', 9 *Yearbook of European Law*, 1 (1990)

THE OBJECT AND EFFECT OF THE KNOW-HOW LICENCE REGULATION

The Commission has propounded a threefold objective underlying the block exemption for know-how licences. This is:

> to ensure that innovation is developed and spread as quickly and as widely as possible on the Community's large market, to ensure effective competition for technically new or improved products and permit their free movement *in so far as this is compatible with the first objective*, and to give firms the legal certainty to which they are entitled.

The term 'innovation', used here in its Schumpeterian sense, includes the development and marketing of a new product or process, rather than merely its invention. It has been suggested above that the Commission's clear indication that effective competition and free movement are to be subverted to the needs of innovation, is reflected in the provisions of the block exemption.

The effect of the grant of territorial exclusivity, sanctioned by the Know-How Licence Regulation, is to permit a virtual elimination of competition between licensees (and between the licensees and the licensor) in respect of a vast range of technology transfers. The Regulation will apply even where the absence of such competition is not balanced by the presence of vigorous competition between the licensor or licensees and firms with access to alternative know-how. Where highly innovative products are involved, the time lag in the development of substitute products will give the licensor and licensees an opportunity to exploit the prohibition on active and passive sales outside the licensed territories. Except in cases where the exclusive territory is the entire common market, there will inevitably be geographical restraints on the free movement of the products of new technology. Passive sales may be prevented for up to five years, and active extra-territorial sales for up to ten years. This may be contrasted with recent Commission decisions in *Jus-Rol and Rich Products* and *DDD Ltd and Delta Chemie*, where the know-how licences specifically provided for the possibility of parallel imports. In the latter decision the Commission expressly referred to the downward pressure on price provided by inter-brand competition and parallel imports.

In *Bussois and Interpane*, however, the Commission adopted the policy now enshrined in the Regulation. The exempted agreement provided for a prohibition on active and passive sales in the territories of other licensees. It was highly relevant that no other licensees had in fact been appointed and that the particular structure of the demand and supply markets meant that a prohibition on active sales only would have been ineffective. As mentioned above, this decision influenced the terms of the Regulation; the circumstances pertaining to that decision are reflected in the preamble to the Know-How Licence Regulation dealing with the five year exemption for prohibitions on passive sales. This states that

> '[t]he users of technologically new or improved products requiring major investment are often not final consumers but intermediate industries which are well informed about prices and alternative sources of supply of the products within the Community. Hence, protection against active competition only would not afford the parties and other licensees the security they needed . . .'.

The Commission's readiness – in both the Know-How Licence Regulation and the Patent Licence Regulation – to assume that a ban on passive sales is justified in relation to technology agreements is in sharp contrast to its earlier policy in relation to exclusive sales and purchase agreements.

The Patent Licence Regulation, on which the Know-How Licence Regulation is based, is regarded as the definitive statement on the place of industrial property agreements within EEC competition policy. Article 36 and 222 of the EEC Treaty remove all debate on the desirability of a patent system from the agenda of the EEC. The system of national patents, even though obstructive to the free movement of goods, must be tolerated by the Community. The grant of patents under the national systems is based on the assumption that the benefits of dynamic efficiency, achieved through the provision of the patent incentive, will outweigh the short term cost of providing the patentee with a monopoly right. But, as [. . .] others have argued, there is no reliable way of testing this cost/benefit hypothesis.

Nevertheless, on the basis that the existence of national intellectual property rights must be accepted, exclusive licences are permitted because either they are no more than a means whereby the licensor apportions its legitimate property rights or because they provide an incentive to licensees to invest in innovation. In that know-how is not recognized as having property protection, the property-based justification for exclusive know-how licences is not compelling. Indeed, the fact that know-how is secured through secrecy rather than property excludes the 'social bargain' justification associated with patent rights which takes account of the immediate dissemination of inventive technology as a counterweight to the temporary monopoly granted to the inventor.

Justification for the apparently anti-competitive provisions of exclusive know-how licences may therefore be sought by reference to the incentive argument. This argument is used as the basis both for the negative clearance of exclusive intellectual property licences and for their exemption under Article 85(3). The incentive argument was used as the basis of the exemption of a pure know-how licence in *Jus-Rol and Rich Products*. In addition, the Commission held that the effect of restricting the licensee to the exclusive territory was to oblige it to 'focus its production and sales efforts in the [territory] and to concentrate on improving the quality of the products manufactured and increasing the quantity produced'. A similar statement was included in the *DDD and Delta Chemie* decision. In neither case, however, did the Commission explain why the territorial limit on the manufacturing licence would necessarily lead to improvement in quality and quantity; the licensee-incentive supposition is therefore the stronger basis for the exemptions. The rule in *Maize Seeds* did not apply to either of these licences. In *Jus-Rol and Rich Products*, the product could be produced by means of alternative know-how, even though that know-how was not 'easily accessible' and in *DDD and Delta Chemie* the licensee had been marketing the product under an exclusive distribution licence for two years prior to the grant of the know-how licence. In *Bussois and Interpane*, the rule was not available because the licence provided for a ban on active and passive sales, and could not therefore be described as 'open'.

The basis of the incentive argument is that firms will be willing to invest in invention and innovation only if protected from competition from firms with access to the same know-how. The assumption is made that such protection will lead to greater competition with firms with access to alternative know-how as firms struggle constantly to compete through technology. The problem with such an assertion is that, although attractive, it is not possible to prove its accuracy in all cases. It is not possible to say whether firms will be willing to take the risks of innovation without territorial protection, or whether licensors will be willing to diffuse information in the absence of the considerable protection afforded to them by the Regulation. Further, it may not be the case that licensing is used as a vehicle for competition through technology. It may, rather, be used as a means of concentrating the market for innovation and thereby chilling competition.

The assertion that territorial protection is essential to the willingness to take risks takes no account of other incentives to risk-taking. Comparative advantages in terms of features such as management and production talent, learning effects from previous projects, geographical location, production capacity, access to cheap inputs, marketing skills, and brand loyalty will be taken into account by a firm when making investment decisions. Even in the absence of territorial protection, therefore, a firm may use its comparative advantages to innovate more successfully than other firms with access to the same know-how. In such circumstances, that firm will not restrict its decision on the purchase of know-how simply to the question of exclusivity. Indeed, the decision on whether to purchase know-how will not only involve a consideration of the benefits of the purchase, but will also take account of the disadvantages of failing to acquire the know-how. The threat of losing market share through a failure to innovate will be a powerful incentive to firms to acquire know-how, either by in-house research and development, or through its purchase by way of licence. The choice open to a potential licensee in a dynamic sector will not be 'invest on the basis of an exclusive territory or do not invest at all', but will be 'invest in technology on the best terms available or lose market share'. Indeed, the assertion of the Economic and Social Committee, quoted above, that the acquisition of know-how is the 'most economical – and often the sole – way of keeping abreast of technical progress' underlines the idea that it is essential for firms to acquire know-how to survive in dynamic markets. Licensees may prefer to have exclusive territories for extended periods, but it is not possible to say that such protection is a necessary precondition to the diffusion of technology.

CONCLUSION

The purpose of the regime protected by the Patent Licence and Know-How Licence Regulations is to provide an hospital environment for innovation so that Community firms can compete effectively on *world* markets, an objective which currently enjoys higher status than the market-integrating objective of EEC competition policy. The relationship between competition and technology policies was clearly expressed by the Commission in its analysis of the economic effects of the completion of the internal market:

> The relationship between competition and innovation is not linear and indeed there exists an optimum level of competition beyond which competition has an adverse effect on innovation because of the difficulty of allocating gains and the greater risks which obtain in highly competitive markets. The optimum market structure from the standpoint of innovation ought rather to promote strategic rivalry between a limited number of firms.

There is a subtle but important change of emphasis in this statement, compared to an earlier Commission statement on the place of technology in competition policy. In the introduction to its *Fifteenth Report on Competition Policy*, the Commission looked forward to the creation of a 'technology Community'. The key to this was seen to be innovative competition, and hence a system which encouraged innovation. The Commission then stated:

> For this purpose, on the one hand, cooperation between enterprises needs to be facilitated and the fruits of innovation should be given a certain degree of protection. On the other hand, a satisfactory level of competition must be maintained between innovators . . . Only effective competition can ensure that innovation does not degenerate into monopolistic rigidity, but leads to dynamic economic activity and growth.

This statement emphasized the importance of effective competition to the significance of innovation as a benefit to the public interest. The later statement, however, predicts the necessity of structural changes to safeguard for innovators the (supracompetitive) returns on innovation.

The permissive attitude of the Commission towards exclusive know-how licences, revealed in the later statement, has its basis in industrial policy rather than competition policy. Under such industrial policy Community undertakings are able to use exclusive know-how licences to concentrate the markets for innovative technology. This will, it is assumed, reduce competition to the level optimal to the successful introduction and diffusion of technology in the Community. The consequent improvement in production and marketing efficiency will permit Community firms to gain a greater share of world markets. Meanwhile, the Commission places its faith in a view of oligopoly in which 'a strategic rivalry' will emerge 'between a limited number of firms'. It is to be hoped that such a view will accurately reflect commercial practices. An alternative view is that oligopoly leads not to strategic rivalry but to tacit co-ordination akin to shared monopoly – the 'monopolistic rigidity' of the Commission's earlier statement.

The circumstances concerning the *Tetra-Pak* decision are instructive. This decision concerned an exclusive patent licence, falling wholly within the terms of the Patent Licence Regulation, which was found to have an exclusionary rather than a competitive effect. The licensee was dominant in the market for the product which was the subject of the technology transfer. The incentive argument, pleaded in favour of the exclusive grant, was found to be insufficient to overcome the disadvantages created by the loss of competition. Potential competitors were prevented from using the technology to gain access to the market, thereby eliminating inter-brand competition. Intra-brand competition was eliminated because of the licensor's inability to appoint other licensees or to produce the product. The Commission therefore proposed to withdraw the benefit of the block exemption on the basis that there was 'a possibility that the concentration of market power in [the licensee's] hands will be detrimental to the improvement of production and distribution and may hinder promotion of technical and economic progress: conditions which normally thrive best in a competitive environment'.

It is encouraging to see that the Commission is prepared to act where the circumstances do not justify an exemption. However, *TetraPak* illustrates the danger that technology transfers may be used as exclusionary rather than competitive vehicles. The generous nature of the Know-How Licence Regulation enhances such danger. It is not realistic to expect the Commission to be able to monitor such exclusionary circumstances, or to have the resources to act in all such cases. Indeed, where the effect of technology transfers is to concentrate the market, it is not clear whether the Treaty gives the Commission the power to control the emerging oligopolies. The Commission has shown itself to be ready to assess the behaviour of tight oligopolies and shared dominance under Article 86. The European Court of Justice has not yet demonstrated an equal enthusiasm. The ability of competition law to deal with the effects of structural changes encouraged in the name of technology is therefore far from clear.

14.5 Commission Regulation (EEC) No. 556/89 on the application of Article 85(3) of the Treaty to certain categories of know-how licensing agreements OJ 1989 No. L61/1

THE COMMISSION OF THE EUROPEAN COMMUNITIES,

[. . .]

Whereas:

(1) Regulation No. 19/65/EEC empowers the Commission to apply Article 85(3) of the Treaty by Regulation to certain categories of bilateral agreements and concerted practices falling within the scope of Article 85(1) which include restrictions imposed in relation to the acquisition or use of industrial property rights, in particular patents, utility models, design or trade marks, or to the rights arising out of contracts for assignment of, or the right to use, a method of manufacture or knowledge relating to the use or application of industrial processes.

The increasing economic importance of non-patented technical information (e.g. descriptions of manufacturing processes, recipes, formulae, designs or drawings), commonly termed 'know-how', the large number of agreements currently being concluded by undertakings including public research facilities solely for the exploitation of such information (so-called 'pure' know-how licensing agreements) and the fact that the transfer of know-how is, in practice, frequently irreversible make it necessary to provide greater legal certainty with regard to the status of such agreements under the competition rules, thus encouraging the dissemination of technical knowledge in the Community. In the light of experience acquired so far, it is possible to define a category of such know-how licensing agreements covering all or part of the common market which are capable of falling within the scope of Article 85(1) but which can normally be regarded as satisfying the conditions laid down in Article 85(3), where the licensed know-how is secret, substantial and identified in any appropriate form ('the know-how'). These definitional requirements are only intended to ensure that the communication of the know-how provides a valid justification for the application of the present Regulation and in particular for the exemption of obligations which are restrictive of competition.

A list of definitions for the purposes of this Regulation is set out in Article 1.

(2) As well as pure know-how agreements, mixed know-how and patent licensing agreements play an increasingly important role in the transfer of technology. It is therefore appropriate to include within the scope of this Regulation mixed agreements which are not exempted by Commission Regulation (EEC) No. 2349/84 (Article 1, 2 or 4) and in particular the following:

- mixed agreements in which the licensed patents are not necessary for the achievement of the objects of the licensed technology containing both patented and non-patented elements; this may be the case where such patents do not afford effective protection against the exploitation of the technology by third parties;
- mixed agreements which, regardless of whether or not the licensed patents are necessary, for the achievement of the objects of the licensed technology, contain obligations which restrict the exploitation of the relevant technology by the licensor or the licensee in Member States without patent protection, in so far and as long as such obligations are based in whole or in part on the exploitation of the licensed know-how and fulfil the other conditions set out in this Regulation.

It is also appropriate to extend the scope of this Regulation to pure or mixed agreements containing ancillary provisions relating to trade marks and other intellectual property rights where there are no obligations restrictive of competition other than those also attached to the know-how and exempted under the present Regulation.

However, such agreements, too, can only be regarded as fulfilling the conditions of Article 85(3) for the purpose of this Regulation where the licensed technical knowledge is secret, substantial and identified.

(3) The provisions of the present Regulation are not applicable to agreements covered by Regulation (EEC) No. 2349/84 on patent licensing agreements.

(4) Where such pure or mixed know-how licensing agreements contain not only obligations relating to territories within the common market but also obligations relating to non-member countries, the presence of the latter does not prevent the present Regulation from applying to the obligations relating to territories within the common market.

However, where know-how licensing agreements for non-member countries or for territories which extend beyond the frontiers of the Community have effects within the common market which may fall within the scope of Article 85(1), such agreements should be covered by the Regulation to the same extent as would agreements for territories within the common market.

(5) It is not appropriate to include within the scope of the Regulation agreements solely for the purpose of sale, except where the licensor undertakes for a preliminary period before the licensee himself commences production using the licensed technology to supply the contract products for sale by the licensee. Also excluded from the scope of the Regulation are agreements relating to marketing know-how communicated in the context of franchising arrangements or to know-how agreements entered into in connection with arrangements such as joint ventures or patent pools and other arrangements in which the licensing of the know-how occurs in exchange for other licences not related to improvements to or new applications of that know-how, as such agreements pose different problems which cannot at present be dealt with in one Regulation (Article 5).

(6) Exclusive licensing agreements, i.e. agreements in which the licensor undertakes not to exploit the licensed technology in the licensed territory himself or to grant further licences there, may not be in themselves incompatible with Article 85(1) where they are concerned with the introduction and protection of a new technology in the licensed territory, by reason of the scale of the research which has been undertaken and of the increase in the level of competition, in particular interbrand competition, and in the competitiveness of the undertakings concerned resulting from the dissemination of innovation within the Community.

In so far as agreements of this kind fall in other circumstances within the scope of Article 85(1), it is appropriate to include them in Article 1, in order that they may also benefit from the exemption.

(7) Both these and the other obligations listed in Article 1 encourage the transfer of technology and thus generally contribute to improving the production of goods and to promoting technical progress, by increasing the number of production facilities and the quality of goods produced in the common market and expanding the possibilities of further development of the licensed technology. This is true, in particular, of an obligation on the licensee to use the licensed product only in the manufacture of its own products, since it gives the licensor an incentive to disseminate the technology in various applications while reserving the separate sale of the licensed product to himself or other licensees. It is also true of obligations on the licensor and on the licensee to refrain not only from active but also from passive competition, in the licensed territory, in the case of the licensor, and in the territories reserved for the licensor or other licensees in the case of the licensee. The users of technologically new or improved products requiring major investment are often not final consumers but intermediate industries which are well informed about prices and alternative sources of supply of the products within the Com-

munity. Hence, protection against active competition only would not afford the parties and other licensees the security they needed, especially during the initial period of exploitation of the licensed technology when they would be investing in tooling up and developing a market for the product and in effect increasing demand.

In view of the difficulty of determining the point at which know-how can be said to be no longer secret, and the frequent licensing of a continuous stream of know-how, especially where technology in the industry is rapidly evolving, it is appropriate to limit to a fixed number of years the periods of territorial protection, of the licensor and the licensee from one another, and as between licensees, which are automatically covered by the exemption. Since, as distinguished from patent licences, know-how licences are frequently negotiated after the goods or services incorporating the licensed technology have proved successful on the market, it is appropriate to take for each licensed territory the date of signature of the first licence agreement entered into for that territory by the licensor in respect of the same technology as the starting point for the permitted periods of territorial protection of the licensor and licensee from one another. As to the protection of a licensee from manufacture, use, active or passive sales by other licensees the starting point should be the date of signature of the first licence agreement entered into by the licensor within the EEC. The exemption of the territorial protection shall apply for the whole duration of such allowed periods as long as the know-how remains secret and substantial, irrespective of when the Member States in question joined the Community and provided that each of the licensees, the restricted as well as the protected one, manufactures the licensed product himself or has it manufactured.

Exemption under Article 85(3) of longer periods of territorial protection, in particular to protect expensive and risky investment or where the parties were not already competitors before the grant of the licence, can only be granted by individual decision. On the other hand, parties are free to extend the term of their agreement to exploit any subsequent improvements and to provide for the payment of additional royalties. However, in such cases, further periods of territorial protection, starting from the date of licensing of the improvements in the EEC, may be allowed only by individual decision, in particular where the improvements to or new applications of the licensed technology are substantial and secret and not of significantly less importance than the technology initially granted or require new expensive and risky investment.

(8) However, it is appropriate in cases where the same technology is protected in some Member States by necessary patents within the meaning of recital 9 of Regulation (EEC) No. 2349/84 to provide with respect to those Member States an exemption under this Regulation for the territorial protection of the licensor and licensee from one another and as between licensees against manufacture, use and active sales in each other's territory for the full life of the patents existing in such Member States.

(9) The obligations listed in Article 1 also generally fulfil the other conditions for the application of Article 85(3). Consumers will as a rule be allowed a fair share of the benefit resulting from the improvement in the supply of goods on the market. Nor do the obligations impose restrictions which are not indispensable to the attainment of the abovementioned objectives. Finally, competition at the distribution stage is safeguarded by the possibility of parallel imports, which may not be hindered by the parties in any circumstances. The exclusivity obligations covered by the Regulation thus do not normally entail the possibility of eliminating competition in respect of a substantial part of the products in question. This also applies in the case of agreements which grant exclusive licences for a territory covering the whole of the common market where there is the possibility of parallel imports from third countries, or where there are other competing technologies on the market, since then the territorial exclusivity may lead to greater market

integration and stimulate Community-wide interbrand competition.

(10) It is desirable to list in the Regulation a number of obligations that are commonly found in know-how licensing agreements but are normally not restrictive of competition and to provide that in the event that because of the particular economic or legal circumstances they should fall within Article 85(1), they also would be covered by the exemption. This list, in Article 2, is not exhaustive.

(11) The Regulation must also specify what restrictions or provisions may not be included in know-how licensing agreements if these are to benefit from the block exemption. The restrictions, which are listed in Article 3, may fall under the prohibition of Article 85(1), but in their case there can be no general presumption that they will lead to the positive effects required by Article 85(3), as would be necessary for the granting of a block exemption, and consequently an exemption can be granted only on an individual basis.

(12) Agreements which are not automatically covered by the exemption because they contain provisions that are not expressly exempted by the Regulation and not expressly excluded from exemption, including those listed in Article 4(2) of the Regulation, may nonetheless generally be presumed to be eligible for application of the block exemption. It will be possible for the Commission rapidly to establish whether this is the case for a particular agreement. Such agreements should therefore be deemed to be covered by the exemption provided for in this Regulation where they are notified to the Commission and the Commission does not oppose the application of the exemption within a specified period of time.

(13) If individual agreements exempted by this Regulation nevertheless have effects which are incompatible with Article 85(3), the Commission may withdraw the benefit of the block exemption (Article 7).

(14) The list in Article 2 includes among others obligations on the licensee to cease using the licensed know-how after the termination of the agreement ('post-term use ban') (Article 2(1)(3)) and to make improvements available to the licensor (grant-back clause) (Article 2(1)(4)). A post-term use ban may be regarded as a normal feature of the licensing of know-how as otherwise the licensor would be forced to transfer his know-how in perpetuity and this could inhibit the transfer of technology. Moreover, undertakings by the licensee to grant back to the licensor a licence for improvements to the licensed know-how and/or patents are generally not restrictive of competition if the licensee is entitled by the contract to share in future experience and inventions made by the licensor and the licensee retains the right to disclose experience acquired or grant licences to third parties where to do so would not disclose the licensor's know-how.

On the other hand, a restrictive effect on competition arises where the agreement contains both a post-term use ban and an obligation on the licensee to make his improvements to the know-how available to the licensor, even on a non-exclusive and reciprocal basis, and to allow the licensor to continue using them even after the expiry of the agreement. This is so because in such a case the licensee has no possibility of inducing the licensor to authorize him to continue exploiting the originally licensed know-how, the hence the licensee's own improvements as well, after the expiry of the agreement.

(15) The list in Article 2 also includes an obligation on the licensee to keep paying royalties until the end of the agreement independently of whether or not the licensed know-how has entered into the public domain through the action of third parties (Article 2(1)(7)). As a rule, parties do not need to be protected against the foreseeable financial consequences of an agreement freely entered into and should therefore not be restricted in their choice of the appropriate means of financing the technology transfer. This applies especially where know-how is concerned since here there can be no question of an abuse of a legal monopoly and, under the legal systems of the Member States, the licensee may have a remedy in an action under the

applicable national law. Furthermore, provisions for the payment of royalties in return for the grant of a whole package of technology throughout an agreed reasonable period independently of whether or not the know-how has entered into the public domain, are generally in the interest of the licensee in that they prevent the licensor demanding a high initial payment up front with a view to diminishing his financial exposure in the event of premature disclosure. Parties should be free, in order to facilitate payment by the licensee, to spread the royalty payments for the use of the licensed technology over a period extending beyond the entry of the know-how into the public domain. Moreover, continuous payments should be allowed throughout the term of the agreement in cases where both parties are fully aware that the first sale of the product will necessarily disclose the know-how. Nevertheless, the Commission may, where it was clear from the circumstances that the licensee would have been able and willing to develop the know-how himself in a short period of time, in comparison with which the period of continuing payments is excessively long, withdraw the benefit of the exemption under Article 7 of this Regulation.

Finally, the use of methods of royalties calculation which are unrelated to the exploitation of the licensed technology or the charging of royalties on products whose manufacture at no stage includes the use of any of the licensed patents or secret techniques would render the agreement ineligible for the block exemption (Article 3(5)). The licensee should also be freed from his obligation to pay royalties, where the know-how becomes publicly known through the action of the licensor. However, the mere sale of the product by the licensor or an undertaking connected with him does not constitute such an action (Article 2(1)(7) and Article 3(5)).

(16) An obligation on the licensee to restrict his exploitation of the licensed technology to one or more technical fields of application ('fields of use') or to one or more product markets is also not caught by Article 85(1) (Article 2(1)8)). This obligation is not restrictive of competition since the licensor can be regarded as having the right to transfer the know-how only for a limited purpose. Such a restriction must however not constitute a disguised means of customer sharing.

(17) Restrictions which give the licensor an unjustified competitive advantage, such as an obligation on the licensee to accept quality specifications, other licences or goods and services that the licensee does not want from the licensor, prevent the block exemption from being applicable. However, this does not apply where it can be shown that the licensee wanted such specifications, licences, goods or services for reasons of his own convenience (Article 3(3)).

(18) Restrictions whereby the parties share customers within the same technological field of use or the same product market, either by an actual prohibition on supplying certain classes of customer or an obligation with an equivalent effect, would also render the agreement ineligible for the block exemption (Article 3(6)).

This does not apply to cases where the know-how licence is granted in order to provide a single customer with a second source of supply. In such a case, a prohibition on the licensee from supplying persons other than the customer concerned may be indispensable for the grant of a licence to the second supplier since the purpose of the transaction is not to create an independent supplier in the market. The same applies to limitations on the quantities the licensee may supply to the customer concerned. It is also reasonable to assume that such restrictions contribute to improving the production of goods and to promoting technical progress by furthering the dissemination of technology. However, given the present state of experience of the Commission with respect to such clauses and the risk in particular that they might deprive the second supplier of the possibility of developing his own business in the fields covered by the agreement it is appropriate to make such clauses subject to the opposition procedure (Article 4(2)).

(19) Besides the clauses already mentioned, the list of restrictions precluding application of the block exemption in Article 3 also includes restrictions regarding the selling prices of the licensed product or the quantities to be manufactured or sold, since they limit the extent to which the licensee can exploit the licensed technology and particularly since quantity restrictions may have the same effect as export bans (Article 3(7) and (8)). This does not apply where a licence is granted for use of the technology in specific production facilities and where both a specific know-how is communicated for the setting-up, operation and maintenance of these facilities and the licensee is allowed to increase the capacity of the facilities or to set up further facilities for its own use on normal commercial terms. On the other hand, the licensee may lawfully be prevented from using the licensor's specific know-how to set up facilities for third parties, since the purpose of the agreement is not to permit the licensee to give other producers access to the licensor's know-how while it remains secret (Article 2(1)(12)).

(20) To protect both the licensor and the licensee from being tied into agreements whose duration may be automatically extended beyond their initial term as freely determined by the parties, through a continuous stream of improvements communicated by the licensor, it is appropriate to exclude agreements with such a clause from the block exemption (Article 3(10)). However, the parties are free at any time to extend their contractual relationship by entering into new agreements concerning new improvements.

(21) The Regulation should apply with retroactive effect to know-how licensing agreements in existence when the Regulation comes into force where such agreements already fulfil the conditions for application of the Regulation or are modified to do so (Articles 8 to 10). Under Article 4(3) of Regulation No. 19/65/EEC, the benefit of these provisions may not be claimed in actions pending at the date of entry into force of this Regulation, nor may it be relied on as grounds for claims for damages against third parties.

(22) Agreements which come within the terms of Articles 1 and 2 and which have neither the object nor the effect of restricting competition in any other way need no longer be notified. Nevertheless, undertakings will still have the right to apply in individual cases for negative clearance under Article 2 of Council Regulation No. 17 or for exemption under Article 85(3),

HAS ADOPTED THIS REGULATION:

Article 1

(1) Pursuant to Article 85(3) of the Treaty and subject to the provisions of this Regulation, it is hereby declared that Article 85(1) of the Treaty shall not apply to pure know-how licensing agreements and to mixed know-how and patent licensing agreements not exempted by Regulation (EEC) No. 2349/84, including those agreements containing ancillary provisions relating to trademarks or other intellectual property rights, to which only two undertakings are party and which include one or more of the following obligations:

1. an obligation on the licensor not to license other undertakings to exploit the licensed technology in the licensed territory;
2. an obligation on the licensor not to exploit the licensed technology in the licensed territory himself;
3. an obligation on the licensee not to exploit the licensed technology in territories within the common market which are reserved for the licensor;
4. an obligation on the licensee not to manufacture or use the licensed product, or use the licensed process, in territories within the common market which are licensed to other licensees;
5. an obligation on the licensee not to pursue an active policy of putting the licensed product on the market in the territories within the common market which are licensed to other licensees, and in particular not to engage in advertising specifically aimed at those territories or to establish any branch or maintain any distribution depot there;

6. an obligation on the licensee not to put the licensed product on the market in the territories licensed to other licensees within the common market;
7. an obligation on the licensee to use only the licensor's trademark or the get-up determined by the licensor to distinguish the licensed product during the term of the agreement, provided that the licensee is not prevented from identifying himself as the manufacturer of the licensed products;
8. an obligation on the licensee to limit his production of the licensed product to the quantities he requires in manufacturing his own products and to sell the licensed product only as an integral part of or a replacement part for his own products or otherwise in connection with the sale of his own products, provided that such quantities are freely determined by the licensee.

(2) The exemption provided for the obligations referred to in paragraph 1(1)(2) and (3) shall extend for a period not exceeding for each licensed territory within the EEC 10 years from the date of signature of the first licence agreement entered into by the licensor for that territory in respect of the same technology.

The exemption provided for the obligations referred to in paragraph 1(4) and (5) shall extend for a period not exceeding 10 years from the date of signature of the first licence agreement entered into by the licensor within the EEC in respect of the same technology.

The exemption provided for the obligation referred to in paragraph 1(6) shall extend for a period not exceeding five years from the date of the signature of the first licence agreement entered into by the licensor within the EEC in respect of the same technology.

(3) The exemption provided for in paragraph 1 shall apply only where the parties have identified in any appropriate form the initial know-how and any subsequent improvements to it, which become available to the parties and are communicated to the other party pursuant to the terms of the agreement and for the purpose thereof, and only for as long as the know-how remains secret and substantial.

(4) In so far as the obligations referred to in paragraph 1(1) to (5) concern territories including Member States in which the same technology is protected by necessary patents, the exemption provided for in paragraph 1 shall extend for those Member States as long as the licensed product or process is protected in those Member States by such patents, where the duration of such protection exceeds the periods specified in paragraph 2.

(5) The exemption of restrictions on putting the licensed product on the market resulting from the obligations referred to in paragraph 1(2), (3), (5) and (6) shall apply only if the licensee manufactures or proposes to manufacture the licensed product himself or has it manufactured by a connected undertaking or by a subcontractor.

(6) The exemption provided for in paragraph 1 shall also apply where in a particular agreement the parties undertake obligations of the types referred to in that paragraph but with a more limited scope than is permitted by the paragraph.

(7) For the purposes of the present Regulation the following terms shall have the following meanings:

1. 'know-how' means a body of technical information that is secret, substantial and identified in any appropriate form;
2. the term 'secret' means that the know-how package as a body or in the precise configuration and assembly of its components is not generally known or easily accessible, so that part of its value consists in the lead-time the licensee gains when it is communicated to him; it is not limited to the narrow sense that each individual component of the know-how should be totally unknown or unobtainable outside the licensor's business;
3. the term 'substantial' means that the know-how includes information which is of importance for the whole or a significant part of (i) a manufacturing process of (ii) a product or service, or (iii) for the development thereof and excludes information which is trivial.

Such know-how must thus be useful, i.e. can reasonably be expected at the date of conclusion of the agreement to be capable of improving the competitive position of the licensee, for example by helping him to enter a new market or giving him an advantage in competition with other manufacturers or providers of services who do not have access to the licensed secret know-how or other comparable secret know-how;

4. the term 'identified' means that the know-how is described or recorded in such a manner as to make it possible to verify that it fulfils the criteria of secrecy and substantiality and to ensure that the licensee is not unduly restricted in his exploitation of his own technology. To be identified the know-how can either be set out in the licence agreement or in a separate document or recorded in any other appropriate form at the latest when the know-how is transferred or shortly thereafter, provided that the separate document or other record can be made available if the need arises;
5. 'pure know-how licensing agreements' are agreements whereby one undertaking, the licensor, agrees to communicate the know-how, with or without an obligation to disclose any subsequent improvements, to another undertaking, the licensee, for exploitation in the licensed territory;
6. 'mixed know-how and patent licensing agreements' are agreements not exempted by Regulation (EEC) No. 2349/84 under which a technology containing both non-patented elements and elements that are patented in one or more Member States is licensed;
7. the terms 'licensed know-how' or 'licensed technology' mean the initial and any subsequent know-how communicated directly or indirectly by the licensor to a licensee by means of pure or mixed know-how and patent licensing agreements; however, in the case of mixed know-how and patent licensing agreements the term 'licensed technology' also includes any patents for which a licence is granted besides the communication of the know-how;
8. the term 'the same technology' means the technology as licensed to the first licensee and enhanced by any improvements made thereto subsequently, irrespective of whether and to what extent such improvements are exploited by the parties or the other licensees and irrespective of whether the technology is protected by necessary patents in any Member States;
9. 'the licensed products' are goods or services the production or provision of which requires the use of the licensed technology;
10. the term 'exploitation' refers to any use of the licensed technology in particular in the production, active or passive sales in a territory even if not coupled with manufacture in that territory, or leasing of the licensed products;
11. 'the licensed territory' is the territory covering all or at least part of the common market where the licensee is entitled to exploit the licensed technology;
12. 'territory reserved for the licensor' means territories in which the licensor has not granted any licences and which he has expressly reserved for himself;
13. 'connected undertakings' means:
    (*a*) undertakings in which a party to the agreement, directly or indirectly;
    - owns more than half the capital or business assets, or
    - has the power to exercise more than half the voting rights, or
    - has the power to appoint more than half the members of the supervisory board, board of directors or bodies legally representing the undertaking, or
    - has the right to manage the affairs of the undertaking;

    (*b*) undertakings which directly or indirectly have in or over a party to the agreement the rights or powers listed in (*a*);
    (*c*) undertakings in which an undertak-

ing referred to in (*b*) directly or indirectly has the rights or powers listed in (*a*);

(*d*) undertakings in which the parties to the agreement or undertakings connected with them jointly have the rights or powers listed in (*a*): such jointly controlled undertakings are considered to be connected with each of the parties to the agreement.

Article 2

(1) Article 1 shall apply notwithstanding the presence in particular of any of the following obligations, which are generally not restrictive of competition:

1. an obligation on the licensee not to divulge the know-how communicated by the licensor; the licensee may be held to this obligation after the agreement has expired;
2. an obligation on the licensee not to grant sub-licences or assign the licence;
3. an obligation on the licensee not to exploit the licensed know-how after termination of the agreement in so far and as long as the know-how is still secret;
4. an obligation on the licensee to communicate to the licensor any experience gained in exploiting the licensed technology and to grant him a non-exclusive licence in respect of improvements to or new applications of that technology, provided that:
   (*a*) the licensee is not prevented during or after the term of the agreement from freely using his own improvements, in so far as these are severable from the licensor's know-how, or licensing them to third parties where licensing to third parties does not disclose the know-how communicated by the licensor that is still secret; this is without prejudice to an obligation on the licensee to seek the licensor's prior approval to such licensing provided that approval may not be withheld unless there are objectively justifiable reasons to believe that licensing improvements to third parties will disclose the licensor's know-how, and
   (*b*) the licensor has accepted an obligation, whether exclusive or not, to communicate his own improvements to the licensee and his right to use the licensee's improvements which are not severable from the licensed know-how does not extend beyond the date on which the licensee's right to exploit the licensor's know-how comes to an end, except for termination of the agreement for breach by the licensee; this is without prejudice to an obligation on the licensee to give the licensor the option to continue to use the improvements after that date, if at the same time he relinquishes the post-term use ban or agrees, after having had an opportunity to examine the licensee's improvements, to pay appropriate royalties for their use;
5. an obligation on the licensee to observe minimum quality specifications for the licensed product or to procure goods or services from the licensor or from an undertaking designated by the licensor, in so far as such quality specifications, products or services are necessary for:
   (*a*) a technically satisfactory exploitation of the licensed technology, or
   (*b*) for ensuring that the production of the licensee conforms to the quality standards that are respected by the licensor and other licensees,

   and to allow the licensor to carry out related checks;
6. obligations:
   (*a*) to inform the licensor of misappropriation of the know-how or of infringements of the licensed patents, or
   (*b*) to take or to assist the licensor in taking legal action against such misappropriation or infringements,

   provided that these obligations are without prejudice to the licensee's right to challenge the validity of the licensed patents or to contest the secrecy of the licensed know-how except where he himself has in some way contributed to its disclosure;

7. an obligation on the licensee, in the event of the know-how becoming publicly known other than by action of the licensor, to continue paying until the end of the agreement the royalties in the amounts, for the periods and according to the methods freely determined by the parties, without prejudice to the payment of any additional damages in the event of the know-how becoming publicly known by the action of the licensee in breach of the agreement;
8. an obligation on the licensee to restrict his exploitation of the licensed technology to one or more technical fields of application covered by the licensed technology or to one or more product markets;
9. an obligation on the licensee to pay a minimum royalty or to produce a minimum quantity of the licensed product or to carry out a minimum number of operations exploiting the licensed technology;
10. an obligation on the licensor to grant the licensee any more favourable terms that the licensor may grant to another undertaking after the agreement is entered into;
11. an obligation on the licensee to mark the licensed product with the licensor's name;
12. an obligation on the licensee not to use the licensor's know-how to construct facilities for third parties; this is without prejudice to the right of the licensee to increase the capacity of its facilities or to set up additional facilities for its own use on normal commercial terms, including the payment of additional royalties.

(2) In the event that, because of particular circumstances, the obligations referred to in paragraph 1 fall within the scope of Article 85(1), they shall also be exempted even if they are not accompanied by any of the obligations exempted by Article 1.

(3) The exemption provided for in paragraph 2 shall also apply where in an agreement the parties undertake obligations of the types referred to in paragraph 1 but with a more limited scope than is permitted by the paragraph.

Article 3

Articles 1 and 2(2) shall not apply where:

1. the licensee is prevented from continuing to use the licensed know-how after the termination of the agreement where the know-how has meanwhile become publicly known, other than by the action of the licensee in breach of the agreement;
2. the licensee is obliged either:
   (*a*) to assign in whole or in part to the licensor rights to improvements to or new applications of the licensed technology;
   (*b*) to grant the licensor an exclusive licence for improvements to or new applications of the licensed technology which would prevent the licensee during the currency of the agreement and/or thereafter from using his own improvements in so far as these are severable from the licensor's know-how, of from licensing them to third parties, where such licensing would not disclose the licensor's know-how that is still secret; or
   (*c*) in the case of an agreement which also includes a post-term use ban, to grant back to the licensor, even on a non-exclusive and reciprocal basis, licenses for improvements which are not severable from the licensor's know-how, if the licensor's right to use the improvements is of a longer duration than the licensee's right to use the licensor's know-how, except for termination of the agreement for breach by the licensee;
3. the licensee is obliged at the time the agreement is entered into to accept quality specifications or further licences or to procure goods or services which

he does not want, unless such licences, quality specifications, goods or services are necessary for a technically satisfactory exploitation of the licensed technology or for ensuring that the production of the licensee conforms to the quality standards that are respected by the licensor and other licensees;

4. the licensee is prohibited from contesting the secrecy of the licensed know-how or from challenging the validity of licensed patents within the common market belonging to the licensor or undertakings connected with him, without prejudice to the right of the licensor to terminate the licensing agreement in the event of such a challenge;
5. the licensee is charged royalties on goods or services which are not entirely or partially produced by means of the licensed technology or for the use of know-how which has become publicly known by the action of the licensor or an undertaking connected with him;
6. one party is restricted within the same technological field of use or within the same product market as to the customers he may serve, in particular by being prohibited from supplying certain classes of user, employing certain forms of distribution or, with the aim of sharing customers, using certain types of packaging for the products, save as provided in Article 1(1)(7) and Article 4(2);
7. the quantity of the licensed products one party may manufacture or sell or the number of operations exploiting the licensed technology he may carry out are subject to limitations, save as provided in Article 1(1)(8) and Article 4(2);
8. one party is restricted in the determination of prices, components of prices or discounts for the licensed products;
9. one party is restricted from competing with the other party, with undertakings connected with the other party or with other undertakings within the common market in respect of research and development, production or use of competing products and their distribution, without prejudice to an obligation on the licensee to use his best endeavours to exploit the licensed technology and without prejudice to the right of the licensor to terminate the exclusivity granted to the licensee and cease communicating improvements in the event of the licensee's engaging in any such competing activities and to require the licensee to prove that the licensed know-how is not used for the production of goods and services other than those licensed;
10. the initial duration of the licensing agreement is automatically prolonged by the inclusion in it of any new improvements communicated by the licensor, unless the licensee has the right to refuse such improvements or each party has the right to terminate the agreement at the expiry of the initial term of the agreement and at least every three years thereafter;
11. the licensor is required, albeit in separate agreements, for a period exceeding that permitted under Article 1(2) not to license other undertakings to exploit the same technology in the licensed territory, or a party is required for periods exceeding those permitted under Article 1(2) or 1(4) not to exploit the same technology in the territory of the other party or of other licensees;
12. one or both of the parties are required:
    (*a*) to refuse without any objectively justified reason to meet demand from users or resellers in their respective territories who would market products in other territories within the common market;
    (*b*) to make it difficult for users or resellers to obtain the products from other resellers within the common market, and in particular to exercise intellectual property rights or take measures so as to prevent users or resellers from obtaining outside, or from putting on the market in the licensed territory products which have been lawfully put on the market within the common market by the licensor or

with his consent; or do so as a result of a concerted practice between them.

Article 4

(1) The exemption provided for in Articles 1 and 2 shall also apply to agreements containing obligations restrictive of competition which are not covered by those Articles and do not fall within the scope of Article 3, on condition that the agreements in question are notified to the Commission in accordance with the provisions of Commission Regulation No. 27 and that the Commission does not oppose such exemption within a period of six months.

(2) Paragraph 1 shall in particular apply to an obligation on the licensee to supply only a limited quantity of the licensed product to a particular customer, where the know-how licence is granted at the request of such a customer in order to provide him with a second source of supply within a licensed territory.

This provision shall also apply where the customer is the licensee and the licence, in order to provide a second source of supply, provides for the customer to make licensed products or have them made by a subcontractor.

(3) The period of six months shall run from the date on which the notification is received by the Commission. Where, however, the notification is made by registered post, the period shall run from the date shown on the postmark of the place of posting.

(4) Paragraphs 1 and 2 shall apply only if:

(*a*) express reference is made to this Article in the notification or in a communication accompanying it; and

(*b*) the information furnished with the notification is complete and in accordance with the facts.

(5) The benefit of paragraphs 1 and 2 may be claimed for agreements notified before the entry into force of this Regulation by submitting a communication to the Commission referring expressly to this Article and to the notification. Paragraphs 3 and 4(*b*) shall apply *mutatis mutandis*.

(6) The Commission may oppose the exemption. It shall oppose exemption if it receives a request to do so from a Member State within three months of the transmission to the Member State of the notification referred to in paragraph 1 or of the communication referred to in paragraph 5. This request must be justified on the basis of considerations relating to the competition rules of the Treaty.

(7) The Commission may withdraw the opposition to the exemption at any time. However, where the opposition was raised at the request of a Member State and this request is maintained, it may be withdrawn only after consultation of the Advisory Committee on Restrictive Practices and Dominant Positions.

(8) If the opposition is withdrawn because the undertakings concerned have shown that the conditions of Article 85(3) are fulfilled, the exemption shall apply from the date of notification.

(9) If the opposition is withdrawn because the undertakings concerned have amended the agreement so that the conditions of Article 85(3) are fulfilled, the exemption shall apply from the date on which the amendments take effect.

(10) If the Commission opposes exemption and the opposition is not withdrawn, the effects of the notification shall be governed by the provisions of Regulation No. 17.

Article 5

(1) This Regulation shall not apply to:

1. agreements between members of a patent or know-how pool which relate to the pooled technologies;
2. know-how licensing agreements between competing undertakings which hold interests in a joint venture, or between one of them and the joint venture, if the licensing agreements relate to the activities of the joint venture;
3. agreements under which one party grants the other a know-how licence

and the other party, albeit in separate agreements or through connected undertakings, grants the first party a patent, trademark or know-how licence or exclusive sales rights, where the parties are competitors in relation to the products covered by those agreements;

4. agreements including the licensing of intellectual property rights other than patents (in particular trade-marks, copyright and design rights) or the licensing of software except where these rights or the software are of assistance in achieving the object of the licensed technology and there are no obligations restrictive of competition other than those also attached to the licensed know-how and exempted under the present Regulation.

(2) This Regulation shall nevertheless apply:

(*a*) to agreements to which paragraph 1(2) applies, under which a parent undertaking grants to the joint venture a know-how licence, provided that the contract products and the other products of the participating undertakings which are considered by users to be equivalent in view of their characteristics, price and intended use represent:
- in case of an exploitation licence limited to production not more than 20 per cent;
- in case of an exploitation licence covering production and distribution not more than 10 per cent.

of the market for all such products in the Common Market or a substantial part thereof;

(*b*) to reciprocal licences within the meaning of point 3 of paragraph 1, provided that the parties are not subject to any territorial restriction within the Common Market with regard to the manufacture, use or putting on the market of the contract products or on the use of the licensed processes;

(3) This Regulation shall continue to apply where the market shares referred to in point (*a*) of paragraph 2 are exceeded during any period of two consecutive financial years by not more than one-tenth. Where this latter limit is also exceeded, this Regulation shall continue to apply for a period of six months following the end of the financial year during which it was exceeded.

Article 6

This Regulation shall also apply to:

1. pure know-how agreements or mixed agreements where the licensor is not the developer of the know-how or the patentee but is authorized by the developer or the patentee to grant a licence or a sub-licence;
2. assignments of know-how or of know-how and patents where the risk associated with exploitation remains with the assignor, in particular where the sum payable in consideration of the assignment is dependent upon the turnover attained by the assignee in respect of products made using the know-how or the patents, the quantity of such products manufactured or the number of operations carried out employing the know-how or the patents;
3. pure know-how agreements or mixed agreements in which rights or obligations of the licensor or the licensee are assumed by undertakings connected with them.

Article 7

The Commission may withdraw the benefit of this Regulation, pursuant to Article 7 of Regulation No. 19/65/EEC, where it finds in a particular case that an agreement exempted by this Regulation nevertheless has certain effects which are incompatible with the conditions laid down in Article 85(3) of the Treaty, and in particular where:

1. such effects arise from an arbitration award;
2. the effect of the agreement is to prevent the licensed products from being exposed to effective competition in the

licensed territory from identical products or products considered by users as equivalent in view of their characteristics, price and intended use;

3. the licensor does not have the right to terminate the exclusivity granted to the licensee at the latest five years from the date the agreement was entered into and at least annually thereafter if, without legitimate reason, the licensee fails to exploit the licensed technology or to do so adequately;
4. without prejudice to Article 1(1)(6), the licensee refuses, without objectively valid reason, to meet unsolicited demand from users or resellers in the territory of other licensees;
5. one or both of the parties:
   (*a*) without objectively justified reason, refuse to meet demand from users or resellers in their respective territories who would market the products in other territories within the common market; or
   (*b*) make it difficult for users or resellers to obtain the products from other resellers within the common market, and in particular where they exercise intellectual property rights or take measures so as to prevent resellers or users from obtaining outside, or from putting on the market in the licensed territory products which have been lawfully put on the market within the common market by the licensor or with his consent;
6. the operation of the post-term use ban referred to in Article 2(1)(3) prevents the licensee from working an expired patent which can be worked by all other manufacturers;
7. the period for which the licensee is obliged to continue paying royalties after the know-how has become publicly known by the action of third parties, as referred to in Article 2(1)(7), substantially exceeds the lead time acquired because of the head-start in production and marketing and this obligation is detrimental to competition in the market;
8. the parties were already competitors before the grant of the licence and obligations on the licensee to produce a minimum quantity or to use his best endeavours as referred to in Article 2(1)(9) and Article 3(9) have the effect of preventing the licensee from using competing technologies.

Article 8

(1) As regards agreements existing on 13 March 1962 and notified before 1 February 1963 and agreements, whether notified or not, to which Article 4(2)(2)(*b*) of Regulation No. 17 applies, the declaration of inapplicability of Article 85(1) of the Treaty contained in this Regulation shall have retroactive effect from the time at which the conditions for application of this Regulation were fulfilled.

(2) As regards all other agreements notified before this Regulation entered into force, the declaration of inapplicability of Article 85(1) of the Treaty contained in this Regulation shall have retroactive effect from the time at which the conditions for application of this Regulation were fulfilled, or from the date of notification, whichever is the later.

Article 9

If agreements existing on 13 March 1962 and notified before 1 February 1963 or agreements to which Article 4(2)(2)(*b*) of Regulation No. 17 applies and notified before 1 January 1967 are amended before 1 July 1989 so as to fulfil the conditions for application of this Regulation, and if the amendment is communicated to the Commission before 1 October 1989 the prohibition in Article 85(1) of the Treaty shall not apply in respect of the period prior to the amendment. The communication shall take effect from the time of its receipt by the Commission. Where the communication is sent by registered post, it shall take effect from the date shown on the postmark of the place of posting.

Article 10

(1) As regards agreements to which Article 85 of the Treaty applies as a result of the accession of the United Kingdom, Ireland and Denmark, Articles 8 and 9 shall apply except that the relevant dates shall be 1 January 1973 instead of 13 March 1962 and 1 July 1973 instead of 1 February 1963 and 1 January 1967.

(2) As regards agreements to which Article 85 of the Treaty applies as a result of the accession of Greece, Articles 8 and 9 shall apply except that the relevant dates shall be 1 January 1981 instead of 13 March 1962 and 1 July 1981 instead of 1 February 1963 and 1 January 1967.

(3) As regards agreements to which Article 85 of the Treaty applies as a result of the accession of Spain and Portugal, Articles 8 and 9 shall apply except that the relevant dates shall be 1 January 1986 instead of 13 March 1962 and 1 July 1986 instead of 1 February 1963 and 1 January 1967.

Article 11

(1) Information acquired pursuant to Article 4 shall be used only for the purposes of the Regulation.

(2) The Commission and the authorities of the Member States, their officials and other servants shall not disclose information acquired by them pursuant to this Regulation of the kind covered by the obligation of professional secrecy.

(3) The provisions of paragraphs 1 and 2 shall not prevent publication of general information or surveys which do not contain information relating to particular undertakings or associations of undertakings.

Article 12

This Regulation shall enter into force on 1 April 1989.

It shall apply until 31 December 1999.

[. . .]

FURTHER READING

See also the following articles on intellectual property licensing and antitrust.

Abell, M. (1990), 'Japanese anti-trust law and patent and know-how licensing', 12 *European Intellectual Property Review*, 413.

Chu, M. (1992), 'An antitrust solution to the new wave of predatory patent infringement litigation', 33 *William and Mary Law Review*, 1341.

Flynn, J. (1992), 'Intellectual property and anti-trust: EC attitudes', 14 *European Intellectual Property Review*, 49.

Gold, M. (1992), 'European patent law and the exhaustion principle', *University of Chicago Legal Forum*, 441.

Herrington, W. (1992), 'Issues at the interface of international trade and intellectual property', 18 *Brooklyn Journal of International Law*, 759.

Hoerner, R. (1991/92), 'The antitrust significance of a patent's exclusionary power', 60 *Antitrust Law Journal*, 867.

Jones, B. (1992), 'An introduction to the European Economic Community and intellectual properties', 18 *Brooklyn Journal of International Law*, 665.

Koelemay, J. (1991), 'Patent-antitrust problems: commentary', 59 *Antitrust Law Journal*, 749.

Note (1991), 'Field-of-use restrictions as procompetitive elements in patent and know-how licensing agreements in the United States and the European Communities', 12 *Northwestern Journal of International Law and Business*, 364.

Note (1991), 'Patent-antitrust: dead or alive?', 59 *Antitrust Law Journal*, 657.

Piraino, T. (1992), 'A reformed antitrust approach to distributor terminations', 68 *Notre Dame Law Review*, 271.

Rosen, N. (1991), 'Developments in European Community licensing law', 59 *Antitrust Law Journal*, 717.

Rule, C. (1991), 'Patent-antitrust policy: looking back and ahead', 59 *Antitrust Law Journal*, 729.

See also the following works on economic issues in intellectual property rights.

Dasgupta, P. and Stiglitz, J. (1980), 'Industrial structure and the nature of innovative activity', 90 *Economic Journal*, 266.

Gilbert, R. and Newbery, D. (1982), 'Preemptive patenting and the persistence of monopoly', 72 *American Economic Review*, 514.

15

VERTICAL AGREEMENTS: FRANCHISE DISTRIBUTION

15.1 *Pronuptia de Paris GmbH, Frankfurt am Main* v. *Rosalinde Irmgard Schillgalis, carrying on business under the name Pronuptia de Paris Irmgard Schillgalis, Hamburg* Case 161/84 Court of Justice of the European Communities [1986] ECR 353, [1986] 1 CMLR 414

[. . .]

Pronuptia de Paris GmbH, Frankfurt am Main, the franchisor, argues that a system of franchise agreements makes it possible to combine the advantages offered by a form of distribution which presents a uniform image to the public (such as a system of subsidiaries) with the distribution of goods by independent retailers who themselves bear the risks associated with selling. The system is made up of a network of vertical agreements intended to ensure uniform presentation to the public and reinforces the franchisor's competitive power at the horizontal level, that is to say, with regard to other forms of distribution. It makes it possible for an undertaking which would not otherwise have the necessary financial resources to establish a distribution network beyond the confines of its own region, a network which enables small undertakings to participate as franchisees while retaining their independence. In view of those advantages Article 85(1) does not apply where the franchise agreements do not include restrictions on the liberty of the contracting parties which go beyond those which are the necessary concomitants of the franchise system. Exclusive delivery and supply obligations, in so far as they are intended to ensure a standard selection of goods, uniform advertising and shop layout and a prohibition on selling goods supplied under the contract in other shops, are inherent in the very nature of the franchise contract and are outside the scope of Article 85(1).

Mrs Schillgalis, the franchisee, submits that the first question should be answered in the affirmative. The most significant characteristic of the contracts in question is the territorial protection given to the franchisee. They cannot be compared with agency agreements, since franchisees, unlike agents, act in their own name and on their own account and bear all trading risks. The system of franchise agreements at issue gives rise to significant restrictions of competition, having regard to the fact that Pronuptia is, as it itself asserts, the world's leading French supplier of wedding dresses and accessories.

The French Government states that Article 85(1) may be applicable to franchise agreements for the distribution of a product but should not necessarily be applied to such agreements, in view of their positive aspects.

The Commission emphasizes that the scope of Article 85(1) is not restricted to particular types of contracts, and infers that in appropriate circumstances Article 85(1) applies also to contracts for the assignment of business names and trade-marks, registered or not, and the provision of services, as well as the supply of goods.

It should be pointed out first of all that franchise agreements, the legality of which has not previously been put in issue before the Court, are very diverse in nature. It appears from what was said in argument before the Court, that a distinction must be drawn between different varieties of franchise agreements. In particular, it is necessary to distinguish between (i) service franchises, under which the franchisee offers a service under the business name or symbol and sometimes the trade-mark of the franchisor, in accordance with the franchisor's instructions, (ii) production franchises, under which the franchisee manufactures products according to the instructions of the franchisor and sells them under the franchisor's trade-mark, and (iii) distribution franchises, under which the franchisee simply sells certain products in a shop which bears the franchisor's business name or symbol. In this judgment the Court is concerned only with this third type of contract [. . .].

In a system of distribution franchises of that kind an undertaking which has established itself as a distributor on a given market and thus developed certain business methods grants independent traders, for a fee, the right to establish themselves in other markets using its business name and the business methods which have made it successful. Rather than a method of distribution, it is a way for an undertaking to derive financial benefit from its expertise without investing its own capital. Moreover, the system gives traders who do not have the necessary experience access to methods which they could not have learned without considerable effort and allows them to benefit from the reputation of the franchisor's business name. Franchise agreements for the distribution system, which do not involve the use of a single business name, the application of uniform business methods or the payment of royalties in return for the benefits granted. Such a system, which allows the franchisor to profit from his success, does not in itself interfere with competition. In order for the system to work two conditions must be met.

First, the franchisor must be able to communicate his know-how to the franchisees and provide them with the necessary assistance in order to enable them to apply his methods, without running the risk that that know-how and assistance might benefit competitors, even indirectly. It follows that provisions which are essential in order to avoid that risk do not constitute restrictions on competition for the purpose of Article 85(1). That is also true of a clause prohibiting the franchisee, during the period of validity of the contract and for a reasonable period after its expiry, from opening a shop of the same or a similar nature in an area where he may compete with a member of the network. The same may be said of the franchisee's obligation not to transfer his shop to another party without the prior approval of the franchisor; that provision is intended to prevent competitors from indirectly benefiting from the know-how and assistance provided.

Secondly, the franchisor must be able to take the measures necessary for maintaining the identity and reputation of the network bearing his business name or symbol. It follows that provisions which establish the means of control necessary for that purpose do not constitute restrictions on competition for the purposes of Article 85(1).

The same is true of the franchisee's obligation to apply the business methods developed by the franchisor and to use the know-how provided.

That is also the case with regard to the franchisee's obligation to sell the goods covered by the contract only in premises laid out and decorated according to the franchisor's instructions, which is intended to ensure uniform presentation in conformity with certain requirements. The same requirements apply to the location of the shop, the choice of which is also likely to affect the network's reputation. It is thus understandable that the franchisee cannot transfer his shop to another location without the franchisor's approval.

The prohibition of the assignment by the franchisee of his right and obligations under the contract without the franchisor's approval protects the latter's right freely to choose the franchisees, on whose business qualifications the establishment and maintenance of the network's reputation depend.

By means of the control exerted by the franchisor on the selection of goods offered by the franchisee, the public is able to obtain goods of the same quality from each franchisee. It may in certain cases – for instance, the distribution of fashion articles – be impractical to lay down objective quality specifications. Because of the large number of franchisees it may also be too expensive to ensure that such specifications are observed. In such circumstances a provision requiring the franchisee to sell only products supplied by the franchisor or by suppliers selected by him may be considered necessary for the protection of the network's reputation. Such a provision may not however have the effect of preventing the franchisee from obtaining those products from other franchisees.

Finally, since advertising helps to define the image of the network's name or symbol in the eyes of the public, a provision requiring the franchisee to obtain the franchisor's approval for all advertising is also essential for the maintenance of the network's identity, so long as that provision concerns only the nature of the advertising. It must be emphasized on the other hand that, far from being necessary for the protection of the know-how provided or the maintenance of the network's identity and reputation, certain provisions restrict competition between the members of the network. That is true of provisions which share markets between the franchisor and franchisees or between franchisees or prevent franchisees from engaging in price competition with each other.

In that regard [. . .] attention [. . .] should be drawn to the provision which obliges the franchisee to sell goods covered by the contract only in the premises specified therein. That provision prohibits the franchisee from opening a second shop. Its real effect becomes clear if it is examined in conjunction with the franchisor's undertaking to ensure that the franchisee has the exclusive use of his business name or symbol in a given territory. In order to comply with that undertaking the franchisor must not only refrain from establishing himself within that territory but also require other franchisees to give an undertaking not to open a second shop outside their own territory. A combination of provisions of that kind results in a sharing of markets between the franchisor and the franchisees or between franchisees and thus restricts competition within the network. As is clear from the judgment of 13 July 1966 (Joined Cases 56 and 58/64, *Consten and Grundig* v. *Commission* [1966] ECR 299), a restriction of that kind constitutes a limitation of competition for the purposes of Article 85(1) if it concerns a business name or symbol which is already well-known. It is of course possible that a prospective franchisee would not take the risk of becoming part of the chain, investing his own money, paying a relatively high entry fee and undertaking to pay a substantial annual royalty, unless he could hope, thanks to a degree of protection against competition on the part of the franchisor and other franchisees, that his business would be profitable. That consideration, however, is relevant only to an examination of the agreement in the light of the conditions laid down in Article 85(3).

Although provisions which impair the franchisee's freedom to determine his own prices are restrictive of competition, that is not the case where the franchisor simply provides franchisees with price guidelines, so long as there is no concerted practice between the franchisor and the franchisees or between the franchisees themselves for the actual application of such prices. It is for the national court to determine whether that is indeed the case.

Finally, it must be added that franchise

agreements for the distribution of goods which contain provisions sharing markets between the franchisor and the franchisees or between the franchisees themselves are in any event liable to affect trade between Member States, even if they are entered into by undertakings established in the same Member State, in so far as they prevent franchisees from establishing themselves in another Member State.

15.2 Commission Regulation (EEC) No. 4087/88 on the application of Article 85(3) of the Treaty to categories of franchise agreements OJ 1988 No. L359/46

THE COMMISSION OF THE EUROPEAN COMMUNITIES,

Having regard to the Treaty establishing the European Economic Community,

Having regard to Council Regulation No. 19/65/EEC of 2 March 1965 on the application of Article 85(3) of the Treaty to certain categories of agreements and concerted practices, as last amended by the Act of Accession of Spain and Portugal, and in particular Article 1 thereof,

Having published a draft of this Regulation,

Having consulted the Advisory Committee on Restrictive Practices and Dominant Positions,

Whereas:

(1) Regulation No. 19/65/EEC empowers the Commission to apply Article 85(3) of the Treaty by Regulation to certain categories of bilateral exclusive agreements falling within the scope of Article 85(1) which either have as their object the exclusive distribution or exclusive purchase of goods, or include restrictions imposed in relation to the assignment or use of industrial property rights.

(2) Franchise agreements consist essentially of licences of industrial or intellectual property rights relating to trade marks or signs and know-how, which can be combined with restrictions relating to supply or purchase of goods.

(3) Several types of franchise can be distinguished according to their object: industrial franchise concerns the manufacturing of goods, distribution franchise concerns the sale of goods, and service franchise concerns the supply of services.

(4) It is possible on the basis of the experience of the Commission to define categories of franchise agreements which fall under Article 85(1) but can normally be regarded as satisfying the conditions laid down in Article 85(3). This is the case for franchise agreements whereby one of the parties supplies goods or provides services to end users. On the other hand, industrial franchise agreements should not be covered by this Regulation. Such agreements, which usually govern relationships between producers, present different characteristics than the other types of franchise. They consist of manufacturing licences based on patents and/or technical know-how, combined with trade-mark licences. Some of them may benefit from other block exemptions if they fulfil the necessary conditions.

(5) This Regulation covers franchise agreements between two undertakings, the franchisor and the franchisee, for the retailing of goods or the provision of services to end users, or a combination of these activities, such as the processing or adaptation of goods to fit specific needs of their customers. It also covers cases where the relationship between franchisor and franchisees is made through a third undertaking, the master franchisee. It does not cover wholesale franchise agreements because of the lack of experience of the Commission in that field.

(6) Franchise agreements as defined in this Regulation can fall under Article 85(1).

They may in particular affect intra-Community trade where they are concluded between undertakings from different Member States or where they form the basis of a network which extends beyond the boundaries of a single Member State.

(7) Franchise agreements as defined in this Regulation normally improve the distribution of goods and/or the provision of services as they give franchisors the possibility of establishing a uniform network with limited investments, which may assist the entry of new competitors on the market, particularly in the case of small and medium-sized undertakings, thus increasing interbrand competition. They also allow independent traders to set up outlets more rapidly and with higher chance of success than if they had to do so without the franchisor's experience and assistance. They have therefore the possibility of competing more efficiently with large distribution undertakings.

(8) As a rule, franchise agreements also allow consumers and other end users a fair share of the resulting benefit, as they combine the advantage of a uniform network with the existence of traders personally interested in the efficient operation of their business. The homogeneity of the network and the constant cooperation between the franchisor and the franchisees ensures a constant quality of the products and services. The favourable effect of franchising on interbrand competition and the fact that consumers are free to deal with any franchisee in the network guarantees that a reasonable part of the resulting benefits will be passed on to the consumers.

(9) This Regulation must define the obligations restrictive of competition which may be included in franchise agreements. This is the case in particular for the granting of an exclusive territory to the franchisees combined with the prohibition on actively seeking customers outside that territory, which allows them to concentrate their efforts on their allotted territory. The same applies to the granting of an exclusive territory to a master franchisee combined with the obligation not to conclude franchise agreements with third parties outside that territory. Where the franchisees sell or use in the process of providing services, goods manufactured by the franchisor or according to its instructions and or bearing its trade mark, an obligation on the franchisees not to sell, or use in the process of the provision of services, competing goods, makes it possible to establish a coherent network which is identified with the franchised goods. However, this obligation should only be accepted with respect to the goods which form the essential subject-matter of the franchise. It should notably not relate to accessories or spare parts for these goods.

(10) The obligations referred to above thus do not impose restrictions which are not necessary for the attainment of the abovementioned objectives. In particular, the limited territorial protection granted to the franchisees is indispensable to protect their investment.

(11) It is desirable to list in the Regulation a number of obligations that are commonly found in franchise agreements and are normally not restrictive of competition and to provide that if, because of the particular economic or legal circumstances, they fall under Article 85(1), they are also covered by the exemption. This list, which is not exhaustive, includes in particular clauses which are essential either to preserve the common identity and reputation of the network or to prevent the know-how made available and the assistance given by the franchisor from benefiting competitors.

(12) The Regulation must specify the conditions which must be satisfied for the exemption to apply. To guarantee that competition is not eliminated for a substantial part of the goods which are the subject of the franchise, it is necessary that parallel imports remain possible. Therefore, cross deliveries between franchisees should always be possible. Furthermore, where a franchise network is combined with another distribution system, franchisees should be free to obtain supplies from authorized distributors. To better inform consumers, thereby helping to ensure that they receive a fair share of the resulting benefits, it must be provided that the franchisee shall be

obliged to indicate its status as an independent undertaking, by any appropriate means which does not jeopardize the common identity of the franchised network. Furthermore, where the franchisees have to honour guarantees for the franchisor's goods, this obligation should also apply to goods supplied by the franchisor, other franchisees or other agreed dealers.

(13) The Regulation must also specify restrictions which may not be included in franchise agreements if these are to benefit from the exemption granted by the Regulation, by virtue of the fact that such provisions are restrictions falling under Article 85(1) for which there is no general presumption that they will lead to the positive effects required by Article 85(3). This applies in particular to market sharing between competing manufacturers, to clauses unduly limiting the franchisee's choice of suppliers or customers, and to cases where the franchisee is restricted in determining its prices. However, the franchisor should be free to recommend prices to the franchisees, where it is not prohibited by national laws and to the extent that it does not lead to concerted practices for the effective application of these prices.

(14) Agreements which are not automatically covered by the exemption because they contain provisions that are not expressly exempted by the Regulation and not expressly excluded from exemption may nonetheless generally be presumed to be eligible for application of Article 85(3). It will be possible for the Commission rapidly to establish whether this is the case for a particular agreement. Such agreements should therefore be deemed to be covered by the exemption provided for in this Regulation where they are notified to the Commission and the Commission does not oppose the application of the exemption within a specified period of time.

(15) If individual agreements exempted by this Regulation nevertheless have effects which are incompatible with Article 85(3), in particular as interpreted by the administrative practice of the Commission and the case law of the Court of Justice, the Commission may withdraw the benefit of the block exemption. This applies in particular where competition is significantly restricted because of the structure of the relevant market.

(16) Agreements which are automatically exempted pursuant to this Regulation need not be notified. Undertakings may nevertheless in a particular case request a decision pursuant to Council Regulation No. 17 as last amended by the Act of Accession of Spain and Portugal.

(17) Agreements may benefit from the provisions either of this Regulation or of another Regulation, according to their particular nature and provided that they fulfil the necessary conditions of application. They may not benefit from a combination of the provisions of this Regulation with those of another block exemption Regulation.

HAS ADOPTED THIS REGULATION:

Article 1

1. Pursuant to Article 85(3) of the Treaty and subject to the provisions of this Regulation, it is hereby declared that Article 85(1) of the Treaty shall not apply to franchise agreements to which two undertakings are party, which include one or more of the restrictions listed in Article 2.

2. The exemption provided for in paragraph 1 shall also apply to master franchise agreements to which two undertakings are party. Where applicable, the provisions of this Regulation concerning the relationship between franchisor and franchisee shall apply *mutatis mutandis* to the relationship between franchisor and master franchisee and between master franchisee and franchisee.

3. For the purposes of this Regulation:

(*a*) 'franchise' means a package of industrial or intellectual property rights relating to trade marks, trade names, shop signs, utility models, designs, copyrights, know-how or patents, to be exploited for the resale of goods or the provision of services to end users;

(*b*) 'franchise agreement' means an agreement whereby one undertaking, the

franchisor, grants the other, the franchisee, in exchange for direct or indirect financial consideration, the right to exploit a franchise for the purposes of marketing specified types of goods and/or services; it includes at least obligations relating to:
- the use of a common name or shop sign and a uniform presentation of contract premises and/or means of transport,
- the communication by the franchisor to the franchisee of know-how,
- the continuing provision by the franchisor to the franchisee of commercial or technical assistance during the life of the agreement;

(*c*) 'master franchise agreement' means an agreement whereby one undertaking, the franchisor, grants the other, the master franchisee, in exchange of direct or indirect financial consideration, the right to exploit a franchise for the purposes of concluding franchise agreements with third parties, the franchisees;

(*d*) 'franchisor's goods' means goods produced by the franchisor or according to its instructions, and/or bearing the franchisor's name or trade mark;

(*e*) 'contract premises' means the premises used for the exploitation of the franchise or, when the franchise is exploited outside those premises, the base from which the franchisee operates the means of transport used for the exploitation of the franchise (contract means of transport);

(*f*) 'know-how' means a package of non-patented practical information, resulting from experience and testing by the franchisor, which is secret, substantial and identified;

(*g*) 'secret' means that the know-how, as a body or in the precise configuration and assembly of its components, is not generally known or easily accessible; it is not limited in the narrow sense that each individual component of the know-how should be totally unknown or unobtainable outside the franchisor's business;

(*h*) 'substantial' means that the know-how includes information which is of importance for the sale of goods or the provision of services to end users, and in particular for the presentation of goods for sale, the processing of goods in connection which the provision of services, methods of dealing with customers, and administration and financial management; the know-how must be useful for the franchisee by being capable, at the date of conclusion of the agreement, of improving the competitive position of the franchisee, in particular by improving the franchisee's performance or helping it to enter a new market;

(*i*) 'identified' means that the know-how must be described in a sufficiently comprehensive manner so as to make it possible to verify that it fulfils the criteria of secrecy and substantiality; the description of the know-how can either be set out in the franchise agreement or in a separate document or recorded in any other appropriate form.

Article 2

The exemption provided for in Article 1 shall apply to the following restrictions of competition:

(*a*) an obligation on the franchisor, in a defined area of the common market, the contract territory, not to:
- grant the right to exploit all or part of the franchise to third parties,
- itself exploit the franchise, or itself market the goods or services which are the subject-matter of the franchise under a similar formula,
- itself supply the franchisor's goods to third parties;

(*b*) an obligation on the master franchisee not to conclude franchise agreement with third parties outside its contract territory;

(*c*) an obligation on the franchisee to exploit the franchise only from the contract premises;

(*d*) an obligation on the franchisee to refrain, outside the contract territory, from seeking customers for the goods or services which are the subject-matter of the franchise;

(*e*) an obligation on the franchisee not to manufacture, sell or use in the course of the provision of services, goods competing with the franchisor's goods which are the subject-matter of the franchise; where the subject-matter of the franchise is the sale or use in the course of the provision of services both certain types of goods and spare parts or accessories therefor, that obligation may not be imposed in respect of these spare parts or accessories.

Article 3

1. Article 1 shall apply notwithstanding the presence of any of the following obligations on the franchisee, in so far as they are necessary to protect the franchisor's industrial or intellectual property rights or to maintain the common identity and reputation of the franchised network:

(*a*) to sell, or use in the course of the provision of services, exclusively goods matching minimum objective quality specifications laid down by the franchisor;

(*b*) to sell, or use in the course of the provision of services, goods which are manufactured only by the franchisor or by third parties designed by it, where it is impracticable, owing to the nature of the goods which are the subject-matter of the franchise, to apply objective quality specifications;

(*c*) not to engage, directly or indirectly, in any similar business in a territory where it would compete with a member of the franchised network, including the franchisor; the franchisee may be held to this obligation after termination of the agreement, for a reasonable period which may not exceed one year, in the territory where it has exploited the franchise;

(*d*) not to acquire financial interests in the capital of a competing undertaking, which would give the franchisee the power to influence the economic conduct of such undertaking;

(*e*) to sell the goods which are the subject-matter of the franchise only to end users, to other franchisees and to resellers within other channels of distribution supplied by the manufacturer of these goods or with its consent;

(*f*) to use its best endeavours to sell the goods or provide the services that are the subject-matter of the franchise; to offer for sale a minimum range of goods, achieve a minimum turnover, plan its orders in advance, keep minimum stocks and provide customer and warranty services;

(*g*) to pay to the franchisor a specified proportion of its revenue for advertising and itself carry out advertising for the nature of which it shall obtain the franchisor's approval.

2. Article 1 shall apply notwithstanding the presence of any of the following obligations on the franchisee:

(*a*) not to disclose to third parties the know-how provided by the franchisor; the franchisee may be held to this obligation after termination of the agreement;

(*b*) to communicate to the franchisor any experience gained in exploiting the franchise and to grant it, and other franchisees, a non-exclusive licence for the know-how resulting from that experience;

(*c*) to inform the franchisor of infringements of licensed industrial or intellectual property rights, to take legal action against infringers or to assist the franchisor in any legal actions against infringers:

(*d*) not to use know-how licensed by the franchisor for purposes other than the exploitation of the franchise; the franchisee may be held to this obligation after termination of the agreement;

(*e*) to attend or have its staff attend training courses arranged by the franchisor;

(*f*) to apply the commercial methods devised by the franchisor, including any subsequent modification thereof, and use the licensed industrial or intellectual property rights;

(*g*) to comply with the franchisor's standards for the equipment and presentation of the contract premises and/or means of transport;

(*h*) to allow the franchisor to carry out checks of the contract premises and/or means of transport, including the goods sold and the services provided, and the inventory and accounts of the franchisee;

(*i*) not without the franchisor's consent to change the location of the contract premises;

(*j*) not without the franchisor's consent to assign the rights and obligations under the franchise agreement.

3. In the event that, because of particular circumstances, obligations referred to in paragraph 2 fall within the scope of Article 85(1), they shall also be exempted even if they are not accompanied by any of the obligations exempted by Article 1.

Article 4

The exemption provided for in Article 1 shall apply on condition that:

(*a*) the franchisee is free to obtain the goods that are the subject-matter of the franchise from other franchisees; where such goods are also distributed through another network of authorized distributors, the franchisee must be free to obtain the goods from the latter;

(*b*) where the franchisor obliges the franchisee to honour guarantees for the franchisor's goods, that obligation shall apply in respect of such goods supplied by any member of the franchised network or other distributors which give a similar guarantee, in the common market;

(*c*) the franchisee is obliged to indicate its status as an independent undertaking; this indication shall however not interfere with the common identity of the franchised network resulting in particular from the common name or shop sign and uniform appearance of the contract premises and/or means of transport.

Article 5

The exemption granted by Article 1 shall not apply where:

(*a*) undertakings producing goods or providing services which are identical or are considered by users as equivalent in view of their characteristics, price and intended use, enter into franchise agreements in respect of such goods or services;

(*b*) without prejudice to Article 2(*e*) and Article 3(1)(*b*), the franchisee is prevented from obtaining supplies of goods of a quality equivalent to those offered by the franchisor;

(*c*) without prejudice to Article 2(*e*), the franchisee is obliged to sell, or use in the process of providing services, goods manufactured by the franchisor or third parties designated by the franchisor and the franchisor refuses, for reasons other than protecting the franchisor's industrial or intellectual property rights, or maintaining the common identity and reputation of the franchised network, to designate as authorized manufacturers third parties proposed by the franchisee;

(*d*) the franchisee is prevented from continuing to use the licensed know-how after termination of the agreement where the know-how has become generally known or easily accessible, other than by breach of an obligation by the franchisee;

(*e*) the franchisee is restricted by the franchisor, directly or indirectly, in the determination of sale prices for the goods or services which are the subject-matter of the franchise, without prejudice to the possibility for the franchisor of recommending sale prices;

(*f*) the franchisor prohibits the franchisee from challenging the validity of the industrial or intellectual property rights which form part of the franchise, without prejudice to the possibility for the franchisor of terminating the agreement in such a case;

(*g*) franchisees are obliged not to supply within the common market the goods or services which are the subject-matter of the franchise to end users because of their place of residence.

Article 6

1. The exemption provided for in Article 1 shall also apply to franchise agreements which fulfil the conditions laid down in Article 4 and include obligations restrictive of competition which are not covered by Articles 2 and 3(3) and do not fall within the scope of Article 5, on condition that the agreements in question are notified to the Commission in accordance with the provisions of Commission Regulation No. 27 and that the Commission does not oppose such exemption within a period of six months.

2. The period of six months shall run from the date on which the notification is received by the Commission. Where, however, the notification is made by registered post, the period shall run from the date shown on the postmark of the place of posting.

3. Paragraph 1 shall apply only if:

(*a*) express reference is made to this Article in the notification or in a communication accompanying it; and

(*b*) the information furnished with the notification is complete and in accordance with the facts.

4. The benefit of paragraph 1 can be claimed for agreements notified before the entry into force of this Regulation by submitting a communication to the Commission referring expressly to this Article and to the notification. Paragraphs 2 and 3(*b*) shall apply *mutatis mutandis*.

5. The Commission may oppose exemption. It shall oppose exemption if it receives a request to do so from a Member State within three months of the forwarding to the Member State of the notification referred to in paragraph 1 or the communication referred to in paragraph 4. This request must be justified on the basis of considerations relating to the competition rules of the Treaty.

6. The Commission may withdraw its opposition to the exemption at any time. However, where that opposition was raised at the request of a Member State, it may be withdrawn only after consultation of the advisory Committee on Restrictive Practices and Dominant Positions.

7. If the opposition is withdrawn because the undertakings concerned have shown that the conditions of Article 85(3) are fulfilled, the exemption shall apply from the date of the notification.

8. If the opposition is withdrawn because the undertakings concerned have amended the agreement so that the conditions of Article 85(3) are fulfilled, the exemption shall apply from the date on which the amendments take effect.

9. If the Commission opposes exemption and its opposition is not withdrawn, the effects of the notification shall be governed by the provisions of Regulation No. 17.

Article 7

1. Information acquired pursuant to Article 6 shall be used only for the purposes of this Regulation.

2. The Commission and the authorities of the Member States, their officials and other servants shall not disclose information acquired by them pursuant to this Regulation of a kind that is covered by the obligation of professional secrecy.

3. Paragraphs 1 and 2 shall not prevent publication of general information or surveys which do not contain information relating to particular undertakings or associations of undertakings.

Article 8

The Commission may withdraw the benefit of this Regulation, pursuant to Article 7 of Regulation No. 19/65/EEC, where it finds in a particular case that an agreement exempted by this Regulation nevertheless has certain effects which are incompatible with the conditions laid down in Article 85(3) of the EEC Treaty, and in particular where territorial protection is awarded to the franchisee and:

(*a*) access to the relevant market or competition therein is significantly restricted by the cumulative effect of parallel networks of similar agreements established by competing manufacturers or distributors;
(*b*) the goods or services which are the subject-matter of the franchise do not face, in a substantial part of the common market, effective competition from goods or services which are identical or considered by users as equivalent in view of their characteristics, price and intended use;
(*c*) the parties, or one of them, prevent end users, because of their place of residence, from obtaining, directly or through intermediaries, the goods or services which are the subject-matter of the franchise within the common market, or use differences in specifications concerning those goods or services in different Member States, to isolate markets;
(*d*) franchisees engage in concerted practices relating to the sale prices of the goods or services which are the subject-matter of the franchise;
(*e*) the franchisor uses its right to check the contract premises and means of transport, or refuses its agreement to requests by the franchisee to move the contract premises or assign its rights and obligations under the franchise agreement, for reasons other than protecting the franchisor's industrial or intellectual property rights, maintaining the common identity and reputation of the franchised network or verifying that the franchisee abides by its obligations under the agreement.

Article 9

This Regulation shall enter into force on 1 February 1989.

It shall remain in force until 31 December 1999.

This Regulation shall be binding in its entirety and directly applicable in all Member States.

Done at Brussels, 30 November 1988.

FURTHER READING

For further analysis of the regulation of franchise agreements, see the following works.

Abell, M. (1992), 'Termination of international franchise agreements', 136 *Solicitors Journal*, 144.

Aubin, J. (1991), 'Franchise tie-ins: the state of the law', 26 *New England Law Review*, 1.

Brickley, J., Dark, F. and Weisbach, M. (1991), 'The economic effects of franchise termination laws', 34 *The Journal of Law and Economics*, 101.

Choi, Dong Shik (1990), 'Franchising in Korea', 58 *Antitrust Law Journal*, 997.

D'Aloisio, T. (1990), 'Franchising in Australia', 58 *Antitrust Law Journal*, 949.

Denger, M. (1991), 'Resale pricing issues in distribution and franchisor operations', 60 *Antitrust Law Journal*, 419.

Han, A. and Oechsli, C. (1990), 'Franchising in mainland China', 58 *Antitrust Law Journal*, 1013.

Hanson, R. (1991), 'The franchising dilemma: franchisor liability for actions of a local franchisee', 19 *North Carolina Central Law Journal*, 190.

Herbers, P. (1992), 'Franchise terminations: forum selection and choice of law', 48 *Journal of the Missouri Bar*, 531.

Korah, V. (1989), *Franchising and the EEC Competition Rules: Regulation 4087/88* (ESC Publishing, Oxford).

Miyake, N. (1990), 'Franchising in Japan', 58 *Antitrust Law Journal*, 975.

Note (1991), 'Pricing issues in dealer and franchise relationships', 60 *Antitrust Law Journal*, 417.

Note (1993), 'Dealer/franchisee collaboration', 61 *Antitrust Law Journal*, 389.

Parker, R. (1990), 'Franchising in Taiwan: transferring technology for the marketplace', 58 *Antitrust Law Journal*, 1007.

Rau, L. (1992), 'Implied obligations in franchising: beyond terminations', 47 *Business Law*, 1053.

Scher, I. (1991), 'Franchising and the Robinson–Patman Act: some problems and solutions', 60 *Antitrust Law Journal*, 479.

PART FOUR

MONOPOLY

16

THE MONOPOLY PROBLEM

The monopoly problem is not a problem of structure but of behaviour; at least, that is the broadly accepted view. Otherwise, there would again be the conflict we have noted between competing and competition. A firm with a good product and a sound strategy would be prevented from using this to attain a pre-eminent position in the industry, so would have to curtail competitive activity. Thus the monopoly problem is one of what a powerful firm may do, and the implications of its actions.

In a sense, some aspects of this topic have already arisen, in considering the behaviour of cartels and of powerful firms putting restraints on others. The general welfare framework, covered in **Waterson**, has underlain the economic and legal judgments. However the importance of scale economies and their influence on welfare outcomes, also discussed in the extract, now comes to the fore.

This leads on to two issues. One, sketched briefly in the extract from **Posner**, concerns the interaction between deadweight loss, opportunities to obtain monopoly positions and (wasteful) competition for the position. The argument is relevant to government-imposed restrictions, for example licences on taxicabs or public houses, as well as to the cases he cites. The other issue, where technology becomes crucial, is in situations where the only efficient or feasible industry structure is monopolistic or nearly so, 'natural monopoly'. The extract from **Sharkey** develops these ideas.

16.1 M. Waterson, 'Allocative efficiency and monopoly as a basis for regulation', in R. Sugden (ed.), *Industrial Economic Regulation* (Routledge, London, 1993)

WHAT IS MEANT BY ALLOCATIVE EFFICIENCY?

The first and second theorems of welfare economics essentially say, respectively, that every competitive equilibrium is Pareto efficient (no one can be made better off without making someone else worse off), and that every Pareto-efficient allocation can be achieved as a competitive equilibrium for some distribution of the endowments. [. . .] Clearly then, *if* distribution of endowments is satisfactory (and this is a big question), it is best to go for a competitive economy. This is one clear way in which we can ensure that the economy operates as efficiently as possible, given total endowments and current state of technological knowledge. Then it is allocatively, and by assumption also technically, efficient.

Allocative efficiency implies the equation of relative marginal benefits of goods between consumers, and the equation of these marginal rates of substitution to ratios of prices or marginal (social) costs of production. In symbols:

$$\frac{mu_x^i}{mu_y^i} = \frac{mu_x^j}{mu_y^j} = \frac{mc_x}{mc_y} \qquad (1)$$

where x and y are two sample goods, i and j are two representative consumers, mu is marginal utility, and mc is marginal cost. [. . .]

MONOPOLY AND ALLOCATIVE EFFICIENCY

Assuming a monopoly sets price above marginal cost, it will obviously violate condition (1) for allocative efficiency. Suppose there is a monopoly in the sale of product x, we would then have:

$$\frac{mu_x^i}{mu_y^i} = \frac{mu_x^j}{mu_y^j} = \frac{p_x}{p_y} > \frac{mc_x}{mc_y} \qquad (2)$$

(where p's are prices). Considering good y as a numeraire, each consumer would be purchasing insufficient of good x (more generally, relatively too much of good y compared with good x) by comparison with its marginal cost. The next unit of good x would cost less to produce than the benefit a consumer would obtain from its use. In the spirit of the partial analysis we are pursuing, Figure 16.1 rephrases the loss of allocative efficiency from monopoly in good x in terms of its cost and demand curves, and consumer surplus.

Here (and this is a crucial assumption) constant returns to scale and fixed factor prices are assumed. Hence, each firm's long-run average cost curve is horizontal and coincides with the marginal cost curve. The supply curve for each firm if good x were to be supplied by a perfectly competitive industry would be at the level of each firm's long-run marginal cost (*LRMC*), so the industry supply curve (*S*), being the horizontal sum of the firms' supply curves, would also be at that level. Therefore setting supply equal to demand (*D*), consumers pay p_c and total output is x_c. The monopolist faces the same industry demand curve *D* but, being the only firm, realises that demand is downward sloping, and therefore that at any level of output marginal revenue is below price (average revenue). Thus, in setting marginal revenue equal to marginal cost to maximise profits, the monopolist chooses an output x_m which is sold at price p_m. As a result of the high price and consequent restriction in output, monopoly profits of an amount $p_m ABp_c$ are earned.

In the perfectly competitive industry, a consumer at *Z* on the demand curve is willing to pay up to a price p_z for the good. Under the competitive regime, the consumer only pays p_c. Hence, she experiences consumer surplus, of an amount $p_z - p_c$, the difference between the maximum she would be willing to pay and what she actually pays. The same sort of thing can be said for consumers at every point on the demand curve. Therefore, the total amount of consumer surplus obtained from consumption of the good in the competitive case is the large triangular area EFp_c – the area under the demand curve but above price. Similarly under monopoly, consumer surplus of the smaller triangle EAp_m is earned. But notice that the monopolist, in making super-normal profits, has deprived consumers of more surplus than it has itself gained. The difference, the triangle *ABF*, is known as monopoly welfare loss. (Of course, if the demand curve is non-linear the area is only roughly triangular.)

Measuring monopoly welfare loss by reference to consumer surplus is not entirely accurate. The reason is that we have not taken into account income effects, and so

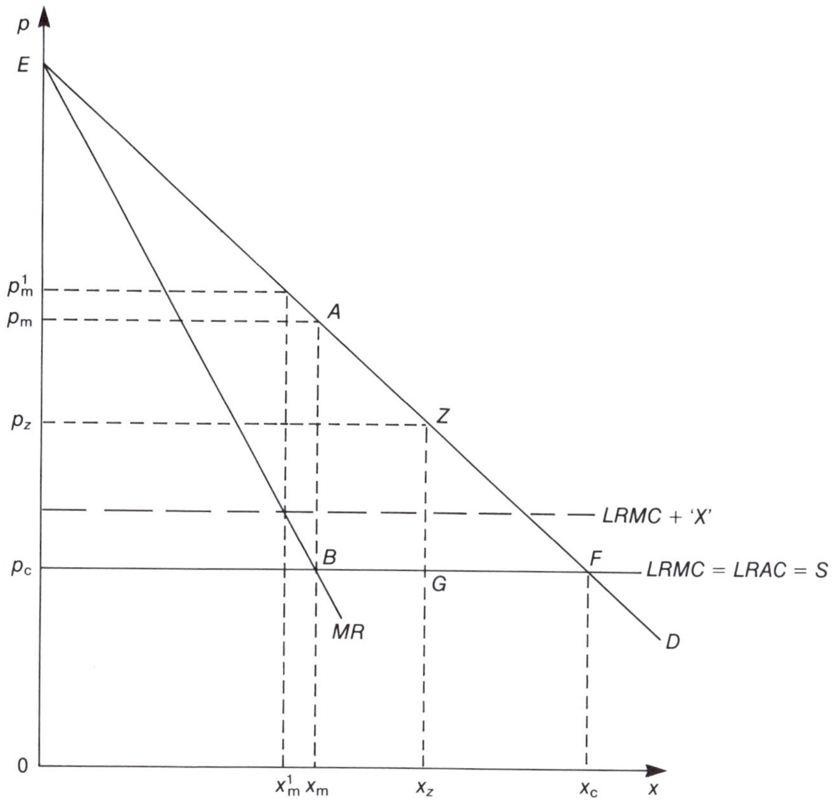

Figure 16.1

changes in the demand for other goods engendered by the distortion in the market for good x. However Willig [. . .] has shown that if the income elasticity of demand for x is low, or if expenditure on the good takes a relatively small proportion of income, then consumers' surplus is a rather good approximation to the underlying change in welfare, whatever prices are taken to measure the true valuation. We shall assume Willig's conditions to be met, and hence assume monopoly welfare loss is well measured by the triangular reduction in consumer surplus.

The concept of consumer surplus and the loss described might seem esoteric. To make it more concrete, you experience consumer surplus when you go, say, to buy a pair of trousers and expect to pay £35 but the shop has just the pair you want at £27. A consumer surplus loss arises for those people who go with £25 in their pocket to buy a pair of trousers and can find none they like at less than £27. Thus if the trousers were supplied by a monopolist at a price of £27, and the competitive price were £20, the first consumer would lose some consumer surplus as a result of trousers being in monopoly supply, but there would be no monopoly welfare loss. The second consumer, who would have experienced some consumer surplus if buying under competition, is not able to experience it under monopoly and therefore illustrates

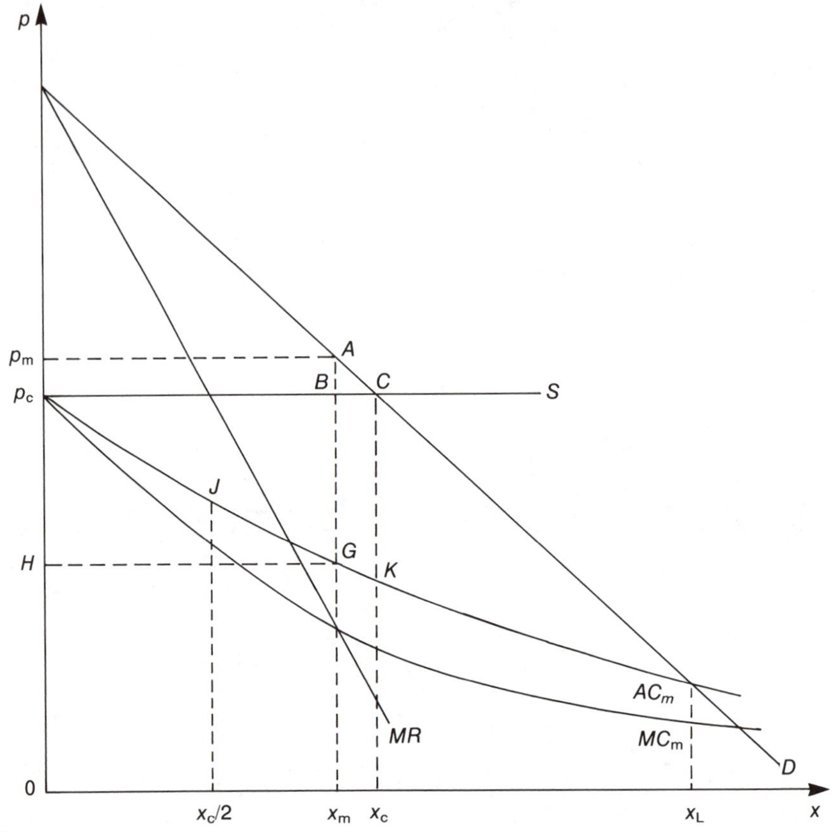

Figure 16.2

the source of monopoly welfare loss. Furthermore, in the simple situation depicted in Figure 16.1, since monopoly welfare loss is a triangle with the same height and same length base as the monopoly profit rectangle ($BF = p_cB$ since MR has twice the slope of D), it can be evaluated at half monopoly profit, a potentially substantial sum.

The situation so far described is rather more straightforward than the case where there are increasing returns to scale. [. . .] [I]f firms' production sets are not convex due to increasing returns, then the second welfare theorem is not satisfied. An industry with increasing returns cannot have perfect competition as an equilibrium market structure. To see this, suppose there were a large number of firms in the market each selling at a price equal to (what would be a rather high) marginal cost. A firm willing to expand output could reduce its costs and so do better than break even by charging the same price as the others. As it expanded output, price would fall slightly and some firms would be forced to increase output to reduce costs themselves, or drop out. It is not necessarily true that the industry equilibrium structure would be a monopoly (we would have to specify the process of competition in more detail in order to say what the eventual outcome would be). But it would be far short of perfectly competitive.

In this case monopoly welfare loss is

rather a misnomer since competition is not an available option. Nevertheless, allocative efficiency can sensibly be discussed.

An industry in which it is most efficient for one firm to be the producer is called a natural monopoly. As just implied, this does not necessarily mean there will be only one producer in practice. Natural monopolies arise (in the single product case), where scale economies are very extensive relative to demand. Thus the simplest example (and a sufficient condition) would be an industry where average cost falls continuously, perhaps because there are important facilities used over a wide range of output levels.

In such a case, a monopoly produces benefits to allocative efficiency unavailable through competition although also, so it would seem, allocative inefficiencies as a result of prices being above marginal cost due to the absence of competition. Figure 16.2 illustrates this – the competitive price may be assumed to be at p_c, whilst monopoly price is higher, so reducing consumer surplus but resulting in substantial resource savings due to increasing returns, which emerge as that part p_cBGH of monopoly profits p_mAGH.

[. . .]

There is another factor which should be raised here. It has so far been assumed that, whatever the structure of industry, the underlying cost curves are the same. But some people [. . .] take the view that firms are typically not technically efficient and that losses from technical inefficiency can easily outweigh losses from allocative inefficiency. It is easily seen for example in Figure 16.1 (curve $LRMC + 'X'$) that the former will essentially be represented by a rectangular area whereas the latter is a triangular area. In addition an increase in costs due to technical inefficiency will create an addition to allocative inefficiency if a markup is applied to actual costs. Further it has been argued [. . .] that X-inefficiency will be prevalent in conditions of monopoly, whereas under perfect competition, inefficient firms will be driven out of the industry. Therefore if these arguments are correct, technical inefficiency is likely to be higher under monopoly.

16.2 R. Posner, 'The social costs of monopoly and regulation', 83 *Journal of Political Economy*, 807 (1975)

[. . .]

When market price rises above the competitive level, consumers who continue to purchase the sellers' product at the new, higher price suffer a loss L[p_mABp_c in Waterson's Figure 16.1 in the previous extract] exactly offset by the additional revenue that the sellers obtain at the higher price. Those who stop buying the product suffer a loss D [ABF in Waterson's figure] not offset by any gain to the sellers. This is the 'deadweight loss' from supracompetitive pricing and in traditional analysis its only social cost, L being regarded merely as a transfer from consumers to producers. Loss D, however, underestimates the social costs of monopoly. The existence of an opportunity to obtain monopoly profits will attract resources into efforts to obtain monopolies, and the opportunity costs of those resources are social costs of monopoly too. [. . .] Theft provides an instructive analogy. The transfer of wealth from victim to thief involves no artificial limitation of output, but it does not follow that the social cost of theft is zero. The opportunity for such transfers draws resources into thieving and in turn into protection against theft, and the opportunity costs of the resources consumed are social costs of theft. [. . .]

This sort of analysis has long been familiar in a few special contexts. Plant's criticism of the patent system, made more than a generation ago, was based on the effect of the patent monopoly in drawing greater resources into invention than into activities that yield only competitive returns [. . .]. Telser's theory of resale price maintenance is in the same vein [. . .] as is the literature on non-price competition among members of a cartel [. . .]. But, while the tendency of monopoly rents to be transformed into costs is no longer a novel insight, its implications both for the measurement of the aggregate social costs of monopoly and for a variety of other important issues relating to monopoly and public regulation [. . .] continue for the most part to be ignored. [. . .]

[. . .]

16.3 W. Sharkey, *The Theory of Natural Monopoly* (Cambridge University Press, Cambridge, 1982)

[. . .]

In 1887 Henry Carter Adams discussed natural monopoly in *Relation of the State to Industrial Action*. Industries were classified into three types according to whether they had constant, decreasing, or increasing returns to scale. Although competition is workable in the first two classes, industries with increasing returns require regulation by the state.

> [W]here the law of increasing returns works with any degree of intensity, the principle of free competition is powerless to exercise a healthy regulating influence. This is true, because it is easier for an established business to extend its facilities for satisfactorily meeting a new demand than for a new industry to spring into competitive existence . . . The control of the state over industries should be coextensive with the application of the law of increasing returns in industries . . . Such businesses are by nature monopolies . . . If it is for the interest of men to combine, no law can make them compete.

Adams simplifies the definition of natural monopoly to the purely technical condition of scale economies in the industry. In addition, he is one of the first to suggest direct regulation of natural monopoly as a means of maximizing the social welfare. Regulation was viewed by Adams as a device that would allow a single firm to secure all the advantages of larger scale production but which would protect consumers from the abuse of monopoly power.

A fundamentally different view of natural monopoly is presented by Richard T. Ely [. . .]. Ely identified three classes of natural monopoly. (1) Those dependent on unique sources of supply (such as Cournot's mineral spring); (2) Those based on secrecy or special privilege (patents); (3) Those arising from 'peculiar properties' inherent in the business. Ely considered the most important natural monopolies, such as the railroad industry and public utilities, to be of the third class. He explained this class in more detail as follows:

> Natural monopolies of this third class are, however, more often rooted in conditions that make competition self-destructive. These conditions are three in number, and the presence of all three is generally necessary to create monopoly: (1) The commodity or service rendered must be of such a nature that a small difference in price will lead buyers to purchase from one producer rather than from another. (2) The business must be of such a nature as to make the creation of a large number of competitive plants impossible. Either because the business is one in which special advantages attach to large-scale production or because there are actual physical difficulties in the way of the multiplication of competing plants, there must be fairly definite limits to the possible increase of the number of plants among which the business might be divided. (3) The proportion of fixed to variable expenses of production must be high.

Thus, for Ely, natural monopoly is defined as the 'unsuitability of competition'. The unsuitability of competition may arise from conditions of economies of scale in production; but Ely believed that there may also be other conditions – those that make competition self-destructive. Here there appears for the first time a second major trend of thought in the theory of natural monopoly. Monopoly may be a superior source of supply because it is more stable as well as more efficient.

Although Adams and Ely are not the only, or even the most prominent, economists to develop a theory of natural monopoly, together they managed to establish the most important characteristics of natural monopoly industries. [. . .]

[. . .]

This survey may be summarized as follows.

1. All authors agree that natural monopolies are primarily industries in which there are pervasive economies of scale. Some have noted that there can be natural monopoly if a single firm can produce more efficiently than two or more firms even in the absence of economies of scale.
2. Most authors have recognized that competition may be unstable and that the conditions for destructive competition are related to the conditions for natural monopoly (although there is no agreement on the precise relationship).
3. Most authors would agree that it is difficult or impossible to label a given industry a natural monopoly by a simple measure of economies of scale (or any other easily quantified measure). Instead, account must be taken of other relevant conditions such as definition of the market and the nature of demand in the industry.

FURTHER READING

See the following works on the issues raised in Part 4, Chapter 16.

Bain, J. (1956), *Barriers to New Competition* (Harvard University Press, Cambridge, MA).

Baumol, W. J., Panzar, J. C. and Willig, R. D. (1988), *Contestable Markets and the Theory of Industry Structure* (Harcourt, Brace, Jovanovich, New York).

Bulow, J., Geanakoplos, J. and Klemperer, P. (1985), 'Multi-market oligopoly, strategic complements and substitutes', 93 *Journal of Political Economy*, 488.

Crew, M. A., Jones-Lee, M. W. and Rowley, C. K. (1971), 'X-theory versus management discretion theory', 38 *Southern Economic Journal*, 173.

Dixit, A. K. (1982), 'Recent developments in oligopoly theory', 72 *American Economic Review* (papers and proceedings), 12.

Fudenberg, D. and Tirole, J. (1984), 'The fat-cat effect, the puppy-dog ploy, and the lean and hungry look', 74 *American Economic Review*, 361.

Sutton, J. (1991), *Sunk Costs and Market Structure* (MIT Press, London).

von Weizsäcker, C. (1980), 'A welfare analysis of barriers to entry', 11 *Bell Journal of Economics*, 399.

17

THE DEFINITION OF MONOPOLY

The extract from West's definition of monopoly in ***The New Palgrave*** provides a historical perspective which extends some of the arguments of the previous chapter regarding the difficulty of a definitive structural test of monopoly. Hence arises the need for policy to be based upon actions taken.

17.1 J. Eatwell, M. Milgate and P. Newman (eds), *The New Palgrave Dictionary of Economics* (Macmillan, London, 1987)

Monopoly. Irving Fisher [. . .] once defined monopoly simply as an 'absence of competition'. From this point of view various attitudes to, or criticisms of, monopoly are connected with the particular vision of competition that each writer has in mind. To the neoclassical economist monopoly is the polar opposite to the now familar 'perfect competition' of the textbooks. Modern writers in the classical tradition, on the other hand, complain that perfect competition neglects the *process* of competitive activity, overlooks the importance of time to competitive processes and assumes away transaction or information costs.

In effect, 'perfect competition' to the neoclassical implies perfect decentralization wherein exchange costs happen to be zero. But the modern critics insist that exchange is not costless. And for this reason competition can be consistent with a wide variety of institutions that are employed to accommodate time, uncertainty and the costs of transacting [. . .]. Such arrangements include, for example, tie-in sales, vertical integration and manufacturer-sponsored resale price maintenance. Such price-making behaviour means that in the real world decentralization is imperfect. And it is imperfect decentralization that is embodied in the classical paradigm of *laissez faire*. Consequently many phenomena that are automatically treated by the neoclassical as the absence of perfect competition or the presence of behaviour that *looks* monopolistic, are often viewed approvingly by those in the classical tradition.

It is widely believed that, historically, Adam Smith's *Wealth of Nations* provided the most sustained and devastating attack on monopoly. It is true that he speaks of 'monopoly' quite frequently, but typically he uses the term in a wide 18th-century sense to include all kinds of political restrictions. Monopoly under the modern meaning of a single uncontested firm was not Smith's usual target. He employed the term most often to refer to multi-firm industries enjoying statutory protection. Thus, 'the law gave a monopoly to our boot-makers and shoe-makers, not only against our graziers, but against our tanners' [. . .]. Again, the whole system of mercantilism was condemned as monopolistic: 'Monopoly of one kind or another, indeed, seems to be the sole engine of the mercantile system' [. . .].

The Ricardians too were more concerned with general restrictions, and especially with the fixed supply of land. Ricardo's *Principles of Political Economy and Taxation* in fact has only five pages out of 292 that discuss monopoly, while John Stuart Mill's *Principles of Political Economy* has only two out of 1004. Following the Ricardians, the development of Darwinian philosophy in the mid-19th century only served to reinforce the classical emphasis on the necessity, if not inevitability, of competition. It is true that the 'modern' and more rigorous theory of monopoly, showing equilibrium to be determined by the equality of marginal revenue with marginal cost, was introduced by Cournot in 1838. But it received very little attention until much later.

In America the classical *laissez-faire* view of competition and imperfect decentralization prevailed at least to the end of the 19th century. When the Sherman Antitrust Act was passed in 1890, economists were almost unanimously opposed to it. Thus, despite his general disposition for widespread government intervention, the founder of the American Economic Association, Richard T. Ely [. . .], firmly rejected the politically popular policy of 'trust busting'. In the late 1880s John Bates Clark similarly feared that antitrust laws would involve a loss of the efficiency advantages of combination or trusts. Combination itself was often necessary to generate adequate capital and to insure against adversity during the depressing period of the business cycle. Other contemporary economists, including Simon N. Patten, David A. Wells and George Gunton, had similar views. The last argued that the concentration of capital does not drive small producers out of business, 'but simply integrates them into a larger and more complex system of production, in which they are enabled to produce wealth more cheaply for the community and obtain a larger income for themselves'. Instead of the concentration of capital tending to destroy competition, the reverse was true: 'By the use of large capital, improved machinery and better facilities, the trust can and does undersell the corporation' (Gunton) [. . .].

17.2 Fair Trading Act 1973

6 MONOPOLY SITUATION IN RELATION TO SUPPLY OF GOODS

(1) For the purposes of this Act a monopoly situation shall be taken to exist in relation to the supply of goods of any description in the following cases, that is to say, if:

(*a*) at least one-quarter of all the goods of that description which are supplied in the United Kingdom are supplied by one and the same person, or are supplied to one and the same person, or

(*b*) at least one-quarter of all the goods of that description which are supplied in the United Kingdom are supplied by members of one and the same group of interconnected bodies corporate, or are supplied to members of one and the same group of interconnected bodies corporate, or

(*c*) at least one-quarter of all the goods of that description which are supplied in the United Kingdom are supplied by members of one and the same group consisting of two or more such persons as are mentioned in subsection (2) of this section, or are supplied to members of one and the same group consisting of two or more such persons, or

(*d*) one or more agreements are in operation, the result or collective result of which is that goods of that description are not supplied in the United Kingdom at all.

(2) The two or more persons referred to in subsection (1)(c) of this section, in relation to goods of any description, are any two or more persons (not being a group of interconnected bodies corporate) who whether voluntarily or not, and whether by agreement or not, so conduct their respective affairs as in any way to prevent, restrict or distort competition in connection with the production or supply of goods of that description, whether or not they themselves are affected by the competition and whether the competition is between persons interested as producers or suppliers or between persons interested as customers of producers or suppliers.

7 MONOPOLY SITUATION IN RELATION TO SUPPLY OF SERVICES

(1) For the purposes of this Act a monopoly situation shall be taken to exist in relation to the supply of services of any description in the following cases, that is to say, if:

(*a*) the supply of services of that description in the United Kingdom is, to the extent of at least one-quarter, supply by one and the same person, or supply for one and the same person, or

(*b*) the supply of services of that description in the United Kingdom is, to the extent of at least one-quarter, supply by members of one and the same group of interconnected bodies corporate, or supply for members of one and the same group of interconnected bodies corporate, or

(*c*) the supply of services of that description in the United Kingdom is, to the extent of at least one-quarter, supply by members of one and the same group consisting of two or more such persons as are mentioned in subsection (2) of this section, or supply for members of one and the same group consisting of two or more such persons, or

(*d*) one or more agreements are in operation, the result or collective result of which is that services of that description are not supplied in the United Kingdom at all.

(2) The two or more persons referred to in subsection (1)(*c*) of this section, in relation to services of any description, are any two or more persons (not being a group of interconnected bodies corporate) who whether voluntarily or not, and whether by agreement or not, so conduct their respective affairs as in any way to prevent, restrict or distort competition in connection with the supply of services of that description, whether or not they themselves are affected by the competition, and whether the competition is between persons interested as persons by whom, or as persons for whom, services are supplied.

(3) In the application of this section for the purposes of a monopoly reference, the Commission, or the person or persons making the reference, may, to such extent as the Commission, or that person or those persons, think appropriate in the circumstances, treat services as supplied in the United Kingdom if the person supplying the services:

(*a*) has a place of business in the United Kingdom, or

(*b*) controls the relevant activities from the United Kingdom, or

(*c*) being a body corporate, is incorporated under the law of Great Britain or of Northern Ireland.

and may do so whether or not those services would otherwise be regarded as supplied in the United Kingdom.

8 MONOPOLY SITUATION IN RELATION TO EXPORTS

(1) For the purposes of this Act a monopoly situation shall be taken to exist in relation to exports of goods of any description from the United Kingdom in the following cases, that is to say, if:

(*a*) at least one-quarter of all the goods of that description which are produced in the United Kingdom are produced by one and the same person, or
(*b*) at least one-quarter of all the goods of that description which are produced in the United Kingdom are produced by members of one and the same group of interconnected bodies corporate;

and in those cases a monopoly situation shall for the purposes of this Act be taken to exist both in relation to exports of goods of that description from the United Kingdom generally and in relation to exports of goods of that description from the United Kingdom to each market taken separately.

(2) In relation to exports of goods of any description from the United Kingdom generally, a monopoly situation shall for the purposes of this Act be taken to exist if:

(*a*) one or more agreements are in operation which in any way prevent or restrict, or prevent, restrict or distort competition in relation to, the export of goods of that description from the United Kingdom, and
(*b*) that agreement is or (as the case may be) those agreements collectively are operative with respect to at least one-quarter of all the goods of that description which are produced in the United Kingdom.

(3) In relation to exports of goods of any description from the United Kingdom to any particular market, a monopoly situation shall for the purposes of this Act be taken to exist if:

(*a*) one or more agreements are in operation which in any way prevent or restrict, or prevent, restrict or distort competition in relation to, the supply of goods of that description (whether from the United Kingdom or not) to that market, and
(*b*) that agreement is or (as the case may be) those agreements collectively are operative with respect to at least one-quarter of all the goods of that description which are produced in the United Kingdom.

9 MONOPOLY SITUATION LIMITED TO PART OF UNITED KINGDOM

(1) For the purposes of a monopoly reference, other than a reference relating to exports of goods from the United Kingdom, the person or persons making the reference may, if it appears to him or them to be appropriate in the circumstances to do so, determine that consideration shall be limited to a part of the United Kingdom.

(2) Where such a determination is made, then for the purposes of that monopoly reference the provisions of sections 6 and 7 of this Act, or such of those provisions as are applicable for those purposes, shall have effect as if, wherever those provisions refer to the United Kingdom, they referred to that part of the United Kingdom to which, in accordance with that determination, consideration is to be limited.

(3) The preceding provisions of this section shall have effect subject to subsection (4) of section 50 of this Act in cases to which that subsection applies.

10 SUPPLEMENTARY PROVISIONS RELATING TO ss 6 to 9

(1) In the application of any of the provisions of sections 6 to 9 of this Act for the purposes of a monopoly reference, those provisions shall have effect subject to the following provisions of this section.

(2) No account shall for those purposes be taken of any provisions of an agreement in so far as they are provisions by virtue of which it is an agreement to which [the Act of 1976] applies.

(3) In relation to goods or services of any description which are the subject of different forms of supply:

(*a*) references in paragraph (*a*) to (*d*) of subsection (1), and in subsection (2), of section 6 or in section 8(3) of this Act to the supply of goods, or
(*b*) references in paragraphs (*a*) to (*d*) of subsection (1), and in subsection (2), of section 7 of this Act to the supply of services, shall for those purposes be

construed in whichever of the following ways the Commission, or the person or persons making the monopoly reference, think appropriate in all the circumstances, that is to say, as references to any of those forms of supply taken separately, to all those forms of supply taken together, or to any of those forms of supply taken in groups.

(4) For the purposes of subsection (3) of this section the Commission, or the person or persons making the monopoly reference in question, may treat goods or services as being the subject of different forms of supply whenever the transactions in question differ as to their nature, their parties, their terms or their surrounding circumstances, and the difference is one which, in the opinion of the Commission, or the person or persons making the reference, ought for the purposes of that subsection to be treated as a material difference.

(5) For the purposes of a monopoly reference made by the Director, subsections (3) and (4) of this section shall have effect subject to section 50(3) and (4) of this Act.

(6) In determining, for the purposes of a monopoly reference, whether the proportion of one-quarter mentioned in any provision of section 6, section 7 or section 8 of this Act is fulfilled with respect to goods or services of any description, the Commission, or the person or persons making the reference, shall apply such criterion (whether it be value or cost or price or quantity or capacity or number of workers employed or some other criterion, of whatever nature) or such combination of criteria as may appear to them or him to be most suitable in all the circumstances.

(7) The criteria for determining when goods or services can be treated, for the purposes of a monopoly reference, as goods or services of a separate description shall be such as the person or persons making the reference may think most suitable in the circumstances.

(8) In construing the provisions of section 7(3) and section 9 of this Act and the provisions of subsections (1) to (7) of this section, the purposes of a monopoly reference shall be taken to include the purpose of enabling the Director, or the Secretary of State or any other Minister, to determine in any particular circumstances:

(*a*) whether a monopoly reference could be made under Part IV of this Act, and
(*b*) if so, whether in those circumstances such a reference could be made by the Director

and references in those provisions to the person or persons making a monopoly reference shall be construed accordingly.

11 MEANING OF 'COMPLEX MONOPOLY SITUATION'

(1) In this Act 'complex monopoly situation' means circumstances in which, in accordance with the preceding provisions of this Act, a monopoly situation is for the purposes of this Act to be taken to exist in relation to the supply of goods or services of any description, or in relation to exports of goods of any description from the United Kingdom, by reason that the condition specified in paragraph (*c*) or in paragraph (*d*) of section 6(1) or of section 7(1) of this Act is fulfilled, or that the conditions specified in subsection (2) or in subsection (3) of section 8 of this Act are fulfilled.

(2) Any reference in the preceding subsection to paragraph (*c*) or paragraph (*d*) of section 6(1) or of section 7(1) of this Act shall be construed as including a reference to that paragraph as modified by section 9(2) of this Act.

In the Green Paper, **Abuse of Market Power**, Cm. 2100 (1992), extracted below (Section 18.1), the Department of Trade and Industry made much of the flexibility of the definition of monopoly. This flexibility is achieved to a great extent through the Act's definition of a complex monopoly position in sections 6 and 7. The scope of 'complex monopoly' was explored – and widened – in the **Visa** case.

17.3 *R.* v. *Monopolies and Mergers Commission, Secretary of State for Trade and Industry, Director General of Fair Trading ex parte Visa International Services Association* (1991) Trad L. R. 97 Court of Appeal (Civil Division)

Dillon LJ:

[. . .]

[I]f one endeavours to discern what Parliament had in mind in enacting section 7(2) [of the Fair Trading Act 1973], it is necessary to remember that under section 10(2) of the Act as amended, in the application of the provisions of section 6 to 9 of the Act, no account is to be taken of any provisions of an agreement in so far as they are provisions by virtue of which it is an agreement to which Part I of the Restrictive Trade Practices Act 1976 applies. It seems therefore that 7(1)(*c*) and 7(2) are dealing with something other than crude infringement of the 1976 Act. It is a complex monopoly situation under 7(1)(*c*) and 7(2) that the MMC claims to have identified in relation to the Visa credit card.

It is plain that the word 'group' in 7(1)(*c*) means something other than 'group of bodies corporate' in 7(1)(*b*). There is a definition of 'group' in section 137(2) of the Act, the general interpretation section, but I have not found it very helpful. There is also a definition in section 137(2) of the phrase 'uncompetitive practices' as meaning 'practices having the effect of preventing, restricting or distorting competition in connection with any commercial activities in the United Kingdom'. The wording of section 7(2) is obviously intended to reflect that definition.

I turn now to how the Visa credit card scheme operates. The Visa company itself (the appellant), does not issue Visa credit cards or directly perform any of the reference services, but it owns the copyright and trademark rights in the well-known Visa name and logo which are fundamental to the operation of the scheme and it also provides machinery for worldwide settlement, which it is unnecessary to examine, with ancillary computer facilities. The members of Visa are numerous worldwide. They include the various banks and other financial institutions worldwide which issue Visa credit cards to their customers. In the United Kingdom there were at the date of the MMC report [*Credit Card Services*, Cm. 718 (1989)] 19 banks and building societies which issued Visa cards and they are named in paragraph 7.19 of the MMC report.

The customers to whom the Visa credit cards are issued are referred to as cardholders. They present their cards to traders, suppliers of goods or services, and on the card being accepted sign vouchers in payment of the goods and services.

The trader who accepts Visa credit cards will first have entered into a contract, in accordance with Visa's operating regulations, with a member of Visa who, in the jargon of the scheme (for which the court accepts no responsibility) is called 'a merchant acquirer' [. . .].

The trader who has accepted a Visa credit card in payment for goods or services will send the voucher, signed by the cardholder, to the merchant acquirer with whom that trader has a contract and the merchant acquirer will pay the trader the amount specified in the voucher, less a discount provided for by the contract between the trader and the merchant acquirer in accordance with Visa's operating regulations. That discount is in effect the price for the trader being allowed to accept Visa credit cards and to get the benefit of the Visa credit card scheme and the custom of those cardholders who want to settle their liabilities for goods or services by the use of their Visa credit cards.

Having paid the trader the merchant acquirer will then recover the full amount specified in the voucher, less a smaller discount, from the bank or other body which had issued to the cardholder the Visa credit card which the cardholder has used in the particular transaction with the trader and that bank will recover the full amount, immediately or by deferred payment with interest, from the cardholder.

The MMC found in their report that a monopoly situation existed in relation to the supply in the United Kingdom of credit card services. In relation to Visa the persons in the monopoly situation were the appellant and the 19 banks and building societies named in paragraph 7.19 of the report. Barclays Bank, which was one of those persons, was also in a separate individual monopoly situation under section 7(1)(*a*) or (*b*) of the Act because of the volume of the Visa credit card work which it transacted. With that we are not concerned. There was also a separate monopoly situation in relation to the credit card variously known as MasterCard, Eurocard or Access, but with that also we are not concerned.

The MMC also found in their report that there were two separate aspects of the Visa scheme which operated against the public interest. That was a finding under section 49(1)(*b*). We are not concerned with its correctness, since it was a matter for the MMC and not the courts to decide. The two aspects were as follows.

In the first place the Visa operating regulations, which are binding on all traders who accept Visa cards, include a 'No Discrimination' clause which precludes the trader from imposing any surcharge when a Visa credit card is used, and which also, in the view of Visa and it seems on the findings of the MMC, precludes the trader from offering any discount to a customer who is prepared to pay in cash rather than by a Visa or other credit card. This was held by the MMC in paragraphs 7.94 to 7.96 of their report to be undesirable and to operate against the public interest, because it restricts the freedom of traders to set their own prices. In particular it prevents the trader from offering a discount for cash, or from imposing a charge for the use of credit cards.

In the second place, although not included in the operating regulations or bylaws of Visa, there is a rule of practice of Visa, referred to as the 'Merchant Acquirer' rule, which is to the effect that banks or other bodies which become members of Visa and issue Visa credit cards to their customers do not automatically become merchant acquirers with power to negotiate their own terms of discount with traders. Visa requires that before they can become acquirers they must demonstrate their commitment to card issuing. As it is put in paragraph 7.19 of the report, 'No Visa member is free to become a merchant acquirer in a country in which it does not issue an acceptable number of Visa cards.'

This restriction on the number of merchant acquirers was held by the MMC to be against the public interest. It was a cause of higher, and indeed excessive, interest rates being charged against cardholders, and also of course it reduced the chances of traders negotiating more favourable contracts, involving less discount, with merchant acquirers.

I agree with the judge that since the 'Merchant Acquirer' rule is a practice which is applied by Visa with the concurrence of all its members who issue Visa credit cards, it matters not for the purposes of the Act that it is not actually contained in the regulations or by-laws of Visa.

Against that background I turn to the specific points raised by Visa on this appeal, and first to the points taken under section 7(1)(*c*) and 7(2) which are concerned with the first issue the MMC had to enquire into, namely whether a monopoly situation existed in relation to the Visa credit cards.

There is no doubt that if the MMC was entitled to treat Visa and the 19 banks and building societies named in paragraph 7.19 of the report as constituting a group for the purposes of section 7(1)(*c*), the one quarter requirement of that subsection was satisfied because the Visa credit card services supplied by the members of that group taken as a whole did amount to at least one quarter of the supply of credit card services in the United Kingdom. It is said however that section 7(2) has been misconstrued by the MMC and the judge and the identification of the group by the MMC is consequently impermissible.

There are two related points taken. Firstly, it is said that the two or more persons mentioned in subsection 7(2) and referred to in subsection 7(1)(*c*) must each be persons who themselves supply the relevant services, that is, the reference services, and the group as identified by the MMC does not satisfy that criterion because the Visa company itself, the appellant, does not supply any of the reference services to anyone. Indeed the really relevant services are those referred to in subhead 1 of the reference, that is to say the undertaking and performance of engagements with suppliers of goods or services, and it is said that those services were only provided by those three members of the supposed group which were merchant acquirers – that is, Barclays, Lloyds and the TSB. They were not even provided by the card issuing banks which are not merchant acquirers, because those banks had no direct relationship with the traders.

In the second place it is said that to satisfy the condition of section 7(2) every member of the group must so conduct its respective affairs, whether voluntarily or not and whether by agreement or not, as to prevent, restrict or distort in any way competition in connection with the supply of the reference services. It is said that the card issuing banks which were not merchant acquirers did not satisfy that condition because they did not impose the 'No Discrimination' clause on the traders, and they were, if anything, the victims of the 'Merchant Acquirer' rule. It was urged that it could not be right to say that a card issuing bank, which had no desire to become a merchant acquirer, was so conducting its affairs as to prevent, restrict or distort competition in connection with the supply of reference services in subhead 1 of the reference since those services were only provided, and could only be provided, by merchant acquirers. It was pointed out [. . .] in argument that the relationship between Visa and its members, or between the members *inter se*, was not one of the recognised legal relationships such as principal and agent or master and servant, where one person's acts can be treated as being in law the acts of another person.

I see no reason however to limit the construction of section 7(2) by reference to the conceptions of principal and agent or master and servant, or for that matter partnership, which are not mentioned in the subsection at all. The language used in the subsection is broad. It must have been intended to be applicable in complex situations and its application, and indeed the whole application of the Act, will raise commercial and economic issues. I agree with the judge that in construing the subsection it is permissible and necessary to give consideration to commercial realities. I agree with him also that the Visa system or Visa scheme is made up of a number of interlocking elements. Each member of the alleged group – Visa itself, the merchant acquirers and the mere card issuing banks and building societies – plays its own part on the basis that each of the others will be playing its part, and each recognises and accepts the limitations of the scheme, including the 'No Discrimination' clause and the 'Merchant Acquirer' rule. The MMC was therefore entitled in my judgment to take the view that each of them so conducted its affairs as to restrict competition in connection with the supply of services in relation to the undertaking and performance of engagements with suppliers to pay for goods or services supplied to credit cardholders against the presentation of a credit card.

This is most obviously so in relation to the 'Merchant Acquirer' rule, which the card issuing banks accept in relying on one of the merchant acquirers to meet the liabilities under the credit cards issued by that bank. The scheme would have no point for the card issuing banks or for Visa itself if the credit cards issued to cardholders were not acceptable to traders, and the cards would not be acceptable to traders if there was no-one to whom the trader could look to meet the voucher signed by the cardholders in payment for the goods and services supplied by the trader. But in my judgment the reason equally extends to the 'No Discrimination' clause, which is part of the terms or conditions of engagements with the traders to pay for goods or services supplied to credit cardholders. The card issuing banks necessarily rely on, and get the benefit of, the 'No Discrimination' clause when they issue the cards to their customers in the expectation that the cards will be used and will be met by the merchant acquirers with the benefit of the 'No Discrimination' clause.

It follows that in my judgment there is no justification for construing subsection 7(2) in the limited sense that each of the persons must itself individually be supplying reference services to the traders.

The relevant finding on this is in paragraph 7.24 of the MMC's report, where it is supported by a reference in a footnote to paragraph 8.7 in an earlier MMC report on *Greyhound Racing* Cmnd. 9834. In paragraph 7.24 of the present report it is said, echoing the paragraph in the Greyhound Racing report:

We consider, and are advised, that section 7(1)(*c*) of the Act does not require that the group should consist solely of persons who supply the services. It requires only that those who supply at least a quarter of the total supply of the services shall be members of the group. This leaves the possibility that there may be others who do not themselves supply the services but are in some way closely enough connected to those who do for all of them together to be regarded as a group.

In the circumstances of the present case the MMC was in my judgment fully entitled to adopt this approach and to hold that Visa, the credit card issuing banks and building societies which were not merchant acquirers and the merchant acquirers were all members of one group for the purposes of section 7(1)(*c*).

The definition of monopoly under Article 86, unlike the Fair Trading Act 1973, does not rely on a threshold market share. Instead, a range of criteria will be taken into account in order to determine whether an undertaking has sufficient independence of action on the market to constitute a dominant position. Market share will, however, comprise an important criterion in that analysis. The **United Brands** case, and the **Napier Brown–British Sugar** decision illustrate the process of defining dominance on the relevant market. For a more systematic approach to the definition of the relevant market, see the provisions of the **Horizontal Merger Guidelines, 1992**, issued by the Department of Justice and the Federal Trade Commission (Section 20).

The **Italian Flat Glass** judgment of the Court of First Instance tackles the question of joint dominance. The approach of the Court, which limited joint dominance to those circumstances in which undertakings have close economic links, was reported in the Department of Trade and Industry's Green Paper, **Abuse of Market Power**, Cm. 2100 (1992) as an example of the narrower remit of Article 86 compared to the definitions of monopoly in the **Fair Trading Act 1973**. On the control of oligopoly markets, see now the decision of the EC Commission in the **Nestlé/Perrier** merger decision (Section 20.6).

17.4 Treaty of Rome, Article 86

Any abuse by one or more undertakings of a dominant position within the common market or in a substantial part of it shall be prohibited as incompatible with the common market in so far as it may affect trade between Member States. Such abuse may, in particular, consist in:

(*a*) directly or indirectly imposing unfair purchase or selling prices or other unfair trading conditions;
(*b*) limiting production, markets or technical development to the prejudice of consumers;
(*c*) applying dissimilar conditions to equivalent transactions with other trading parties, thereby placing them at a competitive disadvantage;
(*d*) making the conclusion of contracts subject to acceptance by the other parties of supplementary obligations which, by their nature or according to commercial usage, have no connection with the subject of such contracts.

17.5 *United Brands Company* v. *Commission of the European Communities*, Case 27/76 Court of Justice of the European Communities [1978] ECR 207, [1978] 1 CMLR 429

[This part of the Court's judgment concerns the question as to whether UBC enjoyed a dominant position on the market for bananas. UBC grew and distributed bananas under the 'Chiquita' trade mark.]

[. . .]

63. Article 86 is an application of the general objective of the activities of the Community laid down by Article 3(*f*) of the Treaty: the institution of a system ensuring that competition in the common market is not distorted.

64. This article prohibits any abuse by an undertaking of a dominant position in a substantial part of the common market in so far as it may affect trade between Member States.

65. The dominant position referred to in this article relates to a position of econonomic strength enjoyed by an undertaking which enables it to prevent effective competition being maintained on the relevant market by giving it the power to behave to an appreciable extent independently of its competitors, customers and ultimately of its consumers.

66. In general a dominant position derives from a combination of several factors which, taken separately, are not necessarily determinative.

67. In order to find out whether UBC is an undertaking in a dominant position on the relevant market it is necessary first of all to examine its structure and then the situation on the said market as far as competition is concerned.

68. In doing so it may be advisable to take account if need be of the facts put forward as acts amounting to abuses without necessarily having to acknowledge that they are abuses.

[. . .]

69. It is advisable to examine in turn UBC's resources for and methods of producing, packaging, transporting, selling and displaying its product.

70. UBC is an undertaking vertically integrated to a high degree.

71. This integration is evident at each of the stages from the plantation to the loading on wagons or lorries in the ports of delivery and after those stages, as far as ripening and sale prices are concerned, UBC even extends its control to ripener/distributors and wholesalers by setting up a complete network of agents.

72. At the production stage UBC owns large plantations in Central and South America.

73. In so far as UBC's own production does not meet its requirements it can obtain supplies without any difficulty from independent planters since it is an established fact that unless circumstances are exceptional there is a production surplus.

74. Furthermore several independent producers have links with UBC through contracts for the growing of bananas which

have caused them to grow the varieties of bananas which UBC has advised them to adopt.

75. The effects of natural disasters which could jeopardize supplies are greatly reduced by the fact that the plantations are spread over a wide geographic area and by the selection of varieties not very susceptible to diseases.

[. . .]

77. At the production stage UBC therefore knows that it can comply with all the requests which it receives.

78. At the stage of packaging and presentation on its premises UBC has at its disposal factories, manpower, plant and material which enable it to handle the goods independently.

79. The bananas are carried from the place of production to the port of shipment by its own means of transport including railways.

80. At the carriage by sea stage it has been acknowledged that UBC is the only undertaking of its kind which is capable of carrying two thirds of its exports by means of its own banana fleet.

81. Thus UBC knows that it is able to transport regularly, without running the risk of its own ships not being used and whatever the market situation may be, two thirds of its average volume of sales and is alone able to ensure that three regular consignments reach Europe each week, and all this guarantees it commercial stability and well being.

82. In the field of technical knowledge and as a result of continual research UBC keeps on improving the productivity and yield of its plantations by improving the draining system, making good soil deficiencies and combating effectively plant disease.

83. It has perfected new ripening methods in which its technicians instruct the distributor/ripeners of the Chiquita bananas.

84. That is another factor to be borne in mind when considering UBC's position since competing firms cannot develop research at a comparable level and are in this respect at a disadvantage compared with the applicant.

[. . .]

87. Th[e] general quality control of a homogeneous product makes the advertising of the brand name effective.

88. Since 1967 UBC has based its general policy in the relevant market on the quality of its Chiquita brand banana.

89. There is no doubt that this policy gives UBC control over the transformation of the product into bananas for consumption even though most of this product no longer belongs to it.

[. . .]

91. UBC has made this product distinctive by large-scale repeated advertising and promotion campaigns which have induced the consumer to show a preference for it in spite of the difference between the price of labelled and unlabelled bananas (in the region of 30 to 40%) and also of Chiquita bananas and those which have been labelled with another brand name (in the region of 7 to 10%).

93. It has thus attained a privileged position by making Chiquita the premier banana brand name on the relevant market with the result that the distributor cannot afford not to offer it to the consumer.

94. At the selling stage this distinguishing factor – justified by the unchanging quality of the banana bearing this label – ensures that it has regular customers and consolidated its economic strength.

95. The effect of its sales networks only covering a limited number of customers, large groups or distributor/ripeners, is a simplification of its supply policy and economies of scale.

96. Since UBC's supply policy consists – in spite of the production surplus – in only meeting the requests for Chiquita bananas parsimoniously and sometimes incompletely UBC is in a position of strength at the selling stage.

[. . .]

97. UBC is the largest banana group having accounted in 1974 for 35% of all banana exports on the world market.

98. In this case however account must only be taken of its operations on the relevant market.

105. [. . .] the Commission states that it estimates UBC's market share at 45%.

106. However UBC points out that this

share dropped to 41% in 1975.

107. A trader can only be in a dominant position on the market for a product if he has succeeded in winning a large part of this market.

108. Without going into a discussion about percentages, which when fixed are bound to be to some extent approximations, it can be considered to be an established fact that UBC's share of the relevant market is always more than 40% and nearly 45%.

109. This percentage does not however permit the conclusion that UBC automatically controls the market.

110. It must be determined having regard to the strength and number of the competitors.

111. It is necessary first of all to establish that on the whole of the relevant market the said percentage represents *grosso modo* a share several times greater than that of its competitor Castle and Cooke which is the best placed of all the competitors, the others coming far behind.

112. This fact together with the others to which attention has already been drawn may be regarded as a factor which affords evidence of UBC's preponderant strength.

113. However an undertaking does not have to have eliminated all opportunity for competition in order to be in a dominant position.

[. . .]

119. Even if the local attacks of some competitors can be described as 'fierce' it can only be placed on record that UBC held out against them successfully either by adapting its prices for the time being [. . .] or by bringing indirect pressure to bear on the intermediaries.

[. . .]

121. UBC's economic strength has thus enabled it to adopt a flexible overall strategy directed against new competitors establishing themselves on the whole of the relevant market.

122. The particular barriers to competitors entering the market are the exceptionally large capital investments required for the creation and running of banana plantations, the need to increase sources of supply in order to avoid the effects of fruit diseases and bad weather (hurricanes, floods), the introduction of an essential system of logistics which the distribution of a very perishable product makes necessary, economies of scale from which newcomers to the market cannot derive any immediate benefit and the actual cost of entry made up *inter alia* of all the general expenses incurred in penetrating the market such as the setting up of an adequate commercial network, the mounting of very large-scale advertising campaigns, all those financial risks, the costs of which are irrecoverable if the attempt fails.

123. Thus, although, as UBC has pointed out, it is true that competitors are able to use the same methods of production and distribution as the applicant, they come up against almost insuperable practical and financial obstacles.

124. That is another factor peculiar to a dominant position.

125. However UBC takes into account the losses which its banana division made from 1971 to 1973 – whereas during this period its competitors made profits – for the purpose of inferring that, since dominance is in essence the power to fix prices, making losses is inconsistent with the existence of a dominant position.

126. An undertaking's economic strength is not measured by its profitability; a reduced profit margin or even losses for a time are not incompatible with a dominant position, just as large profits may be compatible with a situation where there is effective competition.

127. The fact that UBC's profitability is for a time moderate or non-existent must be considered in the light of the whole of its operations.

128. The finding that, whatever losses UBC may make, the customers continue to buy more goods from UBC which is the dearest vendor, is more significant and this fact is a particular feature of the dominant position and its verification is determinative in this case.

129. The cumulative effect of all the advantages enjoyed by UBC thus ensures that it has a dominant position on the relevant market.

17.6 *Napier Brown – British Sugar*, Decision of the Commission of the European Communities OJ L 284, 19.10.88, p. 41; [1990] 4 CMLR 196

[. . .]
(40) Under Article 86 any abuse by one or more undertakings of a dominant position within the common market or a substantial part of it is prohibited as incompatible with the common market in so far as it may affect trade between Member States.

A. THE RELEVANT MARKET

(41) In order for the Commission to determine whether [British Sugar 'BS'] occupies a dominant position within the meaning of Article 86 it is necessary first to define the relevant market. This constitutes the area and product sector in which the economic power of the undertaking in question *vis-à-vis* its customers and competitors is to be judged.

The relevant product market

(42) The relevant product market is granulated sugar. This market may be subdivided into two sub-markets of sugar for sale to retail and industrial clients. Speciality sugars, liquid sugars and syrups, being used for different purposes than granulated sugars, do not meet the same needs and are not therefore part of the relevant product market because they are not substitutable from the customer's point of view.

Industrially produced sugar substitutes such as saccharin, cyclamates or aspartame only compete with natural sugar in limited uses such as 'diet' products, and thus do not form part of the same relevant product market as granulated sugar. (For fuller details of the different sweeteners available, and their particular characteristics, see paragraphs 2.59–2.75 of the Monopolies and Mergers Commission report on the existing and proposed mergers between *Tate & Lyle plc* or *Ferruzzi Finanziaria SpA* and *S. & W. Berisford* (HMSO Cmd. 89) (hereinafter the 'second MMC report').)

The relevant geographical market

(43) In the Community (for a more in-depth analysis of the mechanisms and regulations constituting the EEC sugar regime, see the Monopolies and Mergers Commission report on the proposed merger between S. & W. Berisford and the British Sugar Corporation Limited, 25 March 1981 (ISBN 0 10 2241813 3) hereinafter the 'first MMC report', and the second MMC report) each Member State is given a basic quantity of beet-origin sugar, which it divides up into quotas between its beet processing companies. This sugar is known as A/B sugar. BS receives all the United Kingdom basic quantity (currently 1,144,000 tonnes per annum), being the only United Kingdom beet processing company. This 'quota' is the maximum amount of sugar produced by BS that it may sell in the Community, as an intervention price system operates for sugar sold in the Community. This quota of sugar may also be sold outside the Community with an export refund. Any sugar produced above this quota must be exported outside the Community without export refund (C sugar) or carried over to the next year's A/B quota. Certain companies dealing in sugar which store sugar qualify for a Community sugar storage rebate. Such a rebate is only granted on storage of beet-origin sugar.

The United Kingdom basic quantity covers approximately half the country's total sugar requirements. The balance is largely made good by the import of cane raws from ACP countries pursuant to a Lomé protocol (protocol 3 on ACP sugar annexed to the ACP–EEC Convention of Lomé, signed on 28 February 1975, and contained in Protocol 7 of the third ACP–EEC Convention signed at Lomé on 8 December 1984). This is refined by Tate & Lyle plc (hereinafter T & L). Taking account of the production of both BS and T & L, enough sugar is produced in the United Kingdom to cover domestic demand.

(44) During the previous few years, imports have made up approximately 5 to 10% of total British sugar consumption. This amount appears to be to a large extent a structural limit to imports, which are unlikely to exceed this figure for the following reasons:

(i) Because of the natural barrier of the English Channel, which gives rise to additional transport costs, United Kingdom producers of sugar are able to charge a premium on the price of sugar compared with Continental prices. The United Kingdom price is generally set by BS at slightly under that at which sugar may be profitably imported and sold from the Continent. This was recognized by the House of Lords Select Committee Report on Sugar Policy (House of Lords session 1979/1980, 44th Report Select Committee on the European Communities *EEC Sugar Policy*, 19 March 1980.) which states (paragraph 9) that: 'It is these (EEC) imports which set the level of market prices in the United Kingdom and mean that both beet and cane sugar are priced at just under these levels. There is a consequent lack of price competition, as Tate and Lyle's full refining margin is covered from the UK market premium, and it cannot afford to cut prices significantly, while BS cuts prices to the extent necessary to sell its increasing throughput, but no more. Faced with this situation, industrial sugar users have been willing to import from the continent as a third source of supply.' This conclusion was supported by the MMC in paragraph 16.25 of its second report;

(ii) Importation of sugar for retail sale from other Member States is even more difficult than the importation of industrial sugar, because English-language bags must be specifically printed for the operation, and because transport is even more expensive as 'drop sizes' are generally smaller for retail compared to industrial sales. This was recognized by the MMC in both of its reports;

(iii) In addition to the cost of freight, a further relevant factor is the strength or weakness of sterling. If sterling is strong against other Community currencies imports will be cheaper. If sterling is weak, imports will be more expensive. Currency fluctuations can affect the price by up to £15 per tonne either way. Although the Community's system of monetary compensatory amounts is designed to minimize the effect of currency fluctuations it does not remove all distortions. For example, in the first three months of 1986 sterling weakened against the currencies of other Member States so that imports were expensive. Thus no company, taking account of the large variations in price of imported sugar, will rely to any large extent on imports for its supply of sugar. However, during certain periods, largely as a result of currency fluctuations, the importation of sugar becomes profitable, and during these periods merchants undertake such imports;

(iv) Many customers who require large, frequent and rapid deliveries upon order would have to be supplied from stocks of imported sugar stored in Great Britain; an additional cost would thereby be incurred;

(v) Furthermore, as the MMC pointed out in its second report, in order to secure a substantial amount of imports a considerably higher price in Britain than on the Continent would be necessary because potential exporters may require a large premium to persuade them to export large quantities of sugar to Britain for fear of retaliatory exports by the British producers.

(45) Because of these features, BS has a margin between which it may set British prices, between the Community intervention price for sugar, and the price at which imports would enter Britain in large quantities. It may set these prices just below the level at which imports from the Continent are (aside from periods where currency fluctuations make imports profitable) not competitive and, in fact, during the period

under consideration, has done so.

(46) Imports do, however, enter the United Kingdom each year, varying between 5 and 10% of total sales per annum. These enter because many major purchasers of sugar demand a third source of supply from outside the United Kingdom, to ensure continuity of supplies should a shortage of sugar develop as happened in the 1974/75 season, and to act as a competitive threat to British producers. Furthermore, merchants import sugar when conditions are favourable.

(47) Thus, as a result of these features, the role of imports on the British market has been as a complement to domestic sugar, rather than as a fully competitive alternative.

(48) The only part of the United Kingdom in which different conditions prevail is Northern Ireland, which does not form part of the relevant geographical market for the purposes of this case. No sugar is produced in Northern Ireland and, because of transport costs, most supplies are imported from Ireland. This conclusion is supported by the second MMC report (see paragraph 16.27).

(49) The Commission therefore concludes that for the purposes of Article 86 the relevant market is that of retail and industrial granulated sugar in Great Britain, which is a significant part of the common market.

B. DOMINANT POSITION

BS holds a dominant position on the British sugar market.

(50) The factors which must be taken into account in deciding whether or not BS has a dominant position on the British market for industrial and retail granulated sugar are as follows:

(i) Market shares on the British sugar market

According to figures supplied by NB, BS held, in the 1984/85 season, 58% of the relevant market (granulated sugars in Great Britain), Tate & Lyle 37%, and imports 5%. This estimated market share conforms to BS's own estimation of its market share (contained in the notification of BS's compliance programme), which BS states to be approximately 58% in the 1984/85 season.

In the second MMC report, it was estimated that BS enjoyed a market share of between 57 and 61% of the total white granulated sugar section of the market (see paragraph 2.66 of the report).

(ii) Ability of the other forces upon the relevant market to compete

Tate & Lyle

(51) T & L's position as a cane refiner places it at a considerable disadvantage compared to BS. Because of the Community pricing structure it has a cost disadvantage on refining cane sugar compared to the processing of beet sugar, resulting in T & L being a price follower. This was recognized by the House of Lords Select Committee on EEC Sugar Policy in 1980:

> There is already a lack of price competition in the UK market, as the Communities institutional pricing structure means that Tate & Lyle gets too small a margin to enable it to continue refining and selling cane sugar in the UK unless there is a substantial market premium above intervention price, whereas the same pricing structure allows the BSC a very handsome margin (£13 per tonne on the 1978–79 crop as against £2 per tonne for Tate & Lyle).
>
> The Committee have noted the sugar users' complaint about the lack of price competition in the UK market as, despite claims of rigorous price competition within the market, it appears that UK market prices are dictated by the price at which Continental sugar can be landed. It also appears to them that one of the two principal sugar supplies in the market is unable to compete effectively on cost grounds because of the inadequacy of the refining margin allowed to cane refineries in the EEC's institutional structure of support prices for sugar beet.

(52) The Commission agrees with the opinions of the House of Lords and considers that the facts lying behind these opin-

ions have not materially changed since 1981. The fact that BS is a price leader and T & L, due to the relatively low cane refining margin, is a price follower, was also noted by the MMC in its second report (see paragraphs 16.37 and 16.59).

(53) Thus the Commission concludes that BS acts as a price leader on the relevant market, and T & L as a price follower. The Commission accepts, as the MMC pointed out, that T & L – with sales of sugar similar in quantity to those of BS – provides BS with competition for individual accounts; but considers that this marginal competition, taking account of the fact that T & L 'is unable to implement price increases on its own and is unwilling because of its financial position to initiate general price reductions (the second MMC report, paragraph 16.6), does not prevent BS from enjoying a dominant position on the relevant market.

Imports

(54) Imported sugar acts as a limit to the price that BS may charge for its domestically produced sugar, thus giving BS a margin within which it may set United Kingdom sugar prices. During the period under consideration, BS has set British prices just under that at which it would be consistently profitable to undertake imports. The role of imports on the British market has therefore been as a complement to domestic sugar, rather than as a fully competitive alternative. In the light of this, the Commission considers that competition afforded by imported sugar did not, during the period in question, prevent BS from enjoying a dominant position within the meaning of Article 86.

(iii) Ability of BS unilaterally to increase prices, which the market follows

(55) On 1 July 1986 BS increased its retail sugar price to all its clients by £10 per tonne. BS subsequently made a further increase in its retail sugar price by £10 per tonne on 20 October 1986. BS has been able to maintain these price rises, and the other producers of retail sugar have also increased their price by similar amounts.

This indicates that BS has 'the power to determine prices . . . for a significant part of the products in question' (see the European Court of Justice's definition of a dominant position in the case of *Continental Can*, Case 6/72 ECR (1973), 215), and furthermore has 'the power to behave to an appreciable extent independently of its competitors, customers and ultimately of the consumers' (see the European Court's decision in *United Brands*, ECR (1978), 207).

(iv) Barriers to entry

Beet-origin sugar

Under Council Regulations (EEC) No 1785/81 (OJ No L 177, 1.7. 1981, p. 4), as last amended by Regulation (EEC) No 1107/88 (OJ No L 110, 29.4. 1988, p. 20), and (EEC) No 193/82 (OJ No L 21, 29.1. 1982, p. 3), the United Kingdom Government has the ability but not the obligations to reallocate the basic quantity of sugar received by United Kingdom producers amongst varying producers. At present BS receives all the United Kingdom basic quantity. It appears unlikely that the United Kingdom Government would give part of the allocation to a new producer, taking account of the fact that BS already has sufficient modern and efficient capacity to produce all the United Kingdom basic quantity of sugar.

(56) BS has a well-developed integrated production system and is responsible for all stages of production, from the provision of seed to the growers to the sale of the finished product. Such established, advanced and integrated operations make it difficult for a new producer, which produces on only one level of production, to operate.

(57) Thus considerable barriers to entry exist regarding the production of beet-origin sugar. Indeed, the fact that no new producer of sugar from beet origin has set up in the United Kingdom since 1936 despite the fact that BS has consistently been profitable indicates that these barriers to entry are real and appreciable.

Cane-origin sugar
(58) It appears unlikely that any new company will enter the market importing and refining cane-origin sugar due to the cost disadvantage presently suffered by cane-sugar producers compared to beet-sugar producers.

Imports
(59) As explained above, imports act as a complement to British domestic sugar rather than as a fully competitive alternative.

CONCLUSION

(60) The Commission concludes that, taking account of BS's high market share on the relevant market, the inability of its main competitors to compete fully and effectively with it, the barriers to entry existing on the British sugar market, and BS's proven ability to influence the price at which sugar is sold in Britain by unilateral action, BS holds a dominant position within the meaning of Article 86 on the relevant market – white granulated sugar for both retail and industrial sale in Great Britain [. . .].

17.7 *Re Italian Flat Glass: Società Italiano Vetro SpA and others* v. *Commission of the European Communities*, Cases T-68/69 & T77-78/89 Court of First Instance of the European Communities (1st Chamber) [1992] 5 CMLR 302

[. . .]

APPLICATION OF ARTICLE 86 EEC

In the opinion of the United Kingdom [which intervened in the case], it is only in very special circumstances that two or more undertakings may jointly hold a dominant position within the meaning of Article 86, namely, when the undertakings concerned fall to be treated as a single economic unit in which the individual undertakings do not enjoy a genuine autonomy in determining their conduct on the market and are not to be treated as economically independent of one another. The United Kingdom refers in that regard to *Suiker Unie* [. . .] together with the Opinion of Mayras AG; Case 85/76, *Hoffmann-La Roche* v. *EC Commission* ([1979] ECR 461, [1979] 3 CMLR 211); Case 172/80, *Zuchner* ([1981] ECR 2021, [1982] 1 CMLR 313), together with the Opinion of Slynn AG; Case 298/83, *CICCE* v. *EC Commission* ([1985] ECR 1105, [1986] 1 CMLR 486), together with the Opinion of Lenz AG; Case 75/84, *Metro* v. *EC Commission* ([1986] ECR 3021, [1987] 1 CMLR 118); and Case 247/86, *Alsatel* ([1988] ECR 5987, [1990] 4 CMLR 434).

The United Kingdom points out that, according to the case law of the Court of Justice, Article 85 does not apply to an agreement between a parent and its subsidiary which, although having separate legal personality, enjoys no economic independence [. . .]. When undertakings form part of one and the same economic unit, their conduct must be considered under Article 86 [. . .]. The Court considers that that view is supported by Case 66/86, *Ahmed Saeed* ([1989] ECR 803, [1990] 4 CMLR 102).

According to the United Kingdom, the only matters relied on by the Commission to show that the three undertakings form a 'single entity' are the very same matters as the Commission relies on as constituting infringements of Article 85. The Commission has not demonstrated either the existence of institutional links between the undertakings analogous to those that exist between parent and subsidiary nor the loss of their individual autonomy nor the absence of competition among them.

As regards the abuse of dominant position, the United Kingdom considers the Commission to be in error in holding that the very agreements on which the finding of a collective dominant position is based also constitute an abuse of that collective dominant position [. . .]. It is only the abuse of a dominant position, that is to say abusive conduct by the dominant undertaking, that is prohibited. The abuse is separate from the dominant position itself Case 27/76, *United Brands* v. *EC Commission* ([1978] ECR 207, [1978] 1 CMLR 429) and Case 6/72, *Continental Can* v. *EC Commission* ([1973] ECR 215, [1973] CMLR 199) [. . .].

The Commission [stated that it] in no way intended to apply the concept of collective dominant position to the undertakings in question solely on the ground that they form part of a tight oligopoly controlling more than 80 per cent of the Italian market in flat glass. It applied the concept of collective dominant position to the undertakings in question because, not only did they hold collectively a very large share of the market, they presented themselves on the market as a single entity and not as individuals. That emerges not from the structure of the oligopoly but from the agreements and concerted practices which led the three producers to create structural links amongst themselves, such as, in particular, the systematic exchanges of products. The Commission defends itself for having adopted the position that Article 86 may be applied to undertakings in an oligopolistic position regardless of whether or not there are agreements or concerted practices among them.

The Commission adds that, even if there were certain differences in behaviour, such as in the case of VP which especially favoured processing wholesalers, those differences did not prevent the producers from observing one and the same global market strategy: they, in fact, conducted themselves as undertakings belonging to a single group [. . .].

According to the Commission, in the present case the producers' behaviour is certainly caught by the prohibition laid down in Article 85 in view of the agreements found to exist, which resulted in concerted price changes and in market sharing. That is the objective factual situation in which the three producers found themselves by reason of those agreements which gave them a collective dominant position. Accordingly, that situation of dominance is the result of the unlawful agreements. However, in order to establish the existence of a collective dominant position, the Commission took into consideration, not the restrictive aim of the unlawful agreements, but their effect, which was to unite the three producers into a single entity on the market.

According to the Commission, the Community's other producers in the market in question were practically excluded because of the crystallisation of the market by the three producers in the collective dominant position. It is irrelevant, in the Commission's view, whether the companies were controlled by the private sector [. . .] or the public sector [. . .] since the undertakings were managed according to the same economic criteria. The groups in question had more than 50 per cent of all the Community's production and supply of flat glass and, given the nature of the market, in which the proximity of the place of delivery for the product plays a significant role, they managed to protect themselves from competition from other Community producers which might have had an interest in selling their flat glass in Italy.

The three producers abused their dominant position by agreeing on fixed prices and sharing market quotas among themselves. They thus denied customers the possibility of bringing into play competition on prices between suppliers and also deprived them of choice as to their sources of supply, it being impossible for other producers to enter the Italian market in so far as the three producers in question controlled a market which they had divided among themselves.

The Court notes that the very words of Article 86(1) provide that 'one or more undertakings' may abuse a dominant position. It has consistently been held, as indeed all the parties acknowledge, that the concept of agreement or concerted practice between undertakings does not cover agreements or concerted practices among undertakings belonging to the same group if the undertakings form an economic unit (see, for example, Case 15/74, *Centrafarm*, [*Centrafarm BV* v. *Sterling Drug, Inc.* (15.74) [1974] 2 CMLR 480]). It follows that when Article 85 refers to agreements or concerted practices between 'undertakings', it is referring to relations between two or more economic entities which are capable of competing with one another.

The Court considers that there is no legal or economic reason to suppose that the term 'undertaking' in Article 86 has a different meaning from the one given to it in the context of Article 85. There is nothing, in principle, to prevent two or more independent economic entities from being, on a specific market, united by such economic links that, by virtue of that fact, together they hold a dominant position *vis-à-vis* the other operators on the same market. This could be the case, for example, where two or more independent undertakings jointly have, through agreements or licences, a technological lead affording them the power to behave to an appreciable extent independently of their competitors, their customers and ultimately of their consumers (*Hoffmann-La Roche* [*Hoffmann-La Roche and Co. AG* v. *EC Commission* (85/76) [1979] 3 CMLR 211]).

[. . .] [I]t should be pointed out that for the purposes of establishing an infringement of Article 86 EEC, it is not sufficient, as the Commission's agent claimed at the hearing, to 'recycle' the facts constituting an infringement of Article 85, deducing from them the finding that the parties to an agreement or to an unlawful practice jointly hold a substantial share of the market, that by virtue of that fact alone they hold a collective dominant position, and that their unlawful behaviour constitutes an abuse of that collective dominant position. Among other considerations, a finding of a dominant position, which is in any case not in itself a matter of reproach, presupposes that the market in question has been defined (Case 6/72, *Continental Can*, cited above, paragraph [32]; Case 322/81, *Michelin* v. *EC Commission* [1983] ECR 3461, [1985] 1 CMLR 282). The Court must therefore examine, first, the analysis of the market made in the decision and, secondly, the circumstances relied on in support of the finding of a collective dominant position.

18

THE PROCESS OF ASSESSMENT

The proposals of the UK government to introduce restrictive practices control on the basis of the effects-based system of Article 85 of the Treaty of Rome (Department of Trade and Industry. **Opening Markets: New Policy on Restrictive Trade Practices** Cm. 729 (1989)) were not proceeded with as expeditiously as had been anticipated. In the meantime, the government examined the advantages of undertaking a simultaneous reform of monopoly control. The Green Paper **Abuse of Market Power**, put forward three possible reform packages, two of which would adopt the prohibition system of Article 86.

18.1 Department of Trade and Industry, *Abuse of Market Power: A Consultative Document on Possible Legislative Options*, Cm. 2100. (HMSO, London, 1992)

THE CURRENT UK LEGISLATION

2.1 The existing UK legislation on abuse of market power comprises controls on monopolies under the monopoly provisions of the Fair Trading Act 1973 and on anti-competitive practices under the Competition Act 1980.

Scope

Monopoly Provisions of the Fair Trading Act (FTA)

2.2 The monopoly provisions of the FTA apply to scale and complex monopoly situations. A *scale monopoly* exists where one company (or corporate group) accounts for at least 25 per cent of supply or purchase of particular goods or services in the UK or part of the UK; and a *complex monopoly* where a number of separate companies together account for at least 25 per cent of a market and engage in similar but not collusive conduct which restricts competition. The FTA provides the flexibility to investigate the behaviour of single dominant companies; oligopolists; or several companies which are acting in parallel. It can cover both anti-competitive conduct (aimed at other companies in the market) and exploitative conduct (using market power to take advantage of customers or suppliers).

2.3 The procedure involves a case-by-case investigation by the Monopolies and Mergers Commission (MMC) of the relevant market to establish whether there is a monopoly and, if so, whether it is operating against the public interest. These investigations are initiated by a reference by the Director General of Fair Trading (DGFT) or the Secretary of State for Trade and Industry.

2.4 In determining whether a monopoly is operating against the public interest the FTA requires the MMC to take account of all matters which appear to them in the circumstances to be relevant. In practice, the most important considerations for the MMC are the maintenance and promotion of effective competition in the UK and the promotion of the interests of UK consumers. The most frequently occurring adverse findings in reports published since 1980 have been monopoly pricing, discriminatory pricing, restrictions on supply to certain outlets and restrictions on sales of competitors' goods.

2.5 If the MMC find adverse effects the Secretary of State has powers to remedy them. He can either ask the DGFT to obtain undertakings (which are legally enforceable) or can make an order to prevent or remedy the particular adverse effects. His powers include the ability to impose price controls or to order divestment of a business. However, there are no powers to impose penalties for past conduct or to provide interim or final relief for injured parties. An order for divestment requires approval by Parliament, and the other remedies may be annulled by Parliament if imposed by order.

Competition Act

2.6 The Competition Act was enacted with a view to providing a speedier and more focused means of dealing with anti-competitive conduct by individual companies. It addresses anti-competitive practices; an anti-competitive practice being defined as a 'course of conduct which ... has ... the effect of restricting, distorting or preventing competition ...'. The procedure is concerned with practices of single companies or corporate groups; separate companies engaged in similar practices must be investigated separately. There is no market share threshold for investigation under the Act but conduct of a company with annual turnover of less than £5 million is outside the scope of the Act unless the company has at least 25 per cent of a market in the UK.

2.7 The procedures involve a two stage case-by-case investigation of specific practices. First, the DGFT investigates and reports whether there is an anti-competitive practice; if so, he can refer the matter to the MMC who consider whether there is such a practice and whether it operates against the public interest. Before moving to the second stage, the DGFT may accept any undertakings offered by the party involved. If undertakings are obtained they are legally enforceable and no further investigation is necessary.

2.8 If the MMC reach adverse findings, the Secretary of State can ask the DGFT to obtain undertakings to remedy the adverse findings or can use his order-making powers. These are similar to his powers in relation to monopolies (although they exclude divestment) and enable him to prohibit any anti-competitive practice which the MMC have found to be against the public interest. As with the FTA there is no power to penalise past conduct, or to provide relief for injured parties.

Advantages

Flexibility and Scope for Action

2.9 The current legislation is wide ranging and flexible. The FTA monopoly provisions, in particular, permit the MMC to consider all aspects of a market under investigation including structural issues (e.g. barriers to entry) as well as conduct. They allow for investigation of the conduct of oligopolists as well as that of single dominant companies. This results from the low threshold for the existence of a scale monopoly (25 per cent), which allows for the possibility of two or three scale monopolists in the same market; and the complex monopoly provisions which permit the investigation of similar anti-competitive conduct by several companies.

2.10 The importance of this flexibility can be seen from an analysis of the 37 reports on references made to the MMC since 1980. Scale monopolies were found to exist in 20 cases and complex monopolies in 12 cases. In a further five cases both scale and complex monopolies were found. In seven cases the MMC found that there was more than one scale monopolist in the same market. Less than half of the MMC's investigations during this period were concerned solely with the exercise of market power by a single company.

2.11 Both the FTA and the Competition Act provide for in depth case-by-case investigation by the MMC, which is an independent body. Nothing is unlawful unless it is prohibited by the Secretary of State following an adverse finding by the MMC.

Remedies

2.12 The monopoly provisions of the FTA provide for a wide range of remedial action including behavioural remedies (e.g. termination of agreements or anti-competitive practices), structural remedies (e.g. divestment) and regulation (e.g. price control). Divestment may be more appropriate than a behaviourial remedy in a situation where a company is likely to continue abusing its market power and where that market power cannot be reduced in other ways (e.g. due to regulatory barriers to entry, such as a restrictive licensing regime). Price controls may be the only effective way of dealing with natural monopolies. Since 1980 four MMC monopoly reports have recommended some form of divestment (*Domestic Gas Appliances*, 1980, *Roadside Advertising*, 1981, *Artificial Lower Limbs*, 1989 and *Beer*, 1989) and four have recommended price controls (*Contraceptive Sheaths*, 1982, *White Salt*, 1986, *Opium Derivatives*, 1989 and *Matches*, 1992).

Shortcomings

Relatively Weak Deterrent

2.13 The case-by-case, public interest assessment under current UK legislation, and the absence of a prohibition on abuse of market power, mean that nothing is in itself unlawful. There are no penalties for past conduct or relief for injured parties, even where similar conduct by another company has been prohibited. As a result there is relatively little deterrent effect.

Absence of Third Party Rights

2.14 Third parties who are injured by abuse of market power do not have the right to obtain damages in the courts for past injury. Nor is there any provision for them to obtain interim relief, i.e. temporary orders restraining alleged harmful conduct until an investigation has been completed. This is a particular problem where there is the risk that injured parties may be forced to cease trading before anti-competitive practices can be stopped. Monopoly investigations now normally take 9–12 months, but a major study can take longer. A Competition Act investigation may take up to six months for each of the two stages. In addition, there may be a significant period before an investigation is launched during which the Office of Fair Trading (OFT) seek to establish whether there is *prima facie* evidence of anti-competitive conduct. The procedures are further extended by the time taken while remedies are considered and put into place. No interim relief may be obtained by injured parties during this time. Competitors can – and do – go out of business before action is taken against anti-competitive conduct. Final relief from an adverse practice is dependent upon the remedies chosen by Ministers.

Powers of Investigation

2.15 Under both the FTA and the Competition Act, the OFT have very limited powers to investigate complaints and establish whether there is a *prima facie* case of abuse. Once formal preliminary investigation under the Competition Act has been initiated the OFT have stronger powers to obtain evidence. The MMC believe that they generally have sufficient powers to conduct their enquiries under the Competition Act and the FTA.

Property Rights

2.16 The current legislation addresses problems of competition in the supply of goods and services only. With a few exceptions it does not cover problems of competition which can arise from the supply or acquisition of other tangible property or rights in such property, such as the use of land. As regards the licensing of intellectual property related to goods and services, there are provisions in other legislation (such as the Patents Act 1977, the Registered Designs Act 1949 and the Copyrights, Designs and Patents Act 1988) which are capable of dealing with competition problems which can arise in relation to the intellectual property rights under these Acts.

A PROHIBITION SYSTEM

3.1 In contrast with the existing UK legislation, under which abuses of market power may be prohibited only after they have been found to operate against the public interest, EC competition law (Article 86 of the EEC Treaty) prohibits dominant companies from abusing their dominant position. The essence of a prohibition system is that conduct amounting to an abuse is automatically unlawful, without the need for a prior finding by the competition authorities. The 1989 White Paper signalled the Government's intention to introduce an RTP prohibition system. The possible scope of a parallel prohibition on abuse of market power, the advantages of such a prohibition and the perceived weaknesses of the EC regime are discussed in the remainder of this chapter.

Article 86 of the EEC Treaty

3.2 Article 86 of the EEC Treaty prohibits the abuse of a dominant position in the Common Market, or a substantial part thereof, which affects trade between EC Member States. It is aimed primarily at the conduct of single dominant companies and covers both anti-competitive and exploitative conduct. A *dominant position* has been defined as the ability to operate substantially independently of competitors. This implies a very high market share (normally in excess of 40 per cent), although other factors including relative strength of competitors and barriers to new market entry are also taken into account. [. . .]

3.3 The EC Commission have extensive powers to investigate complaints of abuse of dominant position, including power to obtain information and power to carry out on-site inspections of business records. The Commission also have powers to conduct general sectoral enquiries where there are circumstances such as inflexibility of prices which indicate that competition is being restricted or distorted. Where a company is found to be infringing Article 86 the Commission can require the infringement to be terminated and can impose fines of up to 10 per cent of turnover.

3.4 Article 86 is directly applicable in the UK and will continue to be so regardless of whether or not national competition law is changed in any way. 'Directly applicable' means that it is possible to bring private actions in the UK courts in respect of possible infringement of Article 86. The OFT currently have no powers to enforce Article 86 directly. Legislation could be introduced to give them these powers. However, since Article 86 applies only to abuse of a dominant position in the Common Market or a substantial part of it, which affects trade between Member States, there will inevitably be cases in which abuse of market power in the UK would not be covered by Article 86. It might therefore be desirable to introduce a national prohibition system, similar in form to Article 86.

A national prohibition system

Scope

3.5 A national prohibition would address abuse of market power in the UK as a whole or in distinct local or regional markets. It would be framed in general terms, rather than as a ban on specific conduct, but would include an illustrative list of practices liable to infringe the prohibition similar to that in Article 86 [. . .]. Advice would also be provided through guidance notes issued by the competition authorities. This guidance would include advice on the anticipated dividing line between action by the EC Commission under Article 86 and by the national competition authorities under a national prohibition.

Powers

3.6 The DGFT would be empowered to investigate suspected infringements of the prohibition. He would have powers to obtain information similar to those proposed in relation to the RTP prohibition. These would include a power to enter and search business premises with a magistrate's warrant if information was not supplied on request or if there were grounds to suspect that evidence might be interfered with.

Penalties
3.7 Behaviour which infringed the prohibition would be unlawful and could be subject to penalties. As under the proposed RTP prohibition these would take the form of civil penalties of up to 10 per cent of turnover.

Third Party Actions
3.8 Breach of the prohibition would be actionable as a breach of statutory duty. There would therefore be scope for private actions through the courts for damages and for injunctive relief (including temporary relief pending the outcome of an investigation) to be brought by parties who were adversely affected by conduct of a dominant company.

Advantages

More Effective Deterrent
3.9 A prohibition, backed up by penalties, increased powers of investigation and the possibility of third party actions, would generally provide a more effective deterrent to anti-competitive and exploitative conduct than is provided under the FTA and Competition Act. If introduced in conjunction with an RTP prohibition it would ensure that the competition authorities could take equivalent, effective action against both restrictive agreements and concerted practices, and anti-competitive or exploitative behaviour by individual companies.

Alignment with Europe
3.10 The introduction of prohibitions similar to Article 85 (prohibiting anti-competitive agreements and concerted practices) and Article 86 of the EEC Treaty would more closely align UK and EC competition law and reduce the risks of differing decisions, which can arise for UK companies currently subject to two very different legal systems under national and EC law. There is a strong trend in Europe to align national laws more closely on Community law. Most other EC Member States now have prohibitions either closely modelled on Articles 85 and 86 or based on the same principles. [. . .] There might be more scope for cases affecting UK companies to be referred back for action under a national prohibition, rather than at Community level, if the UK competition authorities had investigatory powers and the ability to impose penalties equivalent to those available to the EC Commission.

Third Party Redress
3.11 The position of parties injured or threatened by abuse of market power would be strengthened if there were a right to private action for damages and the possibility of interim relief. At present, the facility for victims to secure these is extremely limited.

Property Rights
3.12 A prohibition would address anti-competitive and exploitative behaviour by dominant companies in any sphere of economic activity. Unlike the FTA and Competition Act it would not be limited to the supply and acquisition of goods and services. Hence, it could address abuses resulting from the exercise of property rights.

Shortcomings

Joint Dominance
3.13 Article 86 prohibits the abuse of a dominant position by *one or more* undertakings. While it clearly addresses single dominant companies, the European Court of First Instance has ruled that the conduct of two or more companies is covered by the prohibition only where they are structurally linked in a group or are economically linked (e.g. by a technology licensing agreement).

3.14 In contrast, the FTA monopoly provisions allow for the investigation of markets where two or more companies have a strong market position or where several companies are acting in a similar way which prevents, restricts or distorts competition (see paragraph 2.9). Certain MMC reports on monopolies have found the conduct of two or more companies, which together accounted for a large part of the relevant market, to be against the public interest (e.g. concrete roofing tiles, postal franking machines and white salt) and made recommendations to address the adverse findings.

3.15 Such action would probably not be possible under a prohibition in identical or very similar terms to Article 86. The practices which would not be caught include price leadership without collusion and strategic anti-competitive behaviour by duopolists. An example of such behaviour would be each member of a duopoly restricting output and raising prices above the competitive level on the assumption that the other's output will remain unchanged. Some agreements and parallel practices which the MMC have investigated under the complex monopoly provisions (e.g. in their reports on cars, credit cards and carbonated drinks) would probably fall under the proposed RTP prohibition. Investigations under an RTP prohibition would, however, have a narrower focus than the sectoral investigations undertaken under the monopoly provisions.

Excessive Pricing and Other Exploitative Behaviour

3.16 Article 86 applies to the exploitation of market power at the expense of customers or suppliers, as well as anti-competitive practices which have the effect of damaging competitors or restricting competition. Such exploitation can include charging excessive prices: the European Court of Justice has confirmed that charging a price which is excessive in relation to the economic value of the product or service supplied may be an abuse of a dominant position. In practice, however, there have been very few cases in which high prices have been found to infringe Article 86. This partly reflects the difficulty of establishing in any particular case whether a supplier is earning a reasonable or unreasonable return. The problem of assessing whether profits and prices are excessive is not confined to a prohibition system. Nevertheless, it is likely to be more difficult to establish that a pricing practice is abusive, and therefore unlawful, than to find that such a practice is operating against the public interest and should be controlled for the future.

Remedies

3.17 Article 86 is concerned with the conduct of dominant companies. Regulation 17/62, which lays down rules for implementation of Article 86, gives the EC Commission power to require termination of infringements and to impose financial penalities. It does not include provision equivalent to that in the FTA for structural remedies (e.g. divestment) or regulatory remedies (e.g. price controls). Where a company is dominant, it may be able to pass the expected cost of penalties and damages on to its customers and may not be deterred from further abuse of market power. Therefore the only effective remedies may be to reduce market power by dividing up an undertaking or, where there is limited prospect of introducing competition, to regulate prices.

The **Competition Act 1980** provides an alternative control system for the regulation of firms having market power. It allows for a less burdensome process, particularly where the market power is limited to a small geographical area, or where the anticompetitive activity is confined to one, or a few, firms. The activities of the Director General of Fair Trading and the Monopolies and Mergers Commission under these provisions are reviewed by **Utton** in section 19.7. The 1980 Act also introduced a system for the review of the efficiencies of nationally owned or controlled bodies, a feature which was unavailable under the Fair Trading Act 1973.

18.2 COMPETITION ACT 1980

2 ANTI-COMPETITIVE PRACTICES

(1) The provisions of sections 3 to 10 below have effect with a view to the control of anti-competitive practices, and for the purposes of this Act a person engages in an anti-competitive practice if, in the course of business, that person pursues a course of conduct which, of itself or when taken together with a course of conduct pursued by persons associated with him, has or is intended to have or is likely to have the effect of restricting, distorting or preventing competition in connection with the production, supply or acquisition of goods in the United Kingdom or any part of it or the supply or securing of services in the United Kingdom or any part of it.

(2) To the extent that a course of conduct is required or envisaged by a material provision of, or a material recommendation in, an agreement which is registered or subject to registration under the Restrictive Trade Practices Act 1976, that course of conduct shall not be regarded as constituting an anti-competitive practice for the purposes of this Act; and for the purposes of this subsection:

(*a*) a provision of an agreement is a material provision if, by virtue of the existence of the provision (taken alone or together with other provisions) the agreement is one to which that Act applies; and

(*b*) a recommendation is a material recommendation in an agreement if it is one to which a term implied into the agreement by any provision of section 8 or section 16 of that Act (terms implied into trade association agreements and services supply association agreements) applies.

(3) For the purposes of this Act, a course of conduct does not constitute an anti-competitive practice if it is excluded for those purposes by an order made by the Secretary of State; and any such order may limit the exclusion conferred by it by reference to a particular class of persons or to particular circumstances.

(4) Without prejudice to the generality of subsection (3) above, an order under that subsection may exclude the conduct of any person by reference to the size of his business, whether expressed by reference to turnover, as defined in the order, or to his share of a market, as so defined, or in any other manner.

(5) For the purpose only of enabling the Director General of Fair Trading (in this Act referred to as 'the Director') to establish whether any person's course of conduct is excluded by virtue of any such provision of an order under subsection (3) above as is referred to in subsection (4) above, the order may provide for the application, with appropriate modifications, of any provisions of sections 44 and 46 of the Fair Trading Act 1973 (power of Director to require information).

(6) For the purposes of this section any two persons are to be treated as associated:

(*a*) if one is a body corporate of which the other directly or indirectly has control either alone or with other members of a group of interconnected bodies corporate of which he is a member, or

(*b*) if both are bodies corporate of which one and the same person or group of persons directly or indirectly has control;

and for the purposes of this subsection a person or group of persons able directly or indirectly to control or materially to influence the policy of a body corporate, but without having a controlling interest in that body corporate, may be treated as having control of it.

(7) In this section 'the supply or securing of services' includes providing a place or securing that a place is provided other than on a highway, or in Scotland a public right of way, for the parking of a motor vehicle (within the meaning of the Road Traffic Act 1988).

(8) For the purposes of this Act any question whether, by pursuing any course

of conduct in connection with the acquisition of goods or the securing of services by it, a local authority is engaging in an anti-competitive practice shall be determined as if the words 'in the course of business' were omitted from subsection (1) above; and in this subsection 'local authority' means:

(*a*) in England and Wales, a local authority within the meaning of the Local Government Act 1972, the Common Council of the City of London or the Council of the Isles of Scilly,
[. . .]

3 PRELIMINARY INVESTIGATION BY DIRECTOR OF POSSIBLE ANTI-COMPETITIVE PRACTICE

(1) If it appears to the Director that any person has been or is pursuing a course of conduct which may amount to an anti-competitive practice, the Director may in accordance with this section carry out an investigation with a view to establishing whether that person has been or is pursuing a course of conduct which does amount to such a practice.

(2) Before carrying out an investigation under this section, the Director shall:

(*a*) give to the Secretary of State and the person or persons whose conduct is to be investigated notice of the proposed investigation, together with an indication of the matters to be investigated, the person or persons concerned and the goods or services to which the investigation is to relate; and
(*b*) arrange for notice of the proposed investigation, together with an indication of the matters to be investigated, the person or persons concerned and the goods or services to which the investigation is to relate, to be published in such manner as the Director considers most suitable for bringing the proposed investigation to the attention of any other persons who, in the opinion of the Director, would be affected by or be likely to have an interest in the investigation.

(3) The Secretary of State may by regulations prescribe the manner in which any notice is to be given under subsection (2) above, and the evidence which is to be sufficient evidence of its having been given, and of its contents and authenticity.

(4) Subject to the following provisions of this section, where notice of a proposed investigation has been given in accordance with paragraph (*a*) and published in accordance with paragraph (*b*) of subsection (2) above, the Director shall proceed with the investigation as expeditiously as possible.

(5) If, before the end of the period of two weeks beginning with the day on which the Secretary of State receives notice of a proposed investigation under paragraph (*a*) of subsection (2) above, the Secretary of State directs the Director not to proceed with the investigation the Director shall take no further action under this section with respect to the matters referred to in the notice; but nothing in this subsection shall prevent the Director from proceeding with a subsequent investigation, notwithstanding that it relates wholly or partly to the same matters.

(6) Where the Secretary of State gives a direction under subsection (5) above, he shall:

(*a*) give notice of the direction to the person or persons whose conduct was to be investigated; and
(*b*) arrange for the direction to be published in such manner as he considers most suitable for bringing it to the attention of any other person who, in his opinion, would have been affected by, or likely to have had an interest in, the direction.

(7) For the purposes of an investigation under this section the Director may, by notice in writing signed by him:

(*a*) require any person to produce, at a time and place specified in the notice, to the Director or to any person appointed by him for the purpose, any documents which are specified or described in the notice and which are documents in his custody or under his control and relating to any matter relevant to the investigation; or

(*b*) require any person carrying on any business to furnish to the Director such estimates, returns or other information as may be specified or described in the notice, and specify the time, the manner and the form in which any such estimates, returns or information are to be furnished;

but no person shall be compelled for the purpose of any such investigation to produce any document which he could not be compelled to produce in civil proceedings before the High Court or, in Scotland, the Court of Session or, in complying with any requirement for the furnishing of information, to give any information which he could not be compelled to give in evidence in such proceedings.

(8) Subsections (6) to (8) of section 85 of the Fair Trading Act 1973 (enforcement provisions relating to notices under subsection (1) of that section requiring production of documents, etc.) shall appply in relation to a notice under subsection (7) above as they apply in relation to a notice under subsection (1) of that section but as if, in subsection (7) of that section, for the words from 'any one' to 'the Commission' there were substituted 'the Director'.

(9) At any time before the completion of an investigation under this section the Director may, with the consent of the Secretary of State, determine not to proceed with the investigation and, in that event, he shall:

(*a*) give notice of his determination to the person or persons whose conduct was being investigated; and

(*b*) arrange for the determination to be published in such manner as he considers most suitable for bringing it to the attention of any other person who, in his opinion, would have been affected by, or likely to have had an interest in, the investigation.

(10) As soon as practicable after the completion of an investigation under this section the Director shall, in such manner as he considers appropriate, publish a report stating, with reasons, whether in his opinion any course of conduct described in the report constituted or constitutes an anti-competitive practice and, if so:

(*a*) specifying the person or persons concerned and the goods or services in question; and

(*b*) stating, with reasons, whether he considers that it is appropriate for him to make a reference under section 5 below.

4 UNDERTAKINGS IN CONSEQUENCE OF DIRECTOR'S REPORTS

(1) Where a report is published under section 3 above stating, in accordance with subsection (10)(*b*) of that section, that it is appropriate for the Director to make a reference under section 5 below, the Director shall consider any representations in writing which are made to him by a person specified in the report as a person who was or is engaged in an anti-competitive practice and which contain proposals as to what should be done in consequence of the conclusions of the report so far as they relate to that person.

(2) Any such representations may include an undertaking by which the person who makes the representations agrees to be bound, if the undertaking is accepted by the Director, for a period specified in the representations.

(3) At any time before the Director makes a reference under section 5 below in relation to a report under section 3 above, the Director may, by notice given to the person concerned, accept an undertaking which is offered by that person by reference to that report.

(4) It shall be the duty of the Director:

(*a*) to arrange for:

(i) any undertaking accepted by him under this section, and

(ii) any variation or release of such an undertaking after the passing of the Companies Act 1989,

to be published in such manner as appears to him to be appropriate,

(*b*) to keep under review the carrying out of any such undertaking and from time to time to consider whether, by reason of any change of circumstances, the undertaking is no longer appropriate and either the person concerned can be released from the undertaking or the undertaking needs to be varied or superseded by a new undertaking, and

(*c*) if it appears to him that the person by whom an undertaking was given has failed to carry it out, to give that person notice of that fact.

(5) If at any time the Director concludes under subsection (4)(*b*) above:

(*a*) that any person can be released from an undertaking, or

(*b*) that an undertaking needs to be varied or superseded by a new undertaking,

he shall give notice to that person stating that he is so released, or specifying the variation or, as the case may be, the new undertaking which in his opinion is required.

(6) Where a notice is served on any person under subsection (5) above specifying a variation or new undertaking, the notice shall state the change of circumstances by virtue of which the notice is served.

(7) Subject to subsection (8) below, the Director may at any time, by notice given to the person concerned:

(*a*) agree to the continuation of an undertaking in relation to which he has given notice under subsection (5) above specifying a variation or new undertaking, or

(*b*) accept a new or varied undertaking which is offered by that person as a result of such a notice.

(8) If the Director makes a reference under section 5 below in relation to a notice under subsection (5) above, he shall not, after the reference has been made, agree to the continuation of the undertaking in relation to which that notice was given or accept a new or varied undertaking which is offered as a result of that notice.

(9) The Secretary of State may by regulations prescribe the manner in which any notice is to be given under this section, and the evidence which is to be sufficient evidence of its having been given, and of its contents and authenticity.

5 COMPETITION REFERENCES

(1) In any case where:

(*a*) a report has been published under section 3 above stating, in accordance with subsection (10)(*b*) of that section, that it is appropriate for the Director to make a reference under this section and the Director has not accepted from each of the persons specified in the relevant report such undertaking or undertakings as, in his opinion, covers or cover every course of conduct which is described in the report as constituting an anti-competitive practice, or

(*b*) the Director has given notice to any person under section 4(4)(*c*) above with respect to an undertaking given by that person, or

(*c*) the Director has given notice to any person under section 4(5) above specifying either a variation of an undertaking or a new undertaking which is required and has neither accepted a new or varied undertaking from that person nor agreed upon the continuation of the original undertaking, then, subject to the following provisions of this section, the Director may make a reference under this section to the Monopolies and Mergers Commission (in the following provisions of this Act referred to as a 'competition reference').

(2) In this section a competition reference is referred to:

(*a*) as a 'report reference' if it is made by virtue of subsection (1)(*a*) above; and
(*b*) as a 'notice reference' if it is made by virtue of subsection (1)(*b*) or subsection (1)(*c*) above.

(3) No competition reference may be made within the period of four weeks beginning with the relevant date nor, subject to subsection (4) below, may such a reference be made after the expiry of the period of eight weeks beginning on that date; and in this subsection 'the relevant date' means:

(*a*) in the case of a report reference, the date on which was first published, in accordance with section 3(10) above, the report of the Director to which the reference relates; and
(*b*) in the case of a notice reference, the date on which notice was given as mentioned in subsection (1)(*b*) or, as the case may be, subsection (1)(*c*) above.

(4) If the Secretary of State so directs, subsection (3) above shall have effect in relation to a competition reference of a description specified in the direction as if for the period of eight weeks specified in that subsection there were substituted such longer period not exceeding twelve weeks as may be specified in the direction; but the Secretary of State shall not give a direction under this subsection unless, upon representations made to him by the Director, it appears to the Secretary of State that it would be appropriate in the case in question to allow the Director a longer period in which to negotiate one or more undertakings under section 4 above.

(5) In this section and section 6 below 'the relevant report' means:

(*a*) in the case of a report reference, the report referred to in subsection (1)(*a*) above;
(*b*) in the case of a notice reference made by virtue of subsection (1)(*b*) above, the report by reference to which the person to whom the notice was given under section 4(4)(*c*) above gave the undertaking to which that notice refers; and
(*c*) in the case of a notice reference made by virtue of subsection (1)(*c*) above, the report by reference to which the person to whom the notice was given under section 4(5) above gave the undertaking which the Director proposes should be varied or superseded.

6 SCOPE OF COMPETITION REFERENCES

(1) In a competition reference the Director shall specify:

(*a*) the person or persons whose activities are to be investigated by the Commission (in this section referred to as the person or persons 'subject to the reference'),
(*b*) the goods or services to which the investigation is to extend, and
(*c*) the course or courses of conduct to be investigated.

(2) The Director may not under subsection (1) above specify in a competition reference any person who is not specified in the relevant report nor any goods or services which are not so specified nor any course of conduct which is not described in that report but, subject to that and subsection (3) below, the Director may under subsection (1) above specify such person or persons, such goods or services and such course or courses of conduct as he considers appropriate.

(3) To the extent that the Director is of the opinion that an undertaking accepted by him under section 4 above covers the activities of any person specified in the relevant report, or any goods or services so specified, or any course of conduct described in that report, the Director shall exclude that person, those goods or services or, as the case may require, that course of conduct from the reference.

(4) In subsection (3) above the reference

to an undertaking accepted by the Director under section 4 above does not include:

(*a*) an undertaking in respect of which notice has been served under subsection (4)(*c*) of that section, or
(*b*) an undertaking in respect of which the Director has given notice under subsection (5)(*b*) of that section specifying a new or varied undertaking, unless he has agreed upon its continuation with or without variation.

(5) Subject to subsection (6) below, on a competition reference the Commission shall investigate and report on the following questions, namely:

(*a*) whether any person subject to the reference was at any time during the period of twelve months ending on the date of the reference pursuing, in relation to goods or services specified in the reference, a course of conduct so specified or any other course of conduct which appears to be similar in form and effect to the one so specified; and
(*b*) whether, by pursuing any such course of conduct, a person subject to the reference was at any time during that period engaging in an anti-competitive practice; and
(*c*) whether, if any person was so engaging in an anti-competitive practice, the practice operated or might be expected to operate against the public interest.

(6) The Director may at any time, by notice given to the Commission, restrict the scope of a competition reference by excluding from the reference:

(*a*) some or all of the activities of any person subject to the reference,
(*b*) any goods or services specified in the reference, or
(*c*) any course of conduct so specified.

and, subject to section 7 below, on the receipt of such notice the Commission shall discontinue their investigation so far as it relates to any matter so excluded and shall make no reference to any such matter in their report.

8 CONCLUSIONS AND REPORTS OF THE COMMISSION

(1) A report of the Commission on a competition reference shall be made to the Secretary of State.

(2) Subject to section 6(6) above and subsection (3) below, a report on a competition reference shall state, with reasons, the conclusions of the Commission with respect to the following matters:

(*a*) whether any person whose activities were investigated was at any time during the period of twelve months referred to in paragraph (*a*) of subsection (5) of section 6 above pursuing any such course of conduct as is referred to in that paragraph; and
(*b*) if so, whether by pursuing such a course of conduct any such person was at any time during that period engaging in an anti-competitive practice; and
(*c*) if so, whether that anti-competitive practice operated or might be expected to operate against the public interest; and
(*d*) if so, what are, or are likely to be, the effects adverse to the public interest.

(3) If, on a competition reference, the Commission conclude that any person was pursuing such a course of conduct as is referred to in section 6(5)(*a*) above but that, by virtue of section 2(2) above, that course of conduct does not, in whole or in part, constitute an anti-competitive practice, the Commission shall state their conclusion in their report and shall not make any recommendation under subsection (4) below with respect to things done as mentioned in section 2(2) above.

(4) If, on a competition reference, the Commission conclude that any person was at any time during the period of twelve months referred to in section 6(5)(*a*) above engaging in an anti-competitive practice which operated or might be expected to operate against the public interest, the Commission:

(*a*) shall, as part of their investigations, consider what action (if any) should be taken for the purpose of remedying or preventing the adverse effects of that practice; and

(*b*) may, if they think fit, include in their report recommendations as to such action including, where appropriate, action by one or more Ministers (including Northern Ireland departments) or other public authorities.

(5) A copy of every report of the Commission on a competition reference shall be transmitted by the Commission to the Director; and the Secretary of State shall take account of any advice given to him by the Director with respect to any such report.

9 UNDERTAKINGS FOLLOWING REPORT ON COMPETITION REFERENCE

(1) In any case where:

(*a*) the report of the Commission on a competition reference concludes that any person specified in the report was engaging in an anti-competitive practice which operated or might be expected to operate against the public interest, and

(*b*) it appears to the Secretary of State that the effects of that practice which are adverse to the public interest might be remedied or prevented if that person or any other person specified in the report took or refrained from taking any action,

the Secretary of State may by notice in writing request the Director to seek to obtain from the person or, as the case may be, each of the persons specified in the notice an undertaking to take or refrain from taking any action with a view to remedying or preventing those adverse effects.

(2) Where the Secretary of State makes a request under subsection (1) above:

(*a*) he shall at the same time send a copy of the notice by which the request is made to the person or, as the case may be, each of the persons from whom an undertaking is to be sought; and

(*b*) it shall be the duty of the Director to seek to obtain an undertaking or undertakings of the description requested.

(3) In any case where:

(*a*) the Director is satisfied that a person from whom he has been requested to seek to obtain an undertaking is unlikely to give a suitable undertaking within a reasonable time, or

(*b*) having allowed such time as in his opinion is reasonable for the purpose, he is satisfied that a suitable undertaking has not been given by the person in question,

the Director shall give such advice to the Secretary of State as he may think proper in the circumstances.

(4) Where, following a request under subsection (1) above, an undertaking has been accepted by the Director, it shall be his duty:

(*a*) to give a copy of the undertaking and of any variation of it after the passing of the Companies Act 1989 to the Secretary of State;

(*b*) to arrange for the undertaking and any variation or release of it after that time to be published in such manner as appears to him to be appropriate;

(*c*) to keep under review the carrying out of the undertaking and from time to time to consider whether, by reason of any change of circumstances, the undertaking is no longer appropriate and either the person concerned can be released from the undertaking or the undertaking needs to be varied or to be superseded by a new undertaking; and

(*d*) if it appears to him that any person can be so released or that an undertaking has not been or is not being fulfilled, or needs to be varied or superseded, to give such advice to the Secretary of State as he may think proper in the circumstances.

(5) If, following advice from the Director that a person can be released from an

undertaking, the Secretary of State considers that it is appropriate for the Director to release him from it:

(*a*) the Secretary of State shall request the Director to do so, and

(*b*) the Director shall give the person concerned notice that he is released from the undertaking;

and regulations under subsection (9) of section 4 above shall apply in relation to such a notice as they apply to a notice under subsection (5) of that section.

(6) The Secretary of State shall take account of any advice given to him by the Director under this section (including advice as to the exercise by the Secretary of State of any of his powers under this Act).

10 ORDERS FOLLOWING REPORT ON COMPETITION REFERENCE

(1) If, in any case where the report of the Commission on a competition reference concludes that any person specified in the report was engaged in an anti-competitive practice which operated or might be expected to operate against the public interest:

(*a*) the Secretary of State has not under section 9(1) above requested the Director to seek to obtain undertakings from one or more of the persons so specified, or

(*b*) following a request under subsection (1) of section 9 above, the Director has informed the Secretary of State that he is satisfied as mentioned in paragraph (*a*) or pragraph (*b*) of subsection (3) of that section, or

(*c*) the Director has informed the Secretary of State that an undertaking accepted by him under section 9 above from a person specified in the report has not been or is not being fulfilled, the Secretary of State may, if he thinks fit, make an order under this section.

(2) Subject to the following provisions of this section, an order under this section may do either or both of the following, that is to say:

(*a*) prohibit a person named in the order from engaging in any anti-competitive practice which was specified in the report or from pursuing any other course of conduct which is similar in form and effect to that practice; and

(*b*) for the purpose of remedying or preventing any adverse effects which are specified in the report as mentioned in section 8(2)(*d*) above, exercise one or more of the powers specified in Part I of Schedule 8 to the Fair Trading Act 1973 to such extent and in such manner as the Secretary of State considers necessary for that purpose.

(3) No order may be made by virtue of paragraph (*a*) of subsection (2) above in respect of any person unless he is a person specified in the Commission's report and either:

(*a*) he has not given an undertaking which the Director sought to obtain from him in pursuance of a request under section 9(1) above; or

(*b*) the Director was not requested under section 9(1) above to seek to obtain an undertaking from him; or

(*c*) the Director has informed the Secretary of State that an undertaking given by him and accepted by the Director under section 9 above has not been or is not being fulfilled.

(4) In the Fair Trading Act 1973:

(*a*) section 90 (general provisions as to orders under section 56 etc.) except subsection (2),

(*b*) section 91(2) (publication of proposals to make an order),

(*c*) section 93 (enforcement of certain orders), and

(*d*) Part I of Schedule 8 (powers exercisable by orders under section 56 etc.),

shall have effect as if any reference in those provisions to an order under section 56 of that Act included a reference to an order under this section.

11 REFERENCES OF PUBLIC BODIES AND CERTAIN OTHER PERSONS TO THE COMMISSION

(1) The Secretary of State may at any time refer to the Commission any question relating to:

(*a*) the efficiency and costs of,
(*b*) the service provided by, or
(*c*) possible abuse of a monopoly situation by,

a person falling within subsection (3) below and specified in the reference, including any question whether, in relation to a matter falling within paragraph (*a*), (*b*) or (*c*) above, the person is pursuing a course of conduct which operates against the public interest.

(2) For the purposes of subsection (1)(*c*) above 'monopoly situation' includes a monopoly situation which is limited to a part of the United Kingdom and, accordingly, for those purposes references to the United Kingdom in sections 6 and 7 of the Fair Trading Act 1973 shall be taken to include references to a part of the United Kingdom.

(3) The persons referred to in subsection (1) above are:

(*a*) any body corporate:
  (i) which supplies goods or services by way of business,
  (ii) the affairs of which are managed by its members, and
  (iii) the members of which hold office as such by virtue of their appointment to that or another office by a Minister under any enactment; or
(*b*) any person (not falling within paragraph (*a*) above) who provides in Northern Ireland a bus service within the meaning of section 14 of the Finance Act (Northern Ireland) 1966; or
(*bb*) any person who provides a railway passenger service in pursuance of an agreement entered into by London Regional Transport by virtue of section 3(2) of the London Regional Transport Act 1984; or
(*c*) the National Rivers Authority; or
(*d*) any board administering a scheme under the Agricultural Marketing Act 1958 or the Agricultural Marketing (Northern Ireland) Order 1982; or
(*e*) any body corporate with a statutory duty to promote and assist the maintenance and development of the efficient supply of any goods or services by a body falling within paragraphs (*a*) to (*d*) above; or
(*f*) any subsidiary, within the meaning of section 736 of the Companies Act 1985, of a body falling within paragraphs (*a*) to (*e*) above.

(4) The Secretary of State may by order exclude from subsection (3)(*b*) or (*bb*) above persons of such descriptions as may be specified in the order.

(5) No question concerning a person falling within subsection (3)(*b*) or (*bb*) or a subsidiary of a body falling within either of those paragraphs may be referred to the Commission under this section unless it relates to the carriage of passengers by the person or, as the case may be, the subsidiary.

(6) The Secretary of State may at any time by notice given to the Commission vary a reference under this section.

(7) On making a reference under this section or on varying such a reference under subsection (6) above the Secretary of State shall arrange for the reference or, as the case may be, the variation to be published in such manner as he considers most suitable for bringing it to the attention of persons who in his opinion would be affected by it or be likely to have an interest in it.

(8) On a reference under this section the Commission shall investigate and report on any question referred to them but shall exclude from their investigation and report consideration of:

(*a*) any question relating to the appropriateness of any financial obligations or guidance as to financial objectives (however expressed) imposed on or given to the person in question by or under any enactment, or otherwise by a Minister; and

(*b*) the question whether any course of conduct required or envisaged as mentioned in section 2(2) above operates against the public interest.

(9) Sections 70 (time limit for report on merger reference), 84 (public interest) and 85 (attendance of witnesses and production of documents) of the Fair Trading Act 1973 and Part II of Schedule 3 to that Act (performance of functions of Commission) shall apply in relation to a reference under this section as if:

(*a*) the functions of the Commission under this section were functions under that Act;

(*b*) the expression 'merger reference' included a reference to the Commission under this section;

(*c*) in paragraph 11 of that Schedule, the reference to section 71 of that Act were a reference to subsection (6) above; and

(*d*) in paragraph 16(2) of that Schedule, the reference to section 56 of that Act were a reference to section 12 below.

(10) A report of the Commission on a reference under this section shall be made to the Secretary of State and shall state, with reasons, the conclusions of the Commission with respect to any question referred to them and, where the Commission conclude that the person specified in the reference is pursuing a course of conduct which operates against the public interest, the report may include recommendations as to what action (if any) should be taken by the person for the purpose of remedying or preventing what the Commission consider are the adverse effects of that course of conduct.

(11) In this section 'Minister' includes a Northern Ireland department and the head of such a department.

12 ORDERS FOLLOWING REPORT UNDER SECTION 11

(1) This section applies where a report of the Commission on a reference under section 11 above concludes that the person specified in the reference is pursuing a course of conduct which operates against the public interest.

(2) If it appears to the Secretary of State that any other Minister has functions directly relating to the person specified in the reference or, in the case of a reference only concerning the activities of the person in a part of the United Kingdom, functions directly relating to the person in respect of his activities in that part, he shall send a copy of the report of the Commission on the reference to that Minister; and in subsection (3) below 'the relevant Minister' means:

(*a*) in a case where it appears to the Secretary of State that any Minister (including himself) has such functions, that Minister, and

(*b*) in a case where it appears to the Secretary of State that no Minister has such functions, the Secretary of State.

(3) If:

(*a*) the relevant Minister considers it appropriate for the purpose of remedying or preventing what he considers are the adverse effects of the course of conduct specified in the report of the Commission as operating against the public interest, and

(*b*) the person specified in the reference does not fall within paragraph (*d*) of section 11(3) above and is not a subsidiary of a body falling within that paragraph,

he may by order direct the person to prepare within such time, if any, as may be specified in the order a plan for remedying or preventing such of those effects as are so specified; but where there is more than one relevant Minister no such order shall be made except by all the relevant Ministers acting jointly and where none of the relevant Ministers is the Secretary of State no such order shall be made except after consultation with him.

(4) It shall be the duty of a person to whom a direction is given under subsection (3) above to prepare such a plan as is

mentioned in that subsection and to send a copy of that plan to the Minister or Ministers by whom the order containing the direction was made who shall lay it before Parliament; and, in a case where the plan involves the use by a body of its powers in relation to any subsidiary within the meaning of section 736 of the Companies Act 1985, the plan shall specify the manner in which the body proposes using those powers.

(5) Whether or not an order has been or may be made under subsection (3) above, the Secretary of State may, if he considers it appropriate for the purpose of remedying or preventing what he considers are the adverse effects of the course of conduct specified in the report of the Commission as operating against the public interest, by order exercise one or more of the powers specified in Part I, excluding paragraph 10, of Schedule 8 to the Fair Trading Act 1973, to such extent and in such manner as he considers appropriate.

(6) In the Fair Trading Act 1973:

(*a*) section 90 (general provisions as to orders under section 56 etc.) except subsections (2) and (3).
(*b*) section 91(2) (publication of proposals to make an order),
(*c*) section 93 (enforcement of certain orders), and
(*d*) Part I (except paragraph 10) of Schedule 8 (powers exercisable by orders under section 56 etc.),

shall have effect as if any reference in those provisions to an order under section 56 of that Act included a reference to an order under subsection (5) above.

18.3 Anti-Competitive Practices (Exclusions) Order 1980 (SI 1980 No. 979)

[. . .]

2. For the purposes of the Act, a course of conduct is excluded from constituting an anti-competitive practice if it is:

(*a*) a course of conduct described in Schedule 1 to this Order, or
(*b*) the course of conduct of a person (not being a local authority within the meaning of section 2(8) of the Act):
    (i) whose relevant annual turnover in the United Kingdom is less than £5 million, and
    (ii) who enjoys less than one quarter of a relevant market, and
    (iii) who is not a member of a group of interconnected bodies corporate which has an aggregate annual turnover in the United Kingdom of £5 million or more or which enjoys one quarter or more of a relevant market;

and the provisions of Schedule 2 to this Order shall have effect for the purpose of determining whether a person is such a person as is described in subparagraph (*b*) above.

SCHEDULE 1

1. Any course of conduct which consists of:

(*a*) the inclusion in contracts for the supply of goods of conditions relating solely to the supply of those goods outside the United Kingdom, or
(*b*) the refusal to supply goods except upon such conditions.

2. Any course of conduct required or envisaged by any provision of an agreement or arrangement made under section 24 of the Transport Act 1968 or section 1 or 3 of the Transport Act 1978, being a provision the inclusion of which in the agreement or arrangement was pursuant to a duty imposed by the provision of those Acts under which the agreement or arrangement was made.

3.
(1) Any course of conduct pursued by an operator of international sea transport services in respect of such services or in respect of the acquisition of any goods or the securing of any other services in connection with the operation of such services.

(2) Any course of conduct pursued by any person solely in respect of the securing by him of international sea transport services.

(3) In this paragraph, 'international sea transport services' means the international carriage of passengers or goods wholly by sea or (where the carriage is not wholly by sea and the carriage by sea and the carriage otherwise than by sea form part of the same service) partly by sea, and includes carriage by hovercraft.

4.
(1) Any course of conduct pursued by an air transport undertaking solely in respect of international carriage by air otherwise than on a charter flight.

(2) Any course of conduct required or envisaged by a restriction accepted under an agreement described in paragraph 3(2) of the Schedule to the Restrictive Trade Practices (Services) Order 1976, being a course of conduct pursued solely in respect of international carriage by air otherwise than on a charter flight.

(3) In this paragraph, 'air transport undertaking' has the same meaning as in the Air Navigation Order 1980 and 'charter flight' means a flight on which the whole capacity of the aircraft is available for purchase by one or more charterers for his or their own use or for resale.

5.
(1) Any course of conduct required or envisaged by any agreement entered into between the Treasury (or the Treasury and the Secretary of State) and building societies which relates solely to the raising of funds or the making of loans.

(2) In this paragraph, a 'building society' means a society incorporated under the Building Societies Act 1962 or any enactment repealed by that Act (and includes a Northern Ireland society as defined in section 134 of that Act).

6. Any course of conduct required or envisaged by an agreement described in paragraph 6 of the Schedule to the said Order of 1976.

[. . .]

7.
(1) Any course of conduct pursued by a member of an association to which section 33 of the Restrictive Trade Practices Act 1976 applies, being a course of conduct required or envisaged by an agreement to which, by virtue of that section, the said Act does not apply.

(2) Any course of conduct pursued by such an association which is required or envisaged by such an agreement, not being an agreement made between the association and a person who is a member neither of the association nor of a constituent association.

8. Any course of conduct pursued by a parish or community council within the meaning of the Local Government Act 1972 or a community council established under Part IV of the Local Government (Scotland) Act 1973.

SCHEDULE 2

1. In this Schedule: 'relevant date' means:

(*a*) in a case in which notice has been given under section 3(2)(*a*) of the Act to the person in respect of whose course of conduct the question arises whether it is excluded by Article 2(*b*) above from constituting an anti-competitive practice:
  - (i) the first day of April last preceding the day on which notice was so given if that day was not the first day of April in any year, or
  - (ii) the day on which notice was so given if that day was the first day of April in any year, and

(*b*) in a case in which no notice has been given to the said person under the said section:
  - (i) the first day of April last preceding the day on which the said question arises if that day is not the first day of April in any year, or

(ii) the day on which the said question arises if that day is the first day of April in any year;

'relevant goods or services' means, in any particular case, goods or services of the description in relation to which the person in respect of whose course of conduct the question arises whether it is excluded by Article 2(b) above from constituting an anti-competitive practice was or is pursuing that course of conduct;

'relevant period' means, in relation to any particular person:

(*a*) where that person has, within the two years ending immediately before the relevant date, completed an accounting period of more than six months, the last such period so to be completed, or
(*b*) where that person has not so completed such a period but has, within the six months ending immediately before the relevant date, completed an accounting period of six months or less, so much of the period of twelve months ending on the last day of the last such period so to be completed as during which that person was carrying on a business of supplying goods or services in the United Kingdom or otherwise carrying on business in the United Kingdom, or
(*c*) in any other case, so much of the period of twelve months ending immediately before the relevant date as during which that person was carrying on a business of supplying goods or services in the United Kingdom or otherwise carrying on business in the United Kingdom; and

'turnover in the United Kingdom' during any particular period means the total amount charged for the supply of goods and services in the United Kingdom during that period in the ordinary course of a person's business, after deduction:

(*a*) of trade discounts, rebates and other allowances;
(*b*) of Value Added Tax and other taxes directly related to turnover; and
(*c*) of any amount charged for any such supply where both the person supplying the goods or services and the person to whom they were supplied were members of one and the same group of interconnected bodies corporate at the time of supply:

Provided that in a case in which the total amount of revenue receivable by a person during any particular period in the ordinary course of his business in the United Kingdom, after deduction:

(i) of amounts receivable in respect of the supply by him of goods or services;
(ii) of trade discounts, rebates and other allowances;
(iii) of Value Added Tax and other taxes directly related to turnover; and
(iv) of any amount receivable from any other person where both he and that other person were members of one and the same group of interconnected bodies corporate when payment fell due.

equals one third or more of the total amount charged for the supply of goods and services in the United Kingdom during the said period in the ordinary course of his business, after the deductions mentioned in subparagraphs (*a*), (*b*) and (*c*) above, 'turnover in the United Kingdom' during that period means the aggregate of the two said total amounts after the aforementioned respective deductions.

2. For the purposes of Article 2(*b*)(i) above, the relevant annual turnover in the United Kingdom of a person in any particular case is:

(*a*) where the relevant period equals twelve months, the turnover in the United Kingdom of that person during that period, and
(*b*) where the relevant period does not equal twelve months, the amount which bears the same proportion to the turnover in the United Kingdom of that person during that period as twelve months does to that period.

3. For the purposes of Article 2(*b*)(ii) above, a person enjoys less than one quarter of a relevant market unless, during the relevant period, he

supplied, or there were supplied to him, at least one quarter (whether determined by value, by cost, by price or by quantity) of all the relevant goods or services supplied in the United Kingdom or any part of it during that period, no account being taken of any goods or services supplied when both the person supplying the goods or services and the person to whom they were supplied were members of one and the same group of interconnected bodies corporate at the time of supply.

4. For the purposes of Article 2(*b*)(iii) above, a person is a member of a group of interconnected bodies corporate if he is a member of the group on the relevant date.

5. For the purposes of Article 2(*b*)(iii) above, the aggregate annual turnover in the United Kingdom of a group of interconnected bodies corporate in any particular case is the aggregate of the relevant annual turnover in the United Kingdom (within the meaning of paragraph 2 above) of each person who is a member of the group on the relevant date.

6. For the purposes of Article 2(*b*)(iii) above, a group of interconnected bodies corporate enjoys one quarter or more of a relevant market if, during the relevant period, the persons who are members of the group on the relevant date supplied in total, or there were supplied to such persons in total, at least one quarter (whether determined by value, by cost, by price or by quantity) of all the relevant goods or services supplied in the United Kingdom or any part of it during that period, no account being taken of any goods or services supplied when both the person supplying the goods or services and the person to whom they were supplied were members of one and the same group of interconnected bodies corporate at the time of supply.

19

MONOPOLY PRACTICES AND THE PUBLIC INTEREST

The following extracts from monopoly reports of the Monopolies and Mergers Commission demonstrate the approach of the MMC to the 'public interest'. The definition of the public interest in **section 84 of the Fair Trading Act 1973** is very wide and permissive. The MMC is thereby enabled to adopt a bespoke formulation of the public interest in each report. Although the terms of section 84 are not confined to questions of competition, the MMC will treat the competitive impact of the monopoly as the most important aspect in its review of the public interest. The following three reports concern prices and profitability. In **White Salt**, the market took the form of a highly protected duopoly in which the firms refrained from price competition. A form of price regulation was recommended to mimic, and encourage, competition.

In **Soluble Coffee**, the apparently excessive profitability of the market leader was found not to be contrary to the public interest because it did not signify ineffective competition.

In **Plasterboard**, the MMC examined the distinction between competitive and anti-competitive 'predatory' pricing. The UK approach to predatory pricing is also discussed by **Utton** in the extract in section 19.7.

19.1 Fair Trading Act 1973

84 PUBLIC INTEREST

(1) In determining for any purposes to which this section applies whether any particular matter operates, or may be expected to operate, against the public interest, the Commission shall take into account all matters which appear to them in the particular circumstances to be relevant and, among other things, shall have regard to the desirability:

(*a*) of maintaining and promoting effective competition between persons supplying goods and services in the United Kingdom;

(*b*) of promoting the interests of consumers, purchasers and other users of goods and services in the United Kingdom in respect of the prices charged for them and in respect of their quality and the variety of goods and services supplied;

(*c*) of promoting, through competition, the reduction of costs and the development and use of new techniques and new products, and of facilitating the entry of new competitors into existing markets;

(*d*) of maintaining and promoting the balanced distribution of industry and employment in the United Kingdom; and
(*e*) of maintaining and promoting competitive activity in markets outside the United Kingdom on the part of producers of goods, and of suppliers of goods and services, in the United Kingdom.

(2) This section applies to the purposes of any functions of the Commission under this Act other than functions to which section 59(3) of this Act applies.

19.2 Monopolies and Mergers Commission, *White Salt*, Cm. 9778 (HMSO, London, 1986)

The monopoly situation

9.1. We are required by our terms of reference to investigate and report whether a monopoly situation exists in relation to the supply of white salt in the United Kingdom by producers of such salt.

[. . .] In 1984 Imperial Chemical Industries PLC (ICI), through the salt business of its Mond Division, supplied 45 per cent by volume of the total supply of white salt in the United Kingdom; and [. . .] British Salt Ltd. (British Salt), a wholly-owned subsidiary of Staveley Industries PLC (Staveley), supplied 50 per cent. The separate shares of ICI and British Salt each exceeded 25 per cent of the total supply. We therefore conclude that a monopoly situation exists under the provisions of section 6(1)(*a*) of the Fair Trading Act 1973 in favour of ICI and under section 6(1)(*b*) of the Act in favour of British Salt and Staveley, the ultimate parent of British Salt.

The public interest

9.3. Having concluded that a monopoly situation exists in favour of ICI and Staveley and British Salt our terms of reference require us to state whether any steps by way of uncompetitive practices or otherwise are being taken by the monopoly producers to maintain that situation; whether any action or omission on the part of the monopoly producers is attributable to the existence of the monopoly situation; and whether there is anything that we have found that operates or may be expected to operate against the public interest.

The market

9.4. ICI and Staveley have been established in this market since the 1920s. We explained in Chapters 2 and 3 how they owe their monopoly positions in part to having acquired by different routes nearly all the numerous and fragmented salt businesses that used to make up the market. They have also acquired the necessary mineral rights, brinefields and reserves of salt in Cheshire, the area of the United Kingdom best suited logistically to the manufacture of salt. In order to establish and maintain this position the two companies introduced important economies by investment in plant and technology. They each operate one of the very few six-effect salt evaporation plants in the world. ICI has developed the controlled method of brine-winning which appears to have overcome the traditional problem of land subsidence from 'wild' brine pumping. At present this is the only method of controlled brine extraction approved by the Cheshire County Council.

9.5. From a peak of 1.5 million tonnes in 1979 the United Kingdom white salt market has shrunk to just over one million tonnes today. The decline can be attributed mainly to the fall in industrial demand, particularly in the chemical industry, and this has borne most heavily on UV salt. One might expect some rise in demand again as industrial output increases. Moreover the demand for salt in the water softening sector is on the increase. However, there are factors militating against a general rise. First there has been a permanent loss to the salt market of about 180,000 tonnes following the closure of BP Chemicals' chlorine plant in South Wales in 1982. (ICI which has taken over this production uses brine instead of salt to produce chlorine.) Secondly the campaign to reduce human consumption of salt on health grounds is growing, resulting in a fall in demand in the food sector. We doubt therefore whether demand for salt will return in the foreseeable future to its level in 1979 which the production capacities of the two companies were designed to meet.

Competition

9.6. In a market such as salt in which firms are producing broadly standardised products we would expect prices to be similar. However, depending on the particular circumstances, this similarity of prices may reflect active price competition or the lack of it. In the case of white salt we conclude that it is the latter.

9.7. [. . .] With this history parallel pricing without any formal agreement was more likely to be achieved than in an industry without such a history.

9.8. The most striking feature of the pricing behaviour of the two monopoly producers over the last ten years is the absence of a single instance of one company failing to follow the lead of the other in setting list prices.

[. . .]

Barriers to entry

9.15. The market for white salt has been dominated for many years by ICI and British Salt and we see no prospect of the position changing in the foreseeable future. It is true that there are in the country substantial salt deposits not controlled by ICI or British Salt. ICI has also indicated its willingness to license its controlled brine-winning technology to a new entrant and to provide brine in reasonable quantities and at a reasonable price while a new brinefield is being developed.

9.16. There are several factors which, taken together, suggest that new entry on a significant scale is unlikely. First, the economies of scale in the development of a brinefield and in the production of salt mean that an entrant would need to capture a substantial share of the United Kingdom market in order to avoid operating at a cost disadvantage. Second, even if a new entrant was able to secure brine in adequate quantities (and this would depend in part on its location) and on acceptable terms from ICI it would face a cost disadvantage until its own boreholes were fully developed and capable of producing strong brine. (This would take three to five years [. . .]). Third, although salt deposits exist in many areas of the country, Cheshire has certain advantages which make it the most likely centre for any future development of white salt production and the country's planning proposals favour the existing producers [. . .]. Fourth, a large part of the salt market may well be fore-closed to a new entrant as a result of the long-term relationships which ICI and British Salt have with major customers. Finally, a major feature of the industry in recent years has been a large measure of excess capacity caused by the downturn in demand. Neither company forecasts a sharp reversal in the recent trend in demand. A market dominated by two producers, with substantial excess capacity and with little prospect of a strong upturn in demand, is unlikely to prove attractive to potential entrants.

[. . .]

CONCLUSIONS

9.30. The evidence that we have found leads us to the conclusion that price competition in the United Kingdom white salt market has been extremely limited. British Salt, as the low cost producer, could have put more competitive pressure on ICI, and still have achieved a good return on capital employed. Instead in recent years it has chosen to follow the price increases of ICI, whose United Kingdom costs per tonne are significantly higher than its own. This has resulted in domestic price increases made by the two companies being significantly greater than they would have been in effective competition. Neither of the producers faces a high degree of risk. There is little threat of new imports or of new entry into the market; neither producer foresees any change in technology which might put its own process at a disadvantage; and although demand may not revert to its 1979 level, a substantial market for salt looks assured. British Salt's return on capital over the past five years, far from being inadequate, has been high by comparison with the average for manufacturing industry generally [. . .]; and it is notable that British Salt has succeeded in increasing its profits despite a diminishing volume of sales.

9.31. The reasons advanced by British Salt for so persistently matching ICI's price increases are that British Salt considered that its own costs and competitive presence influenced ICI's decisions on price increases, and that if British Salt has sought to undercut ICI this would have provoked a damaging retaliation. We do not accept that these reasons demonstrate the existence of a competitive market. If anything they merely serve to show the lack of effective competition by a company well placed to offer it.

9.32. We have not found evidence to suggest that the two monopoly producers have taken steps to exclude potential competitors from the market nor any other steps by way of uncompetitive practices or otherwise to maintain the monopoly situation. However, we do find that the lack of price competition in the United Kingdom white salt market is an omission and the pricing of white salt in that market is an action on the part both of ICI and of British Salt, and that this action and this omission are attributable to the existence of the monopoly situation. We further conclude that this action and this omission operate and may be expected to operate against the public interest. The particular effect adverse to the public interest is that the United Kingdom prices of white salt are higher than they would be in conditions of effective price competition.

POSSIBLE REMEDIES

9.33. We have considered three ways in which the adverse effect of the conduct of monopoly producers might be reduced. One would be to increase the effectiveness of the market mechanisms by, for instance, creating conditions that are more conducive to new entry or increasing the degree of competition from imports. Another would be to enhance the buying power of customers. A third way would be action by the Secretary of State including price control.

9.34. For the reasons set out in paragraphs 9.15 and 9.16 we judge new entry to be unlikely, and we do not see imports posing a substantial threat to the home producers. Some of the information in our report may increase the buying power of some customers but we do not consider that this will in itself be a sufficient remedy for the adverse effect which we have identified. Since we cannot promote the effective competition we would like to see in this market by either of the first two of these methods, we have to look to the third (action by the Secretary of State). And since the adverse effect which we wish to remedy is that United Kingdom prices are higher than they would be in conditions of effective competition, we consider that some form of control on United Kingdom prices is necessary. In the white salt market prices have been set for the last five years by the high cost producer (ICI) and have been matched by British Salt. The system of control that we seek is one which will break the link between ICI's high costs and British Salt's prices, and which will have the effect of reducing the rate of price increases below what might otherwise have been expected.

9.35. In principle it would be possible to control prices by reference to a measure of profitability. This might seem particularly relevant in the case of British Salt which, as we have shown, has been able to achieve a consistently high return on capital employed and a high margin on sales in the face of declining sales volume. However this form of control might have the possible disadvantage of weakening incentives to increase efficiency. In any case our objective can be achieved more directly by relating permitted price increases to an appropriate index relevant to the *input* costs of the salt business. We believe that this would have the effect of reducing the importance of the adverse effect which we have identified without weakening incentives to improve efficiency.

9.36. We explored the possibility of applying a single composite index which would be applicable to the salt industry as a whole. However because of the substantial differences in the product mix of the two leading producers and because ICI's key variable costs are reflections of transfer prices or rolled through costs, this approach proved to be impractical. We also discussed with British Salt and ICI the possibility of a price control system based on two indices one for each producer and related to each producer's own input costs in the salt business. However we could not derive an appropriate index for ICI which reflected its own costs and at the same time was likely to be effective in controlling prices, since such an index would reflect unduly its own internal transfer prices rather than input costs which were outside its control.

9.37. We believe that price control by means of an index based on the structure of British Salt's costs and applied to British Salt is the most appropriate and effective means of remedying the adverse effect on the market that we have identified in paragraph 9.31 – namely that white salt prices are higher than they would be in conditions of effective price competition. This system of control will restrain both the level of British Salt's prices and the level of prices in the salt market as a whole. The practical effect of applying the index to British Salt's prices is that a limit is imposed beyond which no other producer will be able to raise its prices without jeopardising its market share. It will break the present link between British Salt's prices and ICI's costs and will also increase the pressure on ICI to improve its efficiency. At the same time it will not weaken British Salt's incentive to continue to improve its efficiency.

9.38. Dendritic and granular salt will not be affected by our proposed system of control because these products are not produced by British Salt. However, we do not consider this to be a serious weakness. Very little dendritic salt is sold in the United Kingdom. As for granular salt, prices are unlikely to move far out of line with those of UV and PDV. Some substitution between granular salt and PDV is possible and there is also competition from imported rock salt and salt tablets.

9.39. It may seem paradoxical to apply controls only to one company and moreover to the one we have commended for its efficiency. We have discussed price control with the main producers and New Cheshire Salt Works Ltd. Their views are summarised in Appendix 9.1. ICI recognises that these controls will effectively set the domestic price levels for ICI and the other producers as well as for British Salt. ICI expressed concern at the possibility of being constrained by a system related to the different operating regime of another producer. However, this would apply whether there were two separate indices or one relating to British Salt only. For in a two-index system the price level would tend to be determined by the index reflecting the lower increases in cost and therefore the smaller increases in price. Although we have looked at other possibilities (see paragraph 9.36), we have found them wanting in some respect or other. In all the circumstances therefore an index applied to British Salt alone but with the wider purpose described in paragraph 9.37 is our favoured option.

9.40. The index would be derived from the main components of British Salt's production costs weighted according to the contribution each makes to its total costs. Movement in the cost of the individual inputs would be based on movements in published price indices. [. . .]

9.41. We have stated that the aim of price control in accordance with this index is to reduce the level of future prices below what otherwise might have been expected while not undermining incentives to maintain efficiency. Also in a properly functioning competitive market, where there is effective price competition, part of any gain in efficiency is passed on to the consumer and part retained as profit as a proper reward for that efficiency.

[. . .]

9.42. We do not think therefore that British Salt should be allowed to increase its prices fully in line with the cost index. We believe that the maximum level of United Kingdom prices overall should be determined by the increase in the index in each year abated by one percentage point. In the first year of operation (1986) the maximum permitted level of prices relative to that of the base date 31 January 1985 should be determined by the increases in the cost index relative to their January 1985 level, less one percentage point. The maximum permitted level each year would form the starting point for calculating the permitted prices for the following year which would be determined by the further increases in the cost index less one percentage point.

9.43. The relevant increase in the input cost index to be used in implementing the price control system will be the increase in the 12 months prior to the proposed date of implementation of the price increase. The increase in the input cost index will in part be based on the known increases in the component indices [. . .] say for six months, and in part on estimated increases for the remainder of the 12-month period. The estimated increases in each of the components should be at the same average monthly rate as are available from the published data covering part of the year. Any differences which may emerge when data for the full 12 months are published would be dealt with by adjusting the base allowable level from which the subsequent increase is to be calculated.

9.44. We recommend that British Salt's domestic prices should be limited in this way for a period of five years as amplified in paragraph 9.45(*b*), and that thereafter the matter should be reviewed. We aim to minimise the burdensome effect which controls inevitably have and suggest that the system be operated with a degree of flexibility. Provided that British Salt and Staveley (as the parent of British Salt) have given appropriate undertakings (see below) we see no need for prior notification of intended price increases. If during the period that price control is in operation there were a major change in circumstances which resulted in the special index ceasing to control prices in the way that is intended, the index should be re-examined. And, if there were to be major structural changes in the market which no longer required the existence of an external price regulator, then consideration should be given to terminating the system of controls sooner than five years. We recommend that in the absence of appropriate undertakings, the Secretary of State should make an order to regulate the prices concerned.

19.3 Monopolies and Mergers Commission, *Soluble Coffee*, Cm. 1459 (HMSO, London, 1991)

THE PUBLIC INTEREST ISSUES

7.52. The central issue of our inquiry is whether the profits and prices of Nestlé, the scale monopolist, result from its exploitation of its monopoly position in a market where there is inadequate competition, or reflect its success in conditions of effective competition.

The profitability of Nestlé

7.53. [. . .] Nestlé's return on tangible capital employed in 1989 was some 114 per cent, considerably above the average rate of profitability elsewhere in the economy, or in the food, drink and tobacco sector industry in particular [. . .].

[. . .]

7.55. [. . .] Even allowing for both the age profile of Nestlé's assets, and the possibly abnormally low value of its coffee stocks, its return on capital employed would still be in the order of 70 per cent, a high rate of return by any criteria.

7.56. A further argument raised by Nestlé was that the accounting measure of capital employed excluded the value of its brands. Goodwill, including brand values, arising on acquisition is sometimes included in published balance sheets, but it is not the general practice to attribute a value to brands where it has been internally generated, although a number of well-known companies have started to do so in recent years. Nestlé provided us with a valuation of its brands by Interbrands UK Ltd, made for the purpose of our inquiry [. . .]. This valuation, it emphasised, was not intended to arrive at an arm's length value of what the brands might fetch if sold, as it was intended to exclude any element that might represent the capitalisation of monopoly profits.

7.57. We must clearly accept that successful brands do have value to their owner and indeed are helpful to consumers, who may prefer to choose branded products for their assurance of reliable quality. There are doubts, however, as to whether brands can be valued with any accuracy in the absence of the evidence provided by an arm's length sale. It is also difficult to distinguish to what extent profits result from the development of a successful brand in a competitive market, and to what extent they result from monopoly profits in a market that is not fully competitive. Although Nestlé believed that the brand valuation it provided to us avoided any circularity of approach – by which the value of 'monopoly' profits would be capitalised, thus reducing the return on capital to a normal level – any approach to the measurement of profitability by reference to a capital base that includes brand values or goodwill must, in our view, introduce an element of circularity, in so far as it places a value on the ability of the business to earn profits in excess of the normal return on its tangible capital. Moreover the criteria that were used in evaluating the strength of the brands themselves depended on the extent to which the products were 'market leaders'. An alternative approach used by Nestlé, which involved capitalising and then amortising advertising expenditure, is also subjective in that it depends heavily on the rate of amortisation used.

7.58. A further difficulty in including brand values is that to do so would invalidate comparisons with the profitability of industry generally, or with other firms in the food, drink and tobacco manufacturing sector, the profitability statistics for which do not take account of the value of brands. To the extent, therefore, that other firms in the sector have successful brands, figures for the average profitability of the sector, with which it would seem appropriate to compare Nestlé's profits, would be correspondingly overstated. We have not, therefore, felt it appropriate, in considering Nestlé's profitability for the purpose of this inquiry, to take account of the value of Nestlé brands, but have considered its profitability on the basis of its tangible capital employed.

7.59. Nestlé also argued that the profitability of its reference business could not be considered in isolation from the rest of its business. [. . .] [I]ts overall return on capital employed in 1989 was over 40 per cent, considerably higher than for industry generally, but well below that of its reference business. Nestlé suggested that any food manufacturer would have a mix of more and less successful activities. Although it did not believe that there was any intentional cross-subsidisation, it argued that high returns were necessary on the more successful activities, if a company was to risk investing across the range of its activities, and was to develop new products. It further argued that the profitability it achieved on its most successful brands should be compared with the profitability achieved by other food companies on their successful brands and indeed Nestlé gave us examples of some of its other successful brands in competitive markets with returns on capital employed similar to that on soluble coffee. In this connection, Nestlé emphasised that Nescafé is one of a relatively small number of uniquely successful products in the food market, and that its profitability reflects that. In turn, Nescafé's profitability is a major contributor to the profitability of Nestlé's coffee business [. . .].

7.60. We, however, have to examine only the soluble coffee market and have available to us only aggregate information on other companies. In these circumstances, therefore, we seem to have little alternative but to consider Nestlé's profits on its reference business alone compared with those in the economy in general, or the food manufacturing industry in particular.

7.61. Nestlé also argued that we should not have regard only to the more recent levels of profitability on its reference business. Average returns on capital on soluble coffee over the period 1976 to 1989 were around 50 per cent, regardless of whether historical or replacement costs are used; Nestlé believed that profitability was currently at a peak (although maintained in 1990) and that such high profits were unlikely to recur. It would, however, seem wrong to us to discount the very high profitability – of about 100 per cent or more over the last three years – by reference to its lower profitability of the earlier ten years.

7.62. In our view, therefore, we have to consider the recent profitability of Nestlé's reference business as measured in accordance with principles adopted in preparing its accounts, while acknowledging that this may be overstated to an extent by the present age profile of its assets and possibly the current low coffee bean prices. On this basis Nestlé's profitability is high, relative both to other industries and to other enterprises in its own industry. High profits can, however, be viewed as the reward for success in a competitive industry; we have to consider whether this is so in Nestlé's case, or whether its high profitability reflects its monopoly position in the market, possibly in conjunction with the ineffectiveness of competition, or potential competition, in that market.

[. . .]

7.64. [. . .] [T]here are well in excess of 200 types of soluble coffee available in the United Kingdom produced by a dozen or more suppliers. [. . .] Nescafé itself was sold at a premium of some 5p per 100 grammes on the Maxwell House price, and at a significantly larger premium on own-label granulated coffee prices. Consumer preference for the leading Nestlé brands, particularly for Nescafé, the main contributor to its profitability, reflects therefore the outcome of consumer choice among a wide range of alternatives and a preference for a perceived higher quality at a somewhat higher price.

7.65. Although there is a wide range of choice available, and a number of competing suppliers, we still, however, have to consider whether Nestlé's market position is such as to limit the effectiveness of this competition, or enable Nestlé, for example, to set the overall level of prices in the industry.

7.66. [. . .] [C]ompetition between soluble coffees has been described as in 'value for money', encompassing quality improvements, price and brand image, supported by advertising. The market research studies we have seen confirm that quality has improved over time, and that most participants in the market are continuing to improve the quality of their products. Given the continuing choice available to consumers, with a wide spectrum of price and quality alternatives, these improvements in quality would appear to accord with consumer preferences. Nestlé has indeed increased its market share at the expense of own label by offering higher quality and better value for money, despite higher prices. The increasing success of its brands, particularly of Nescafé, given the extent of choice available reflects Nestlé's success as a competitor in offering a reliable product at a quality and price in accordance with consumer preference.

7.67. We have considered to what extent the emphasis on quality has reduced price competition. We have noted the similar movements in the list prices of Nescafé and Maxwell House. There is, however, a greater variation in manufacturers' prices, taking account of discounts, and more intensive price competition in supplying own-label coffees. Own-label price movements have not therefore always followed the lead of the main brands, and competition from own label would seem to provide at least some further constraint on the pricing policies of both Nestlé and GFL [the manufacturer of Maxwell House], particularly as retailers establish a higher quality image for their own-label soluble coffees. Despite the wide range of retail prices, there has, however, been little aggressive price competition to Nestlé from soluble coffees of comparable quality.

7.68. Competition may strengthen further. GFL has acknowledged that its performance in the past has not been as effective as it could have been, but is clearly determined to continue to improve the quality of its products. The quality of several own-label soluble coffees is also being improved so that they will offer a quality more comparable with that of Nestlé or GFL but at lower prices.

The position of Nestlé's competitors

7.69. We have also considered the extent to which the other suppliers in the market are in a position to compete effectively with Nestlé. Their soluble coffee businesses are clearly much less profitable than that of Nestlé, but the main competitors are part of larger groups in a position to support their activities in this market, and there are a number of other major food companies (such as Douwe Egberts) whose presence in the market is at present only limited. It is indeed possible that present price levels have encouraged some of these competitors to stay in the market, thus improving the outlook for competition in the longer term.

7.70. Nestlé's success would, however, appear to have given it a number of competitive advantages. Its lower unit costs, both of production and of advertising, may in part reflect the scale economies given by a market share at least twice the size of its biggest competitor. It clearly has a strong brand image, well supported by advertising, which may benefit from the umbrella 'Nescafé' branding it employs, but is also sustained by the reliability of its product.

7.71. Nestlé is not, however, in an unchallengeable position: it pointed to GFL's experience in the United States, where the market share of Maxwell House declined from 40 per cent to 20 per cent over a 25-year period. A similar major change could in our view occur in the United Kingdom market, should the quality of Nestlé's product or its competitive performance deteriorate, its prices increase beyond a competitive level, or its competitors equal or surpass its present quality or performance.

The position of retailers

7.72. We also believe that retailers' own-label coffees are in a strong competitive position, despite their decline in market share in the last ten years. Retailers are able to determine the allocation of shelf space, and thus the positioning of their and their competitors' products: retailers have also attempted, in so far as they are able, to adopt some of the features of the Nestlé brands. Any improvement in the quality of retailers' own-label coffees would, in our view, improve their competitive position further.

7.73. Nestlé would appear to derive some advantage from the lower retail margins on its products as a result of which the differences in manufacturers' prices between Nestlé and its competitors are not fully reflected in price differences at retail level. This advantage arises in turn from Nestlé's market position and competition between retailers themselves: Nestlé cannot be regarded as imposing such lower margins, or determining retail prices.

7.74. The lower retail margins on Nestlé's products may in part reflect their higher stockturn, a further advantageous consequence of its strong position in the market. Retailers would, however, also seem unable to exert any significant countervailing power over Nestlé. Given the strength of its brands in the marketplace they are not in a position to refuse to stock Nescafé. Given that Nescafé is one of a number of 'known value items' on which competition between retailers is most intensive, retailers also have little option but to accept lower margins on the Nestlé brands.

7.75. Retailers are, by contrast, able to obtain lower manufacturers' prices and thus earn higher margins, on lesser brands and on own-label soluble coffees, which indeed provides them with an inducement to stock such products. The other manufacturers to whom we spoke agreed that the higher retail margins on their products put them at some disadvantage compared with Nestlé: but did not believe that this disadvantage was sufficient to prevent them from offering effective competition to Nestlé.

Entry

7.76. Nestlé's success is establishing its position in the market and its strong brand image also give it some advantage over new entrants to the market. New entrants have to offer retailers higher margins if their products are to be stocked, and retailers may require new brands to perform well in a short time if they are to continue to be stocked, and adequate advertising of such brands to ensure their good performance.

7.77. Such advertising costs would not, however, seem particularly high for branded grocery products. There is also no shortage in the supply of soluble coffee for import into the United Kingdom. The disadvantages would not therefore seem to be so great as to deter entry to the market, and a number of new entrants have built up niche market positions. There may be less prospect of new entrants competing with Nestlé head-on although we have not come across any case where Nestlé has aggressively retaliated against competition. Any deterioration in Nestlé's performance would, however, in our view be expected to lead to more sustained competition from new entrants into the industry.

Whether Nestlé's profitability reflects ineffective competition

7.78. While we can point to a number of advantages to Nestlé that arise from its market position, and various weaknesses in the position of its competitors, we do not believe that competition can be characterised as 'ineffective'. Competition has brought the benefits of considerable consumer choice, and of improvements in quality and, in our view, while there may have been little aggressive price competition, there is sufficient competition or potential competition on prices to set a ceiling to the prices that can be charged by Nestlé. Nestlé's very advantages stem from its success as a competitor; it has increased its market share by offering a good quality product, its advertising is more effective, its leading brands stronger, and in a number of other ways it appears to have been more efficient than its competitors. Its position reflects its success: it cannot disregard its competitors who are either members of major food groups, or retailers with own-label coffee, the latter being well placed to promote their products at the expense of Nestlé's.

7.79. It may be regretted that no other firm has to date proved as effective a competitor as Nestlé, but this is no reason, we feel, to conclude that Nestlé's performance is against the public interest, or to intervene in the market. Nestlé is, in our view, a highly effective and successful competitor in this market: its high profitability need not lead us to penalise that success in a market characterised by such a wide degree of choice. Its high profitability should indeed be seen as an incentive for other firms to compete in this lucrative market.

7.80. Regulatory intervention, in the event of an adverse finding, could offer some short-term benefits in the form of price reductions, but – particularly given the poorer profitability of Nestlé's competitors – it would carry the considerable risk of there being less choice, poorer quality and weaker competition in the long run. The interests of consumers, who already have the option of purchasing cheaper coffee should they so choose, are in our view best served by the maintenance of competition. Only if there were to be a significant deterioration in the competitive structure of the market – such as, for example, the withdrawal of all or some of Nestlé's competitors or the abandonment by retailers of their own-label coffees – do we believe that intervention should be considered. In the present market situation intervention would itself be likely to cause such a deterioration in market structure, and cause the withdrawal of some suppliers from the market with adverse consequences in the longer term.

19.4 Monopolies and Mergers Commission, *Plasterboard*, Cm. 1224 (HMSO, London, 1990)

9.9. The supply of plasterboard was previously referred to the Monopolies Commission for investigation and report on 4 September 1972. The Commission reported on 12 October 1973 and the report was published in January 1974. At that time BPB was the only manufacturer of plasterboard within the United Kingdom. BPB supplied Northern Ireland, as it does now, with imports from its subsidiary in the Republic of Ireland. There were no other significant imports into the United Kingdom.

9.10. The report found that BPB's system of uniform delivered prices for most of the United Kingdom market, its practice of discouraging collection by the customer, including particularly its inadequate collection allowance, and its practice of selling only through merchants and not direct to users operated, and might be expected to operate, against the public interest [. . .].

[. . .]

9.11. Following the report, BPB gave undertakings to the Secretary of State [. . .] to the effect that it, and its subsidiaries, would:

(*a*) allow collection from, and charge the same ex-works prices at, its different plants;
(*b*) charge delivered prices which enabled BG to recoup the cost of transport within any delivery zone [. . .]; and
(*c*) allow users to buy direct from the company at the same prices as charged to merchants.

[. . .]

9.12. The Office of Fair Trading (OFT) told us it believed that BPB had breached the undertakings, by reducing prices in South-West England and South Wales [. . .].

[. . .]

9.64. [. . .] The central issue is whether, in the light of current and expected competition in the supply of plasterboard, the undertakings should continue to apply to BPB, either in their present form or otherwise. [. . .]

[. . .]

9.66. All the evidence we have received in this inquiry shows that there has been vigorous competition in the British plasterboard market since the entry of the two new manufacturers, RPL and Knauf, whose advent coincided with a recession in the building industry.

9.67. BPB's prices for its main products have fallen sharply since January 1989. [. . .]

9.68. The strategy of the new entrants has been to offer list prices below those of BPB, supplemented in RPL's case by selective discounts to individual customers. These lower prices have been allied with a considerable marketing effort. The results are demonstrated by the growth of market share of the new entrants, the number of customers which they have gained and the recognition which they have achieved, even among those customers not purchasing from them, that they are realistic alternatives to BPB as plasterboard suppliers. In a period of about two years, RPL and Knauf have together achieved a 28 per cent market share.

9.69. Apart from price competition,

many customers consider that, in response to the arrival of the new entrants, BPB's quality of service has improved.

9.70. BPB's pricing strategy has included some price cutting which is selective in effect, in particular through its two quantity discount schemes, under which it has offered substantial discounts to its major customers. It has retained all, or the major part of, the plasterboard business of many of its largest customers.

9.71. The increased discounts introduced by BPB in June 1990 brought a prompt response from RPL and Knauf, who both increased their own discounts. If the new lower general level of prices in the industry is maintained, the public will benefit. There will be further pressure on all the suppliers to improve their quality of service.

[. . .]

9.72. RPL has claimed that BPB's June 1990 discounts are predatory in intent on the grounds that they are not sustainable in the long run and can therefore only be aimed at driving the new entrants out of the market, so that BPB can then raise prices again unhindered by competition.

9.73. There are three interrelated factors in this case which we consider to be relevant in determining the distinction between, on the one hand, acceptable competitive pricing aimed at preserving or increasing market share, and on the other hand, predatory pricing, by which we mean pricing at a level which is not sustainable in the long run and which is designed to drive out competitors and thus enable prices subsequently to be raised. These are:

(*a*) the relationship between prices and costs;
(*b*) the intentions of the firm accused of predation; and
(*c*) the structure of the market.

(*a*) The relationship between prices and costs

9.74. BPB has provided us with evidence that its latest realised prices exceed total average costs (including depreciation). An analysis of BPB's average set sales realisation and average cost of sales at the different levels of discount offered showed that even for a customer obtaining the best terms available, BPB's net profit margin on the plasterboard sold at this maximum discount would still be positive. These best terms would include the maximum merchants' discount of 22.5 per cent, a prompt settlement discount of 2.5 per cent, and the maximum available discount under the Gyproc Super Stockist Scheme of [*] per cent. Even allowing for some uncertainty in BPB's estimates of modest cost savings resulting from the changes in the pattern of sales brought about by the new discount structure, we are satisfied that BPB's latest realised prices are all above total average costs. Knauf for its part has told us that it considers the latest prices to be sustainable in the long term by BPB and itself.

(*b*) Intentions of BPB

9.75. BPB has told us that the purpose of its latest price cuts is to stem the steep decline in its sales volumes and thus its profitability which has resulted from the lower prices offered by its competitors. Its aim is to defend a 'base-load' level of sales at which it believes it could operate profitably. In March 1990 its capacity utilisation was about 55 per cent, well below the level at which its unit costs start to rise, further threatening profitability. We accept that the June 1990 price cuts can be reasonably explained in terms of BPB's tactics to defend itself in a market which is subject to considerable overcapacity and in which its position is being eroded. Further evidence of BPB's intentions can be deduced from the structure of the market, which we discuss below.

(*c*) Structure of the market

9.76. We have shown that there is vigorous competition in the plasterboard market in Britain. Whether this competition will continue depends in part on the willingness and ability of RPL and Knauf to continue manufacturing plasterboard at their British plants.

9.77. BPB has put it to us that Knauf must be regarded as established in the

United Kingdom market as they have expended substantial sums in the building of their plants and in the establishment of a United Kingdom sales force.

9.78. The sinking of substantial capital in new manufacturing plants is clearly evidence of an intention not only to enter but to remain in a market. RPL and Knauf have between them committed some £75 million on the three new plants at Bristol, Sittingbourne and Immingham, which will have a combined capacity of about 93 million square metres.

9.79. We have already shown [. . .] that both RPL and Knauf have succeeded in building up a sound customer base. We estimate RPL's current market share as 18 per cent and Knauf's as 10 per cent. Towards the beginning of our inquiry a number of large merchants, who were buying plasterboard from the two new producers as well as from BPB, told us [. . .] that they regarded RPL and Kanuf as established in the market and, once any teething troubles had been diposed of, able to compete fully with BPB on price, quality and delivery.

9.80. As to the financial standing of the two new entrants, RPL is owned by two powerful parents, both prominent suppliers of building materials, whose interests include plasterboard manufacture in Australia, France, the Netherlands and Norway. One of the parents, Redland, is a major force in the British market for building materials other than plasterboard. RPL seems in a position to withstand sustained price competition from BPB.

[. . .]

9.82. Knauf has stated that it is prepared to wait many years before it achieves a profitable operation in Britain and we accept this statement. Although we do not have access to details of the finances of Knauf's parent, Knauf OHG, which as a West German *Offene Handelsgesellschaft* is not required to publish accounts, it is generally accepted in the industry that the parent is strong and could therefore sustain losses that might arise from the need to respond to vigorous price cutting by BPB for a substantial period of time. Moreover, in West Germany Knauf OHG is the major producer of plasterboard and is in a position to retaliate against price competition in Britain by cutting prices in West Germany and thereby depressing the margins of BPB's West German subsidiary.

9.84. We therefore conclude that, even in the face of keen competition by BPB, RPL and Knauf may be expected to remain viable competitors. They have invested substantial capital in starting up manufacture in Great Britain; the financial position of their parents is strong; and each of them has built up a sound customer base.

9.85. In the light of the relevant considerations, we conclude that BPB's latest price custs were not predatory. BPB's resulting realised prices are expected to exceed total average costs; the cuts are explicable as a competitive action by BPB in a market in which it is under threat, particularly at a time of excess capacity; and having regard to the structure of the market it is implausible to suppose that BPB considered that the cuts were likely to drive out either RPL or Knauf.

The nature of control under Article 86 is not directed at a broad approach to the public interest. It is, rather, a prohibition of such conduct of a dominant undertaking as amounts to an abuse of its dominance, in so far as such abuse may affect trade between Member States. Although the purpose of control differs in this way, the nature of the dominant undertaking's conduct will not. The Monopolies and Mergers Commission report on **Plasterboard** was informed by a prior decision of the European Commission under Article 86; the European Commission's decision in **Napier Brown–British Sugar** relied heavily on the findings of the MMC in two mergers reports concerning the same relevant market. In the latter decision, the Commission dealt with a number of price-related abuses as well as abuse comprising in a refusal to supply. In the **Tetra Pak** decision, the Court of First Instance determined the relationship of Article 85 and Article 86 in the context of the control of abusive conduct.

19.5 *Napier Brown–British Sugar*, Decision of the Commission of the European Communities OJ L 284, 19.10.88, p. 41; [1990] 4 CMLR 196

(1) This Decision arises from an application pursuant to Article 3 of Regulation No. 17 by Napier Brown and Company Ltd. (hereinafter NB) and certain other United Kingdom sugar merchants – a complaint that was extended and enlarged by NB in mid-1985. NB alleged that British Sugar plc, part of the large multinational group S. & W. Berisford had, contrary to Article 86 of the EEC Treaty, abused the dominant position which it holds in the United Kingdom granulated sugar market.

[. . .]

C. ABUSE OF A DOMINANT POSITION

Refusal to supply

(61) BS refused to supply NB with industrial sugar. NB requested 30,000 tonnes of industrial sugar during 1985/86 sugar year, and BS was only prepared to offer NB 7,148 tonnes or to offer NB 30,000 tonnes of 'special grain' sugar at a price so high that NB would be unable to use the sugar. BS claims that its refusal to meet NB's request is justified by the necessity of it implementing a quota scheme.

(62) However, the evidence outlined above shows that the quota scheme implemented by BS was not necessary and was put forward only in order to justify BS's refusal to supply.

BS refused to supply NB with the objective of removing NB as a producer of retail sugar; it is clear that the natural and foreseeable consequence of the refusal to supply NB would be to precipitate NB's withdrawal from the retail sugar market. Indeed, the handwritten document of BS's marketing executive director, proposing to refuse to supply NB, and the documents found at BS relating to BS's de-listing policy, indicate that BS's refusal to supply was made with just such an intention.

(63) NB cannot be considered to be a new client of BS in relation to this refusal to supply. BS had supplied NB with industrial sugar before, e.g. 30,000 tonnes in 1984/85, a similar amount and type of sugar that NB was requesting in the present case. The fact that NB intended to package a part of this into retail bags, selling the rest to industrial clients as it had done in the past cannot result in NB being considered as a new client for the purposes of this case.

(64) The Commission considers that BS has abused its dominant position by refusing to supply industrial sugar to NB without objective necessity, the intention or foreseeable result of which would have been to precipitate the removal of NB from the United Kingdom retail sugar market, thereby reducing competition on that market.

This conclusion is supported by the judgment of the European Court in Joined Cases 6 and 7/73: *ICI and CSC* v. *Commission* ('Commercial Solvents') (6 March 1974, ECR [1974], 223, at point 25 (also *United Brands* v. *Commission*, Case 22/76; 14 February 1978, ECR [1978], 207).). In this case the European Court held that:

> an undertaking being in a dominant position as regards the production of raw material and therefore able to control the supply to manufacturers of derivatives, cannot, just because it decides to start manufacturing these derivatives (in competition with its former customers) act in such a way as to

eliminate their competition which in the case in question, would amount to eliminating one of the principal manufacturers of ethambutol in the common market.

Since such conduct is contrary to the objectives expressed in Article 3(*f*) of the Treaty and set out in greater detail in Article 85 and 86, it follows that an undertaking which has a dominant position in the market in raw materials and which, with the object of reserving such raw material for manufacturing its own derivatives, refuses to supply a customer, which is itself a manufacturer of these derivatives and therefore risks eliminating all competition on the part of this customer, is abusing his dominant position within the meaning of Article 86 . . .

BS's pricing policy

(i) The pricing policy of BS regarding its sales of retail sugar since NB's entry onto the retail sugar market

(65) The pricing information indicated above shows that BS has engaged in a price cutting campaign leaving an insufficient margin for a packager and seller of retail sugar, as efficient as BS itself in its packaging and selling operations, to survive in the long term.

(66) The maintaining, by a dominant company, which is dominant in the markets for both a raw material and a corresponding derived product, of a margin between the price which it charges for a raw material to the companies which compete with the dominant company in the production of the derived product and the price which it charges for the derived product, which is insufficient to reflect that dominant company's own costs of transformation (in this case the margin maintained by BS between its industrial and retail sugar prices compared to its own repackaging costs) with the result that competition in the derived product is restricted, is an abuse of dominant position (for a similar case under the ECSC Treaty, see *National Carbonising Company* v. *Commission*, Case 109/75, 22 October 1975, [1976] 2 CMLR 457).

In the present case, BS's action of reducing the margin between its industrial and retail sugar prices such that it sold retail sugar at a price which no longer reflected its own transformation costs resulted in an abuse of a dominant position and a restriction of competition within the meaning of Article 86. It is clear from the facts as set out above that should BS have maintained this margin in the long term, NB, or any company equally efficient in repackaging as BS without a self-produced source of industrial sugar, would have been obliged to leave the United Kingdom retail sugar market. Thus, taken in the context of the other abuses as outlined above, and of the fact that the intention or natural and foreseeable consequence of the maintenance of this pricing policy by BS would be the removal of NB from the British retail sugar market, the Commission considers that BS's pricing policy constitutes an abuse of a dominant position within the meaning of Article 86.
[. . .]

(ii) Ex factory pricing

(69) BS has accepted that, before the end of 1986, it refused to supply sugar to its customers unless the customer also accepted that BS itself (whether BS delivered the sugar itself or did so through third parties acting under contract for BS being irrelevant) supplied the service of delivery of the sugar. It was thus reserving for itself the separate but ancillary activity of delivering the sugar which could, under normal circumstances be undertaken by an individual contractor acting alone (e.g. acting as a real merchant delivering the sugar to a third party customer using his own transport facilities). As the MMC stated in paragraph 2.104 of its second report 'merchants also sell on their own account sugar purchased from the two United Kingdom producers. This form of competition can be expected to restrain the United Kingdom producers from charging excessively for distribution (although not if they refuse to supply sugar on an ex-factory basis.)'

(70) The Commission is not aware of any objective necessity requiring BS to reserve such an activity to itself, and the fact that following BS's undertaking it has offered a

choice to its clients between ex factory or delivered sugar, indicates that no such objective necessity exists.

(71) The Commission considers that BS has abused its dominant position on the sugar market by refusing to grant to its customers an option between purchasing sugar on an ex factory or delivered price basis, thereby reserving for itself the ancillary activity of the delivery of that sugar, thus eliminating all competition in relation to the delivery of the products.

(72) This conclusion is supported by the judgment of the European Court in the Case *Centre Belge d'Etudes de Marché-Télé-Marketing SA* v. *Compagnie Luxembourgeoise de Télédiffusion SA and Information Publicité Benelux SA* (Case 311/84) [1985] ECR 3261, [1986] 2 CMLR 558. In this case, the Court held that:

> an abuse within the meaning of Article 86 is committed where, without any objective necessity, an undertaking holding a dominant position on a particular market reserves to itself or to an undertaking belonging to the same group, an ancillary activity which might be carried out by another undertaking as part of its activities on a neighbouring but separate market, with the possibility of eliminating all competition from such undertaking.

Beet origin; discrimination

(73) The Commission considers that BS has applied 'discriminatory conditions to equivalent transactions with other trading parties, thereby placing them at a competitive disadvantage' (Article 86(*c*) EEC.), and has thus abused its dominant position, by denying exclusively beet-origin sugar to NB, while supplying it to others.

Group commitment, or loyalty bonuses

(74) BS made an offer to the [. . .] which involved the granting by BS of a rebate on the price it was willing to offer the members of the buying group at that time purchasing exclusively from BS if, in future, all the members of [. . .] agreed to purchase exclusively from BS.

Such an offer, which has the effect of requiring certain existing BS customers to 'tie-in' other companies to purchase exclusively from BS in order to receive a reduced price for retail sugar, is, in a manner similar to the operation of a loyalty rebate, designed to deprive the purchasers in question of, or restrict their possible choices of, sources of supply and furthermore to deny other producers, and in this case specifically NB, access to the market.

Due to the commitment bonus, pressure was put upon the members of [. . .] not purchasing from BS to recommence purchasing from BS, not only because they would benefit from the bonus themselves but also because, should they wish to purchase elsewhere for price or quality reasons, the remaining members of the group would thereafter be obliged to pay a higher price for their sugar. As a result of BS's offer, one member of the group, [. . .] which was previously purchasing from NB, switched to purchasing sugar from BS.

(75) The Commission considers that BS has abused its dominant position by offering to conclude, and subsequently concluding, a contract which included a provision for a group commitment bonus.

(76) This conclusion is confirmed by the judgment of the European Court in the case *Hoffman-La Roche* v. *Commission* (ECR [1979] 461, paragraph 89. Also *United Brands* v. *Commission*, ECR [1978] 207.), in which the European Court of Justice considered the application of Article 86 to exclusive purchasing contracts and fidelity rebates involving a dominant undertaking.

D. EFFECT ON TRADE BETWEEN MEMBER STATES

(77) The Commission considers that the facts as outlined above establish that BS engaged in practices which had the foreseeable result that NB would have been forced to withdraw from the retail sugar market. Indeed, in this case, evidence (e.g. the documents regarding 'de-listing') shows that the alleged abuses were carried out with the intention of removing NB from that market.

The removal of NB from the British retail sugar market would have had clear effects upon trade between Member States, and furthermore, would have affected the structure of competition and trade within the common market.

(78) A United Kingdom sugar merchant such as NB has two sources of sugar, domestic and imports, and will import sugar for resale whenever, for example, currency fluctuations make such imports profitable. Thus, NB has purchased in the past, and intends to purchase in the future, sugar from other Member States for both its retail and industrial operations whenever conditions are favourable. Contrary to BS's arguments, these imports cannot be considered to be abnormal and artificial but are part of the normal pattern of trade.

Imports of sugar into the United Kingdom have in the past been almost exclusively of industrial sugar (imports of retail sugar are difficult not only because English language bags must be specifically printed for such an operation, but furthermore because drop sizes are generally smaller for retail than for industrial sugar) (see, for example, paragraph 5.8 of the first MMC report).

NB entered the market using, and intending to continue using, both domestic and imported industrial sugar for its repackaging operations. As a result of NB's entry onto the market, an avenue was opened whereby imported industrial sugar would for the first time be used for retail repackaging whenever conditions favoured the use of such sugar – NB, being the only British repackager without its own domestically produced source of sugar, is thus the only repackager free to choose to source its sugar for repackaging from either domestic or imported sugar, whichever is cheaper at any moment in time. Should NB have been removed from the market, this avenue through which imported sugar could freely and easily be sold upon the British retail market, would have been effectively closed.

NB entered the British retail sugar market because it believed that the differential between the selling price of packet sugar and that of bulk sugar greatly exceeded the cost of an efficient packaging operation (see paragraph 2.104 of the first MMC report). This large differential occurred because although, as recognized above, imported sugar effectively limits the price that may be charged for industrial sugar in Britain, such imported sugar could not effectively limit retail prices due to the difficulties in importing retail sugar which are outlined above. NB's entry onto the retail market established the first link, independent from domestically produced industrial sugar, between the price of industrial sugar which is limited by the price of imports, and retail sugar, the price of which has not to the same extent, been limited by the price of imported sugar. Should NB have been removed from the retail sugar market, this independent link between British retail and industrial sugar prices, and thus between imported industrial and British retail sugar prices, would have been effectively closed.

Thus the Commission concludes that an effect on trade between Member States would have resulted from NB's removal from the market. This is confirmed by the following argument put forward by BS before the MMC in 1981, in which BS recognizes the importance of sugar imported by merchants as a real restraint to the maximum prices that BS may charge on the British market:

> Since BS was the price leader in the UK and Tate & Lyle (because of its low margins) was a price follower, imported continental sugar was the key to price competition. As long as there was a substantial surplus of sugar in the EEC, the continental price could effectively set a ceiling on the price in this country and it was the merchants' commercial interest in selling imports (on which they earned a margin and not merely a handling allowance) which provided competition between merchants and BS.

(79) As the Court of Justice held in Case 27/62 *United Brands* (at ground 201), where the occupier of a dominant position established in the common market aims at eliminating a competitor also established in the common market, it is immaterial whether this behaviour relates directly to trade between Member States once it has been

shown that such elimination will have repercussions on the patterns of competition within the common market.

This is particularly the case when a dominant company attempts, as in the present case, to remove a competitor whose activities include the import, transformation and resale of a product.

As shown above, BS's actions, having the intention or foreseeable result of precipitating NB's removal from the retail sugar market, had a potential effect on the structure of competition and trade within the common market, and thus on trade between Member States within the meaning of Article 86.

(80) The refusal of BS to sell industrial sugar to NB had direct and appreciable effects on inter-State trade. Because NB could not purchase beet-origin sugar from BS, it purchased such sugar (under 1986 market conditions more expensively) from other Community producers in France, Denmark and the Netherlands. Until 5 June 1986, NB was unable to use T & L industrial sugar for repackaging because [. . .]. Even if NB had been able to purchase T & L sugar for repackaging, it would still have been unwilling to use such sugar for this purpose, because it cannot receive the Community sugar storage rebate for the storage of cane-origin sugar. In this respect, it is notable that NB ordered more than twice as much Continental sugar for import between October 1985 and June 1986 compared with the amounts purchased between October 1984 and September 1985.

Thus an artificial pattern of trade between Member States was created because, had it not been for BS's refusal to supply, NB would not have undertaken a large part of these imports, rather purchasing cheaper sugar from BS. The fact that BS's refusal to supply effectively increased the level of trade between Member States does not prevent BS's action from affecting trade within the meaning of Article 86. As the European Court stated in *Consten and Grundig* v. *Commission* (ECR [1966] 299.):

> what is particularly important is whether the agreement is capable of constituting a threat, either direct or indirect, actual or potential, to freedom of trade between Member States in a manner which might harm the attainment of the objectives of a single market between states. Thus, the fact that an agreement encourages an increase, even a large one, in the volume of trade between states, is not sufficient to exclude the possibility that the agreement may 'affect' such trade in the above-mentioned manner.

BS's refusal to supply industrial sugar to NB therefore had an effect on trade between Member States within the meaning of Article 86.

The Commission therefore concludes that BS's above-mentioned behaviour had an effect on trade within the meaning of Article 86 of the Treaty of Rome.

E. CONCLUSION

(81) On the basis of the considerations set out above, the Commission considers that BS infringed Article 86 of the EEC Treaty in the following ways:

1. By refusing to supply industrial granulated sugar to NB;
2. By reducing its prices for retail sugar to the extent that an insufficient margin existed between its prices for retail and industrial sugar;
3. By refusing to sell sugar unless it was on a delivered-price basis;
4. By discriminating against NB in refusing to supply exclusively beet-origin sugar to NB whereas it supplied exclusively beet-origin sugar to other purchasers at their request;
5. By offering 'group commitment' bonuses.

[. . .]

Remedies

(a) Fines

(83) Under Article 15 of Regulation No. 17, infringements of Article 86 may be sanctioned by fines of up to 1 million ECU or 10% of the turnover of the undertaking

in the preceding business year, whichever is the greater. Regard must be had to both the gravity and the duration of the infringement.

(84) The evidence demonstrates that BS abused its dominant position in several important ways. These several abuses were all designed to have the same effects; namely, to severely damage the position of, or even eliminate, a newly established competitor on the market.

BS sought, as a result of this behaviour, to maintain or reinforce its dominant position.

In fact, the infringements in question were designed to have an adverse effect on the structure of competition in a substantial part of the common market. Moreover, had the Commission not issued a Statement of Objections that led to BS's undertaking, a competitor could have been irreversibly removed from the market.

(85) In the light of this, the Commission takes the view that it should impose a fine on BS. In setting the level of this fine, the Commission takes account not only of BS's abusive behaviour, as outlined above, but also of the exemplary manner in which BS has conducted itself following its receipt of the interim measures Statement of Objections.

(86) As the present Decision relates solely to BS's actions in the past, the fine is set taking account of the fact that the abuses in question occurred in the period between the events leading up to NB's packaging of sugar for retail sale and the adoption by BS of its undertaking and subsequent Community compliance programme – between approximately April 1985 and early August 1986.

(87) It is the practice of the Commission, in setting a fine, to take account of whether or not the rules of competition of the EEC Treaty have been sufficiently developed by the Decisions of the Commission in any particular area (see, for example, Commission Decision 78/252/EEC (IV/29.176 – *Vegetable Parchment*, OJ No. L 70, 13.3 1978, p. 54, paragraph 83).) As stated above, the Commission has decided that BS, in selling sugar exclusively on a delivered price bases, abused its dominant position under Article 86. Such a decision constitutes the first time that the Commission has stated that the maintenance of a delivered-price-only system by a dominant company may constitute an abuse of a dominant position within the meaning of Article 86. In the light of this, the Commission has not fined BS in relation to this particular abuse.

In relation to BS's retail-sugar pricing practices, BS argues that the competition rules have been insufficiently developed when the abuse occurred to justify the imposition of a fine. The Commission considers that such pricing practices, adopted with the intention or foreseeable result of removing NB from the retail sugar market, are types of predatory practices clearly envisaged by Article 86, and thus considers that BS intentionally or at least negligently abused its dominant position in this respect. The imposition of a fine for this abuse is therefore justified. The Commission does, however, accept that the law relating to such an abuse has been less fully clarified by Commission Decision and Court ruling than in respect to the other abuses committed by BS, and has taken this into account in fixing the level of the fine.

(88) However, the Commission considers that, as regards the other abuses outlined above, BS undertook these abuses intentionally or at least negligently. Furthermore, the rules of competition of the EEC Treaty have been sufficiently developed by previous Decisions of the Commission and the European Court of Justice, or are sufficiently clear from the provisions of the Treaty of Rome in the areas covered by those abuses, in order to justify the imposition of a fine in relation thereto [. . .].

[. . .] [A] fine of 3 million ECU is hereby imposed on British Sugar plc.

19.6 *Tetra Pak Rausing SA* v. *Commission of the European Communities*, Court of First Instance of the European Communities Case T-51/89 [1991] 4 CMLR 334

[. . .]

By decision of 26 July 1988 ('the Decision') the Commission found that, by acquiring, through its purchase of the Liquipak Group, the exclusivity of the patent licence granted on 27 August 1981 by the National Research and Development Council to Novus Corp, a company in the Liquipak group, Tetra Pak Rausing SA was in breach of Article 86 of the EEC Treaty from the date of that acquisition until the exclusivity came to an end.

The decision involves the sector concerned with the packaging of liquid foods, especially milk, in cartons. There are two distinct types of such packaging. Ultra-high-temperature (UHT) treated milk is filled by special machines into cartons which are sterilised, then sealed immediately after filling, by the machines under strictly aseptic conditions. The packaging of fresh pasteurised milk does not require the same degree of sterility and so calls for less sophisticated equipment.

The company to which the Decision is addressed, Tetra Pak Rausing SA (Tetra Pak), whose registered office is in Switzerland, co-ordinates the policy of a group of companies world-wide specialising mainly in equipment for the packaging of milk in cartons. Tetra Pak's activities cover the sector concerned with the packaging of fresh and UHT-treated milk. They consist essentially of manufacturing cartons and carton-filling machines using the group's own technology. In the field of aseptic packaging, Tetra Pak supplies the 'Tetrabrik' system. In the field of fresh products, it also distributes machines made by a number of other manufacturers.

In 1985 the group, which has manufacturing and distribution subsidiaries in all EEC Member States except Luxembourg and Greece, had nearly half its total turnover – amounting to approximately 2,000 million ECUs – in the European Economic Community. In the same year the group's share of the Community market was approximately 90 per cent in the field of aseptic packaging and 50 per cent in fresh milk packaging.

Before it was taken over by Tetra Pak, the Liquipak group was owned or controlled by the Allpak group of Canada and a private individual. It specialises in the development and manufacture of filling equipment for liquid food products.

The Elopak group is Norwegian in origin and is mainly engaged in Europe. In 1987, it had a turnover of around 300 million ECUs.

Although its activities are essentially in the fresh milk sector, particularly in the supply of 'gable-top' cartons where its main competitor is Tetra Pak, Elopak was also Liquipak's exclusive distributor for its machines for pasteurised milk and also for any machine to be developed for UHT-treated milk. Elopak helped Liquipak in its efforts to develop a new packaging machine incorporating the process protected by the exclusive licence at issue in this case.

That exclusive licence relates to a new UHT milk-packaging process involving the use of ultra-violet light which makes it possible to use a weak solution of hydrogen peroxide in combination with heat, as opposed to the processes hitherto applied in the Community which use a combination of concentrated hydrogen peroxide and heat. Unlike the processes used in the aseptic packaging machines currently on the market, this technique for use in carton-filling machines can be adapted for both 'brick' and 'gable-top' cartons. The current machines are not suitable for use with gable-top cartons on which, as the Decision says, Elopak has concentrated its development efforts and for which it has the most know-how.

The exclusive licence at issue was granted, with effect from 27 August 1981, to Novus Corp by the National Research and Development Council, whose activities have been taken over by the British Technology Group (BTG). The licence relates to the patents covering BTG's new sterilisation technique and the relevant know-how. Within the Community, patents have been granted in Ireland, Spain and Belgium. A patent application is pending in Italy and an application has been filed under the European Patent Convention for, *inter alia*, the United Kingdom, France, the Federal Republic of Germany and the Netherlands.

The exclusive licence qualified for block exemption under Commission Regulation 2349/84 of 23 July 1984 on the application of Article 85(3) of the Treaty to certain categories of patent licensing agreements, subject always to Article 9 of that regulation, which provides that the Commission may withdraw exemption where the conditions laid down in Article 85(3) of the Treaty are not fulfilled.

In 1986 Tetra Pak acquired the United States company Liquipak International Inc. As part of the same transaction, it also acquired the companies in the Liquipak group to which Novus Corp had in 1983 assigned the BTG licence. At the time of Liquipak's takeover by Tetra Pak, the new version of the machine incorporating the BTG process, developed by Liquipak with the assistance of Elopak, had not yet been tested in practice. Following the announcement of Tetra Pak's takeover of Liquipak, Elopak brought its collaboration to an end. Elopak considered that the machine was very nearly operational. Tetra Pak considered that further major and costly research was required before the BTG technique could be exploited.

As regards the companies' position on the market, it appears from the Decision that at the material time only two undertakings – Tetra Pak and PKL, a subsidiary of the German group Rheinmetall AG – were to any significant extent in a position to market aseptic milk-packaging machines in the Community. For the technical reasons mentioned above and also because, in practice, the manufacturers of aseptic machines also manufacture the cartons for their own machines, possession of an aseptic-filling technique is the key to market entry both for packaging equipment and for cartons.

[. . .] [T]he Elopak group made a complaint to the Commission [. . .] with a view to establishing that Tetra Pak had infringed Articles 85 and 86 of the EEC Treaty. After service of a statement of objections by the Commission [. . .] and a hearing [. . .] Tetra Pak informed the Commission [. . .] that it was abandoning all claims to exclusivity in the BTG licence. Although the infringement to which objection had been taken was brought to an end in the course of administrative procedure, the Commission considered that a finding of infringement should be made by formal Decision with a view, *inter alia*, to clarifying its position on the relevant point of law. But since the point raised was unprecedented, no fine was imposed on Tetra Pak. In its Decision, the Commission considers in turn the application of Article 86 and of Article 85. With regard to Article 85, the Commission sets out the reasons which would have entitled it to withdraw the benefit of exemption from the exclusive licence for so long as there was an infringement of Article 86.

At the end of its discussion of Article 86, the Commission concludes that 'Tetra abused its dominant position by the acquisition of [the BTG] exclusive licence which had the effect of strengthening its already dominant position, further weakening existing competition and rendering even more difficult the entry of any new competition' (paragraph 60 of the Decision).

[. . .]

Tetra Pak challenges the decision on the grounds that it is contrary to Article 85(3) and Article 86 that the Commission should treat an agreement enjoying block exemption under Article 85(3) as prohibited under Article 86. The challenge is developed under three heads. The applicant relies, first, on a schematic analysis of the relevant rules of the Treaty and secondary sources; second, on the principle of legal certainty; and third, on the principle of uniform application of Community law.

(a) Schematic analysis of Articles 85 and 86 of the Treaty and of secondary legislation

The applicant maintains that the Commission cannot apply Article 86 to behaviour exempt under Article 85(3) because Articles 85 and 86 both pursue the same objective. The applicant relies on the judgment of the Court of Justice in *Continental Can* [*Euremballage Corp. and Continental Can Co. Inc.* v. *EC Commission* (6/72) [1973] CMLR 199] where it was stated that 'Articles 85 and 86 cannot be interpreted in such a way that they contradict each other, because they serve to achieve the same aim'. Conduct cannot both be expressly authorised under Article 85(3) and prohibited under Article 86 since exemption involves 'positive action', as the Court put it in Walt Wilhelm [*Walt Wilhelm* v. *Bundeskartelamt* (14/68) [1969] CMLR 100], though that case was concerned with the relationship between Article 85(3) and national rules on competition.

In support of that argument, the applicant claims that the finding against it in the Decision relates essentially to the exclusivity granted by the licensing agreement. The applicant goes on to argue that the Commission based the application of Article 86 on a distinction, for which there is no justification in competition law, between an exclusive licence enjoying block exemption on the one hand and, on the other, acquisition of the exclusivity afforded by the licence through takeover of a competing company (in this case Liquipak) such acquisition having been held in the Decision to constitute infringement of Article 86. Both, according to the applicant, have the same restrictive effects on competition.

The applicant further argued at the hearing that since, on this view, Article 86 cannot be applied to an agreement enjoying exemption under Article 85(3), the fact that an undertaking in a dominant position becomes party to an agreement enjoying such exemption cannot constitute an abuse within the meaning of Article 86 unless a supplementary element, extrinsic to the agreement and attributable to the undertaking, is present. The applicant relied in this connection on Ahmed Saeed [*Ahmed Saeed and Silver Line Reisebüro GmbH* v. *Zentrale zur Bekampfung Unlauteren Wettbewerbs* (66/86) [1990] 4 CMLR 102] where the Court of Justice said that there may be abuse of a dominant position where, in particular, an undertaking in a dominant position succeeds in imposing unfair contractual conditions on competitors or customers.

The applicant points out that the inapplicability of Article 86 to an exempt agreement does not jeopardise achievement of the objectives of Article 86 since it is always within the discretion of the Commission to withdraw the exemption. In support of its view that the application of Article 86 is conditional on the prior withdrawal of exemption, Tetra Pak cites Article 7(2) of Council Regulation 3976/87 of 14 December 1987 on the application of Article 85(3) of the Treaty to certain categories of agreements and concerted practices in the air transport sector and Article 8(2) of Council Regulation 4056/86 of 22 December 1986 laying down detailed rules for the application of Articles 85 and 86 of the Treaty to maritime transport. Under these regulations, where an agreement enjoying block exemption nevertheless has effects prohibited by Article 86, the Commission may withdraw the benefit of exemption and take all appropriate steps to bring the infringement of Article 86 to an end.

The applicant [. . .] accepts that there is no express exemption for the prohibition under Article 86 [. . .] But in support of its view that Article 86 is inapplicable to conduct exempt under Article 85(3), it puts forward an interpretation of the conditions for applying Article 86 based on the general scheme of Article 85. This interpretation leads in reality to accepting that there can be an implied exemption in respect of abuse of a dominant position. In determining whether conduct constitutes an abuse, one must, the applicant argues, 'impliedly undertake the two-stage process which is made explicit in Article 85, namely [. . .] ask does the conduct have the object or effect of preventing, restricting or distorting competition within the common market, and, if so, does the conduct nevertheless have overall a pro-competitive effect because it contributes to promoting technical or economic progress'.

In reply to this schematic analysis developed by Tetra Pak, the Commission deploys an argument based on a different interpretation of Articles 85 and 86. In particular, referring to the Advocate General's Opinion in *Ahmed Saeed*, the Commission argues that since no abuse can be authorised in a Community governed by the rule of law, there can be no derogation from the prohibition of abuse of a dominant position. The Commission points out that in the judgment in that case the Court of Justice expressly stated that no exemption may be granted in respect of an abuse of a dominant position. It concludes that the applicant's argument, that Article 86 is inapplicable to an agreement exempt under Article 85(3) so long as the Commission has not withdrawn the exemption, cannot be accepted since that would be tantamount to recognising the existence of exemption for abuse of a dominant position, withdrawal of exemption being effective only *ex nunc*.

This Court notes at the outset that the problem of reconciling application of Article 86 with enjoyment of block exemption, which is the crux of the present case and arises because of the need for logical coherence in the implementation of Articles 85 and 86, has not yet been expressly determined by the Community court. However, it must be borne in mind that the relationship between Articles 85 and 86 has, to an extent, been clarified by the Court of Justice, in that the Court has expressly said that the applicability to an agreement of Article 85 does not preclude application of Article 86. The Court held that in such a case the Commission may apply either of the two provisions to the act in question: 'the fact that agreements [. . .] might fall within Article 85 and in particular within paragraph [3] thereof does not preclude the application of Article 86 [. . .] so that in such cases the Commission is entitled, taking into account the nature of the reciprocal undertakings entered into and the competitive position of the various contracting parties on the market or markets on which they operate, to proceed on the basis of Article 85 or Article 86. The Court of Justice confirmed that position in *Ahmed Saeed* where it said that, in certain circumstances, 'the possibility that Articles 85 and 86 may both be applicable cannot be ruled out'). But the problem raised in *Ahmed Saeed*, as far as the relationship between Articles 85 and 86 is concerned, was the question of principle as to whether implementation of an agreement capable of falling under Article 85(1) can also constitute abuse of a dominant position (paragraph [34]). The relationship between exemption under Article 85(3) and the applicability of Article 86 was not at issue.

Resolution of the problem of reconciling application of Article 86 with exemption under Article 85(3) must therefore start from the Treaty system for the protection of competition, in particular as laid down by those two Articles of the Treaty and their implementing regulations. Articles 85 and 86 are complementary inasmuch as they pursue a common general objective, set out in Article 3(*f*) of the Treaty, which provides that the activities of the Community are to include 'the institution of a system ensuring that competition in the common market is not distorted'. But they none the less constitute, in the scheme of the Treaty, two independent legal instruments addressing different situations. This was emphasised by the Court of Justice in Continental Can where, having said that 'Article 85 concerns agreements between undertakings, decisions of associations of undertakings and concerted practices, while Article 86 concerns unilateral activity of one or more undertakings', the Court held that Articles 85 and 86 seek to achieve the same aim on different levels, viz. the maintenance of effective competition within the Common Market.

Turning to the specific nature of the conduct whose compatibility with Article 86 is considered in the Decision, this Court holds that the mere fact that an undertaking in a dominant position acquires an exclusive licence does not *per se* constitute abuse within the meaning of Article 86. For the purpose of applying Article 86, the circumstances surrounding the acquisition, and in particular its effects on the structure of competition in the relevant market, must be taken into account. This interpretation is borne out by the case law of the Court of Justice, in which the concept of abuse is defined as

> an objective concept relating to the behaviour of an undertaking in a dominant position which is such as to influence the structure of a market where, as a result of the very presence of the undertaking in question, the degree of competition is weakened and which, through recourse to methods different from those which condition normal competition in products or services on the basis of the transactions of commercial operators, has the effect of hindering the maintenance of the degree of competition still existing in the market or the growth of that competition.

So, here, the Commission was right not to put in issue the exclusive licence as such, but rather to object specifically under Article 86 to the anti-competitive effect of its being acquired by the applicant. It is plain from the reasoning and conclusions of the Decision that the infringement of Article 86 found by the Commission stemmed precisely from Tetra Pak's acquisition of the exclusive licence 'in the specific circumstances of this case'. The specific context to which the Commission refers is expressly characterised as being the fact that acquisition of the exclusivity of the licence not only 'strengthened Tetra's very considerable dominance but also had the effect of preventing, or at the very least considerably delaying, the entry of a new competitor into a market where very little if any competition is found' [. . .] The decisive factor in the finding that acquisition of the exclusive licence constituted an abuse therefore lay quite specifically in the applicant's position in the relevant market and in particular, as appears from the Decision (paragraph 27), in the fact that at the material time the right to use the process protected by the BTG licence was alone capable of giving an undertaking the means of competing effectively with the applicant in the field of the aseptic packaging of milk. The takeover of Liquipak was no more than the means – to which the Commission has attached no particular significance in applying Article 86 – by which the applicant acquired the exclusivity of the BTG licence, the effect of which was to deprive other undertakings of the means of competition with the applicant.

Similarly, the applicant's argument that there must be a supplementary element, external to the agreement, cannot be accepted. In this connection, it is relevant to note that in *Ahmed Saeed* to which the applicant refers the Court of Justice held that 'the application of tariffs for scheduled flights on the basis of bilateral or multilateral agreements may, in certain circumstances, constitute an abuse of a dominant position on the market in question, in particular where an undertaking in a dominant position has succeeded in imposing on other carriers the application of excessively high or excessively low tariffs or the exclusive application of only one tariff on a given route'. It is true that the Court of Justice justified the concurrent application of Articles 85 and 86 to the tariff agreements there at issue by referring to the existence of a supplementary element, which in that case took the form of pressure brought to bear by the undertaking on its competitors. But the Decision in the present case does refer to the additional element that constituted an abuse within the meaning of Article 86 and justified its application. The additional element lies in the very context of the case – in the fact that Tetra Pak's acquisition of the exclusive licence had the practical effect of precluding all competition in the relevant market. This was emphasised in the Decision and was not put in issue by the applicant.

In these circumstances, this Court holds that in the scheme for the protection of competition established by the Treaty the grant of exemption, whether individual or block exemption, under Article 85(3) cannot be such as to render inapplicable the prohibition set out in Article 86. This principle follows both from the wording of

Article 85(3) which permits derogation, through a declaration of inapplicability, only from the prohibition of agreements, decisions and concerted practices set out in Article 85(1), and also from the general scheme of Articles 85 and 86 which, as noted above, are independent and complementary provisions designed, in general, to regulate distinct situations by different rules. Application of Article 85 involves two stages: a finding that Article 85(1) has been infringed followed, where appropriate, by exemption from that prohibition if the agreement, decision or concerted practice in question satisfies the conditions laid down in Article 85(3). Article 86, on the other hand, by reason of its very subject-matter (abuse), precludes any possible exception to the prohibition it lays down. If the Commission were required in every case to take a decision withdrawing exemption before applying Article 86, this would be tantamount, in view of the non-retroactive nature of the withdrawal of exemption, to accepting that an exemption under Article 85(3) operates in reality as a concurrent exemption from the prohibition of abuse of a dominant position. For the reasons just given, that would be consistent with the very nature of the infringement prohibited by Article 86. Moreover, in the view of the principles governing the hierarchical relationship of legal rules, grant of exemption under secondary legislation could not, in the absence of any enabling provision in the Treaty, derogate from a provision of the Treaty, in this case Article 86.

Having established that, in principle, the grant of exemption cannot preclude application of Article 86, the question remains whether, in practice, findings made with a view to the grant of exemption under Article 85(3) preclude application of Article 86.

Under Article 85(3), the prohibition laid down in Article 85(1) may be declared inapplicable to agreements, decisions or concerted practices, or to categories thereof, which fulfil the conditions set out in Article 85(3). Article 85(3) provides *inter alia* that the agreement must not afford the undertakings the possibility of eliminating competition in respect of a substantial part of the products in question.

The way in which the question of exemption arises may in practice be different depending on whether an individual or block exemption is involved. The grant of individual exemption presupposes that the Commission has found that the agreement in question complies with the conditions set out in Article 85(3). So, where an individual exemption decision has been taken, characteristics of the agreement which would also be relevant in applying Article 86 may be taken to have been established. Consequently, in applying Article 86, the Commission must take account, unless the factual and legal circumstances have altered, of the earlier findings made when exemption was granted under Article 85(3).

Now it is true that regulations granting block exemption, like individual exemption decisions, apply only to agreements which, in principle, satisfy the conditions set out in Article 85(3). But unlike individual exemptions, block exemptions are, by definition, not dependent on a case-by-case examination to establish that the conditions for exemption laid down in the Treaty are in fact satisfied. In order to qualify for a block exemption, an agreement has only to satisfy the criteria laid down in the relevant block-exemption regulation. The agreement itself is not subject to any positive assessment with regard to the conditions set out in Article 85(3). So a block exemption cannot, generally speaking, be construed as having effects similar to negative clearance in relation to Article 86. The result is that, where agreements to which undertakings in a dominant position are parties fall within the scope of a block-exemption regulation (that is, where the regulation is limited in scope), the effects of block exemption on the applicability of Article 86 must be assessed solely in the context of the scheme of Article 86.

Lastly, the possibility of applying Article 86 to an agreement covered by a block exemption is confirmed by analysis of the scheme of the block-exemption regulations. First, those regulations do not, in principle, exclude undertakings in a dominant position from qualifying for the exemption and therefore do not take account of the position on the relevant markets of the parties to any given agreement. That is particularly so in the case of Regulation 2349/84 on exemptions in respect of patent licensing agreements (cited above) which is relevant in this case. Second, the possibility of applying Article 85(3) and Article 86 concurrently is expressly confirmed by certain of the block-exemption regulations where it is provided that enjoyment of block exemption does not preclude application of Article 86 – in particular, the three block-exemption regulations in the field of air transport adopted by the Commission on the 26 July 1988, each of which states expressly in the preamble that group exemption does not preclude the application of Article 86. (The relevant regulations are Regulation 2671/88 on the application of Article 85(3) of the Treaty to certain categories of agreements between undertakings, decisions of associations of undertakings and concerted practices concerning joint planning and co-ordination of capacity, sharing of revenue and consultations on tariffs on scheduled air services and slot allocation at airports, Regulation 2672/88 on the application of Article 85(3) of the Treaty to certain categories of agreements between undertakings relating to computer reservation systems for air transport services and regulation 2673/88 on the application of Article 85(3) of the Treaty to certain categories of agreements between undertakings, decisions of associations of undertakings and concerted practices concerning ground handling services.) Similarly, Article 8(1) of Council Regulation 4056/86, cited above, states expressly that abuse of a dominant position within the meaning of Article 86 is prohibited, no prior decision to that effect being required [. . .].

19.7 M. Utton, 'Anticompetitive practices and the Competition Act 1980', 38 *Antitrust Bulletin* (1993)

[. . .]

[. . .] [I]n 23 out of the first 29 cases considered by the OFT [under the Competition Act 1980], the conclusion by the DG was that anticompetitive practices had occurred. In the remaining six cases the behaviour investigated was not considered anticompetitive and no further action was taken. In five cases [*British Railways Board – Motorail* (1983), *British Railways Board – Godfrey Davis* (1983), *Sealink Harbours* (1987), *South Yorkshire Transport* (1989), and *Oracle Teletext* (1990)] no further action was taken despite an 'anticompetitive' finding either because the impact on competition was considered slight (e.g. *Sealink Harbours*, *British Railways Board – Godfrey Davis*) or too much time had elapsed since the ending of the practice, for a reference to the MMC to be made (e.g. *South Yorkshire Transport* and *Oracle Teletext*). In ten cases the DG accepted undertakings from the firms concerned and in eight, the second part of the procedure was brought into play and references to the MMC were made.

[. . .] [A]pproximately half of the cases involved 'local' or 'regional' markets rather than 'national'. While some of these are important and may raise questions of wide applicability (e.g. competition in local bus services following deregulation) others have involved very small markets and appear to have little general importance for competitive issues (e.g. *British Railways Board* [reports]). Where resources devoted to competition policy are limited it can be argued that they should be deployed in those areas where the gains to consumers are potentially the largest. Judging by the size of some the markets involved in the anticompetitive practices enquiries it is not clear that such considerations have played a prominent part in the selection process. [. . .]

[. . .]

ANTICOMPETITIVE PRACTICES AND THE PUBLIC INTEREST

[. . .] [T]hree different types of market conduct appear to have raised the most important and controversial issues. Each has been the subject of several reports under section 3 and each has also involved references to the MMC. The reports involve: selective distribution systems but in particular *refusal to sell* by a manufacturer to retailers; the conflict between competition policy and *intellectual property rights*; and *predatory pricing* to eliminate a new entrant.

Refusal to sell. In its very first enquiry under section 3 the OFT had to consider the issues raised by a firm with the largest market share refusing to supply its products to distributors who were known for their price cutting policies. Nine years later in another important case almost exactly the same issues arose and the conclusions of the OFT and the MMC remained unchanged. Central to both cases was the question of market power. Our contention is that because the MMC has adopted a very woolly notion of market power it arrived at the wrong decision in both cases.

[. . .] Both cases [*Raleigh Bicycles* (OFT, 1981 and HC 67, 1981) and *Black and Decker* (OFT, 1989 and Cm 805)] involved leading manufacturers of major brands pursuing a policy of refusing to sell to an important group of retailers on the grounds that they were known to cut or had been cutting prices to low levels. Both companies were suffering a decline in market share and the policy appears, if anything, to have worsened the situation, although in both cases they remained the largest single sellers in their respective markets [. . .].

[. . .]

[. . .] B. and D.'s action was triggered by a threatened boycott by some of its leading retail customers. They judged that B. and D.'s products were being used for promotional purposes and that as a result margins had become too slim [. . .]. In contrast Raleigh had made its decision not to supply certain retailers known for their price cutting to protect what it saw as the most important part of its distribution network, specialist Raleigh dealers and bicycle stores.

The point is particularly interesting in view of the discussion in an earlier MMC report into the specific issues of refusal to sell [MMC, *Refusal to Supply*, Cmnd 4372, 1978]. In the conclusion of that report three situations are identified where refusal to sell may be against the public interest: (i) where it involves known or suspected price cutters (ii) where it is in response to a boycott threatened by other distributors, and (iii) where the supplier does not operate in reasonably competitive conditions. [. . .] As we have seen situations (i) and (ii) prevailed in *B. and D.*, whereas (i) occurred in *Raleigh*. In relation to *B. and D.* we might add that it is especially surprising that the MMC did *not* refer to its earlier report where it effectively concludes that *any* refusal to supply in the face of a threatened boycott by other distributors will deny consumers the benefit of a choice which the supplier was prepared to make available to them and is in itself therefore against the public interest. [. . .].

We come now to what should have been the focus of both the *Raleigh* and *B. and D.* cases, namely situation (iii), the requirement that suppliers have to be operating in an uncompetitive market for the practice of refusing to sell to be potentially against the public interest. In both *Raleigh* and *B. and D.* the MMC had little doubt that the relevant markets were *not* very competitive and in particular that both companies wielded considerable market power. In other words condition (iii) was present in both cases. In view of the evidence and on a reasonable definition of market power this conclusion is difficult to sustain.

The MMC appears to have taken a much too static and woolly view of what constitutes market power in both of the cases under consideration. It was relatively easy to establish and was not disputed by either company that they had the largest individual shares in the markets concerned: 40 per cent in the case of Raleigh and 67 per cent for B. and D. In the *Raleigh* report the market share alone *appears* to have been taken as sufficient evidence of an uncompetitive market and *presumably* of Raleigh's market power. Our caution is emphasized by the italics because there is no substantive discussion of Raleigh's market power in the report. In view of the facts outlined in the second chapter of the report this is hardly surprising because they all point to the conclusion that partly because of Raleigh's distribution policy and partly for other reasons of general management, Raleigh was unable to exercise market power. Against the background of a strongly growing market although Raleigh was much larger than other UK producers it had lost and was continuing to lose both its domestic and foreign market share. [. . .]

Market power consists of the ability of a firm (or group of firms) persistently to hold prices above competitive levels *without a substantial loss of sales* [. . .]. Except in the very extreme case of a complete monopolist it depends on a number of factors: the market share of the firm (or firms) concerned, the market elasticity of demand and the elasticity of supply from 'fringe' producers. The MMC appears to have identified market power or market dominance with market share alone. At one point it recognises the adverse consequences for Raleigh of its distribution policy.

> The increase in imports which has taken place at Raleigh's expense may be to some extent attributable to its existing distribution policy rather than have occurred in spite of it. If Raleigh had adopted a different attitude towards modern retailing methods and had been more disposed to deal with some of the retailing chains to whom it as hitherto refused supplies, we wonder whether it might be trading more successfully now. (para. 6.26)

It does not, however, follow through this analysis by drawing the inference that Raleigh was unable to exercise market power. The retailers to whom it had denied supplies had ready alternatives available from foreign firms which over a decade had built up their share of the UK market to more than a third of the total at the time of the report. Thus at the level of prices that Raleigh was trying to sustain the market was highly competitive and its current market share although not irrelevant was not the most important factor in any consideration of market power. There is general agreement that where a market is competitive refusal to supply is ineffective and thus cannot be against the public interest [. . .]. The 1970 MMC report seems to catch more or less precisely the situation prevailing in Raleigh: 'we concern ourselves with such refusals under competitive conditions and we see no reason to regard their effects as harmful to the consumer or user. Of course, a supplier may be mistaken in his judgement but we do not consider normal commercial fallibility in these matters to raise an issue of public interest' (para. 28).

Thus by not paying sufficient attention to the central characteristics of market power the MMC was led to an erroneous conclusion. [. . .]

[The same may be said about the] MMC's consideration of market power in the B. and D. case. [. . .] [A]lthough at the time of the report B. and D. had a larger share of the relevant market than Raleigh (66 per cent as against 40 per cent) it too had been losing its share fairly steadily for a decade largely at the hands of a highly successful international competitor (Bosch). [. . .]

[. . .]

The MMC recognised that the development of the market was likely to be in the direction of higher quality products as incomes rose and that Bosch catered for this market whereas 'B and D has a low-price, high volume strategy' [. . .]. Nevertheless the MMC identified B and D's market power in terms of the strength of its brand image in the eyes of consumers and many retailers who felt that they *had* to supply B. and D.'s products and therefore accept their terms and conditions [. . .]. As in the *Raleigh* case there is a strong indication that as far as the MMC is concerned the firm currently with the largest market share and with a widely known product must therefore have market power. There is no discussion of B. and D.'s ability or otherwise to hold prices persistently above competitive levels. Indeed the whole case arose over B. and D.'s inability in the short run to hold prices at levels it considered satisfactory. Retailers apparently were able to find alternative supplies in the face of B. and D.'s policy, just as they were in the *Raleigh* case. As a result B. and D. had lost a substantial share of the market [. . .].

The most clear cut cases of where refusal to sell is likely to impede competition and be against the public interest are where a well established firm with identifiable market power uses it against new entrants who have no alternative sources of supply. However if any of these conditions are not met a firm attempting to coerce others by refusing to sell is likely to damage its own interests more than those of other firms or consumers.

[. . .]

Predatory pricing. An aspect of market conduct which has been as prominent in section 3 reports as refusal to supply has been the complex issue of predatory pricing. It has featured in five cases with four relating to the newly deregulated local bus industry. [. . .]

[. . .]

Since the mid-1970s the issue of predatory pricing and then, more broadly, predatory behaviour, has generated an enormous economic and legal literature largely in the US but increasingly in Europe. The size of the literature is a good indication that many of the issues raised by predatory behaviour are, as yet, unresolved. After all if the central questions were all answered and agreed there would be little need for further comment and analysis.

The notion of predatory pricing is usually taken to involve some reductions of price and sacrifice in profits in the short run with the intent of undermining and eliminating a rival, in the expectation that prices will be raised and profits recouped in the long run. The action is frequently but not exclusively alleged to take place in the face of new entry to markets with an established and dominant incumbent firm. From a policy perspective the central difficulty is to distinguish accurately between price reductions which merely reflect the normal and healthy process of competition from those that destroy competition and then harm consumers in the long term. If policy is too harsh, established firms will be unwilling to reduce prices and pass on the effects, say, of additional scale economies to consumers, whereas if it is too tolerant the competitive process will be impaired and consumers forced to pay monopoly prices.

Much of the discussion in the recent literature has concerned the *level* to which prices must fall before they can properly be judged 'predatory' rather than competitive. Largely to provide a benchmark for use by US antitrust courts, Areeda and Turner proposed that prices at or above short-run marginal cost (in practice its proxy, average variable cost) should be regarded as competitive and prices below this level as predatory. A central point emerging from the large response provoked by their suggestion, was that the proposed rule was far too narrow and would allow many incumbent firms to price strategically above their own variable costs and even above average total costs, but with the effect of sacrificing some short-term profit and the intent of eliminating new entry. Many other factors had therefore to be taken into account to establish whether predatory pricing had occurred.

In its treatment of predatory pricing in section 3 cases the OFT has attempted to incorporate elements of both approaches. The framework used was initially set out in *Becton–Dickinson* [OFT, 1988] but was subsequently used in the bus industry cases. It has three elements: (i) are the market conditions such as to make predatory pricing feasible; (ii) have prices below average variable costs or average total costs been charged, and if they have, what were the circumstances in the market; and (iii) is there any evidence about the intent of the firm in reducing its prices? We discuss each of these elements in turn, drawing on the five cases mentioned above.

Predatory pricing will only be feasible where the firm concerned is confident that the strategy of low prices and losses – possibly large losses – in the short run will be at least compensated by high profits in the long run. To have such confidence, as the OFT stressed in *Becton–Dickinson*, 'the predator would normally need a strong market position; the ability to sustain loss making in the product concerned from another area of operation, or substantial reserves so as to withstand short-term losses; competitors who were unwilling or unable to sustain similar short-term losses; little likelihood of competitors re-entering the market once prices were raised substantially; and a lack of countervailing buyer power' [. . .]. For the first part of this rather complex condition the OFT has generally relied on the market share of the firm concerned and its overall size and financial resources. Thus *Becton–Dickinson's* share of the National Health Service market was approximately 45 per cent and as it was part of a much larger group 'the potential exists for cross-subsidisation from profits earned in other markets or countries' [. . .]. In *Highland Scottish Omnibuses* [OFT, 1989] the company was the sole supplier of services until the entry of a new competitor and more significantly was, at the time, part of a public corporation which allowed it costless access to a fund of £300,000 in addition to its own accumulated reserves. The OFT was therefore satisfied that it could finance a predatory campaign and that this course of action was not open to a new entrant solely dependent on the market concerned.

The second part of the feasibility condition which concerns the impact and reaction of competitors, has caused more difficulty both to those writing on the subject and the OFT in its section 3 enquiries. Clearly for a campaign of predatory pricing to be successful the predator has to be fairly certain that entrants vanquished in the short term will remain so and not reappear, perhaps in a different guise, once prices are raised in the long run. For this to be true some barrier to successful entry has to be erected, otherwise the cycle will simply be repeated and the predator will never recoup the forgone profits. [. . .]

[. . .]

[. . .] Entry on a very small scale may occur and may even persist but it should not be inferred that entry conditions are therefore 'easy'. Quite apart from the point that it may serve the purpose of a dominant firm to tolerate the presence of peripheral competition, the fact that such entrants make very little headway in the market but simply hang on to an insignificant share is more likely to signify *high* entry barriers. Such an inference has been made by the OFT in its analysis of the bus industry. Thus in *South Yorkshire Transport Ltd.* [OFT, 1989] the OFT concluded that the 'development of the local bus market in the Sheffield area since deregulation supports the view that barriers to entry remain. The share of the new entrants in 1988 remained at around 4% of registered commercial services. . . Furthermore, competition between existing operators has been muted, as in many other parts of the country' [. . .]. This is in line with a similar general assessment about entry conditions made by Schmalensee. He argued that economists may recently have taken an overly optimistic view of the ease with which small firms can overcome intangible entry barriers. The mere presence of small scale entrants who remain small should not be interpreted as signifying a lack of barriers.

In the bus industry the physical restrictions which had been in place for 50 years were removed by the 1985 Transport Act which aimed to deregulate local bus services and allow open competition from new entrants (as long as they met specified safety and financial requirements). It was then argued by companies subsequently investigated under section 3 (of the 1980 Act) that predatory pricing was infeasible because entry was now open and easy. The OFT rejected this argument on a number of grounds largely dependent on information asymmetries. Because regulations had been in place for so long customers expected services of a certain kind from companies that they easily recognised and this gave an advantage (at least in the short term) to incumbents. In addition, potential entrants would be unsure about the precise cost levels of incumbent firms and, more importantly, in the midst of claims about predatory pricing, would be uncertain about the reaction of incumbent firms to new entry. Recent theoretical analysis also suggested that a strong incumbent would have an incentive to use predatory tactics in order to establish a reputation for toughness to deter any future entrants. In other words the OFT was quite sure that in the immediate aftermath of deregulation physical or legal entry barriers had been replaced by more intangible but no less effective barriers which owed much to the previous regulated environment.

There are a number of comments that can be made about the OFT's view of entry barriers in the bus industry. By definition potential entrants have no recent competitive history of the industry to draw on in making their assessment of the market, precisely because there is none. However, what most of the *actual* entrants to the market did have was knowledge and experience of operating, not necessarily in a managerial capacity, in the industry. Thus in *West Yorkshire Road Car Company* [OFT, 1989] the main competing company was founded by an ex-employee of the incumbent; in *Highland Scottish Omnibuses* the new entrant was a co-operative formed by ex-employees of the incumbent; in *South Yorkshire Transport* the entrant had experience in providing coach services; and in *Kingston upon Hull City Transport* [OFT, 1990] the entrant was also a private hire coach company. Their knowledge was therefore probably at least as good as any new entrant to other markets. As far as possible reactions of the incumbent are concerned, all new entrants have to make an assessment as to their likelihood and form. Small entrants with limited resources are more vulnerable than entrants which belong to a larger grouping with sizeable financial resources. In short the notion that asymmetric information was playing a *special* role in the bus industry following deregulation is dubious, and it is questionable whether it constituted anything like the formidible barrier assigned to it by the OFT.

Since, however, in all four cases the OFT concluded that barriers to entry were high enough to make predatory pricing feasible, it proceded to the second element in its analysis concerning the relationship between prices and costs. In *Becton–Dickinson* where the issue of predatory pricing under section 3 was first systematically discussed, the OFT made it clear that it did not accept the narrow interpretation proposed by Areeda and Turner. While recognising that 'there is no rational, non-predatory reason why a firm should choose to make out-of-pocket losses' (i.e. by selling below short-run marginal cost, srmc) nevertheless 'the Office's view is that *prices can be predatory even when above srmc.* If a firm is able to maintain prices which are above that level but do not contribute fully to its fixed (overhead) costs and to the minimum return necessary to remunerate investment in its plant and other fixed facilities by drawing on financial resources generated elsewhere in the business, other firms which are just as efficient in supplying the product(s) on which losses (in such an accounting sense) are incurred may be forced out of business' [. . .]. However because prices between short-run marginal cost and average total cost cannot unambiguously be ascribed to predatory behaviour, additional evidence (e.g. on intent) was required before a complete assessment was made.

Without actually using the terms this interpretation of predatory pricing would allow the OFT in theory to include strategic pricing behaviour by a dominant enterprise, i.e. behaviour which allowed it (but not the entrant) to make more than normal returns, while undermining the position of the entrant. In practice the OFT has settled for a less sophisticated interpretation based essentially on the notion of normal returns. The position was spelt out in *Kingston upon Hull City Transport.* Having reiterated that prices above short run variable cost can be predatory, the report continues: 'If a firm is able to maintain prices *below those necessary to contribute fully to overheads and the minimum return necessary to remunerate investment*, then other firms in the industry which are just as efficient may be forced out of business [. . .]'. However, as Areeda and Turner realised, and as the OFT cases have now demonstrated, it may be especially difficult, to determine with any degree of accuracy and agreement whether an apparent price–cost configuration meant that the firm's prices were covering average total cost or fell some way below it and therefore may be predatory. In *Becton–Dickinson* the OFT was satisfied that on the basis of one year's figures the company was not making a loss, and the price–cost data therefore gave no support to the allegation of predatory pricing. In *West Yorkshire Road Car Company* on the other hand, the assessment depended on the allocation by the OFT of revenues and overheads to parts of a route where the incumbent encountered competition. It found that revenues were sufficient to cover variable costs but insufficient to cover overheads and 'given that such a position is not sustainable in the long-run it could therefore be evidence of predatory behaviour' [. . .]. The fragility of the analysis, which depends entirely on what assumptions are made about overheads attributable to part of the contested route, is obvious. The OFT were aware of this and therefore went on to consider any evidence of predatory intent. Two months later, in *South Yorkshire Transport*, the OFT had to consider cost allocations on a particular route. Everything hinged on the treatment of so called 'platform staff' costs for the service. When these were included costs exceeded revenues during the period of competition. The position was rather similar in *Highland Scottish Omnibuses* where costs and revenues were considered over the whole network of services which had been subject to new competition. In this case revenues more than covered 'strictly variable costs' (wages, fuel and lubricants, and tyres) but when 'semi-variable costs' (cleaning, maintenance and vehicle depreciation) were included costs exceeded revenues during the period when competition had occurred [. . .].

Of the four bus enquiries only in *Hull City Transport* was the OFT satisfied that on each relevant route 'revenue exceeded not only variable and semi-variable costs but also total costs, including an allocation of depot costs and overheads. A substantial operating profit was achieved on each route' [. . .]. It was therefore clear to the OFT that no predatory pricing had occurred. In the other three cases price seemed to lie between average variable and average total cost but as we have indicated very much depended on what items were treated as variable and how overhead expenses were allocated to determine whether 'full' costs were covered. It is probable that all three cases would have passed the Areeda–Turner test which according to some authorities had been widely adopted by antitrust judges seeking a respectable but clear-cut rule to guide them through an analytical and empirical morass.

The OFT, in contrast, found in favour of one company but against two. The explanation for the different outcomes rests on the third element of the OFT's procedure, namely evidence of intent. The pitfalls of inferring predatory intent from the actions or documents of a dominant firm have been well described by Posner: 'the availability of evidence of improper intent is often a function of luck and of the defendant's legal sophistication, not of the underlying reality. A firm with executives sensitized to antitrust problems will not leave any documentary trail of improper intent; one whose executives lack this sensitivity will often create rich evidence of such intent simply by the clumsy choice of words to describe innocent behaviour' [. . .]. So far in its section 3 reports the OFT has attempted to avoid such difficulties by drawing its inferences from the actual behaviour of the companies concerned rather than 'the inveterate tendency of sales executives to brag to their supervisors about their competitive prowess' [. . .]. However it is not always clear why inferences should differ in cases where the facts are very similar. For example in both *West Yorkshire Road Car* and *South Yorkshire Transport* the OFT placed particular emphasis on the highly selective nature of the incumbents' price cuts. In both cases these were targetted precisely on the routes where new competition had emerged. In the former case the tactic was apparently unsuccessful and it is noted that the incumbent firm did *not* respond to the new competitor's subsequent expansion. The West Yorkshire company was found *not* to have acted anti-competitively. In the latter case the competitor withdrew from the market and the incumbent promptly raised its prices. 'This suggests that SYT has been willing to resort to selective action to discourage competition' [. . .]. The incumbent was found to have acted anticompetitively. The *intent* of both companies may have been similar but in one case the tactic was successful whereas in the other it was not. The comparative strength and tenacity of the entrants seems to have been the main difference between the two cases rather than the intent of the incumbents. It is thus difficult to avoid the conclusion that in relation to these cases the OFT was inferring intent from outcomes.

In neither case, however, did the incumbent respond to new entry by substantially increasing its services on the routes concerned. This was a major feature of the remaining case *Highland Scottish Omnibuses* where the company was found to have acted anticompetitively and was referred to the MMC. In response to entry by a company formed by ex-employees, the incumbent had reduced its fares to the level of those charged by its new competitor (except in one case where it went lower and to which we refer below). As we have mentioned the OFT judged revenues to be below costs for the incumbent when 'semi-variables' were included. However in this case the incumbent's increase in (mainly unregistered) services on routes served by the entrant amounting to a 60 per cent expansion in its weekly mileage was interpreted as evidence of predatory intent by the OFT. The MMC agreed and ruled that the incumbent's behaviour was against the public interest. If Highland Scottish has been more restrained in the expansion of its services, it seems likely (although neither the OFT nor the MMC reports actually say as much) that by merely *matching* the entrant's lower prices its action would not have been interpreted as restricting competition. Both the OFT and the MMC recognised that the appearance of a new competitor on a number of key routes required a response from Highland Scottish. Since prices were lower *some* expansion of mileage was to be expected to meet the increased demand. It was the *disproportionate* response which appeared to carry most weight with both antitrust bodies. The point is reinforced by the MMC's conclusion about the one route where Highland Scottish had undercut the new entrant. They interpreted this as a reasonable competitive response in view of the entrant's common price for other routes. The MMC thus rejected the OFT's conclusion that this particular action was predatory.

The Highland Scottish case is particularly interesting in that it illustrates most clearly how the 'three element' approach works. First, the incumbent was not only well established but as explained above had access to substantial funds. Secondly, it cut its prices to a level between average variable and average total costs which is non-sustainable in the long-run. Thirdly, it greatly increased its services on routes covered by the entrant. Each element was necessary and taken together the three elements were sufficient to constitute predatory behaviour in the judgment of both the OFT and MMC.

In the analysis, however, one factor appears to have been overlooked. For predatory behaviour to be rational the predator has to be confident that having successfully killed off current entrants, no others will appear when prices are raised to recoup previous losses. In *Becton–Dickinson*, as we have observed the OFT was explicit on this point: amongst other things there must be 'little likelihood of competitors re-entering the market once prices were raised substantially' [. . .]. For policy purposes the key question is clearly what kind of 'competitors' are meant in this context? It is not part of competition policy to protect or encourage weak sellers. There is some evidence in the MMC report that Traction, the original entrant, fell into this category. At various points the MMC refers to the lack of managerial skill and experience [. . .] and under-capitalisation [. . .]. Its pricing strategy was based on a wildly optimistic forecast of the market share it could capture which appeared to depend on

Highland Scottish taking no retaliatory action to its entry [. . .]. Since Traction itself had cut prices it did not have the option, when Highland Scottish reacted, to sit out the storm by, for example, persuading its bankers that current price levels were artificially low and bound to rise sooner or later.

If Highland Scottish relied on its retaliatory strategy and the subsequent demise of Traction to dissuade further entry, is miscalculated. At first in the month after Traction went into receivership (April 1989) its goodwill and assets were purchased by another small company, Alexanders, which continued to compete until November 1989 when it, too, failed. However, the assets then passed to Magicbus Scotland, a subsidiary of Stagecoach Holdings which, according to the MMC was the biggest private bus company in Western Europe [. . .]. The MMC was unable to comment in detail on the behaviour of the two companies after the entry of Stagecoach because the time period involved fell outside its terms of reference.

It observed, however, that Highland Scottish's reaaction had been more muted than when confronted by Traction and that the companies were moving towards a 'less hectic form of competition' [. . .]. In principle Highland Scottish could have reacted to the new entrant in exactly the same way as it had to Traction. The financial resources were still available, as was the capacity to increase service miles substantially. The reason it did not was simply that it recognised in Stagecoach a much more formidable competitor [. . .]. The fact that first Alexanders and then Stagecoach entered suggests that the market was large enough to accommodate at least two companies. At the time of writing [. . .] there is no sign that Stagecoach intends to leave the market.

Thus despite the reservations by the OFT about entry conditions, barriers are not high for well managed and properly funded companies. It is doubtful whether a company of this kind whatever its overall size, is vulnerable to the strategy employed by Highland Scottish because it would have planned for 'shakedown' losses normally incurred when entering a new market and would have a good idea what level of prices was sustainable. In the face of the threat of *renewed* entry from equally efficient companies whenever prices were raised by the incumbent to recoup previous losses, a predatory policy becomes unprofitable.

The implication of this analysis is that it should be possible under the 1980 Act for both the OFT and the MMC to pay more attention to the viability of the complainant or 'prey'. The current procedure is for the OFT to investigate complaints *against* a company which is usually well established and with a large market share. It is much more difficult to examine in some detail the economic credentials of an entrant. In *Highland Scottish*, therefore, there is a detailed discussion of the incumbent's costs but no information at all about Traction's costs. We do not know, for example, whether the prices charged covered average variable or average total costs, or at what share of the market revenues would have been greater than costs. Unless more is known about entrant firms, section 3 may be turned into a mechanism for protecting 'competitors', however vulnerable, rather than competition. As the OFT itself said in *Kingston Upon Hull City Transport* the competitive entry that should be protected is by firms that are of equal efficiency to the incumbent. [. . .]

Section 2 of the Sherman Act, a criminal provision, is directed against 'monopolization'. The meaning of this offence combines the nature of monopoly and its acquisition and maintenance. In the **Berkey** case, below, the US Court of Appeals (Second Circuit) provides a thorough analysis of the history, purpose and meaning of section 2.

19.8 United States Code Title 15. Commerce and Trade Chapter 1. Monopolies and Combinations in Restraint of Trade (Sherman Act)

2. MONOPOLIZATION

Every person who shall monopolize, or attempt to monopolize, or combine or conspire with any other person or persons, to monopolize any part of the trade or commerce among the several States, or with foreign nations, shall be deemed guilty of a felony, and, on conviction thereof, shall be punished by fine not exceeding $10,000,000 if a corporation, or, if any other person, $350,000, or by imprisonment not exceeding three years, or by both said punishments [. . .].

19.9 *Berkey Photo, Inc.* v. *Eastman Kodak Company*, United States Court of Appeals for the Second Circuit 603 F.2d 263; 53 A.L.R. Fed. 768; 1979-1 Trade Cas. (CCH) P62,718

Kaufman, Chief Judge:

[. . .]

To millions of Americans, the name Kodak is virtually synonymous with photography. Founded over a century ago by George Eastman, the Eastman Kodak Company has long been the preeminent firm in the amateur photographic industry. It provides products and services covering every step in the creation of an enduring photographic record from an evanescent image. Snapshots may be taken with a Kodak camera on Kodak film, developed by Kodak's Color Print and Processing Laboratories, and printed on Kodak photographic paper. The firm has rivals at each stage of this process, but in many of them it stands, and has long stood, dominant. It is one of the giants of American enterprise, with international sales of nearly $6 billion in 1977 and pre-tax profits in excess of $1.2 billion.

This action, one of the largest and most significant private antitrust suits in history, was brought by Berkey Photo, Inc., a far smaller but still prominent participant in the industry. Berkey competes with Kodak in providing photo finishing services – the conversion of exposed film into finished prints, slides, or movies. Until 1978, Berkey sold cameras as well. It does not manufacture film, but it does purchase Kodak film for resale to its customers, and it also buys photo finishing equipment and supplies, including color print paper, from Kodak.

The two firms thus stand in a complex, multifaceted relationship, for Kodak has been Berkey's competitor in some markets and its supplier in others. In this action, Berkey claims that every aspect of the association has been infected by Kodak's monopoly power in the film, color print paper, and camera markets, wilfully acquired, maintained, and exercised in violation of [section] 2 of the Sherman Act. [. . .] It also charges that Kodak conspired with flash lamp manufacturers in violation of [section] 1 of the Act [. . .] Berkey alleges that these violations caused it to lose sales in the camera and photo finishing markets and to pay excessive prices to Kodak for film, color print paper, and photo finishing equipment [. . .] A number of the charges arise from Kodak's 1972 introduction of the 110 photographic system, featuring a 'Pocket Instamatic' camera and a new color print film, Kodacolor II, but the case is not limited to that episode. It embraces many of Kodak's activities for the last decade and, indeed, from preceding years as well.

[. . .]

After deliberating for eight days on liability and five on damages, the jury found for

Berkey on virtually every point [. . .] Kodak now appeals this judgment, as well as the two forms of equitable relief that we shall discuss below. It challenges virtually every aspect of the district court proceedings, from the theories of liability and damages presented to the jury to the sufficiency of the evidence to sustain them [. . .]. Resolution of [this appeal] requires us to settle a number of important and novel issues concerning [section] 2 of the Sherman Act. We believe that the district Court committed several significant errors as it charted its course through the complexities of this case, and we are therefore compelled to reverse the judgment below in certain major respects [. . .].

I. THE AMATEUR PHOTOGRAPHIC INDUSTRY

Before plunging into the welter of issues raised in this appeal, we must understand the industry out of which the litigation arose. It is, of course, a basic principle in the law of monopolization that the first step in a court's analysis must be a definition of the relevant markets. See, e.g. *United States* v. *E.I. du Pont de Nemours and Co.*, 351 U.S. 377, 391-93 (1956). Although Kodak does not now challenge the jury's delineation of the markets a survey of this terrain remains essential. The jury found monopolization or other anticompetitive conduct in no fewer than five distinct markets within the amateur photographic industry, and in several instances Kodak was held to have misused its control over one market to disadvantage rivals in another. Accordingly, to evaluate the verdicts, it is necessary to describe not only the individual markets but also the interrelationships among them.

The principal markets relevant here, each nationwide in scope, are amateur conventional still cameras, conventional photographic film, photo finishing services, photo finishing equipment, and color print paper. The numerous technological interactions among the products and services constituting these markets are manifest. To take an obvious example, not only are both camera and film required to produce a snapshot, but the two must be in compatible 'formats'. This means that the film must be cut to the right size and spooled in a roll or cartridge that will fit the camera mechanism. Berkey charges that Kodak refused to supply on economical terms film usable with camera formats designed by other manufacturers, thereby exploiting its film monopoly to obstruct its rivals in the camera market. Similarly, Berkey contends, since the emulsions and other constituents of a film determine the chemicals and processes required to develop it, Kodak was able to project its power over film into the photo finishing market as well.

These and other market interactions will be discussed in depth as we analyze the verdicts and rulings below. First, however, we must describe in detail the individual markets themselves.

A. The Camera Market

The 'amateur conventional still camera' market now consists almost entirely of the so-called 110 and 126 instant-loading cameras. These are the direct descendants of the popular 'box' cameras, the best-known of which was Kodak's so-called 'Brownie'. Small, simple, and relatively inexpensive, cameras of this type are designed for the mass market rather than for the serious photographer [. . .].

Kodak has long been the dominant firm in the market thus defined. Between 1954 and 1973 it never enjoyed less than 61% of the annual unit sales, nor less than 64% of the dollar volume, and in the peak year of 1964, Kodak cameras accounted for 90% of market revenues. Much of this success is no doubt due to the firm's history of innovation. In 1963 Kodak first marketed the 126 'Instamatic' instant-loading camera [. . .] and in 1972 it came out with the much smaller 110 'Pocket Instamatic'. Not only are these cameras small and light, but they employ film packaged in cartridges that can simply be dropped in the back of the camera, thus obviating the need to load and position a roll manually. Their introduction triggered successive revolutions in the industry. Annual amateur still camera sales in the United States averaged 3.9 million units between 1954 and 1963, with little annual variation. In the first full year after Kodak's introduction of the 126, industry sales leaped 22%, and they took an even larger quantum jump when the 110 came to market. Other camera manufacturers, including Berkey, copied both these inventions, but for several months after each introduction anyone desiring to purchase a camera in the new format was perforce remitted to Kodak.

Berkey has been a camera manufacturer since its 1966 acquisition of the Keystone Camera Company, a producer of movie cameras and equipment [. . .]. In 1968 Berkey began to sell amateur still cameras made by other firms, and the following year the Keystone Division commenced manufacturing such cameras itself. From 1970 to 1977, Berkey accounted for 8.2% of the sales in the camera market in the United States, reaching a peak of 10.2% in 1976. In 1978, Berkey sold its camera division and thus abandoned this market.

B. The Film Market

The relevant market for photographic film comprises color print, color slide, color movie, and black-and-white film [. . .]. Kodak's grip on this market is even stronger than its hold on cameras. Since 1952, its annual sales have always exceeded 82% of the nationwide volume on a unit basis, and 88% in revenues. Foreign competition has recently made some inroads into Kodak's monopoly, but the Rochester firm concedes that it dominated film sales throughout the period relevant to this case. Indeed, in his summation, Kodak's trial counsel told the jury that 'the film market . . . has been a market where there has not been price competition and where Kodak has been able to price its products pretty much without regard to the products of competitors'.

The jury included movie film and 35-millimeter film in this market, presumably because they are substantially identical to the film used in amateur still cameras. Instant film, however, a product chemically distinct from laboratory-processed film, was excluded.

Kodak's monopoly in the film market is particularly important to this case, because the jury accepted Berkey's contention, noted above, that it had been used to disadvantage rivals in cameras, photo finishing equipment, and other markets. Of special relevance to this finding is the color print film segment of the industry, which Kodak has dominated since it introduced 'Kodacolor', the first amateur color print film, in 1942. In 1963, when Kodak announced the 126 Instamatic camera, it also brought out a new, faster color print film – Kodacolor X – which was initially available to amateur photographers only in the 126 format. Nine years later, Kodak repeated this pattern with the simultaneous introduction of the 110 Pocket Instamatic and Kodacolor II film. For more than a year, Kodacolor II was made only for 110 cameras, and Kodak has never made any other color print film in the 110 size.

C. Photofinishing Services and Photofinishing Equipment

Before 1954, Kodak's Color Print and Processing Laboratories (CP&P) had a nearly absolute monopoly of color photo finishing maintained by a variety of practices. Accounting for over 95% of color film sales, Kodak sold every roll with an advance charge for processing included. Consumers had little choice but to purchase Kodak film, and in so doing they acquired the right to have that film developed and printed by CP&P at no further charge. Since few customers would duplicate their costs to procure the services of a non-Kodak photo finisher, Kodak was able to parlay its film monopoly to achieve equivalent market power in photo finishing [. . .] This film/processing 'tie-in' attracted the attention of the Justice Department, and in 1954 a consent decree changed the structure of the color photo finishing market drastically. Kodak was forbidden to link photo finishing to film sales, and it agreed to make its processing technology, chemicals, and paper available to rivals at reasonable rates. As a result, CP&P's share of the market plummeted from 96% in 1954 to 69% two years later, and it has declined sharply ever since. In 1970, CP&P accounted for but 17% of the market, and by 1976 its share reached a low of 10%. There are now approximately 600 independent photo finishers in the United States.

Berkey is one of the largest of these processors. It has been a photo finisher since 1933, but until 1954 its principal business was developing and printing black-and-white film. In addition, Berkey purchased Kodak black-and-white film, which was sold without a processing tie-in, for resale to its photo finishing customers. After the 1954 decree, Berkey applied to Kodak for the appropriate licenses and in 1956 began to process significant amounts of color film. It now finishes more 126 and 110 color print film than does Kodak. Prior to 1954 a small part of Berkey's business consisted of processing Anscocolor film – manufactured by a rival of Kodak's, Ansco – into both slides and color prints. Using paper and chemicals supplied by Ansco, Berkey was also able to produce color prints from Kodachrome slides.

A variety of equipment is used to process film, and the Kodak Apparatus Division (KAD) designs and produces most of the machinery used by CP&P. Kodak also sells some equipment to other photo finishers, but this is an insignificant portion of its business; indeed, until the introduction of the 110 system, Kodak made still film processing equipment for its own use only. Several other firms supply photo finishing equipment to the rival processors, and Berkey does not contend that Kodak monopolized or attempted to monopolize this market.

D. The Color Paper Market

The market for color paper – that is, paper specially treated so that images from color film may be printed on it – effectively came into being after entry of the 1954 consent decree. Before then, Kodak was for all practical purposes the only color photo finisher, and its requirements for color paper were met entirely by the paper division of Kodak Park Works in Rochester. The remaining processors, who dealt with non-Kodak color film and used non-Kodak paper, occupied only 4% of the color photo finishing market. Consequently, the vertical foreclosure created by CP&P's lock on photo finishing and its exclusive use of Kodak color paper was virtually complete.

Although the 1954 decree steadily loosened Kodak's grip in photo finishing, it did not immediately affect the firm's control of color paper. For more than a decade, the independent photo finishers that sprang up after the decree was entered looked only to Kodak for their paper supplies. Indeed, although entry by both foreign and domestic paper manufacturers has reduced Kodak's share substantially, to a low of 60% in 1976, the firm's color paper operations have remained remarkably profitable. Between 1968 and 1975, while its market share was falling from 94% to 67%, Kodak's earnings from operations as a percentage of sales remained virtually constant, averaging 60% for the period. Moreover, the most recent telling event in the market has not been entry but exit: GAF Corporation announced in 1977 that it was abandoning its effort to sell color paper, leaving Kodak with only one domestic and two foreign competitors.

Kodak, then, is indeed, a titan in its field, and accordingly has almost inevitably invited attack under [section] 2 of the Sherman Act. Few, if any, cases have presented so many diverse and difficult problems of [section] 2 analysis. It is appropriate, therefore, to elucidate some fundamental principles of law relating to that statutory provision.

[SECTION] 2 OF THE SHERMAN ACT

The Sherman Antitrust Act of 1890 has been characterized as 'a charter of freedom': *Appalachian Coals, Inc.* v. *United States*, 288 U.S. 344, 359 (1933). For nearly ninety years it has engraved in law a firm national policy that the norm for commercial activity must be robust competition. The most frequently invoked section of the Act is the first, which forbids contracts, combinations, or conspiracies in restraint of trade. But the prohibition of [section] 1 is incomplete (*Standard Oil Co. of New Jersey* v. *United States*, 221 U.S. 1, 60-61 (1911)), for it only applies to conduct of two or more actors. If sufficiently powerful, however, a single economic entity may also stifle competition: R. Callmann, *The Law of Unfair Competition, Trademarks, and Monopolies* 341–42 (3d edn. 1967). Accordingly, in [section] 2 of the Sherman Act, Congress made it unlawful to 'monopolize, or attempt to monopolize, or combine or conspire . . . to monopolize' any part of interstate or foreign commerce. It is [section] 2 to which we give our principal attention in analyzing this case.

In passing the Sherman Act, Congress recognized that it could not enumerate all the activities that would constitute monopolization. Section 2, therefore, in effect conferred upon the federal courts 'a new jurisdiction to apply a "common law" against monopolizing': P. Areeda and D. Turner, *Antitrust Law* 40 (1978). In performing that task, the courts have enunciated certain principles that by now seem almost elementary to any student of antitrust law. But, because [section] 2 must reconcile divergent and sometimes conflicting policies, it has been difficult to synthesize the parts into a coherent and consistent whole. To provide a framework for deciding the issues presented by this case, therefore, we begin by stating what we conceive to be the fundamental doctrines of [section] 2.

A. Monopoly Power as the Essence of the [Section] 2 Violation

The gravamen of a charge under [section] 1 of the Sherman Act is conduct in restraint of trade; no fundamental alteration of market structure is necessary. Thus, certain restrictive practices among competitors, such as price fixing, are illegal *per se*. That the conspirators lack the market power to affect prices is immaterial: *United States* v. *Socony-Vacuum Oil Co.*, 310 U.S. 150, 224 n.59 (1940). Section 2, by contrast, is aimed primarily not at improper conduct but at a pernicious market structure in which the concentration of power saps the salubrious influence of competition.

Indeed, there is little argument over the principle that existence of monopoly power – 'the power to control prices or exclude competition' *E. I. du Pont de Nemours and Co.*, *supra*, 351 U.S. at 391) – is 'the primary requisite to a finding of monopolization': M. Handler, *Twenty-five Years of Antitrust*, 691 (1973). The Supreme Court has informed us that 'monopoly power, whether lawfully or unlawfully acquired, may itself constitute an evil and stand condemned under [section] 2 even though it remains unexercised': *United States* v. *Griffith*, 334 U.S. 100, 107 (1948).

This tenet is well grounded in economic analysis. There is little disagreement that a profit-maximizing monopolist will maintain his prices higher and his output lower than the socially optimal levels that would prevail in a purely competitive market: e.g. F. Scherer, *Industrial Market Structure and Economic Performance*, 13-19 (1970) [see now later editions of this work]. The price excess represents not a reasonable return on investment but the spoils of the monopolist's power: e.g. L. Sullivan, *Handbook of the Law of Antitrust*, 25-26 (1977); P. Areeda and D. Turner, *supra*, at 323-34.

It is not a defense to liability under [section] 2 that monopoly power has not been used to charge more than a competitive price or extract greater than a reasonable profit. Learned Hand stated the rationale in the Alcoa case, *United States* v. *Aluminum Co. of America*, 148 F.2d 416, 427 (2d Cir. 1945). He said in his incisive manner that the Sherman Act is based on the belief: that possession of unchallenged economic power deadens initiative, discourages thrift and depresses energy; that immunity from competition is a narcotic, and rivalry is a stimulant, to industrial progress; that the spur of constant stress is necessary to counteract an inevitable disposition to let well enough alone. Judge Hand explained, in addition, that Congress was not 'actuated by economic motives alone' in enacting [section 2]. (*ibid.*) Considerations of political and social policy form a major part of our aversion to monopolies, for concentration of power in the hands of a few obstructs opportunities for the rest. Because, like all power, it is laded with the possibility of abuse; because it encourages sloth rather than the active quest for excellence; and because it tends to damage the very fabric of our economy and our society, monopoly power is 'inherently evil': *United States* v. *United Shoe Machinery Corp.*, 110 F. Supp. 295, 345 (D. Mass. 1953), 347 U.S. 521 (1954); see *United States* v. *Grinnell Corp.*, 236 F. Supp. 244, 258 (D.R.I. 1964), 384 U.S. 563 (1966). If a finding of monopoly power were all that were necessary to complete a violation of [section] 2, our task in this case would be considerably lightened. Kodak's control of the film and color paper markets clearly reached the level of a monopoly. And, while the issue is a much closer one, it appears that the evidence was sufficient for the jury to find that Kodak possessed such power in the camera market as well [. . .]. But our inquiry into Kodak's liability cannot end there.

B. The Requirement of Anticompetitive Conduct

Despite the generally recognized evils of monopoly power, it is 'well settled', see J. von Kalinowski, *Antitrust Laws and Trade Regulation* P802(3), at 8-41 (1979), that [section] 2 does not prohibit monopoly *simpliciter* – or, as the Supreme Court phrased it in the early landmark case of Standard Oil Co. of New Jersey, *supra*, 221 U.S. at 62, 'monopoly in the concrete'.

Thus, while proclaiming vigorously that monopoly power is the evil at which [section] 2 is aimed, courts have declined to take what would have appeared to be the next logical step – declaring monopolies unlawful *per se* unless specifically authorized by law. To understand the reason for this, one must comprehend the fundamental tension – one might almost say the paradox – that is near the heart of [section] 2. This tension creates much of the confusion surrounding [section] 2. It makes the cryptic *Alcoa* opinion a litigant's wishing well, into which, it sometimes seems, one may peer and find nearly anything he wishes.

The conundrum was indicated in characteristically striking prose by Judge Hand, who was not able to resolve it. Having stated that Congress 'did not condone "good trusts" and condemn "bad" ones; it forbad all' (Alcoa, *supra*, 148 F.2d at 427), he declared with equal force, 'The successful competitor, having been urged to compete, must not be turned upon when he wins' (*ibid.*, at 430). Hand, therefore, told us that it would be inherently unfair to condemn success when the Sherman Act itself mandates competition. Such a wooden rule, it was feared, might also deprive the leading firm in an industry of the incentive to exert its best efforts. Further success would yield not rewards but legal castigation. The antitrust laws would thus compel the very sloth they were intended to prevent. We must always be mindful lest the Sherman Act be invoked perversely in favor of those who seek protection against the rigors of competition: e.g. *Buffalo Courier-Express, Inc.* v. *Buffalo Evening News, Inc.*, No. 77-7617, slip op. at 2196 (2d Cir. Apr. 16, 1979).

In Alcoa the crosscurrents and pulls and tugs of [section] 2 law were reconciled by noting that, although the firm controlled the aluminum ingot market, 'it may not have achieved monopoly; monopoly may have been thrust upon it': 148 F.2d at 429. In examining this language, which would condemn a monopolist unless it is 'the passive beneficiary of a monopoly' (*ibid.*, at 430), we perceive Hand the philosopher. As an operative rule of law, however, the 'thrust upon' phrase does not suffice. It has been criticized by scholars (P. Areeda and D. Turner, *supra*, at 20; L. Sullivan, *supra*, at 96-97; Handler, 'Some Unresolved Problems of Antitrust', 62 *Columbia Law Review*, 930, 934 (1962)), and the Supreme Court appears to have abandoned it: see *United States* v. *Grinnell Corp.*, 384 U.S. 563, 570-71 (1966); M. Handler, *supra*, at 692. Grinnell instructs that after possession of monopoly power is found, the second element of the [section] 2 offense is 'the willful acquisition or maintenance of that power as distinguished from growth or development as a consequence of a superior product, business acumen, or historic accident': 384 U.S. at 570-71.

This formulation appears to square with the understanding of the draftsmen of the Sherman Act that [section] 2 does not condemn one 'who merely by superior skill and intelligence . . . got the whole business because nobody could do it as well': *United Shoe Machinery Corp.*, *supra*, 110 F. Supp. at 341 (quoting legislative history). Thus the statement in *Alcoa* that even well-behaved monopolies are forbidden by [section] 2 must be read carefully in context. Its rightful meaning is that, if monopoly power has been acquired or maintained through improper means, the fact that the power has not been used to extract improper benefits provides no succor to the monopolist.

But the law's hostility to monopoly power extends beyond the means of its acquisition. Even if that power has been legitimately acquired, the monopolist may not wield it to prevent or impede competition. Once a firm gains a measure of monopoly power, whether by its own superior competitive skill or because of such actions as restrictive combinations with others, it may discover that the power is capable of being maintained and augmented merely by using it: e.g. *Lorain Journal Co.* v. *United States*, 342 U.S. 143 (1951). That is, a firm that has achieved dominance of a market must find its control sufficient to preserve and even extend its market share by excluding or preventing competition. A variety of techniques may be employed to achieve this end – predatory pricing, lease-only policies, and exclusive buying arrangements, to list a few.

Even if the origin of the monopoly power was innocent, therefore, the Grinnell rule recognizes that maintaining or extending market control by the exercise of that power is sufficient to complete a violation of [section] 2. As we have explained, only considerations of fairness and the need to preserve proper economic incentives prevent the condemnation of [section] 2 from extending even to one who has gained his power by purely competitive means. The district court judge correctly indicated that such a monopolist is tolerated but not cherished. Thus, the rule of Grinnell must be read together with the teaching of Griffith, that the mere existence of monopoly power 'whether lawfully or unlawfully acquired', is in itself violative of [section] 2, 'provided it is coupled with the purpose or intent to exercise that power': 334 U.S. at 107.

The key to analysis, it must be stressed, is the concept of market power. Although power may be derived from size, e.g. *United States* v. *Swift and Co.*, 286 U.S. 106, 116 (1932), the two are not identical: F. Scherer, *supra*, at 352. A firm that has lawfully acquired a monopoly position is not barred from taking advantage of scale economies by constructing, for example, a large and efficient factory. These benefits are a consequence of size and not an exercise of power over the market [. . .]. Nevertheless, many anticompetitive actions are possible or effective only if taken by a firm that dominates its smaller rivals: see *Telex Corp.* v. *International Business Machines Corp.*, 510 F.2d 894, 925-26 (10th Cir.), cert. dismissed, 423 U.S. 802 (1975). A classic illustration is an insistence that those who wish to secure a firm's services cease dealing with its competitors: see, e.g. *Lorain Journal Co.*, *supra*. Such conduct is illegal when taken by a monopolist because it tends to destroy competition, although in the hands of a smaller market participant it might be considered harmless, or even 'honestly industrial': *Alcoa*, *supra*, 148 F.2d at 431.

In sum, although the principles announced by the [section] 2 cases often appear to conflict, this much is clear. The mere possession of monopoly power does not *ipso facto* condemn a market participant. But, to avoid the proscriptions of [section] 2, the firm must refrain at all times from conduct directed at smothering competition. This doctrine has two branches. Unlawfully acquired power remains anathema even when kept dormant. And it is no less true that a firm with a legitimately achieved monopoly may not wield the resulting power to tighten its hold on the market.

C. Monopoly Power as a Lever in Other Markets

It is clear that a firm may not employ its market position as a lever to create – or attempt to create – a monopoly in another market: see, e.g. *Griffith*, *supra*; *Smith-Kline Corp*. v. *Eli Lilly and Co*., 575 F.2d 1056 (3d Cir.), cert. denied, 99 S. Ct. 123 (1978). Kodak, in the period relevant to this suit, was never close to gaining control of the markets for photo finishing equipment or services and could not be held to have attempted to monopolize them. Berkey nevertheless contends that Kodak illicitly gained an advantage in these areas by leveraging its power over film and cameras.

Accordingly, we must determine whether a firm violates [section] 2 by using its monopoly power in one market to gain a competitive advantage in another, albeit without an attempt to monopolize the second market. We hold, as did the lower court, that it does [. . .]. The *Griffith* case confirms this view. There, a chain of motion picture exhibitors operated the only theaters in a number of towns, and used its concomitant buying power to extract from distributors certain exclusive rights in other localities where it faced challengers. The Court held that monopoly power had been illegally used 'to beget monopoly': 334 U.S. at 108. Its rationale swept more broadly, however, for it admonished that 'the use of monopoly power, however lawfully acquired, to foreclose competition, to gain a competitive advantage, or to destroy a competitor, is unlawful': *ibid*., at 107.

This rule is linked to the prohibition against tying arrangements in the sale of goods and services: see P. Areeda and D. Turner, *supra*, at 223–24. Indeed, in *Northern Pacific Railway* v. *United States*, 356 U.S. 1, 11 (1958), the Supreme Court described the 'vice' of ties in language evocative of Griffith: 'the use of economic power in one market to restrict competition on the merits of another'. And to condemn a tie, the market for the tied product need not be monopolized. It suffices that a 'substantial' amount of competition is foreclosed: *Times-Picayune Publishing Co*. v. *United States*, 345 U.S. 594, 608-09 (1953); *International Salt Co*. v. *United States*, 332 U.S. 392, 396 (1947).

We need not rely solely on policy considerations or an analysis of the Griffith dictum to support the view asserted here. Indeed, whatever problems of murkiness may plague the *Alcoa* opinion, on this point is it pellucid. The defendant had employed its monopoly power in the ingot market to impose a price squeeze on the manufacturers of aluminum sheet. Although this court expressly noted that there was no attempt to monopolize the sheet market, it held the challenged practice to be 'an unlawful exercise of "Alcoa's" power': 148 F.2d at 438. A more recent case arriving at the same conclusion is *Sargent-Welch Scientific Co*. v. *Ventron Corp*., 567 F.2d 701, 711–13 (7th Cir.), cert. denied, 99 S.Ct. 87 (1978). There a manufacturer of precision scientific instruments with a monopoly in the market for electromagnetic microbalances allegedly threatened to refuse to sell these devices to retailers who did not stock its millibalances as well. The court ruled that this practice would violate [section] 2, even though Ventron did not seek or gain a monopoly in the market for millibalances [. . .].

Accordingly, the use of monopoly power attained in one market to gain a competitive advantage in another is a violation of [section] 2, even if there has not been an attempt to monopolize the second market. It is the use of economic power that creates the liability. But, as we have indicated, a large firm does not violate [section] 2 simply by reaping the competitive rewards attributable to its efficient size, nor does an integrated business offend the Sherman Act whenever one of its departments benefits from association with a division possessing a monopoly in its own market. So long as we allow a firm to compete in several fields, we must expect it to seek the competitive advantages of its broad-based activity – more efficient production, greater ability to develop complementary products, reduced transaction costs, and so forth. These are gains that accrue to any integrated firm, regardless of its market share, and they cannot by themselves be considered uses of monopoly power [. . .].

FURTHER READING

See also the following articles on the regulation of market power.

Armentano, D. (1991), 'Antitrust and monopoly: anatomy of a policy failure', 32 *Santa Clara Law Review*, 1171.

Blair, R. and Harrison, J. (1992), 'The measurement of monopsony power', 37 *Antitrust Bulletin*, 133.

Daltrop, J. and Ferry, J. (1991), 'The relationship between Articles 85 and 86: *Tetra Pak*', 13 *European Intellectual Property Review*, 31.

Easterbrook, F. (1992), 'Monopolization: past, present, future', 61 *Antitrust Law Journal*, 99.

Jacobson, J. and Dorman, G. (1992), 'Monopsony revisited: a comment on Blair and Harrison', 37 *Antitrust Bulletin*, 151.

Smith G. (1991), 'From monopoly to competition: the transformations of Alcoa, 1888-1986', 36 *Antitrust Bulletin*, 267.

See the following works on the economic issues raised in Chapter 19.

Areeda, P. E. and Turner, D. F. (1975), 'Predatory pricing and related practices under Section 2 of the Sherman Act', 88 *Harvard Law Review*, 697.

Brander, J. A. and Eaton, J. (1984), 'Product line rivalry', 74 *American Economic Review*, 323.

Comanor, W. S. and Frech, III, H. E. (1984), 'Strategic behavior and antitrust analysis', 74 *American Economic Review*, 372.

Dixit, A. K. (1980), 'The role of investment in entry deterrence', 90 *Economic Journal*, 95.

Dixon, H. (1989), 'Oligopoly theory made simple', in S. Davies, B. Lyons with H. Dixon, P. Geroski, *Economics of Industrial Organisation* (Longman, London).

Eaton, B. C. and Lipsey, R. (1980), 'Exit barriers are entry barriers: the durability of capital as a barrier to entry', 11 *Bell Journal of Economics*, 721.

Fudenberg, D. and Tirole, J. (1983), 'Capital and commitment: strategic investment to deter mobility', 31 *Journal of Economic Theory*, 227.

Geroski, P. A. (1991), *Market Dynamics and Entry* (Basil Blackwell, Oxford).

Judd, K. (1985), 'Credible Spatial Preemption', 16 *Rand Journal of Economics*, 153.

Klemperer, P. (1987), 'Entry deterrence in markets with consumer switching costs', 97 *Economic Journal* (supplement), 99.

Mankiw, N. G. and Whinston, M. D. (1986), 'Free-entry and social inefficiency', 17 *Rand Journal of Economics*, 48.

Milgrom, P. and Roberts, J. (1982), 'Limit pricing and entry under incomplete information: an equilibrium analysis', 50 *Econometrica*, 443.

Salop, S. and Sheffman, D. (1983), 'Raising rivals' costs', 73 *American Economic Review*, (papers and proceedings), 267.

Schmalensee, R. (1978), 'Entry deterrence in the ready-to-eat breakfast cereal industry', 9 *Bell Journal of Economics*, 305.

Schmalensee, R. (1987), 'Standards for dominant firm conduct: what can economists contribute?', in D. Hay and J. Vickers (eds), *The Economics of Market Dominance* (Basil Blackwell, Oxford).

Shaw, R. and Simpson, P. (1985), 'The Monopolies Commission and the process of competition', 6(1) *Fiscal Studies*, 82.

PART FIVE

MERGERS

20

MERGER TRANSACTIONS

20.1 Fair Trading Act 1973

63 Mergers references to which ss 64 to 75 apply

[. . .]

(2) In the following provisions of this Part of this Act 'enterprise' means the activities, or part of the activities, of a business.

64 Merger situation qualifying for investigation

(1) A merger reference may be made to the Commission by the Secretary of State where it appears to him that it is or may be the fact that two or more enterprises (in this section referred to as 'the relevant enterprises'), of which one at least was carried on in the United Kingdom or by or under the control of a body corporate incorporated in the United Kingdom, have, at a time or in circumstances falling within subsection (4) of this section, ceased to be distinct enterprises, and that either:

(*a*) as a result, the condition specified in subsection (2) or in subsection (3) of this section prevails, or does so to a greater extent, with respect to the supply of goods or services of any description, or

(*b*) the value of the assets taken over exceeds £30 million.

(2) The condition referred to in subsection (1)(*a*) of this section, in relation to the supply of goods of any description, is that at least one-quarter of all the goods of that description which are supplied in the United Kingdom, or in a substantial part of the United Kingdom, either:

(*a*) are supplied by one and the same person or are supplied to one and the same person, or

(*b*) are supplied by the persons by whom the relevant enterprises (so far as they continue to be carried on) are carried on, or are supplied to those persons.

(3) The condition referred to in subsection (1)(*a*) of this section, in relation to the supply of services of any description, is that the supply of services of that description in the United Kingdom, or in a substantial part of the United Kingdom, is, to the extent of at least one-quarter, either:

(*a*) supply by one and the same person, or supply for one and the same person, or

(*b*) supply by the persons by whom the relevant enterprises (so far as they continue to be carried on) are carried on, or supply for those persons.

(4) For the purposes of subsection (1) of this section enterprises shall be taken to have ceased to be distinct enterprises at a time or in circumstances falling within this subsection if either:

(*a*) they did so not earlier than six months before the date on which the merger reference relating to them is to be made, or (*b*) they did so under or in consequence of arrangements or transactions which were entered into without prior notice being given to the Secretary of State or to the Director of material facts about the proposed arrangements or transactions and in circumstances in which those facts had not been made public, and notice of those facts was not given to the Secretary of State or to the Director or made public more than six months before the date mentioned in the preceding paragraph.

(5) In determining whether to make a merger reference to the Commission the Secretary of State shall have regard, with a view to the prevention or removal of uncertainty, to the need for making a determination as soon as is reasonably practicable.

(6) On making a merger reference, the Secretary of State shall arrange for it to be published in such manner as he thinks most suitable for bringing it to the attention of persons who in his opinion would be affected by it.

(7) The Secretary of State may by order made by statutory instrument provide, subject to any transitional provisions contained in the order, that for the sum specified in subsection (1)(*b*) of this section (whether as originally enacted or as previously varied by an order under this subsection) there shall be substituted such other sum (not being less than £5 million) as is specified in the order.

(8) The fact that two or more enterprises have ceased to be distinct enterprises in the circumstances described in subsection (1) of this section (including in those circumstances the result specified in paragraph (*a*), or fulfilment of the condition specified in paragraph (*b*), of that subsection) shall, for the purposes of this Act, be regarded as creating a merger situation qualifying for investigation; and in this Act 'merger situation qualifying for investigation' and any reference to the creation of such a situation shall be construed accordingly.

(9) In this section 'made public' means so publicised as to be generally known or readily ascertainable.

65 Enterprises ceasing to be distinct enterprises

(1) For the purposes of this Part of this Act any two enterprises shall be regarded as ceasing to be distinct enterprises if either:

(*a*) they are brought under common ownership or common control (whether or not the business to which either of them formerly belonged continues to be carried on under the same or different ownership or control), or
(*b*) either of the enterprises ceases to be carried on at all and does so in consequence of any arrangements or transaction entered into to prevent competition between the enterprises.

(2) For the purposes of the preceding subsection enterprises shall (without prejudice to the generality of the words 'common control' in that subsection) be regarded as being under common control if they are:

(*a*) enterprises of interconnected bodies corporate, or
(*b*) enterprises carried on by two or more bodies corporate of which one and the same person or group of persons has control, or
(*c*) an enterprise carried on by a body corporate and an enterprise carried on by a person or group of persons having control of that body corporate.

(3) A person or group of persons able, directly or indirectly, to control or materially to influence the policy of a body corporate, or the policy of any person in carrying on an enterprise, but without having a controlling interest in that body corporate or in that enterprise, may for the purposes of subsections (1) and (2) of this section be treated as having control of it.

(4) For the purposes of subsection (1)(*a*) of this section, in so far as it relates to bringing two or more enterprises under common control, a person or group of persons may be treated as bringing an enterprise under his or their control if:

(*a*) being already able to control or materially to influence the policy of the person carrying on the enterprise, that person or group of persons acquires a controlling interest in the enterprise or, in the case of an enterprise carried on by a body corporate, acquires a controlling interest in that body corporate, or

(*b*) being already able materially to influence the policy of the person carrying on the enterprise, that person or group of persons becomes able to control that policy.

66 Time when enterprises cease to be distinct

(1) Where under or in consequence of the same arrangements or transaction, or under or in consequence of successive arrangements or transactions between the same parties or interests, successive events to which this subsection applies occur within a period of two years, then for the purposes of a merger reference those events may, if the Secretary of State or the Commission thinks fit, be treated as having occurred simultaneously on the date on which the latest of them occurred.

(2) The preceding subsection applies to any event whereby, under or in consequence of the arrangements or the transactions in question, any enterprises cease as between themselves to be distinct enterprises.

(3) For the purposes of subsection (1) of this section any arrangements or transactions may be treated by the Secretary of State or the Commission as arrangements or transactions between the same interests if it appears to him to be appropriate that they should be so treated, having regard to the persons who are substantially concerned in them.

(4) Subject to the preceding provisions of this section and to section 66A of this Act, the time at which any two enterprises cease to be distinct enterprises, where they do so under or in consequence of any arrangements or transaction not having immediate effect, or having immediate effect in part only, shall be taken to be the time when the parties to the arrangements or transaction become bound to such extent as will result, on effect being given to their obligations, in the enterprises ceasing to be distinct enterprises.

(5) In accordance with subsection (4) of this section (but without prejudice to the generality of that subsection) for the purpose of determining the time at which any two enterprises cease to be distinct enterprises no account shall be taken of any option or other conditional right until the option is exercised or the condition is satisfied.

66A Obtaining control by stages

(1) Where an enterprise is brought under the control of a person or group of persons in the course of two or more transactions (referred to in this section as a 'series of transactions') falling within subsection (2) of this section, those transactions may, if the Secretary of State or, as the case may be, the Commission thinks fit, be treated for the purposes of a merger reference as having occurred simultaneously on the date on which the latest of them occurred.

(2) The transactions falling within this subsection are:

(*a*) any transaction which:
  (i) enables that person or group of persons directly or indirectly to control or materially to influence the policy of any person carrying on the enterprise,
  (ii) enables that person or group of persons to do so to a greater degree, or
  (iii) is a step (whether direct or indirect) towards enabling that person or group of persons to do so, and

(*b*) any transaction whereby that person or group of persons acquires a controlling interest in the enterprise or, where the enterprise is carried on by a body corporate, in that body corporate.

(3) Where a series of transactions includes a transaction falling within subsection (2)(*b*) of this section, any transaction occurring after the occurrence of that trans-

action is to be disregarded for the purposes of subsection (1) of this section.

(4) Where the period within which a series of transactions occurs exceeds two years, the transactions that may be treated as mentioned in subsection (1) of this section are any of those transactions that occur within a period of two years.

(5) Sections 65(2) to (4) and 77(1) and (4) to (6) of this Act apply for the purposes of this section to determine whether an enterprise is brought under the control of a person or group of persons and whether a transaction falls within subsection (2) of this section as they apply for the purposes of section 65 of this Act to determine whether enterprises are brought under common control.

(6) In determining for the purposes of this section the time at which any transaction occurs, no account shall be taken of any option or other conditional right until the option is exercised or the condition is satisfied.

67 Valuation of assets taken over

(1) The provisions of this section shall have effect for the purposes of section 64(1)(*b*) of this Act.

(2) Subject to subsection (4) of this section, the value of the assets taken over:

(*a*) shall be determined by taking the total value of the assets employed in, or appropriated to, the enterprises which cease to be distinct enterprises, except:
  (i) any enterprise which remains under the same ownership and control, or
  (ii) if none of the enterprises remains under the same ownership and control, the enterprise having the assets with the highest value, and

(*b*) shall be so determined by reference to the values at which, on the enterprises ceasing to be distinct enterprises or (if they have not then done so) on the making of the merger reference to the Commission, the assets stand in the books of the relevant business, less any relevant provisions for depreciation, renewals or diminution in value.

(3) For the purposes of subsection (2) of this section any assets of a body corporate which, on a change in the control of the body corporate or of any enterprise of it, are dealt with in the same way as assets appropriated to any such enterprise shall be treated as appropriated to that enterprise.

(4) Where in accordance with subsection (1) of section 66 or subsection (1) of section 66A of this Act events to which either of those subsections applies are treated as having occurred simultaneously, subsection (2) of this section shall apply with such adjustments as appears to the Secretary of State or to the Commission to be appropriate.

68 Supplementary provisions as to merger situations qualifying for investigation

(1) In relation to goods or services of any description which are the subject of different forms of supply:

(*a*) references in subsection (2) of section 64 of this Act to the supply of goods, or

(*b*) references in subsection (3) of that section to the supply of services,

shall be construed in whichever of the following ways appears to the Secretary of State or the Commission, as the case may be, to be appropriate in all the circumstances, that is to say, as references to any of those forms of supply taken separately, to all those forms of supply taken together, or to any of those forms of supply taken in groups.

(2) For the purposes of the preceding subsection the Secretary of State or the Commission may treat goods or services as being the subject of different forms of supply whenever the transactions in question differ as to their nature, their parties, their terms or their surrounding circumstances, and the difference is one which, in the opinion of the Secretary of State or of the Commission, as the case may be, ought for the purposes of that subsection to be treated as a material difference.

(3) For the purpose of determining whether the proportion of one-quarter

mentioned in subsection (2) or subsection (3) of section 64 of this Act is fulfilled with respect to goods or services of any description, the Secretary of State or the Commission, as the case may be, shall apply such criterion (whether it be value or cost or price or quantity or capacity or number of workers employed or some other criterion, of whatever nature) or such combination of criteria as may appear to the Secretary of State or the Commission to be most suitable in all the circumstances.

(4) The criteria for determining when goods or services can be treated, for the purposes of section 64 of this Act, as goods or services of a separate description shall be such as in any particular case the Secretary of State or, as the case may be, the Commission thinks most suitable in the circumstances of that case.

69 Different kinds of merger references

(1) Subject to the following provisions of this Part of this Act, on a merger reference the Commission shall investigate and report on the questions:

(*a*) whether a merger situation qualifying for investigation has been created, and
(*b*) if so, whether the creation of that situation operates, or may be expected to operate, against the public interest.

(2) A merger reference may be so framed as to require the Commission, in relation to the question whether a merger situation qualifying for investigation has been created, to exclude from consideration paragraph (*a*) of subsection (1) of section 64 of this Act, or to exclude from consideration paragraph (*b*) of that subsection, or to exclude one of those paragraphs if the Commission find the other satisfied.

(3) In relation to the question whether any such result as is mentioned in section 64(1)(*a*) of this Act has arisen, a merger reference may be so framed as to require the Commission to confine their investigation to the supply of goods or services in a specified part of the United Kingdom.

(4) A merger reference may require the Commission, if they find that a merger situation qualifying for investigation has been created, to limit their consideration thereafter to such elements in, or possible consequences of, the creation of that situation as may be specified in the reference, and to consider whether, in respect only of those elements or possible consequences, the situation operates, or may be expected to operate, against the public interest.

70 Time-limit for report on merger reference

(1) Every merger reference shall specify a period (not being longer than six months beginning with the date of the reference) within which a report on the reference is to be made; and a report of the Commission on a merger reference shall not have effect, and no action shall be taken in relation to it under this Act, unless the report is made before the end of that period or of such further period (if any) as may be allowed by the Secretary of State in accordance with the next following subsection.

(2) The Secretary of State shall not allow any further period for a report on a merger reference except on representations made by the Commission and on being satisfied that there are special reasons why the report cannot be made within the period specified in the reference; and the Secretary of State shall allow only one such further period on any one reference, and no such further period shall be longer than three months.

71 Variation of certain merger references

(1) Subject to the following provisions of this section, the Secretary of State may at any time vary a merger reference.

[. . .]

(3) Without prejudice to the powers of the Secretary of State under section 70 of this Act, a merger reference shall not be varied so as to specify a period within which a report on the reference is to be made which is different from the period specified in the reference in accordance with that section.

72 Report of Commission on merger reference

(1) In making their report on a merger reference, the Commission shall include in it definite conclusions on the questions comprised in the reference, together with:

(*a*) such an account of their reasons for those conclusions, and
(*b*) such a survey of the general position with respect to the subject-matter of the reference, and of the developments which have led to that position.

as is their opinion are expedient for facilitating a proper understanding of those questions and of their conclusions.

(2) Where on a merger reference the Commission find that a merger situation qualifying for investigation has been created and that the creation of that situation operates or may be expected to operate against the public interest (or, in a case falling within subsection (4) of section 69 of this Act, find that one or more elements in or consequences of that situation which were specified in the reference in accordance with that subsection so operate or may be expected so to operate) the Commission shall specify in their report the particular effects, adverse to the public interest, which in their opinion the creation of that situation (or, as the case may be, those elements in or consequences of it) have or may be expected to have; and the Commission:

(*a*) shall, as part of their investigations, consider what action (if any) should be taken for the purpose of remedying or preventing those adverse effects, and
(*b*) may, if they think fit, include in their report recommendations as to such action.

(3) In paragraph (*a*) of subsection (2) of this section the reference to action to be taken for the purpose mentioned in that paragraph is a reference to action to be taken for that purpose either:

(*a*) by one or more Ministers (including Ministers or departments of the Government of Northern Ireland) or other public authorities, or
(*b*) by one or more persons specified in the report as being persons carrying on, owning or controlling any of the enterprises which, in accordance with the conclusions of the Commission, have ceased to be distinct enterprises.

73 Order of Secretary of State on report on merger reference

(1) The provisions of this section shall have effect where a report of the Commission on a merger reference has been laid before Parliament in accordance with the provisions of Part VII of this Act, and the conclusions of the Commission set out in the report, as so laid:

(*a*) include conclusions to the effect that a merger situation qualifying for investigation has been created and that its creation, or particular elements in or consequences of it specified in the report, operate or may be expected to operate against the public interest, and
(*b*) specify particular effects, adverse to the public interest, which in the opinion of the Commission the creation of that situation, or (as the case may be) those elements in or consequences of it, have or may be expected to have.

(2) In the circumstances mentioned in the preceding subsection the Secretary of State may by order made by statutory instrument exercise such one or more of the powers specified in Parts I and II of Schedule 8 to this Act as he may consider it requisite to exercise for the purpose of remedying or preventing the adverse effects specified in the report as mentioned in the preceding subsection; and those powers may be so exercised to such extent and in such manner as the Secretary of State considers requisite for that purpose.

(3) In determining whether, or to what extent or in what manner, to exercise any of those powers, the Secretary of State shall take into account any recommendations included in the report of the Commission in pursuance of section 72(2)(*b*) of this Act and any advice given by the Director under section 88 of this Act.

74 Interim order in respect of merger reference

(1) Where a merger reference has been made to the Commission, then, with a view to preventing action to which this subsection applies, the Secretary of State, subject to subsection (3) of this section, may by order made by statutory instrument:

(*a*) prohibit or restrict the doing of things which in his opinion would constitute action to which this subsection applies, or
(*b*) impose on any person concerned obligations as to the carrying on of any activities or safeguarding of any assets, or
(*c*) provide for the carrying on of any activities or the safeguarding of any assets either by the appointment of a person to conduct or supervise the conduct of any activities (on such terms and with such powers as may be specified or described in the order) or in any other manner, or
(*d*) exercise any of the powers which, by virtue of paragraphs 12 and 12A of Schedule 8 to this Act, are exercisable by an order under section 73 of this Act.

(2) In relation to a merger reference the preceding subsection applies to any action which might prejudice the reference or impede the taking of any action under this Act which may be warranted by the Commission's report on the reference.

(3) No order shall be made under this section in respect of a merger reference after whichever of the following events first occurs, that is to say:

(*a*) the time (including any further period) allowed to the Commission for making a report on the reference expires without their having made such a report;
(*b*) the period of forty days beginning with the day on which a report of the Commission on the reference is laid before Parliament expires.

(4) An order under this section made in respect of a merger reference (if it has not previously ceased to have effect) shall cease to have effect on the occurrence of whichever of those events first occurs, but without prejudice to anything previously done under the order.

(5) Subsection (4) of this section shall have effect without prejudice:

(*a*) to the operation, in relation to any such order, of section 134(1) of this Act, or
(*b*) to the operation of any order made under section 73 of this Act which exercises the same or similar powers to those exercised by the order under this section.

75 Reference in anticipation of merger

(1) A merger reference may be made to the Commission by the Secretary of State where it appears to him that it is or may be the fact that arrangements are in progress or in contemplation which, if carried into effect, will result in the creation of a merger situation qualifying for investigation.

(2) Subject to the following provisions of this section, on a merger reference under this section the Commission shall proceed in relation to the prospective and (if events so require) the actual results of the arrangements proposed or made as, in accordance with the preceding provisions of this Part of this Act, they could proceed if the arrangements in question had actually been made, and the results in question had followed immediately before the date of the reference under this section.

(3) A merger reference under this section may require the Commission, if they find that a merger situation qualifying for investigation has been created, or will be created if the arrangements in question are carried into effect, to limit their consideration thereafter to such elements in, or possible consequences of, the creation of that situation as may be specified in the reference, and to consider whether, in respect only of those elements or possible consequences, the situation might be expected to operate against the public interest.

(4) In relation to a merger reference under this section, sections 66, 66A, 67, 69,

71, 72, 73 and 74 of this Act shall apply subject to the following modifications, that is to say:

(*a*) section 66 shall apply, where an event by which any enterprises cease as between themselves to be distinct enterprises will occur if the arrangements are carried into effect, as if the event had occurred immediately before the date of the reference;
(*aa*) section 66A shall apply, where a transaction falling within subsection (2) of that section will occur if the arrangements are carried into effect, as if the transaction had occurred immediately before the date of the reference;
(*b*) in section 67(4) the references to subsection (1) of section 66 and subsection (1) of section 66A shall be construed as references to those subsections as modified in accordance with paragraph (*a*) or (*aa*) of this subsection;
(*c*) in section 69, subsection (1) shall be construed as modified by subsection (2) of this section; in subsections (2) and (3) any reference to the question whether a merger situation qualifying for investigation has been created, or whether a result mentioned in section 64(1)(*a*) of this Act has arisen, shall be construed as including a reference to the question whether such a situation will be created or such a result will arise if the arrangements in question are carried into effect; and subsection (4) of that section shall not apply;
(*d*) in section 71, in section 72(2) and in section 74(1), the references to section 69(4) of this Act shall be construed as references to subsection (3) of this section; and
(*e*) in section 73(1), the reference to conclusions to the effect that a merger situation qualifying for investigation has been created shall be construed as including a reference to conclusions to the effect that such a situation will be created if the arrangements in question are carried into effect.

(4A) Where a merger reference is made under this section, it shall be unlawful, except with the consent of the Secretary of State under subsection (4C) of this section:

(*a*) for any person carrying on any enterprise to which the reference relates or having control of any such enterprise or for any subsidiary of his, or
(*b*) for any person associated with him or for any subsidiary of such a person,

directly or indirectly to acquire, at any time during the period mentioned in subsection (4B) of this section, an interest in shares in a company if any enterprise to which the reference relates is carried on by or under the control of that company.

(4B) The period referred to in subsection (4A) of this section is the period beginning with the announcement by the Secretary of State of the making of the merger reference concerned and ending:

(*a*) where the reference is laid aside at any time, at that time,
(*b*) where the time (including any further period) allowed to the Commission for making a report on the reference expires without their having made such a report, on the expiration of that time,
(*c*) where a report of the Commission on the reference not including such conclusions as are referred to in section 73(1)(*b*) of this Act is laid before Parliament, at the end of the day on which the report is so laid,
(*d*) where a report of the Commission on the reference including such conclusions is laid before Parliament, at the end of the period of forty days beginning with the day on which the report is so laid,

and where such a report is laid before each House on different days, it is to be treated for the purposes of this subsection as laid on the earlier day.

(4C) The consent of the Secretary of State:

(*a*) may be either general or special,
(*b*) may be revoked by the Secretary of State, and
(*c*) shall be published in such way as, in the

opinion of the Secretary of State, to give any person entitled to the benefit of it an adequate opportunity of getting to know of it, unless in the Secretary of State's opinion publication is not necessary for that purpose.

(4D) Section 93 of this Act applies to any contravention or apprehended contravention of subsection (4A) of this section as it applies to a contravention or apprehended contravention of an order to which section 90 of this Act applies.

(4E) Subsections (4F) to (4K) of this section apply for the interpretation of subsection (4A).

(4F) The circumstances in which a person acquires an interest in shares include those where:

(*a*) he enters into a contract to acquire the shares (whether or not for cash),
(*b*) not being the registered holder, he acquires a right to exercise, or to control the exercise of, any right conferred by the holding of the shares, or
(*c*) he acquires a right to call for delivery of the shares to himself or to his order or to acquire an interest in the shares or assumes an obligation to acquire such an interest.

but does not include those where he acquires an interest in pursuance of an obligation assumed before the announcement by the Secretary of State of the making of the merger reference concerned.

(4G) The circumstances in which a person acquires a right mentioned in subsection (4F) of this section:

(*a*) include those where he acquires a right or assumes an obligation the exercise or fulfilment of which would give him that right, but
(*b*) does not include those where he is appointed as proxy to vote at a specified meeting of a company or of any class of its members or at any adjournment of the meeting or he is appointed by a corporation to act as its representative at any meeting of the company or of any class of its members,

and references to rights and obligations in this subsection and subsection (4F) of this section include conditional rights and conditional obligations.

(4H) Any reference to a person carrying on or having control of any enterprise includes a group of persons carrying on or having control of an enterprise and any member of such a group.

(4J) Sections 65(2) to (4) and 77(1) and (4) to (6) of this Act apply to determine whether any person or group of persons has control of any enterprise and whether persons are associated as they apply for the purposes of section 65 of this Act to determine whether enterprises are brought under common control.

(4K) 'Subsidiary' has the meaning given by section 736 of the Companies Act 1985, but that section and section 736A of that Act also apply to determine whether a company is a subsidiary of an individual or of a group of persons as they apply to determine whether it is a subsidiary of a company and references to a subsidiary in subsections (8) and (9) of section 736A as so applied are to be read accordingly.

(4L) In this section: 'company' includes any body corporate, and 'share' means share in the capital of a company, and includes stock.

(4M) Nothing in subsection (4A) of this section makes anything done by a person outside the United Kingdom unlawful unless he is:

(*a*) a British citizen, a British Dependent Territories citizen, a British Overseas citizen or a British National (Overseas),
(*b*) a body corporate incorporated under the law of the United Kingdom or of a part of the United Kingdom, or
(*c*) a person carrying on business in the United Kingdom, either alone or in partnership with one or more other persons.

(5) If, in the course of their investigations on a merger reference under this section, it appears to the Commission that the proposal to make arrangements such as

are mentioned in the reference has been abandoned, the Commission:

(*a*) shall, if the Secretary of State consents, lay the reference aside, but
(*b*) shall in that case furnish to the Secretary of State such information as he may require as to the results until then of the investigations.

75A General rule where notice given by acquirer and no reference made within period for considering notice

(1) Notice may be given to the Director by a person authorised by regulations to do so of proposed arrangements which might result in the creation of a merger situation qualifying for investigation.

(2) The notice must be in the prescribed form and state that the existence of the proposal has been made public.

(3) If the period for considering the notice expires without any reference being made to the Commission with respect to the notified arrangements, no reference may be made under this Part of this Act to the Commission with respect to those arrangements or to the creation or possible creation of any merger situation qualifying for investigation which is created in consequence of carrying those arrangements into effect.

(4) Subsection (3) of this section is subject to sections 75B(5) and 75C of this Act.

(5) A notice under subsection (1) of this section is referred to in sections 75B to 75F of this Act as a 'merger notice'.

75B The role of the Director

(1) The Director shall, when the period for considering any merger notice begins, take such action as he considers appropriate to bring the existence of the proposal, the fact that the merger notice has been given and the date on which the period for considering the notice may expire to the attention of those who in his opinion would be affected if the arrangements were carried into effect.

(2) The period for considering a merger notice is the period of twenty days, determined in accordance with subsection (9) of this section, beginning with the first day after:

(*a*) the notice has been received by the Director, and
(*b*) any fee payable to the Director in respect of the notice has been paid.

(3) The Director may, and shall if required to do so by the Secretary of State, by notice to the person who gave the merger notice:

(*a*) extend the period mentioned in subsection (2) of this section by a further ten days, and
(*b*) extend that period as extended under paragraph (*a*) of this subsection by a further fifteen days.

(4) The Director may by notice to the person who gave the merger notice request him to provide the Director within such period as may be specified in the notice with such information as may be so specified.

(5) If the Director gives to the person who gave the merger notice (in this subsection referred to as 'the relevant person') a notice stating that the Secretary of State is seeking undertakings under section 75G of this Act, section 75A(3) of this Act does not prevent a reference being made to the Commission unless:

(*a*) after the Director has given that notice, the relevant person has given a notice to the Director stating that he does not intend to give such undertakings, and
(*b*) the period of ten days beginning with the first day after the notice under paragraph (*a*) of this subsection was received by the Director has expired.

(6) A notice by the Director under subsection (3), (4) or (5) of this section must either be given to the person who gave the merger notice before the period for considering the merger notice expires or be sent in a properly addressed and pre-paid letter posted to him at such time that, in the ordinary course of post, it would be delivered to him before that period expires.

(7) The Director may, at any time before the period for considering any merger notice expires, reject the notice if:

(*a*) he suspects that any information given in respect of the notified arrangements, whether in the merger notice or otherwise, by the person who gave the notice or any connected person is in any material respect false or misleading,
(*b*) he suspects that it is not proposed to carry the notified arrangements into effect, . . .
(*c*) any prescribed information is not given in the merger notice or any information requested by notice under subsection (4) of this section is not provided within the period specified in the notice or,
(*d*) it appears to him that the notified arrangements are, or if carried into effect would result in, a concentration with a Community dimension within the meaning of Council Regulation (EEC) No. 4064/89 of 21st December 1989 on the control of the concentrations between undertakings.

(8) If:

(*a*) under subsection (3)(*b*) of this section the period for considering a merger notice has been extended by a further fifteen days, but
(*b*) the Director has not made any recommendation to the Secretary of State under section 76(*b*) of this Act as to whether or not it would in the Director's opinion be expedient for the Secretary of State to make a reference to the Commission with respect to the notified arrangements, then, during the last five of those fifteen days, the power of the Secretary of State to make a reference to the Commission with respect to the notified arrangements is not affected by the absence of any such recommendation.

(9) In determining any period for the purposes of subsections (2), (3) and (5) of this section no account shall be taken of:

(*a*) Saturday, Sunday, Good Friday and Christmas Day, and
(*b*) any day which is a bank holiday in England and Wales.

75C Cases where power to refer unaffected

(1) Section 75A(3) of this Act does not prevent any reference being made to the Commission if:

(*a*) before the end of the period for considering the merger notice, it is rejected by the Director under section 75B(7) of this Act,
(*b*) before the end of that period, any of the enterprises to which the notified arrangements relate cease to be distinct from each other,
(*c*) any information (whether prescribed information or not) that:
   (i) is, or ought to be, known to the person who gave the merger notice or any connected person, and
   (ii) is material to the notified arrangements;

   is not disclosed to the Secretary of State or the Director by such time before the end of that period as may be specified in regulations,
(*d*) at any time after the merger notice is given but before the enterprises to which the notified arrangements relate cease to be distinct from each other, any of those enterprises ceases to be distinct from any enterprise other than an enterprise to which those arrangements relate,
(*e*) the six months beginning with the end of the period for considering the merger notice expires without the enterprises to which the notified arrangements relate ceasing to be distinct from each other,
(*f*) the merger notice is withdrawn, or
(*g*) any information given in respect of the notified arrangements, whether in the merger notice or otherwise, by the person who gave the notice or any connected person is in any material respect false or misleading.

(2) Where:

(*a*) two or more transactions which have occurred or, if any arrangements are carried into effect, will occur may be treated for the purposes of a merger reference as having occurred simultaneously on a particular date, and
(*b*) subsection (3) of section 75A of this Act does not prevent such a reference with respect to the last of those transactions,

that subsection does not prevent such a reference with respect to any of those transactions which actually occurred less than six months before:

(i) the date, or
(ii) the actual occurrence of another of those transactions with respect to which such a reference may be made (whether or not by virtue of this subsection).

(3) In determining for the purposes of subsection (2) of this section the time at which any transaction actually occurred, no account shall be taken of any option or other conditional right until the option is exercised or the condition is satisfied.

75D Regulations

(1) The Secretary of State may make regulations for the purposes of sections 75A to 75C of this Act.

(2) The regulations may, in particular:

(*a*) provide for section 75B(2) or (3) or section 75C(1)(*e*) of this Act to apply as if any reference to a period of days or months were a reference to a period specified in the regulations for the purposes of the provision in question,
(*b*) provide for the manner in which any merger notice is authorised or required to be given, rejected or withdrawn, and the time at which any merger notice is to be treated as received or rejected,
(*c*) provide for the manner in which any information requested by the Director or any other material information is authorised or required to be provided or disclosed, and the time at which such information is to be treated as provided or disclosed,
(*d*) provide for the manner in which any notice under section 75B of this Act is authorised or required to be given,
(*e*) provide for the time at which any notice under section 75B(5)(*a*) of this Act is to be treated as received,
(*f*) provide for the address which is to be treated for the purposes of section 75B(6) of this Act and of the regulations as a person's proper address,
(*g*) provide for the time at which any fee is to be treated as paid, and
(*h*) provide that a person is, or is not, to be treated, in such circumstances as may be specified in the regulations, as acting on behalf of a person authorised by regulations to give a merger notice or a person who has given such a notice.

(3) The regulations may make different provision for different cases.

(4) Regulations under this section shall be made by statutory instrument.

75E Interpretation of sections 75A to 75D

In this section and sections 75A to 75D of this Act: 'connected person', in relation to the person who gave a merger notice, means:

(*a*) any person who, for the purposes of section 77 of this Act, is associated with him, or
(*b*) any subsidiary of the person who gave the merger notice or of any person so associated with him,

'merger notice' is to be interpreted in accordance with section 75A(5) of this Act; 'notified arrangements' means the arrangements mentioned in the merger notice or arrangements not differing from them in any material respect, 'prescribed' means prescribed by the Director by notice having effect for the time being and published in the *London, Edinburgh* and *Belfast Gazettes*, 'regulations' means regulations under section 75D of this Act, and 'subsidiary' has the meaning given by section 75(4K) of this Act, and references to the enterprises to which the notified arrangements relate are references to those enterprises that would have ceased to be distinct from one another if the arrangements mentioned in the merger notice in question had been carried into effect at the time when the notice was given.

[. . .]

75G Acceptance of undertakings

(1) Where:

(*a*) the Secretary of State has power to make a merger reference to the Commission under section 64 or 75 of this Act,

(*b*) the Director has made a recommendation to the Secretary of State under section 76 of this Act that such a reference should be made, and

(*c*) the Director has (in making that recommendation or subsequently) given advice to the Secretary of State specifying particular effects adverse to the public interest which in his opinion the creation of the merger situation qualifying for investigation may have or might be expected to have,

the Secretary of State may, instead of making a merger reference to the Commission, accept from such of the parties concerned as he considers appropriate undertakings complying with subsections (2) and (3) of this section to take specified action which the Secretary of State considers appropriate to remedy or prevent the effects adverse to the public interest specified in the advice.

(2) The undertakings must provide for one or more of the following:

(*a*) the division of a business by the sale of any part of the undertaking or assets or otherwise (for which purpose all the activities carried on by way of business by any one person or by any two or more interconnected bodies corporate may be treated as a single business),

(*b*) the division of a group of interconnected bodies corporate, and

(*c*) the separation, by the sale of any part of the undertaking or assets concerned or other means, of enterprises which are under common control otherwise than by reason of their being enterprises of interconnected bodies corporate.

(3) The undertakings may also contain provision:

(*a*) preventing or restricting the doing of things which might prevent or impede the division or separation,

(*b*) as to the carrying on of any activities or the safeguarding of any assets until the division or separation is affected,

(*c*) for any matters necessary to effect or take account of the division or separation, and

(*d*) for enabling the Secretary of State to ascertain whether the undertakings are being fulfilled.

(4) If the Secretary of State has accepted one or more undertakings under this section, no reference may be made to the Commission with respect to the creation or possible creation of the merger situation qualifying for investigation by reference to which the undertakings were accepted, except in a case falling within subsection (5) of this section.

(5) Subsection (4) of this section does not prevent a reference being made to the Commission if material facts about the arrangements or transactions, or proposed arrangements or transactions, in consequence of which the enterprises concerned ceased or may cease to be distinct enterprises were not:

(*a*) notified to the Secretary of State or the Director, or

(*b*) made public,

before the undertakings were accepted.

(6) In subsection (5) of this section ‘made public’ has the same meaning as in section 64 of this Act.

75H Publication of undertakings

(1) The Secretary of State shall arrange for:

(*a*) any undertakings accepted by him under section 75G of this Act,

(*b*) the advice given by the Director for the purposes of subsection (1)(*c*) of that section in any case where such an undertaking has been accepted, and
(*c*) any variation or release of such an undertaking, to be published in such manner as he may consider appropriate.

(2) In giving advice for the purposes of section 75G(1)(*c*) of this Act the Director shall have regard to the need for excluding, so far as practicable, any matter to which subsection (4) of this section applies.

(3) The Secretary of State shall exclude from any such advice as published under this section:

(*a*) any matter to which subsection (4) of this section applies and in relation to which he is satisfied that its publication in the advice would not be in the public interest, and
(*b*) any other matter in relation to which he is satisfied that its publication in the advice would be against the public interest.

(4) This subsection applies to:

(*a*) any matter which relates to the private affairs of an individual, where publication of that matter would or might, in the opinion of the Director or the Secretary of State, as the case may be, seriously and prejudicially affect the interests of that individual, and
(*b*) any matter which relates specifically to the affairs of a particular body of persons, whether corporate or unincorporate, where publication of that matter would or might, in the opinion of the Director or the Secretary of State, as the case may be, seriously and prejudicially affect the interests of that body, unless in his opinion the inclusion of that matter relating specifically to that body is necessary for the purposes of the advice.

(5) For the purposes of the law relating to defamation, absolute privilege shall attach to any advice given by the Director for the purposes of section 75G(1)(*c*) of this Act.

75J Review of undertakings

When an undertaking has been accepted by the Secretary of State under section 75G of this Act, it shall be the duty of the Director:

(*a*) to keep under review the carrying out of that undertaking, and from time to time consider whether, by reason of any change of circumstances, the undertaking is no longer appropriate and either:
   (i) one or more of the parties to it can be released from it, or
   (ii) it needs to be varied or to be superseded by a new undertaking, and
(*b*) if it appears to him that the undertaking has not been or is not being fulfilled, that any person can be so released or that the undertaking needs to be varied or superseded, to give such advice to the Secretary of State as he may think proper in the circumstances.

75K Order of Secretary of State where undertaking not fulfilled

(1) The provisions of this section shall have effect where it appears to the Secretary of State that an undertaking accepted by him under section 75G of this Act has not been, is not being or will not be fulfilled.

(2) The Secretary of State may by order made by statutory instrument exercise such one or more of the powers specified in paragraphs 9A and 12 to 12C and Part II of Schedule 8 to this Act as he may consider it requisite to exercise for the purpose of remedying or preventing the adverse effects specified in the advice given by the Director for the purposes of section 75G(1)(*c*) of this Act; and those powers may be so exercised to such extent and in such manner as the Secretary of State considers requisite for that purpose.

(3) In determining whether, or to what extent or in what manner, to exercise any of those powers, the Secretary of State shall take into account any advice given by the Director under section 75J(*b*) of this Act.

(4) The provision contained in an order

under this section may be different from that contained in the undertaking.

(5) On the making of an order under this section, the undertaking and any other undertaking accepted under section 75G of this Act by reference to the same merger situation qualifying for investigation are released by virtue of this section.

76 Functions of Director in relation to merger situations

(1) it shall be the duty of the Director:

(*a*) to take all such steps as are reasonably practicable for keeping himself informed about actual or prospective arrangements or transactions which may constitute or result in the creation of merger situations qualifying for investigation, and

(*b*) to make recommendations to the Secretary of State as to any action under this Part of this Act which in the opinion of the Director it would be expedient for the Secretary of State to take in relation to any such arrangements or transactions.

(2) In exercising his duty under this section the Director shall take into consideration any representations made to him by persons appearing to him to have a substantial interest in any such arrangements or transactions or by bodies appearing to him to represent substantial numbers of persons who have such an interest.

For a definition of 'a substantial part of the United Kingdom', see the House of Lords judgment in ***R. v. MMC ex p. South Yorkshire Transport*** following. For examples of the ability materially to influence the policy of a body corporate, see the MMC reports on *Elders IXL/Scottish & Newcastle* Cm. 654; *British Airways/ Sabena* Cm. 1155; and *Stora/Swedish Match/Gillette* Cm. 1473.

The merger provisions of the Fair Trading Act do not contain anything equivalent to the 'local monopoly' facility of section 9. A merger situation will qualify for investigation by satisfying the asset value test of section 64(1)(*b*), or by creating or enhancing a scale monopoly situation in the United Kingdom or 'in a substantial part of the United Kingdom' (section 64(3)). The meaning of this phrase was eventually clarified by the House of Lords in the **South Yorkshire Transport** case. The Lords effectively extended the legislation to permit the regulation of 'local mergers', a move which may have important consequences for the nature of merger control in the United Kingdom.

20.2 R. v. *Monopolies and Mergers Commission and Another ex parte South Yorkshire Transport Limited and Others* House of Lords. (*The Times*, 17 December 1992.)

Lord Mustill:

My Lords,

On 22 March 1990 the Secretary of State for Trade and Industry referred to the Monopolies and Mergers Commission for investigation and report the acquisition of the present respondents, South Yorkshire Transport Company Ltd., of certain companies operating local bus services in South Yorkshire and in parts of Derbyshire and Nottinghamshire. Upon the reference the Commission had two distinct tasks. First, to decide whether the 'merger situation', as it is known, was one which satisfied the criteria for investigation established by section 64(3) of the Fair Trading Act 1973. If it did not the Commission had no jurisdiction to proceed. The Commission decided that the criteria were satisfied, and went on to investigate the merger. On 1 August 1990 the Commission published its report, to the effect that the merger might be expected to operate against the public interest, and that the most effective means to restore competition would be to require the respondents to divest themselves of the assets and business acquired. On the same day the Secretary of State announced that he had accepted the conclusions and recommendation of the report.

The respondents disagreed with the Commission on both issues, but recognised that the conclusions and recommendations on the question of public interest were not open to effective challenge in the courts. They did however contest by judicial review the finding of the Commission, crucial to its jurisdiction, that the geographical area by reference to which the existence of a merger situation had to be ascertained ('the reference area') was a 'substantial part' of the United Kingdom, within the meaning of section 64(3) of the Act of 1973. The application for judicial review was heard by Otton J, who in a valuable and comprehensive judgment held that the respondents' challenge was well-founded, that the Commission had acted without jurisdiction, and that accordingly the conclusions and recommendations in the report, and the decision of the Secretary of State to accept them, were unlawful and of no effect. The Commission appealed to the Court of Appeal [1992] 1 WLR 291 which by a majority (Lord Donaldson of Lymington MR and Butler-Sloss LJ, Nourse LJ dissenting) dismissed the appeal. The Commission appeals to your Lordships' House.

[. . .]

[T]he reference area [lies] [. . .] roughly between the Leeds/Bradford conurbation to the North, Lincolnshire to the East, Derby/Nottingham to the South and Greater Manchester to the North-West. More exactly, the spine of the area, some 45 miles long at its greatest extent, runs from just north of Derby through Matlock, and then continues through Chesterfield, Sheffield and Barnsley to a point a few miles south of the line joining Huddersfield, Wakefield and Pontefract. To the west the area encompasses the Derbyshire Dales and the Peak District. On the eastern side of the spine there are found at the northern end the industrial areas of Doncaster and Rotherham. Further south a space of more open country extends to within about ten miles of Lincoln. The total surface area is rather more than 1500 square miles. About 1.8 million people live there. These figures represent 1.65 per cent and 3.2 per cent of the totals for the United Kingdom as a whole.

[. . .]

The following are the material paragraphs of Chapter 2 [of the report now under review] ((1990) Cmnd. 1166)].

2.5 We further consider that the phrase additionally involves both a quantitative and a qualitative assessment. In considering what quantitative and qualitative elements should be taken into account for this purpose, we had regard to the size of the reference area, its population; its social political, economic, financial and geographic significance; and whether it had any particular characteristics that might render the area special or significant. These featured too in the previous reports and no additional relevant elements have occurred to us.

2.6 As to the quantitative elements relating to the reference area, it is roughly 1.65 per cent of the total area, and has a population of some 1.8 million, or 3.2 per cent of the total population of the United Kingdom.

2.7 In considering the elements that give the reference area its particular characteristics, we noted that the area includes Sheffield, the third largest metropolitan district in England on the basis of population, one of the great cities of the United Kingdom, and the towns of Barnsley, Doncaster, Rotherham and Chesterfield. As well as traditional industries based on mining and steel, the area also has a range of other manufacturing and service activities, significant academic and sports facilities, and parts of the Peak District favoured for recreation.

2.8 Having taken into consideration the

various factors, general and specific, mentioned previously and having done so in the context of the United Kingdom as a whole, we conclude that the area may be properly and correctly described as 'a substantial part of the United Kingdom', for the purpose of section 64(3) of the Act.

In the Divisional Court Otton J reached a different conclusion. After an extensive review of the authorities, in which he clearly demonstrated that the word 'substantial' is (as he aptly put it) like a chameleon, taking its colour from its environment, he concluded that 'substantial' in this context was not to be equated with something greater than merely nominal; and, that the right approach was to draw a contrast between the United Kingdom as a whole and the reference area, as regards the surface extent, the population and the relevant economic activity, here measured in terms of kilometres travelled by passenger buses. Inspecting the reasons given by the Commission for assuming jurisdiction the learned judge found that it had misdirected itself by adopting the interpretation of substantial as meaning 'more than *de minimis*' which he had himself rejected. He went on to hold that if the Commission had applied the approach which he considered right the answer would inevitably have been that the reference area was not a substantial part of the United Kingdom.

In the Court of Appeal the majority of the court adopted a standpoint which, although rather differently expressed, was broadly the same as that of Otton J. By contrast, Nourse LJ held that the amount necessary to satisfy the test of substantiality depends on the purpose of the Act in which the word is found; it is a variable, whose meaning expands or contrasts so far as to give effect to that purpose. His Lordship [1992] 1 WLR, 291, 301G saw no *a priori* reason for interpreting 'a substantial part' in section 64(3) as meaning a big or large part of the United Kingdom; it means 'a considerable part, that is, a part of such dimensions as to make it worthy of consideration for the purpose of the Act'. The percentages might not for other purposes be regarded as being substantial but in his opinion it was worthy of consideration for the purposes of the Act of 1973.

Arriving now at the present appeal I believe that the interpretation of section 64(3) must proceed by two stages. First, a general appreciation of what 'substantial' means in its present context. Second, a consideration of the elements to be taken into account when deciding whether the requirements of the word, so understood, are satisfied in the individual case.

Approaching the first stage as a matter of common language no recourse need be made to dictionaries to establish that 'substantial' accommodates a wide range of meanings. At one extreme there is 'not trifling'. At the other, there is 'nearly complete', as where someone says that he is in substantial agreement with what has just been said. In between, there exist many shades of meaning, drawing colour from their context.

That the protean nature of the word has been reflected in the decided cases is, I believe, made quite clear by the judgment of Otton J, in which the authorities are so thoroughly discussed as to make it unnecessary to go through them again. It is sufficient to say that although I do not accept that 'substantial' can never mean 'more than *de minimis*' [. . .]. I am satisfied that in section 64(3) the word does indeed lie further up the spectrum than that. To say how far up is another matter. The courts have repeatedly warned against the dangers of taking an inherently imprecise word, and by redefining it thrusting on it a spurious degree of precision. I will try to avoid such an error. Nevertheless I am glad to adopt, as a means of giving a general indication of where the meaning of the word in section 64(3) lies within the range of possible meanings, the expression of Nourse LJ [1992] 1 WLR 291, 301G 'worthy of consideration for the purpose of the Act' [. . .].

There remains however the question whether, even if the Commission had placed the test in broadly the right part of the spectrum of possible meanings it nevertheless failed to apply the test correctly. Here, the contest is between three methods of approach: (1) An arithmetical proportion should be struck between the reference area of the United Kingdom as a whole, as regards surface area, population and volume of the economic activity with which the reference is concerned. If the proportion(s) are too low, the area does not qualify. (2) An assessment in absolute terms of the size and importance of the area, independent of proportions. (3) A mixture of the two kinds of criterion.

The respondents contend for the first, proportionate, approach. At one stage of the passage of this case through the courts they placed the weight of their arguments on the collocation of 'a substantial part' with 'of the United Kingdom'. On this view, one should look at the United Kingdom as a geographical feature of the map, and see how much of the map is occupied by the reference area. At other stages more significance was attached to the proportion which the economic activity in question (here, the operation of local bus services) in the reference area bore to the United Kingdom as a whole. Throughout, however, the respondents relied on the fact that whatever comparison one chose to make the proportion was too low.

My Lords, although I agree that the relationship of the part to the whole is not to be ignored, I am unable to accept that proportionality is the beginning and end of the matter. As regards geographical extent the reference to a substantial part of the United Kingdom is enabling, not restrictive. Its purpose is simply to entitle the Secretary of State to refer to the Commission mergers whose effect is not nationwide. Like the asset-value criterion of section 64(1)(*b*), the epithet 'substantial' is there to ensure that the expensive, laborious and time-consuming mechanism of a merger reference is not set in motion if the effort is not worthwhile. The reference area is thus enabled to be something less than the whole. But I cannot see why its relationship to the whole is the only measure of the Commission's jurisdiction. Nor does the contrast with section 9, which omits the word 'substantial', yield any other result. As Nourse LJ pointed out the introduction of this new jurisdiction for monopoly references in 1973 cannot have been intended to alter the meaning of an expression which had been in use since 1948. It may be that sections 9 and 64 involve different tests. The question is not for decision here. What does seem to me clear is that there is no cut-off point fixed by reference to geography and arithmetic alone.

I have reached the same conclusion as regards the argument which came to the forefront of the respondents' case in this House, namely that the decisive factor consists of a comparison between the number of bus-miles run by the services under investigation and those in the country as a whole. I find this interpretation very hard to square with the words '[. . .] part of the United Kingdom' which are surely intended to relate to the area itself, and not (at any rate primarily) to the market share of the area. Furthermore, the suggested criterion would produce odd practical results, for a sparsely populated area of great extent would automatically fail the test if poorly served by buses. Whereas, by contrast, a tiny area such as Inner London which would fail the respondents' test of geographical proportionality would easily qualify if bus-mileage were the criterion. Moreover, as was pointed out in argument, since local bus-services are by their nature both limited in their field of operation and in total mileage run, it is hard to see how on an uncritical application of an arithmetical test they could ever qualify for investigation under the Act. It seems to me that where the task is to interpret an enabling provision, designed to confer on the Commission the power to investigate mergers believed to be against the public interest the court should lean against the interpretation which would give the Commission jurisdiction over references of the present kind in only a small minority of cases. This is the more so in the particular context of local bus services, since the provision of adequate services is a matter of importance to the public, as witness the need felt by Parliament to make special provision for them in the Transport Act 1985.

Accordingly, although I readily accept that the Commission can, and indeed should, take into account the relative proportions of the area by comparison with the United Kingdom as a whole, as regards surface area, population, economic activities and (it may be) in some cases other factors as well, when reaching a conclusion on jurisdiction, neither each of them on its own, nor all of them together, can lead directly to the answer. The parties could reasonably expect that since the test for which the respondents contend has been rejected another would be proposed in its place. I am reluctant to go far in this direction because it would substitute non-statutory words for the words of the Act which the Commission is obliged to apply, and partly because it is impossible to frame a definition which would not unduly fetter the judgment of the Commission in some future situation not now foreseen. Nevertheless I believe that, subject to one qualification, it will be helpful to endorse the formulation of Nourse LJ already mentioned, as a general guide: namely that the reference area must be of such dimensions as to make it worthy of consideration for the purposes of the Act. The qualification is that the word 'dimensions' might be thought to limit the enquiry to matters of geography. Accordingly I would prefer to state that the part must be 'of such size, character and importance as to make it worth consideration for the purposes of the Act'. To this question an enquiry into proportionality will often be material but it will not lead directly to a conclusion [. . .].

Merger control was introduced into EEC law considerably more recently than in UK or USA law. The Council's **Merger Regulation** introduced a requirement to pre-notify 'concentrations having a Community dimension' to the EC Commission. Such transactions are then assessed by the Commission for their compatibility with the Treaty of Rome. Those provisions detailing the processes of merger control are extracted in Section 21.2. The following provisions provide a definition of those transactions which amount to 'concentrations having a Community dimension'. In keeping with other systems of merger control, the **Regulation** covers transactions which give rise to either ownership or control.

The nature of joint ventures provides a particular difficulty of definition. Cooperative joint ventures are to be regarded, not as concentrations, but as analogous to a restrictive agreement: they continue to be regulated by Article 85. Concentrative joint ventures are, however, regulated by the **Regulation**. The distinction between these two transactions is both difficult and essential. The Commission's guidelines on applying the distinction are contained in the **Notice** extracted in Section 20.4. The extract from the article by **Sibree** discusses the consequences of the distinction.

FURTHER READING

See the following works on the **EEC Merger Regulation.**

Bourgeois, J. and Langeheine, B. (1990/91), 'Jurisdictional issues: the EEC Merger Control Regulation, Member State laws, and Articles 85 and 86', 14 *Fordham International Law Journal*, 387.

Hawk, B. (1990), 'The EEC merger regulation: the first step toward one-stop merger control', 59 *Antitrust Law Journal*, 195.
Jones, C. (1990/91), 'The scope of application of the Merger Control Regulation', 14 *Fordham International Law Journal*, 359.

20.3 Council Regulation (EEC) No. 4064/89 of 21 December 1989 on the control of concentrations between undertakings OJ 1989 No. L 395/1

THE COUNCIL OF THE EUROPEAN COMMUNITIES

[. . .]

(1) Whereas, for the achievement of the aims of the Treaty establishing the European Economic Community, Article 3(*f*) gives the Community the objective of instituting 'a system ensuring that competition in the common market is not distorted';

(2) Whereas this system is essential for the achievement of the internal market by 1992 and its further development;

(3) Whereas the dismantling of internal frontiers is resulting and will continue to result in major corporate reorganizations in the Community, particularly in the form of concentrations;

(4) Whereas such a development must be welcomed as being in line with the requirements of dynamic competition and capable of increasing the competitiveness of European industry, improving the conditions of growth and raising the standard of living in the Community;

(5) Whereas, however, it must be ensured that the process of reorganization does not result in lasting damage to competition; whereas Community law must therefore include provisions governing those concentrations which may significantly impede effective competition in the common market or in a substantial part of it;

(6) Whereas Articles 85 and 86, while applicable, according to the case-law of the Court of Justice, to certain concentrations, are not, however, sufficient to control all operations which may prove to be incompatible with the system of undistorted competition envisaged in the Treaty;

(7) Whereas a new legal instrument should therefore be created in the form of a Regulation to permit effective control of all concentrations from the point of view of their effect on the structure of competition in the Community and to be the only instrument applicable to such concentrations;

(8) Whereas this Regulation should therefore be based not only on Article 87 but, principally, on Article 235 of the Treaty, under which the Community may give itself the additional powers of action necessary for the attainment of its objectives, including with regard to concentrations on the markets for agricultural products listed in Annex (ii) to the Treaty;

(9) Whereas the provisions to be adopted in this Regulation should apply to significant structural changes the impact of which on the market goes beyond the national borders of any one member-State;

(10) Whereas the scope of application of this Regulation should therefore be defined according to the geographical area of activity of the undertakings concerned and be limited by quantitative thresholds in order to cover those concentrations which have a Community dimension; whereas, at the end of an initial phase of the application of this Regulation, these thresholds should be reviewed in the light of the experience gained;

(11) Whereas a concentration with a Community dimension exists where the combined aggregate turnover of the under-

takings concerned exceeds given levels worldwide and within the Community and where at least two of the undertakings concerned have their sole or main fields of activities in different member-States or where, although the undertakings in question act mainly in one and the same member-State, at least one of them has substantial operations in at least one other member-State; whereas that is also the case where the concentrations are effected by undertakings which do not have their principal fields of activities in the Community but which have substantial operations there;

(12) Whereas the arrangements to be introduced for the control of concentrations should, without prejudice to Article 90(2) of the Treaty, respect the principle of non-discrimination between the public and the private sectors; whereas, in the public sector, calculation of the turnover of an undertaking concerned in a concentration needs, therefore, to take account of undertakings making up an economic unit with an independent power of decision, irrespective of the way in which their capital is held or of the rules of administrative supervision applicable to them;

(13) Whereas it is necessary to establish whether concentrations with a Community dimension are compatible or not with the common market from the point of view of the need to maintain and develop effective competition in the common market; whereas, in so doing, the Commission must place its appraisal within the general framework of the achievement of the fundamental objectives referred to in Article 2 of the Treaty, including that of strengthening the Community's economic and social cohesion, referred to in Article 130(*a*);

(14) Whereas this Regulation should establish the principle that a concentration with a Community dimension which creates or strengthens a position as a result of which effective competition in the common market or in a substantial part of it is significantly impeded is to be declared incompatible with the common market;

(15) Whereas concentrations which, by reason of the limited market share of the undertakings concerned, are not liable to impede effective competition may be presumed to be compatible with the common market; whereas, without prejudice to Articles 85 and 86 of the Treaty, an indication to this effect exists, in particular, where the market share of the undertakings concerned does not exceed 25% either in the common market or in a substantial part of it;

(16) Whereas the Commission should have the task of taking all the decisions necessary to establish whether or not concentrations with a Community dimension are compatible with the common market, as well as decisions designed to restore effective competition;

(17) Whereas to ensure effective control undertakings should be obliged to give prior notification of concentrations with a Community dimension and provision should be made for the suspension of concentrations for a limited period, and for the possibility of extending or waiving a suspension where necessary; whereas in the interests of legal certainty the validity of transactions must nevertheless be protected as much as necessary;

(18) Whereas a period within which the Commission must initiate proceedings in respect of a notified concentration and periods within which it must give a final decision on the compatibility or incompatibility with the common market of a notified concentration should be laid down;

(19) Whereas the undertakings concerned must be afforded the right to be heard by the Commission when proceedings have been initiated; whereas the members of the management and supervisory bodies and the recognized representatives of the employees of the undertakings concerned, and third parties showing a legitimate interest, must also be given the opportunity to be heard;

(20) Whereas the Commission should act in close and constant liaison with the competent authorities of the member-States from which it obtains comments and information;

(21) Whereas, for the purposes of this Regulation, and in accordance with the case-law of the Court of Justice, the Commission must be afforded the assistance of

the member-States and must also be empowered to require information to be given and to carry out the necessary investigations in order to appraise concentrations;

(22) Whereas compliance with this Regulation must be enforceable by means of fines and periodic penalty payments; whereas the Court of Justice should be given unlimited jurisdiction in that regard pursuant to Article 172 of the Treaty;

(23) Whereas it is appropriate to define the concept of concentration in such a manner as to cover only operations bringing about a lasting change in the structure of the undertakings concerned; whereas it is therefore necessary to exclude from the scope of this Regulation those operations which have as their object or effect the coordination of the competitive behaviour of undertakings which remain independent, since such operations fall to be examined under the appropriate provisions of the Regulations implementing Articles 85 and 86 of the Treaty; whereas it is appropriate to make this distinction specifically in the case of the creation of joint ventures;

(24) Whereas there is no coordination of competitive behaviour within the meaning of this Regulation where two or more undertakings agree to acquire jointly control of one or more other undertakings with the object and effect of sharing amongst themselves such undertakings or their assets;

(25) Whereas this Regulation should still apply where the undertakings concerned accept restrictions directly related and necessary to the implementation of the concentration;

(26) Whereas the Commission should be given exclusive competence to apply this Regulation, subject to review by the Court of Justice;

(27) Whereas the member-States may not apply their national legislation on competition to concentrations with a Community dimension, unless this Regulation makes provision therefor; whereas the relevant powers of national authorities should be limited to cases where, failing intervention by the Commission, effective competition is likely to be significantly impeded within the territory of a member-State and where the competition interests of that member-State cannot be sufficiently protected otherwise by this Regulation; whereas the member-States concerned must act promptly in such cases; whereas this Regulation cannot, because of the diversity of national law, fix a single deadline for the adoption of remedies;

(28) Whereas, furthermore, the exclusive application of this Regulation to concentrations with a Community dimension is without prejudice to Article 223 of the Treaty, and does not prevent the member-States from taking appropriate measures to protect legitimate interests other than those pursued by this Regulation, provided that such measures are compatible with the general principles and other provisions of Community law;

(29) Whereas concentrations not covered by this Regulation come, in principle, within the jurisdiction of the member-States; whereas, however, the Commission should have the power to act, at the request of a member-State concerned, in cases where effective competition could be significantly impeded within that member-State's territory;

(30) Whereas the conditions in which concentrations involving Community undertakings are carried out in non-member countries should be observed, and provision should be made for the possibility of the council giving the Commission an appropriate mandate for negotiation with a view to obtaining non-discriminatory treatment for Community undertakings;

(31) Whereas this Regulation in no way detracts from the collective rights of the employees as recognized in the undertakings concerned,

HAS ADOPTED THIS REGULATION:

Article 1 Scope

1. Without prejudice to Article 22 this Regulation shall apply to all concentrations with a Community dimension as defined in paragraph 2.

2. For the purposes of this Regulation, a

concentration has a Community dimension where:

(*a*) the combined aggregate worldwide turnover of all the undertakings concerned is more than ECU 5,000 million; and
(*b*) the aggregate Community-wide turnover of each of at least two of the undertakings concerned is more than ECU 250 million,

unless each of the undertakings concerned achieves more than two-thirds of its aggregate Community-wide turnover within one and the same member-State.

3. The thresholds laid down in paragraph 2 will be reviewed before the end of the fourth year following that of the adoption of this Regulation by the Council acting by a qualified majority on a proposal from the Commission.

[. . .]

Article 3 Definition of Concentration

1. A concentration shall be deemed to arise where:

(*a*) two or more previously independent undertakings merge, or
(*b*) one or more persons already controlling at least one undertaking, or one or more undertakings acquire, whether by purchase of securities or assets, by contract or by any other means, direct or indirect control of the whole or part of one or more other undertakings.

2. An operation, including the creation of a joint venture, which has as its object or effect the coordination of the competitive behaviour of undertakings which remain independent shall not constitute a concentration within the meaning of paragraph 1 (*b*). The creation of a joint venture performing on a lasting basis all the functions of an autonomous economic entity, which does not give rise to coordination of the competitive behaviour of the parties amongst themselves or between them and the joint venture, shall constitute a concentration within the meaning of paragraph 1(*b*).

3. For the purposes of this Regulation, control shall be constituted by rights, contracts or any other means which, either separately or in combination and having regard to the considerations of fact or law involved, confer the possibility of exercising decisive influence on an undertaking, in particular by:

(*a*) ownership or the right to use all or part of the assets of an undertaking;
(*b*) rights or contracts which confer decisive influence on the composition, voting or decisions of the organs of an undertaking.

4. Control is acquired by persons or undertakings which:

(*a*) are holders of the rights or entitled to rights under the contracts concerned; or
(*b*) while not being holders of such rights or entitled to rights under such contracts, have the power to exercise the rights deriving therefrom.

5. A concentration shall not be deemed to arise where:

(*a*) credit institutions or other financial institutions or insurance companies, the normal activities of which include transactions and dealing in securities for their own account or for the account of others, hold on a temporary basis securities which they have acquired in an undertaking with a view to reselling them, provided that they do not exercise voting rights in respect of those securities with a view to determining the competitive behaviour of that undertaking or provided that they exercise such voting rights only with a view to preparing the disposal of all or part of that undertaking or of its assets or the disposal of those securities and that any such disposal takes place within one year of the date of the acquisition; that period may be extended by the Commission on request where such institutions or companies can show that the disposal was not reasonably possible within the period set;
(*b*) control is acquired by an office-holder according to the law of a member-State relating to liquidation, winding up, in-

solvency, cessation of payments, compositions or analogous proceedings;

(*c*) the operations referred to in paragraph 1(*b*) are carried out by the financial holding companies referred to in Article 5(3) of the Fourth Council Directive 78/660/EEC of 25 July 1978 on the annual accounts of certain types of companies, as last amended by Directive 84/569/EEC, provided however that the voting rights in respect of the holding are exercised, in particular in relation to the appointment of members of the management and supervisory bodies of the undertakings in which they have holdings, only to maintain the full value of those investments and not to determine directly or indirectly the competitive conduct of those undertakings [. . .].

[. . .]

Article 5 Calculation of Turnover

1. Aggregate turnover within the meaning of Article 1(2) shall comprise the amounts derived by the undertakings concerned in the preceding financial year from the sale of products and the provision of services falling within the undertakings' ordinary activities after deduction of sales rebates and of value added tax and other taxes directly related to turnover. The aggregate turnover of an undertaking concerned shall not include the sale of products or the provision of services between any of the undertakings referred to in paragraph 4. Turnover, in the Community or in a member-State, shall comprise products sold and services provided to undertakings or consumers, in the Community or in that member-State as the case may be.

2. By way of derogation from paragraph 1, where the concentration consists in the acquisition of parts, whether or not constituted as legal entities, of one or more undertakings, only the turnover relating to the parts which are the subject of the transaction shall be taken into account with regard to the seller or sellers. However, two or more transactions within the meaning of the first subparagraph which take place within a two-year period between the same persons or undertakings shall be treated as one and the same concentration arising on the date of the last transaction.

3. In place of turnover the following shall be used:

(*a*) for credit institutions and other financial institutions, as regards Article 1(2)(*a*), one-tenth of their total assets.

As regards Article 1(2)(*b*) and the final part of Article 1(2), total Community-wide turnover shall be replaced by one-tenth of total assets multiplied by the ratio between loans and advances to credit institutions and customers in transactions with Community residents and the total sum of those loans and advances. As regards the final part of Article 1(2), total turnover within one member-State shall be replaced by one-tenth of total assets multiplied by the ratio between loans and advances to credit institutions and customers in transactions with residents of that member-State and the total sum of those loans and advances;

(*b*) for insurance undertakings, the value of gross premiums written which shall comprise all amounts received and receivable in respect of insurance contracts issued by or on behalf of the insurance undertakings, including also outgoing reinsurance premiums, and after deduction of taxes and parafiscal contributions or levies charged by reference to the amounts of individual premiums or the total volume of premiums; as regards Article 1(2)(*b*) and the final part of Article 1(2), gross premiums received from Community residents and from residents of one Member-State respectively shall be taken into account.

4. Without prejudice to paragraph 2, the aggregate turnover of an undertaking concerned within the meaning of Article 1(2) shall be calculated by adding together the respective turnovers of the following:

(*a*) the undertaking concerned;

(*b*) those undertakings in which the under-

taking concerned, directly or indirectly:
- owns more than half the capital or business assets, or
- has the power to exercise more than half the voting rights, or
- has the power to appoint more than half the members of the supervisory board, the administrative board or bodies legally representing the undertakings, or
- has the right to manage the undertakings' affairs;

(*c*) those undertakings which have in the undertaking concerned the rights or powers listed in (*b*);

(*d*) those undertakings in which an undertaking as referred to in (*c*) has the rights or powers listed in (*b*);

(*e*) those undertakings in which two or more undertakings as referred to in (*a*) to (*d*) jointly have the rights or powers listed in (*b*).

5. Where undertakings concerned by the concentration jointly have the rights or powers listed in paragraph 4(*b*), in calculating the aggregate turnover of the undertakings concerned for the purposes of Article 1(2):

(*a*) no account shall be taken of the turnover resulting from the sale of products or the provision of services between the joint undertaking and each of the undertakings concerned or any other undertaking connected with any one of them, as set out in paragraph 4(*b*) to (*e*);

(*b*) account shall be taken of the turnover resulting from the sale of products and the provision of services between the joint undertaking and any third undertakings. This turnover shall be apportioned equally amongst the undertakings concerned.

20.4 Commission of the European Communities, *Commission notice regarding the concentrative and cooperative operations under Council Regulation (EEC) No. 4064/89 of 21 December 1989 on the control of concentrations between undertakings OJ 1990 No. C203/10*

I. INTRODUCTION

1. Article 3(1) of Council Regulation (EEC) No. 4064/89 ('the Regulation') contains an exhaustive list of the factual circumstances which fall to be considered as concentrations. In accordance with the 23rd recital, this term refers only to operations that lead to a lasting change in the structure of the participating undertakings.

By contrast, the Regulation does not deal with operations whose object or effect is the coordination of the competitive activities of undertakings that remain independent of each other. Situations of this kind are cooperative in character. Accordingly, they fall to be assessed under the provisions of Regulations (EEC) No. 17, (EEC) No. 1017/68 No. 4056/86 or No. 3975/87. The same applies to an operation which includes both a lasting structural change and the coordination of competitive behaviour, where the two are inseparable.

If the structural change can be separated from the coordination of competitive behaviour, the former will be assessed under the Regulation and the latter, to the extent that it does not amount to an ancillary restriction within the meaning of Article 8(2), second subparagraph of the Regulation, falls to be assessed under the other Regulations implementing Articles 85 and 86 of the EEC Treaty.

2. The purpose of this notice is to define as clearly as possible, in the interests of legal certainty, concentrative and coopera-

tive situations. This is particularly important in the case of joint ventures. The same issue is raised in other forms of association between undertakings seen as unilateral or reciprocal shareholdings and common directorships, and of certain operations involving more than one undertaking, such as unilateral or reciprocal transfers of undertakings or parts of undertakings, or joint acquisition of an undertaking with a view to its division. In all these cases, operations may not fall within the scope of the Regulation, where their object or effect is the coordination of the competitive behaviour of the undertakings concerned.

3. This notice sets out the main considerations which will determine the Commission's view to what extent the aforesaid operations are or are not caught by the Regulation. It is not concerned with the assessment of these operations, whether under the Regulation or any other applicable provisions, in particular Articles 85 and 86 of the EEC Treaty.

4. The principles set out in this notice will be followed and further developed by the Commission's practice in individual cases. As the operations considered are generally of a complex nature, this notice cannot provide a definitive answer to all conceivable situations.

5. This notice is without prejudice to the interpretation which may be given by the Court of Justice or the Court of First Instance of the European Communities.

II. JOINT VENTURES WITHIN ARTICLE 3 OF THE REGULATION

6. The Regulation in Article 3(2) refers to two types of joint venture: those which have as their object or effect the coordination of the competitive behaviour of undertakings which remain independent (referred to as 'cooperative joint ventures') and those which perform on a lasting basis all the functions of an autonomous economic entity and which do not give rise to coordination amongst themselves or between them and the joint venture (referred to as 'concentrative joint ventures'). The latter are concentrations and as such are caught by the Regulation. Cooperative joint ventures fall to be considered under other regulations implementing Articles 85 and 86.

A. Concept of joint venture

7. To define the term 'joint venture' within the meaning of Article 3(2), it is necessary to refer to the provision of Article 3(1)(*b*) of the Regulation. According to the latter, JVs are undertakings that are jointly controlled by several other undertakings, the parent companies. In the context of the Regulation the term JV thus implies several characteristics:

1. Undertaking

8. A JV must be an undertaking. That is to be understood as an organized assembly of human and material resources, intended to pursue a defined economic purpose on a long-term basis.

2. Control by other undertakings

9. In the context of the Regulation, a JV is controlled by other undertakings. Pursuant to Article 3(3) of the Regulation, control means the possibility of exercising, directly or indirectly, a decisive influence on the activities of the JV; whether this condition is fulfilled can only be decided by reference to all the legal and factual circumstances of the individual case.

10. Control of a JV can be based on legal, contractual or other means, within which the following elements are especially important:

- ownership or rights to the use of all or some of the JV's assets,
- influence over the composition, voting or decisions of the managing or supervisory bodies of the JV,
- voting rights in the managing or supervisory bodies of the JV,
- contracts concerning the running of the JV's business.

3. Joint control

11. A JV under the Regulation is jointly controlled. Joint control exists where the

parent companies must agree on decisions concerning the JV's activities, either because of the rights acquired in the JV or because of contracts or other means establishing the joint control. Joint control may be provided for in the JV's constitution (memorandum or articles of association). However, it need not be present from the beginning, but may also be established later, in particular by taking a share in an existing undertaking.

12. There is no joint control where one of the parent companies can decide alone on the JV's commercial activities. This is generally the case where one company owns more than half the capital or assets of the undertaking, has the right to appoint more than half of the managing or supervisory bodies, controls more than half of the votes in one of those bodies, or has the sole right to manage the undertaking's business. Where the other parent companies either have completely passive minority holdings or, while able to have a certain influence on the undertaking, cannot, individually or together, determine its behaviour, a relative majority of the capital or of the votes or seats on the decision-making bodies will suffice to control the undertaking.

13. In many cases, the joint control of the JV is based on agreements or concertation between the parent companies. Thus, a majority shareholder in a JV often extends to one or more minority shareholders a contractual right to take part in the control of the JV. If two undertakings each hold half of a JV, even if there is no agreement between them, both parent companies will be obliged permanently to cooperate so as to avoid reciprocal blocking votes on decisions affecting the JV's activity. The same applies to JV's with three or more parents, where each of them has a right of veto. A JV can even be controlled by a considerable number of undertakings that can together muster a majority of the capital or the seats or votes on the JV's decision-making bodies. However, in such cases, joint control can be presumed only if the factual and legal circumstances – especially a convergence of economic interests – support the notion of a deliberate common policy of the parent companies in relation to the JV.

14. If one undertaking's holding in another is, by its nature or its extent, insufficient to establish sole control, and if there is no joint control together with third parties, then there is no concentration within the meaning of Article 3(1)(*b*) of the Regulation. Articles 85 or 86 of the EEC Treaty may however be applicable on the basis of Regulation (EEC) No. 17 or other implementing Regulations (see III.1).

B. Concentrative joint ventures

15. For a joint venture to be regarded as concentrative it must fulfil all the conditions of Article 3(2), subparagraph 2, which lays down a positive condition and a negative condition.

1. Positive condition; joint venture performing on a lasting basis all of the functions of an autonomous economic entity

16. To fulfil this condition, a JV must first of all act as an independent supplier and buyer on the market. JVs that take over from their parents only specific partial responsibilities are not to be considered as concentrations where they are merely auxiliaries to the commercial activities of the parent companies. This is the case where the JV supplies its products or services exclusively to its parent companies, or when it meets its own needs wholly from them. The independent market presence can even be insufficient if the JV achieves the majority of its supplies or sales with third parties, but remains substantially dependent on its parents for the maintenance and development of its business.

17. A JV exists on a lasting basis if it is intended and able to carry on its activity for an unlimited, or at least for a long, time. If this is not the case there is generally no long-term change in the structures of the parent companies. More important than the agreed duration are the human and material resources of the JV. They must be of such nature and quantity as to ensure the JV's existence and independence in the

long term. This is generally the case where the parent companies invest substantial financial resources in the JV, transfer an existing undertaking or business to it, or give it substantial technical or commercial know-how, so that after an initial starting-up period it can support itself by its own means.

18. A decisive question for assessing the autonomous character of the JV is whether it is in a position to exercise its own commercial policy. This requires, within the limits of its company objects, that it plans, decides and acts independently. In particular, it must be free to determine its competitive behaviour autonomously and according to its own economic interests. If the JV depends for its business on facilities that remain economically integrated with the parent companies' businesses, that weakens the case for the autonomous nature of the JV.

19. The JV's economic independence will not be contested merely because the parent companies reserve to themselves the right to take certain decisions that are important for the development of the JV, namely those concerning alterations of the objects of the company, increases or reductions of capital, or the application of profits. However, if the commercial policy of the JV remains in the hands of the parent undertakings, the JV may take on the aspect of an instrument of the parent undertakings' market interests. Such a situation will usually exist where the JV operates in the market of the parent undertakings. It may also exist where the JV operates in markets neighbouring, or upstream or downstream of, those of the parent undertakings.

2. *Negative condition: absence of coordination of competitive behaviour*

20. Subject to what is said in the first paragraph of this notice a JV can only be considered to be concentrative within the meaning of Article 3(2), subparagraph 2 of the Regulation, if it does not have as its object or effect the coordination of the competitive behaviour of undertakings that remain independent of each other. There must not be such coordination either between the parent companies themselves or between any or all of them on the one hand and the JV on the other hand. Such coordination must not be an object of the establishment or operation of the JV, nor may it be a consequence thereof. The JV is not to be regarded as concentrative if as a result of the agreement to set up the JV or as a result of its existence or activities it is reasonably foreseeable that the competitive behaviour of a parent or of the JV on the relevant market will be influenced. Conversely, there will normally be no foreseeable coordination when all the parent companies withdraw entirely and permanently from the JV's market and do not operate on markets neighbouring those of the JV's.

21. Not every cooperation between parent companies with regard to the JV prevents a JV from being considered concentrative. Even concentrative JVs generally represent a means for parent companies to pursue common or mutually complementary interests. The establishment and joint control of a JV is, therefore, inconceivable without an understanding between the parent companies as concerns the pursuit of those interests. Irrespective of its legal form, such a concordance of interests is an essential feature of a JV.

22. As regards the relations of the parent undertakings, or any one of them, with the JV, the risk of coordination within the meaning of Article 3(2) will not normally arise where the parent undertakings are not active in the markets of the JV or in neighbouring or upstream or downstream markets. In other cases, the risk of coordination will be relatively small where the parents limit the influence they exercise to the JV's strategic decisions, such as those concerning the future direction of investment, and when they express their financial, rather than their market-oriented, interests. The membership of the JV's managing and supervisory bodies is also important. Common membership of the JV's and the parent companies' decision-making bodies may be an obstacle to the development of the JV's autonomous commercial policy.

23. The dividing line between the concordance of interests in a JV and a coordination of competitive behaviour that is incompatible with the notion of concentration cannot be laid down for all conceivable kinds of case. The decisive factor is not the legal form of the relationship between the parent companies and between them and the JV. The direct or indirect, actual or potential effects of the establishment and operation of the JV on market relationships, have determinant importance.

24. In assessing the likelihood of coordination of competitive behaviour, it is useful to consider some of the different situations which often occur:

(*a*) JVs that take over pre-existing activities of the parent companies;
(*b*) JVs that undertake new activities on behalf of the parent companies;
(*c*) JVs that enter the parent companies' markets;
(*d*) JVs that enter upstream, downstream or neighbouring markets.

(a) JVs that take over pre-existing activities of the parent companies

25. There is normally no risk of coordination where the parent companies transfer the whole of certain business activities to the JV and withdraw permanently from the JV's market so that they remain neither actual nor potential competitors – of each other nor of the JV. In this context, the notion of potential competition is to be interpreted realistically, according to the Commission's established practice. A presumption of a competitive relationship requires not only that one or more of the parent companies could re-enter the JV's market at any time; this must be a realistic option and represent a commercially reasonable course in the light of all objective circumstances.

26. Where the parent companies transfer their entire business activities to the JV, and thereafter act only as holding companies, this amounts to complete merger from the economic viewpoint.

27. Where the JV takes on only some of the activities that the parent companies formerly carried on independently, this can also amount to a concentration. In this case, the establishment and operation of the JV must not lead to a coordination of the parent companies' competitive behaviour in relation to other activities which they retain. Coordination of competitive behaviour between any or all of the parent companies and the JV must also be excluded. Such coordination is likely where there are close economic links between the areas of activity of the JV on one side and of the parent companies on the other. This applies to upstream, downstream and neighbouring product markets.

28. The withdrawal of the parent companies need not be simultaneous with the establishment of the JV. It is possible – so far as necessary – to allow the parent companies a short transitional period to overcome any starting-up problems of the JV, especially bottlenecks in production or supplies. This period should not normally exceed one year.

29. It is even possible for the establishment of a JV to represent a concentration situation where the parent companies remain permanently active on the JV's product or service market. In this case, however, the parent companies' geographic market must be different from that of the JV. Moreover, the markets in question must be so widely separated, or must present structures so different, that, taking account of the nature of the goods or services concerned and of the cost of (first or renewed) entry by either into the other's market, competitive interaction may be excluded.

30. If the parent companies' markets and the JV's are in different parts of the Community or neighbouring third countries, there is a degree of probability that either, if it has the necessary human and material resources, could extend its activities from the one market to the other. Where the territories are adjacent or very close to each other, this may even be assumed to be the case. At least in this last case, the actual allocation of markets gives reason to suppose that it follows from a coordination

of competitive behaviour between parent companies and the JV.

(b) JVs that undertake new activities on behalf of the parent companies

31. There is normally no risk of coordination in the sense described above where the JV operates on a product or service market which the parent companies individually have not entered and will not enter in the foreseeable future, because they lack the organizational, technical or financial means or because, in the light of all the objective circumstances, such a move would not represent a commercially reasonable course. An individual market entry will also be unlikely where, after establishing the JV, the parent companies no longer have the means to make new investments in the same field, or where an additional individual operation on the JV's market would not make commercial sense. In both cases there is no competitive relationship between the parent companies and the JV. Consequently, there is no possibility of coordination of their competitive behaviour. However, this assessment is only true if the JV's market is neither upstream nor downstream of, nor neighbouring, that of the parent companies.

32. The establishment of a JV to operate in the same product or service market as the parent companies but in another geographic market involves the risk of coordination if there is competitive interaction between the parent companies' geographic market and that of the JV.

(c) JVs that enter the parent companies' market

33. Where the parent companies, or one of them, remain active on the JV's market or remain potential competitors of the JV, a coordination of competitive behaviour between the parent companies or between them and the JV must be presumed. So long as this presumption is not rebutted, the Commission will take it that the establishment of the JV does not fall under Article 3(2), subparagraph 2 of the Regulation.

(d) JVs that operate in upstream, downstream or neighbouring markets

34. If the JV is operating in a market that is upstream or downstream of that of the parent companies, then, in general, coordination of purchasing or, as the case may be, sales policy between the parent companies is likely where they are competitors on the upstream or downstream market.

35. If the parent companies are not competitors, it remains to be examined whether there is a real risk of coordination of competitive behaviour between the JV and any of the parents. This will normally be the case where the JV's sales or purchases are made in substantial measure with the parent companies.

36. It is not possible to lay down general principles regarding the likelihood of coordination of competitive behaviour in cases where the parent companies and the JV are active in neighbouring markets. The outcome will depend in particular on whether the JV's and the parent companies' products are technically or economically linked, whether they are both components of another product or are otherwise mutually complementary, and whether the parent companies could realistically enter the JV's market. If there are no concrete opportunities for competitive interaction of this kind, the Commission will treat the JV as concentrative.

III. OTHER LINKS BETWEEN UNDERTAKINGS

1. Minority shareholdings

37. The taking of a minority shareholding in an undertaking can be considered a concentration within the meaning of Article 3(1)(*b*) of the Regulation if the new shareholder acquires the possibility of exercising a decisive influence on the undertaking's activity. If the acquisition of a minority shareholding brings about a situation in which there is an undertaking jointly controlled by two or more others, the principles described above in relation to JVs apply.

38. As long as the threshold of individual or joint decisive influence has not been reached, the Regulation is not in any event applicable. Accordingly, the assessment under competition law will be made only in relation to the criteria laid down in Articles 85 and 86 of the EEC Treaty and on the basis of the usual procedural rules for restrictive practices and abuses of dominant position.

39. There may likewise be a risk of coordination where an undertaking acquires a majority or minority interest in another in which a competitor already has a minority interest. If so, this acquisition will be assessed under Articles 85 and 86 of the EEC Treaty.

2. Cross-shareholding

40. In order to bring their autonomous and hitherto separate undertakings or groups closer together, company owners often cause them to exchange shareholdings in each other. Such reciprocal influences can serve to establish or to secure industrial or commercial cooperation between the undertakings or groups. But they may also result in establishing a 'single economic entity'. In the first case, the coordination of competitive behaviour between independent undertakings is predominant; in the second, the result may be a concentration. Consequently, reciprocal directorships and cross-shareholdings can only be evaluated in relation to their foreseeable effects in each case.

41. The Commission considers that two or more undertakings can also combine without setting up a parent-subsidiary relationship and without either losing its legal personality. Article 3(1) of the Regulation refers not only to legal, but also to economic concentrations. The condition for the recognition of a concentration in the form of a combined group is, however, that the undertakings or groups concerned are not only subject to a permanent, single economic management, but are also amalgamated into a genuine economic unit, characterized internally by profit and loss compensation between the various undertakings within the groups and externally by joint liability.

3. Representation on controlling bodies of other undertakings

42. Common membership of managing or supervisory boards of various undertakings is to be assessed in accordance with the same principles as cross-shareholdings.

43. The representation of one undertaking on the decision-making bodies of another is usually the consequence of an existing shareholding. It reinforces the influence of the investing undertaking over the activities of the undertaking in which it holds a share, because it affords it the opportunity of obtaining information on the activities of a competitor or of taking an active part in its commercial decisions.

44. Thus, common membership of the respective boards may be the vehicle for the coordination of the competitive behaviour of the undertakings concerned, or for a concentration of undertakings within the meaning of the Regulation. This will depend on the circumstances of the individual case, among which the economic link between the shareholding and the personal connection must always be examined. This is equally true of unilateral and reciprocal relationships between undertakings.

45. Personal connections not accompanied by shareholdings are to be judged according to the same criteria as shareholding relationships between undertakings. A majority of seats on the managing or supervisory board of an undertaking will normally imply control of the latter; a minority of seats at least a degree of influence over its commercial policy, which may further entail a coordination of behaviour. Reciprocal connections justify a presumption that the undertakings concerned are coordinating their business conduct. A very wide communality of membership of the respective decision-making bodies – that is, up to half of the members or more – may be an indication of a concentration.

4. Transfers of undertakings or parts of undertakings

46. A transfer of assets or shares falls within the definition of a concentration, according to Article 3(1)(*b*) of the Regulation, if it results in the acquirer gaining control of all or of part of one or more

undertakings. However, the situation is different where the transfer conferring control over part of an undertaking is linked with an agreement to coordinate the competitive behaviour of the undertakings concerned, or where it necessarily leads to or is accompanied by coordination of the business conduct of undertakings which remain independent. Cases of this kind are not covered by the Regulation; they must be examined according to Articles 85 and 86 of the EEC Treaty and under the appropriate implementing Regulations.

47. The practical application of this rule requires a distinction between unilateral and reciprocal arrangements. A unilateral acquisition of assets or shares strongly suggests that the Regulation is applicable. The contrary needs to be demonstrated by clear evidence of the likelihood of coordination of the parties' competitive behaviour. A reciprocal acquisition of assets or shares, by contrast, will usually follow from an agreement between the undertakings concerned as to their investments, production or sales, and thus serves to coordinate their competitive behaviour. A concentration situation does not exist where a reciprocal transfer of assets or shares forms part of a specialization or restructuring agreement or other type of coordination. Coordination presupposes in any event that the parties remain at least potential competitors after the exchange has taken place.

5. Joint acquisition of an undertaking with a view to its division

48. Where several undertakings jointly acquire another, the principles for the assessment of a joint venture are applicable, provided that within the acquisition operation, the period of joint control goes beyond the very short term. In this case the Regulation may or may not be applicable, depending on the concentrative or cooperative nature of the JV. If, by contrast, the sole object of the agreement is to divide up the assets of the undertaking and this agreement is put into effect immediately after the acquisition, then, in accordance with the 24th recital, the Regulation applies.

20.5 W. Sibree, 'EEC merger control and joint ventures', 17 *European Law Review*, 91 (1992)

Much was said at the time of the adoption of Regulation 4064/89 ('the Merger Regulation') of the benefits of one-stop shopping under the new regulation. Now that the Merger Regulation has been in operation for over a year, though, it is becoming a matter of increasing concern that the clarity and simplicity which we were to expect does not exist in the case of joint ventures; and further that the expectation that the Merger Regulation should lead to control over only substantial transactions in Community terms was misfounded.

Of particular concern are: a somewhat inconsistent analysis of joint ventures; the uncertain status now of the Commission's own interpretative notice; and the fact that transactions which do not appear to be concentrations or have a real Community dimension are falling under the Community jurisdiction. The net effect of this has been the opposite of one-stop shopping. Parties to joint ventures have found themselves obliged to go through national, as well as Community, authorities and the position is exacerbated by the fact that national authorities feel unable to take decisions on the substance until they have had the Commission's decision on jurisdiction. This problem has now been alleviated somewhat by the setting up of an informal screening committee procedure within the Merger Task Force to deal with jurisdictional issues prior to notification. The long term worry is that the Commission is unlikely in practice to be subject to any effective judicial control on mergers. Appeal to the Court of First Instance, with a likely time lag of at least 12 months, is not a realistic possibility in most cases.

It has to be admitted that some of the confusion is due to the rather rigid distinction made by the Merger Regulation between concentrative and coordinative transactions. No doubt the Commission would have been happier with a more flexible and pragmatic test of what constitutes a merger such as exists in the United Kingdom and Germany. It may also be the case that the Merger Task Force has been encouraged in this direction by the parties. There are often practical advantages in bringing a joint venture under the Merger Regulation: rapid decision-making relative to procedures under Article 85 EEC; a more easily satisfied test of compatibility with the common market; and, once jurisdiction is taken, the avoidance of the necessity for additional national clearances.

THE COMMISSION'S PRACTICE UNDER THE MERGER REGULATION

The background

The starting point under the Merger Regulation is the second paragraph of Article 3(2):

> The creation of a joint venture performing on a lasting basis all the functions of an autonomous economic entity, which does not give rise to co-ordination of the competitive behaviour of the parties amongst themselves or between them and the joint venture, shall constitute a concentration within the meaning of paragraph 1(*b*).

The two major problems from a practitioner's viewpoint are firstly, what constitutes 'performing . . . all the functions of an autonomous economic entity'; and secondly, in what circumstances is it likely that co-ordination between the parents or parents and joint venture will be found. These are indeed the points on which the Commission's interpretative notice concentrates.

The nub of what is said in the notice appears in paragraphs 18–19 and 33–34. First, on the question of autonomy;

> A decisive question for assessing the autonomous character of the JV is whether it is in a position to exercise its own commercial policy. This requires, within the limits of its company objects, that it plans, decides and acts independently. In particular, it must be free to determine its competitive behaviour autonomously and according to its own economic interest. If the JV depends for its business on facilities that remain economically integrated with the parent companies' businesses, that weakens the case for the autonomous nature of the JV.
>
> The JV's economic independence will not be contested merely because the parent companies reserve to themselves the right to take certain decisions that are important for the development of the JV, namely those concerning alterations of the objects of the company, increases or reductions of capital, or the application of profits. However, if the commercial policy of the JV remains in the hands of the parent undertakings, the JV may take on the aspect of an instrument of the parent undertakings' market interests. Such a situation will usually exist where the JV operates in the market of the parent undertakings. It may also exist where the JV operates in markets neighbouring, or upstream or downstream of, those of the parent undertakings.

As a practical commercial matter, it is very doubtful whether there are any joint ventures where the parents abandon all influence over commercial policy, any more than they would over wholly-owned subsidiaries. It is a question of degree. But there is also an important point of interpretation here. The regulation does *not* say that the joint venture 'must be an autonomous economic entity': it says it must *perform all the functions* of such an entity. That is rather a different concept. The parents may well have influence, for example, through their appointees to the Board, but the joint venture must act *as if* it were autonomous. In substance it must be free-standing; it must be an independent 'undertaking' within the meaning of Article 85 EEC.

Turning to the second point of substance, namely lack of co-ordination, the notice says this:

> Where the parent companies, or one of

them, remain active on the JV's market or remain potential competitors of the JV, a co-ordination of competitive behaviour between the parent companies or between them and the JV must be presumed. So long as this presumption is not rebutted, the Commission will take it that the establishment of the JV does not fall under Article 3(2), subparagraph 2 of the Regulation. If the JV is operating in a market that is upstream or downstream of that of the parent companies, then, in general, co-ordination of purchasing or, as the case may be, sales policy between the parent companies is likely where they are competitors on the upstream or downstream market.

[. . .]

That statement [. . .] does of course give rise to the anomaly that concentrative cases will benefit from the higher threshold (creation or enhancement of a dominant position) even though they may be more anti-competitive than co-operative joint ventures which fall to be measured against the lower threshold of Article 85 EEC (appreciable restriction of competition). That, however, is endemic in the substantive test for compatibility adopted by the Council in the Merger Regulation.

LEGAL AND POLICY ISSUES

A review of the joint venture cases to date raises a number of legal and policy issues which can be summarised as follows. Firstly, the decisions have not dispelled the uncertainty surrounding the application of the regulation to joint ventures. In some areas they may have increased the uncertainty. It is to be hoped that the pre-notification screening process will, however, smooth the path on jurisdictional issues. Secondly, the Commission has effectively reversed some of the jurisprudence under Article 85 EEC and departed from aspects of its own published notice. That is unsatisfactory: the Court of Justice is rarely, if ever, going to have the opportunity to redirect the Commission's practice because appeals in merger cases are inherently unlikely (particularly where a clearance is ultimately given). Thirdly, Community jurisdiction has been exercised over some relatively small transactions, often centred on a single Member State, which are perhaps more appropriately dealt with by national authorities. The unfortunate compromise drafting of the Merger Regulation is in part responsible for this; but it is submitted that this still allowed a degree of latitude to decline jurisdiction in appropriate cases. In particular, Article 5(2) of the Merger Regulation could have been interpreted more liberally in appropriate cases so as to cede jurisdiction to national authorities; and the concept of a concentration could have been applied in such a way as to exclude start-up joint ventures with no impact within the Community. These are dealt with more fully below.

Uncertainty

Practitioners in this area may, except in clear cases, be forced to advise clients that there is little option but to file Form CO to determine whether a joint venture is concentrative or co-operative. Much depends on how effective the Merger Task Force's pre-notification screening procedure proves on difficult jurisdictional issues, although the difficulty here is that the jurisdictional analysis will often turn on substantive issues such as market definition, competitive overlaps and possibilities for co-ordination. The early decisions tend to follow the guidelines in the notice. The most recent decisions – particularly *Elf/BC CEPSA, ABC/Générale des Eaux* and *Thomson/Pilkington* – appear to have departed from that analysis without substituting any clear new guidelines. It may be possible to ignore certain competing activities of the parent and joint ventures either by defining them as separate markets or by categorising them as insignificant. It appears that upstream and downstream activities of the parents may not be of any great relevance.

It cannot be expected that the Court of Justice will have the opportunity to remove the uncertainty. In the circumstances the Commission should withdraw its current notice and issue a revised notice as soon as possible. In the interim, it has shown itself readier to give informal guidance to parties so as to avoid the expense (and possible duplication of work required) of filing Form CO and making clearance applications to national authorities.

Previous case law

There appear to be three main points here. First, the Commission now appears to accept that, provided one parent withdraws from the joint venture's market entirely, the transaction will be regarded as concentrative. This is consistent with *Kaiser/Estel* but contradicts paragraph 33 of its own notice:

> Where the parent companies, *or one of them*, remain active on the JV's market or remain potential competitors of the JV, a co-ordination of competitive behaviour . . . must be presumed.

Secondly, the earlier case law and paragraph 34 of the notice make it plain that there must be no co-ordination between parents and joint venture and that such co-ordination is likely where they are in upstream or downstream markets. The reason behind this proposition is that one or other will coordinate its purchasing, to the detriment of third-party suppliers. It is at best unclear from the text of a number of recent decisions whether the Commission has made a close analysis of this possibility.

Thirdly, there is no authority in the earlier case law for the proposition that a newly formed joint venture to which neither parent contributes business assets can constitute a concentration. Article 3(2) of the Merger Regulation may on its face suggest that such operations are within its scope; but, read in the light of the spirit of the regulation and in particular recital (23), it is submitted that it was not intended to catch such operations. Yet in *BNP Dresdner Bank – Czechoslovakia* that was the finding. This appears to be an excess of jurisdiction, perhaps encouraged by the parties themselves.

The conclusion to be drawn from these points is that there should be closer scrutiny of the Commission's policy in this area. The Merger Task Force plainly has to exercise a degree of autonomy in its own sphere and a number of decisions may correspond with the wishes of the notifying parties; but viewed objectively there is cause for concern if its decisions undermine established principles or encroach on the jurisdiction of other branches of DGIV, particularly as the tests under the Merger Regulation are much more generous than under Article 85 EEC. Certainly there is a need for effective judicial control. That might be achieved by establishing some form of expedited procedure before the Court of First Instance which would enable appeals to be decided within an acceptably short period.

Size and nature of transaction

Difficulties in the wording of the Regulation, combined in some degree with the manner of the Commission's interpretation, have resulted in the Commission examining a number of transactions where Community supervision seems inappropriate either because of the modest size of the transaction or because it has no real Community dimension. This is because in most joint venture cases the Commission is obliged to take into account the turnover of both parents and that may well exceed the ECU five billion threshold even if the joint venture's turnover is minute. One solution would be to alter the rules for calculating turnover, perhaps by requiring the joint venture to be of a certain size, but the chances of amendments being got through the Council of Ministers must be remote, given how difficult it was to get agreement on a regulation at all. In the case of start-up joint ventures, it is submitted that the Commission could and should have interpreted the notion of a concentration more narrowly. The two *BNP/Dresdner Bank* decisions will have the extraordinary result of making notifiable a joint venture between two non-Community companies (who happen to have sufficient turnover within Community) even where that joint venture's operations are to be conducted wholly outside the Community. In the case of an existing company in which a stake is bought, the Commission could make more liberal use of Article 5(2) of the Merger Regulation and treat the transaction as the acquisition of part. That is to say, it could treat the transaction as in substance an acquisition rather than a joint venture and take into account only the turnover of the company in which a stake is to be bought. Instead it has taken a stricter reading of Article 5(2) and argued that where there is joint control as a matter of law then both parents are participating undertakings whose turnover must be taken into account.

The ability of Article 86 to regulate oligopoly markets was curtailed by the decision of the European Court of First Instance in the **Italian Flat Glass** case (Section 17.7). However, in the **Nestlé/Perrier** merger decision, the EC Commission made an important contribution to the control of oligopoly through merger control. Paying due regard to the approach of legal systems such as those in the USA and the UK (**section 6(2), Fair Trading Act 1973**, Section 17.2), the Commission determined that the Merger Regulation was intended to apply not only to concentrations which created or enhanced single-undertaking dominance, but also to those creating or enhancing oligopoly.

20.6 *Nestlé/Perrier* Decision of the Commission of the European Communities OJ 1992 No. L 356/1

THE COMMISSION OF THE EUROPEAN COMMUNITIES

Having regard to the Treaty establishing the European Economic Community,

Having regard to Council Regulation (EEC) No. 4064/89 of 21 December 1989 on the control of concentrations between undertakings, and in particular Article 8(2) thereof,

Having regard to the Commission decision of 25 March 1992 to initiate proceedings in this case,

Having given the undertakings concerned the opportunity to make known their views on the objections raised by the Commission.

Having regard to the opinion of the Advisory Committee on Concentrations,

Whereas:

I. BACKGROUND

(1) On 25 February 1992, Nestlé SA notified a public bid for 100% of the shares of Source Perrier SA which was launched by Demilac, a jointly controlled subsidiary of Nestlé and Banque Indosuez. Nestlé has an option to purchase the shareholding of Banque Indosuez in Demilac, which it has announced it will take up. On 30 January 1992, Nestlé concluded an agreement with BSN following which the Volvic source of Perrier will be sold to BSN if Nestlé acquires control over Perrier.

(2) By decision dated 17 March 1992, the Commission continued the suspension of the concentration pursuant to Article 7(2) of Council Regulation No. 4064/89 (the Merger Regulation). Nestlé has acquired the majority of the shares in Perrier but is refrained from exercising the voting rights attached to these shares pursuant to Article 7(3) of the Merger Regulation.

(3) By decision dated 25 March 1992, the Commission declared that the proposed concentration raised serious doubts as to its compatibility with the common market. The Commission therefore initiated proceedings in this case pursuant to Article 6(1)(*c*) of the Merger Regulation.

[. . .]

(i) Application of Article 2(3) of the Merger Regulation to oligopolies

(110) Article 2(3) of the Merger Regulation stipulates: A concentration which creates or strengthens a dominant position as a result of which effective competition would be significantly impeded in the common market or in a substantial part of it shall be declared incompatible with the common market.

The question is whether this provision covers only a market situation where effective competition is significantly impeded by one firm which alone has the power to behave to an appreciable extent independently of its competitors, customers and consumers, or whether this provision also covers market situations where effective competition is significantly impeded by more than one firm which together have the power to behave to an appreciable extent independently of the remaining competitors, of customers and ultimately of consumers.

(111) Nestlé has not denied the fact that from an economic point of view, both single firm dominance and oligopolistic dominance can significantly impede effective competition under certain market structure conditions [. . .].

(112) The Commission considers that the distinction between single firm dominance and oligopolistic dominance cannot be decisive for the application or non-application of the Merger Regulation because both situations may significantly impede effective competition under certain market structure conditions. This is in particular the case if there is already before the merger weakened competition between the oligopolists which is likely to be further weakened by a significant increase in concentration and if there is no sufficient price-constraining competition from actual or potential competition coming from outside the oligopoly.

(113) Article 3(*f*) of the EEC Treaty provides for the institution of a system ensuring that competition in the common market is not distorted. One of the principal goals of the Treaty is thus the maintenance of effective competition. The restriction of effective competition which is prohibited if it is the result of a dominant position held by one firm cannot become permissible if it is the result of more than one firm. If, for instance, as a result of a merger, two or three undertakings acquire market power and are likely to apply excessive prices this would constitute an exercise of a collective market power which the Merger Regulation is intended to prevent by the maintenance of a competitive market structure. The dominant position is only the means by which effective competition can be impeded. Whether this impediment occurs through single firm power or collective power cannot be decisive for the application or non-application of Article 2(3) of the Merger Regulation.

(114) In the absence of explicit exclusion of oligopolistic dominance by Article 2(3) it cannot be assumed that the legislator intended to permit the impediment of effective competition by two or more undertakings holding the power to behave together to an appreciable extent independently on the market. This would create a loophole in the fundamental Treaty objective of maintaining effective competition at all times in order not to jeopardize the proper functioning of the common market. If, in order to avoid the application of the Merger Regulation, it sufficed to divide the dominant power between for instance two companies in order to escape the prohibition of Article 2(3), then, in contradiction to the basic principles of the common market, effective competition could be significantly impeded. In such a hypothesis the objective of Article 3(*f*) of the EEC Treaty could be overturned.

(115) Seen in the light of these legal and economic considerations, Article 2(3) must be interpreted as covering both single firm and oligopolistic dominance. It is also significant to note that all other major antitrust systems with a merger control system apply or can apply their rules to both single firm and oligopolistic dominance, e.g. the American system, the French law (Article 38 of the Law of 1 December 1986); German law (22 GWB) and UK law (Fair

Trading Act, Section 6(2)). In most of these systems, it is an established practice to control mergers raising a problem of oligopolistic dominance. It cannot be the case that following the adoption of the Merger Regulation mergers which previously were subject to such control would now be subject only to single firm dominance control. The Merger Regulation would not only have transferred the national merger control powers to the Community but those Member States which had a system with oligopolistic dominance control would at the same time have abandoned such control altogether without any substitute for it at Community level. In the absence of any express provisions to that effect, such a cession of control cannot be assumed.

(116) The argument of BSN that the Commission would be violating the principle of legal certainty because this case would be the first case to apply the oligopolistic dominance concept cannot be accepted. As explained above, the correct interpretation of the Merger Regulation leads to the conclusion that Article 2(3) has always covered dominance which significantly impedes effective competition independently of whether such situation is the result of one or more than one firm. Furthermore, if the argument of BSN was right, it would mean that the Commission could never develop any of its administrative case law. Although BSN's argument could under other circumstances have some relevance in particular where *a posteriori* control takes place and involves interference in acquired rights, the merger control system is an *a priori* control system which by definition does not allow the implementation of mergers without prior authorization by the Commission.

[. . .]

The approach in the USA to the definition of a merger transaction, and the market in which it is to be assessed, is more structured and systematic, but also more complex. The new joint **Horizontal Merger Guidelines, 1992** of both regulatory agencies (the Department of Justice and the Federal Trade Commission) require a definition of the relevant market and its participants according to the 'five percent test'. The concentration of the market must then be assessed according to the Herfindahl–Hirschman Index to determine whether merger control is warranted.

20.7 *Horizontal Merger Guidelines, 1992*, Department of Justice and Federal Trade Commission April 2, 1992 Statement of the US Department of Justice and the Federal Trade Commission, Accompanying Release of Revised Merger Guidelines

The US Department of Justice (Department) and Federal Trade Commission (Commission) today jointly issued *Horizontal Merger Guidelines* revising the Department's 1984 *Merger Guidelines* and the Commission's 1982 *Statement Concerning Horizontal Merger Guidelines*. The release marks the first time that the two federal agencies that share antitrust enforcement jurisdiction have issued joint guidelines.

Central to the 1992 Department of Justice and Federal Trade Commission Horizontal Merger Guidelines is a recognition that sound merger enforcement is an essential component of our free enterprise system benefiting the competitiveness of

American firms and the welfare of American consumers. Sound merger enforcement must prevent anticompetitive mergers yet avoid deterring the larger universe of procompetitive or competitively neutral mergers. The 1992 *Horizontal Merger Guidelines* implement this objective by describing the analytical foundations of merger enforcement and providing guidance enabling the business community to avoid antitrust problems when planning mergers.

The Department first released *Merger Guidelines* in 1968 in order to inform the business community of the analysis applied by the Department to mergers under the federal antitrust laws. The 1968 *Merger Guidelines* eventually fell into disuse, both internally and externally, as they were eclipsed by the developments in legal and economic thinking about mergers.

In 1982, the Department released revised *Merger Guidelines* which, reflecting those developments, departed dramatically from the 1968 version. Relative to the Department's actual practice, however, the 1982 *Merger Guidelines* represented an evolutionary not revolutionary change. On the same date, the Commission released its *Statement Concerning Horizontal Mergers* highlighting the principal considerations guiding the Commission's horizontal merger enforcement and noting the 'considerable weight' given by the Commission to the Department's 1982 *Merger Guidelines*. The Department's current *Merger Guidelines*, released in 1984, refined and clarified the analytical framework of the 1982 *Merger Guidelines*. Although the agencies' experience with the 1982 *Merger Guidelines* reaffirmed the soundness of its underlying principles, the Department concluded that there remained room for improvement.

The revisions embodied in the 1992 *Horizontal Merger Guidelines* reflect the next logical step in the development of the agencies' analysis of mergers. They reflect the Department's experience in applying the 1982 and 1984 *Merger Guidelines* as well as the Commission's experience in applying those *Guidelines* and the Commission's 1982 *Statement*. Both the Department and the Commission believed that their respective *Guidelines* and *Statement* presented sound frameworks for antitrust analysis of mergers, but that improvements could be made to reflect advances in legal and economic thinking. The 1992 *Horizontal Merger Guidelines* accomplish this objective and also clarify certain aspects of the *Merger Guidelines* that proved to be ambiguous or were interpreted by observers in ways that were inconsistent with the actual policy of the agencies. The 1992 *Horizontal Merger Guidelines* do not include a discussion of horizontal effects from non-horizontal mergers (e.g. elimination of specific potential entrants and competitive problems from vertical mergers). Neither agency has changed its policy with respect to non-horizontal mergers. Specific guidance on non-horizontal mergers is provided in Section 4 of the Department's 1984 *Merger Guidelines*, read in the context of today's revisions to the treatment of horizontal mergers.

A number of today's revisions are largely technical or stylistic. One major objective of the revisions is to strengthen the document as an analytical road map for the evaluation of mergers. The language, therefore, is intended to be burden-neutral, without altering the burdens of proof or burdens of coming forward as those standards have been established by the courts. In addition, the revisions principally address two areas.

The most significant revision to the *Merger Guidelines* is to explain more clearly how mergers may lead to adverse competitive effects and how particular market factors relate to the analysis of those effects. These revisions are found in Section 2 of the *Horizontal Merger Guidelines*. The second principal revision is to sharpen the distinction between the treatment of various types of supply responses and to articulate the framework for analyzing the timeliness, likelihood and sufficiency of entry. These revisions are found in Sections 1.3 and 3.

The new *Horizontal Merger Guidelines* observe, as did the 1984 *Guidelines*, that because the specific standards they set out must be applied in widely varied factual circumstances, mechanical application of those standards could produce misleading results. Thus, the *Guidelines* state that the agencies will apply those standards reasonably and flexibly to the particular facts and circumstances of each proposed merger.

0. PURPOSE, UNDERLYING POLICY ASSUMPTIONS AND OVERVIEW

These *Guidelines* outline the present enforcement policy of the Department of Justice and the Federal Trade Commission (the Agency) concerning horizontal acquisitions and mergers (mergers) subject to section 7 of the Clayton Act,[1] to section 1 of the Sherman Act,[2] or to section 5 of the FTC Act.[3] They describe the analytical framework and specific standards normally used by the Agency in analyzing mergers.[4] By stating its policy as simply and clearly as possible, the Agency hopes to reduce the uncertainty associated with enforcement of the antitrust laws in this area.

Although the *Guidelines* should improve the predictability of the Agency's merger enforcement policy, it is not possible to remove the exercise of judgment from the evaluation of mergers under the antitrust laws. Because the specific standards set forth in the *Guidelines* must be applied to a broad range of possible factual circumstances, mechanical application of those standards may provide misleading answers to the economic questions raised under the antitrust laws. Moreover, information is often incomplete and the picture of competitive conditions that develops from historical evidence may provide an incomplete answer to the forward-looking inquiry of the *Guidelines*. Therefore, the Agency will apply the standards of the *Guidelines* reasonably and flexibly to the particular facts and circumstances of each proposed merger.

0.1 Purpose and Underlying Policy Assumptions of the *Guidelines*

The *Guidelines* are designed primarily to articulate the analytical framework the Agency applies in determining whether a merger is likely substantially to lessen competition, not to describe how the Agency will conduct the litigation of cases that it decides to bring. Although relevant in the latter context, the factors contemplated in the *Guidelines* neither dictate nor exhaust the range of evidence that the Agency must or may introduce in litigation. Consistent with their objective, the *Guidelines* do not attempt to assign the burden of proof, or the burden of coming forward with evidence, on any particular issue. Nor do the *Guidelines* attempt to adjust or reapportion burdens of proof or burdens of coming forward as those standards have been established by the courts.[5] Instead, the Guidelines set forth a methodology for analyzing issues once the necessary facts are available. The necessary facts may be derived from the documents and statements of both the merging firms and other sources.

Throughout the *Guidelines*, the analysis is focused on whether consumers or producers 'likely would' take certain actions, that is, whether the action is in the actor's economic interest. References to the profitability of certain actions focus on economic profits rather than accounting profits. Economic profits may be defined as the excess of revenues over costs where costs include the opportunity cost of invested capital.

Mergers are motivated by the prospect of financial gains. The possible sources of the financial gains from mergers are many, and the *Guidelines* do not attempt to identify all possible sources of gain in every merger. Instead, the *Guidelines* focus on the one potential source of gain that is of concern under the antitrust laws: market power.

The unifying theme of the *Guidelines* is that mergers should not be permitted to create or enhance market power or to facilitate its exercise. Market power to a seller is the ability profitably to maintain prices above competitive levels for a significant period of time.[6] In some circumstances, a sole seller (a 'monopolist') of a product with no good substitutes can maintain a selling price that is above the level that would prevail if the market were competitive. Similarly, in some circumstances, where only a few firms account for most of the sales of a product, those firms can exercise market power, perhaps even approximating the performance of a monopolist, by either explicitly or implicitly coordinating their actions. Circumstances also may permit a single firm, not a monopolist, to exercise market power through unilateral or non-coordinated conduct – conduct the success of which does not rely on the concurrence of other firms in the market or on coordinated responses by those firms. In any case, the result of the exercise of market power is a transfer of wealth from buyers to sellers or a misallocation of resources.

Market power also encompasses the ability of a single buyer (a 'monopsonist'), a coordinating group of buyers, or a single buyer, not a monopsonist, to depress the price paid for a product to a level that is below the competitive price and thereby depress output. The exercise of market power by buyers ('monopsony power') has adverse effects comparable to those associated with the exercise of market power by sellers. In order to assess potential monopsony concerns, the Agency will apply an analytical framework analogous to the framework of these *Guidelines*.

While challenging competitively harmful mergers, the Agency seeks to avoid unnecessary interference with the larger universe of mergers that are either competitively beneficial or neutral. In implementing this objective, however, the *Guidelines* reflect the congressional intent that merger enforcement should interdict competitive problems in their incipiency.

0.2 Overview

The *Guidelines* describe the analytical process that the Agency will employ in determining whether to challenge a horizontal merger. First, the Agency assesses whether the merger would significantly increase concentration and result in a concentrated market, properly defined and measured. Second, the Agency assesses whether the merger, in light of market concentration and other factors that characterize the market, raises concern about potential adverse competitive effects. Third, the Agency assesses whether entry would be timely, likely and sufficient either to deter or to counteract the competitive effects of concern. Fourth, the Agency assesses any efficiency gains that reasonably cannot be achieved by the parties through other means. Finally the Agency assesses whether, but for the merger, either party to the transaction would be likely to fail, causing its assets to exit the market. The process of assessing market concentration, potential adverse competitive effects, entry, efficiency, and failure is a tool that allows the Agency to answer the ultimate inquiry in merger analysis: whether the merger is likely to create or enhance market power or to facilitate its exercise.

1. MARKET DEFINITION, MEASUREMENT AND CONCENTRATION

1.0 Overview

A merger is unlikely to create or enhance market power or to facilitate its exercise unless it significantly increases concentration and results in a concentrated market, properly defined and measured. Mergers that either do not significantly increase concentration or do not result in a concentrated market ordinarily require no further analysis. The analytical process described in this section ensures that the Agency evaluates the likely competitive impact of a merger within the context of economically meaningful markets – i.e. markets that could be subject to the exercise of market power. Accordingly, for each product or service (hereafter product) of each merging firm, the Agency seeks to define a market in which firms could effectively exercise market power if they were able to coordinate their actions.

Market definition focuses solely on demand substitution factors – i.e. possible consumer responses. Supply substitution factors – i.e. possible production responses – are considered elsewhere in the *Guidelines* in the identification of firms that participate in the relevant market and the analysis of entry. See Sections 1.3 and 3. A market is defined as a product or group of products and a geographic area in which it is produced or sold such that a hypothetical profit-maximizing firm, not subject to price regulation, that was the only present and future producer or seller of those products in that area likely would impose at least a 'small but significant and nontransitory' increase in price, assuming the terms of sale of all other products are held constant. A relevant market is a group of products and a geographic area that is no bigger than necessary to satisfy this test. The 'small but significant and non-transitory' increase in price is employed solely as a methodological tool for the analysis of mergers: it is not a tolerance level for price increases.

Absent price discrimination, a relevant market is described by a product or group of products and a geographic area. In determining whether a hypothetical monopolist would be in a position to exercise market power, it is necessary to evaluate the likely demand responses of consumers to a price increase. A price increase could be made unprofitable by consumers either switching to other products or switching to the same product produced by firms at other locations. The nature and magnitude of these two types of demand responses respectively determine the scope of the product market and the geographic market.

In contrast, where a hypothetical monopolist likely would discriminate in prices charged to different groups of buyers, distinguished, for example, by their uses or locations, the Agency may delineate different relevant markets corresponding to each such buyer group. Competition for sales to each such group may be affected differently by a particular merger and markets are delineated by evaluating the demand response of each such buyer group. A relevant market of this kind is described by a collection of products for sale to a given group of buyers.

Once defined, a relevant market must be measured in terms of its participants and concentration. Participants include firms currently producing or selling the market's products in the market's geographic area. In addition, participants may include other firms depending on their likely supply responses to a 'small but significant and nontransitory' price increase. A firm is viewed as a participant if, in response to a 'small but significant nontransitory' price increase, it likely would enter rapidly into production or sale of a market product in the market's area, without incurring significant sunk costs of entry and exit. Firms likely to make any of these supply responses are considered to be 'uncommitted' entrants because their supply response would create new production or sale in the relevant market and because that production or sale could be quickly terminated without significant loss.[7] Uncommitted entrants are capable of making such quick and uncommitted supply responses that they likely influenced the market premerger, would influence it post-merger, and accordingly are considered as market participants at both times. This analysis of market definition and market measurement applies equally to foreign and domestic firms.

If the process of market definition and market measurement identifies one or more relevant markets in which the merging firms are both participants, then the merger is considered to be horizontal. Sections 1.1 through 1.5 describe in greater detail how product and geographic markets will be defined, how market shares will be calculated and how market concentration will be assessed.

1.1 Product Market Definition

The Agency will first define the relevant product market with respect to each of the products of each of the merging firms.[8]

[. . .]

1.11 General Standards

Absent price discrimination, the Agency will delineate the product market to be a product or group of products such that a hypothetical profit-maximizing firm that was the only present and future seller of those products ('monopolist') likely would impose at least a 'small but significant and nontransitory' increase in price. That is, assuming that buyers likely would respond to an increase in price for a tentatively identified product group only by shifting to other products, what would happen? If the alternatives were, in the aggregate, sufficiently attractive at their existing terms of sale, an attempt to raise prices would result in a reduction of sales large enough that the price increase would not prove profitable, and the tentatively identified product group would prove to be too narrow.

Specifically, the Agency will begin with each product (narrowly defined) produced or sold by each merging firm and ask what would happen if a hypothetical monopolist of that product imposed at least a 'small but significant and nontransitory' increase in price, but the terms of sale of all other products remained constant. If, in response to the price increase, the reduction in sales of the product would be large enough that a hypothetical monopolist would not find it profitable to impose such an increase in price, then the Agency will add to the product group the product that is the next-best substitute for the merging firm's product.[9]

In considering the likely reaction of buyers to a price increase, the Agency will take into account all relevant evidence, including, but not limited to, the following:

(1) evidence that buyers have shifted or have considered shifting purchases between products in response to relative changes in price or other competitive variables;
(2) evidence that sellers base business decisions on the prospect of buyer substitution between products in response to relative changes in price or other competitive variables;
(3) the influence of downstream competition faced by buyers in their output markets; and
(4) the timing and costs of switching products.

The price increase question is then asked for a hypothetical monopolist controlling the expanded product group. In performing successive iterations of the price increase test, the hypothetical monopolist will be assumed to pursue maximum profits in deciding whether to raise the prices of any or all of the additional products under its control. This process will continue until a group of products is identified such that a hypothetical monopolist over that group of products would profitably impose at least a 'small but significant and nontransitory' increase, including the price of a product of one of the merging firms. The Agency generally will consider the relevant product market to be the smallest group of products that satisfies this test.

In the above analysis, the Agency will use prevailing prices of the products of the merging firms and possible substitutes for such products, unless premerger circumstances are strongly suggestive of coordinated interaction, in which case the Agency will use a price more reflective of the competitive price.[10] However, the Agency may use likely future prices, absent the merger, when changes in the prevailing prices can be predicted with reasonable reliability. Changes in price may be predicted on the basis of, for example, changes in regulation which affect price either directly or indirectly by affecting costs or demand.

In general, the price for which an increase will be postulated will be whatever is considered to be the price of the product at the stage of the industry being examined.[11] In attempting to determine objectively the effect of a 'small but significant and nontransitory' increase in price, the Agency, in most contexts, will use a price increase of five percent lasting for the foreseeable future. However, what constitutes a 'small but significant and nontransitory' increase in price will depend on the nature of the industry, and the Agency at times may use a price increase that is larger or smaller than five percent.

1.12 Product Market Definition in the Presence of Price Discrimination

The analysis of product market definition to this point has assumed that price discrimination – charging different buyers different prices for the same product, for example – would not be profitable for a hypothetical monopolist. A different analysis applies where price discrimination would be profitable for a hypothetical monopolist.

Existing buyers sometimes will differ significantly in their likelihood of switching to other products in response to a 'small but significant and nontransitory' price increase. If a hypothetical monopolist can identify and price differently to those buyers ('targeted buyers') who would not defeat the targeted price increase by substituting to other products in response to a 'small but significant and nontransitory' price increase for the relevant product, and if other buyers likely would not purchase the relevant product and resell to targeted buyers, then a hypothetical monopolist would profitably impose a discriminatory price increase on sales to targeted buyers. This is true regardless of whether a general increase in price would cause such significant substitution that the price increase would not be profitable. The Agency will consider additional relevant product markets consisting of a particular use or uses by groups of buyers of the product for which a hypothetical monopolist would profitably and separately impose at least a 'small but significant and nontransitory' increase in price.

1.2 Geographic Market Definition

For each product market in which both merging firms participate, the Agency will determine the geographic market or markets in which the firms produce or sell. A single firm may operate in a number of different geographic markets.

1.21 General Standards

Absent price discrimination, the Agency will delineate the geographic market to be a region such that a hypothetical monopolist that was the only present or future producer of the relevant product at locations in that region would profitably impose at least a 'small but significant and nontransitory' increase in price, holding constant the terms of sale for all products produced elsewhere. That is, assuming that buyers likely would respond to a price increase on products produced within the tentative indentified region only by shifting to products produced at locations of production outside the region, what would happen? If those locations of production outside the region were, in the aggregate, sufficiently attractive at their existing terms of sale, an attempt to raise price would result in a reduction in sales large enough that the price increase would not prove profitable, and the tentatively identified geographic area would prove to be too narrow.

In defining the geographic market or markets affected by a merger, the Agency will begin with the location of each merging firm (or each plant of a multiplant firm) and ask what would happen if a hypothetical monopolist of the relevant product at that point imposed at least a 'small but significant and nontransitory' increase in price, but the terms of sale at all other locations remained constant. If, in response to the price increase, the reduction in sales of the product at that location would be large enough that a hypothetical monopolist producing or selling the relevant product at the merging firm's location would not find it profitable to impose such an increase in price, then the Agency will add the location from which production is the next-best substitute for production at the merging firm's location.

In considering the likely reaction of buyers to a price increase, the Agency will take into account all relevant evidence, including, but not limited to, the following:

(1) evidence that buyers have shifted or have considered shifting purchases between different geographic locations in response to relative changes in price or other competitive variables;
(2) evidence that sellers base business decisions on the prospect of buyer substitution between geographic locations in response to relative changes in price or other competitive variables;
(3) the influence of downstream competition faced by buyers in their output markets; and

(4) the timing and costs of switching suppliers.

The price increase question is then asked for a hypothetical monopolist controlling the expanded group of locations. In performing successive iterations of the price increase test, the hypothetical monopolist will be assumed to pursue maximum profits in deciding whether to raise the price at any or all of the additional locations under its control. This process will continue until a group of locations is identified such that a hypothetical monopolist over that group of locations would profitably impose at least a 'small but significant and nontransitory' increase, including the price charged at a location of one of the merging firms.

The 'smallest market' principle will be applied as it is in product market definition. The price for which an increase will be postulated, what constitutes a 'small but significant and nontransitory' increase in price, and the substitution decisions of consumers all will be determined in the same way in which they are determined in product market definition.

1.22 Geographic Market Definition in the Presence of Price Discrimination

The analysis of geographic market definition to this point has assumed that geographic price discrimination – charging different prices net of transportation costs for the same product to buyers in different areas, for example – would not be profitable for a hypothetical monopolist. However, if a hypothetical monopolist can identify and price differently to buyers in certain areas ('targeted buyers') who would not defeat the targeted price increase by substituting to more distant sellers in response to a 'small but significant and nontransitory' price increase for the relevant product, and if other buyers likely would not purchase the relevant product and resell to targeted buyers,[12] then a hypothetical monopolist would profitably impose a discriminatory price increase. This is true even where a general price increase would cause such significant substitution that the price increase would not be profitable. The Agency will consider additional geographic markets consisting of particular locations of buyers for which a hypothetical monopolist would profitably and separately impose at least a 'small but significant and nontransitory' increase in price.

1.3 Identification of Firms that Participate in the Relevant Market

1.31 Current Producers or Sellers

The Agency's identification of firms that participate in the relevant market begins with all firms that currently produce or sell in the relevant market. This includes vertically integrated firms to the extent that such inclusion accurately reflects their competitive significance in the relevant market prior to the merger. To the extent that the analysis under Section 1.1 indicates that used, reconditioned or recycled goods are included in the relevant market, market participants will include firms that produce or sell such goods and that likely would offer those goods in competition with other relevant products.

1.32 Firms That Participate Through Supply Response

In addition, the Agency will identify other firms not currently producing or selling the relevant product in the relevant area as participating in the relevant market if their inclusion would more accurately reflect probable supply responses. The firms are termed 'uncommitted entrants.' These supply responses must be likely to occur within one year and without the expenditure of significant sunk costs of entry and exit, in response to a 'small but significant and nontransitory' price increase. If a firm has the technological capability to achieve such an uncommitted supply response, but likely would not (e.g. because difficulties in achieving product acceptance, distribution, or production would render such a response unprofitable), that firm will not be considered to be a market participant. The competitive significance of supply responses that require more time or that require firms to incur significant sunk costs of entry and exit will be considered in entry analysis. See Section 3.[13]

Sunk costs are the acquisition costs of tangible and intangible assets that cannot be recovered through the redeployment of these assets outside the relevant market, i.e. costs uniquely incurred to supply the relevant product and geographic market. Examples of sunk costs may include market-specific investments in production facilities, technologies, marketing (including product acceptance), research and development, regulatory approvals, and testing. A significant sunk cost is one which would not be recouped within one year of the commencement of the supply response, assuming a 'small but significant and nontransitory' price increase in the relevant market. In this context, a 'small but significant and nontransitory' price increase will be determined in the same way in which it is determined in product market definition, except the price increase will be assumed to last one year. In some instances, it may be difficult to calculate sunk costs with precision. Accordingly, when necessary, the Agency will make an overall assessment of the extent of sunk costs for firms likely to participate through supply responses.

These supply responses may give rise to new production of products in the relevant product market or new sources of supply in the relevant geographic market. Alternatively, where price discrimination is likely so that the relevant market is defined in terms of a targeted group of buyers, these supply responses serve to identify new sellers to the targeted buyers. Uncommitted supply responses may occur in several different ways: by the switching or extension of existing assets to production or sale in the relevant market; or by the construction or acquisition of assets that enable production or sale in the relevant market.

1.32.1 Production Substitution and Extension: The Switching or Extension of Existing Assets to Production or Sale in the Relevant Market

The productive and distributive assets of a firm sometimes can be used to produce and sell either the relevant products or products that buyers do not regard as good substitutes. Production substitution refers to the shift by a firm in the use of assets from producing and selling one product to producing and selling another. Production extension refers to the use of those assets, for example, existing brand names and reputation, both for their current production and for the production of the relevant product. Depending upon the speed of that shift and the extent of sunk costs incurred in the shift or extension, the potential for production substitution or extension may necessitate treating as market participants firms that do not currently produce the relevant product.[14]

If a firm has existing assets that likely would be shifted or extended into production and sale of the relevant product within one year, and without incurring significant sunk costs of entry and exit, in response to a 'small but significant and nontransitory' increase in price for only the relevant product, the Agency will treat that firm as a market participant. In assessing whether a firm is such a market participant, the Agency will take into account the costs of substitution or extension relative to the profitability of sales at the elevated price, and whether the firm's capacity is elsewhere committed or elsewhere so profitably employed that such capacity likely would not be available to respond to an increase in price in the market.

1.32.2 Obtaining New Assets for Production or Sale of the Relevant Product

A firm may also be able to enter into production or sale in the relevant market within one year and without the expenditure of significant sunk costs of entry and exit, in response to a 'small but significant and nontransitory' increase in price for only the relevant product, even if the firm is newly organized or is an existing firm without products or productive assets closely related to the relevant market. If new firms, or existing firms without closely related products or productive assets, likely would enter into production or sale in the relevant market within one year without the expenditure of significant sunk costs of entry and exit, the Agency will treat those firms as market participants.

1.4 Calculating Market Shares

1.41 General Approach

The Agency normally will calculate market shares for all firms (or plants) identified as market participants in Section 1.3 based on the total sales or capacity currently devoted to the relevant market together with that which likely would be devoted to the relevant market in response to a 'small but significant and nontransitory' price increase. Market shares can be expressed either in dollar terms through measurement of sales, shipments, or production, or in physical terms through measurement of sales, shipments, production, capacity, or reserves.

Market shares will be calculated using the best indicator of firms' future competitive significance. Dollar sales or shipments generally will be used if firms are distinguished primarily by differentiation of their products. Unit sales generally will be used if firms are distinguished primarily on the basis of their relative advantages in serving different buyers or groups of buyers. Physical capacity or reserves generally will be used if it is these measures that most effectively distinguish firms.[15] Typically, annual data are used, but where individual sales are large and infrequent so that annual data may be unrepresentative, the Agency may measure market shares over a longer period of time.

In measuring a firm's market share, the Agency will not include its sales or capacity to the extent that the firm's capacity is committed or so profitably employed outside the relevant market that it would not be available to respond to an increase in price in the market.

1.42 Price Discrimination Markets

When markets are defined on the basis of price discrimination (Sections 1.12 and 1.22), the Agency will include only sales likely to be made into, or capacity likely to be used to supply, the relevant market in response to a 'small but significant and nontransitory' price increase.

1.4 Special Factors Affecting Foreign Firms

Market shares will be assigned to foreign competitors in the same way in which they are assigned to domestic competitors. However, if exchange rates fluctuate significantly, so that comparable dollar calculations on an annual basis may be unrepresentative, the Agency may measure market shares over a period longer than one year.

If shipments from a particular country to the United States are subject to a quota, the market shares assigned to firms in that country will not exceed the amount of shipments by such firms allowed under the quota.[16] In the case of restraints that limit imports to some percentage of the total amount of the product sold in the United States (i.e. percentage quotas), a domestic price increase that reduced domestic consumption also would reduce the volume of imports into the United States. Accordingly, actual import sales and capacity data will be reduced for purposes of calculating market shares. Finally, a single market share may be assigned to a country or group of countries if firms in that country or group of countries act in coordination.

1.5 Concentration and Market Shares

Market concentration is a function of the number of firms in a market and their respective market shares. As an aid to the interpretation of market data, the Agency will use the Herfindahl–Hirschman Index (HHI) of market concentration. The HHI is calculated by summing the squares of the individual market shares of all the participants.[17] Unlike the four-firm concentration ratio, the HHI reflects both the distribution of the market shares of the top four firms and the composition of the market outside the top four firms. It also gives proportionately greater weight to the market shares of the larger firms, in accord with their relative importance in competitive interactions.

The Agency divides the spectrum of market concentration as measured by the HHI into three regions that can be broadly characterized as unconcentrated (HHI below 1000), moderately concentrated (HHI between 1000 and 1800), and highly concentrated (HHI above 1800). Although the resulting regions provide a useful framework for merger analysis, the numerical divisions suggest greater precision than is possible with the available economic tools and information. Other things being equal, cases falling just above and just below a threshold present comparable competitive issues.

1.51 General Standards

In evaluating horizontal mergers, the Agency will consider both the post-merger market concentration and the increase in concentration resulting from the merger.[18] Market concentration is a useful indicator of the likely potential competitive effect of a merger. The general standards for horizontal mergers are as follows:

(*a*) Post-merger HHI below 1000. The Agency regards markets in this region to be unconcentrated. Mergers resulting in unconcentrated markets are unlikely to have adverse competitive effects and ordinarily require no further analysis.

(*b*) Post-merger HHI between 1000 and 1800. The Agency regards markets in this region to be moderately concentrated. Mergers producing an increase in the HHI of less than 100 points in moderately concentrated markets post-merger are unlikely to have adverse competitive consequences and ordinarily require no further analysis. Mergers producing an increase in the HHI of more than 100 points in moderately concentrated markets post-merger potentially raise significant competitive concerns depending on the factors set forth in sections 2–5 of the *Guidelines*.

(*c*) Post-merger HHI above 1800. The Agency regards markets in this region to be highly concentrated. Mergers producing an increase in the HHI of less than 50 points, even in highly concentrated markets post-merger, are unlikely to have adverse competitive consequences and ordinarily require no further analysis. Mergers producing an increase in the HHI of more than 50 points in highly concentrated markets post-merger potentially raise significant competitive concerns, depending on the factors set forth in sections 2–5 of the *Guidelines*. Where the post-merger HHI exceeds 1800, it will be presumed that mergers producing an increase in the HHI of more than 100 points are likely to create or enhance market power or facilitate its exercise. The presumption may be overcome by a showing that factors set forth in sections 2–5 of the *Guidelines* make it unlikely that the merger will create or enhance market power or facilitate its exercise, in light of market concentration and market shares.

1.52 Factors Affecting the Significance of Market Shares and Concentration

The post-merger level of market concentration and the change in concentration resulting from a merger affect the degree to which a merger raises competitive concerns. However, in some situations, market share and market concentration data may either understate or overstate the likely future competitive significance of a firm or firms in the market or the impact of a merger. The following are examples of such situations.

1.52.1 Changing Market Conditions

Market concentration and market share data of necessity are based on historical evidence. However, recent or ongoing changes in the market may indicate that the current market share of a particular firm either understates or overstates the firm's future competitive significance. For example, if a new technology that is important to long-term competitive viability is available to other firms in the market, but is not available to a particular firm, the Agency may conclude that the historical market share of that firm overstates its future competitive significance. The Agency will consider reasonably predictable effects of recent or ongoing changes in market conditions in interpreting market concentration and market share data.

1.52.2 Degree of Difference Between the Products and Locations in the Market and Substitutes Outside the Market

All else equal, the magnitude of potential competitive harm from a merger is greater if a hypothetical monopolist would raise price within the relevant market by substantially more than a 'small but significant and nontransitory' amount. This may occur when the demand substitutes outside the relevant market, as a group, are not close substitutes for the products and locations within the relevant market. There thus may be a wide gap in the chain of demand substitutes at the edge of the product and geographic market. Under such circumstances, more market power is at stake in the relevant market than in a market in which a hypothetical monopolist would raise price by exactly five percent.

NOTES

1 15 U.S.C. @ 18 (1988). Mergers subject to section 7 are prohibited if their effect 'may be substantially to lessen competition, or to tend to create a monopoly'.

2 15 U.S.C. @ 1 (1988). Mergers subject to section 1 are prohibited if they constitute a 'contract, combination [. . .] or conspiracy in restraint of trade'.

3 15 U.S.C. @ 45 (1988). Mergers subject to section 5 are prohibited if they constitute an 'unfair method of competition'.

4 These *Guidelines* update the *Merger Guidelines* issued by the US Department of Justice in 1984 and the *Statement of Federal Trade Commission Concerning Horizontal Mergers* issued in 1982. *The Merger Guidelines* may be revised from time to time as necessary to reflect any significant changes in enforcement policy or to clarify aspects of any existing policy.

5 For example, the burden with respect to efficiency and failure continues to reside with the proponents of the merger.

6 Sellers with market power also lessen competition on dimensions other than price, such as product quality, service, or innovation.

7 Probable supply responses that require the entrant to incur significant sunk costs of entry and exit are not part of market measurement, but are included in the analysis of the significance of entry. See Section 3. Entrants that must commit substantial sunk costs are regarded as 'committed' entrants because those sunk costs make entry irreversible in the short term without forgoing that investment; thus the likelihood of their entry must be evaluated with regard to their long-term profitability.

8 Although discussed separately, product market definition and geographic market definition are interrelated. In particular, the extent to which buyers of a particular product would shift to other products in the event of a 'small but significant and nontransitory' increase in price must be evaluated in the context of the relevant geographic market.

9 Throughout the *Guidelines*, the term 'next best substitute' refers to the alternative which, if available in unlimited quantities at constant prices, would account for the greatest value of diversion of demand in response to a 'small but significant and nontransitory' price increase.

10 The terms of sale of all other products are held constant in order to focus market definition on the behavior of consumers. Movements in the terms of sale for other products, as may result from the behavior of producers of those products, are accounted for in the analysis of competitive effects and entry. See Sections 2 and 3.

11 For example, in a merger between retailers, the relevant price would be the retail price of a product to consumers. In the case of a merger among oil pipelines, the relevant price would be the tariff – the price of the transportation service.

12 This arbitrage is inherently impossible for many services and is particularly difficult where the product is sold on a delivered basis and where transportation costs are a

significant percentage of the final cost.

13 If uncommitted entrants likely would also remain in the market and would meet the entry tests of timeliness, likelihood and sufficiency, and thus would likely deter anticompetitive mergers or deter or counteract the competitive effects of concern (see Section 3), the Agency will consider the impact of those firms in the entry analysis.

14 Under other analytical approaches, production substitution sometimes has been reflected in the description of the product market. For example, the product market for stamped metal products such as automobile hub caps might be described as 'light metal stampings', a production process rather than a product. The Agency believes that the approach described in the text provides a more clearly focused method of incorporating this factor in merger analysis. If production substitution among a group of products is nearly universal among the firms selling one or more of those products, however, the Agency may use an aggregate description of those markets as a matter of convenience.

15 Where all firms have, on a forward-looking basis, an equal likelihood of securing sales, the Agency will assign firms equal shares.

16 The constraining effect of the quota on the importer's ability to expand sales is relevant to the evaluation of potential adverse competitive effects. See Section 2.

17 For example, a market consisting of four firms with market shares of 30 percent, 30 percent, 20 percent and 20 percent has an HHI of 2600 (30<2> + 30<2> + 20<2> + 20<2> = 2600). The HHI ranges from 10,000 (in the case of a pure monopoly) to a number approaching zero (in the case of an atomistic market). Although it is desirable to include all firms in the calculation, lack of information about small firms is not critical because such firms do not affect the HHI significantly.

18 The increase in concentration as measured by the HHI can be calculated independently of the overall market concentration by doubling the product of the market shares of the merging firms. For example, the merger of firms with shares of 5 percent and 10 percent of the market would increase the HHI by 100 ($5 \times 10 \times 2 = 100$). The explanation for this technique is as follows: In calculating the HHI before the merger, the market shares of the merging firms are squared individually: (*a*)<2> + (*b*)<2>. After the merger, the sum of those shares would be squared: (*a* + *b*)<2>, which equals *a*<2> + 2*ab* + *b*<2>. The increase in the HHI therefore is represented by 2*ab*.

FURTHER READING

See the following works on the ***Horizontal Merger Guidelines.***

Arquit, K. (1992), 'Perspectives on the 1992 US government *Horizontal Merger Guidelines*', 61 *Antitrust Law Journal*, 121.

Ordover, J. A. and Baker, J. (1992), 'Entry analysis under the 1992 *Horizontal Merger Guidelines*', 61 *Antitrust Law Journal*.

Pitofsky, R. (1992), 'Merger analysis in the '90s: the *Guidelines* and beyond', 61 *Antitrust Law Journal*, 147.

Weiss, A. (1992), 'Using the efficiencies defense in horizontal mergers', 37 *Antitrust Bulletin*, 123.

Yao, D. and De Santi, S. S. (1993), 'Innovation issues under the 1992 *Merger Guidelines*', 61 *Antitrust Law Journal*, 505.

See also the following works on merger law.

Afonso, M. (1992), 'A catalogue of merger defenses under European and United States antitrust law', 33 *Harvard International Law Journal*, 1.

American Bar Association (1986), *Horizontal Mergers: Law and Policy* (American Bar Association, Chicago).

Brittan, L. (1991), *Competition Policy and Merger Control in the Single European Market* (Grotius, Cambridge).

Collins, W. and Loftis, J. (1988), *Non-Horizontal Mergers: Law and Policy* (American Bar Association, Chicago).

Coopers and Lybrand (1989), *Barriers to Takeovers in the European Community: A Study by Coopers & Lybrand for the DTI (HMSO, London).*

Espen Eckbo, B. (1990) 'Competition and wealth effects of horizontal mergers', in F. Mathewson, M. Trebilcock and M. Walker (eds). *The Law and Economics of Competition Policy* (The Fraser Institute, Vancouver).

Fairburn, J. and Kay, J. (eds) (1989), *Mergers and Merger Policy*, Oxford University Press, Oxford).

Langeheine, B. (1992), 'Judicial review in the field of merger control', *Journal of Business Law*, 121.

Lipworth, S. (1990), 'Development of merger control in the UK and the European Community', The Denning Lecture 1990, reproduced in R. Miller (ed.), *The Monopolies and Mergers Yearbook* (Blackwell, London).

Miller, R. (ed.) (1992), *The Monopolies and Mergers Yearbook: March 1989 to December 1990* (Blackwell, Oxford).

Monopolies and Mergers Commission, *The Role of the Commission*, 4th edn (HMSO London).

Morris, J. and Mosteller, G. (1991), 'Defining markets for merger analysis', 36 *Antitrust Bulletin*, 599.

Morse, G. (1991), 'The city code on takeovers and mergers: self-regulation or self-protection?', *Journal of Business Law*, 509.

Note (1992), 'From the United States to Europe: a comparative study of production joint ventures', 2 *Duke Journal of Comparative and International Law*, 163.

Office of Fair Trading (1983), *Mergers: A Guide to the Procedures under the Fair Trading Act 1973*, 2nd edn (HMSO, London).

Ordover, J. and Baker, J. (1992), 'Entry analysis under the 1992 *Horizontal Merger Guidelines*', 61 *Antitrust Law Journal*, 139.

Peacock, A. and Bannock, G. (1991), *Corporate Takeovers and the Public Interest: Report of an Inquiry Conducted for the Joseph Rowntree Foundation by the David Hume Institute* (Aberdeen University Press, Aberdeen).

Praeger, B. (1991), *Premerger Notification Practice Manual*, (ABA, Chicago).

Rowley, J. W. and Baker, D. I. (1991) *International Mergers: The Antitrust Process* (Sweet and Maxwell, London).

Veljanovski, C. and Darcey, M. (1992), Econometrics and the Commission', 142 *New Law Journal*.

21

THE PROCESS OF ASSESSMENT

The Trade and Industry Committee of the House of Commons conducted an enquiry into the effectiveness of merger control in the UK. This enquiry followed a **Blue Paper** issued by the Department of Trade and Industry in 1988 (section 22.6) and consequent reforms to the Fair Trading Act 1973, introduced through the Companies Act 1989 (included in the provisions extracted above (section 20.1). The Trade and Industry Committee took a great deal of evidence from those concerned with merger control. Its **first report** was published in 1992. Although the government response to the first report did not signify an intention to make any further changes to the legislation in the short term, the report – extracted below – provides a useful critical guide to the processes of merger control.

21.1 Trade and Industry Committee, *First Report on Takeovers and Mergers*, HC Paper 90, Session 1991–92

THE WORK OF THE OFFICE OF FAIR TRADING

76. Work on mergers accounted for only 7.6% of the OFT's resources of £14.7 million and 360 permanent staff in 1990 [. . .]. Thus £1.1 million was spent on examining 261 qualifying mergers involving assets of target companies worth £100,000 million. The OFT has a separate Estimate (Class IV Vote 8) in the Supply Estimates. Expenditure is planned to grow to £20.5 million and staff to 488 in 1993–94. Since 1st October 1990 fees have to be paid to the OFT by companies involved in mergers.

[. . .]

77. The Office of Fair Trading has told us 'the UK system is . . . an administrative one with a considerable degree of discretion for the DGFT, the MMC and the Secretary of State'. The OFT is the first of the competition authorites to be involved in any proposed merger. Companies can inform the OFT of their intentions under the 'confidential guidance' procedure. Under the Companies Act 1989 a system of voluntary pre-notification was introduced.

78. If the merging companies notify the OFT in advance they can normally expect to be told within a month whether a reference to the MMC will be made. Otherwise the Secretary of State has up to six months, from the time a merger proposal has been made public, to decide whether to make a reference. Since 1 April 1990, 67 cases have been dealt with under the pre-notification procedure, a fifth of all cases considered by the OFT. Of these, 60% were cleared by the OFT within the minimum period of 20 working days.

PRE-NOTIFICATION

79. We have also considered whether pre-notification should be made mandatory. Pre-notification of large mergers to the European Commission is mandatory. In the USA all mergers above the set thresholds have to be notified. Sir Gordon Borrie, when asked about this, told us 'I do not think it would be necessary or useful . . . because I cannot think of any merger or takeover in recent years that we have not known about anyway'. We feel, however, that this complicates the process by making it informal and uncertain.

80. **We recommend that pre-notification of mergers involving assets of more than £30 million should be made mandatory.**

UNDERTAKINGS IN LIEU OF REFERENCE

81. Another recent development enables companies to avoid a reference to the MMC by agreeing to dispose of particular enterprises. The Companies Act 1989 gave the OFT powers to accept undertakings from companies to divest themselves of certain enterprises in order to avoid undue anti-competitive overlap following the merger and thereby avoid reference to the MMC. This provision has been used in only three cases. Sir Gordon Borrie told us that this procedure could work in only a small number of cases 'because there simply are not that many mergers where there are bits of this business or bits of that business which can be hived off, sold off, as an entity'.

82. The practice of seeking undertakings in lieu of further proceedings by the competition authorities is a very normal practice in Canada and indeed is seen as a key function of Canada's Bureau of Competition Policy. An insistence on undertakings, as a condition of approval of a merger, should not become an excuse for determining how a company should be run, but we see great merit in developing such a route to the speedy resolution of potential mergers, to avoid a reference to the MMC. Much evidence favoured this and in particular that the OFT should notify companies privately of a provisional intention to refer, thereby initiating negotiations with the bidding company to try to resolve the matter without a reference.

CRITERIA FOR OFT CONSIDERATION

84. Mergers qualify for consideration by the OFT if they create or enhance a 25% market share or if the value of assets taken over exceeds £30 million. The assets test threshold has not been raised in line with inflation since 1984. In 1990 eight references were recommended on the grounds that a market share of more than 25% would be created, five on the grounds that assets of more than £30 million were involved and 12 on both grounds combined [. . .]. GKN told us that the OFT 'often seem reluctant to use the 25% market share criterion . . . because this test is more open to dispute'.

85. The European Commission, the US competition authorities and the Canadian competition authorities all use thresholds based on turnover or assets rather than market share when deciding whether to investigate mergers. They do of course use market share tests when subsequently deciding the effect on competition of a proposed merger.

86. Professor Kay told us that there was a fair degree of consistency about what size of market share would cause problems with UK authorities:

> if the combined market shares of the two firms involved are under 20%, it is unlikely that there will be a negative verdict but if it is over 30% there is a high and increasing possibility of a negative verdict.

87. It has been put to us by Coopers & Lybrand Deloitte that too much attention has been given by the OFT to very small markets. They argue that the economic impact of any reduction in competition in small markets is very limited. In 1988–90 there were 12 references involving markets of less than £65 million, including one of less than £7 million.

89. A reference to the MMC is expensive and time consuming for the companies concerned. Companies need a degree of predictability. 'It remains exceedingly difficult for businesses to ascertain whether a proposed merger is likely to be contrary to government competition policy', we were told by Scottish & Newcastle. Nestlé said: 'the benefits of . . . flexibility, in national terms, are somewhat offset from a corporate perspective by the uncertainty to which it gives rise'.

90. On the other hand, Professor Kay told us that 'after a slightly rocky period in the early 1980s, after the guidelines for making references were clarified in 1984, there has been a fair degree of predictability about what bids were likely to be referred and what bids were not likely to be referred'. The DTI witnesses acknowleged that there was a long-standing debate between the relative advantages of predictability and flexibility in any competition or anti-trust system:

> The remaining flexibility of the system is very much to everyone's advantage, rather than having a mechanistic system which could lead to unnecessary references at enormous burden to industry as well as to the authorities concerned.

UNDERSTANDING OF OFT CRITERIA

91. Predictability of how authorities are likely to act in any given set of circumstances depends on knowledge and understanding of the reasons for the past decisions of those authorities. Several witnesses commented on the need for the regular publication of an analysis of the basis on which cleared cases have not required further investigation and of a comprehensive set of reasoned OFT decisions. Although the various competition authorities have distinct tasks, it appears that the criteria under which they operate are not clearly understood. A poll of senior executives of UK companies revealed that a slim majority found the OFT grounds for reference well-known; the position was reversed on the MMC's ground rules [. . .].

[. . .]

92. In both the USA and Canada the competition authorities have published extensive guidelines on mergers, a practice we feel is overdue for introduction in the UK. Since the United States procedure is conducted through public hearings in court or before the Federal Trade Commission, the whole process is more open and therefore better understood. The position in the market of the merging companies is analysed in the USA by reference to a statistical index called the Herfindahl–Hirschman Index (HHI). While not above criticism on other grounds, this index does provide an objective way of calculating unconcentrated, moderately concentrated and concentrated markets for the purpose of deciding the effect of a proposed merger on a particular market. We note that the MMC, in evidence to the Committee, has now set out the factors it takes into account in assessing competition.

93. After we had finished taking evidence the MMC published a booklet on *Assessing Competition*. This sets out the factors the MMC takes into account in considering individual merger cases. We understand that this booklet is based on existing MMC internal guidance. We welcome its publication as a useful step in improving general understanding of how mergers are considered by the regulatory authorities and in providing practitioners with a firm framework in which they can present their case to the competition authorities.

94. The MMC's reasons are published in specific reports on each case referred to it. A brief explanation of the reason to refer is made by the DTI, but no reasons are given for a decision not to refer. In each case the DTI announces whether the decision was in accordance with the DGFT's advice. By contrast with the systems in the USA and Canada, the UK arrangements will seem too secretive. While we favour greater openness, we recognise that it may not be without risk.

95. Some reasons may be based, in part

at least, on commercially confidential information supplied by the parties, partial disclosure of which could be misleading. The actions of the OFT and the Secretary of State can, in limited circumstances, be challenged in the courts through an application for judicial review. Full declaration of the reasons for a reference might be construed as prejudging the case and fettering the Secretary of State's discretion when he eventually comes to consider the MMC's report.

96. The Secretary of State defended the refusal to give reasons for non-reference by analogy to the treatment of the release from custody of a suspected criminal. We recognize the public policy implicit in the general prohibition on the criminal law agencies from stating why a suspect has been discharged, but find the analogy with the administrative regulation of mergers quite inappropriate. There is often great public awareness of a particular proposed merger and strongly-held beliefs in some quarters that the transaction merits reference to the MMC on public interest grounds. We believe that public confidence and understanding would be improved if more detailed reasons for reference were given and if reasons for non-reference were stated in appropriate cases.

97. **We recommend that the Secretary of State should give a more detailed explanation of the grounds for his decision to refer a merger to the MMC and that a statement of the reasons for a decision not to refer should be made in respect of the larger and more important transactions where there is a significant public interest in the Secretary of State's decision.**

98. Not only is there no general disclosure of reasons for OFT decisions, but the parties in particular cases are not given full reasons for a reference to the MMC. This makes them wonder what they could have done to avoid a reference and what issues they have to address in the forthcoming MMC hearings. Courage Ltd. thought that the OFT should give clearer guidance on possible concerns in respect of a proposed transaction and should enter into informal discussion which might avert a reference to the MMC.

99. The OFT does occasionally give confidential guidance to companies under a procedure which requires the OFT to get the approval of the Secretary of State. In such cases the OFT has to give a view without allowing other affected parties the opportunity to state their case. We were told that the OFT is reluctant to give guidance except in straightforward cases. The National Consumer Council called for greater transparency about confidential guidance and recommended that an annual analysis of confidential guidance by OFT should be produced.

MERGERS PANEL

100. There is one little known stage in the process between the OFT's own consideration of a proposed merger and the DGFT's advice to the Secretary of State. A Mergers Panel, comprising representatives of different government departments with an interest in the particular merger, meets under the chairmanship of the DGFT. It is questionable whether this stage should be conducted under the aegis of the theoretically independent DGFT or whether it belongs in the DTI as part of the ministerial decision-making machinery. [. . .]

101. The Mergers Panel also appears to have a role in collating the views of different government departments on large takeovers before the Government's attitude is communicated to the European Commission. The Secretary of State told us that the DGFT would gather views from interested parties on the competition and other aspects so that 'any representations about a large European-scale merger would be fully and carefully considered and an expression of our understanding of the facts would be made to the European Commission'. The lack of clarity over the role of the Mergers Panel is a potential source of problems. We would like to see a clarification of the role and status of the Mergers Panel.

[. . .]

THE WORK OF THE MONOPOLIES AND MERGERS COMMISSION

110. A significant proportion of all UK mergers qualify for reference to the MMC. Mergers can only be blocked by the Secretary of State, or have conditions imposed for their clearance, if they have been referred to the MMC and found to be against the public interest. Members of the Commission are appointed for renewable three-year terms. Apart from the full-time Chairman, there are three Deputy Chairmen who work 2.5 days a week and 32 part-time Commissioners who are expected to work for 1.5 days a week. [. . .] The Chairman told us that most members have wide professional and business experience. Only four are qualified scientists or engineers. This appears to us to leave the MMC with too few Commissioners qualified to judge the technical merits of cases involving manufacturing companies and issues concerning research and development. An MMC inquiry usually takes three months and is conducted by a panel of four or five members of the Commission.

111. The Commission's proceedings are conducted in formal hearings before a panel of Commissioners. According to the Chairman 'our role is both investigative and judicial'. He made it plain to us that he regards himself as bound by section 84 of the Fair Trading Act 1973 and not by the policy of the incumbent Secretary of State. The DGFT told us that the MMC only makes an adverse finding if there really is a high probability that the merger will be adverse to the public interest.

112. The MMC investigatory process has been described to us as 'slow and inflexible' and 'cumbersome and outdated'. Another witness said that the MMC seeks large quantities of information, some of which has already been supplied to OFT and that the MMC should tell the parties the areas of concern and the areas on which no further evidence is needed. A firm of solicitors said that the scope of questioning at MMC hearings leaves parties uncertain as to where main concerns lie. A firm of accountants added that the lack of focus makes it difficult to anticipate MMC's concerns.

113. We were also told, on the one hand, that the MMC should be more critically searching of third party evidence and, on the other, that there is some doubt about the fairness of MMC procedures to third parties. A company which has seen both sides of the MMC procedure told us that at present there does not seem to be any uniform fact-gathering procedure and that both parties should be required to submit certain basic information in a common format. Grand Metropolitan, with considerable experience of the MMC, made the practical proposal that proofs of evidence, with commercially sensitive information deleted, should be exchanged in advance to enable parties to exercise a right of reply and to save time at formal Commission hearings.

114. The MMC must observe the rules of natural justice and therefore currently the MMC seeks to inform the principal parties in a reference of any adverse contentions put forward by other parties. Nonetheless, particularly in strongly contested cases, a principal party may be able more effectively to rebut the opponent's case if the opposing submissions are exchanged, and, subject to the question of business secrets, we see no reason in principle why a more open procedure of this kind should not be adopted.

[. . .]

MMC RESOURCES

[. . .]

125. We accept that Commissioners with relevant experience and sufficient seniority are a vary scarce resource. We are also concerned at the relatively poor representation of people with direct industrial experience and the difficulty of recruiting active businessmen from the regions of the UK. One possible remedy would be to have more full-time and professionally qualified Commissioners. Another would be to have a larger panel of Commissioners, with a

wider range of professional experience, who would be called on less frequently but used for inquiries where their own experience was relevant (as is the case with the telecommunications and newspaper panels of the MMC).

126. **We recommend that the three Deputy Chairmanships of the MMC become full-time appointments and that the panel of qualified people from which Commissioners can be drawn for part-time work should be broadened.**

127. We recognise that there is a problem of consistency in the judgments reached by the Commission. This would be to some extent overcome by our proposal that there should be four full-time Commissioners (Chairman and three deputies) who would chair all inquiries and who would act collegiately in approving every report. The five Commissioners of the US Federal Trade Commission, the role of which has similarities with the MMC's, work full-time. They are political nominees appointed, subject to the consent of the US Senate, for a period of seven years. The Chairman holds office during the President's pleasure.

[. . .]

284. Throughout our inquiry we have considered whether, under the current government policy in which competition is seen as almost the only criterion when judging mergers, it is necessary to have three separate decision-making bodies: the Secretary of State, the OFT and the MMC. We believe that the final decision-making role of the Secretary of State should be retained. We have already stated our support for wider considerations than just competition being taken into account in UK policy on takeovers and mergers. The key issue is how the public interest should best be represented in the process, while seeking to avoid a regulatory system which is too cumbersome.

[. . .]

A SINGLE BODY?

286. The DGFT told us 'there could be certain advantages in the two bodies being joined together'. The Secretary of State, however, told us 'there is an advantage . . . in having a separate body deciding on referral from the one that is to make the judgement'. The Competition Law Working Party of the UK Bars and Law Societies favoured keeping the two stages separate. We note also that a majority of senior executives of UK companies surveyed preferred keeping the MMC independent from policiticans and civil servants and did not favour combining it with the OFT.

[. . .]

287. It must remain questionable whether the present separate process is an efficient way of handling matters. It seems that the OFT's examination is rather superficial. We do not believe that it has the necessary resources to undertake more than a cursory examination of the competition consequences of a proposed merger. It certainly is not well-enough equipped to judge other public interest factors, even should the Director General be more inclined than at present to give greater consideration to such aspects. We were offered many alternative models.

288. Scottish & Newcastle Breweries plc argued that the DTI's role of promoting industry and protecting the consumer interest should be separated. Ernst and Young suggested a model in which the MMC would be the neutral arbiter, hearing not just the parties and outside interests, but also hearing the DTI putting the case for economic development and the OFT as the 'advocate of competition'. The DGFT himself, BAT, the National Consumer Council and Kingfisher suggested that the OFT's role be confined to assessing competition issues, with wider public interest matters left to the Secretary of State for consideration.

289. The remaining issue is whether other public interest issues should be examined at the same time as competition. If it is decided that the existing structure be kept, then it should be made clear that the DGFT will consider all public interest issues equally with competition. The Secretary of State would not have powers to prevent reference from the DGFT to the MMC but

he would retain the final decision on the merger. Nonetheless, we favour a change in the structure: the creation of a single body.

290. Therefore we suggest for consideration a new structure for handling mergers. This would be to separate from the OFT the relatively small proportion of its work that relates to mergers and confine the OFT to its wider consumer protection role. The merger work, including confidential guidance, prenotification and undertakings in lieu of a reference would be combined with the existing MMC into a single new Authority. We suggest that it might be called the Competition and Mergers Authority. It seems more appropriate that all competition issues, including the responsibilities currently exercised by the OFT and MMC in relation to restrictive practices, Competition Act cases and monopolies, as well as mergers, should be considered by the same body.

291. Combining both the preliminary examination and the more detailed scrutiny of competition issues in one body provides an opportunity for expertise to be built up: knowledge of the companies, the appropriate industrial sectors and the nature of the market. Consideration of non-competition issues by the same body would enable that expertise to be drawn on, with a consequential saving of time and costs in the investigation. A two-stage process within one body is now what happens for large scale mergers dealt with by the European Commission, but it differs in that the European Commission deals almost entirely with competition issues.

292. One argument in favour of the present structure is that consideration of the competition and other issues by two separate bodies (the OFT and the MMC) ensures greater fairness. The Committee is concerned that any change in the structure must not substantially reduce the fairness of the merger procedures. It believes that within a single authority there could well be a division of function. One task force within the Competition and Mergers Authority could be responsible for gathering the evidence and forming a prima facie view on the merits of the merger. If a full investigation was initiated, the Authority itself, assisted by a separate task force and after formal hearings, would make its recommendation to the Secretary of State.

21.2 Council Regulation (EEC) No. 4064/89 on the control of concentrations between undertakings OJ 1989 No. L 395/1

[Preamble and remaining articles, see section 20.3]

[. . .]

ARTICLE 2 APPRAISAL OF CONCENTRATIONS

1. Concentrations within the scope of this Regulation shall be appraised in accordance with the following provisions with a view to establishing whether or not they are compatible with the common market. In making this appraisal, the Commission shall take into account:

(*a*) the need to maintain and develop effective competition within the common market in view of, among other things, the structure of all the markets concerned and the actual or potential competition from undertakings located either within or outwith the Community;

(*b*) the market position of the undertakings concerned and their economic and financial power, the alternatives available to suppliers and users, their access to supplies or markets, any legal or other barriers to entry, supply and demand trends for the relevant goods and services, the interests of the intermediate and ultimate consumers, and the development of technical and economic progress provided that it is to consumers' advantage and does not form an obstacle to competition.

2. A concentration which does not create or strengthen a dominant position as a result of which effective competition would be significantly impeded in the common market or in a substantial part of it shall be declared compatible with the common market.

3. A concentration which creates or strengthens a dominant position as a result of which effective competition would be significantly impeded in the common market or in a substantial part of it shall be declared incompatible with the common market.

[. . .]

ARTICLE 4 PRIOR NOTIFICATION OF CONCENTRATIONS

1. Concentrations with a Community dimension defined in this Regulation shall be notified to the Commission not more than one week after the conclusion of the agreement, or the announcement of the public bid, or the acquisition of a controlling interest. That week shall begin when the first of those events occurs.

2. A concentration which consists of a merger within the meaning of Article 3(1)(*a*) or in the acquisition of joint control within the meaning of Article 3(1)(*b*) shall be notified jointly by the parties to the merger or by those acquiring joint control as the case may be. In all other cases, the notification shall be effected by the person or undertaking acquiring control of the whole or parts of one or more undertakings.

3. Where the Commission finds that a notified concentration falls within the scope of this Regulation, it shall publish the fact of the notification, at the same time indicating the names of the parties, the nature of the concentration and the economic sectors involved. The Commission shall take account of the legitimate interest of undertakings in the protection of their business secrets.

[. . .]

ARTICLE 6 EXAMINATION OF THE NOTIFICATION AND INITIATION OF PROCEEDINGS

1. The Commission shall examine the notification as soon as it is received:

(*a*) where it concludes that the concentration notified does not fall within the scope of this Regulation, it shall record that finding by means of a decision.

(*b*) where it finds that the concentration notified, although falling within the scope of this Regulation, does not raise serious doubts as to its compatibility with the common market, it shall decide not to oppose it and shall declare that it is compatible with the common market.

(*c*) if, on the other hand, it finds that the concentration notified falls within the scope of this Regulation and raises serious doubts as to its compatibility with the common market, it shall decide to initiate proceedings.

2. The Commission shall notify its decision to the undertakings concerned and the competent authorities of the member-States without delay.

ARTICLE 7 SUSPENSION OF CONCENTRATIONS

1. For the purposes of paragraph 2 a concentration as defined in Article 1 shall not be put into effect either before its notification or within the first three weeks following its notification.

2. Where the Commission, following a preliminary examination of the notification within the period provided for in paragraph 1, finds it necessary in order to ensure the full effectiveness of any decision taken later pursuant to Article 8(3) and (4), it may decide on its own initiative to continue the suspension of a concentration in whole or in

part until it takes a final decision, or to take other interim measures to that effect.

3. Paragraphs 1 and 2 shall not prevent the implementation of a public bid which has been notified to the Commission in accordance with Article 4(1), provided that the acquirer does not exercise the voting rights attached to the securities in question or does so only to maintain the full value of those investments and on the basis of a derogation granted by the Commission under paragraph 4.

4. The Commission may, on request, grant a derogation from the obligations imposed in paragraphs 1, 2 or 3 in order to prevent serious damage to one or more undertakings concerned by a concentration or to a third party. That derogation may be made subject to conditions and obligations in order to ensure conditions of effective competition. A derogation may be applied for and granted at any time, even before notification or after the transaction.

5. The validity of any transaction carried out in contravention of paragraph 1 or 2 shall be dependent on a decision pursuant to Article 6(1)(*b*) or Article 8(2) or (3) or on a presumption pursuant to Article 10(6). This Article shall, however, have no effect on the validity of transactions in securities including those convertible into other securities admitted to trading on a market which is regulated and supervised by authorities recognized by public bodies, operates regularly and is accessible directly or indirectly to the public, unless the buyer and seller knew or ought to have known that the transaction was carried out in contravention of paragraph 1 or 2.

ARTICLE 8 POWERS OF DECISION OF THE COMMISSION

1. Without prejudice to Article 9, all proceedings initiated pursuant to Article 6(1)(*c*) shall be closed by means of a decision as provided for in paragraphs 2 to 5.

2. Where the Commission finds that, following modification by the undertakings concerned if necessary, a notified concentration fulfils the criterion laid down in Article 2(2), it shall issue a decision declaring the concentration compatible with the common market. It may attach to its decision conditions and obligations intended to ensure that the undertakings concerned comply with the commitments they have entered into *vis-à-vis* the Commission with a view to modifying the original concentration plan. The decision declaring the concentration compatible shall also cover restrictions directly related and necessary to the implementation of the concentration.

3. Where the Commission finds that a concentration fulfils the criterion laid down in Article 2(3), it shall issue a decision declaring that the concentration is incompatible with the common market.

4. Where a concentration has already been implemented, the Commission may, in a decision pursuant to paragraph 3 or by separate decision, require the undertakings or assets brought together to be separated or the cessation of joint control or any other action that may be appropriate in order to restore conditions of effective competition.

5. The Commission may revoke the decision it has taken pursuant to paragraph 2 where:

(*a*) the declaration of compatibility is based on incorrect information for which one of the undertakings is responsible or where it has been obtained by deceit; or

(*b*) the undertakings concerned commit a breach of an obligation attached to the decision.

6. In the cases referred to in paragraph 5, the Commission may take a decision under paragraph 3, without being bound by the deadline referred to in Article 10(3).

ARTICLE 9 REFERRAL TO THE COMPETENT AUTHORITIES OF THE MEMBER-STATES

1. The Commission may, be means of a decision notified without delay to the undertakings concerned and the competent

authorities of the other member-States, refer a notified concentration to the competent authorities of the member-State concerned in the following circumstances.

2. Within three weeks of the date of receipt of the copy of the notification a member-State may inform the Commission, which shall inform the undertakings concerned, that a concentration threatens to create or to strengthen a dominant position as a result of which effective competition would be significantly impeded on a market, within that member-State, which presents all the characteristics of a distinct market, be it a substantial part of the common market or not.

3. If the Commission considers that, having regard to the market for the products or services in question and the geographical reference market within the meaning of paragraph 7, there is such a distinct market and that such a threat exists, either:

(*a*) it shall itself deal with the case in order to maintain or restore effective competition on the market concerned; or

(*b*) it shall refer the case to the competent authorities of the member-State concerned with a view to the application of that state's national competition law. If, however, the Commission considers that such a distinct market or threat does not exist it shall adopt a decision to that effect which it shall address to the member-State concerned.

4. A decision to refer or not to refer pursuant to paragraph 3 shall be taken:

(*a*) as a general rule within the six-week period provided for in Article 10(1), second subparagraph, where the Commission, pursuant to Article 6(1)(*b*), has not initiated proceedings; or

(*b*) within three months at most of the notification of the concentration concerned where the Commission has initiated proceedings under Article 6(1)(*c*), without taking the preparatory steps in order to adopt the necessary measures under Article 8(2), second subparagraph, (3) or (4) to maintain or restore effective competition on the market concerned.

5. If within the three months referred to in paragraph 4(*b*) the Commission, despite a reminder from the member-State concerned, has not taken a decision on referral in accordance with paragraph 3 nor has taken the preparatory steps referred to in paragraph 4(*b*), it shall be deemed to have taken a decision to refer the case to the member-State concerned in accordance with paragraph 3(*b*).

6. The publication of any report or the announcement of the findings of the examination of the concentration by the competent authority of the member-State concerned shall be effected not more than four months after the Commission's referral.

7. The geographical reference market shall consist of the area in which the undertakings concerned are involved in the supply and demand of products or services, in which the conditions of competition are sufficiently homogeneous and which can be distinguished from neighbouring areas because, in particular, conditions of competition are appreciably different in those areas. This assessment should take account in particular of the nature and characteristics of the products or services concerned, of the existence of entry barriers or of consumer preferences, of appreciable differences of the undertakings' market shares between the area concerned and neighbouring areas or of substantial price differences.

8. In applying the provisions of this Article, the member-State concerned may take only the measures strictly necessary to safeguard or restore effective competition on the market concerned.

9. In accordance with the relevant provisions of the Treaty, any member-State may appeal to the Court of Justice, and in particular request the application of Article 186, for the purpose of applying its national competition law.

10. This Article will be reviewed before the end of the fourth year following that of the adoption of this Regulation.

ARTICLE 10 TIME LIMITS FOR INITIATING PROCEEDINGS AND FOR DECISIONS

1. The decisions referred to in Article 6(1) must be taken within one month at most. That period shall begin on the day following that of the receipt of a notification or, if the information to be supplied with the notification is incomplete, on the day following that of the receipt of the complete information. That period shall be increased to six weeks if the Commission receives a request from a member-State in accordance with Article 9(2).

2. Decisions taken pursuant to Article 8(2) concerning concentrations must be taken as soon as it appears that the serious doubts referred to in Article 6(1)(*c*) have been removed, particularly as a result of modifications made by the undertakings concerned, and at the latest by the deadline laid down in paragraph 3.

3. Without prejudice to Article 8(6), decisions taken pursuant to Article 8(3) concerning notified concentrations must be taken within not more than four months of the date on which proceedings are initiated.

4. The period set by paragraph 3 shall exceptionally be suspended where, owing to circumstances for which one of the undertakings involved in the concentration is responsible, the Commission has had to request information by decision pursuant to Article 11 or to order an investigation by decision pursuant to Article 13.

5. Where the Court of Justice gives a judgment which annuls the whole or part of a Commission decision taken under this Regulation, the periods laid down in this Regulation shall start again from the date of the judgment.

6. Where the Commission has not taken a decision in accordance with Article 6(1)(*b*) or (*c*) or Article 8(2) or (3) within the deadlines set in paragraphs 1 and 3 respectively, the concentration shall be deemed to have been declared compatible with the common market, without prejudice to Article 9.

ARTICLE 11 REQUESTS FOR INFORMATION

1. In carrying out the duties assigned to it by this Regulation, the Commission may obtain all necessary information from the governments and competent authorities of the member-States, from the persons referred to in Article 3(1)(*b*), and from undertakings and associations of undertakings.

2. When sending a request for information to a person, an undertaking or an association of undertakings, the Commission shall at the same time send a copy of the request to the competent authority of the member-State within the territory of which the residence of the person or the seat of the undertaking or association of undertakings is situated.

3. In its request the Commission shall state the legal basis and the purpose of the request and also the penalties provided for in Article 14(1)(*c*) for supplying incorrect information.

4. The information requested shall be provided, in the case of undertakings, by their owners or their representatives and, in the case of legal persons, companies or firms, or of associations having no legal personality, by the persons authorized to represent them by law or by their statutes.

5. Where a person, an undertaking or an association of undertakings does not provide the information requested within the period fixed by the Commission or provides incomplete information, the Commission shall by decision require the information to be provided. The decision shall specify what information is required, fix an appropriate period within which it is to be supplied and state the penalties provided for in Articles 14(1)(*c*) and 15(1)(*a*) and the right to have the decision reviewed by the Court of Justice.

6. The Commission shall at the same time send a copy of its decision to the competent authority of the member-State within the territory of which the residence of the person or the seat of the undertaking or association of undertakings is situated.

ARTICLE 12 INVESTIGATIONS BY THE AUTHORITIES OF THE MEMBER STATES

1. At the request of the Commission, the competent authorities of the member-States shall undertake the investigations which the Commission considers to be necessary under Article 13(1), or which it has ordered by decision pursuant to Article 13(3). The officials of the competent authorities of the member-States responsible for conducting those investigations shall exercise their powers upon production of an authorization in writing issued by the competent authority of the member-State within the territory of which the investigation is to be carried out. Such authorization shall specify the subject matter and purpose of the investigation.

2. If so requested by the Commission or by the competent authority of the member-State within the territory of which the investigation is to be carried out, officials of the Commission may assist the officials of that authority in carrying out their duties.

ARTICLE 13 INVESTIGATIVE POWERS OF THE COMMISSION

1. In carrying out the duties assigned to it by this Regulation, the Commission may undertake all necessary investigations into undertakings and associations of undertakings. To that end the officials authorized by the Commission shall be empowered

(*a*) to examine the books and other business records;
(*b*) to take or demand copies of or extracts from the books and business records;
(*c*) to ask for oral explanations on the spot;
(*d*) to enter any premises, land and means of transport of undertakings.

2. The officials of the Commission authorized to carry out the investigations shall exercise their powers on production of an authorization in writing specifying the subject matter and purpose of the investigation and the penalties provided for in Article 14(1)(*d*) in cases where production of the required books or other business records is incomplete. In good time before the investigation, the Commission shall inform, in writing, the competent authority of the member-State within the territory of which the investigation is to be carried out of the investigation and of the identities of the authorized officials.

3. Undertakings and associations of undertakings shall submit to investigations ordered by decision of the Commission. The decision shall specify the subject matter and purpose of the investigation, appoint the date on which it shall begin and state the penalties provided for in Articles 14(1)(*d*) and 15(1)(*b*) and the right to have the decision reviewed by the Court of Justice.

4. The Commission shall in good time and in writing inform the competent authority of the member-State within the territory of which the investigation is to be carried out of its intention of taking a decision pursuant to paragraph 3. It shall hear the competent authority before takings its decision.

5. Officials of the competent authority of the member-State within the territory of which the investigation is to be carried out may, at the request of that authority or of the Commission, assist the officials of the Commission in carrying out their duties.

6. Where an undertaking or association of undertakings opposes an investigation ordered pursuant to this Article, the member-State concerned shall afford the necessary assistance to the officials authorized by the Commission to enable them to carry out their investigation. To this end the member-States shall, after consulting the Commission, take the necessary measures within one year of the entry into force of this Regulation.

ARTICLE 14 FINES

1. The Commission may by decision impose on the persons referred to in Article 3(1)(*b*), undertakings or associations of undertakings fines of from ECU 1,000 to 50,000 where intentionally or negligently:

(*a*) they fail to notify a concentration in accordance with Article 4;
(*b*) they supply incorrect or misleading information in a notification pursuant to Article 4;
(*c*) they supply incorrect information in response to a request made pursuant to Article 11 or fail to supply information within the period fixed by a decision taken pursuant to Article 11;
(*d*) they produce the required books or other business records in incomplete form during investigations under Article 12 or 13, or refuse to submit to an investigation ordered by decision taken pursuant to Article 13.

2. The Commission may by decision impose fines not exceeding 10% of the aggregate turnover of the undertakings concerned within the meaning of Article 5 on the persons or undertakings concerned where, either intentionally or negligently, they:

(*a*) fail to comply with an obligation imposed by decision pursuant to Article 7(4) or 8(2), second subparagraph;
(*b*) put into effect a concentration in breach of Article 7(1) or disregard a decision taken pursuant to Article 7(2);
(*c*) put into effect a concentration declared incompatible with the common market by decision pursuant to Article 8(3) or do not take the measures ordered by decision pursuant to Article 8(4).

3. In setting the amount of a fine, regard shall be had to the nature and gravity of the infringement.

4. Decisions taken pursuant to paragraphs 1 and 2 shall not be of a criminal law nature.

ARTICLE 15 PERIODIC PENALTY PAYMENTS

1. The Commission may by decision impose on the persons referred to in Article 3(1)(*b*), undertakings or associations of undertakings concerned periodic penalty payments of up to ECU 25,000 for each day of delay calculated from the date set in the decision, in order to compel them:

(*a*) to supply complete and correct information which it has requested by decision pursuant to Article 11;
(*b*) to submit to an investigation which it has ordered by decision pursuant to Article 13.

2. The Commission may by decision impose on the persons referred to in Article 3(1)(*b*) or on undertakings periodic penalty payments of up to ECU 100,000 for each day of delay calculated from the date set in the decision, in order to compel them:

(*a*) to comply with an obligation imposed by decision pursuant to Article 7(4) or Article 8(2), second subparagraph, or
(*b*) to apply the measures ordered by decision pursuant to Article 8(4).

3. Where the persons referred to in Article 3(1)(*b*), undertakings or associations of undertakings have satisfied the obligation which it was the purpose of the periodic penalty payment to enforce, the Commission may set the total amount of the periodic penalty payments at a lower figure than that which would arise under the original decision.

ARTICLE 16 REVIEW BY THE COURT OF JUSTICE

The Court of Justice shall have unlimited jurisdiction within the meaning of Article 172 of the Treaty to review decisions whereby the Commission has fixed a fine or periodic penalty payments; it may cancel, reduce or increase the fine or periodic penalty payments imposed.

ARTICLE 17 PROFESSIONAL SECRECY

1. Information acquired as a result of the application of Article 11, 12, 13 and 18 shall be used only for the purposes of the relevant request, investigation or hearing.

2. Without prejudice to Articles 4(3), 18 and 20, the Commission and the competent

authorities of the member-States, their officials and other servants shall not disclose information they have acquired through the application of this Regulation of the kind covered by the obligation of professional secrecy.

3. Paragraphs 1 and 2 shall not prevent publication of general information or of surveys which do not contain information relating to particular undertakings or associations of undertakings.

ARTICLE 18 HEARING OF THE PARTIES AND OF THIRD PERSONS

1. Before taking any decision provided for in Articles 7(2) and (4), Article 8(2), second subparagraph, and (3) to (5) and Articles 14 and 15, the Commission shall give the persons, undertakings and associations of undertakings concerned the opportunity, at every stage of the procedure up to the consultation of the advisory committee, of making known their views on the objections against them.

2. By way of derogation from paragraph 1, a decision to continue the suspension of a concentration or to grant a derogation from suspension as referred to in Article 7(2) or (4) may be taken provisionally, without the persons, undertakings or associations of undertakings concerned being given the opportunity to make known their views beforehand, provided that the Commission gives them that opportunity as soon as possible after having taken its decision.

3. The Commission shall base its decision only on objections on which the parties have been able to submit their observations. The rights of the defence shall be fully respected in the proceedings. Access to the file shall be open at least to the parties directly involved, subject to the legitimate interest of undertakings in the protection of their business secrets.

4. In so far as the Commission or the competent authorities of the member-States deem it necessary, they may also hear other natural or legal persons. Natural or legal persons showing a sufficient interest and especially members of the administrative or management bodies of the undertakings concerned or the recognized representatives of their employees shall be entitled, upon application, to be heard.

ARTICLE 19 LIAISON WITH THE AUTHORITIES OF THE MEMBER-STATES

1. The Commission shall transmit to the competent authorities of the member-States copies of notifications within three working days and, as soon as possible, copies of the most important documents lodged with or issued by the Commission pursuant to this Regulation.

2. The Commission shall carry out the procedures set out in this Regulation in close and constant liaison with the competent authorities of the member-States, which may express their views upon those procedures. For the purposes of Article 9 it shall obtain information from the competent authority of the member-State as referred to in paragraph 2 of that Article and give it the opportunity to make known its views at every stage of the procedure up to the adoption of a decision pursuant to paragraph 3 of that Article; to that end it shall give it access to the file.

3. An advisory committee on concentrations shall be consulted before any decision is taken pursuant to Article 8(2) to (5), 14 or 15, or any provisions are adopted pursuant to Article 23.

4. The advisory committee shall consist of representatives of the authorities of the member-States. Each member-State shall appoint one or two representatives; if unable to attend, they may be replaced by other representatives. At least one of the representatives of a member-State shall be competent in matters of restrictive practices and dominant positions.

5. Consultation shall take place at a joint meeting convened at the invitation of and chaired by the Commission. A summary of the case, together with an indication of the most important documents and a preliminary draft of the decision to be taken for each case considered, shall be sent with the

invitation. The meeting shall take place not less than 14 days after the invitation has been sent. The Commission may in exceptional cases shorten that period as appropriate in order to avoid serious harm to one or more of the undertakings concerned by a concentration.

6. The advisory committee shall deliver an opinion on the Commission's draft decision, if necessary by taking a vote. The advisory committee may deliver an opinion even if some members are absent and unrepresented. The opinion shall be delivered in writing and appended to the draft decision. The Commission shall take the utmost account of the opinion delivered by the committee. It shall inform the committee of the manner in which its opinion has been taken into account.

7. The advisory committee may recommend publication of the opinion. The Commission may carry out such publication. The decision to publish shall take due account of the legitimate interest of undertakings in the protection of their business secrets and of the interest of the undertakings concerned in such publication's taking place.

ARTICLE 20 PUBLICATION OF DECISIONS

1. The Commission shall publish the decisions which it takes pursuant to Article 8(2) to (5) in the official journal of the European Communities.

2. The publication shall state the names of the parties and the main content of the decision; it shall have regard to the legitimate interest of undertakings in the protection of their business secrets.

ARTICLE 21 JURISDICTION

1. Subject to review by the Court of Justice, the Commission shall have sole jurisdiction to take the decisions provided for in this Regulation.

2. No member-State shall apply its national legislation on competition to any consideration that has a Community dimension. The first subparagraph shall be without prejudice to any member-State's power to carry out any enquiries necessary for the application of Article 9(2) or after referral, pursuant to Article 9(3), first subparagraph, indent (*b*), or (5), to take the measures strictly necessary for the application of Article 9(8).

3. Notwithstanding paragraphs 1 and 2, member-States may take appropriate measures to protect legitimate interests other than those taken into consideration by this Regulation and compatible with the general principles and other provisions of Community law.

Public security, plurality of the media and prudential rules shall be regarded as legitimate interests within the meaning of the first subparagraph.

Any other public interest must be communicated to the Commission by the member-State concerned and shall be recognized by the Commission after an assessment of its compatibility with the general principles and other provisions of Community law before the measures referred to above may be taken. The Commission shall inform the member-State concerned of its decision within one month of that communication.

ARTICLE 22 APPLICATION OF THE REGULATION

1. This Regulation alone shall apply to concentrations as defined in Article 3.

2. Regulations No. 17, (EEC) No. 1017/68, (EEC) No. 4056/86 and (EEC) No. 3975/87 shall not apply to concentrations as defined in Article 3.

3. If the Commission finds, at the request of a member-State, that a concentration as defined in Article 3 that has no Community dimension within the meaning of Article 1 creates or strengthens a dominant position as a result of which effective competition would be significantly impeded within the territory of the member-State concerned it may, in so far as the concentration affects trade between member-States, adopt the decisions provided for in Article 8(2), second subparagraph, (3) and (4).

4. Articles 2(1)(*a*) and (*b*), 5, 6, 8 and 10 to 20 shall apply. The period within which proceedings may be initiated pursuant to Article 10(1) shall begin on the date of the receipt of the request from the member-State. The request must be made within one month at most of the date on which the concentration was made known to the member-State or effected. This period shall begin on the date of the first of those events.

5. Pursuant to paragraph 3 the Commission shall take only the measures strictly necessary to maintain or store effective competition within the territory of the member-State at the request of which it intervenes.

6. Paragraphs 3 to 5 shall continue to apply until the thresholds referred to in Article 1(2) have been reviewed.

ARTICLE 23 IMPLEMENTING PROVISIONS

The Commission shall have the power to adopt implementing provisions concerning the form, content and other details of notifications pursuant to Article 4, time limits pursuant to Article 10, and hearings pursuant to Article 18.

ARTICLE 24 RELATIONS WITH NON-MEMBER COUNTRIES

1. The member-States shall inform the Commission of any general difficulties encountered by their undertakings with concentrations as defined in Article 3 in a non-member country.

2. Initially not more than one year after the entry into force of this Regulation and thereafter periodically the Commission shall draw up a report examining the treatment accorded to Community undertakings, in the terms referred to in paragraphs 3 and 4, as regards concentrations in non-member countries. The Commission shall submit those reports to the Council, together with any recommendations.

3. Whenever it appears to the Commission, either on the basis of the reports referred to in paragraph 2 or on the basis of other information, that a non-member country does not grant Community undertakings treatment comparable to that granted by the Community to undertakings from that non-member country, the Commission may submit proposals to the Council for an appropriate mandate for negotiation with a view to obtaining comparable treatment for Community undertakings.

4. Measures taken under this Article shall comply with the obligations of the Community or of the member-States, without prejudice to Article 234 of the Treaty, under international agreements, whether bilateral or multilateral.

ARTICLE 25 ENTRY INTO FORCE

1. This Regulation shall enter into force on 21 September 1990.

2. This Regulation shall not apply to any concentration which was the subject of an agreement or announcement or where control was acquired within the meaning of Article 4(1) before the date of this Regulation's entry into force and it shall not in any circumstances apply to any concentration in respect of which proceedings were initiated before that date by a member-State's authority with responsibility for competition.

This Regulation shall be binding in its entirety and directly applicable in all member-States.

Done at Brussels, 21 December 1989.

22

MERGERS AND THE PUBLIC INTEREST

One of the most vexed questions in competition policy is that of the public interest in mergers or takeovers. There is a respectable argument for the proposition that mergers can *enhance* efficiency – this is the primary focus of the extract from **Waterson**. On the other hand, whether these benefits extend to practice is somewhat dubious: the summary of evidence from the **Blue Paper** suggests a rather pessimistic view (though one not carried forward into proposals!). Moreover it is clear that private and social benefits need not coincide. The interests of consumers are not amongst those considered by a takeover raider (or merging parties), nor may be the interests of the target firm's pensioners or current employees. Consumers, in particular, may suffer through a reduction in competition in the case of horizontal mergers – hence the **Statement of Policy**.

22.1 M. Waterson, 'Takeovers', 7 *The Economic Review*, 2 (1989)

THE ECONOMIC RATIONALE

[. . .] [W]hat are the potential benefits of takeovers? Broadly speaking, there are two: to enable economic rationalisation and to correct inefficient management. In many industries, technological change moves in the direction of increasing the importance of economies of scale [. . .]. Firms in such an industry can be faced with the problem that either they grow and so, hopefully, survive, or they are forced to become a minor player in the market, seeking niches or, at worst, collapsing. Buying a rival is one route to rationalisation. To take another case, a firm may require an efficient distribution network to achieve full potential, or may need reliable access to a crucial input, but might be sceptical of the continuing likelihood of being able to use the normal market mechanisms. Thus it decides to purchase a firm further forward or backward in the production process in order to achieve rationalisation as a vertically integrated firm.

So far, I have been describing the case for mergers as achieving 'industrial logic' as the market sometimes puts it, that is horizontal (buying the rival) and vertical (buying into another stage of production) merger respectively. There are two points to take issue with here. For one thing, there is a clear alternative to takeover, namely internal growth; for another, a substantial minority of takeovers are neither horizontal nor vertical in nature.

The advantages of internal growth, as opposed to merger, are that a company only grows if it is successful. If it has something important to offer then this can be translated to a larger scale, and internal growth is generally less disruptive than takeovers. On the other hand, in a market already saturated with product, internal growth can lead to overcapacity in an industry, so creating a poor trading position from the company's point of view (though probably a good one for consumers).

But what of mergers that are neither horizontal or vertical, the so-called conglomerate mergers? Why should benefits stem from the merger of a match company and a razorblade company, or a rubber products company and a glassmaker? This is where the second general reason advanced for takeovers as an efficiency-enhancing device is relevant: that they act as a constraint on managers. An extensive literature in the 1960s and early 1970s argued that managers of large companies were able to indulge their own whims, within limits. Shareholders, who in theory own a company, are commonly so numerous that any one of them has but a small stake. The individual shareholder has a rather limited incentive to put time and effort into discovering the firm's inefficiencies because there is what is known as a *free rider problem*. If inefficiencies are discovered and corrected, profits and profit expectations should increase. Given even a reasonably efficient capital market, this will be reflected in the firm's share price. At this stage, our heroic shareholder gets his or her reward. But so do all those others who sat back and did nothing (the free riders). At the very least this dulls the individual shareholder's incentive to be an active monitor of company management's behaviour. How then could the diligent shareholder internalise the external benefits he or she confers on others? Simply by keeping the information secret, buying up shares cheaply, then taking over the firm and instituting efficiency improvements.

Of course it is not quite as straightforward as this in practice. For a start, it is difficult to discover whether a firm is poorly managed, or is being as well managed as possible given poor prevailing trading conditions. Rumours of a takeover are often enough to raise the share price, so making a takeover more expensive. The *City Takeover Code* forces early disclosure of substantial interests, and intentions to acquire. (However, it also acts to prevent minority shareholders holding on to their shares and so free riding on the successful change in management without risk, because it triggers compulsory acquisition once the bidder's equity stake reaches 90%.)

A particularly problematic event for the potential acquirer is the development of an auction, in which two or more companies both bid for the same target firm. Costly newspaper advertising, circulars to shareholders and so on ensue, and at least one company (Guinness, pursuing Distillers) seems to have been rather over-enthusiastic in its attempt to make its offer attractive, by aiming to boost up its own share price. Moreover, defence weapons against takeovers have ben developed, particularly in the US. Going by exotic names such as 'poison pills', 'shark repellants' and 'golden parachutes', the aim is to make a company less attractive to potential acquirers by saddling any acquirer with burdensome obligations, or at least ensuring that the outgoing management gets a handsome payoff.

If takeovers or the threat of takeovers do provide management with an important push towards acting efficiently, to rule them out without appeal would be to neglect a *potentially* important efficiency-generating force. [. . .]

THE EFFECTS OF TAKEOVERS

At the outset, it must be said that efficiency cannot be expected to provide the complete explanation for takeover activity. Otherwise, why should this activity display such a markedly cyclical pattern? This perhaps has more to do with the availability of finance than anything else. More generally, empirical work *explaining* takeover activity is much less advanced than work on the effects of takeover. [. . .]

[The latter is discussed in the extract from the Blue Paper later in this chapter.]

[. . .]

The results on post-merger performance in the UK suggest that shareholders in the acquired company commonly have a once-for-all gain in the form of a premium paid for their shares over the prevailing stock price. By contrast, the acquirer's shareholders experience neutral or adverse effects from acquisition. [. . .]. Moreover it should be noted that what these studies measure is gains to the firms' shareholders. Studies based upon accounting data are more pessimistic regarding the benefits. In the case of horizontal mergers, any benefits to the firms concerned can be at the cost of reduced competition, higher prices, etc., to consumers. And in any takeover it is possible for the acquired firm's shareholders to benefit at the expense of employees' pension rights, etc. Thus private benefits to the shareholders are necessary but not sufficient for social benefits, and may be expected to overstate the benefits to society as a whole.

[. . .]

[. . .] [W]e should first remember that takeover decisions are made under conditions of uncertainty. Acquiring firms do not know the full truth about the firms they attempt to acquire, nor do they know the future conditions that will face the combined firm. We would therefore expect some takeovers to be failures, just as we expect some new firms to fail or some investment projects to fail. The real question is whether the failure rate in takeovers is unusually high and whether the social costs of takeovers might outweigh the private benefits even for the 'successful' takeovers.

The detailed reasons for failure of an acquisition will vary from case to case. Two brief examples will have to suffice. In 1952 the car manufacturer Austin merged with Morris to form the British Motor Corporation. Yet economies of rationalisation appear never to have been pursued particularly rigorously, so that the Mini launched in 1959 was produced both at the Austin plant, Longbridge, and the Morris factory at Cowley. Separate Boards of Directors existed until 1966. The two companies continued to pursue separate design philosophies, and even when taken over in turn by Leyland in 1968, full integration of the existing facilities to capture scale benefits had not occurred. Indeed, rationalisation of their extensive franchised dealership networks was long overdue.

A rather different case is presented by the Imperial group and the Howard Johnson chain of motels in the US. The Imperial group, like all tobacco-based companies, engaged heavily in diversification into other areas of activity. In 1980 it bought the motel chain for £280 million, but its subsidiary consistently made losses – largely because the parent company was not in touch with US consumer tastes. Finally in 1985 it sold the chain at around half the price that it paid. Diversification clearly does not yield sure-fire success. (Imperial was itself subsequently purchased by Hanson Trust, who then disposed of many of its businesses.)

22.2 Monopolies and Mergers Commission, *Report on the Proposed Joint Venture: Allied-Lyons PLC/Carlsberg A/S* CM. 2029 (HMSO, London, 1992)

THE TRANSACTION

8.16. the merger would bring together Allied's United Kingdom brewing and drinks wholesaling business with Carlsberg's brewing and distribution business in the United Kingdom. The latter represents the whole of Carlsberg's existing operations in the United Kingdom, whereas Allied retains numerous other activities outside the joint venture, notably its retail pub estate. Allied and Carlsberg would grant exclusive perpetual licences (subject to certain existing licences) enabling the joint venture to brew and sell all the brands currently owned and brewed by each company in the United Kingdom, and Allied would pass on the benefit of its licences to brew and sell third-party brands. In addition to injecting its United Kingdom business, Carlsberg would make a cash payment of £135 million to the joint venture which would be used to repay external loans transferred in from elsewhere in the Allied group of companies.

8.17. The details of the corporate reorganisation are complex but in essence the joint venture would be operated by a company named Carlsberg-Tetley Brewing Ltd. (CTL) which would be owned by the holding company, Carlsberg-Tetley. Allied Breweries and Carlsberg would each own 50 per cent of the shares in Carlsberg-Tetley and appoint an equal number of directors to its board. For at least the first three years of the agreement Allied would retain management control by having an additional vote, but a number of important matters to do with arrangements between Carlsberg-Tetley and its shareholders, substantial acquisitions and disposals by Carlsberg-Tetley, the appointment and removal of certain directors, and changes to Carlsberg-Tetley's auditors would have to be decided jointly. CTL would be responsible for day-to-day operations working within guidelines established by Carlsberg-Tetley.

8.18. CTL would enter into a seven-year beer supply agreement with the Allied group company which now owns and runs Allied's pub estate (referred to in this report as Allied Retail). CTL would make available an agreed range of beers, including some third-party brands, and Allied Retail would obtain 100 per cent of its beer requirements – subject only to the guest beer provisions of the Tied Estate Order – from CTL, of which up to 15 per cent by volume could be third-party brands. CTL would take orders from, deliver to and invoice the individual pubs as agent for Allied Retail. The price invoiced to the pubs would be CTL's wholesale list price but the price paid by Allied Retail to CTL would be at a discount to the list price (the discounts and related arrangements are laid down in the supply agreement). Thus the pubs would pay Allied Retail the full list price and Allied Retail would retain the value of the discount.

PUBLIC INTEREST ISSUES

8.21. In considering the issues which the merger raises for the public interest we consider first the state of competition in the beer market as a whole and in the supply of lager in particular. We then consider the effect of the merger on competition in brewing and wholesaling, and the effects on two groups of participants in the market, namely regional and local brewers and independent wholesalers. Finally we examine the effects on vertical links and on efficiency and employment.

[. . .]

The state of the beer market

8.43. Our overall view is that while some aspects of the market are [. . .] becoming more competitive, the position of the national brewers remains very strong. This strength creates difficulties for regional and local brewers and independent wholesalers and there are continuing signs of competitive weakness, notably in the behaviour of retail prices. The supply of lager is already slightly more concentrated that ale and the importance of strong, nationally advertised brands is putting pressure on smaller brewers' ability to compete with the nationals.

The effect of the merger on competition in brewing and wholesaling

[. . .]

8.55. Our analysis of the effect of the merger has to be made in the context of the view we have taken of the state of the market [. . .]. We have also had regard to the considerations which were taken into account by our predecessors in the last MMC report on a merger in the beer industry, namely the Elders/Grand Met case.

8.56. As regards the increase in market

share, the effect of the merger depends very much on a judgment as to which criterion should be used to measure it. Taking the increase in share of final sales of all beer as the criterion, Carlsberg would add only 1 per cent to Allied's existing share of 13 per cent, leaving CTL well behind Bass and Courage, and not far ahead of Whitbread and S&N [. . .]. Taking the other end of the scale, namely shares of production of lager alone, Carlsberg would add 8 per cent to Allied's 13 per cent. On this measure CTL would be nearly on a par with Bass and Courage, which have 24 per cent and 22 per cent respectively of lager production.

8.57. In the light of the view we have taken that lager is a distinct product, we consider it appropriate to assess the merger primarily by reference to its effect on lager. Moreover in this case, where we are dealing with a brewer (Carlsberg) which sells mainly through other brewers, we believe that final sales, although relevant, is inadequate as a measure. Carlsberg, as owner of one of the leading lager brands, exercises its influence on the market not only by its sales to independent wholesalers and retailers but also by its sales to other brewers. The fact that regional and local brewers can look to Carlsberg as a source of lagers affects, at least potentially, their ability to negotiate terms with suppliers. Equally the fact that several different brewers may buy Carlsberg beers not only for sale through their tied estates but also in the free on-trade is a contribution to a competitive market. Moreover Carlsberg's expenditure on promoting its brands, which the company told us is unusually high because of the need to compensate for the lack of a distribution network, has a direct effect in influencing consumer demand regardless of the channels of distribution used.

8.58. We consider therefore that the effect of the merger on market share with respect to lager is broadly equivalent to the Elders/Grand Met case – in which Grand Met's 11 per cent share of the beer market by final sales, the appropriate measure in that case, was added to Courage's 10 per cent.

8.59. In contrast to Elders/Grand Met, which was a merger of two of the six national brewers, there is in the present case no reduction in the number of national brewers, but instead the elimination of one of the two large brewers without a tied estate (the other being Guinness) as an independent player, and a significant strengthening of one of the five remaining national brewers. Taking the latter point first, we have expressed the view [. . .] that the position of the national brewers remains very strong despite the reductions in the size of their tied estates. While it is still too early to judge the full impact of the Beer Orders, certain trends are emerging. We see the aim of the merger, as indeed the parties put it to us, as equipping CTL to compete successfully in the new market conditions by winning a greater share of free on-trade business. This has both benefits and drawbacks for competition. On the one hand we believe it would be beneficial that CTL would be able to compete more effectively against Bass and Courage, in that a market structure in which there are three leading suppliers rather than two is less likely to lead to uncompetitive practices. On the other hand the gap in competitive strength between the national brewers taken together and the regional and local brewers would be widened further with the leading independent lager brand coming under the control of a national brewer [. . .].

8.60. As to the loss of Carlsberg as an independent player, we believe this would harm competition at the wholesale level. Having no tied estate, no ale brands and no extensive distribution system, Carlsberg has different interests from the national brewers and behaves differently from them. This is particularly so as regards attitudes to smaller brewers and independent wholesalers [. . .].

8.61. Another factor which weighed in the Elders/Grand Met case was the effect on competition of an accumulation of strong brands by Courage, matching those already held by Bass. Both Allied and Carlsberg are believers in the importance of brands. It is significant that Skol, which is still Allied's top-selling beer, is regarded by both companies as a weak brand because it has to be sold more on price than other brands with a better image such as Castlemaine and Carlsberg. The merger would bring together three of the seven top-selling lager brands in the United Kingdom, giving CTL a powerful position in what is still expected to be the growth sector of the market. We would expect CTL to compete to a significant extent by means of advertising and other forms of promotion. We accept that the parties are unlikely to phase out a major brand such as Skol in the near future but some rationalisation of lager brands in the enlarged portfolio seems likely in due course, with a consequent reduction in choice. Moreover, with Carlsberg lager in its portfolio, CTL will have less need than Allied has had to achieve sales of Skol by cutting prices to compensate for its weakness as a brand.

Effects on regional and local brewers

8.62. In 1991 some 15 per cent of Carlsberg's sales were to regional and local brewers. Of this, half went to three companies to which Carlsberg has provided loan subsidies and half went in small quantities to over 50 other brewers. We would expect this element of Carlsberg's sales to increase, if Carlsberg remained independent, because of its need to achieve additional sales to make up for the reduced barrelage going to Courage, since September 1991, as compared with the quantities taken by Grand Met under the old agreement. Carlsberg told us that in general it had difficulties in selling to these brewers because they would prefer to brew Carlsberg lager themselves – which Carlsberg could not agree to – or to enter an ale-for-lager agreement, which was also impossible because Carlsberg had no network through which to sell ales.

8.63. The parties told us that CTL would continue to supply Carlsberg products to regional and local brewers on reasonable terms so there would be no effect. We find it difficult to accept that there would be no effect. As an independent company selling very little direct to retailers, Carlsberg does not come into competition much with regional and local brewers, whose strength is in any case in ale rather than lager. CTL would be competing with them directly in selling to the free on-trade and the off-trade. Carlsberg's absorption into CTL is likely to affect the terms of supply to some customers, as CTL could be expected to adopt a different marketing strategy from Carlsberg, for example by competing directly with some of Carlsberg's existing customers as a full-line wholesaler. These considerations also apply to brewers for which Carlsberg is at present a potential rather than actual source of supply, but whose negotiating ability as buyers is assisted by Carlsberg's presence in the market. The fact that Carlsberg lagers may be available to smaller brewers from other national brewers, notably Courage, as well as from Carlsberg direct qualifies, but does not undermine, this assessment.

8.64. Regional and local brewers will also lose indirectly as a result of CTL's enhanced ability to compete for business in the free on-trade [. . .]. In particular it would become more difficult for these brewers to continue to promote their own lager brands successfully in the face of CTL's strength in lager – which would enable it to focus its advertising spend more effectively than Allied and Carlsberg separately – alongside that of Bass, Courage and the other nationals.

Effects on independent wholesalers

8.65. In 1991 18 per cent of Carlsberg's sales were to independent wholesalers, representing around 23 per cent of their lager requirements. Carlsberg told us that this latter percentage has now fallen to around 13 per cent as a result of Courage's appointment as exclusive distributor of Carlsberg lager to the off-trade.

8.70. We find it difficult to believe that CTL, whose management other than at senior level will be carried on by existing Allied personnel, would continue to behave towards wholesalers in exactly the same way as Carlsberg, a company with a very different position in the market. We accept that much of the wholesalers' existing business would not be of interest to CTL as a direct supplier and that CTL would be happy to continue supplying Carlsberg beers for wholesalers to supply to smaller accounts. Wholesalers may also be able to obtain Carlsberg products from Courage and perhaps other brewers. It is to be expected, however, that CTL will increasingly want to take over the final sales of Carlsberg beers rather than supplying through other brewers or wholesalers, and that the terms on which it would supply independent wholsesalers would, over a period, worsen compared with those now available from Carlsberg. The effect of the merger will be an increasing dependence of independent wholesalers on national brewers, which is likely to diminish their prospects of becoming a more significant force in the market.

The effects on vertical links

8.74. [. . .] [W]e do not consider that the introduction of Carlsberg into the structure will greatly affect the substance of the links with the Allied tied estate. Carlsberg's interest as half-owner of the brewing and wholesaling operation will be similar to Allied's as regards the importance of the secure outlets provided by the retail estate. Moreover, the fact that Allied, the owner of the estate, will have 50 per cent rather than 100 per cent of the brewing business will not materially affect Allied Retail's incentive to buy beer and other drinks from CTL.

8.75. The separation of the management of the brewing and retail operations may result in a more focused approach to each business and hence to some divergence of views. This, however, is a matter of degree and we would not expect major differences to develop which would be such as to disturb the central supply relationship. Equally, while the formalisation of the relationship into a supply agreement gives Allied Retail more independence in choice of brands, this too does not affect the basic relationship. Apart from the modest increase in the proportion of third-party beers which Allied Retail may buy, the protected market which the estate provides will be unchanged in size. While the ownership link is diluted by the joint venture, we would expect that, as things stand at present, the ownership relationship would continue to provide an incentive for maintaining the trading links. The situation might be different if there were significant changes in the market, or in the shareholdings in either CTL or Allied Retail.

8.76. As to the argument that the merger extends vertical integration by giving Carlsberg access to Allied's tied estate, we accept the parties' contention that sales of Carlsberg beers to Allied Retail will be largely at the expense of existing Allied brands. While the improved portfolio may bring Allied Retail some increase in market share, we would not expect this effect to be material in the context of the market as a whole. Consequently both the amount of business going through the tied estate and the amount of beer for which markets outside the estate are needed will be broadly unchanged.

8.77. The displacement argument applies to the prospect of Carlsberg gaining access to Allied's loan-tied and supply agreement business, with the important difference that the size of that business is not fixed. As noted above, we expect the merger to enable CTL to win more business in these two categories. While not equivalent to ownership ties, loan ties and long-term supply agreements have some features which we regard as anti-competitive in that, at least in the short run, they foreclose or sharply reduce the availability of the particular outlets' business to competing suppliers [. . .].

8.78. We have attempted to examine the combined effect of Allied's tied estate, loan ties and supply agreements at local level, i.e. by Petty Sessional Division (PSD). This is straightforward as regards the tied estate and reasonably so as regards loan ties, which are normally with individual pubs, at any particular time. There are 27 PSDs in which more than 20 per cent of full on-licences will be tied to Allied by ownership after November 1992. This number rises to 60 if full on-licences tied by loan are added to the owned estate. This compares with a total of some 520 PSDs in Great Britain.

8.79. Assessing the geographical impact of supply agreements is much more difficult, and would require a detailed investigation which was outside the scope of this inquiry. This is because the terms of supply agreements vary widely, in particular as regards the proportion of the purchaser's beer requirements that is covered. If the proportion is significantly less than 100 per cent, one would have to establish to which individual pubs the supplier's beer was going. There is also a conceptual question as to how to treat pubs which are taking beer from two or more brewers, albeit under the terms of supply agreements.

8.80. The most we can say, therefore, is that the extent of local concentration arising from ownership and loan ties may be exacerbated by the effects of supply agreements with independent retail chains, particularly as these tend to be regionally based, and that this effect will increase if such supply agreements become a more common feature of the market, as appears to be happening. The merger may contribute to an increase in local concentration in so far as it enables CTL to win more loan-tied and supply agreement business than Allied alone would have, but it is very difficult to identify the particular effect in any one PSD.

Effects on efficiency and employment

8.81. The parties said that the merger would bring efficiency gains for both Allied and Carlsberg. The addition of Carlsberg's products to Allied's portfolio would reduce unit costs in marketing, selling and distribution. Allied would achieve production savings through Carlsberg's efficient Northampton brewery, the subsequent rationalisation of brewing operations, and the application of Carlsberg's know-how to its own production centres. For Carlsberg the main benefit was that its products would be distributed through Allied's wholesale network, giving them direct access to retail outlets on a national scale for the first time. The parties forecast significant savings in administration and marketing and more modest savings in production and distribution by year five. The savings would clearly be useful but they are not large in the context of projected net beer sales revenue of over £1 billion (see paragraph 2.19 and Table 2.2).

8.82. The parties estimated that some [*] jobs or [*] per cent of the combined workforce would be lost as a result of the merger. These would be additional to jobs which would be lost from Allied's operation whether the merger went ahead or not, including those at the Romford brewery whose closure had already been announced. Although the incidence of some of the job losses has already been decided, the overall pattern would be influenced by the merger if it proceeded [. . .]. The extent of the incremental loss of jobs reflects the fact that there is not much overlap between the two companies' distribution networks, and appears to be a necessary consequence if the efficiency gains from the merger are to be realised [. . .].

CONCLUSIONS

8.84. In reviewing the state of the market we have found that, while the market is changing in some respects, there are persistent indications of a lack of competitiveness. The strength of the national brewers is undiminished, particularly in lager [. . .].

8.85. Against this background we find that the merger is likely to aggravate existing weaknesses in market structure. It would eliminate Carlsberg, which is a useful force for competition at wholesale level in the lager sector, as an independent supplier and significantly strengthen Allied, the third-ranking of the national brewers. These effects would increase the competitive advantages which the national brewers collectively enjoy over other brewers, and their relative strength *vis-à-vis* all other parties in the market.

8.86. There would be particular adverse effects on regional and local brewers and on independent wholesalers [. . .]. These parties play a valuable, albeit currently modest, role in providing competition and choice and we consider it important that their potential to grow should not be weakened as a result of merger activity involving the national brewers.

8.87. The merger would in our judgment have little direct effect on vertical links but would put CTL in a good position to win more loan-tied and supply agreement business. Although not equivalent to ownership ties – which even after November 1992 will cover around 30 per cent of the beer market – loan ties and supply agreements further reduce, during their period of operation, the proportion of the market which is open to free competition.

8.88. On the other hand the merger would yield benefits in the form of efficiency gains for the parties, an improved portfolio of brands in Allied's tied estate, and the creation, in CTL, of a stronger potential competitor against Bass and Courage (and against Bass and S&N in Scotland). In our judgment, made against the market background which we have described, these benefits would not effectively offset the adverse effects which we have found. Rather, we believe that the merger would on balance represent a backward step in the process of moving towards a more competitive structure in the beer industry.

8.89. We therefore conclude that the merger may be expected to operate against the public interest with the particular adverse effect that competition for the supply of beer, particularly lager, at wholesale level would be reduced and that this could be expected to lead to wholesale prices being higher than they would be in the absence of the merger.

The Tebbit Guidelines, issued in 1984 by the then Secretary of State for Trade and Industry, indicated a government intention to refer mergers to the Monopolies and Mergers Commission only where issues of competition were involved, except in exceptional cases. The Fair Trading Act 1973 provides for a reference on any aspect of the public interest. The Tebbit Guidelines reflected not only the government's views on intervention, but also a need for greater certainty in merger control. That policy has been reiterated by subsequent Secretaries of State. Section 84 of the Fair Trading Act does allow the Monopolies and Mergers Commission a wide discretion in the assessment of mergers referred to it. However, the major part of the MMC's assessment remains a consideration of its horizontal competitive effects. Although non-competition concerns will be examined, they will not be used to block a merger which does not have anticompetitive implications. The report of the MMC in the **Allied-Lyons PLC/Carlsberg A/S** merger indicates the approach of the MMC, and continues the regulation of the industry commenced by the two **Beer Orders** (sections 11.6 and 11.7).

The Tebbit Guidelines were supplemented by the Lilley Guidelines in 1990. This statement of the Secretary of State indicated an intention to refer mergers where the acquiring firm is state controlled, even where the merger does not raise any competition concerns. This statement appears below, together with the MMC's assessment (in the **Crédit Lyonnais and Woodchester** report) of the relevance of state control to the process of merger control.

22.3 Secretary of State for Trade and Industry, *Statement of Policy*, 26 July 1990

On 26 July 1990, in a written reply to a Parliamentary Question, the Secretary of State for Trade and Industry said:

> In deciding whether to refer merger situations to the Monopolies and Mergers Commission, I shall in future pay particularly close attention to the degree of state control, if any, of the acquiring company.
>
> One of the government's fundamental policy objectives has been to allow market forces to determine the most efficient allocation of resources in the interests of industry, commerce and the consumer. We have taken many important steps towards this objective over the last decade including an extensive programme of privatisation, deregulation and the vigorous application of competition policy. This objective could be undermined by nationalisation by the back door.
>
> State-controlled companies are not subject to the same disciplines as those in the private sector. They tend to have the assurance of government backing for their business activities and consequently they do not compete on even terms with private sector companies which operate under the threat of financial failure. Their managements may be motivated to make non-commercial decisions. They may not deploy resources efficiently; and an increase in the resources they manage may well reduce competitive forces. It is important that the MMC should have the chance to consider in detail mergers involving state-controlled companies.
>
> All bids by state-controlled companies, whether United Kingdom or foreign, will be treated evenhandedly. I shall, of course, continue to exercise my discretion in deciding whether to refer any particular case to the MMC, after receiving advice from the Director General of Fair Trading. But among the factors to which I shall give particularly close attention will be the degree of state control, if any, of the acquiring company.
>
> The MMC will, of course, continue to weigh up each case on its merits. Referring a merger to the MMC does not prejudge whether it may be expected to operate against the public interest.

22.4 Monopolies and Mergers Commission, *Report on the Proposed Merger between Crédit Lyonnais and Woodchester*, Cm. 1404 (HMSO, London, 1991)

STATE CONTROL: POTENTIAL ISSUES

8.15. This reference, like three others concurrently under investigation, raises a set of issues beyond the normal competition criteria. These are issues surrounding the concept of state ownership or state control of at least one of the enterprises involved.

8.16. The Department of Trade and Industry (DTI) has suggested to us a number of propositions against which the circumstances of any case involving state ownership or state control might be tested [. . .]. These proceed from the basic assumption that state control inevitably distorts the natural condition of the market. State-controlled companies, the argument runs, are likely to behave in a fundamentally different way from other companies because the state as a shareholder is unlike private enterprise shareholders. The state may have objectives distinct from the normal commercial objective of maximising the financial return on a shareholder's investment. State-controlled companies do not face the threat of financial failure, they are not financially accountable in the same way as a quoted company, and they may have access to cheaper forms of finance. Because their objectives (or actions) may not be, or may not be perceived to be, strictly commercial, their behaviour is apt to be unpredictable by the normal standards of the market place. This creates uncertainty among companies operating in the same area. To the extent that competitors in the private sector adjust their own behaviour as a result of the involvement of a state-controlled company, there may be a misallocation of resources in the market leading to overall loss of efficiency in the production of the goods or services concerned. In the case of acquisitions by foreign state-owned companies, the state concerned might be seeking to control a sector of the economy in order to pursue some objective inimical to the national interests of the United Kingdom. Furthermore, in addition to the distortion of the product market, the market for corporate control will be adversely affected because state-controlled companies themselves will usually be immune from take-over and from take-over pressures.

8.17. DTI further argues that, taken together, these possible consequences lead to a general presumption that acquisitions by state-controlled companies are likely to have adverse effects on the public interest unless there are offsetting benefits.

8.18. We fully appreciate the importance which is attached by DTI to these propositions and the possible consequences suggested. We accept that, in some investigations including the present one, these and other matters arising in connection with state control are among the relevant issues. As regards some merger situations qualifying for investigation, the fact of state control, taken alone or in conjunction with other relevant facts, might indeed be the basis of a conclusion that the creation of the situation operated or might be expected to operate against the public interest.

8.19. Nevertheless, we are unable to accept that we can look at these matters in terms, as has been suggested, of a general presumption. Our approach to the public interest, or to any aspect of it, is governed by section 84(1) of the Act. This provision requires the MMC 'to take into account all matters which appear to them in the particular circumstances to be relevant'. The subsection goes on to require the MMC to have regard to the desirability of five specific matters or objectives. The language of the subsection appears to us to exclude any presumptions, whether of fact or of law.

8.20. It is the MMC's duty to approach each case according to its facts. Whether any particular issue, including as to state control, arises, and the weight to be attached to it for the purpose of section 84(1), will depend on an evaluation of all the relevant evidence against the background of the circumstances of the case in question.

[. . .]

8.39. In reaching our conclusions, we emphasise that we make no judgment on the general propositions advanced by DTI. Our conclusions are confined exclusively to the case before us. The circumstances will vary in each case. In this instance we have found that the two companies have only a small presence in the market, with little overlap, and singly or together exert little market power. We are satisfied that the merged company would not exert its position in the market in an anti-competitive manner. We have also taken into consideration the statement by Crédit Lyonnais that it intends to leave the Woodchester management to conduct its day-to-day business without interference, and that one of its main purposes in entering into partnership with the Woodchester management was to obtain the benefit of the latter's skills and experience in the leasing business in order to develop its own leasing business more effectively in France and other parts of Europe.

8.40. Clearly there can be circumstances in which the fact of state control could, on investigation, be expected to operate against the public interest. For this to be our conclusion in the present case, each of several conditions would need to be fulfilled. Not only would the French government have to be in a position to control the policy of the banks it owned, and in particular that of Crédit Lyonnais, but it would also have to be able to do so effectively.

This would mean that Crédit Lyonnais would have insufficient autonomy of direction and management to withstand what might in some instances need to be quite significant interference in its normal commercial operations. Furthermore, the effect of adding the United Kingdom operations of Woodchester to those of the French state-owned banks (particularly, in this case, those of Crédit Lyonnais) would need to be significant enough, or otherwise to give rise to sufficient market power in the United Kingdom markets affected by the merger, that any such state interference, with its possible immediate or potential future distorting effects on competition and efficiency, was or might be expected to be adverse to the United Kingdom public interest. In this particular case we are clear that none of those conditions except the first is fulfilled.

8.41. We have accordingly concluded that the competitive status of Crédit Lyonnais and Woodchester together is too small directly to affect competition in the large and vigorous United Kingdom markets concerned [. . .], and that in the circumstances of the market the fact of state control may be expected not to have an adverse effect [. . .]. Hence we conclude that the proposed merger may be expected not to operate against the public interest.

The Monopolies and Mergers Commission will assess a merger by having regard to its probable impact on the public interest. Many studies have been made of the actual effects of mergers, in terms of their competitive impact, efficiencies and profitability. One such widely regarded study was G. Meeks, *Disappointing Marriage: A Study of the Gains from Merger* (Cambridge University Press, Cambridge, 1977). A Green Paper published in 1978 abstracted this study and several similar ones (*A Review of Monopolies and Mergers Policy*, Cmnd. 7198, HMSO, London, 1978). The Department of Trade and Industry's more recent **Blue Paper**, abstracted below, considered more recent studies which used different methodologies.

22.5 Department of Trade and Industry, *Merger Policy: A Department of Trade and Industry Paper on the policy and procedures of merger control*, (HMSO, London, 1988)

[. . .]

POST-MERGER PERFORMANCE: THE EVIDENCE

I. Introduction

1. The 1978 Green Paper (Cmnd. 7198) considered several studies that attempted to evaluate the benefits of mergers by looking at post-merger profitability in comparison with profitability before the mergers took place. These studies produced the finding that in roughly half the cases examined, the merger had resulted in an unfavourable or neutral effect on the profitability of the companies concerned. The failure of the evidence to show improved profitability following mergers was interpreted as strong evidence that mergers were failing to generate economic benefits.

2. It was recognised that there were a number of limitations to these studies of post-merger performance. In particular, there were difficulties in estimating how the firms concerned would have performed in the absence of the merger and thus in attributing any change in profitability to the

merger itself. The force of this criticism was reduced by the fact that other studies adopting quite different approaches had arrived at results similarly showing disappointing post-merger performance. A further problem with the studies is that they measure performance by profitability, a weak test of efficiency gains because mergers may produce higher profits through the exploitation of increased market power. Thus this limitation serves, if anything, to reinforce the findings of poor post-merger performance.

II. Subsequent evidence

3. Since Cmnd. 7198 was prepared, a number of empirical studies of merger performance have been conducted using several different approaches. These include detailed case studies, accounting studies of pre- and post-merger performance and stock market studies that assess whether mergers create value for shareholders. The findings of a number of these studies are summarised below:

(*a*) *Cowling (1980):* using an in-depth case study approach of nine mergers that occurred between 1965 and 1970, this attempts to assess the overall contribution of mergers to economic efficiency of firms, thus avoiding the shortcomings associated with profit performance. Efficiency was measured using the unit factor requirement index that estimates total input requirements per unit of output. The results showed no general efficiency gains forthcoming. However, there were one or two instances of efficiency gains, notably when superior management gained control of more resources, but these were not sufficient to suggest that efficiency gains typically apply.

(*b*) *Mueller* et al. *(1980):* this major empirical investigation was designed as an international comparison covering seven countries – UK, USA, Germany, France, Belgium, Holland and Sweden. One of the objectives of the research was to ascertain whether mergers increased the efficiency of the companies concerned. This also recognised the inadequacy of the profit test and measured performance using growth and share prices as well as profitability. The results using after-tax profits were mixed, with four countries, including the UK, showing slightly improved performance and the other three showing declines. The tests on growth were uniformly negative. Returns to shareholders in four countries including the UK, improved in the immediate post-merger period, but this difference disappeared after three years. The results of this comprehensive investigation tended to reinforce the doubts felt about mergers as generators of improved company performance.

(*c*) *Hughes* et al. *(1986):* this study focused on the relationship between financial institutions' holdings and companies' economic performance. Data was used on institutional holdings for a sample of 300 UK industrial companies over the period 1971–80. Overall the results showed a decline in profitability following merger. However, it was small in magnitude and only statistically significant in one year. The results for acquirers with large institutional holdings were different, showing some improvement in profitability, though again the results were not significant.

(*d*) *Kumar (1984):* this study investigated issues relating to the growth of firms over the period 1960 to 1976, using data for 2,000 UK quoted companies. As part of this wider examination, some analysis of post-merger performance, examining the impact on investment as well as profitability was conducted. The results were rather mixed, showing some tendency towards a worsening in profitability performance and an improvement in investment post-merger. However, there was a significant minority of mergers showing a worsening of investment performance and an improvement in profit. Disaggregating the sample, Kumar's results showed that non-horizontal (i.e. vertical and conglomerate mergers) led to a clear improvement in performance while the results of horizontal mergers were more mixed with no pronounced trend.

(*e*) *Holl and Pickering (1986):* the aim of this study was to discover the determinants of successful and unsuccessful takeover bids. Performance was measured using profitability and growth and the data consisted of a matched sample of 50 abandoned and 50 consummated UK mergers. Overall, the results showed that mergers appeared to have an adverse effect on profits and medium-term growth. Of particular interest is the result that both bidding and target companies of abandoned mergers performed better than the matched sample of successful bidders. The conclusion of the study was twofold:
  (i) that the threat of takeover was an effective spur to efficiency and
  (ii) that consummated mergers do not, on balance, lead to efficiency gains.

(*f*) *Ravenscraft and Scherer (1986):* the aim of this study was to assess whether acquired companies showed superior post-merger profit performance relative to control groups and their pre-merger performance. The study covered the mid-1970s and used US data. The results showed that in just over half the sample, profits improved compared with the pre-merger period. In those cases where profits declined, the counter-factual question of whether this would have happened if the merger had not taken place was addressed. It was found that the profits of merged companies fell more rapidly than those of the control group. One interesting conclusion is that in contrast to Kumar's findings, conglomerate mergers performed less well than horizontal mergers.

(*g*) *Sturgess and Wheale (1984):* this study used annual shareholders' rates of return as a measure of post-merger performance. 52 UK firms were assessed over the period 1961–70, including 26 firms that had grown through acquisition and 26 through internal growth. The results were inconclusive with neither the merger intensive group nor the internally growing group consistently out-performing the other.

(*h*) *Firth (1980):* the approach used in this study was similar to that of Sturgess and Wheale, involving an assessment of gains and losses to stockholders. A sample of 224 successful UK takeover bids over the period 1972–74 was used. On average, the stock market took a slightly pessimistic view of these mergers, with gains and losses fairly evenly balanced. The author concluded that mergers were not value creating and were more likely to be motivated by maximisation of management utility reasons than by maximisation of shareholder wealth.

(*i*) *Franks and Harris (1986):* this again examined shareholder wealth effects of corporate takeovers, using data on almost 2,000 acquisitions over the period 1955 to 1985. The results showed large returns to acquiree shareholders in the form of large acquiree bid premiums, which were even higher in the case of contested bids. Post-merger performance of acquirors over the two years following the merger, showed returns comparable to general stock market prices, but insufficient to keep pace with the acquiror's own pre-merger performance.

III. Conclusions

4. Evidence on post-merger performance that has emerged since the Green Paper supports the earlier findings of disappointing or inconclusive performance. Indeed, the consistency of the results of the various studies and the wide range of approaches used tends to reduce the force of the methodological limitations and to increase the robustness of the findings.

The Commission of the European Communities has not sought to prohibit or modify many of the concentrations notified to it under the Merger Regulation. The decision in **Aerospatiale-Alenia/de Havilland** in which a concentration was declared to be incompatible with the common market, is not therefore typical. It does, however, demonstrate the nature of the Commission's assessment of a concentration's anticompetitive peril.

22.6 *Aerospatiale-Alenia/de Havilland* Decision of the Commission of the European Communities OJ 1991 No. L 334/42

THE COMMISSION OF THE EUROPEAN COMMUNITIES:

I. BACKGROUND

The nature of the proceedings

(1) These proceedings concern a proposed operation which was notified on 13 May 1991 pursuant to Article 4 of Council Regulation (EEC) No. 4064/89 (the 'Merger Regulation') consisting of the joint acquisition by Aerospatiale SNI (Aerospatiale) and Alenia-Aeritalia e Selenia SpA (Alenia) of the assets of the de Havilland division (de Havilland) from Boeing Company (Boeing).

[. . .]

The parties

(3) Aerospatiale is a French company active in the aerospace industries. Its product range includes civil and military aircraft and helicopters, missiles, satellites, space systems and avionics. Alenia is an Italian company predominantly active also in the aerospace industries. Its product range includes civil and military aircraft, satellites, space systems, avionics, and air and maritime traffic control systems. Aerospatiale and Alenia jointly control the Groupement d'Intérêt Économique (GIE) Avions de Transport Régional (ATR) which was set up in 1982 in order jointly to design, develop, manufacture and sell regional transport aircraft. There are currently two ATR regional turbo-prop aircraft on the market.

(4) De Havilland, which is a Canadian division of Boeing, only manufactures regional turbo-prop aircraft. The former de Havilland Corporation (DHC) was nationalized by the Candian Government in 1982 and sold to Boeing in 1986. There are currently two de Havilland regional turbo-prop aircraft on the market.

II. THE CONCENTRATION

(5) The notified operation is a concentration in the form of a concentration joint venture within the meaning of Article 3 of the Merger Regulation since:

- de Havilland will be run by an operating company which will be jointly controlled by Aerospatiale and Alenia, and
- the actions of Aerospatiale and Alenia in regional turbo-prop aircraft (commuters) have already been concentrated in the GIE ATR since 1982.

III. COMMUNITY DIMENSION

(6) The combined aggregate worldwide turnover of Aerospatiale, Alenia and de Havilland exceeds ECU 5 billion [. . .]. Aerospatiale and Alenia each achieve a Community-wide turnover of more than ECU 250 million. Furthermore, the undertakings concerned do not achieve more than two-thirds of their Community-wide turnover within one and the same Member State. Thus the concentration has a Community

dimension within the meaning of Article 1(2) of the Merger Regulation.

IV. ASSESSMENT PURSUANT TO ARTICLE 2 OF THE MERGER REGULATION

(7) The operation has as its effect that Aerospatiale and Alenia, which control the world and European leading manufacturer of regional aircraft (ATR), acquire the world and European number two (de Havilland) [. . .]. Regional aircraft (commuters) are aircraft in a range of between 20 and 70 seats intended for regional carriers and have an average flight duration of approximately one hour. The regional transport market is mainly characterized by low density traffic where turbo-prop engined aircraft are, as a general rule, less expensive to operate than jet aircraft. Although the market has for the time being and will have until the mid-90s a relatively high growth rate, the commuter market is comparatively small in terms of aerospace markets generally (total worldwide value of deliveries of new commuter aircraft in 1990: US$2.3 billion, which is estimated at less than 2% of the value of the total aerospace industry).

1. Relevant product markets

(8) The relevant product markets affected by the proposed concentration are those of regional turbo-prop aircraft.

Regional jet aircraft currently being developed (Canadair's 50-seat CL601 RJ jet) cannot be included in these markets. The commuter manufacturers and the airlines questioned on this issue have stated almost unanimously that it is unlikely that regional jet aircraft will compete with traditional turbo-props of a similar capacity. Regional jet aircraft have significantly higher acquisition and operating costs, and furthermore the time saving which a regional jet would offer compared to turbo-props is not significant until routes of 400 to 500 nautical miles are involved. The average distance operated by turbo-props is less than half of this, and according to the parties' own figures as many as 85% of all regional transport aircraft flights are in fact below 400 nautical miles. It is considered therefore that there is no significant overlap of tubo-props and regional jets.

Jet aircraft of around 100 seats developed for short- and medium-haul flights (in particular the Boeing 737, the Fokker 100 and the British Aerospace BAe 146) are also not in competition with regional turbo-prop aircraft. These jet aircraft cost around twice as much as the largest turbo-prop aircraft, and are used on longer routes or routes with high density. The Commission has therefore followed the market definition of the parties, and all the competitors and customers contacted, by excluding jet aircraft from the relevant product markets.

(10) The parties in the notification, the customers and the competitors in their replies to the Commission's enquiry all identified distinct markets within the overall commuter market of 20 to 70-seat aircraft. The division into different relevant markets within the overall market is considered correct by the Commission.

A relevant product market comprises in particular all those products which are regarded as interchangeable or substitutable by the consumer, by reason of the products' characteristics, their prices and their intended use.

It would not appear, for example, that a 60-seat commuter is interchangeable or substitutable with a 30-seat commuter. They are used on routes with a significantly different density. The prices vary significantly [. . .].

(11) According to the Commission's analysis three relevant product markets exist. The segmentation which realistically reflects the different conditions of competition in the overall market distinguishes between commuters with 20 to 39 seats, 40 to 59 seats and 60 seats and over.

(13) This analysis is based in particular on the following:

- The segmentation above is generally consistent with the view of the overwhelming majority of customers and competitors who replied to the Commission's enquiries.

(14) As to possible supply-side substitutability between segments, there may be some possibility in the medium term for the commuter manufacturers to modify existing types (to 'stretch'), so as to develop a new competing product in a higher segment, e.g. ATR 42 to ATR 72. This does not affect the analysis that a type in one segment would not be substitutable for a type in another segment. Furthermore, according to a study carried out for the parties, it would take considerable time, longer than three or four years, for manufacturers for example of 30-seat aircraft to switch their facilities to produce 50-seat aircraft, to the extent that these facilities already exist.

2. Geographical reference market

(20) The commuter markets from an ecomic point of view are considered to be world markets. There are no tangible barriers to the importation of these aircraft into the Community and there are negligible costs of transportation.

There is a significant mutual penetration in particular between the markets of North America and Europe. European commuter manufacturers compete successfully in North America, and the one North American competitor, de Havilland, has a strong market position within the Community.

In their analyses, the parties exclude China and the eastern European countries from the overall world market. This would appear correct since there is no interpenetration between the markets of China and the eastern European countries and the overall world markets, and it is not expected that there will be such interpenetration in the foreseeable future.

It is considered therefore that the geographical market to be taken into account is the world market excluding China and eastern Europe.

[. . .]

3. Market structure

(26)

- in the relevant product market of 40 to 59 seats the new entity would obtain about 64% of the world market and about 72% in the Community,
- in the relevant product market of 60 seats and above, the new entity would have about 76% of the world market and about 74% in the Community,
- ATR and DHC after a merger would obtain worldwide a share of about 50% of the overall commuter market and about 65% in the Community.

4. Impact of the concentration

A. *Effect on ATR's position*

(27) The proposed concentration would significantly strengthen ATR's position on the commuter markets, for the following reasons in particular:

- high combined market share on the 40 to 59-seat market, and of the overall commuter market
- elimination of de Havilland as a competitor
- coverage of the whole range of commuter aircraft
- considerable extension of the customer base.

B. *Assessment of the strength of the remaining competition*

(34) In order to be able to assess whether the new combined entity would be able to act independently of its competitors, in view of its strengthened position, it is necessary to assess the current and expected future strength of the remaining competitors.

(35) As to the competitors, a distinction can be drawn between those which are medium-sized specialists and those which belong to large groups in which commuters form a relatively small part of their overall aerospace activity.

[. . .]

(42) [. . .] [E]ffective competition for the combined entity would only be maintained in the market of 20 to 39-seat commuters, although even here the ability of the competitors to compete with the combined entity would lessen to a certain extent given the overall advantages to ATR/de Havilland arising from a broad sales base

and coverage of all the markets. In the markets for commuters of 40 seats and over, apart from the limited competition from the Saab 2000, it is questionable whether the other existing competitors could provide effective competition in the medium to long term.

C. *Assessment of the customers*

(43) In order to be able to assess whether the new combined entity would be able to act independently of customers, in view of its strong position and the relative weakness of the competitors, the position of customers in the commuter markets must be examined.

(48) [. . .] [F]or most established airlines a direct negative effect from the proposed concentration would only appear over time. The impact would be immediate for airlines which will come on to the market in the future, in particular following deregulation in the community.

(49) Even if in general terms customers would want to switch to a significant extent to the competitors of ATR/de Havilland, there is only a limited possibility given that the existing capacity of each competitor on average is estimated to be capable only of an increase of some 15 to 20% in one to two years. This amounts to under 10% of the overall current worldwide commuter production capacity.

D. *Summary of effect of the proposed concentration on the commuter markets*

(51) The combined entity ATR/de Havilland will obtain a very strong position in the world and Community commuter markets of 40 seats and over, and in the overall world and Community commuter market, as a result of the proposed concentration. The competitors in these markets are relatively weak. The bargaining ability of the customers is limited. The combination of these factors leads to the conclusion that the new entity could act to a significant extent independently of its competitors and customers, and would thus have a dominant position on the commuter markets as defined.

(52) [. . .] [T]he market power of ATR/de Havilland in an overall commuter market is even stronger than is reflected in the market shares. In the overall commuter market, there is an identifiable general trend towards larger aircraft in particular in the Community [. . .]. The higher segments therefore have a strategic importance for the overall commuter market both now and in the future. The evaluation of market power must reflect this dynamic of the market and take into account the fact that a competitor is particularly strong in the strategic parts of the overall market. The extremely strong position which would be obtained by ATR/de Havilland in the higher segments together with the other structural factors as outlined above leads to the conclusion that a dominant position would also be created on an overall market of aircraft of 20 to 70 seats.

E. *Potential entry into the market*

(53) In general terms, a concentration which leads to the creation of a dominant position may however be compatible with the common market within the meaning of Article 2(2) of the Merger Regulation if there exists strong evidence that this position is only temporary and would be quickly eroded because of high probability of strong market entry. With such market entry the dominant position is not likely to significantly impede effective competition within the meaning of Article 2(3) of the Merger Regulation. In order to assess whether the dominant position of ATR/de Havilland is likely to significantly impede effective competition therefore, it is necessary to assess the likelihood of new entry into the market.

(54) Any theoretical attractiveness of entry into the commuter market by a new player must be put into perspective taking into account the forecast demand and the time and cost considerations to enter the market.

(56) [. . .] [A] new entrant into the market would face high risk. Furthermore, given the time necessary to develop a new aircraft and the foreseeable development of the market as described above, a new manufacturer may come too late into the market to catch the expected period of

relatively high demand. Any new market entry at this stage could only come when the market would have declined from current levels and have stabilized. It is therefore doubtful whether a break-even level of sales could be achieved by a new entrant since even existing competitors are not yet at break-even point in their product cycles.

(63) It follows that there is no realistic significant potential competition in the commuter markets in the foreseeable future.

F. *Other general considerations*

(65) The parties argue that one of their objectives in acquiring de Havilland is to reduce costs. The potential cost savings arising from the concentration which have been identified amount to only some ECU 5 million per year. According to the estimates of the parties' economic consultants, these cost savings to the combined entity would arise from rationalizing parts procurement, marketing and product support.

Without prejudice as to whether such considerations are relevant for assessment under Article 2 of the Merger Regulation, such cost savings would have a negligible impact on the overall operation of ATR/de Havilland, amounting to around 0.5% of the combined turnover. The parties have identified (although not quantified) cost savings which could be made by better management of certain aspects of de Havilland's internal operation. These cost savings would not arise as a consequence of the concentration *per se*, but are cost savings which could be achieved by de Havilland's existing owner or by any other potential acquirer.

(68) Although some advantage may be obtained from a dollar manufacturing base, it should be noted that no competitor other than de Havilland has such a base. [. . .]

(69) For the above reasons, the Commission does not consider that the proposed concentration would contribute to the development of technical and economic progress within the meaning of Article 2(1)(*b*) of the Merger Regulation. Even if there was such progress, this would not be to the consumers' advantage.

The consumers will be faced with a dominant position which combines the most popular aircraft families on the market. Choice will be significantly reduced. There is a high risk that in the foreseeable future, the dominant position of ATR/de Havilland would be translated into a monopoly.

Having established a monopoly, ATR/de Havilland would be able to increase prices without any competitive check.

(70) With this perspective, the proposed concentration would become even more harmful to the customers over time as the dominant position translates to a monopoly. Higher prices for commuters have a proportionally large impact on regional airlines since the price of an aircraft accounts for some 30 to 40% of their total operating costs.

(71) The proposed concentration would also lead to adverse effects in the adjacent 100-seat jet market. The British Aerospace BAe 146 jet is produced in the same factory as the ATP commuter so that fixed costs are spread over the two aircraft. A similar interdependency exists between the Fokker F100 jet and the Fokker 50 commuter. Removal of the commuter product lines of both companies would therefore weaken their competitiveness in the 100-seat jet market where they are already facing strong competition from the Boeing 737.

V. CONCLUSION

(72) For the reasons outlined above, it is considered that the proposed concentration would lead to a situation whereby the combined entity ATR/de Havilland could act to a significant extent independently of its competitors and customers on the world markets as defined for commuters of 40 to 59 seats and 60 seats and over. The proposed concentration therefore creates a dominant position on the world markets. Furthermore, according to the above analysis, this dominant position is not merely temporary and will therefore significantly impede effective competition. It is considered that such a dominant position is also created even if the relevant product market is the overall 20 to 70-seat market.

The conditions of competition of the Community commuter markets are not appreciably different from those prevailing in the overall world markets. The market shares of the new entity would be similar in both the world and Comunity markets for commuters of 60 seats and over, and even higher in the Community market for commuters of 40 to 59 seats than in the world market. These markets are also relatively more important in the Community than in the rest of the world. As to the overall market of 20 to 70 seats, the market shares of the new entity would be higher in the Community than in the rest of the world. It is considered therefore that the proposed concentration creates a dominant position which significantly impedes effective competition in the common market within the meaning of Article 2(3) of the Merger Regulation.

HAS ADOPTED THIS DECISION:

ARTICLE 1

The proposed concentration between Aerospatiale and Alenia and de Havilland is declared incompatible with the common market.

The **Horizontal Merger Guidelines** of the Department of Justice and Federal Trade Commission recommend the assessment of a merger in terms of its competitive threat. The principal concern of the **Guidelines** is that higher levels of concentration will enhance firms' ability to collude; the ability of a firm to act independently is also taken into account. Although the **Guidelines** and the EEC **Merger Regulation** are both concerned with mergers which lead to oligopoly (see the **Nestlé/Perrier** decision, section 20.6), the **Merger Regulation** requires evidence of a joint or single dominant position, rather than merely an enhanced ability to enter into, and maintain, restrictive agreements.

22.7 *Horizontal Merger Guidelines*, 1992, Department of Justice and Federal Trade Commission, April 2, 1992

[. . .]

2. THE POTENTIAL ADVERSE COMPETITIVE EFFECTS OF MERGERS

2.0 Overview

Other things being equal, market concentration affects the likelihood that one firm, or a small group of firms, could successfully exercise market power. The smaller the percentage of total supply that a firm controls, the more severely it must restrict its own output in order to produce a given price increase, and the less likely it is that an output restriction will be profitable. If collective action is necessary for the exercise of market power, as the number of firms necessary to control a given percentage of total supply decreases, the difficulties and costs of reaching and enforcing an understanding with respect to the control of that supply might be reduced. However, market share and concentration data provide only the starting point for analyzing the competitive impact of a merger. Before determining whether to challenge a merger, the Agency also will assess the other market factors that pertain to competitive effects, as well as entry, efficiencies and failure.

This section considers some of the potential adverse competitive effects of mergers and the factors in addition to market concentration relevant to each. Because an individual merger may threaten to harm competition through more than one of these effects, mergers will be analyzed in terms of as many potential adverse competitive effects as are appropriate. Entry, efficiencies, and failure are treated in Sections 3–5.

2.1 Lessening of competition through coordinated interaction

A merger may diminish competition by enabling the firms selling in the relevant market more likely, more successfully, or more completely to engage in coordinated interaction that harms consumers. Coordinated interaction is comprised of actions by a group of firms that are profitable for each of them only as a result of the accommodating reactions of the others. This behavior includes tacit or express collusion, and may or may not be lawful in and of itself.

Successful coordinated interaction entails reaching terms of coordination that are profitable to the firms involved and an ability to detect and punish deviations that would undermine the coordinated interaction. Detection and punishment of deviations ensure that coordinating firms will find it more profitable to adhere to the terms of coordination than to pursue short-term profits from deviating, given the costs of reprisal. In this phase of the analysis, the Agency will examine the extent to which post-merger market conditions are conducive to reaching terms of coordination, detecting deviations from those terms, and punishing such deviations. Depending upon the circumstances, the following market factors, among others, may be relevant: the availability of key information concerning market conditions, transactions and individual competitors; the extent of firm and product heterogeneity; pricing or marketing practices typically employed by firms in the market; the characteristics of buyers and sellers; and the characteristics of typical transactions.

Certain market conditions that are conducive to reaching terms of coordination also may be conducive to detecting or punishing deviations from those terms. For example, the extent of information available to firms in the market, or the extent of homogeneity, may be relevant to both the ability to reach terms of coordination and to detect or punish deviations from those terms. The extent to which any specific market condition will be relevant to one or more of the conditions necessary to coordinated interaction will depend on the circumstances of the particular case.

It is likely that market conditions are conducive to coordinated interaction when the firms in the market previously have engaged in express collusion and when the salient characteristics of the market have not changed appreciably since the most recent such incident. Previous express collusion in another geographic market will have the same weight when the salient characteristics of that other market at the time of the collusion are comparable to those in the relevant market.

In analyzing the effect of a particular merger on coordinated interaction, the Agency is mindful of the difficulties of predicting likely future behavior based on the types of incomplete and sometimes contradictory information typically generated in merger investigations. Whether a merger is likely to diminish competition by enabling firms more likely, more successfully or more completely to engage in coordinated interaction depends on whether market conditions, on the whole, are conducive to reaching terms of coordination and detecting and punishing deviations from those terms.

2.11 Conditions conducive to reaching terms of coordination

Firms coordinating their interactions need not reach complex terms concerning the allocation of the market output across firms or the level of the market prices but may, instead, follow simple terms such as a common price, fixed price differentials, stable market shares, or customer or territorial restrictions. Terms of coordination need not perfectly achieve the monopoly outcome in order to be harmful to consumers. Instead, the terms of coordination may be imperfect and incomplete – inasmuch as they omit some market participants, omit some dimensions of competition, omit some customers, yield elevated prices short of monopoly levels, or lapse into episodic price wars – and still result in significant competitive harm. At some point, however, imperfections cause the profitability of abiding by the terms of coordination to decrease and, depending on their extent, may make coordinated interaction unlikely in the first instance.

Market conditions may be conducive to or hinder reaching terms of coordination. For example, reaching terms of coordination may be facilitated by product or firm homogeneity and by existing practices among firms, practices not necessarily themselves antitrust violations, such as standardization of pricing or product variables on which firms could compete. Key information about rival firms and the market may also facilitate reaching terms of coordination. Conversely, reaching terms of coordination may be limited or impeded by product heterogeneity or by firms having substantially incomplete information about the conditions and prospects of their rivals' businesses, perhaps because of important differences among their current business operations. In addition, reaching terms of coordination may be limited or impeded by firm heterogeneity, for example, differences in vertical integration or the production of another product that tends to be used together with the relevant product.

2.12 Conditions conducive to detecting and punishing deviations

Where market conditions are conducive to timely detection and punishment of significant deviations, a firm will find it more profitable to abide by the terms of coordination than to deviate from them. Deviation from the terms of coordination will be deterred where the threat of punishment is credible. Credible punishment, however, may not need to be any more complex than temporary abandonment of the terms of coordination by other firms in the market. Where detection and punishment likely would be rapid, incentives to deviate are diminished and coordination is likely to be successful. The detection and punishment of deviations may be facilitated by existing practices among firms, themselves not necessarily antitrust violations, and by the characteristics of typical transactions. For example, if key information about specific transactions or individual price or output levels is available routinely to competitors, it may be difficult for a firm to deviate secretly. If orders for the relevant product are frequent, regular and small relative to the total output of a firm in a market, it may be difficult for the firm to deviate in a substantial way without the knowledge of rivals and without the opportunity for rivals to react. If demand or cost fluctuations are relatively infrequent and small, deviations may be relatively easy to deter.

By contrast, where detection or punishment is likely to be slow, incentives to deviate are enhanced and coordinated interaction is unlikely to be successful. If demand or cost fluctuations are relatively frequent and large, deviations may be relatively difficult to distinguish from these other sources of market price fluctuations, and, in consequence, deviations may be relatively difficult to deter.

In certain circumstances, buyer characteristics and the nature of the procurement process may affect the incentives to deviate from terms of coordination. Buyer size alone is not the determining characteristic. Where large buyers likely would engage in long-term contracting, so that the sales covered by such contracts can be large relative to the total output of a firm in the market, firms may have the incentive to deviate. However, this only can be accomplished where the duration, volume and profitability of the business covered by such contracts are sufficiently large as to make deviation more profitable in the long term that honoring the terms of coordination, and buyers likely would switch suppliers.

In some circumstances, coordinated interaction can be effectively prevented or limited by maverick firms – firms that have a greater economic incentive to deviate from the terms of coordination than do most of their rivals (e.g. firms that are unusually disruptive and competitive influences in the market). Consequently, acquisition of a maverick firm is one way in which a merger may make coordinated interaction more likely, more successful, or more complete. For example, in a market where capacity constraints are significant for many competitors, a firm is more likely to be a maverick the greater is its excess of divertable capacity in relation to its sales or its total capacity, and the lower are its direct and opportunity costs of expanding sales in the relevant market.[1] This is so because a firm's incentive to deviate from price-elevating and output-limiting terms of coordination is greater the more the firm is able profitably to expand its output as a proportion of the sales it would obtain if it adhered to the terms of coordination and the smaller is the base of sales on which it enjoys elevated profits prior to the price cutting deviation.[2] A firm also may be a maverick if it has an unusual ability secretly to expand its sales in relation to the sales it would obtain if it adhered to the terms of coordination. This ability might arise from opportunities to expand captive production for a downstream affiliate.

2.2 Lessening of competition through unilateral effects

A merger may diminish competition even if it does not lead to increased likelihood of successful coordinated interaction, because merging firms may find it profitable to alter their behavior unilaterally following the acquisition by elevating price and suppressing output. Unilateral competitive effects can arise in a variety of different settings. In each setting, particular other factors describing the relevant market affect the likelihood of unilateral competitive effects. The settings differ by the primary characteristics that distinguish firms and shape the nature of their competition.

2.21 Firms distinguished primarily by differentiated products

In some markets the products are differentiated, so that products sold by different participants in the market are not perfect substitutes for one another. Moreover, different products in the market may vary in the degree of their substitutability for one another. In this setting, competition may be non-uniform (i.e. localized), so that individual sellers compete more directly with those rivals selling closer substitutes.[3]

A merger between firms in a market for differentiated products may diminish competition by enabling the merged firm to profit by unilaterally raising the price of one or both products above the premerger level. Some of the sales loss due to the price rise merely will be diverted to the product of the merger partner and, depending on relative margins, capturing such sales loss through merger may make the price increase profitable even though it would not have been profitable premerger. Substantial unilateral price elevation in a market for differentiated products requires that there be a significant share of sales in the market accounted for by consumers who regard the products of the merging firms as their first and second choices, and that repositioning of the non-parties' product lines to replace the localized competition lost through the merger be unlikely. The price rise will be greater the closer substitutes are to the products of the merging firms, i.e. the more the buyers of one product consider the other product to be their next choice.

2.21.1 Closeness of the products of the merging firms

The market concentration measures articulated in Section 1 may help assess the extent of the likely competitive effect from a unilateral price elevation by the merged firm notwithstanding the fact that the affected products are differentiated. The market concentration measures provide a measure of this effect if each product's market share is reflective of not only its relative appeal as a first choice to consumers of the merging firms' products but also its relative appeal as a second choice, and hence as a competitive constraint to the first choice.[4] Where this circumstance holds, market concentration data fall outside the safeharbor regions of Section 1.5, and the merging firms have a combined market share of at least thirty-five percent, the Agency will presume that a significant share of sales in the market are accounted for by consumers who regard the products of the merging firms as their first and second choices.

Purchasers of one of the merging firms' products may be more or less likely to make the other their second choice than market shares alone would indicate. The market shares of the merging firms' products may understate the competitive effect of concern, when, for example, the products of the merging firms are relatively more similar in their various attributes to one another than to other products in the relevant market. On the other hand, the market shares alone may overstate the competitive effects of concern when, for example, the relevant products are less similar in their attributes to one another than to other products in the relevant market.

Where market concentration data fall outside the safeharbor regions of Section 1.5, the merging firms have a combined market share of at least thirty-five percent, and where data on product attributes and relative product appeal show that a significant share of purchasers of one merging firm's product regard the other as their second choice, then market share data may be relied upon to demonstrate that there is a significant share of sales in the market accounted for by consumers who would be adversely affected by the merger.

2.21.2 Ability of rival sellers to replace lost competition

A merger is not likely to lead to unilateral elevation of prices of differentiated products if, in response to such an effect, rival sellers likely would replace any localized competition lost through the merger by repositioning their product lines.[5]

In markets where it is costly for buyers to evaluate product quality, buyers who consider purchasing from both merging parties may limit the total number of sellers they consider. If either of the merging firms would be replaced in such buyers' consideration by an equally competitive seller not formerly considered, then the merger is not likely to lead to a unilateral elevation of prices.

2.22 Firms distinguished primarily by their capacities

Where products are relatively undifferentiated and capacity primarily distinguishes firms and shapes the nature of their competition, the merged firm may find it profitable unilaterally to raise price and suppress output. The merger provides the merged firm a larger base of sales on which to enjoy the resulting price rise and also eliminates a competitor to which customers otherwise would have diverted their sales. Where the merging firms have a combined market share of at least thirty-five percent, merged firms may find it profitable to raise price and reduce joint output below the sum of their premerger outputs because the lost markups on the forgone sales may be outweighed by the resulting price increase on the merged base of sales.

This unilateral effect is unlikely unless a sufficiently large number of the merged firm's customers would not be able to find economical alternative sources of supply, i.e. competitors of the merged firm likely would not respond to the price increase and output reduction by the merged firm with increases in their own outputs sufficient in the aggregate to make the unilateral action of the merged firm unprofitable. Such non-party expansion is unlikely if those firms face binding capacity constraints that could not be economically relaxed within two years or if existing excess capacity is significantly more costly to operate than capacity currently in use.[6]

3. ENTRY ANALYSIS

3.0 Overview

A merger is not likely to create or enhance market power or to facilitate its exercise, if entry into the market is so easy that market participants, after the merger, either collectively or unilaterally could not profitably maintain a price increase above premerger levels. Such entry likely will deter an anticompetitive merger in its incipiency, or deter or counteract the competitive effects of concern.

Entry is that easy if entry would be timely, likely, and sufficient in its magnitude, character and scope to deter or counteract the competitive effects of concern. In markets where entry is that easy (i.e. where entry passes these tests of timeliness, likelihood, and sufficiency), the merger raises no antitrust concern and ordinarily requires no further analysis.

The committed entry treated in this Section is defined as new competition that requires expenditure of significant sunk costs of entry and exit.[7] The Agency employs a three step methodology to assess whether committed entry would deter or counteract a competitive effect of concern.

The second step assesses whether committed entry would be a profitable and, hence, a likely response to a merger having competitive effects of concern. Firms considering entry that requires significant sunk costs must evaluate the profitability of the entry on the basis of long term participation in the market, because the underlying assets will be committed to the market until they are economically depreciated. Entry that is sufficient to counteract the competitive effects of concern will cause prices to fall to their premerger levels or lower. Thus, the profitability of such committed entry must be determined on the basis of premerger market prices over the long term.

A merger having anticompetitive effects can attract committed entry, profitable at premerger prices, that would not have occurred premerger at these same prices. But following the merger, the reduction in industry output and increase in prices associated with the competitive effect of concern may allow the same entry to occur without driving market prices below premerger levels. After a merger that results in decreased output and increased prices, the likely sales opportunities available to entrants at premerger prices will be larger than they were premerger, larger by the output reduction caused by the merger. If entry could be profitable at premerger prices without exceeding the likely sales opportunities – opportunities that include pre-existing pertinent factors as well as the merger-induced output reduction – then such entry is likely in response to the merger.

The third step assesses whether timely and likely entry would be sufficient to return market prices to their premerger levels. This end may be accomplished either through multiple entry or individual entry at a sufficient scale. Entry may not be sufficient, even though timely and likely, where the constraints on availability of essential assets, due to incumbent control, make it impossible for entry profitably to achieve the necessary level of sales. Also, the character and scope of entrants' products might not be fully responsive to the localized sales opportunities created by the removal of direct competition among sellers of differentiated products. In assessing whether entry will be timely, likely, and sufficient, the Agency recognizes that precise and detailed information may be difficult or impossible to obtain. In such instances, the Agency will rely on all available evidence bearing on whether entry will satisfy the conditions of timeliness, likelihood, and sufficiency.

3.1 Entry alternatives

The Agency will examine the timeliness, likelihood, and sufficiency of the means of entry (entry alternatives) a potential entrant might practically employ, without attempting to identify who might be potential entrants. An entry alternative is defined by the actions the firm must take in order to produce and sell in the market. All phases of the entry effort will be considered, including, where relevant, planning, design, and management; permitting, licensing, and other approvals; construction, debugging, and operation of production facilities; and promotion (including necessary introductory discounts), marketing, distribution, and satisfaction of customer testing and qualification requirements.[8] Recent examples of entry, whether successful or unsuccessful, may provide a useful starting point for identifying the necessary actions, time requirements, and characteristics of possible entry alternatives.

3.2 Timeliness of entry

In order to deter or counteract the competitive effects of concern, entrants quickly must achieve a significant impact on price in the relevant market. The Agency generally will consider timely only those committed entry alternatives that can be achieved within two years from initial planning to significant market impact.[9] Where the relevant product is a durable good, consumers, in response to a significant commitment to entry, may defer purchase by making additional investments to extend the useful life of previously purchased goods and in this way deter or counteract for a time the competitive effects of concern. In these circumstances, if entry only can occur outside of the two year period, the Agency will consider entry to be timely so long as it would deter or counteract the competitive effects of concern within the two year period and subsequently.

3.3 Likelihood of entry

An entry alternative is likely if it would be profitable at premerger prices, and if such prices could be secured by the entrant.[10] The committed entrant will be unable to secure prices at premerger levels if its output is too large for the market to absorb without depresssing prices further. Thus, entry is unlikely if the minimum viable scale is larger than the likely sales opportunity available to entrants.

Minimum viable scale is the smallest average annual level of sales that the committed entrant must persistently achieve for profitability at premerger prices.[11] Minimum viable scale is a function of expected revenues, based upon premerger prices,[12] and all categories of costs associated with the entry alternative, including an appropriate rate of return on invested capital given that entry could fail and sunk costs, if any, will be lost.[13]

Sources of sales opportunities available to entrants include: (a) the output reduction associated with the competitive effect of concern,[14] (b) entrants' ability to capture a share of reasonably expected growth in market demand,[15] (c) entrants' ability securely to divert sales from incumbents, for example, through vertical integration or through forward contracting, and (d) any additional anticipated contraction in incumbents' output in response to entry.[16] Factors that reduce the sales opportunities available to entrants include: (a) the prospect that an entrant will share in a reasonably expected decline in market demand, (b) the exclusion of an entrant from a portion of the market over the long term because of vertical integration or forward contracting by incumbents, and (c) any anticipated sales expansion by incumbents in reaction to entry, either generalized or targeted at customers approached by the entrant, that utilizes prior irreversible investments in excess production capacity. Demand growth or decline will be viewed as relevant only if total market demand is projected to experience long-lasting change during at least the two year period following the competitive effect of concern.

3.4 Sufficiency of entry

Inasmuch as multiple entry generally is possible and individual entrants may flexibly choose their scale, committed entry generally will be sufficient to deter or counteract the competitive effects of concern whenever entry is likely under the analysis of Section 3.3. However, entry, although likely, will not be sufficient if, as a result of incumbent control, the tangible and intangible assets required for entry are not adequately available for entrants to respond fully to their sales opportunities. In addition, where the competitive effect of concern is not uniform across the relevant market, in order for entry to be sufficient, the character and scope of entrants' products must be responsive to the localized sales opportunities that include the output reduction associated with the competitive effect of concern. For example, where the concern is unilateral price elevation as a result of a merger between producers of differentiated products, entry, in order to be sufficient, must involve a product so close to the products of the merging firms that the merged firm will be unable to internalize enough of the sales loss due to the price rise, rendering the price increase unprofitable.

4. EFFICIENCIES

The primary benefit of merger to the economy is their efficiency-enhancing potential, which can increase the competitiveness of firms and result in lower prices to consumers. Because the antitrust laws, and thus the standards of the *Guidelines*, are designed to proscribe only mergers that present a significant danger to competition, they do not present an obstacle to most mergers. As a consequence, in the majority of cases, the *Guidelines* will allow firms to achieve available efficiencies through mergers without interference from the Agency.

Some mergers that the Agency otherwise might challenge may be reasonably necessary to achieve significant net efficiencies. Cognizable efficiencies include, but are not limited to, achieving economies of scale, better integration of production facilities, plant specialization, lower transportation costs, and similar efficiencies relating to specific manufacturing, servicing, or distribution operations of the merging firms. The Agency may also consider claimed efficiencies resulting from reductions in general selling, administrative, and overhead expenses, or that otherwise do not relate to specific manufacturing, servicing, or distribution operations of the merging firms, although, as a practical matter, these types of efficiencies may be difficult to demonstrate. In addition, the Agency will reject claims of efficiencies if equivalent or comparable savings can reasonably be achieved by the parties through other means. The expected net efficiencies must be greater the more significant are the competitive risks identified in Sections 1–3.

5. FAILURE AND EXITING ASSETS

5.0 Overview

Notwithstanding the analysis of Sections 1–4 of the *Guidelines*, a merger is not likely to create or enhance market power or to facilitate its exercise, if imminent failure, as defined below, of one of the merging firms would cause the assets of that firm to exit the relevant market. In such circumstances, post-merger performance in the relevant market may be no worse than market performance had the merger been blocked and the assets left the market.

5.1 Failing firm

A merger is not likely to create or enhance market power or facilitate its exercise if the following circumstances are met: (1) the allegedly failing firm would be unable to meet its financial obligations in the near future; (2) it would not be able to reorganize successfully under Chapter 11 of the Bankruptcy Act;[17] (3) it has made unsuccessful good-faith efforts to elicit reasonable alternative offers of acquisition of the assets of the failing firm[18] that would both keep its tangible and intangible assets in the relevant market and pose a less severe danger to competition than does the proposed merger; and (4) absent the acquisition, the assets of the failing firm would exit the relevant market.

5.2 Failing Division

A similar argument can be made for 'failing' divisions as for failing firms. First, upon applying appropriate cost allocation rules, the division must have a negative cash flow on an operating basis. Second, absent the acquisition, it must be that the assets of the division would exit the relevant market in the near future if not sold. Due to the ability of the parent firm to allocate costs, revenues, and intracompany transactions among itself and its subsidiaries and divisions, the Agency will require evidence, not based solely on management plans that could be prepared solely for the purpose of demonstrating negative cash flow or the prospect of exit from the relevant market. Third, the owner of the failing division also must have complied with the competitively-preferable purchaser requirement of Section 5.1.

NOTES

1 But excess capacity in the hands of non-maverick firms may be a potent weapon with which to punish deviations from the terms of coordination.

2 Similarly, in a market where product design or quality is significant, a firm is more likely to be an effective maverick the greater is the sales potential of its products among customers of its rivals, in relation to the sales it would obtain if it adhered to the terms of coordination. The likelihood of expansion responses by a maverick will be analyzed in the same fashion as uncommitted entry or committed entry (see sections 1.3 and 3) depending on the significance of the sunk costs entailed in expansion.

3 Similarly, in some markets sellers are primarily distinguished by their relative advantages in serving different buyers or groups or buyers, and buyers negotiate individually with sellers. Here, for example, sellers may formally bid against one another for the business of a buyer, or each buyer may elicit individual price quotes from multiple sellers. A seller may find it relatively inexpensive to meet the demands of particular buyers or types of buyers, and relatively expensive to meet others' demands. Competition, again, may be localized: sellers compete more directly with those rivals having similar relative advantages in serving particular buyers or groups of buyers. For example, in open outcry auctions, price is determined by the cost of the second lowest-cost seller. A merger involving the first and second lowest-cost sellers could cause prices to rise to the constraining level of the next lowest-cost seller.

4 Information about consumers' actual first and second product choices may be provided by marketing surveys, information from bidding structures, or normal course of business documents from industry participants.

5 The timeliness and likelihood of repositioning responses will be analyzed using the same methodology as used in analyzing uncommitted entry or committed entry (see Sections 1.3 and 3), depending on the significance of the sunk costs entailed in repositioning.

6 The timeliness and likelihood of non-party expansion will be analyzed using the same methodology as used in analyzing uncommitted or committed entry (see Sections 1.3 and 3) depending on the significance of the sunk costs entailed in expansion.

7 Supply responses that require less than one year and insignificant sunk costs to effectuate are analyzed as uncommitted entry in section 1.3.

The first step assesses whether entry can achieve significant market impact within a timely period. If significant market impact would require a longer period, entry will not deter or counteract the competitive effect of concern.

8 Many of these phases may be undertaken simultaneously.

9 Firms which have committed to entering the market prior to the merger generally will be included in the measurement of the market. Only committed entry or adjustments to pre-existing entry plans that are induced by the merger will be considered as possibly deterring or counteracting the competitive effects of concern.

10 Where conditions indicate that entry may be profitable at prices below premerger levels, the Agency will assess the likelihood of entry at the lowest price at which such entry would be profitable.

11 The concept of minimum viable scale (MVS) differs from the concept of minimum efficient scale (MES). While MES is the smallest scale at which average costs are minimized, MVS is the smallest scale at which average costs equal the premerger price.

12 The expected path of future prices, absent the merger, may be used if future price changes can be predicted with reasonable reliability.

13 The minimum viable scale of an entry alternative will be relatively large when the fixed costs of entry are large, when the fixed costs of entry are largely sunk, when the marginal costs of production are high at low levels of output, and when a plant is underutilized for a long time because of delays in achieving market acceptance.

14 Five percent of total market sales typically

is used because where a monopolist profitably would raise price by five percent or more across the entire relevant market, it is likely that the accompanying reduction in sales would be no less than five percent.

15 Entrants' anticipated share of growth in demand depends on incumbents' capacity constraints and irreversible investments in capacity expansion, as well as on the relative appeal, acceptability and reputation of incumbents' and entrants' products to the new demand.

16 For example, in a bidding market where all bidders are on equal footing, the market share of incumbents will contract as a result of entry.

17 11 U.S.C. @@ 1101–1174 (1988).

18 Any offer to purchase the assets of the failing firm for a price above the liquidation value of those assets – the highest valued use outside the relevant market or equivalent offer to purchase the stock of the failing firm – will be regarded as a reasonable alternative offer.

FURTHER READING

Works on Merger Law and Policy

American Bar Association (1986), *Horizontal Mergers: Law and Policy* (American Bar Association, Chicago).

Collins, W. and Loftis, J. (1988), *Non-Horizontal Mergers: Law and Policy* (American Bar Association, Chicago).

Cook, C. and Kerse, C. (1991), *EEC Merger Control: Regulation 4064/89* (Sweet & Maxwell, London).

Coopers and Lybrand (1989), *Barriers to Takeovers in the European Community: A Study by Coopers & Lybrand for the DTI* (HMSO: London).

Downes, T. and Ellison, J. (1990), *The Legal Control of Mergers in the EC* (Blackstone, London).

Fairburn, J. and Kay, J. (eds) (1989), *Mergers and Merger Policy* (Oxford University Press, Oxford).

Fine, F. (1989), *Mergers and Joint Ventures in Europe: The Law and Policy of the EEC* (Graham and Trotman, London).

Jacquemin, A. (1991), *Merger and Competition Policy in the European Community* (Basil Blackwell, Oxford).

Monopolies and Mergers Commission (1992), *The Role of the Commission*, 4th edn (HMSO, London).

Miller, R. (ed.) (1992), *The Monopolies and Mergers Yearbook: March 1989 to December 1990* (Blackwell Business, Oxford).

Office of Fair Trading (1983), *Mergers: A Guide to the Procedures Under the Fair Trading Act 1973*, 2nd edn (HMSO, London).

Peacock, A. and Bannock, G. (1991), *Corporate Takeovers and the Public Interest: Report of an Inquiry Conducted for the Joseph Rowntree Foundation by the David Hume Institute.*

Works on economic issues in vertical mergers and horizontal mergers

Vertical mergers

Allen, B. T. (1971), 'Vertical integration and market foreclosure: the case of cement and concrete', 14 *Journal of Law and Economics*, 251.

Blair, R. D. and Kaserman, D. L. (1983), *Law and Economics of Vertical Integration and Control*, Academic Press, New York.

Greenhut, M. and Ohta, H. (1979), 'Vertical integration of successive oligopolies', 69 *American Economic Review*, 137.

Hart, O. D. and Tirole, J. (1990), 'Vertical integration and market foreclosure', *Brookings Papers on Economic Activity*, *Microeconomics*, 205.

Kaserman, D. L. (1978), 'Theories of vertical integration: implications for antitrust policy', 23 *Antitrust Bulletin*, 483.

Ordover, J. A., Saloner, G. and Salop, S. C. (1990), 'Equilibrium vertical foreclosure', 86 *American Economic Review*, 137.

Salinger, M. A. (1988), 'Vertical merger and market foreclosure', 103 *Quarterly Journal of Economics*, 345.

Schmalensee, R. (1973), 'A note on the theory of vertical integration', 81 *Journal of Policitcal Economy*, 442.

Horizontal mergers

Barker, J. B. and Bresnahan, T. F. (1985), 'The gains from merger and collusion in product-differentiated industries', 33 *Journal of Industrial Economics*, 427.

Caves, R. E. (1989), 'Mergers, takeovers and economic efficiency: foresight vs. hindsight', 9 *International Journal of Industrial Organization*, 151.

Cowling, K., Stoneman, P., Cubbin, J., Cable, J., Hall, G., Domberger, S., Dutton, P. (1980), *Mergers and Economic Performance* (Cambridge University Press).

Dansby, R. E. and Willig, R. D. (1979), 'Industry performance gradient indices', 69 *American Economic Review*, 249.

Fairburn, J. and Kay, J. (eds) (1989), *Mergers and Merger Policy* (Oxford University Press, Oxford).

Hannah, L. and Kay, J. A. (1976), *Concentration in Modern Industry* (Macmillan, London).

Mueller, D. C. (ed.) (1980), *The Determinants and Effects of Mergers: An International Comparison* (Oelgeslayer, Gunn and Mann, London).

Muller, J. (1976), 'The impact of mergers on concentration: a study of eleven West German industries', 25 *Journal of Industrial Economics*, 113.

Ravenscraft, D. J. and Scherer, F. M. (1989), 'The profitability of mergers', 7 *International Journal of Industrial Organization*, 101.

Salant, S. W., Switzer, S. and Reynolds, R. J. (1983). 'Losses from horizontal merger: the effects of an exogenous change in industry structure on Cournot–Nash equilibrium', 98 *Quarterly Journal of Economics*, 185.

Williamson, O. E. (1968), 'Economics as an antitrust defense: The welfare tradeoffs', 58 *American Economic Review*, 18.

Willig, R. D. (1991), Merger analysis, industrial organisation theory, and merger guidelines', *Brookings Papers on Economic Activity, Microeconomics*, 281.

PART SIX

EXTRATERRITORIALITY

23

EXTRATERRITORIALITY

In the **Wood Pulp** cases, over forty manufacturers of bleached sulphate pulp (a product used in the manufacture of paper), all of whom were located outside the territory of the EEC, representing two-thirds of the supply of the product in the EEC, engaged in a price-fixing arrangement. Agreements and concerted practices were used as vehicles for the pricing arrangements. Prices were announced by each producer for the following quarter; over a long period, the producers announced identical or similar prices. The Commission determined that it had sufficient territorial jurisdiction to extend Article 85 to the practices in question. That was disputed before the European Court of Justice. Prior to this case, the Court had relied on the 'single economic entity' doctrine, as developed in the *Dyestuffs* case: *ICI* v. *EC Commission* [1972] CMLR 557, under which the presence of a part of an undertaking (such as a subsidiary) within the EEC was sufficient to found jurisdiction against all parts of the undertaking, even those located outside the EEC.

One convenience of such an approach was to avoid the application of the 'effects doctrine', under which jurisdiction may be claimed in respect of acts, the effect of which are felt on the territory of the prosecuting state. Many states had taken great exception to the adoption of the effects doctrine, which remained controversial in international law. Such objections were forcefully expressed in the *aide-mémoire* sent by the British government to the European Court of Justice on the occasion of the *Dyestuffs* case. The UK's hostile attitude to the effects doctrine was also manifested in the **Protection of Trading Interests Act 1980**, which was enacted as a response to the enthusiastic prosecution by the USA of such extraterritorial jurisdiction.

In that the firms involved in the **Wood Pulp** cases had no corporate location in the EEC, the 'single economic entity' doctrine could not be deployed. The European Court of Justice was therefore presented with an opportunity to review its policy on extraterritorial jurisdiction. Specifically, the Court was invited to support the adoption of the effects doctrine for EEC competition law.

Courts and agencies in the USA now adopt a much more conciliatory approach to claims to jurisdiction, under the influence of the *Antitrust Enforcement Guidelines for International Operations*, published by the Department of Justice in

1988. A 'rule of reason' approach to jurisdiction was supported by the Court of Appeals for the Ninth Circuit in *Timberlane Lumber Co.* v. *Bank of America*, 549 F. 2d 594 (1976). An alternative approach to disputes over jurisdiction was adopted with the publication of an **international agreement** between the USA and the EEC in 1991.

FURTHER READING

Friedberg, J. (1991), 'The convergence of law in an era of political integration: the Wood Pulp case and the Alcoa effects doctrine', 52 *University of Pittsburgh Law Review*, 289.

Note (1990), 'Inconsistent application of the extraterritorial provisions of the Sherman Act: a judicial response based upon the much maligned "effects" test'. 73 *Marquette Law Review*, 435.

23.1 Re Wood Pulp Cartel: *A. Ahlstrom Oy and Others* v. *Commission of the European Communities*, Court of Justice of The European Communities [1988] ECR 5193, [1988] 4 CMLR 901

Opinion of the Advocate General:

[T]he addressees of the Commission's decision – all of which have their registered office outside the Community – [. . .] called in question [. . .] the issue of the Community's jurisdiction to apply the competition rules of the Treaty to undertakings in non-member countries [. . .].

It is the basis on which the Commission relied in its contested decision in order to establish its jurisdiction – namely the location of the effects (paragraph (79) of the contested decision) – which is challenged by the applicants and disapproved of by the United Kingdom. Whatever its position on this matter may have been in other contexts and even if, as some have been at pains to point out, the Commission has tended in its documents to rely at times on the location of the effects and at other times on the location of the anti-competitive conduct, it seems to me that it must be on the basis of the former that the issue of Community jurisdiction is decided.

In that respect, I differ from the United Kingdom, which has asked the Court to resolve this dispute by holding that this case involves the exercise of territorial jurisdiction, which is accepted both by Community law and by international law.

The opponents of the effects doctrine have sought to make out their case against it on the basis of arguments derived from both Community law and international law. Thus the objection to the Commission's decision is that neither Community law nor international law authorises the application of the Community competition rules to undertakings established outside the Community solely by reason of the effects produced within the Community.

Once those two aspects have been considered, it will be necessary to review the principles laid down in the particularly rich United States case law in this field. I shall then suggest the criteria to be adopted as the basis for the Community's jurisdiction over undertakings established outside the Community [. . .].

I. THE EFFECTS DOCTRINE IN THE LIGHT OF COMMUNITY LAW

Whatever the specific features of each of the cases now before the Court, the challenge to the Community's jurisdiction to apply its competition rules to undertakings established outside the Community rests on two considerations. In the first place, it is said that there is nothing in the wording of Article 85 of the Treaty to allow it to be extended to cover undertakings outside the Community solely by reason of anti-competitive effects produced within the territory of the Community. Secondly, it is suggested that the case law of the Court can be construed as rejecting the effects doctrine. Let me state at once that I will advise the Court to uphold neither of those objections.

1. The wording of Article 85

The wording of Article 85 of the Treaty offers general support for the proposition that Community competition law is applicable, by its very essence, whenever anti-competitive effects have been produced within the territory of the Community. The effect on trade between Member States constitutes the demarcating criterion between Community jurisdiction and national jurisdiction in the matter. It is agreements, decisions and concerted practices which have 'as their object or effect the prevention, restriction or distortion of competition within the Common Market' that are prohibited and declared incompatible with the Treaty.

In the light of that provision, the vast majority of academic writers take the view that it is neither the nationality nor the geographical location of the undertaking but the location of the anti-competitive effect which constitutes the criterion for the application of Community competition law (G. Bernini, 'Les règles de concurrence' in *Trente Ans de Droit Communautaire* (Office des Publications Officielles des Communautés Européennes, 1982) p. 345, in particular p. 375; B. Goldman, 'Les champs d'application territoriale des lois sur la concurrence', [1969] III RCADI, 635, in particular p. 676 *et seq.*, and by the same author, 'Les effets juridiques extraterritoriaux de la politique de la concurrence', [1972] RMC 612, in particular pp. 614 and 615; J. M. Bischoff and R. Kovar, 'L'application du Droit Communautaire de la concurrence aux enterprises etablies a l'exterieur de la Communauté, [1975] JDI 675, in particular p. 684; J. Schapira, G. le Tallec, J.-B. Blaise, *Droit Européen des Affaires* (PUF, Themis, 1984) p. 245; J. Megret, J.-V. Louis, D. Vignes, M. Waelbroeck, *Le Droit de la Communauté Economique Européenne*, Vol. 4: *Concurrence* (Editions de l'Université de Bruxelles, 1972) pp. 110 and 111; J. Soufflet, 'Law competence extraterritoriale du droit de la concurrence de la Communauté Economique Européenne', [1971] JDI 487, in particular p. 491.)

In fact, it is uncertain whether the 'effect' referred to in Article 85 of the Treaty constitutes, strictly speaking, a basis of jurisdiction. This concept, like that of 'object' (Focsaneaunu, 'Pour objet ou pur effet', [1966] RMC 862), quite clearly makes it possible to establish an infringement of the substantive law of competition in cases where Community jurisdiction itself is indisputable. However, it may be relied upon to serve a different function, as a criterion of jurisdiction, and its scope is then not necessarily identical to that of the effect in substantive law. I shall return to this point in due course.

2. Principles laid down by the Court in its case law

Although the Court has not, in its decision to date, formally upheld the effects doctrine with regard to the application of competition law to undertakings outside the Community, that does not imply that it rejects the doctrine.

The cases most frequently cited in this connection are the so-called Dyestuffs cases (Case 48/69, *Imperial Chemical Industries* [1972] ECR 619, [1972] CMLR 557; Case 52/69, *JR Geigy AG* [1972] ECR 787, [1972] CMLR 557; Case 53/69, *Sandoz AG* [1972]

ECR 845, [1972] CMLR 557). In its judgment of 14 July 1972, although Mayras AG had suggested that the Court adopted the criterion of the effects, albeit the qualified effects, in order to establish the Community's jurisdiction over undertakings outside its territory, the Court preferred to base such jurisdiction on the unity of the undertaking. But that certainly does not mean that the location of the effects would not constitute a sufficient basis for jurisdiction (see J.-M. Bischoff and R. Kovar, *supra*, p. 684). As Professor Goldman has pointed out, precisely in connection with that judgment, 'no inferences may be drawn from the silences of the Court' (B. Goldman, International Law Association, *Report of the 55th Conference* (New York 1972) p. 128).

Nor is it possible to infer from the Court's judgments in that field conclusive arguments in favour of the effects doctrine, even though some of those judgments contain statements which may go some way towards supporting it. Thus, for instance, when the Court stated in its judgment in Beguelin that 'the fact that one of the undertakings which are parties to the agreement is situate in a third country does not prevent application of [. . .] [Article 85 of the Treaty] [. . .] since the agreement is operative on the territory of the common market (Case 22/71: [1971] ECR 949, [1972] CMLR 81 at paragraph (11) of the decision), the fact must not be altogether disregarded that that case concerned an agreement granting an exclusive concession and that one of the parties to it was established within the Community.

In other words, the case law of the Court concerning competition law is not conclusive either for or against the effects doctrine as the criterion for the applicability of Community law to undertakings situated outside the Community.

Conversely, support for the application of the effects doctrine may be found in *Walrave* v. *Union Cycliste Internationale* (Case 36/74: [1974] ECR 1405). In that judgment, regarding the principle of non-discrimination on grounds of nationality in connection with the Treaty rules in freedom of movement for workers and the provision of services, the Court stated that:

> By reason of the fact that it is imperative, the rule on non-discrimination applies in judging all legal relationships in so far as these relationships, by reason either of the place where they are entered into or of the place where they take effect, can be located within the territory of the Community (Case 36/74: [1974] ECR 1405, [1975] 1 CMLR 277 at paragraph (28) of the decision).

That case was concerned with a rule of the Union Cycliste Internationale, whose seat was in Geneva. In the proceedings before the Court, the Union Cycliste Internationale sought to rely on *Geigy* (Case 52/69 [1972] ECR 787 at 826, [1972] CMLR 557 at 639) and *Continental Can* (Case 6/72 [1973] ECR 215 at 241, [1973] CMLR 199 at 221) against the effects doctrine, on the ground that that criterion had not been adopted by the Court in those judgments.

That argument reveals the full significance of the Court's answer. Some writers have drawn the conclusion that the effects doctrine is a basis for asserting Community jurisdiction which, although enunciated in another context, may be relied upon in the field of competition (P. Delannay, 'Observations sous l'Arrêt 36/74, *Walrave et Koch*', [1976] CDE, 209, in particular p. 224). If the position adopted by the Court in *Walrave* may be transported to competition law, and I see no reason why it should not, it is legitimate to argue that, far from repudiating the effects doctrine, the Court has no hesitation in endorsing it.

However, that finding alone does not suffice. In a matter of this kind, it is necessary to ascertain whether or not such a criterion is in conformity with the requirements and the practice of international law.

II. THE EFFECTS DOCTRINE IN THE LIGHT OF INTERNATIONAL LAW

The two undisputed bases on which State jurisdiction is founded under international law are territoriality and nationality (see, for instance, R. Higgins, 'The legal bases of jurisdiction', in C. J. Olmstead (ed.) *Extra-*

territorial Application of Laws and Responses Thereto (Oxford: ILA and ECS, 1984) p. 3). The former confers jurisdiction on the State in which the person or the goods in question are situated or the event in question took place. The latter confers jurisdiction over nationals of the State concerned.

Territoriality itself has given rise to two distinct principles of jurisdiction:

- subjective territoriality, which permits a State to deal with acts which originated within its territory, even though they were completed abroad;
- objective territoriality, which, conversely, permits a State to deal with acts which originated abroad but which were completed, at least in part, within its own territory.

The principle of objective territoriality has played a decisive role in the extension of national jurisdiction in the field of competition. From it is derived the effects doctrine, which, in order to deal with the effects in question, confers jurisdiction upon a State even if the conduct which produced them did not take place within its territory.

Is the location of effects doctrine, as a basis for jurisdiction, consistent with the rules of international law? In order to answer that question, it is necessary first of all to consider the very nature of international law. Is it law which confers powers, so that a State seeking to exercise its jurisdiction must establish the existence of a permissive rule of international law? Or is it, on the contrary, a law which respects all the powers of the State – a corollary of sovereignty – and merely sets certain limits to the exercise of such sovereignty which, in the absence of prohibitive rules, remains intact?

Academic writers are divided on that point. The discussion has revolved essentially around the significance and scope of the *Lotus* judgement, delivered on 7 September 1927 by the Permanent Court of International Justice ((1927) PCIJ ser A, no 10). That judgment, adopted by the President's casting vote, states in particular that international law does not prohibit a State from exercising jurisdiction in its own territory, in respect of any case which relates to acts which have taken place abroad, and in which it cannot rely on some permissive rule of international law. Such a view would only be tenable if international law contained a general prohibition to States to extend the application of their laws and the jurisdiction of their courts to persons, property and acts outside their territory, and if, as an exception to this general prohibition, it allowed States to do so in certain specific cases. But this is certainly not the case under international law as it stands at present. Far from laying down a general prohibition to the effect that States may not extend the application of their laws and the jurisdiction of their courts to persons, property and acts outside their territory, it leaves them in this respect a wide measure of discretion which is only limited in certain cases by prohibitive rules; as regards other cases, every State remains free to adopt the principle which it regards as best and most suitable.

This discretion left to States by international law explains the great variety of rules which they have been able to adopt without objections or complaints on the part of other States [. . .]

[. . .] [A]ll that can be required of a State is that it should not overstep the limits which international law places upon its jurisdiction; within these limits, its title to exercise jurisdiction rests in its sovereignty.

The full force of that statement becomes apparent if it is read in conjunction with the Permanent Court's declaration that 'international law governs relations between independent States' and that 'restrictions upon the independence of States cannot therefore be presumed'.

The position under international law in that regard was restated and refined by Sir Gerald Fitzmaurice in his Separate Opinion in the judgment of the International Court of Justice of 5 February 1970 in *Barcelona Traction*:

> It is true that, under present conditions, international law does not impose hard and fast rules on States delimiting spheres of

national jurisdiction in such matters (and there are of course others – for instance in the fields of shipping, 'antitrust' legislation, etc.), but leaves to States a wide discretion in the matter. It does however (a) postulate the existence of limits – though in any given case it may be for the tribunal to indicate what these are for the purposes of that case; (b) involve for every State an obligation to exercise moderation and restraint as to the extent of the jurisdiction assumed by its courts in cases having a foreign element, and to avoid undue encroachment on a jurisdiction more properly appertaining to, or more appropriately exercisable by, another State. [1970] ICJ Rep 65 at 105).

Another passage in the *Lotus* judgment has been relied upon by certain writers in order to limit its scope with regard to recognition of the effects doctrine as a basis for State jurisdiction. The Permanent Court pointed out that even the courts of countries which have a strictly territorial conception of their criminal legislation interpret it in such a way as to include within its scope offences, even if committed abroad, if 'one of the constituent elements of the offence, and more especially its effects' have taken place within the national territory. The Permanent Court goes on to point out in its judgment that, in that case, the act and its effects 'are, legally, entirely inseparable', which has led certain writers to argue that only circumstances of that kind permit a State to exercise its jurisdiction by virtue of the principle of objective territoriality.

However, on the assumption that the Permanent Court wished, in so doing, to circumscribe the jurisdiction of the State based on objective territoriality to cases in which the effect produced within its territory was itself a constituent element of the offence, that would have no bearing on the application of the Community competition rules to undertakings established outside the Community. It should be recalled that Article 85 of the Treaty prohibits any agreements, decisions and concerted practices which have as their effect 'the prevention, restriction or distortion of competition within the Common Market'. Is not such an effect necessarily a constituent element of the offence? (M. Akehurst, 'Jurisdiction in international law', [1972–1973] *British Yearbook of International Law* 145, in particular pp. 195 and 196; B. Goldman, 'Les champs d'application territoriale des lois sur la concurrence'. [1969] III RCADI 635, in particular p. 701). That was the view taken by Mayras AG when he stated that 'in competition law the effect of the offence is in fact one of its constituent and probably even the essential element' (opinion of Mayras AG in Cases 48/69, 52/69, and 53/69, *Dyestuffs* [1972] ECR 619 at 694, [1972] CMLR 557 at 604.)

Accordingly, even though, for other reasons, the question has been asked 'is the Lotus still sailing' (P. Julliard, 'L'application extraterritoriale de la loi économique' in *L'Application Extraterritoriale du Droit Economique*, Cahiers du Cedin, *supra* p. 13, in particular p. 24), there would appear to be no doubt that the principle thus laid down, which has admittedly been criticised by academic writers but has not so far been contradicted by international case law, permits the conclusion to be drawn that consideration of the location of the effects as the basis of a State's jurisdiction is in conformity with the rules of international law (In that regard P. Demaret writes: 'The *Lotus* judgment was given with the smallest possible majority. But the dictum cited above corresponds to the true state of international affairs as it was in 1927 and undoubtedly still is today': see L'Extraterritorialité des lois et les relations transatlantiques: une question de droit ou de diplomatie?' [1985] CDE 1, in particular p. 26). And what is thus permissible for States must necessarily also be permissible for the Community, as a subject of international law, where the jurisdiction of the Community has been substituted for that of the Member States.

The jurisdiction thus conferred is 'jurisdiction to prescribe', being the power of the State to 'lay down general or individual rules through its legislative, executive or judicial bodies' (B. Stern, 'Quelques observations sur les règles internationales relatives a l'application extraterritoriale du droit', [1986] AFDI 7, in particular p. 11). It cannot be understood as constituting 'jurisdiction to enforce', which is the 'power of a State to give effect to a general rule or an individual decision by means of substantive implementing measures which may include even coercion by the authorities'. That opinion is widely shared by those academic writers who accept that the effects doctrine may constitute a basis for the assertion of jurisdiction by the State. Moreover, it is essentially against measures taken pursuant to enforcement jurisdiction that some 20 countries have adopted so-called 'blocking statutes' (see, for instance, J. R. Atwood, 'Blocking statutes and sovereign compulsion: recent developments and the proposed restatement', in B. E. Hawk (ed.), *Antitrust and Trade Policies in the United States and the European Community, Annual Proceedings of the Fordham Corporate Law Institute* (New York, Matthew Bender, 1986), Chapter 16, p. 327; L. Collins, 'Blocking and clawback statutes: the United Kingdom approach', [1986] *Journal of Business Law*, pp. 372 and 452). But the question which must then be raised is whether the power to impose a fine comes within the scope of prescriptive jurisdiction or enforcement jurisdiction.

Where an agreement, decision or concerted practice is declared unlawful and a fine is imposed, that is generally agreed to constitute the exercise of prescriptive jurisdiction. The prohibition imposed by international law upon a State is, to adopt the wording used in *Lotus*, that 'failing the existence of a permissive rule to the contrary – it may not exercise its power in any form in the territory of another State'.

Accordingly, it is specific measures of enforcement and coercion that are excluded. However, as others have written before, 'to order is not to compel' (B. Goldman and A. Lyon-Caen, *Droit Commercial Européen* (Dalloz, 4th edn 1983) p. 886). And I, for my part, agree with the following analysis made by Professor Goldman:

> An order to pay a fine, where it penalises events covered by the law of the forum in view of the effects which they produce within the territory of the forum [. . .] is indissolubly linked, like the fact giving rise to it or the finding of nullity, to the application of the law which is by definition the proper law, and to deny the court the power to make such an order would render that 'prescriptive jurisdiction' nugatory. (B. Goldman, 'Observations sur les arrêts "Matières Colorantes"'. [1973] JDI 935).

That was the approach taken by Mayras AG in his Opinion in the *Dyestuffs* cases:

> The imposition of a pecuniary sanction, the purpose of which is to suppress conduct interfering with competition, and also to prevent its continuance or renewal, should be distinguished from the recovery of a fine imposed which can only be effected, should the undertaking penalised refuse to pay, by means of a forcible execution. ([1972] ECR 619 at 695, [1972] CMLR 557 at 606)

That having been said, it is undoubtedly in United States law that are to be found the most far-reaching deliberations and efforts to determine the circumstances permitting a State to exercise its prescriptive jurisdiction in situations involving extraneous elements. That is not surprising. The Sherman Act (for the text of the Act see [1984] ECC 293) dates back to 1890. It has given rise to a very considerable body of case law and academic writing, evidencing the concern to reconcile legitimate national interests with the imperative requirements of international law and international relations. That is why I propose to refer to the most noteworthy decisions of the United States courts.

III. THE PRINCIPLES OF UNITED STATES LAW

Originally, the United States courts confined themselves to the strict application of the territoriality criterion. One of the most celebrated dicta on this point is that of Justice Oliver Wendell Holmes in the *American Banana* case ((1909) 213 US 347): 'All legislation is prima facie territorial'. And he went on to say that, according to a general or universal rule, the legality or illegality of an act is determined exclusively by the law of the country within whose territory the act is done.

It was necessary to wait until 1945 and the *Alcoa* judgment ((1945) 148 F 2d 416) to see the effects doctrine laid down in its most absolute form. Until that judgment was given, undertakings established abroad were penalised in the United States only on account of their conduct within United States territory and the principle of objective territoriality, known in other branches of the law, had not been relied upon in disputes concerning competition (A. D. Neale and M. L. Stephens, *International Business and National Jurisdiction* (Oxford, Clarendon Press, 1988) p. 167). The *Alcoa* case, which was decided by a specially constituted court, gave Judge Learned Hand occasion to state that, with regard to the interpretation of national antitrust legislation, it is appropriate to take into consideration the limitations customarily observed by States upon the exercise of their powers. He went on, using words which still have an impact in view of the extent to which they embody the effects doctrine in its extreme form:

> It is settled law [. . .] that any State may impose liabilities, even upon persons not within its allegiance, for conduct outside its borders which the State reprehends; and these liabilities other States will ordinarily recognise. According to Judge Learned Hand, such an application of the national rules of competition to undertakings established abroad presupposes the existence of both an element of intent and a substantive element. Thus, an act is covered by those rules only if it was intended and if it created effects, regardless of their magnitude.

Decisions of that kind are rare, no doubt because the cases in which there is no connecting factor other than the effect produced are themselves exceptional. However, I would refer to the judgment in *Horlogerie Suisse* ((1965 Trade cases, 71,352; (1963) Trade cases, 70,600). Judge Cashin, relying expressly on the effects doctrine, upheld the jurisdiction of the United States authorities over the defendant which was established abroad, since the conduct of the latter had a substantial and direct effect in the United States. It is worth noting, at this juncture, the court's concern to qualify the effects.

That case law, particularly in its most far-reaching form, as embodied in the terms used by Judge Learned Hand, inevitably provoked reactions and some criticism. In order to prevent conflicts which might arise, in particular, from the exercise of concurrent jurisdiction, and from the unreserved application of the effects doctrine, various proposals have been made in the United States. In that regard, I would cite the *Restatement of Foreign Relations Law of the United States*, published in 1965 by the American Law Institute, and the *Antitrust Guide for International Operations*, which was issued in January 1977 on the initiative of the United States Department of Justice. The latter document refers to the concept of a substantial and forseeable effect. The same concept of a substantial effect appears in the *Tentative Draft of the Restatement* (revised) published in 1985 which requires there to be, in addition, conduct abroad which has or is intended to have a substantial effect within United States territory. The existence of an intent is, according to some writers, equivalent to the requirement of a foreseeable effect (see A. D. Neale and M. L. Stephens, *supra*, p. 167).

In the context of this attempt to circumscribe the effects doctrine, reference should be made to the judgment of Judge Choy in the *Timberlane Lumber* case ((9th Cir 1977) 549 F 2d 597). Whilst endorsing the *Alcoa* and *Horlogerie Suisse* judgments, Judge Choy considered that the efforts made so far to narrow the scope of the effects doctrine were not very satisfactory. In the first place, the concept of a substantial effect appeared to him hard to define in an international context. Secondly, the distinction between direct and indirect effects was, in his view, inappropriate in so far as it did not permit the interests of other countries to be taken into account.

Judge Choy came to the conclusion that, in certain circumstances, the interests of the United States were too weak and the incentive for restraint in order to preserve harmony in its international relations too strong to justify an assertion of extraterritorial jurisdiction. In order to determine whether such jurisdiction must be exercised, he laid down three cumulative criteria, the first two relating to legality, and the third relating to expediency, which he expressed in the form of three questions:

1. Does the alleged restraint of competition affect, or was it intended to affect, the foreign trade of the United States?
2. Is it of such a type and magnitude as to be cognisable as a violation of the Sherman Act?
3. As a matter of international comity and fairness, should the extraterritorial jurisdiction of the United States be asserted to cover it?

That third condition, which is essentially a jurisdictional rule of reason, includes seven elements which do not constitute an exhaustive list. They include:

- the degree of conflict with a foreign rule;
- the nationality of the parties and the locations or principal places of business of the undertakings concerned;
- the relative significance of the effects in the United States as compared with the effects produced elsewhere;
- the extent to which there is an explicit purpose to harm or affect United States trade, and the foreseeability of such effect.

I would also cite the judgment in *Mannington Mills* ((3rd Cir 1979) 595 F 2d 1287), in which Judge Weis, referring to and interpreting *Timberlane Lumber*, adds to the criteria listed therein other factors, some of which are expressly connected with foreign policy considerations. Briefly, it would appear that the position, without challenging the principle of extraterritorial jurisdiction, amplifies the conditions relating to the expediency of exercising it. I would point out, however, that in the same case, Judge Adams gave a different interpretation of the same criteria which, in his view, serve to establish the actual existence of jurisdiction and not to lay down the conditions for its exercise.

In that regard, United States law, as it now stands, rests on two principles. The first is that the United States will assert jurisdiction where the effects on its trade are direct, substantial and foreseeable. According to the second, the courts should assess the 'balance of interests' in order to ensure that the exercise of such jurisdiction is reasonable (A. D. Neal and M. L. Stephens, *supra* p. 177).

The rule of 'judicial interest balancing' with regard to jurisdiction has not escaped critical comment. One of the most striking criticisms is that made by Judge Wilkey in *Laker Airways* ((DC Cir 1984), 731 F 2d 909, [1984] European Commercial Cases 485). Judge Wilkey has also criticised the judicial balancing of interests in 'American antitrust: adjusting conflicts with other legal systems', published in *Private Investors Abroad* (New York, Matthew Bender, 1985) cited by A. D. Neal and M. L. Stephens, *supra*, p. 179, note 14). In his view, the balancing of interests by the courts in order to ensure that the exercise of jurisdiction is in conformity with the rule of reason is an unsuitable approach. It requires the courts to choose between a domestic law, which is designed to protect domestic interests, and a foreign law which is calculated to thwart the application of the domestic law which allegedly threatens foreign interests. Interest balancing in that context is hindered by two factors. In the first place, there are substantial limitations on the courts' ability to make, in such situations, an objective evaluation of the competing interests. Judge Wilkey expresses serious misgivings as to the extent to which a court can adequately assess the competing problems and priorities in question. Secondly, he considers that interest balancing is unlikely to achieve its goal of promoting international comity in so far as its effectiveness, as a means of ascertaining the most reasonable exercise of prescriptive jurisdiction, has not been demonstrated. That approach, he stated in particular, has gained only a temporary foothold in domestic law.

Noting that the United States courts frequently refuse to adopt that approach and that academic criticism thereof has intensified, Judge Wilkey also pointed out that there is no evidence that interest balancing constitutes a rule of international law. International law does not preclude concurrent jurisdiction. If two assertions of jurisdiction are justified under international law, there is no rule of international law which permits one to be displaced in favour of the other on the ground that the latter is 'more reasonable'.

Finally, I would point out that the 1985 *Tentative Draft of the Restatement* lists eight criteria for determining the circumstances in which the exercise of jurisdiction must be regarded as reasonable. Those criteria include the substantial, direct and foreseeable character of the effect, the conformity of the rule with the traditions of the international system, any interest which other States may have and the likelihood of a conflict arising therefrom.

In practice, therefore, it would not appear that the balancing of interests in accordance with the criteria formulated in *Timberlane Lumber* and *Mannington Mills* has made it possible to elicit a jurisdiction rule of reason. With one exception – a United States writer has pointed out – no court has refused to exercise its jurisdiction as a result of the analysis put forward in those judgments (J. P. Griffin, 'Possible resolutions of international disputes over enforcement of US antitrust laws', [1882] 18 *Stanford Journal of International Law* (Issue 2) cited by A. D. Neale and M. L. Stephens, *supra*, p. 76, Note 14). For his part, Professor Mann considers that the balancing of interests is, in law, a 'bad and misleading guide' (F. A. Mann, 'The doctrine of international jurisdiction revisited after twenty years', [1984] III RCADI 12, in particular pp. 30 and 31). In his view, a court cannot have a discretion to decide whether it should exercise its jurisdiction. If, construed in the light of international law, a statute applies, a court is not entitled to reject it. If the rules of international law preclude its application, a court has no discretionary power to apply it. Consequently, the distinction between the existence and the exercise of jurisdiction, on the one hand, and, on the other, the recognition of a discretion to refrain from exercising existing jurisdiction constitute a misleading approach which should not be followed (F. A. Mann, *ibid.*, pp. 87 and 88). However subtle and fertile it may be, therefore, United States law, while casting some light on this problem, evidently does not provide jurisdictional criteria that are sufficiently tried and tested and precise enough to be adopted without further qualification. Hence it is for the Court, with the aid in particular of learned writings on the matter, to define the circumstances in which the Community may assert jurisdiction to apply its competition rules to undertakings established outside its territory.

IV. SUGGESTED JURISDICTIONAL CRITERIA

The difficulties encountered in this area illustrate clearly that territoriality, as a connecting factor, does not make it possible to resolve all the problems connected with the scale and nature of contemporary international trade. According to Professor Mann, an inflexible territoriality principle is no longer suited to the modern world (*supra*, [1964] RCADI 126). The same view is taken by Professor Prosper Weil in the following passage:

> The picture before us is that of an international society made up of adjacent cells, separated by frontiers; the concept of territory, which lies at the very heart of the concept of territoriality, illustrates that division between separate entities by physical and geographical boundaries. But it is clear [. . .] that frontiers are not only barriers but also crossing points and economic life makes light of such barriers. (P. Weil, *L'Application Extraterritoriale du Droit Economique*, Cahiers de Cedin, Montchrestien, 1987, p. 11)

This assessment has led different writers to devise different criteria for the extraterritorial application of laws. Sir Robert Jennings, for example, considers that under international law a State is entitled to exercise extraterritorial jurisdiction where its legitimate interests are concerned but that it may not abuse that right. There is abuse where the exercise of extraterritorial jurisdiction constitutes interference with the exercise of the local territorial jurisdiction (R. Y. Jennings, 'Extraterritorial jurisdiction and the United States antitrust laws', [1957] *British Yearbook of International Law* 146, in particular p. 153). According to Professor Mann, the real problem is that of identifying what he calls the 'legally relevant facts': F. A. Mann, 'The doctrine of jurisdiction in international law', [1964] RCADI 7, in particular p. 45) and the State whose connection with those facts is of such a kind as to render the assertion of jurisdiction fair and reasonable. Advocating that jurisdiction should be based on 'closeness of connection', Professor Mann considers that a State has (legislative) jurisdiction, if its contract with a given set of facts is so close, so substantial, so direct, so weighty, that legislation in respect of them is in harmony with international law and its various aspects (including the practice of States, the principles of non-interference and reciprocity and the demands of interdependence).

Professor Mann points out at the same time that a mere political, economic, commercial or social interest does not constitute a close connection. In the case, more particularly, of the law of competition, he considers that the effect, whether intended, forseeable or, *a fortiori*, unanticipated, cannot establish a connection of that kind.

Other writers suggest that the jurisdiction of the State in which 'the primary effect' of the act is felt should be recognised (in particular, M. Akehurst, *supra*, p. 198). In order to determine whether the effect is primary or secondary, it is necessary to take a twofold factor into consideration: is the effect produced within the State concerned more direct and more substantial than the effect produced in other States. It is suggested that that approach permits jurisdiction to be exercised only by States having a legitimate interest therein. Finally, it is generally acknowledged that international law does not preclude concurrent jurisdiction. I would point out, however, that, according to some writers, the development of customary international law leads to the emergence of certain specific limitations on the extraterritorial application of domestic law where it might give rise to conflicting obligations (P. Julliard, 'L'Application extraterritoriale de la loi economique', in *L'Application Extraterritoriale du Droit Economique*, *supra*, p. 13 and in particular p. 31), or provoke conflicts of jurisdiction (B. Stern, *supra*, p. 15).

In my view, those various concerns are, for the most part, taken into account by the adoption of the criterion of qualified effect. That criterion, which does not conflict with any prohibitive rule of international law, has gained wide acceptance in the practice of States (L. Idot, *Le Contrôle des Pratiques Restrictives de Concurrence dans les Echanges Internationaux* (Université de Droit, d'Economie et des Sciences Sociales de Paris, Paris II, Thèse, 1981 Roneo) in particular p. 89 *et seq*.). Moreover, it is, on objective grounds, particularly appropriate in view of the specific nature of competition law (J. M. Bischoff and R. Kovar, *supra*, p. 700) as a law designed to regulate market conditions and safeguard *ordre public* in the economic context (P. Eeckman, 'L'application de l'Article 85 du Traité de Rome aux ententes étrangerès à la CEE mais causant des restriction à la concurrence à l'Interieur du Marché Commun', [1965] RCDIP 499, in particular p. 519). It is on the basis of those considerations and of the criteria of international law that it is necessary to define the characteristics of an effect whose location justifies the assertion of prescriptive jurisdiction over undertakings established outside the Community.

According to some writers, such effects should correspond to those which are covered where the interference with competition is the result of conduct within the territory of the State which claims jurisdiction (P. Demaret, *supra*, p. 33). However, as I have pointed out, it is unclear whether the concept of effect provided for in Article 85 of the EEC Treaty in order to establish the existence of an infringement of the competition rules is identical to that required by Community law, and accepted by international law, in order to determine whether there is jurisdiction over undertakings established outside the Community.

According to the substantive provisions of Community law, the restriction of competition must be 'perceptible' (J. Megret, J.-V. Louis, D. Vignes, M. Waelbroeck, *Le Droit de la Communauté Economique Européenne* (Editions de l'Université de Bruxelles, 1972) Volume 4, *Concurrence*, p. 20) or 'appreciable'. The adverse affect on competition may be either direct or indirect and objectively or reasonably foreseeable (B. Goldman and A. Lyon-Caen, *Droit Commercial Européen* (Dalloz, 4th edn) p. 551). Those are the characteristics of the effect envisaged as a constituent element of interference with freedom of competition within the Community.

In my view, not all of those characteristics have to be adopted if the effect is taken as the criterion of extraterritorial jurisdiction. The most important reservation in that regard concerns indirect effect (J. M. Bischoff and R. Kovar, *supra*, in particular p. 706 *et seq.*). I would remind the Court that Mayras AG suggested, in his Opinion in the *Dyestuffs* cases, the adoption of the criterion of the direct and immediate, reasonably forseeable and substantial effect ([1972] ECR 619 at 694, [1972] CMLR 557, at 604). I agree with that solution and, for the reasons which he sets forth, I would adopt his analysis which is as follows:

> Surely the Commission would be disarmed if, faced with a concerted practice, the initiative for which was taken and the responsibility for which was assumed exclusively by undertakings outside the Common Market, it was deprived of the power to take any decision against them? This would also mean giving up a way of defending the Common Market and one necessary for bringing about the major objectives of the European Economic Community.

The qualified effects are generally adopted as the criterion conferring jurisdiction. The Restatement refers to substantial and forseeable effect. At its 55th Conference in New York in August 1972, the International Law Association adopted a resolution on the application of the principles of international law in the field of restrictive practices (The International Law Association, *Report of the 55th Conference* held in New York, August 21 to August 26, 1972, p. 138). According to Article 5 of that resolution, a State has jurisdiction to prescribe rules of law governing conduct that takes place outside its territory and causes an effect within its territory provided that three conditions are satisfied: (a) the conduct and its effect are constituent elements of a restrictive practice, (b) the effect within the territory is substantial, and (c) it occurs as a direct and primarily intended result of the conduct outside the territory. It is noteworthy that this resolution was preferred to that submitted by the Committee on the Extra-Territorial Application of Restrictive Trade Practices, according to which international law does not permit a State to assume or exercise extra-territorial prescriptive jurisdiction solely on the basis that conduct which took place abroad produces effects or repercussions within its territory. Hence, within that academic forum, the proposal rejecting the effects doctrine was discarded in favour of a resolution supporting the adoption of the qualified effect criterion.

Admittedly, in its observations, the United Kingdom, referring to the *Aide-Mémoire* of 20 October 1969 which it submitted to the Commission regarding the *Dyestuffs* cases, has maintained that the territorial basis alone can justify the Community's assertion of jurisdiction in these cases. It therefore considers that the principle laid down in the *Dyestuffs* cases must apply not only to subsidiaries but also to other intermediate establishments, situated within the Community, whose conduct within the Community has had an anti-competitive effect there. In those circumstances, according to the United Kingdom, it is merely the exercise of territorial jurisdiction which is involved.

In the light of all the foregoing considerations, I do not believe that I can advise the Court to take that approach. Moreover, the applicants deny that there is a territorial connection with the Community such as to enable it to assume jurisdiction over them. They claim that any conduct which may be attributed to them took place outside the Community. The applicants add that their various representatives acted independently and that none of those representatives' activities may be imputed to the applicants. Be that as it may, it serves no purpose in my view to enter into a discussion on the nature of the legal relationship between the applicant companies and their various establishments within the Community.

As we have seen, there is no rule of international law which is capable of being relied upon against the criterion of the direct, substantial and forseeable effect. Nor does the concept of international comity, in view of its uncertain scope, militate against that criterion either. (On the concept of international comity, see L. Oppenheim, *International Law* (8th edn by H. Lauterpacht, Longmans, Green and Co.) Vol. 1, p. 33 *et seq.*; E. Nys, *Le Droit International* (2nd edn, 1904) Vol. 1, p. 201 *et seq.*; H. E. Yntema, 'The comity doctrine', [1966–1967] *Michigan Law Review*, Vol. 65, p. 1.)

In the absence of any such prohibitive rule and in the light of widespread State practice, I would therefore propose that in view of its appropriateness to the field of competition, it be adopted as a criterion for the jurisdiction of the Community.

[. . .]

DECISION OF THE EUROPEAN COURT OF JUSTICE

[. . .]

All the applicants which have made submissions regarding jurisdiction maintain first of all that by applying the competition rules of the Treaty to them the Commission has misconstrued the territorial scope of Article 85. They note that in its judgment of 14 July 1972 (Case 48/69, *ICI* v. *EC Commission* [1972] ECR 619, [1972] CMLR 557) the Court did not adopt the 'effects doctrine' but emphasised that the case involved conduct restricting competition within the Common Market because of the activities of subsidiaries which could be imputed to the parent companies. The applicants add that even if there is a basis in Community law for applying Article 85 to them, the action of applying the rule interpreted in that way would be contrary to public international law which precludes any claim by the Community to regulate conduct restricting competition adopted outside the territory of the Community merely by reason of the economic repercussions which that conduct produces within the Community [. . .].

In so far as the submission concerning the infringement of Article 85 of the Treaty itself is concerned, it should be recalled that that provision prohibits all agreements between undertakings and concerted practices which may affect trade between Member States and which have as their object or effect the restriction of competition within the Common Market are prohibited.

It should be noted that the main sources of supply of wood pulp are outside the Community, in Canada, the United States, Sweden and Finland and that the market therefore has global dimensions. Where wood pulp producers established in those countries sell directly to purchasers established in the Community and engage in price competition in order to win orders from those customers, that constitutes competition within the Common Market.

It follows that where those producers concert on the prices to be charged to their customers in the Community and put that concertation into effect by selling at prices which are actually co-ordinated, they are taking part in concertation which has the object and effect of restricting competition within the Common Market within the meaning of Article 85 of the Treaty.

Accordingly, it must be concluded that by applying the competition rules in the Treaty in the circumstances of this case to undertakings whose registered offices are situated outside the Community, the Commission has not made an incorrect assessment of the territorial scope of Article 85.

The applicants have submitted that the decision is incompatible with public international law on the grounds that the application of the competition rules in this case was founded exclusively on the economic repercussions within the Common Market of conduct restricting competition which was adopted outside the Community.

It should be observed that an infringement of Article 85, such as the conclusion of an agreement which has had the effect of restricting competition within the Common Market, consists of conduct made up of two elements, the formation of the agreement, decision or concerted practice and the implementation thereof. If the applicability of prohibitions laid down under competition law were made to depend on the place where the agreement, decision or concerted practice was formed, the result would obviously be to give undertakings an easy means of evading those prohibitions. The decisive factor is therefore the place where it is implemented.

The producers in this case implemented their pricing agreement within the Common Market. It is immaterial in that respect whether or not they had recourse to subsidiaries, agents, sub-agents, or branches within the Community in order to make their contacts with purchasers within the Community.

Accordingly the Community's jurisdiction to apply its competition rules to such conduct is covered by the territoriality principle as universally recognised in public international law [. . .].

23.2 *Aide-Mémoire* of the British Government to the Commission of the European Communities, 20 October 1969

The United Kingdom Government have noted in the *Journal Officiel* of the European Communities dated 7 August 1969, the publication of a decision of the Commission of 24 July 1969 (No. IV/26267) concerning proceedings pursuant to Article 85 of the Treaty establishing the European Economic Community in the matter of dyestuffs. Article 1 of this decision declares that 'the concerted practices of fixing the rate of price increases and the conditions of application of these increases in the dyestuffs sector . . . constitute violations of the provisions of Article 85 of the EEC Treaty'. Article 2 of the decision inflicts or purports to inflict certain fines upon the commercial undertakings who are alleged to have participated in these concerted practices. Among the undertakings specified in Articles 1 and 2 of the decision are Imperial Chemical Industries, Limited (hereinafter referred to as 'ICI'), which is a company incorporated and carrying on business in the United Kingdom. Article 4 of the decision declares that 'the present decision is directed to the undertakings mentioned in Article 1'; it then goes on to state that as far as ICI and certain Swiss undertakings are concerned, '[the decision] may likewise be notified to them at the seat of one of their subsidiaries established in the Common Market'.

The United Kingdom Government neither wish nor intend to take issue with the Commission about the merits of this particular case. They accept that it is for the undertakings to whom the decision is directed to pursue whatever remedies are available to them under the EEC Treaty if they desire for their part to challenge the legality or correctness of this measure taken by the Commission. It is in any event their understanding that certain of the undertakings to whom the decision is directed have already indicated their intention to institute proceedings before the European Court of Justice challenging the decision on various grounds.

The concern of the United Kingdom Government in this matter is rather directed towards the more fundamental point concerning the reach and extent of the jurisdiction exercisable by the Commission *vis-à-vis* undertakings which are neither incorporated in the territory of a member State of the European Economic Community, nor carrying on business nor resident therein.

The Commission will be aware that certain claims to exercise extra-territorial jurisdiction in anti-trust proceedings have given rise to serious and continuing disputes between Western European Governments (including the Governments of some EEC Member States) and the United States government, inasmuch as these claims have been based on grounds which the Western European governments consider to be unsupported by public international law.

In particular, the United Kingdom government have for their part consistently objected to the assumption of extra-territorial jurisdiction in antitrust matters by the courts or authorities of a foreign state when that jurisdiction is based upon what is termed the 'effects doctrine' – that is to say, the doctrine that territorial jurisdiction over conduct which has occurred wholly outside the territory of the State claiming jurisdiction may be justified because of the resulting economic 'effects' of such conduct within the territory of that State. This doctrine becomes even more open to objection when, on the basis of the alleged 'effects' within the State claiming jurisdiction of the conduct of foreign corporations abroad (that is to say, conduct pursued outside the territory of that State), such corporations are actually made subject to penal sanctions.

The United Kingdom government are of the view that certain of the 'considerations' advanced in the decision of the Commission of 24 July 1969 conflict with the principles of public international law concerning the basis upon which personal and substantive jurisdiction may be exercised over foreign corporations in anti-trust matters. A summary statement of these principles as seen by the United Kingdom government, is annexed to this *aide-mémoire* for ease of reference.

In particular, it will be noted that the method by which the decision of the Commission was purportedly notified to ICI (Article 4 of the decision) ignores the clear legal distinction between a parent company and its subsidiaries and the separate legal personalities of the latter. The United Kingdom government consider that this attempted 'notification' of a parent company through its subsidiary is designed to support a doctrine of substantive jurisdiction which is itself open to objection as going beyond the limits imposed by the accepted principles of international law.

So far as substantive jurisdiction is concerned, the United Kingdom government are of the view that the decision of the Commission incorporates an interpretation of the relevant provisions of the EEC Treaty which is not justified by the accepted principles of international law governing the exercise of extra-territorial jurisdiction over foreigners in respect of acts committed abroad.

The United Kingdom government deem it necessary to bring these considerations to the attention of the Commission lest there be any misunderstanding as to their position in the matter.

STATEMENT OF PRINCIPLES ACCORDING TO WHICH, IN THE VIEW OF THE UNITED KINGDOM GOVERNMENT, JURISDICTION MAY BE EXERCISED OVER FOREIGN CORPORATIONS IN ANTI-TRUST MATTERS

The basis on which personal jurisdiction may be exercised over foreign corporations

(1) Personal jurisdiction should be assumed only if the foreign company 'carries on business' or 'resides' within the territorial jurisdiction.

(2) A foreign company may be considered to 'carry on business' within the jurisdiction by an agent only if the agent has legal power to enter into contracts on behalf of the principal.

(3) A foreign parent company may not be considered to 'carry on business' within the jurisdiction by a subsidiary company, unless it can be shown that the subsidiary is the agent for the parent in the sense of carrying on the parent's business within the jurisdiction.

(4) The separate legal personalities of a parent company and its subsidiary should be respected. Such concepts as 'enterprise entity' and 'reciprocating partnership' when applied for the purpose of asserting personal jurisdiction over a foreign parent company by reason of the presence within the jurisdiction of a subsidiary (and a foreign subsidiary by reason of the presence of its parent company) are contrary to sound legal principle in that they disregard the distinction of personality between parent and subsidiary.

(5) The normal rules governing the exercise of personal jurisdiction should not be extended in such a manner as to extend beyond proper limits the exercise of substantive jurisdiction in respect of the activities of foreigners abroad. Nor can the assertion of extended personal jurisdiction be justified on the basis that it is necessary for the enforcement of legislation which in itself exceeds the proper limits of substantive jurisdiction.

(6) There is no justification for applying a looser test to methods of personal service in anti-trust matters than is permissible in relation to other matters.

The basis on which substantive jurisdiction may be exercised in anti-trust matters

(1) On general principles, substantive jurisdiction in anti-trust matters should only be taken on the basis of either

(*a*) the territorial principle, or
(*b*) The nationality principle.

There is nothing in the nature of anti-trust proceedings which justifies a wider application of these principles than is generally accepted in other matters; on the contrary there is much which calls for a narrower application.

(2) The territorial principle justifies proceedings against foreigners and foreign companies only in respect of conduct which consists in whole or in part of some activity by them in the territory of the State claiming jurisdiction. A State should not exercise jurisdiction against a foreigner who or a foreign company which has committed no act within its territory. In the case of conspiracies the assumption of jurisdiction is justified:

(*a*) if the entire conspiracy takes place within the territory of the State claiming jurisdiction; or
(*b*) if the formation of the conspiracy takes place within the territory of the State claiming jurisdiction even if things are done in pursuance of it outside its territory; or
(*c*) if the formation of the conspiracy takes place outside the territory of the State claiming jurisdiction, but the person against whom the proceedings are brought has done things within its territory in pursuance of the conspiracy.

(3) The nationality principle justifies proceedings against nationals of the State claiming jurisdiction in respect of their activities abroad only provided that this does not involve interference with the legitimate affairs of other States or cause such nationals to act in a manner which is contrary to the laws of the State in which the activities in question are conducted.

22.3 Protection of Trading Interests Act 1980

1 OVERSEAS MEASURES AFFECTING UNITED KINGDOM TRADING INTERESTS

(1) If it appears to the Secretary of State:

(*a*) that measures have been or are proposed to be taken by or under the law of any overseas country for regulating or controlling international trade; and
(*b*) that those measures, in so far as they apply or would apply to things done or to be done outside the territorial jurisdiction of that country by persons carrying on business in the United Kingdom, are damaging or threaten to dam-

age the trading interests of the United Kingdom.

the Secretary of State may by order direct that this section shall apply to those measures either generally or in their application to such cases as may be specified in the order.

[. . .]

2 DOCUMENTS AND INFORMATION REQUIRED BY OVERSEAS COURTS AND AUTHORITIES

(1) If it appears to the Secretary of State:

(*a*) that a requirement has been or may be imposed on a person or persons in the United Kingdom to produce to any court, tribunal or authority of an overseas country any commercial document which is not within the territorial jurisdiction of that country or to furnish any commercial information to any such court, tribunal or authority; or

(*b*) that any such authority has imposed or may impose a requirement on a person or persons in the United Kingdom to publish any such document or information,

the Secretary of State may, if it appears to him that the requirement is inadmissible by virtue of subsection (2) or (3) below, give directions for prohibiting compliance with the requirement.

[. . .]

5 RESTRICTION ON ENFORCEMENT OF CERTAIN OVERSEAS JUDGMENTS

(1) A judgment to which this section applies shall not be registered under Part II of the Administration of Justice Act 1920 or Part I of the Foreign Judgments (Reciprocal Enforcement) Act 1933 and no court in the United Kingdom shall entertain proceedings at common law for the recovery of any sum payable under such a judgment.

(2) This section applies to any judgment given by a court of an overseas country, being:

(*a*) a judgment for multiple damages within the meaning of subsection (3) below;

(*b*) a judgment based on a provision or rule of law specified or described in an order under subsection (4) below and given after the coming into force of the order;

[. . .]

(3) In subsection (2)(*a*) above a judgment for multiple damages means a judgment for an amount arrived at by doubling, trebling or otherwise multiplying a sum assessed as compensation for the loss or damage sustained by the person in whose favour the judgment is given.

(4) The Secretary of State may for the purposes of subsection (2)(*b*) above make an order in respect of any provision or rule of law which appears to him to be concerned with the prohibition or regulation of agreements, arrangements or practices designed to restrain, distort or restrict competition in the carrying on of business of any description or to be otherwise concerned with the promotion of such competition as aforesaid.

[. . .]

6 RECOVERY OF AWARDS OF MULTIPLE DAMAGES

(1) This section applies where a court of an overseas country has given a judgment for multiple damages within the meaning of section 5(3) above against:

(*a*) a citizen of the United Kingdom and Colonies; or

(*b*) a body corporate incorporated in the United Kingdom or in a territory outside the United Kingdom for whose international relations Her Majesty's Government in the United Kingdom are responsible; or

(*c*) a person carrying on business in the United Kingdom.

(in this section referred to as a 'qualifying defendant') and an amount on account of the damages has been paid by the qualifying defendant either to the party in whose favour the judgment was given or to another party who is entitled as against the qualifying defendant to contribution in respect of the damages.

(2) Subject to subsections (3) and (4) below, the qualifying defendant shall be entitled to recover from the party in whose favour the judgment was given so much of the amount referred to in subsection (1) above as exceeds the part attributable to compensation; and that part shall be taken to be such part of the amount as bears to the whole of it the same proportion as the sum assessed by the court that gave the judgment as compensation for the loss or damage sustained by that party bears to the whole of the damages awarded to that party.

(3) Subsection (2) above does not apply where the qualifying defendant is an individual who was ordinarily resident in the overseas country at the time when the proceedings in which the judgment was given were instituted or a body corporate which had its principal place of business there at that time.

(4) Subsection (2) above does not apply where the qualifying defendant carried on business in the overseas country and the proceedings in which the judgment was given were concerned with activities exclusively carried out in that country.

(5) A court in the United Kingdom may entertain proceedings on a claim under this section notwithstanding that the person against whom the proceedings are brought is not within the jurisdiction of the court.

(6) The reference in subsection (1) above to an amount paid by the qualifying defendant includes a reference to an amount obtained by execution against his property or against the property of a company which (directly or indirectly) is wholly owned by him; and references in that subsection and subsection (2) above to the party in whose favour the judgment was given or to a party entitled to contribution include references to any person in whom the rights of any such party have become vested by succession or assignment or otherwise.

(7) This section shall, with the necessary modifications, apply also in relation to any order which is made by a tribunal or authority of an overseas country and would, if that tribunal or authority were a court, be a judgment for multiple damages within the meaning of section 5(3) above.

(8) This section does not apply to any judgment given or order made before the passing of this Act.

23.4 Agreement Between the Government of the United States of America and the Commission of the European Communities Regarding the Application of their Competition Laws, September 1991

THE GOVERNMENT OF THE UNITED STATES OF AMERICA AND THE COMMISSION OF THE EUROPEAN COMMUNITIES:

Recognizing that the world's economies are becoming increasingly interrelated, and in particular that this is true of the economies of the United States of America and the European Communities;

Noting that the Government of the United States of America and the Commission of the European Communities share the view that the sound and effective enforcement of competition law is a matter of importance to the efficient operation of their respective markets and to trade between them;

Noting that the sound and effective enforcement of the Parties' competition laws would be enhanced by cooperation and, in appropriate cases, coordination between them in the application of those laws;

Noting further that from time to time

differences may arise between the Parties concerning the application of their competition laws to conduct or transactions that implicate significant interests of both Parties;

Having regard to the Recommendation of the Council of the Organization for Economic Cooperation and Development Concerning Cooperation Between Member Countries on Restrictive Business Practices Affecting International Trade, adopted on June 5, 1986; and

Having regard to the Declaration on US–EC Relations adopted on November 23, 1990;

HAVE AGREED AS FOLLOWS:

ARTICLE I PURPOSE AND DEFINITIONS

1. The purpose of this Agreement is to promote cooperation and coordination and lessen the possibility or impact of differences between the Parties in the application of their competition laws.

2. For the purposes of this Agreement, the following terms shall have the following definitions:

(*a*) 'Competition law(s)' shall mean
  (i) for the European Communities, Articles 85, 86, 89 and 90 of the Treaty establishing the European Economic Community, Regulation (EEC) No. 4064/89 on the control of concentrations between undertakings, Articles 65 and 66 of the Treaty establishing the European Coal and Steel Community (ECSC), and their implementing Regulations including High Authority Decision no. 24–54, and
  (ii) for the United States of America, the Sherman Act (15 U.S.C. [sections] 1–7), the Clayton Act (15 U.S.C. [sections] 12–27), the Wilson Tariff Act (15 U.S.C. [sections] 8–11), and the Federal Trade Commission Act (15 U.S.C. [sections] 41–68, except as these sections relate to consumer protection functions),

  as well as such other laws or regulations as the Parties shall jointly agree in writing to be a 'competition law' for purposes of this Agreement;

(*b*) 'Competition authorities' shall mean
  (i) for the European Communities, the Commission of the European Communities, as to its responsibilities pursuant to the competition laws of the European Communities, and
  (ii) for the United States, the Antitrust Division of the United States Department of Justice and the Federal Trade Commission;

(*c*) 'Enforcement activities' shall mean any application of competition law by way of investigation or proceeding conducted by the competition authorities of a Party; and

(*d*) 'Anticompetitive activities' shall mean any conduct or transaction that is impermissible under the competition laws of a Party.

ARTICLE II NOTIFICATION

1. Each Party shall notify the other whenever its competition authorities become aware that their enforcement activities may affect important interests of the other Party.

2. Enforcement activities as to which notification ordinarily will be appropriate include those that:

(*a*) Are relevant to enforcement activities of the other Party;

(*b*) Involve anticompetitive activities (other than a merger or acquisition) carried out in significant part in the other Party's territory;

(*c*) Involve a merger or acquisition in which one or more of the parties to the transaction, or a company controlling one or more of the parties to the transaction, is a company incorporated or organized under the laws of the other Party or one of its States or Member States;

(*d*) Involve conduct believed to have been required, encouraged or approved by the other Party; or
(*e*) Involve remedies that would, in significant respects, require or prohibit conduct in the other Party's territory.

3. With respect to mergers or acquisitions required by law to be reported to the competition authorities, notification under this Article shall be made:

(*a*) In the case of the Government of the United States of America,
   (i) not later than the time its competition authorities request, pursuant to 15 U.S.C. [section] 18*a*(*e*), additional information or documentary material concerning the proposed transaction,
   (ii) when its competition authorities decide to file a complaint challenging the transaction, and
   (iii) where this is possible, far enough in advance of the entry of a consent decree to enable the other Party's views to be taken into account; and
(*b*) In the case of the Commission of the European Communities,
   (i) when notice of the transaction is published in the Official Journal, pursuant to Article 4(3) of Council Regulation No. 4064/89, or when notice of the transaction is received under Article 66 of the ECSC Treaty and a prior authorization from the Commission is required under that provision,
   (ii) when its competition authorities decide to initiate proceedings with respect to the proposed transaction, pursuant to Article 6(1)(*c*) of Council Regulation No. 4064/89, and
   (iii) far enough in advance of the adoption of a decision in the case to enable the other Party's views to be taken into account.

4. With respect to other matters, notification shall ordinarily be provided at the stage in an investigation when it becomes evident that notifiable circumstances are present, and in any event far enough in advance of:

(*a*) the issuance of a statement of objections in the case of the Commission of the European Communities, or a complaint or indictment in the case of the Government of the United States of America, and
(*b*) the adoption of a decision or settlement in the case of the Commission of the European Communities, or the entry of a consent decree in the case of the Government of the United States of America,

to enable the other Party's views to be taken into account.

5. Each Party shall also notify the other whenever its competition authorities intervene or otherwise participate in a regulatory or judicial proceeding that does not arise from its enforcement activities, if the issues addressed in the intervention or participation may affect the other Party's important interests. Notification under this paragraph shall apply only to:

(*a*) regulatory or judicial proceedings that are public,
(*b*) intervention or participation that is public and pursuant to formal procedures, and
(*c*) in the case of regulatory proceeding in the United States, only proceedings before federal agencies.

Notification shall be made at the time of the intervention or participation or as soon thereafter as possible.

6. Notifications under this Article shall include sufficient information to permit an initial evaluation by the recipient Party of any effects on its interests.

ARTICLE III EXCHANGE OF INFORMATION

1. The Parties agree that it is in their common interest to share information that will (a) facilitate effective application of their respective competition laws, or (b)

promote better understanding by them of economic conditions and theories relevant to their competition authorities' enforcement activities and interventions or participation of the kind described in Article II, paragraph 5.2. In furtherance of this common interest, appropriate officials from the competition authorities of each Party shall meet at least twice each year, unless otherwise agreed, to (a) exchange information on their current enforcement activities and priorities, (b) exchange information on economic sectors of common interest, (c) discuss policy changes which they are considering, and (d) discuss other matters of mutual interest relating to the application of competition laws.

3. Each Party will provide the other Party with any significant information that comes to the attention of its competition authorities about anticompetitive activities that its competition authorities believe is relevant to, or may warrant, enforcement activity by the other Party's competition authorities.

4. Upon receiving a request from the other Party, and within the limits of Articles VIII and IX, a Party will provide to the requesting Party such information within its possession as the requesting Party may describe that is relevant to an enforcement activity being considered or conducted by the requesting Party's competition authorities.

ARTICLE IV COOPERATION AND COORDINATION IN ENFORCEMENT ACTIVITIES

1. The competition authorities of each Party will render assistance to the competition authorities of the other Party in their enforcement activities, to the extent compatible with the assisting Party's laws and important interests, and within its reasonably available resources.

2. In cases where both Parties have an interest in pursuing enforcement activities with regard to related situations, they may agree that it is in their mutual interest to coordinate their enforcement activities. In considering whether particular enforcement activities should be coordinated, the Parties shall take account of the following factors, among others:

(*a*) the opportunity to make more efficient use of their resources devoted to the enforcement activities;

(*b*) the relative abilities of the Parties' competition authorities to obtain information necessary to conduct the enforcement activities;

(*c*) the effect of such coordination on the ability of both Parties to achieve the objectives of their enforcement activities; and

(*d*) the possibility of reducing costs incurred by persons subject to the enforcement activities.

3. In any coordination arrangement, each Party shall conduct its enforcement activities expeditiously and, insofar as possible, consistently with the enforcement objectives of the other Party.

4. Subject to appropriate notice to the other Party, the competition authorities of either Party may limit or terminate their participation in a coordination arrangement and pursue their enforcement activities independently.

ARTICLE V COOPERATION REGARDING ANTI-COMPETITIVE ACTIVITIES IN THE TERRITORY OF ONE PARTY THAT ADVERSELY AFFECT THE INTERESTS OF THE OTHER PARTY

1. The Parties note that anticompetitive activities may occur within the territory of one Party that, in addition to violating that Party's competition laws, adversely affect important interests of the other Party. The Parties agree that it is in both their interests to address anticompetitive activities of this nature.

2. If a Party believes that anticompetitive activities carried out on the territory of the other Party are adversely affecting its important interests, the first Party may notify the other Party and may request that the

other Party's competition authorities initiate appropriate enforcement activities. The notification shall be as specific as possible about the nature of the anticompetitive activities and their effects on the interests of the notifying Party, and shall include an offer of such further information and other cooperation as the notifying Party is able to provide.

3. Upon receipt of a notification under paragraph 2, and after such other discussion between the Parties as may be appropriate and useful in the circumstances, the competition authorities of the notified Party will consider whether or not to initiate enforcement activities, or to expand ongoing enforcement activities, with respect to the anticompetitive activities identified in the notification. The notified Party will advise the notifying Party of its decision. If enforcement activities are initiated, the notified Party will advise the notifying Party of their outcome and, to the extent possible, of significant interim developments.

4. Nothing in this Article limits the discretion of the notified Party under its competition laws and enforcement policies as to whether or not to undertake enforcement activities with respect to the notified anticompetitive activities, or precludes the notifying Party from undertaking enforcement activities with respect to such anticompetitive activities.

ARTICLE VI AVOIDANCE OF CONFLICTS OVER ENFORCEMENT ACTIVITIES

Within the framework of its own laws and to the extent compatible with its important interests, each Party will seek, at all stages in its enforcement activities, to take into account the important interests of the other Party. Each Party shall consider important interests of the other Party in decisions as to whether or not to initiate an investigation or proceeding, the scope of an investigation or proceeding, the nature of the remedies or penalties sought, and in other ways, as appropriate. In considering one another's important interests in the course of their enforcement activities, the Parties will take account of, but will not be limited to, the following principles:

1. While an important interest of a Party may exist in the absence of official involvement by the Party with the activity in question, it is recognized that such interests would normally be reflected in antecedent laws, decisions or statements of policy by its competent authorities.

2. A Party's important interests may be affected at any stage of enforcement activity by the other Party. The Parties recognize, however, that as a general matter the potential for adverse impact on one Party's important interests arising from enforcement activity by the other Party is less at the investigative stage and greater at the stage at which conduct is prohibited or penalized, or at which other forms of remedial orders are imposed.

3. Where it appears that one Party's enforcement activities may adversely affect important interests of the other Party, the Parties will consider the following factors, in addition to any other factors that appear relevant in the circumstances, in seeking an appropriate accommodation of the competing interests:

(*a*) the relative significance to the anticompetitive activities involved of conduct within the enforcing Party's territory as compared to conduct within the other party's territory;

(*b*) the presence or absence of a purpose on the part of those engaged in the anticompetitive activities to affect consumers, suppliers, or competitors within the enforcing Party's territory;

(*c*) the relative significance of the effects of the anticompetitive activities on the enforcing Party's interests as compared to the effects on the other Party's interests;

(*d*) the existence or absence of reasonable expectations that would be furthered or defeated by the enforcement activities;

(*e*) the degree of conflict or consistency between the enforcement activities and the other party's laws or articulated economic policies; and (*f*) the extent to which enforcement activities of the other Party with respect to the same persons, including judgments or undertakings resulting from such activities, may be affected.

ARTICLE VII CONSULTATION

1. Each Party agrees to consult promptly with the other Party in response to a request by the other Party for consultations regarding any matter related to this Agreement and to attempt to conclude consultations expeditiously with a view to reaching mutually satisfactory conclusions. Any request for consultations shall include the reasons therefor and shall state whether procedural time limits or other considerations require the consultations to be expedited.

These consultations shall take place at the appropriate level, which may include consultations between the heads of the competition authorities concerned.

2. In each consultation under paragraph 1, each Party shall take into account the principles of cooperation set forth in this Agreement and shall be prepared to explain to the other Party the specific results of its application of those principles to the issue that is the subject of consultation.

ARTICLE VIII CONFIDENTIALITY OF INFORMATION

1. Notwithstanding any other provision of this Agreement, neither Party is required to provide information to the other Party if disclosure of that information to the requesting Party (a) is prohibited by the law of the Party possessing the information, or (b) would be incompatible with important interests of the Party possessing the information.

2. Each Party agrees to maintain, to the fullest extent possible, the confidentiality of any information provided to it in confidence by the other Party under this Agreement and to oppose, to the fullest extent possible, any application for disclosure of such information by a third party that is not authorized by the Party that supplied the information.

ARTICLE IX EXISTING LAW

Nothing in this Agreement shall be interpreted in a manner inconsistent with the existing laws, or as requiring any change in the laws, of the United States of America or the European Communities or of their respective states or member states.

ARTICLE X COMMUNICATIONS UNDER THIS AGREEMENT

Communications under this Agreement, including notifications under Articles II and V, may be carried out by direct oral, telephonic, written or facsimile communication from one Party's competition authority to the other Party's authority. Notifications under Articles II, V and XI, and requests under Article VII, shall be confirmed promptly in writing through diplomatic channels.

ARTICLE XI ENTRY INTO FORCE, TERMINATION AND REVIEW

1. This Agreement shall enter into force upon signature.

2. This Agreement shall remain in force until 60 days after the date on which either Party notifies the other Party in writing that it wishes to terminate the Agreement.

3. The Parties shall review the operation of this Agreement not more than 24 months from the date of its entry into force, with a view to assessing their cooperative activities, identifying additional areas in which they could usefully cooperate and identifying any other ways in which the Agreement could be improved. The Parties agree that this review will include, among other things, an analysis of actual or potential cases to determine whether their interests could be better served through closer cooperation.

IN WITNESS WHEREOF, the undersigned, being duly authorized, have signed this Agreement.

Done at Washington, in duplicate, this twenty-third day of September, 1991 [. . .].

TABLE OF CASES AND DECISIONS

TABLE OF LEGISLATION

UK ACTS

Fair Trading Act 1973

Resale Prices Act 1976

Restrictive Trade Practices Act 1976

Competition Act 1980

UK STATUTORY INSTRUMENTS

TREATY OF ROME

SECONDARY EEC LEGISLATION

USA ACTS

BIBLIOGRAPHY OF GENERAL WORKS ON COMPETITION LAW AND POLICY

American Bar Association (1990), *Compliance Manuals for the New Antitrust Era* (American Bar Association, Section of Antitrust Law, Chicago, Ill).

Bellamy, C. and Child, G. (1993), *Common Market Law of Competition*, 4th edn (Sweet and Maxwell, London).

Burke, T., Genn-Bash, A. and Haines, B. (1988), *Competition in Theory and Practice*, (New York, Croom Helm, London).

Duggan, M. (1981), *Antitrust and the US Supreme Court, 1829–1980: a Compendium of Supreme Court Decisions dealing with Restraint of Trade and Monopoly*, 2nd edn (Federal Legal Publications, New York).

Economic and Social Committee of the European Communities (1987) *Community Competition Policy* (Economic and Social Committee, Brussels).

Frazer, T. (1972), *Monopoly, Competition and the Law: The Regulation of Business Activity in Britain, Europe and America*, 2nd edn (London, Harvester Wheatsheaf, Hemel Hempstead).

Goyder, D. G. (1993) *EEC Competition Law*, 2nd edn (Clarendon, Oxford).

Hawk, B. (1991), *United States, Common Market, and International Antitrust: A Comparative Guide*, 2nd edn (Prentice Hall, Clifton, NJ).

Hay, D. and Morris, D. (1991), *Industrial Economics and Organisation*, 2nd edn (especially Part IV) (Oxford University Press, Oxford).

Korah, V. and Rothnie, W. (1990), *An Introductory Guide to EEC Competition Law and Practice*, 4th edn (ESC Publishing, Oxford).

Kwoka, J. and White, L. (eds) (1989), *The Antitrust Revolution* (Scott Foreman, London).

Maitland-Walker, J. (ed.) (1989) *Towards 1992: The Development of International Anti-Trust* (ESC Publishing, Oxford).

Mathewson, F., Trebilcock, M. and Walker, M. (eds) (1990), *The Law and Economics of Competition Policy* (Fraser Institute, Vancouver, BC).

Matthews, R. (1986) *EEC Anti-Trust Compliance: How to Achieve Corporate Compliance in the EEC Competition Rules* (European Business Publications, London).

Montagnon, P. (ed.) (1990) *European Competition Policy* (Chatham House Papers, Pinter, London).

Neale, A. D. and Goyder, D. G. (1980), *The Antitrust Laws of the United States of*

America: A Study of Competition Enforced by Law, 3rd edn (Cambridge University Press, Cambridge).

Office of Fair Trading (1990) *An Outline of United Kingdom Competition Policy* (Office of Fair Trading, London).

Oxford Review of Economic Policy, vol. 1, no. 2 (1985): issue on Recent Developments in Industrial Economics and their Implications for Policy.

Oxford Review of Economic Policy, vol. 9, no. 3 (1993): issue on Competition Policy.

Scherer, F. and Ross, D. (1990), *Industrial Market Structure and Economic Peformance*, 3rd edn (Houghton Mifflin, Boston, MA).

Schmalensee, R. and Willig, R. (1989) *Handbook of Industrial Organization*, vols I and II (North Holland, Amsterdam).

Tirole, J. (1989) *The Theory of Industrial Organization* (MIT Press, London).

Utton, M. (1986) *The Economics of Regulating Industry* (Basil Blackwell, Oxford).

Veljanovski, C. (ed.) (1989), *Privatisation and Competition: A market prospectus* (Institute of Economic Affairs, London).

Waterson, M. (1984), *Economic Theory of the Industry* (Cambridge University Press, Cambridge).

Whish, R. (1993), *Competition Law*, 3rd edn (Butterworths, London).

SOURCE BOOKS

Livingston, D. and Pouncey, C. (1991), *Competition Law Sources* (Longman, London).

Jones, C., van der Woude, M. and Lewis, X. (1992), *EEC Competition Law Handbook* (Sweet and Maxwell, London).

Lindrup, G. (ed.) (1991), *Butterworths Competition Law Handbook*, 2nd edn (Butterworths, London).

Note: Further bibliographies appear at appropriate places in the text.

INDEX